CW01332843

The Hesilrige/Hazlerigg Family in Great Britain

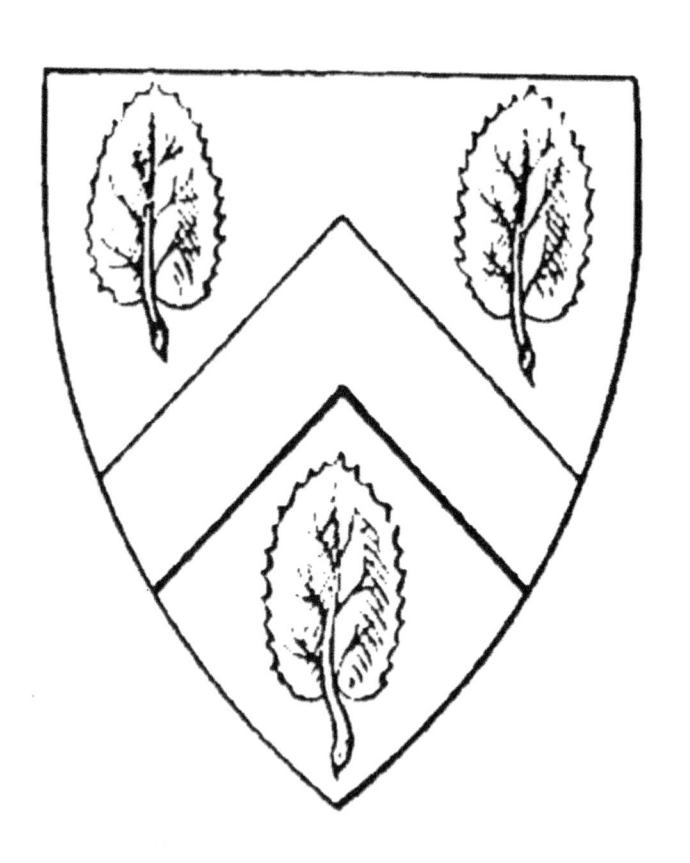

The Hesilrige/Hazlerigg Family in Great Britain, 1066 to the 1900s

corrected edition

Lawrence Hazelrigg

◇|◇|◇|◇|◇|◇|◇|◇|◇

Swiftwind Resources

Tallahassee, Florida

2021

◇|◇|◇|◇|◇|◇|◇|◇|◇

Copyright © 2021 by Lawrence Hazelrigg

ISBN-13: 978-1512114836
ISBN-10: 1512114839

All rights reserved. No part of this book, nor the book as a whole, may be reproduced or transmitted in any form or by any means, electronic or mechanical, including photocopying, recording, or by any information storage and retrieval system, without permission in writing from the copyright owner.

Swiftwind Resources
Tallahassee, Florida, USA

This book was printed in the United States of America.

Contents

List of Exhibits	xi
Preface	xv

1. Beginnings — 1
- Normandy to Hastings — 3
- The Evidence of Public Records — 6
- Some Background, Historical and Ethno-Cultural — 17
- "Came Down from Scotland"? — 23
- Hastings, the Battle — 27
- After Hastings: Northern Resistance to Strong Monarchy — 29

2. The Borders — 39
- The Battle for Sovereignty — 39
- Cumberland Sites — 41
- Northumberland: Known Estates, Early Records — 52
- Early Lineages — 62

3. Building Patrimony — 65
- Fortified Manors — 71
- One of the King's Men — 84
- More Lineage — 95

4. From Swarland to Noseley — 103
- Famine, Black Death, and 150 Years of War along the Way — 105
- More of the Lineage — 120
- Trials of Property Rights — 127
- Swarland and Vicinity — 139
- Swarland Lineage — 146
- Leaving Northumberland, Gradually — 156

5. Leicestershire, the Early Years — 159
- A Local Community in Context — 163
- Another Segment of the Lineage — 183
- Castle Donington, Sutton-Bonington — 211
- Noseley — 223
- Other Leicestershire Estates — 230

6. The Road to Civil Wars, 1601-1641 — 235
    Accepting Knighthood, Rewarded with Baronetcy — 240
    A Seventeenth-Century Segment of Lineage — 244
    And the First Puritan Hesilrige Was … ? — 247
    Thomas, the 1st Bt, and King James I — 253
    London's New Urban World — 258
    Arthur, the 2nd Bt, and King Charles I — 261
    Escape to the New World? — 268
    Seeds of a New Civil War — 278

7. War, Revolution, Republic, 1642-1660 — 299
    The First Civil War — 300
    Revolutionary Politics — 321
    The Second Civil War — 327
    Struggles for a Republic — 333
    The End Game — 347
    Restoration, 1660 — 355

8. A Portrait of Arthur Hesilrige — 357
    A Puritan Household — 358
    Contents of Mind — 367
    Family Man — 376
    Images of Character — 388
    Estate Acquisitions — 396
    A Sample of Sir Arthur's Published Words — 403
    Sir Arthur's Last Thoughts? — 430

9. Recovery and Resumption — 433
    A Segment of Lineage, c1660 to c1770 — 438
    Initial Consequences and Recoveries — 440
    The "Glorious Revolution" of 1688 — 451
    Changing Patterns of Familial Organization — 455
    Northampton's Hazelrigg House — 459
    Arthur and Hannah — 465
    Ringtail — 472

10. Becoming Citizens of the World	475
A Segment of Lineage, c1760 to c1850	479
British North America	482
What to Do with Those Rancorous Colonists	497
An Englishman in India	502
The Fortunes of Noseley Hall	510
11. A Millennium of History in Britain	525
Taking One's Kit into the World, and Back	525
A Concluding Segment of Lineage	529
Vignettes	538
Military	539
Clergy	552
Colonial Civil Service	557
Teaching	561
Estate Management	565
Last Stands	570

List of Exhibits

1.1	Part of a Pipe Roll Sheet, Northumberland, 1194	9
1.2	Hesilrige/Hazlerigg Arms, Four Versions	12
1.3	Quartering of the Hesilrige Shield	13
1.4	Example of Historical Record (mid-1300s)	15
1.5	Maps of Stannington Parish and Vicinity, Northumberland	16
1.6	Map of England, 878	21
1.7	Bust of "Head of a Scotsman"	27
1.8	Field of the Battle of Hastings	28
1.9	Early Norman Outposts in Northumberland	34
2.1	Hazelrigg Beck and Hazel Rigg, near Unthank, Cumberland	43
2.2	Hazelrig, near Unthank, Cumberland	44
2.3	Hazelrigg Footpath near Unthank, Cumberland	45
2.4	Hazelrigg Cottage, Howscales, Cumberland	45
2.5	Old Town, Mansergh, Cumberland	47
2.6	Hazelrigg at Terry Bank, Cumberland	48
2.7	Location of Hazelrigg Farm, near Ulverston	49
2.8	Main House, Hazelrigg Farm, near Ulverston	50
2.9	Hazelrigg Farm, Hazelrigg Lane, near Ellel, Lancashire	51
2.10	Farmhouse, Hazelrigg Farm, near Ellel, Lancashire	52
2.11	Excerpt of Transcript of Pipe Roll, Northumberland, 1187	53
2.12	Heselrig Settlement, Chatton Parish, Northumberland	56
2.13	Four Scenes, Area of Hazelrigg, Northumberland, 1980s & 90s	58
2.14	Some Northumberland Sites, Morpeth to Old Hazelrigg	60
2.15	Northumberland Sites near New Castle	61
3.1	Swarland Old Hall, Northumberland	72
3.2	A Section of Speed's Map of Northumberland, 1610	74
3.3	A Section of Greenwood's Map of Northumberland, 1828	75
3.4	Area North of Newcastle-upon-Tyne, Late 1800s	76
3.5	Plessey Hall	82
3.6	Maps of the Area between Wooler and Yetholm	90
3.7	Map of Approximate Location of Castle Lanark	93
3.8	Extract from Foster's *Some Feudal Coats of Arms*	102
4.1	Selected Forename Counts	119
4.2	Image of a Plea of Covenant, 6 October 1356	122
4.3	Latin Text of a Land Transaction, 20 October 1386	129
4.4	Contested Claims, King's Norton, 1489	135
4.5	Swarland Old Hall, c1904 and c2004	145
4.6	Robert Heselrig Inventory, 15 January 1638/9	154
4.7	Northumberland Inquisition, 1 June 1650	156

5.1	Some Northern and Midland Counties	164
5.2	Some Estates in Three East Midland Counties	165
5.3	Extract from the Calendar of French Rolls, 1445-1446	191
5.4	Thomas Heselrigg Weds Sarah Dixon, 1633	197
5.5	A Pardon for Murder, 1536	202
5.6	Robert and Eleanor Hasylryg Tomb	213
5.7	Robert and Eleanor Hasylryg in Effigy	216
5.8	Haselrigg Road, Clapham, Surrey	222
5.9	Some Sites to the West of Noseley Hall	225
5.10	Two Views of Noseley Hall and Chapel, 1700s	226
5.11	Part of Floor of Chancel, Noseley Chapel	228
5.12	Table Tomb Illustrations from Nichols	230
5.13	Hesilrige Manor, Humberstone	232
5.14	Recent Aerial View of Noseley Hall and Chapel	234
6.1	Sir Thomas Hesilrige, Knight & 1st Baronet	242
6.2	Five Signatures, 1592 to 1642	243
6.3	Ireland, c1450	259
6.4	Record of Thomas Hesilrige, London, 1634	261
6.5	Sir Arthur Hesilrige, Knight & 2nd Baronet	263
6.6	Panoramic Maps of London, c1600	281-284
6.7	Westminster Palace and Abbey, and St Margaret's Church	298
7.1	Cover of Booklet, *Nineteen Propositions*	299
7.2	Banner of Regiment of Horse, Sir Arthur Hesilrige	301
7.3	Robert Greville, 2nd baron Brooke	306
7.4	Sir Arthur Hesilrige in "Lobster" Armor, 1640	307
7.5	Cover of John Milton's *Areopagitica*, 1644	319
7.6	Cover of *An Agreement of the People*, 1647	325
7.7	Part of Faithorne's Map, 1658	351
8.1	Memorial to Children of Sir Arthur Hesilrige, 2nd Bt	378
8.2	Dorothea, Wife, and Daughters Dorothy and Mary of 2nd Bt	379
8.3	Probably Thomas Hesilrige, 1652	384
8.4	Lampooning Sir Arthur Hesilrige, 2nd Bt	392
8.5	An Early Selection from *Rump Songs*, 1662	393
8.6	Hazelrigg Farmhouse, Hazelrigg Lane, near Ulverston	402
8.7	Title Page of Cervantes' *Don Quixote*, 1605	404
8.8	Defense against Treason, 5 January 1641/2	406
8.9	Disposition of Scottish Prisoners, 8 November 1650	414
8.10	Sir Arthur's Speech to Commons, 7 February 1658/9	420

9.1	Plaque at St Margaret's Church, Westminster	434
9.2	Memorial to Catherine ("Kate") Hesilrige Babington	442
9.3	Part of Wenceslaus Hollar's Map of London, 1666	450
9.4	Map of Marefair District, Northampton, c1880	460
9.5	St Peter's Church, Marefair Road, Northampton	461
9.6	Hazelrigg House, 33 Marefair Road, Northampton	462
9.7	Dorothy (*nee* Maynard) and Robert Hesilrige, 6th Bt	465
9.8	Sir Arthur Hesilrige, 7th Bt	466
9.9	Sir Arthur and Hannah (*nee* Sturges) Hesilrige	468
9.10	Title Page, Richardson's *Pamela*, 2nd Edition	470
9.11	Stonework above Front Entrance, Noseley Hall	471
9.12	Painting of Ringtail, Noseley Hall	474
10.1	Memorial to Percival Lowell (1571-1665)	483
10.2	Meeting-House Hill, Roxbury, 1790	484
10.3	Sir Robert Hesilrige, 8th Bt	495
10.4	Map of Central Area of Calcutta, 1893	508
10.5	Col. Grey Hesilrige	513
10.6	Robert Greville Hesilrige's Waterloo Medal	514
10.7	Laurence Sterne to Thomas Hesilrige, 1765	517
10.8	Thomas Maynard Hesilrige, 10th Bt, c1803	519
10.9	Hoxne Hall, c1800	520
10.10	The Hesilrige Seal	521
10.11	Sir Arthur Grey Hazlerigg, 11th Bt, 1819	523
11.1	Major Arthur Grey Hazlerigg & Janet Edith Orr-Ewing	540
11.2	A Tablet of the Mafeking Memorial	544
11.3	Arthur Grey Hazlerigg Shannon, 1916	548
11.4	Jean Marie Hazlerigg, 1943 and 2009	551
11.5	Grey Hazlerigg, c1890	555
11.6	Dorothy Rachel (*nee* Buxton) and A G Hazlerigg, 13th Bt	566
11.7	Edward, Prince of Wales, and Sir Arthur Hazlerigg, 13th Bt	567
11.8	Hazlerigg Hall, Loughborough University	568
11.9	Arthur Grey Hazlerigg, 14th Bt and 2nd baron	569

Preface

This book, a chronological narrative of the life of the Hesilrige/Hazlerigg family across many centuries, has been written primarily with family members on the western side of the Atlantic in mind. Our British kin know their family history, even in its early periods, as well as they wish to know it, I suppose, and surely need no "Yankee" to tell them of it. This is not to say, however, that their readership is discouraged. Nor will their criticisms and corrections be unwelcome.

To say that the book is a chronological narrative is to say that it is not a history, properly speaking (as professional historians would rightly tell you). Although there are pieces of analysis scattered throughout, the pieces are generally brief and in service to the narrative. The word "history" does appear here and there, but it is used in the weak sense of "a story told through the passage of time." The story here ends long before the present day, partly because of my own concern to observe privileges of privacy of the living but also partly because more recent members of the family in Britain have sometimes shown reluctance to participate by sharing records, and I do not intend to abuse the welcome mat or to aggravate discomforts of one branch relative to another.

The pleasures (frustrations included) of working with records that are hundreds, in some cases nearly a thousand, years old have been much greater than one might imagine. The oldest records were written in medieval Latin, which differs considerably from classical (Ciceronian, Horatian) Latin, and differs to some extent from scribe to scribe over time. Most of that record keeping was formulaic, involving a rather limited vocabulary, plus irregular abbreviations (sometimes irregular within a given document). Most of the original manuscripts (all of the oldest) were kept away from me, of course, because of obvious hazards of contact (even human breath). So one must work with transcriptions. But in this context the very notion of "original" is rather different, since in many instances "a document" thought to be identical with itself over time had in fact been copied, and copies copied, by various scribes, not only in order to resist ravages of time but also in order to store the given document in different repositories. Depending on the considered value of a given document during a given period of history, its content could and often did change, usually but not always in casual and unimportant ways.

Just as there are variations by scribe, there are also variations by transcriber, and as one accumulates experience with different transcribers one learns which of them left behind the more careful, reliable work. Unfortunately, because many documents cannot be examined in "original" manuscript, sometimes only a single transcription was available as source. The older transcriptions generally retained the medieval Latin, except that some transcribers made formating changes, intended to ease reading, and added some abbreviations of their own. Usually these differences can be regarded as of no consequence, but they nonetheless add reason for caution. Then, too, some transcriptions are not verbatim copies but only abstracts, some of them rendered with a smooth continuity as if they had been copied word for word.

Another lesson one learns with experience is to be alert to a certain kind of bias about age. The tendency is to assume that, given two transcriptions of what was surely one and the same manuscript, the transcription dating two or three centuries nearer the original will be the more accurate, simply because of fewer intervening copies or separate transcriptions, fewer opportunities for the addition of mistakes. If one does not allow that care of work quality need not correlate well, in one direction of the other, with time, the reasoning behind that assumption is not bad (though still imperfect). Detecting a single instance in which the newer transcription was demonstrably more accurate than the older (such as one discussed in chapter 4) is sufficient to alert one to the importance of that correlation (or lack thereof), and thus to maintain caution about unexamined assumptions.

All of the difficulty of working with ancient records has resulted in a presentation that readers may find rather tendentious. This result is by deliberate decision. It would have been easy to present each record as clear and certain. It would have been easy to offer a "general alert," as here, then to move on without reminders of ambiguities, inconsistencies, and doubts. But skepticism is, I believe, a healthy attitude. As author I write with confidence in judgments, but I do not think these judgments to be beyond questioning; and I recommend the same caution to my readers.

A few words about spelling of the family name are in order. Like most surnames, ours has been rendered in a variety of ways, often with records of one and the same person showing different spellings of that person's surname. In general, I have imposed little restriction of that variation, usually only enough to eliminate risks of confusion. Much of the variation was local and occasional. But two broad patterns can be discerned. During early centuries the first vowel was usually written as "e" (and some of the exceptions to that are probably due to impositions by transcribers during recent centuries). The second pattern began with what linguistic historians sometimes call "the Great Vowel Shift," which occurred mainly during the sixteenth and seventeenth centuries and was part of the hinge from Middle English to Modern English. This shift consisted in the pronunciation of long vowel sounds (short vowels stayed mainly unchanged), with a corresponding change in orthography following the sound change. To illustrate the shift with an example tailored to present purposes, the string of letters "*derk*" in Middle English was pronounced with a sound closer to the vowel sound in the Modern English word "dark." As the vowel sound of that "e" in "*derk*" shifted forward and higher in the mouth, it became the sound of the "a" in the Modern English "dark"; and the spelling followed in due course. Thus, "*he*," which had been pronounced somewhat like the Modern English word "hay," became "ha" (as in "hay," not "ha ha"). The shift occurred more slowly in the northern part of England than in the south, and some regional variations remain in the texture of the vowel shift. Since 1818 the "official" name in Great Britain has been spelled Hazlerigg, and I have generally followed that usage, the main exception being the lineage who have maintained the predominant spelling of the surname as it was during the centuries prior to 1818—Hesilrige. This latter spelling apparently was the spelling preferred by Sir Arthur Hesilrige, 2nd Bt, judging by the fact of his recorded signature; yet some of his published writings carry the surname as "Haselrig" or "Haslerig." For the early centuries the surviving written record seems most often to use a still different spelling, "Heselrig" or something very close to that, and I tend to use that spelling for the early period. However, when reciting a record of a specific person my preference has been to reproduce the spelling used in that record, though here again I impose some restriction (not always announced) in order to avoid confusion.

    Another concern has to do with titular names or dignities, which for some individuals accumulated quite handsomely over time. In formal custom that person would be addressed by his or her latest, most elevated titular name. An illustration taken from part of the history covered in this book will be helpful. Scion of an aristocratic family (and confidant of a king for several years), Edward Montagu was knighted in 1626; thus, he was Sir Edward. A few months later he received his father's dignity of baron Montagu of Kimbolton; thus, he was lord Kimbolton. Next came the courtesy title, viscount Mandeville ("viscount" stands above "baron" but below "earl," which is the British equivalent of "count"); thus, he was lord Mandeville. At his father's death in 1642 he succeeded as 2nd earl of Manchester; thus, he was earl Manchester, or simply Manchester. Also, during the first civil war he held the rank of major-general, head of all parliamentary forces in the eastern counties. Depending on date, he was by tradition referenced in one of at least five ways (or six, if the military context should be foremost in reference). David Cannadine, in his monumental book, *The Decline and Fall of the British Aristocracy*, recommended by example the advice received from Harold Nicolson, biographer of George V: "calling people by the names they possessed at the date of which I am writing." I have opted for a simpler choice. The audience of this book, no doubt very largely North American, are not accustomed to sorting through titles and keeping straight the links of those chains. In deference to that, and without intending any lack of respect for the British tradition of dignities, I have generally named individuals primarily by their birth names, forename and surname, with dignities usually added at least initially but without attending to the chains as Nicolson advised. Thus, Edward Montagu will appear in the pages primarily as Edward Montagu (unless within another writer's citation, in which he might have been named Kimbolton, Mandeville, or Manchester).

  Several persons have taken an interest in and been helpful with the preparation of this book—foremost among them Katherine Hazelrigg and Rose Coster, who offered steadfast support and critical eye and advice. Some persons have been helpful without necessarily knowing of that fact—among them, Chris Phillips, creator and indefatigable overseer of his website, Medieval Genealogy; Darryl Lundy, creator and overseer of another website, The Peerage; Mary Lou Hazelrigg, always alert to new resources; and a few persons whose assistances are acknowledged at specific places in the text. There is also, of course, the long list of predecessors as historians, genealogists, and heraldic scholars (most especially John Hodgson, Frederick Walter Dendy, John Crawford Hodgson, George Farnham, William Fletcher): they harrowed and sorted massive volumes of ancient recordings, along the way building extracts that serve their followers as efficient and usually highly accurate guides. In his 1910 published extract of the plea rolls of the Court of Common Pleas relating to Northumberland during the 250 years from 1308 (an extract that will appear piecemeal in footnotes of this book), Dendy gave indication of the scope of work involved by cautioning against any claim of a complete indexing: the rolls in question—only one of several categories or types of roll—numbered 987, and each roll contained hundreds of "skins" or "membranes," the sheets that were stitched together to form rolled documents. Again, that was for only one category of rolls, for only one county, across a mere 250 years.

To a Northumberland Heselrig by descent who offered a wealth of good advice and information, and requested anonymity, a tip of the hat with much gratitude. And special thanks to Geoffrey Kendal of New South Wales, descendant of Alice Heselrig of Northumberland.

Finally, with special gratitude and remembrance, I thank the late Arthur Hazlerigg, 14th baronet and 2nd baron Hazlerigg, who arranged access to family papers, both those held in hand and those on deposit at the Records Office (now known as The National Archives), and whose spirit kept me to my agreement to write this book. He, as later his son and heir, Arthur, 15th baronet and 3rd baron Hazlerigg, was always gracious host and advisor, allowing free run of Noseley, its history and its legacies.

Lawrence Hazelrigg
St George Island

~ 1 ~
Beginnings

According to the 76th edition of *Burke's Peerage and Baronetage* (page 985), the Hazlerigg family "traces from Roger de Hesilrige, one of the knights who accompanied William the Conqueror to England." Whether the progenitor of the Hazlerigg family in England (and Great Britain) was a member of the expedition cannot be decided in fact. No evidence independent of tradition within the family establishes that he was a participant in this momentous though hardly unprecedented migration of people from the continent to the British Isles. In the larger scheme of history, human beings had been migrating predominantly westward for many centuries prior to 1066; and continue on that trek they would, for centuries thereafter. The expedition that made landfall near Hastings in southeast England can be regarded, with much accuracy, as a family feud—though not involving anyone of the Hazlerigg family except insofar as a family member was in service to William, duke of Normandy, as the tradition says. But for the Hazlerigg family in particular it was momentous in light especially of the family's subsequent fortune.

Whether this man Roger was the family's English progenitor or not, and whether he came as a companion of William, duke of Normandy or not—and in fact neither connection can be successfully proven or disproven—it is unmistakably established that not long after 1066 the family had become significant land holders in England and beneficiary of royal dispositions repeatedly. There is no evidence of any sort that the family had been similarly successful in Normandy or elsewhere on the continent, although if in fact Roger, or an unnamed "stand-in," had come to England as a knight, he had already achieved a level of material success that was rather rare in those days in those places. A battle-ready horse and his maintenance, a lance or broad sword, helmet and body armor, hardly cheap items, were far beyond the possessions of most men.

Time for the tones of skepticism and the evidence of written records comes later. We begin, as above, by honoring the family legend of Roger, and the assumption that it is basically correct of historical presence and circumstance. The time and place, eleventh-century Europe, did not know much of written records. It was an oral culture, very different from our cultures of the *scriptorum*, the scrolls, the codices, the books. To judge, thus, that a corpus of information must not be believed because it was not written in the original time and place but only later, even much later, is to violate something of the integrity of that older culture. It merits evaluation with due respect, even if ultimately for us it remains in some realm of the undecidable.[1]

We begin, thus, in his reputed place of origin, the region of Normandy or lands nearby. There is little information to use, even from family legend. Perspective is important, of course: there is little information to use for *any* family, even royal families, for that early time. For the beginnings of the Hazlerigg family in Normandy, we must look to a time long ago to find any information that could tell us about specific persons and specific events associated with those persons. For this family, "a long time ago" means ten centuries at least—that is to say, 1,000 years. How likely is it that a family, any family, would maintain records of its persons, places, and events across, say, 40 generations? For that matter, how likely is it that any family, defined relative to others by a surname that carried a lineage, would even *survive* across ten centuries? Anyone alive today obviously descends from two individuals who were alive 1,000 years ago, somewhere. But think of the large proportion of families of eleventh-century Normandy, or of twelfth-century England, who have *not a single descendant* alive today, anywhere in the world.

Estimates of the size of William's invasion force vary by as much as a factor of two, but the most considered estimates put the force at 5,000 to 7,000 men, of whom roughly 2,000 were cavalry (of whom, by legend, our Roger was one). This was a remarkable feat of logistics for the day, to sail nearly 800 ships carrying that many men and their equipment, plus enough supplies to sustain them until they could raid local produce, across more than fifty miles of sometimes treacherous water. Who knows how many perished before reaching the English coast, coming ashore the shingle beach at Pevensey Bay, and occupying the old Roman fort before marching east toward Hastings.[2] It was a partly mercenary force, adherents expecting compensation in plunder, favor, and good land, in wake of victory and survival. Such was the recruiter's promise: win for me, and reap your reward, all the fruits of war both in glory and in material goods (*if* you live to see victory). William's men were Norman, of course, but also from various Frankish

---

[1] Anyone who would seek better understanding of these matters would not be shorted by Mary Carruthers' fine study, *The Book of Memory*, 2nd edition (Cambridge: Cambridge University Press, 2008), which follows in the tradition of Frances Yates' *The Art of Memory* (London: Routledge & Kegan Paul, 1966).

[2] A "shingle" beach differs in being covered not by sand but by pebbles and even small cobbles, firmer foundation for horse hooves and narrow-wheeled carts and wagons.

backgrounds (e.g., Flemish), plus some from Gallic lands to the south and east, perhaps some even of Celtic origin (i.e., Breton). Where was Roger in that inventory? We have no way of knowing, beyond the odds from population size. Most of the men were either Norman or Frank; thus, he was probably one or the other--or both, since during their centuries of residence in this part of the world the Normans had intermarried with others, mainly Franks. It remains to be said, of course, that Roger, as one specific person, *could* have come from anywhere, although distance was an important factor. It is unlikely that he hailed from Iberia, for example; but then, too, not impossible.

How old was he? If in fact a knight, he would have been old enough to have assembled the wealth that was precondition: a battle-ready horse, equipment, the means to maintain both during training and testing (e.g., tournaments), plus travel to the point of embarkation. Yet not too old to impress that he himself, along with his stead, was battle-ready. (Duke William was just short of 40 in 1066.) Did Roger leave behind a wife and children? Was he in flight from authorities of some other place? What was his rank among William's knights? Was he part of the Flemish cavalry, the Breton cavalry, or the Norman cavalry? Was the choice his? Had he served the duke before this expedition? Obviously the questions could be multiplied, all without definite answer beyond pleas of ignorance. The most one can do is to turn to a general history of place and time, a history that attends to more than the royal and the noble, providing a general view of what life was like, as best we can know, for persons of various specific ranks.[3]

Normandy to Hastings, 1066

Did Roger arrive as part of the army raised by William of Normandy? Like most other longstanding families who have claimed descent from the invasion, only legend can be brought to bear. In William Betham's *Baronetage of England*,[4] the claim is stated that Roger de Hesilrige came with William the Conqueror "from a place of that name in Normandy, [then] settled in Cumberland, and the place took his name." As we

---

[3] For medieval Normandy, one such resource is Robert Fossier's *The Axe and the Oath: Ordinary Life in the Middle Ages* (trans. Lydia G Cochrane; Princeton: Princeton University Press, 2007/2010).

[4] *The Baronetage of England, or the History of the English Baronets*, etc. (London: William Miller, 1801), volume 1, pages 260-263, at page 260. Betham intended his work as successor of Arthur Collins' 1720 volume, with many corrections and additions (page viii), as well as of later editions such as Wotton's of 1741.

proceed through these early chapters we will see ample reason to doubt all three of the quoted points. Whether Roger did come with William in 1066 remains undecided, the evidence for either reckoning simply not available. On the other hand, Eneas MacKenzie reported in his history of Northumberland that a manorial estate held by the family in the eastern part of the shire, Swarland, was held by the family pre-Conquest.[5] He offered no evidence for it, and in fact the record clearly shows that the estate was acquired by the Hesilrige family long after the eleventh century (see chapter 3). In general, MacKenzie's book merits cautiously attentive reading. Equally, in view of factual records, we can doubt with good reason that Roger came from a place called "Hesilrige" in Normandy, that he then settled at some location in Cumberland, and that his Cumbrian place of settlement then assumed his surname, "Hesilrige." These pieces will fall into place as we proceed.

When on a July day in 1622 the then head of the family, Sir Thomas Hesilrige, having only recently been knighted by James I, was granted baronetage by that same monarch, an official pedigree was declared, and it depended on continuity of line as demonstrated by written record. The pedigree began, and begins yet today, not with Roger but with a later man, Simon de Hesilrige, lord of estates in southeastern Northumberland. There were and are records of the family for the previous century, but the line from those men and their estates to Simon is not continuous in record. These earlier households will be described in the next chapter, to the extent that records permit, and estimates of lineage gaps will be offered. Later chapters will then proceed with the pedigree, beginning with Simon.

The written record of those who later were accorded the honor of "Companions of the Conqueror" consists of three documents that were produced shortly after Hastings: William of Poitiers, *The Deeds of William II, Duke of Normans* (c1075); *The Ecclesiastical History* which Orderic Vitalis produced between 1110 and 1142, parts of which recount the invasion; and the famed Bayeux Tapestry, which identifies a few participants in the battle. Based on these few sources, only twenty-one "companions" have been proven (and of these, five or six are still disputed by interested parties). This is of an army that totaled at least 6,000 men, perhaps as many as 10,000 men, most of them foot soldiers but many of them knights (i.e., with horse and equipment). Subsequent documents such as the "Domesday" survey commissioned by king

---

[5] *An Historical, Topographical, and Descriptive View of the County of Northumberland*, 2nd edition, volume 1 (Newcastle-upon-Tyne: MacKenzie and Dent, 1825), page 489.

William in 1086 (about which, more below) have been cited as proven sources, but none of these addresses the question, "date of arrival." Domesday is typical in mixing landholders who arrived in William's army with those who arrived later, and there is simply no way to separate them. The number of later arrivals is unknown; but if William's army totaled 7,000, probably as many more and perhaps as many as twice that number arrived from Normandy during William's reign as the king of England.

The well-known *Roll of Battle Abbey* was constructed long after Hastings and installed in the famed abbey that William had erected on site of the battle (reportedly on the exact location of king Harold's death, another legend). The original roll was somehow lost, and for long after the surviving copies were cause of considerable dispute among families, because their lists differed. The earliest of those often-examined copies dated to the 1500s. Remarkably, only during the just past century, it appears, did someone realize that an older copy (c1335) exists in the Auchinleck manuscript collection in the National Library of Scotland.[6] Inspection of this copy shows that it, too, does not include the family surname Hesilrige or Heselrig (or other variants). However, one should bear in mind that if Roger's presence was recorded on the Battle Abbey roll or any other document, and if the record stated affiliation with a place, as was common for knights—and, after all, "mere" foot soldiers were unlikely to be recorded individually—the place name need not have been "Heselrig" in any of its variant Old Norse or Middle English spellings. There is reason, in fact, to think that the place name would have been in Norman-French; for, as has been discussed by many, one of the "secrets" of Norman success in territorial conquest was adoption and adaptation of local customs, including naming practices. (Duke William, for instance, was not "William" but "Guillaume" at home in Normandy.)

The claim, as repeated above, that the family came from a place named "Hesilrige" or "Heselrig" (or something like that) in Normandy is highly dubious. Allan Mawer has reported that the surname Heselrig or Hesilrige is in Old English a compound of *hæsel* and *hrycg*.[7] These are in turn of Old Norse derivation, and they mean "hazel" (as in the nut-

---

[6] The reference is to Lord Auchinleck, born Alexander Boswell, father of James Boswell, best known as biographer of Samuel Johnson. Of course, "copy" presumes an "original," which may never have existed. See John Horace Round, "The Companions of the Conqueror," *The Monthly Review*, volume 3 (June 1901), pages 91-111.

[7] Allen Mawer, *The Place-Names of Northumberland and Durham* (Cambridge: Cambridge University Press, 1920), page 107.

bearing small tree or shrub) on the "ridge" (i.e., a topographical ridge line). There were (and are) three counterparts to "hazel" in French: the nut, and by extension the tree, is "noisette" or "avellene" or "coudrier."[8] Neither of the first two candidate place names appears in the list of names in any version of the *Roll of Battle Abbey*. The third name *is* in the list recorded in the oldest known copy of the roll (i.e., the Auchinleck copy of 1335). Was this Roger? There is no way to know. The list consists only of surnames, whether place name or patronym; and even had the entry been written "Roger de Coudrier," we would nonetheless lack means of linking him to a subsequent man named "Roger de Hesilrige." It is at least as likely that he retained "Coudrier" as a surname, perhaps in the format of "de Coudrier," later anglicized to "Cordray" or similar spelling. But again, the simple fact is we do not know. It is possible that this man *was* Roger de Coudrier (but the list, remember, is silent of forename), arrived in England and, following the Conqueror's example, shifted from Norman French to Old English, becoming Roger de Heselrig. Possible; but unlikely.

The Evidence of Public Records
Evidence from legends within a family must not be neglected unless it can be conclusively disproven, and even then such evidence tells us something about the family, even if not what the motivation of the legend intended. Sometimes, of course, stories passed down from the past within a family are all that we have in regard to one or another question. But caution is always warranted. Evidence by legend cannot by itself carry much weight in public discourse. Other sources of evidence must be brought to bear wherever possible on any given question. This is not to say that evidence from other sources automatically trumps evidence by legend within a family. Public sources (e.g., official sources of state or church) offer public records, to be sure, and that is their advantage. However, public records often began as guesses or estimates, and often as guesses or estimates tainted by this or that bias, by specific persons who usually occupied some position of authority yet were anything but infallible and unbiased. One must approach a public record with the same caution that is recommended for a family's legends. Having two or more public records that address a given question agreeably will result in

---

[8] Some refinement: "noisette" mainly names the nut, so it is a less likely candidate; "avellana" gave rise to several names, including Aveline, Avelina, Evelyn, and (in Scots English) Eileen; "coudrier" could be anglicized as Cordry, Courdrey, and so forth, and was.

weightier evidence behind a particular answer to the question only when it is clear that the two or more records were constructed independently of each other. Sometimes that independence cannot be determined. Sometimes, on the other hand, it is apparent that a later record cribbed, in part or in whole, from an earlier record. Indeed, during medieval times the function of a scribe was precisely to copy a written document, in order to preserve the information and/or in order to communicate that information to new territory, new people. Then one must ask about the accuracy and reliability of the scribe, the deliberate shading of meaning, the quality of translating from a Latin to a local vernacular, and so forth.[9] In sum, there is no easy road even when records—familial, public, and otherwise—are relatively plentiful in regard to a given question. Logic, inferential and deductive, usually offers assistance in sifting through possibilities and probabilities, but of course logic must have some substance (evidence) on which to work. The upshot is, here and throughout this book, that stated conclusions are always in some degree tentative, the reasoning on which they depend open, and the evidentiary base explicit.

"Plentiful" is a word seldom used when addressing matters of evidence for the eleventh century—except in description of reasons for doubt and uncertainty. (Likewise for subsequent centuries.) A brief overview of the kinds of sources will provide some orientation. In general, the principal source in the sense of depository is the Public Record Office, directly and through partial holdings by regional record offices, along with the British Library. The overview that follows focuses on records more for the medieval period than for later periods.

The Domesday survey, mentioned earlier, was commissioned by William, king of England, and completed in 1086 as the Domesday Book, a survey of landholders, Norman and Anglo-Saxon. So far as can be determined, the survey was remarkably good for its time (a Norman strength was bureaucratic-governmental organization of territory, aided by its adoption of local customs and language). Because the northern lands remained in dispute between the king's Norman claim to them and old Anglo-Saxon claims of sovereignty (plus periodic raids from Galloway and other parts of Scotland), the survey did not include any of Northumberland, Cumberland, or Westmoreland, and (due mainly to

---

[9] Note the locution, "*a* Latin." Those of us who learned a grammar school Latin years ago may have been left with the misfortune of thinking there is and has been but one Latin. There have been many, over time and across places. In short, Latin has been anything but a "dead language."

William's harrying, discussed below) only sketchy coverage of northern parts of Yorkshire and Lancashire.

Various ecclesiastical surveys were conducted, mostly at the parish level, few of them surviving. Prominent exceptions include two surveys of Durham, which was a county palatine ruled by the bishop of Durham.[10] The first, known as the Boldon Book, was a survey of all the lands under the authority of the bishop of Durham, Hugh du Puiset (aka Pudsey), in 1173. The second, completed c1382, was bishop Hatfield's similar survey.

Scattered commercial records have survived, but these are mostly accounts and, excepting an occasional receipts book, have survived mainly as records of taxation and the like.

The *Rotuli Annales* are also known as the *Rotuli Pipæ*, or "pipe rolls," so-called because they were rolled sheets or scrolls of parchment, typically stacked lengthwise atop one another, looking much like racks of lead pipe. (An example of a segment of one of the sheets is given as Exhibit 1.1.) They are an especially valuable resource for the twelfth and subsequent centuries, mainly because they are virtually alone as country-wide records. While initially intended only as recordings of revenue for the kingdom from land holders, the rolls gradually acquired other sorts of entries, including some paid entries by land holders who wanted a secure reserve copy of a transaction. The rolls are incomplete, however, especially for northern shires, with many gaps both of years and of contents within a given year. Apparently no rolls survived (if made) from Stephen's reign (1135-1154). Transcriptions of records from the original rolls have been made by various historians, sometimes with at least partial translation of the original Latin. John Hodgson's *History of Northumberland*, published early in the nineteenth century, is one of the sources on which the present account has relied. His transcriptions are quite good, considering the state of many of the rolls, but occasionally the result is unclear and perhaps mistaken. While altering format to some extent, Hodgson left the transcriptions mostly in the original Latin, some of which was written in inconsistent and irregular abbreviations.

---

[10] This status derived from claims dating to the Kingdom of Northumbria, c684. As a palatine authority, the bishop enjoyed quasi-royal rights within the palatine territory, though ultimately at the pleasure of the monarch. Palatine ("from the palace") authority was extended to counties that were subject to invasion, granting local rulers greater than usual powers in return for their efforts to quell invading forces. In addition to Durham, Cheshire gained palatine status from William. Lancashire later gained palatine status.

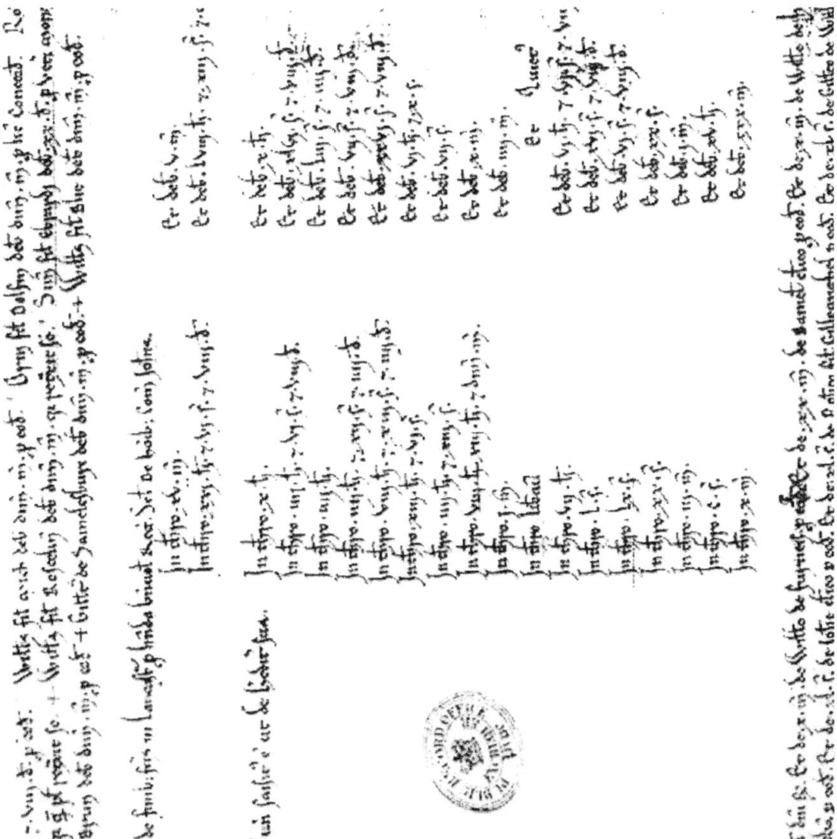

Exhibit 1.1. Part of a Pipe Roll Sheet, Northumberland, 1194

Other kinds of early recording included barons' charters, parish registers, and heraldic visitations that compiled and investigated (in some sense) family pedigrees, arms, and associated documents. These visitations became an official basis of pedigrees, later compiled in works such as *Burke's Peerage and Baronetage*, begun by John Burke in 1826. Also important are maps, although these seldom date earlier than the 1700s. Saxton's 1576 map of Warwickshire and Leicestershire is one exception; it shows the family's estate at Noseley. Another is Speed's map of Northumberland, 1610, which shows the much older estate (designated Heselridge) of the north-central area, as well as the Weteslade and other estates in the southeast near Newcastle-upon-Tyne (discussed in the next chapter).

Much of the large volume of various kinds of historical documents was later assembled and ordered as manuscript collections. One of the most important, the Harleian collection, was undertaken by Robert Harley (1661-1724) and his son Edward (1689-1741), respectively the 1st and 2nd earls of Oxford and Mortimer, and now includes more than 7,000 manuscripts, 14,000 charters, and 500 rolls. All of these collections, together with other sources, formed the basis of the series of shires histories begun under queen Victoria (and still underway).

While most of the recording was verbal text, a small portion was pictorial, the principal instance being, in addition to maps, a family's arms. The oldest known display of arms after the Roman Empire is in the Bayeux Tapestry (not really a tapestry but an embroidered linen cloth some 230 feet long), dating probably to the 1070s. Royal recognition of arms in England began with Henry I in 1127, and an office of heraldry was established soon thereafter. Initially an arms was assigned to a particular person, who could pass it to his or her heir. Late in the twelfth century Richard I declared arms to be hereditary and thus an arms was associated with a family. Also during this period the use of familial surnames became more and more common, especially at first among members of the aristocracy. Identification by place (as in William de Hesilrige), by occupation (as in John the sawyer), by personal trait (as in Charles the Bold) or by similar other means of distinguishing two or more men named William, John, or Charles (etc.) within the same locale, gave way to use of an "extra name" to signify a familial line of descent.

Initially the insignia of arms—in particular, the central element, the shield, such as that for the Hesilrige/Hazlerigg arms, displayed as frontispiece to this book—were adopted most often by knights as a form of identification in battle and in tournaments, displayed on a banner and/or on a cloth tunic or painted on the surface of a helmet or breastplate (thus, "coat of arms"). Once arms became familial, the right to bear a family's arms was in the province of the main hereditary line. Other lines of the family could display "differenced" arms—that is, each differing from the main arms by a slight change in design (e.g., a color change, a difference in an internal proportion, an embellishment, etc.). Sometimes a redesign followed a marriage, with a small version of each line's shield being displayed in the new shield, resulting in quartered and, in a few instances, re-quartered shields.

Four versions of the arms of the Hesilrige/Hazlerigg family are shown in Exhibit 1.2. With reference to any one of these, the main parts are the shield (which consists of parts), the supports, the crest, and the motto (at the bottom of English arms; at the top of Scottish arms). The shield is basically in common across all versions (these four and presumably all others). It was emblazoned above the doorway to Hesilrige Tower, in north-central Northumberland, a stone tower erected as part of a defensive line against brigand raiding parties, and after 1714 incorporated as part of a dwelling in what is now known as Old Hazelrigg (about which, more in chapter 2).[11]

The official description of the shield—and these are matters regulated by heraldic law in England—describes a chevron separating three hazel-leaves against the background of the shield. In English heraldry, colors are of two sorts: "metals," of which there are two, lightly tinctured, *argent* (silver) and *or* (gold); and "colours," of which there are five, darkly tinctured, *azure* (blue), *gules* (red), *purpure* (purple), *sable* (black), and *vert* (green). In all know versions of the Hesilrige/Hazlerigg shield the leaves are green; the chevron is usually black or red, although in at least one description it was given as green (vert)[12]; the background

---

[11] In his *Leicestershire Pedigrees and Royal Descents* (Leicester: Clarke and Hodgson, 1887), page 8, William George Dimock Fletcher mentions the tower as a separate structure in 1714. See also Fletcher's *The Early History of the Family of Hesilrige, of Noseley, co. Leicester* (Leicester: Clarke and Hodgson, 1892).

[12] The two known instances of a green chevron are, first, in Peter Armstrong's *Stirling Bridge and Falkirk 1297-98* (Botley, Oxford: Osprey, 2003), page 31, a sketch of the shield associated with Sir William Heselrig (b. by 1260, d. 1297), sheriff of the Clydesdale and a representative of the English king, Edward I, in Scotland (more about this William in chapter 3); and in a medallion affixed to the wall above the tomb of Thomas Hesilrige, 1st Bt, and his wife, Frances (Gorges) Hesilrige, in Noseley Chapel (and on the cover of this book), although the intent for the latter might have been black.

is silver. Shapes vary. The leaves, for instance, are sometimes ovate or obtuse, other times falcate. The doubly serrated edge of the actual leaf of British hazel is not easy to depict in such small space, but some of the representations clearly made the attempt.

Exhibit 1.2. Hesilrige/Hazlerigg Arms, Four Versions

The two versions on the left side of the exhibit are the more common of the four; either is the oldest of the four (the one at bottom is in Wotton's *Baronetage*, 1741), the differences between them small. In each the supports (to use proper nomenclature) are, left, a hart and, right, a Talbot hound, each figure rampant. The Talbot, now extinct, was a large white or grey-white hunting dog, reportedly in size similar to a modern bloodhound. In the parlance of medieval hunts, the word "hart" referred to a fully mature deer (though some argue that in this depiction it was more specifically an "Irish deer"). Above the shield, the crest features a chapeau dressed in ermine and, above that, "the head of a Scotsman" (more about this below). On a ribbon beneath the shield, the family motto: *Pro Aris et Foci* ("For the Altars and Hearths"). Finally, note in both versions, at the very top portion of the shield, a smaller shield that features a human hand—less distinct in the bottom version but in the top clearly a right hand—and the hand displays what is traditionally described as a "Scottish hex sign." Provenience of this emblem is unknown. It was not part of the shield that was cut into stone above the doorway to Hesilrige Tower, but that absence could well have been due to the small size of the hand relative to stonecutting tools then available.

The version at top right is very similar to the two already discussed. The main variation is substitution of a "Lobster"—a fully armored combatant of the rebel side—and "Cavalier"—a cavalryman of the royal side—from the English civil wars of the seventeenth century, in place of the hart and the hound. Note that the hex-signing hand is absent. Given its historical specificity, this design was probably commissioned by Sir Arthur Hesilrige, the 2nd Bt, during the 1640s or 1650s.

Finally, at bottom right, a version designed by, or at least for, Sir Arthur Grey Hazlerigg, the 13th Bt: dated at about 1914, this one has non-animate supports and a differing crest.

Two examples of shields redesigned in acknowledgement of marriages are displayed in Exhibit 1.3. Collateral families represented in quarterings include (ignoring spelling variations of surname) Heron, Haggerston, Sadington, Martivall, Staunton, Eccleshall, Meignell, Warde, Everden, Entwyssell, Shirley, Gorges, and Oldhall. As the shield on the right side of the exhibit shows, repeated quartering results in smallish component shields. The marriages represented in this one are also part of the written record. They will be addressed in due course.

Exhibit 1.3. Quartering of the Hesilrige Shield

Several sorts of written public records are valuable sources for the present book of family history, and recourse will be made to them according to century and generation.[13] Here a general account will be useful as brief introduction and illustration. Early records, whether a function of royal court or of church, were made in Latin. It was a rather cryptic Latin, consisting of more or less stylized abbreviations and standard phrases, although uses could vary even within one and the same document. Because few people were then literate, and most of these few were official scribes of church or court, thus of the official *lingua franca*, they had soon adopted this "coded" form of recording which made the records more compact and easier to copy for purposes of wide dissemination and preservation. But of course that could not ensure that one scribe would be as assiduous as his predecessor, or as careful in hand script.

An example of the sort of written record that is available from the early period is shown in an extract from page 339 of Hodgson's compilation in his *History of Northumberland*, drawn mainly from pipe rolls beginning in the reign of Henry II (accession 1154).[14] This extract (see Exhibit 1.4) pertains to Stannington Parish and vicinity, mid-1300s, a time when the family held several estates in this area of southeastern Northumberland. At least five different men of the Hazlerigg family are mentioned: Thomas de Heselrigg lord of Heselrigg, William son of Simon de Heselrigg, Thomas son of Simon de Heselrigg, and John de Heselrigg of Shepwash (known also as Sheepwash, which was a small estate, later a village, about four miles east of Morpeth on the south bank of the river Wansbeck, now mostly absorbed by the town of Ashington; see the map in Exhibit 1.5). It is possible that one or more of the other men named in this extract were also of the Hazlerigg family but were named in association with a different estate—for instance here, "Woderington," which was a reference to the manor of Widdrington.

These instances illustrate the fact that use of a family surname had been reintroduced (after the fall of Rome), first among the aristocracy, and by the 1300s had become fairly regular, although inheritance across generations was still sporadic among commoners. The phrase in line 7 in

---

[13] This is ground already cultivated: see, for example, pages 8-14 of William Fletcher's *Leicestershire Pedigrees and Royal Descents* (1887) and his *Early History of the Family of Hesilrige* (1892). Fruits of his work are incorporated into this book.

[14] John Hodgson, *History of Northumberland*, volume 2, part 2 (Newcastle-on-Tyne, 1832). Note that the letter yogh, represented by ȝ , was then used (e.g., second line, fifth line, in Exhibit 1.4).

uersionis sc̃i Pauli anno supradc̃o.—*(Id. 76.)*

28. Omnibȝ &c. Rogerus de Woderington' filius Joh̃is de Woderington militis salt̃m in dño . Noueritis me dedisse—Gerardo de Woderington' . Henrico de Hauerington' militibȝ . Rogero Heron' psona eccl̃ie de fford . Johanne de Burdon' psona eccl̃ie de Routhbury . Will̃mo de Emeldon' psona eccl̃ie de Bottale . Thm̃e de Heselrigg dño de Heselrigg . Rogero de Fenwick . Edmundo de Woderington . Will̃mo fil̃ Symon' de Heselrigg . Thm̃a fil̃ Symon de Heselrigg . Joh̃i fil̃ Ade de Rodum . Joh̃i de Heselrigg de Schepwassh̃ . Rob̃to de Massam . Ranulfo de Malteby . Joh̃i fil̃ Gilb̃ti de Babington' . Joh̃i fil̃ Will̃i fil̃ Ric̃i de Babington' . Gilb̃to Gaumbel de Werkword . Will̃mo fil̃ Will̃i de Swethop . Gilb̃to Heron' fil̃ Rog̃i Heron' militis . Ric̃o fil̃ Joh̃ Heron' militis . maneria mea de Plescys et Schotton' . Habend &c. Hiis testibȝ dñis Rob̃to de la vale . Will̃mo Heron' . Johne Heron militibȝ . Edmundo de Esshet . Will̃mo Whiteheued . Rob̃to de Midleton' . Adm de Lyam . Ricardo de Blakden' et aliis.—*(Id. 118.)* No date; but this deed was probably made in 1350, for John de Burdon, rector of Rothbury, died in 1352.

29. Omnib; Gerardus de Woderington Henric' de Hauerington, &c. (ut Supra, No. 28). Noueritis nos dedisse Rog̃o de Woderington fil̃ Joh̃is de Woderington militis maneria nr̃a de Plescys et Schotton cũ om̃ibȝ suis

Exhibit 1.4. Example of Historical Record (mid-1300s)

the exhibit, "Thme de Heselrigg dño de Heselrigg," means that Thomas de Heselrigg was "lord of the manor of Heselrigg." Likewise, the man

John de Heselrigg de Schepwash was Heselrigg in family surname and living on the estate of Schepwash.

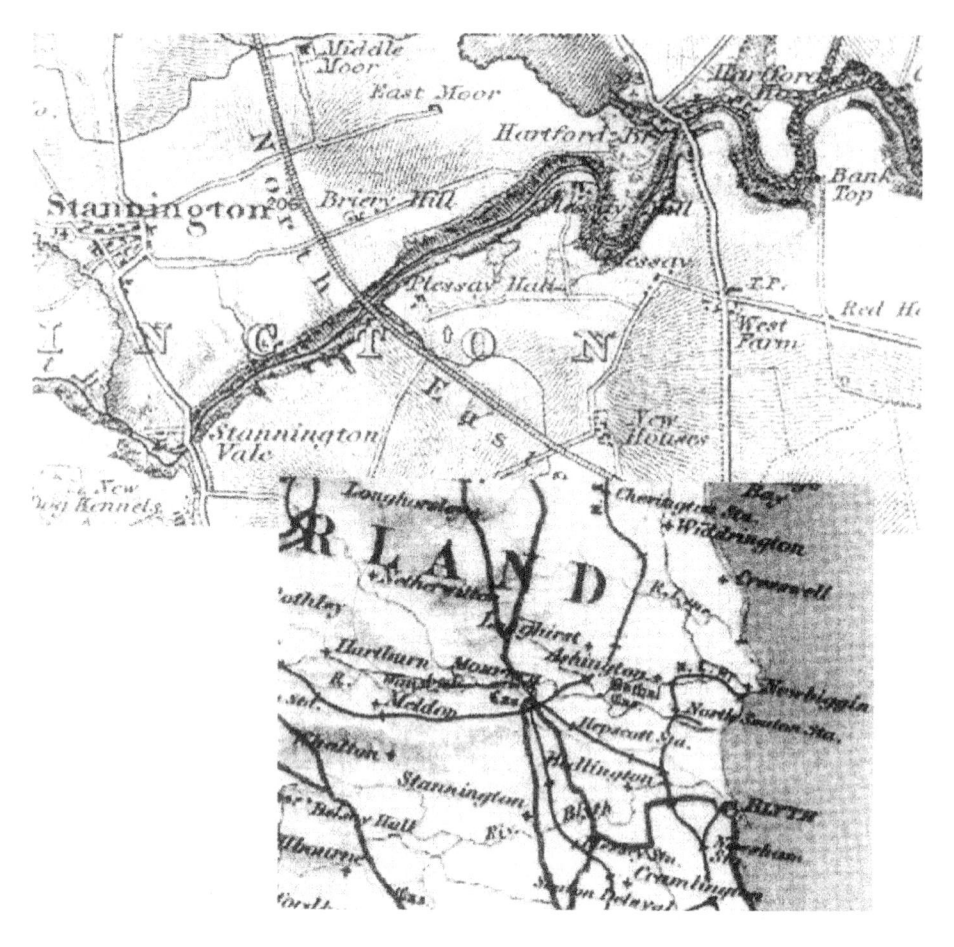

Exhibit 1.5. Maps of Stannington Parish and Vicinity, Northumberland

Filiations were sometimes given for the sake of clarity, examples being William and Thomas, each a son of Simon de Heselrigg. Further, some persons were identified by what we would call occupational position—John de Woderington, a soldier serving the lord of the manor; Roger Heron, a person of the church of Ford—though these positions were actually part of the feudal order of "stations" within the hierarchical relations of fealty and authority, not "occupations" in the modern sense. The Latin *particule* "de" was long retained by aristocratic families as place-of-origin reminder and/or as notice of the family's principal seat. Thus, we know from the record extracted in Exhibit 1.4 that Thomas de Heselrigg was lord of the manor of Heselrigg and that this manor was the main seat of Thomas' ancestral lineage. Unfortunately, we cannot say with certainty how long the manor of Heselrigg had been principal seat, but based on some evidence discussed in the next chapter it seems likely that Thomas inherited from his father, and he from his father. Note that several other families cited in that extract intermarried with the Heselrigg family: for instance, "John son of Gilbert de Babington," "Richard son of Roger Heron soldier."

Some Background, Historical and Ethno-Cultural
We must try to work as best we can, in an impossible task, toward an ever-elusive goal. The world of eleventh-century Europe was different from anything any of us have experienced. It is relatively easy to talk about at least some of the differences; but that is far, far short of having any real experience of any part of that eleventh-century world.

Well, is it? The fact of the matter is, since none of us has actually *lived* in any part of that world, we lack a measuring stick of "experienced world" that would be reasonably fair to that world yet close enough to our own that we could understand the comparisons. Of course, always we must begin where we stand. What we can do reasonably well is to draw up some lists of differences—those that we know about with high confidence, those that we have reason to think are likely, and those that can only be treated as conjectures from the differences that we know with confidence. The lists could be quite long, even the first one. Our world is populated by hordes of material things, many of which we take for granted. Make your own list of material items in your world, your personal world and the broader world beyond about which you have confident knowledge. Amazingly long, isn't it? Yet I see you've left off thumb screws (in our world as well as theirs), paper clips (no, not of theirs; they rarely used paper), tin boxes (yes, they had them, too, but few did; they were expensive); oh, and electrons, quarks, quark-gluon plasma, red corpuscles, amygdalas (part of the structure in our brain, not the nut referenced in Greek), a seventh planet from the sun (for that matter, the notion that the sun rather than earth is the locus from which planets are measured), a machine that pulses light in intervals measured in yoctoseconds (that's a trillionth of a *trillionth* of a second), steam engines, gasoline, moldboard plows, elevators, steel, polyvinyl chloride, and on and on. However long your list when you give up the task—and it is surely incomplete—very nearly all of those things did not exist in eleventh-century Europe. Many of the items mentioned just above, you might protest, *did* exist in the eleventh century—electrons, etc.—but the people alive then just did not know about them. Yes, *we* think that. But they did not. They had no means, no vocabulary, by which to experience them. Moreover, so far we have concentrated on material objects and the corresponding names (words) and concepts. What of beliefs more generally? This becomes especially tricky when we consider beliefs covered by words seemingly the same then and now. Words such as "God" and "evil" and "truth" and "justice" are obvious instances. But there are many, many others: "safe," "cause," "distant," "obedient," and "same" are just a handful; and there are phrases as well, such as "less than nothing" and "lord of the manor" and "phlegmatic character." Comparisons across such an expanse of time as ten centuries are an exercise partly futile, partly treacherous, but also partly inescapable. Under such conditions the severe paucity of information about Roger and his eleventh and early twelfth-century descendants can easily be looked upon as an opportunity for the proverbial lemonade from a lemon. So much then can be fabricated. We must resist that temptation.

    The world Roger entered on that October day of 1066 was very small, though probably not as small as the world he left. After all, he was now a knight in a conquering army, which meant that he had traveled far from home, surely for the first time at this distance. Even had he traveled days within (and perhaps to) Normandy in order to answer the duke's call to raise an army, he almost certainly had come of age within a short compass. That was true of very nearly everyone. A journey of more than four dozen miles was difficult, expensive, often dangerous (disease, injury, brigandage, etc.), and if without horse or oxcart (added expense) very slow. Think of the expense as due not only to provisions along the way but also to labor missing from the person's home production in agriculture. Likewise, that of the horse or ox and cart. Unless a princely figure, the traveler was rarely if ever on a leisurely excursion to survey the countryside. For nearly everyone, geography was measured in small circles. A conquering duke, now king of an expanded realm, had been surveying in much larger circles, however, and Roger no doubt was appreciative of that fact. Where in this new realm would be *his* place? He learned the answer to that question; or his son or sons did, if he did not survive to see the reward of loyal service. We do not know the answer. All we know is, first, from "familial memory," that Roger was awarded some land in Northumberland (Northumbria)—although another version says rather, or also, in Cumberland (Cumbria), a matter that will be addressed later—and, second, from written records long maintained in the Public Record Office, that a man recorded as "William de Herselrig" held a grant of land in Northumberland as early as 1187 (or as the calendar was then kept, 33 Henry 2).[15] That is the earliest date at which a member of the family has been located anywhere by official record—in other words, 121 years, or three, perhaps four generations, after Hastings.[16]

Why Northumberland? By inference, one can guess that the assignee, whether Roger or a son, was known for loyalty and stalwart character. Northumberland was far away from Hastings and London, and this "north country" was still hotly contested by various groups. On the other hand, one could also guess that the outpost was of relatively little importance to the king: if this Heselrig man and his minions could hold it, so much the better; but if not, well, it *was* far away. Finally, a third factor is plausible: if Roger was a Norman or a Frank by parentage, he (or his son) would perhaps have been seen as having a better chance of winning some alliances and allegiance among the native population of Northumberland soon after Hastings. It is this factor that is to be considered here both as context and as background. Contrary to popular thought, England in 1065 had not been a land only of Anglo-Saxons, plus large pockets (in Cornwall, in Wales, and in Scotland) of Celtic refugees from conquests by the Angles and Saxons who had arrived from Germany five centuries before Hastings. A quick review of some invasions and battles will be useful.

A couple of centuries after the arrival of Angles (from a part of present-day Germany that is directly southeast of Denmark) and Saxons (mainly from lower Saxony) sea-faring Norsemen known as Vikings began their explorations and conquests of territory. Vikings were in the Faroe Islands (between Norway and Iceland, almost due north of Scotland) by c800; by the late 800s they had settled the Orkney Islands (10 miles north of the Scottish mainland). Danes and Norse had invaded and ruled eastern England between the rivers Thames and Tees (see the map dated 878 in Exhibit 1.6, below), and were marauding the northwest

---

[15] The transcription reads "Herselrig," not "Heselrig," but there is reason to think the difference was due to error, by scribe or by transcriber. We will return to this case in the next chapter.

[16] Three generations is a stretch. Assume Roger was 25 in 1066 and survived to sire a male heir at age 45 (1086), who survived to sire a male heir at 45 (1131), who survived to age 56 in 1187; all possible, certainly, but unlikely. Assume rather that Roger sired a male heir at age 35 (1076, who sired a male heir at 35 (1111), who sired a male heir at 35 (1146), who sired a male heir at 35 (1181); the last was fourth generation from Roger but only six years old in 1187, too young to have been the landholder. The probable sequence is somewhere between those.

coast of France (Francia, a name derived from the Frankish people). In 911, by treaty with Charles III, king of western Francia, a Norse nobleman remembered as Rollo (c846-c931) gained control of lands that took their name (Normandy, because settled by so many "Normans," a contraction of "Norseman"). One of his great-great-great-grandsons was Guillaume, duke of Normandy—after 1066 known in England as William the Conqueror and William I, king of England.

During the early 1000s a prince of Denmark, later known as Cnut (or Canute) the Great, gained the throne in England, thus expanding the Danish lands of Britain. Cnut ascended to the Danish throne in 1018 and ruled as emperor of a North Sea Empire (Denmark, England, Norway, part of Sweden) until his death in 1035, after which the empire fragmented. A generation later, Harald Hardrada, king of Norway, failed in his efforts to reclaim Cnut's vast domain. In the meantime, England's throne had reverted to an Anglo-Saxon line, in the person of Edward the Confessor. When Edward died in January 1066, Harald Hardrada invaded northeast England. He was killed at the Battle of Stamford Bridge (east Yorkshire) on 25 September 1066, by the Anglo-Saxon army of the man who had just succeeded to the English throne, Harold Godwinson. Anglo-Saxon by main descent, Godwinson was a relative of Cnut by affinal descent; his mother was Cnut's sister-in-law. It was Godwinson who had the misfortune of confronting the Norman duke, Guillaume, at Hastings less than a month after prevailing at Stamford Bridge. Godwinson had known of the impending arrival of the Normans in the south. While preparing that defense, he learned of the Norwegian invasion and rushed to repel Hardrada's force. Having defeated the invaders in the north, he then rushed back to the southeast to repel the second invasion, all within a span of little more than three weeks.

In sum, the presence of Norse influence in much of Britain was pronounced long before duke Guillaume and his Normans arrived, and it lasted long thereafter. Prior to Hastings much of eastern England was taxed for tribute to the Danes, to keep them at bay. This tax was known as the Danegeld. King William I retained the Danegeld even though the Danes had ceased to be a threat; indeed, at times he increased its rate. Record of payment of Danegeld appears in the pipe roll for Northumberland in the fourteenth year of the reign of Henry II (i.e., 1168), though it soon disappeared. An even greater continuance of the Norman influence occurred as the royal lineage of England, of course, in successive monarchs. At least as important as that, however, was the Norman influence in instruments of governance, the organization of territory, and the expansion—slow though it often was, sometimes reversing—of means of sovereignty. The famous Magna Carta of 1215,

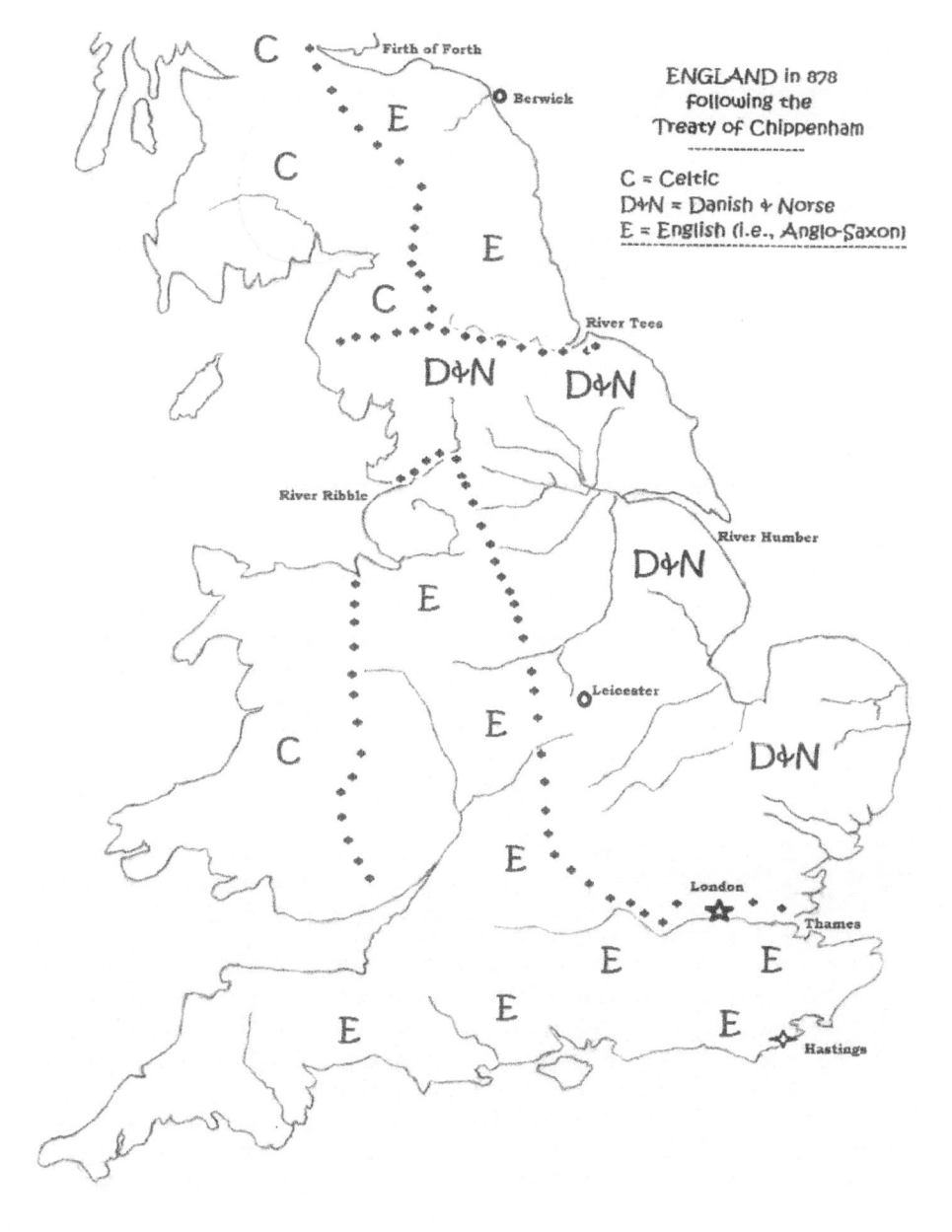

Exhibit 1.6. Map of England, 878

for instance, was due largely to the efforts of some Norman-descended barons. During the Second Barons War against Henry III, Simon de

Montfort, a prominent baron, called together a parliament in 1265 that operated by principles similar to those of the Norse tradition of general assembly (i.e., the *althingi*). The man who defeated the uprising, Henry's son and heir, later adopted much of that design in founding what became known as the Model Parliament of Edward I, 1295.

The map displayed above as Exhibit 1.6 illustrates the main ethnic geography of Britain, south of the Firth of Forth, in the year 878, following the Treaty of Chippenham (also known as the Treaty of Wedmore), a legendary agreement between Alfred, Anglo-Saxon king of Wessex, and Guthrum, leader of Viking forces, after the latter's defeat by Alfred. Guthrum's followers, mainly Danish and Norse, agreed to remain in the areas of East Anglia and East Mercia, plus an extension to the west and Morecambe Bay, north of the river Ribble. This was the territory known as the region of Dane Law (i.e., Danelaw). To the north and along the eastern coast up to the Firth of Forth lay territory of the old Kingdom of Northumbria (which the mapmaker labeled as "English," i.e., Anglo-Saxon). To the west lay Celtic territory of the Strathclyde and Galloway. Wales, too, was Celtic. The mapmaker described the far southwest as "English," even though pockets of a Celtic population remained in Cornwall (then called "West Wales"). King Alfred's territory of Wessex (i.e., "western Saxon") included that southwestern peninsula and lands up to the river Ribble ("English Mercia"), plus the land south of the river Thames.

Place names can be clues to demographic history of places, but they can also mislead if taken uncritically. The name "Mercia," for example, might suggest the English word "mercy," but in fact the proper noun is a Latinized version of an Old English word meaning "people of the border," while the common English noun ("mercy") derives from a Latin word meaning "price paid" or "wages." Likewise, one might scan across maps of the old region known as the Danelaw and see very few place names that "look Nordic." But, aside from the fact that Nordic and Old English languages have common roots (such that words that "look English" could have derived from Nordic words), there is another factor at play: Anglo-Saxons came along after the Danes and restored older names of places or assigned new ones. There are Latin roots around— one of the most often cited instances being the Roman fortified town "Londinium," which after c500 gained the Anglo-Saxon "Lundenburh" (London fort) plus a new settlement called "Lundenwic," the suffix coming from the Latin "vicus" and both meaning "trading town." Norman-French, the language of duke William and his followers (or most of them), was far less Gallic than Frankic in vocabulary, and thus closer to the Nordic and Germanic languages. Linguistic evolution resulted in lots of names that do not immediately disclose their roots in Frankish culture. For example, the names "Lewis" and "Louis," usually broadly considered English and French, respectively, can be traced back to "Ludwig" and "Clovis," thence to the Frankic "Chlodowech," the name of the late fifth-century king more often remembered as Clovis I, who unified all of the Frankic peoples into a single kingdom in the Merovingian dynasty which lasted until the time of Rollo in Normandy. By the same token, some famous names of Scottish history, such as Robert le Bruce and John Balliol, are often thought of as "French" because of the common spelling, when in fact they, too, had Norman roots—cousins, one might say, of duke William.

"Came Down from Scotland"?
Speaking of Scotland, there is an alternative account of the arrival of the family in England. Far less specific than the one reported for our man Roger, it consists only of one simple clause, really just a bald assertion: "the family came down from Scotland." Date of arrival is unsaid. Point of origin in Scotland, whether geographic or ethnic (or both), is left to one's imagination. Likewise, point of first settlement in England. So lacking in specifics, the account can hardly be analyzed in its own terms. But it must be addressed, if only in the end to set it aside.

There are a couple of circumstantial factors that add some plausibility to the assertion.[17] First, as mentioned already, the earliest official record of the family's geographic settlement dates from the 1100s and has them in an area of Northumberland that is very close to the present-day border between Scotland and England, part of an area known as "the Borders" and long disputed between governments in Edinburgh and London. Second, a century later a sheriff of part of the river Clydesdale region around Lanark was a Hesilrige man, Sir William Hesilrige (whom we will meet at greater length in chapter 3). Never mind that this man was in service to the king of England (Edward I); one could argue that William had been selected by the English court precisely because he was "one of the locals," or was scion of one such family, and thus had a better chance of winning over the populace of Lanarkshire, or at least had a better understanding of its people.

---

[17] Also, there are a few sites in Scotland that carry the Hazlerigg name, but these are almost surely of much later date (see chapter 11 for descriptions).

One might object that "de Hesilrige" surely does not look or sound like a Scottish name. But this objection seems far more convincing to an audience in the United States than to one either in Scotland or in England, because of a certain blend of myth and nostalgia found among a Scottish-ethnophile segment of the US population. The people who in the eleventh and twelfth centuries occupied the territory that is today's Scotland were a mix of different ethnic groups, including some who were known as "English," some who were Norse (i.e., from Scandinavia and close cousins of the Normans of France), and Celtic people known as Gaels, who arrived from Ireland. (The earlier inhabitants, the Picts, had been mostly absorbed by Norse and Gaels by the tenth century.) By the time of the reign of Malcolm III (aka Malcolm Cuthnose), the king of Scotland from 1058 to 1093, the southeastern part of his realm was largely English-speaking, while the north and west of Scotland were outside his realm and mainly Norse and Norse-Gaelic, while Galloway, the southwest, was predominantly Gaelic. After the Norman invasion at Hastings, French-Norman people migrated into Scotland—among them, the "le Brus" family who arrived in Scotland during the early twelfth century and whose progeny included Robert le Brus ("Robert the Bruce"), early fourteenth-century king of Scotland who fought for independence from London. So it is conceivable that the de Hesilrige family arrived in Scotland along with, or prior to, the immigration of the le Brus family. Likewise, whereas the mother of Robert le Brus was a woman from Carrick, part of Gaelic-speaking Galloway, it is conceivable that men of the de Hesilrige family also married Gaelic-speaking women. But evidence in support of this latter speculation is lacking.

Efforts to date the origin of some verbal expression are almost always left open-ended, unless the expression is specifically tied to a datable event or person or other such anchorage in the historical stream. The origin of the claim, "came down from Scotland," cannot be discerned. Nor can the circumstances of its first or subsequent utterances. The earliest known record of it dates no earlier than the nineteenth century. That said, a plausible conjecture is that the claim originated in the aftermath of the English Civil Wars of the mid-1600s, and that it was intended as an insult or perhaps as an expiating deprecation. Various reasons could have conspired to that intention. First, as noted above, the family was involved in the long contest over the Borders, and even though the known record indicates that this involvement was in service to London, not Edinburgh, the southern

English tendency to view their neighbors to the north, regardless which side the Border, as rude and uncivil would have counted against the family. Second, the protestant reformation was about as thoroughgoing in Scotland as in Germany and, thus, far more so than in England, where the church of England established by Henry VIII preserved most of the structure of the Roman church hierarchy and ritual, save for the papacy. This settlement was maintained until the mid-1600s. In Scotland the Presbyterians allowed no bishops, very little ritual, no superordination of kingship over the divinity of churchly matters. When, following the death of Elizabeth I, James VI of Scotland was invited to assume the throne in London as James I, thus uniting the crowns of Great Britain, he was both happy to escape the presbyteries of Scotland and eager to impress upon the English, beginning with the Conference at Hampton Court in January 1604,[18] that he did not welcome similar challenge by England's own breed of dissenters and nonconformists, many of whom (including members of the Hesilrige family) came to be known as Puritans. He *was* and *ever would be* head of the church of England, which gave that confession pride of place throughout his realm. Third, one of those members of the family, Sir Arthur Hesilrige, became known increasingly throughout the land, during the 1640s and 1650s, as not only a Puritan but also an Independent and a nascent republican who had strongly opposed claims by Charles I and who was held by many to have been complicit in the execution of king Charles in 1649. After restoration of the monarchy in 1660, not only the persistent monarchists but also many of those who had been in opposition were quick to try to put such ugly events behind them. In these circumstances, attribution of the "crimes" of members of the Hesilrige family to their having "come down from Scotland" could have been seen as a convenience of polite society.[19]

Whatever the actual origin of the "down from Scotland" claim, the family has openly depicted some sort of connection to Scotland by featuring "the head of a Scotsman" atop a chapeau at the crest of the family arms, as mentioned earlier. Again, the origin of that phrase and reference is obscure. Of interest here is the personal version of the family arms which the 13th Bt, Sir Arthur Grey Hazlerigg, designed during the late 1890s or early naughts (see Exhibit 1.2, bottom right):

---

[18] See chapter 3 of Adam Nicolson's *God's Secretaries* (New York: HarperCollins, 2003).
[19] Several of the events mentioned in this paragraph will be addressed in greater detail in later chapters.

among its distinctive features the most prominent is the size and character of that head. Not only is the head rather larger; it is wrapped with a headband that could signify an "untamed" quality, and the whole of the presentation is atop what appears to be a stylized image of a knight's helmet. We lack any verbal record by the 13th Bt of his intent, but it is easy to read in the design some sort of statement of pride in a "Scottish connection." Was it, however, a reminder of descent, or was it a reminder of early service to the English crown in combat against the Scots? It could have been either. (Or, though unlikely, both.) Fletcher, in his *Leicestershire Pedigrees and Royal Descents* (1887, page 14), reported that the head was "said to be given to one of the family who killed a Scotch [sic] champion in the face of the army, and presented his head to the commander." Fletcher also reported that an alternate version of the family's arms displays at top "a woman's head, couped at the shoulders, her hair dishevelled" (see Exhibit 1.3). Note that Fletcher's locution is careful to avoid suggestion that he vouched for either of these references, and he declined to give sources (perhaps Charles Maynard Hesilrige, brother of the 11th Bt).

Fletcher's account of the male head is almost surely a reference to William Wallace, who killed Sir William Heselrig when the latter was serving Edward I as sheriff of Lanarkshire. Perhaps the intended meaning was that Wallace's head was later presented to a member of the family as token of revenge. Perhaps, too, the woman's head was reference to Wallace's alleged soon-to-be wife, who, according to the same legend, the Hesilrige sheriff captured and held as bait to lure Wallace into ambush. (These are still contentious matters to people who identify with Wallace and the "Scottish cause" of that day. We will return to them in chapter 3.) Clearly by this account the presence of the Scotsman's head was not a signal of descent. But because we do not know its origin, or more specifically how old it is, the account does not dictate a choice between interpretations. Fletcher's account might well be the correct one, however. It is worth noting that at some unknown date the family commissioned a bust of the Scotsman (Exhibit 1.7, below). The likeness is similar to the depiction of the head at the crest of the arms in the version associated with Sir Arthur Hesilrige, 2nd Bt (see Exhibit 1.2, top right) and with the quartered arms shown in Exhibit 1.3 (right side).

Exhibit 1.7. Bust of "Head of a Scotsman"

Hastings, the Battle
Battles such as the one at Falkirk, 22 July 1298, which resulted in the defeat of the Scottish army led by William Wallace, would be counted as distinct "wars" but for the fact that they were part of a series of interrelated armed conflicts between the same opposing forces. Thus, the Battle of Falkirk was later remembered as one of the main military contests in what became defined as the First War of Scottish Independence. Other battles were somewhat more isolated events in the larger scheme of politics and sovereignty, and thus could count as separate wars. For the basic definition of "war" is simply "active armed conflict" between opposing parties. In recent times people have come to expect wars to last more than a day or two; rather, a year or two, at least, and sometimes much longer. But for its time, what we remember as the Battle of Hastings could well count as a war, even though it began and ended on the same day. It was a war for sovereign rights to the Kingdom of England, the sitting king having recently died and the claims of at least two of the men aspiring to succeed to the late king Edward's throne having substantial merit. In the event, it proved to be a decisive as well as short war between what we would perhaps call different "nations"—predominantly Anglo-Saxon England versus predominantly Norman forces of an invading duke of Normandy—even though it was also a contest between two men who were kin in the same family tree (via the English king Harold's paternal grandmother), far from the last time two sparks in an old tree would ignite a major war (e.g., World War I).

Although at times during the course of the day the fighting was a close-run contest, by evening Harold's army was spent, bringing to an end the Anglo-Saxon run of kings. It marked the beginning of Norman and then more generally "French" dynasties of monarchy in England—from Norman to Angevin to Plantagenet—and in the process introduced to English soil a system of territorial order, at once economic, political, familial, and personal organization, that properly is called "feudal."

Exhibit 1.8. Field of the Battle of Hastings

The main field of battle is shown above (Exhibit 1.8). One can see in the right background a portion of Battle Abbey, the first version of which the new king William had erected supposedly on the site of the old king's death, depicted in the Bayeux Tapestry as Harold struggling with a arrow to the eye. At the start of battle, mid-morning of the 14th of October, Harold's army was arrayed along the ridge at the top of a hill, while the forces of duke William approached from positions below (even further downhill than can be seen in this photograph). Little is known of either side's planning (and much else, besides), but on the face of it this deployment surely has the markings of a strategic blunder on William's part. Indeed, it could well account for the fact that even though his forces were superior in a number of respects, the two sides were still at draw by early afternoon. Had Harold's subcommanders not made tactical blunders in right wing soon thereafter, William the Conqueror might very well have become William the Conquered.

The battle on this field a few miles north of the village of Hastings unfolded as a clash of two systems of military organization. Harold's army consisted mainly of foot soldiers, centered on his personal bodyguard of "housecarles" (from the Old Norse *huskarl*) and filled out by what amounted to local militias, comprising via the universal levy the "Fyrd," which was led by the local leaders of each shire with their households. Harold instructed them to hold the ridge line at all costs. But discipline was uneven, and some local units, seeing part of the Norman forces in retreat (at first, genuine; then later, it appears, feigned as a tactical manouver), chased after them. William's tacticians, perhaps William himself, saw the breaks as opportunities for the Norman cavalry to achieve what otherwise it had been unable to do. William's forces, by contrast, were a well-disciplined balance of foot soldiers, archers, and cavalry, divided among three component armies: William's Norman army at center (largest of the three), an army of Bretons at left wing, led by a cousin of the ruling count, and an army of Frank and Flemish troops at right wing, led by William fitzOzbern and Eustace of Boulogne. If our Roger was among the knights of one of these armies, he was one of about 2,000 (of whom half were William's Normans). If one of the senior knights, he would have brought with him one or more squires—attendants to assist with horse and equipment, transport, and other duties—as well as some number of foot soldiers from among his followers. If our Roger was there in any capacity, he lived to tell the tale to his heirs. From a quarter to a third of William's forces did not survive (at rough guess). Chronicles of the battle agree that casualties were much greater on the other side, hardly surprising since they lost their king and the entire contest, as many of the victors still had that great advantage known as a war horse.

After Hastings: Northern Resistance to Strong Monarchy
With the October victory in hand, William's immediate task was to pacify the country to his rule. Counting both the surviving members of his army and settlers from Normandy who arrived soon after the battle, he had perhaps 10,000 fellow Normans as aides in the project, amidst one or two

million Anglo-Saxons, Danes, and others. He moved quickly. By 1086, 200 Norman barons had displaced 4,000 thegns (thanes). As the Domesday survey illustrates, pacification of the southern parts of England proceeded rather well. There was resistance in Wales, but it could be isolated and mostly ignored. Because conditions to the north were notably different, William faced stiff resistance in the traditional lands of Northumbria and Cumbria throughout his reign, as did his successors, and, accordingly, the question of a border between England and Scotland as different realms long remained unsettled.

Several factors contributed to the northern resistance. Sheer distance from London was one, of course. Another was that much of the northern land was agriculturally spare and thus of low density in human settlement. Excepting the coastal plains east and west, terrains were hilly-to-mountainous, soils thin, climates cold and windy, and precipitations relatively heavy. Off to the west the lands of Cumbria had usually blended into the lands of Galloway, de facto borders sliding northward or southward depending on strength and tenacity of raiding parties, usually with neither Cumbrians nor Galwegians paying much heed to forces to the east or south owing mainly to the latter's relative indifference.

To the east, however, lay the ancient Kingdom of Northumbria, which stretched from the Humber in the south to the northern boundary of Lothian at the Firth (estuary) of river Forth in the north.[20] A predominantly Anglo-Saxon land until Æthelstan, king of the Wessex (i.e., West Saxons), conquered it in 927, thus uniting all of England under one crown, it maintained a strong sense of independence even then, although with reduced territory. When all other resources of cohesion failed, Northumbrians invoked "the patrimony of St. Cuthbert," the spirit of a mystical cult celebrating the life, deeds, and continued service of a seventh-century Anglo-Saxon monk, Cuthbert, of the monasteries of Lindisfarne and Melrose. To the extent that William I could be said to

---

[20] In other words, from south of York to north of Edinburgh. A couple of technical details are worth noting. A firth is a particular sort of estuary, best denoted by the borrowed word "fjord," which, though sometimes used loosely, applies to an estuary formed by glacial carving and having very steep and rather deep sides. The firth or fjord of the river Firth is a prime example. The Humber, while often mentioned as "river Humber," is in fact a tidal estuary of the rivers Trent and Ouse. To its north lies the East Riding of Yorkshire. (And, appropriately, a third technical note, this one linguistic without geology: there is no "South Riding" of Yorkshire not because of that riverine border but because it would make no sense, for "riding" is devolved from "thriding," a Norse word meaning "a third part.")

have inherited the old Northumbrian kingdom, it was a domain that by Norman standards had known a rather relaxed cohesiveness, but which in more recent times had seen internal strife in wake of Æthelstan's conquest and ensuing contests for control both from without and among the Northumbrian earldom. Skipping most of that history, our attention will begin with the year just prior to Hastings.[21]

To the south of the Humber lay the region of the Danelaw. Suspicion of Danish plans to expand that region had long figured in Northumbrian perceptions of threat (not without reason). Following defeat by Æthelstan, the Northumbrian kingship dissolved and was replaced by the authority structure of an earldom, the holder appointed from without. In 1065 the earl was a man who, though barely Danish in ancestry, was nonetheless viewed in like manner, because he was a leading representative of the Danelaw in eastern England, in particular the land of Yorkshire and of Northumberland. This man, earl Tostig (younger brother of Harold Godwinson), had ruled for a decade, during which time he had managed to alienate virtually every member of the old Anglo-Saxon aristocracy of the region, chiefly by ignoring, even flouting, longstanding customs. One of these customs had been a policy of taxing landholders, the Anglo-Saxon barons, at a rate that was low by southern standards. Earl Tostig imposed taxes at rates considerably higher than had been customary. The combined weight of policies and actions seen as abusive by the barons resulted in a revolt against earl Tostig, which began slightly more than one year before the duke of Normandy invaded England. The barons succeeded locally, and Edward the Confessor, king of England, conceded the victory. One consequence was reduction in the forces of unity, as the barons became individually more competitive toward each other but at the same time remained emboldened in resistance against authority from the south.

When king Edward died and Tostig's brother claimed the London throne as king Harold of England, the northern thegns suspected that Harold would be at least as demanding as Tostig had been. Those concerns were quickly set aside, replaced by a perception of even graver threat after Hastings. King William I stoked that perception when he chose as the new earl of Northumberland a man, Cospig, who had been

---

[21] Of the several accounts of this patch of history in that part of Britain, one of the best, in my judgment, especially from the standpoint of William's and successors' efforts to subdue Northumberland, is William Kapelle, *The Norman Conquest of the North* (Chapel Hill: University of North Carolina Press, 1979). It is a major source of insights for this and the next chapter.

an agent of Tostig. Cospig would be governing in the name of William, king of England. It is fair to ask, as Kapelle did,[22] whether William's choice was primarily from ignorance—of Cospig's background, of Northumberland custom, of recent northern history. The known record offers no answer. However, it is also plausible that William's action was a deliberate message of intent, a warning not only of what his goal was but presumptively of what he was capable of doing to achieve that goal, the subjection of the north.

In any case, before repairing to Normandy to attend his interests in his native land the new king levied the Danegeld in the north as throughout his kingdom—no doubt at least in part as a means of paying off debts to his knights, current accounts for maintenance of the realm, and preparing the first of a chain of castles in defense along the eastern coast against invasion from Norway or Denmark. This chain included, in Northumberland, a "new castle" in 1080 at what became known as the town Newcastle, directed by William's eldest son Robert; at Bamburgh, by 1095, the core of the present castle, which was expanded in 1131; at Alnwick, in 1096; at Morpeth, first a motte-and-bailey in the eleventh century, then rebuilt on the old bailey in the early 1300s; Wark on Tweed (aka Carham castle), in 1136, another motte-and-bailey construction; Warkworth castle, by 1157; and so on until 1550 when Lindisfarne castle was erected on Holy Island. In addition, there had long been problems of brigandage wherever royal power was seen as weak, and this had been especially descriptive of the north. Because Northumberland and parts of Yorkshire had suffered raids from the hills and mountains to their west, as well as from Scottish lands to the north, there was interest in building inland fortifications at passes and other areas of the foothills and along south banks of rivers. While much of this work occurred at later dates, William's intent to plant Norman landholders all through his kingdom surely recognized the need for defensive positions in inland areas as well as along the coast.[23]

---

[22] Kapelle, *The Norman Conquest of the North* (1979), page 106.

[23] Northumberland has been described as a harsh land. Winters can be severe, though more from cold damp winds than from volume of snowfall. But pleasant attractions abound, along the coast as well as inland. The Northumberland Coast Path ambles from Berwick-upon-Tweed southward 64 miles to Cresswell (21 miles north of Newcastle), offering dunes, sandflats, rolling tides, and often a salt-laced wind off the North Sea (which, it has been said, can scour the whiskers from your face); some days clouds shoot past at brisk pace, other days bright sunshine, and still others a grim greyness that hides the boundary between sea and air. Small hotels (e.g., the Blue Bell in Belford, an early favorite) and bed-and-breakfast accommodations can be found all along the route.

Rebellion quickly followed the Danegeld levy. William's response was calculated, harsh, enduring, unambiguous. It has long been known as "the harrying of the north"—in particular, in Yorkshire, Durham, and the southern part of Northumberland, lands that he had not been able to plant successfully with his own Norman loyalists in place of Anglo-Saxon landholders. During the winter of 1069-70 those lands were scoured of crops, stored harvests and seeds, livestock, and many dwellings. His action was designed not merely to "send a message"—though it surely did that—but more pointedly to reduce agricultural means of sustenance, removing both targets of raiders and means of living off the land by any invading force, as well as weakening the bases of economic and thus political power of the Anglo-Saxon thegns. To harry is to lay waste; and that is precisely what William's army accomplished. Immediate consequences included increased rates of starvation, disease, mortality, and migrations of population. Longer term, many peasants fled or entered into slavery as means of survival. Baronial estates were impoverished. The economic base of towns as well as countryside remained in much reduced state for many years. Another fifteen winters passed and still the northern part of Yorkshire was so devastated that Domesday surveyors ignored it, along with Northumberland.[24]

The immediate period of harrying was followed by what Kapelle called "government by punitive expedition."[25] Perhaps during these expeditions, William's knights were encouraged by promised or at least imagined awards of this or that confiscated estate, not an unusual motivator in the scheme of "pacifying" a countryside. But if so, they probably understood from what they saw that much effort would be required to restore most estates, to say nothing of gaining and maintaining peace. No doubt the campaign delayed William's re-assignment of northern estates to Normans. In the shorter run both William and his son and successor, William II (aka William Rufus, a reference apparently to his ruddy complexion), were content to tolerate Anglo-Saxon barons and, at first, an Anglo-Saxon earl, so long as these latter maintained at least a semblance of loyalty. In 1095, after another revolt in the north—this one led by a *Norman* earl, no less—William II vanquished the uprising, abolished the earldom, and thereafter appointed sheriffs as royal governors of Northumberland.

---

[24] Similarly, the northern part of Lancashire was ignored, along with Cumberland, not because of systematic razing but because the lands were relatively poor and in some areas subject to frequent brigandage from the north.
[25] Kapelle, *The Norman Conquest of the North* (1979), page 120.

William I had begun the process of planting a Norman aristocracy in Northumberland as early as 1080, by creating a *network of fees* extending north from the New Castle on the river Tyne to Morpeth, Roxbury, and Wooler. A map of the area, based on part of a more detailed map constructed by Kapelle, is shown below (Exhibit 1.9).[26]

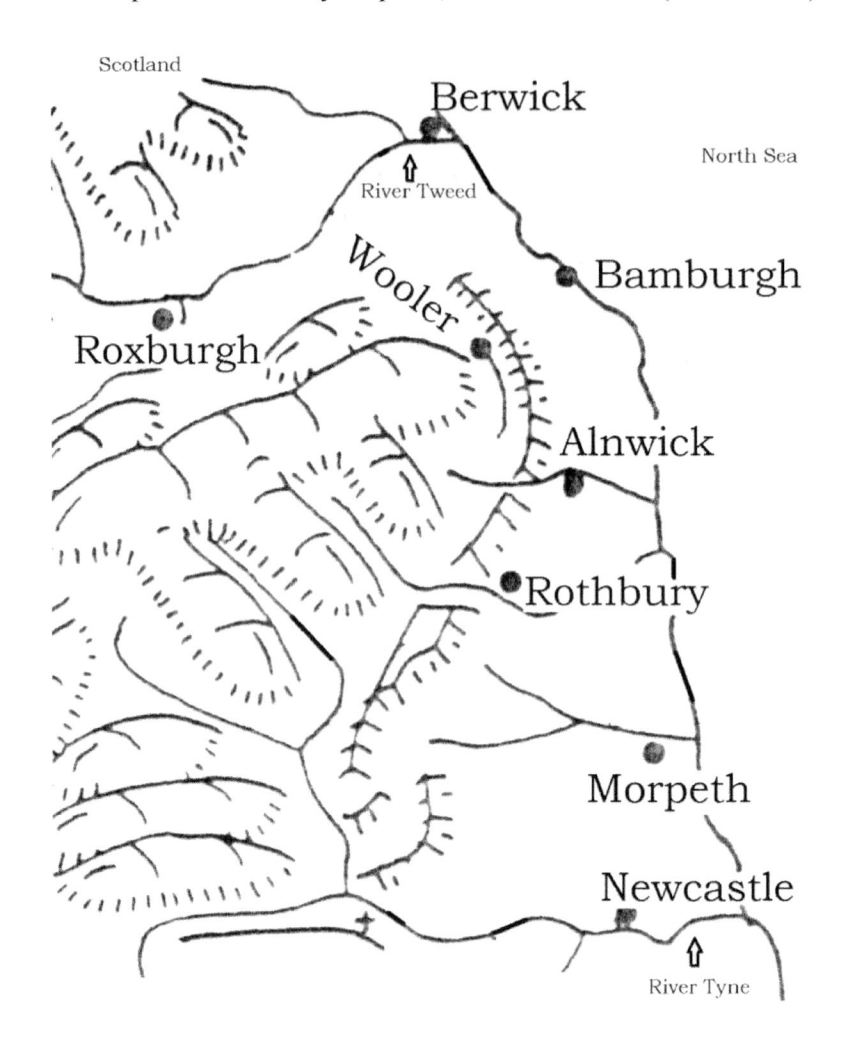

Exhibit 1.9. Early Norman Outposts in Northumberland

The phrase, "network of fees," italicized in the sentence above, prompts an excursion into the feudal system of landholding, which the

---

[26] Kapelle, *The Norman Conquest of the North* (1979), page 143.

Normans introduced into England. Normans sought to impose a centralized organization, with London as capital city; but as was their usual practice, they adapted and incorporated existing forms wherever possible. One prominent example has been cited already, king William's recognition of Durham's longstanding exceptional status by according it the standing of a "county palatine."[27] Another prominent example is that shires in which Anglo-Saxon influence remained strong generally retained their internal organization in probably "enough land to support 100 households headed by 100 men" (the hundred-men), who collectively formed what might be called a "ruling council." A single hundred consisted of 100 hides, a single hide being the amount of land required to support one household. This amount varied from about 60 to about 120 "old acres" (i.e., 15 to 30 modern acres), depending on the quality of the land. (Note that the referent point of measurement was to concrete material need, not to a more abstract system of units such as we use today.) In shires that fell under Danelaw—Derbyshire, Leicestershire, Lincolnshire, Northamptonshire, Nottinghamshire, and Rutland, even Yorkshire and Northumberland to some extent—the organizational counterpart to the hundred was the "wapentake" (but as in Leicestershire, for instance, the unit reverted to the hundred, as we will see later in discussion of the estate at Noseley in the Gartree Hundred). The Normans were content to allow these and other "local variations" so long as they did not interfere with loyalty to the crown. Norman interest in centralized authority would be pursued, and eventually achieved, by a variety of means, some of them direct but many indirect.

In the Norman system political authority or rulership, economy, and territory were all organized by a set of principles known as manorialism, which gradually invaded and dominated territories that had traditionally been organized as hundreds, wapentakes, or otherwise. An estate in land (a phrase to which we will return shortly) would itself be a manor ("manorial estate"), if dominant in an area, with other "dependent estates" falling under its sway. Attached to a manor, and to some dependent estates, would be one or more vills (villages, hamlets, etc.), tenements, a chapel or church, and other facilities such as a mill or waterworks. The "lord of a manor" stood likewise in a hierarchy of lordship, extending up to the monarch.

---

[27] As mentioned above, palatine standing was granted also to Chester and (later) to Lancashire, the understanding being in each case that the earl would have a relatively free hand in defending against incursions from Wales (Chester) and from Cumbria and Galloway as well as Wales (Lancashire).

Now let's return to "network of fees": the word "fee" derives from "fief," which refers to a feudal landholding. To say that the system of landholding was "feudal" is to say that a hierarchy of duties and responsibilities was involved, extending from an "overlord"—ultimately a monarch as overlord—down to the lowest rank of person attached to a piece of land. All land in a territory of monarchy was ultimately the monarch's domain. Parcels of the monarch's domain would be granted, assigned, to subordinate persons. Strictly speaking, it was an *estate* in land, not the land itself, that was granted (and thus can be regarded, in our terms, as an "owned" parcel within certain limits). The most common sort of grant was a *fee*—more specifically a *fee simple*. By accepting the grant of estate in a parcel of land, the grantee is obligated to specified service to the estate overlord, an example being performance in service as a knight (a person with horse and required equipment, skilled in the arts of combat not only for himself and his fellow knights but also in concert with ground troops such as archers and halberd-bearing foot soldiers). In establishing the network of fees northward from Newcastle, William was building a sequence of communication posts and defensive positions that would link into the chain of castles. Knights who had their own retinues of retainers—younger knights and foot soldiers but also masons, carpenters, husbandmen, and the like—were logical choices to build and maintain these outposts on the southeastern coastal plains of Northumberland. As it happens, two of the three outposts named above, Morpeth and Wooler, among the first of the network begun by William I, were also among the earliest known locations of men of the Hazlerigg family. If Roger and/or a son or sons were among them, they remain silent testaments to endurance under circumstances that surely were difficult. (But then at least Roger, by legend, had endured that fast-paced battle in southeastern England, no easy feat.) Indeed, the names of those who materially built, guarded, and expanded those early outposts are unknown in general, not just in this family.

We must remember that, while our present attention has been on Northumberland, the troubles of the northern parts of his new kingdom were far from William's main concern, which was to secure the country south of the Humber. In one sense, he accomplished this remarkably fast, replacing Anglo-Saxon with Norman families in the main baronies of England. That hardly solved all of his problems of authority and power, however. The new barons pursued interests of their own, typically interests of each to extend his own family's land holdings and thus wealth and power, both relative to each other and relative to the centralizing pressure of royal authority. Barons were generally willing to support some level of taxation when it was to advantage of their own interests—for instance, coastal defenses—but they were quick to protest "undue" taxation, whether it was seen as undue in frequency or in level or in both, and they were quick also to discern and protest favoritism, as, for example, when William was thought (sometimes correctly) to levy the Danegeld more heavily against some than against others, or to relieve a few of the obligation altogether. Furthermore, William remained duke of Normandy. In many ways Normandy remained his home. While he could converse in English and agreed to be known as king William of England, the official language of his court was French. He spent much time at home in Normandy, tending interests there, while leaving his kingdom to the authority of his regent. On the one hand, this arrangement could lessen the force of his royal presence in England, leaving the stronger barons to work their own interests to greater advantage relative to their weaker compatriots. On the other hand, the absence threatened to reduce what the barons saw as the proper authority of the monarchy. The absence also left William less sensitive to flows of information, which could make him seem out of touch and even disinterested in English affairs. One example was the revolts of some earls in 1075, ostensibly because one of them sought a marriage that William refused to sanction.

Threats can arrive from members of one's own family as well as from outside, and because of proximity of contacts such threats can be, and be suspected to be, even more serious. During the early years of his reign William left his half-brother, Odo, now earl of Kent, as regent when William was in Normandy. Odo had interests of his own, of course, and while he was successful in leading rebuff to the earls' revolt in 1075, he continued his practice of acquiring many prized estates in southern England for himself. This had aroused resentment, which grew only more intense with the earls' defeat. The following year charges were brought against Odo, and he was tried successfully for offenses against the crown. The earls were appeased, William had reasserted his power and authority, but it was clear that the contest would continue. At one point, William was challenged by his own eldest son, Robert Curthose. As Shakespeare later depicted in more than one play (e.g., *King Lear*), a king, a father, can be "too slow to die."

Eleven years later king William *was* dead. He had decreed that elder son, Robert, would succeed as duke of Normandy; third son, William Rufus, would become king of England. (The second son,

Richard, had died c1075.) As demonstrated by the Rebellion of 1088, arrangements that appear to be fair from one point of view can be seen as quite unfair from another. This one did not satisfy all parties. Probably from the father's point of view, elder son got the better deal: Normandy was rich territory and secure; England, still a brewing kettle. But it seems Robert was disappointed that he had not inherited both domains. From the standpoint of barons who held estates in both domains, moreover, the settlement was less than satisfactory because of clouded fealty: to whom did they owe principal allegiance? How could one satisfy two courts, especially when rivalry between them was clear to most? This rebellion was led by Odo and another half-brother of the dead king, Robert, Count of Mortain. Their object was to unite behind Robert Curthose, overthrowing king William II. The rebellion failed. Invasion from without failed to materialize. William II prevailed. He lived another dozen years, and the English throne passed to his younger brother, Henry I.

~ 2 ~
The Borders

If the legend of Roger de Heselrig, knight in the Conqueror's army at Hastings, is based in fact on main particulars, he surely was not high in the queue—not to say lacking favor entirely with William I or William II, but nonetheless short of favor of an estate in the south of England or even in the Midlands. Whatever the facts of the man, the first record of the family, or at least the first record by recognizable name, appears in the far north, the part of England that passed back and forth between sovereignties of England and Scotland, when not neglected by both and left to memories of the ancient Kingdom of Northumbria. The title of this chapter, "The Borders," is a none-too-subtle reference to standing: when estates in land were handed out, our family's small portion came with geopolitical contentions already made and awaiting new contenders. Here we will try to sort through the possibilities of those assignments, relying on family legend as point of departure but hewing closer and closer to written records as they become available in time.

The Battle for Sovereignty
The existing record of inhabitants in the northern part of England during the eleventh and twelfth centuries is extremely thin, so it should be no surprise to read that only a single record has been found of a member of the Hesilrige family during that period in Northumberland, Cumberland, and Westmoreland. As Kapelle summarized from his own detailed investigations,[1] as of 1070 "the castles at York were the de facto northern limit of William's reign, and fifty miles of empty countryside separated them from Durham," which borders Northumberland south side. Indeed, "there is no evidence whatsoever that North Tynedale"—that is, the north side of the valley of river Tyne—"was part of England until the reign of Henry I [1100-1135] at the earliest and more probably the reign of Henry II." Only with the English reign of Edward I did eventual political settlement begin. Considerable progress was made during the reign of Henry I, but following his death civil war broke out.

The period between the two Henrys was royally tumultuous, because lines of succession were in flux, as were relations between

---
[1] William E Kapelle, *The Norman Conquest of the North* (Chapel Hill: University of North Carolina Press, 1979), pages 122, 127, 130.

England and Normandy. Henry I was himself younger brother of William II. Clear enough, in that; and his own son, William, was his obvious heir and successor—until he died in a ship disaster. Henry I then named his daughter, Matilda ("Maud"), as his heir. In the meantime, Matilda had done well for herself, having married the emperor of the Holy Roman Empire. Following his death she accepted the marriage, arranged by her father, to Geoffrey, count of Anjou,[2] by whom she had the first of her children, Henry of Anjou (later, England's Henry II). Still styled "the Empress Matilda," she carried considerable standing—although, as it turned out, more in France than in England. The beneficiary was Stephen, third son of Stephen, count of Blois, and Adela, daughter of England's William I. Young Stephen was well known in London, as he was reared by his uncle, Henry I. Initially, Stephen agreed to support Matilda's claim to the English throne. But upon the death of Henry I in December 1135, England's nobility became more and more resistant to the idea of an Angevin taking the throne. Stephen, by now in his mid-40s, made his counterclaim with much support, and assumed the throne. Proving to be a weak leader, however, he failed to consolidate that support. In 1138 Matilda's half-brother, Robert, earl of Gloucester, raised an army against Stephen, and Matilda invaded England the following September. Stephen sought to accommodate Matilda, as she gained control of the western part of England, from her seat in Bristol. But civil war ensued. This became the period long remembered as "the Anarchy." Forces gradually arrayed against her, however, and with Stephen prevailing, she returned to France in 1148. Soon thereafter, her son, Henry of Anjou, matured, and in January 1153 he invaded England. Stephen relented, signing a treaty that declared Henry to be his successor. Thus began, with Henry II in 1154, the Angevin house of kings in England.

Main events of the period of anarchy were centered in the south, but effects were felt in the north, mainly as London's lack of attention. Advances made by Henry I stalled. If members of the Hesilrige family gained advantage from those advances, holding on to them would have been difficult. The record is silent. Only with the reign Henry II do we see concrete evidence that the family had gained standing anywhere in

---

[2] Anjou was a part of France, then about equal in size to Normandy, its neighbor to the north. Angevins (as Anjou's inhabitants were called), a predominantly Gallic people, had long been rivals of the Normans, often feeling as prey to Normans (and to their neighbors to the west, Bretagne) as predator. This rivalry would become a factor as well in England.

England, and this was in Northumberland. Then the record becomes nearly as thin again, as the son and successor of Henry II, Richard I, grows pre-occupied with the Crusades during his short reign (1189-1199). Richard's brother, John, was perhaps less venal than the Robin Hood legend depicts, but his behavior during his brother's long absence had not endeared him to the nobility, and his seventeen years as king (1199-1216) were marked by contest with powerful barons who were intent on fashioning checks against excessive monarchal power (e.g., the Magna Carta of 1215). On the other hand, the long reign of John's son, Henry III (1216-1272) glows by comparison for its stable organization of lines of authority across the expanse of England's royal realm, and once again the public record becomes thicker for the north as well as the south. Even during this reign, the northern pipe rolls contain many tax accounts for men who are identified only as (e.g.) "John the son of Robert," and judging from the sums reported it seems clear that some of these men held small estates in land. Which if any of them were Heselrig men cannot be said.

We do know of one man, William de Heselrig, who was prospering as head of a manorial estate in the time of Henry II. We know of another man, also named William de Heselrig, who was prospering as head of a manorial estate in the time of Henry III. These two figures—almost certainly too far apart in time to be the same person, but perhaps father and son—will serve as principals of discussion in this chapter, buttressed by conjectures of "what must have happened" during the gap of two, possibly three, generations, from 1187 to 1248, between records.

From the time of Edward I (son of Henry III), the record becomes more revealing. That will topically furnish the next chapter. Here, we will make the most that we can of the meager records of the twelfth and early thirteenth centuries for two northern territories, Northumberland and Cumberland, each of which figures in legendary claims about the family's benefits of early royal grants of land. We will begin with Cumberland, mostly in order to set it aside. Then the remainder of the chapter will describe early land holdings in Northumberland.

Cumberland Sites

London did not succeed in subduing Cumberland until 1092, when William II achieved a major victory and settled the area around Carlisle with Norman colonists. But even then, Norman sovereignty was frequently disputed, and raids from the north were to continue sporadically for many years to come. During the civil war between forces for Stephen and forces for his cousin, Matilda, Cumberland reverted to Scottish control. Henry II regained control in 1157 and formed two counties: Carliol (later, Cumberland) and Westmoreland. During the reign of his grandson the border between Scotland and England was fixed by the Treaty of York (1237), although this did not stop raids back and forth.

    Did the family gain any early estates in Cumberland? Evidence for it, if any ever existed, has seemingly disappeared. Some old family memories report that the first estates awarded to Roger and/or his descendants were in Cumberland.[3] The only external evidence bearing on that claim consists in some place names, discussed below. The odds are that some of these sites gained their nominal references ("Hazelrigg Beck," "Hazelrig," etc.) at a later, probably much later, date. We know that during the civil wars of the mid-1600s Sir Arthur Hesilrige, 2nd Bt, was in the Carlisle area for a time. Indeed, the 1650 act for the maintenance of Parliament's army names him as one of the commissioners for Cumberland (as well as a commissioner also for each of Durham, Northumberland, and Leicestershire). It is possible that the 2nd Bt nominated himself as commissioner for the northern areas, but in any case he was known by ancestry as well as personal interest as someone having knowledge of the Borders. Cumberland was generally royalist during the wars; the 2nd Bt was often on the hunt for good agricultural land that would yield rental income; he might have acquired farms in the area of those sites. It is worth noting that none of the pedigrees that won approval during heraldic visitations of Cumberland and Westmoreland in 1615 and in 1666 mentioned the family surname directly or via marriage.[4] While the pedigree recorded for the Fleming family of Rydale shows marital ties to two Northumberland families having connections also with the Hesilrige family (Fenwick and Collingwood), the seat of Flemings of Rydale, being in Westmoreland, was a bit distant from the relevant sites in Cumberland. As will be seen in the following discussions, a smattering of evidence suggests that a few of the sites that carry the name "Hazelrigg" might have been connected to the family's surname by one or more persons, whether directly or by

---

[3] As we saw in the previous chapter, this claim was repeated by William Betham, in his *The Baronetage of England, or the History of the English Baronets*, etc. (London: William Miller, 1801), volume 1, page 260.

[4] See Joseph Foster's edition of *Pedigrees Recorded at the Heralds' Visitations of the Counties of Cumberland and Westmoreland ... 1615 and 1666* (Carlisle: Charles Thurnam and Sons, 1891).

marital kin. However, the evidence suggests that most, if not all, of the sites were assigned a place name for botanic-topographic reason, and well before the seventeenth century.[5]

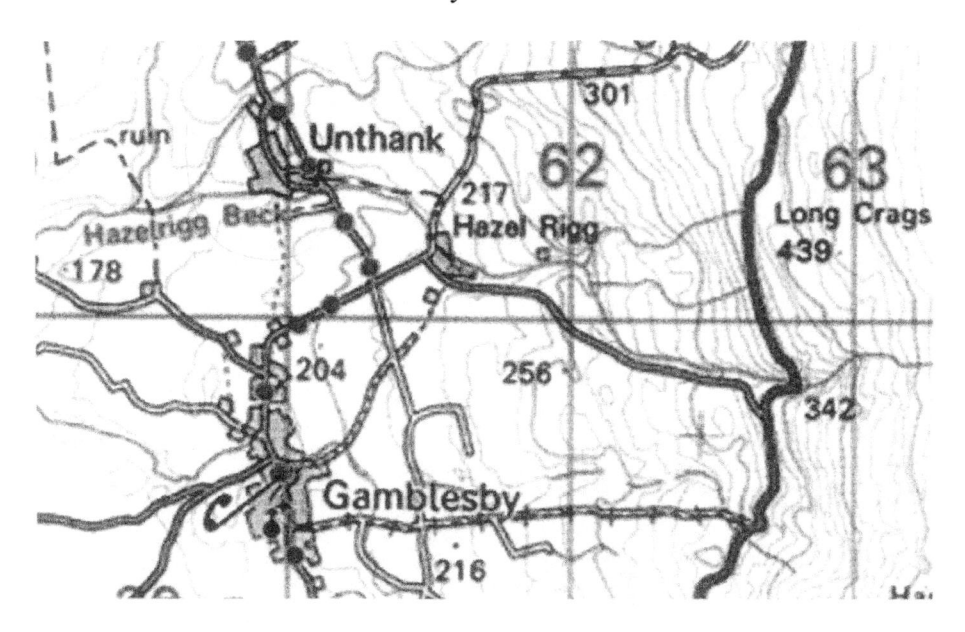

Exhibit 2.1. Hazelrigg Beck and Hazel Rigg, near Unthank, Cumberland

Three of the named sites fit within the compass of a small area, probably no more than three miles in diameter. By present-day maps—in particular, the fine-gauge Ordnance Survey map of Cumberland (see Exhibit 2.1)—the place to begin is a small stream, Hazelrigg Beck, which flows by the north side of Glassonby, emptying into the river Eden from a small watershed of the crags to the east, the Pennine range, which there probably have a maximum elevation of no more than 2,000 feet. The stream shows clearly on old maps of the area (e.g., Saxton's map of 1576) but without name, as the scale of his endeavor allowed room for few words. Hazelrigg Beck collects three feeder streams which converge at a point about 0.7 mile east-southeast of the village of Unthank, which is north of Gamblesby and east of Kirkoswald.[6] Just to the west of that

---

[5] Having visited these sites, and the general area of Cumberland, on several occasions, I can attest that hazel shrubs and trees are anything but rare in hedge rows and along streams.

[6] "Unthank" is from the Old English *unpance*, meaning "without leave" or permit, as in "interloper." There are at least ten places of that name in England; and four in Scotland. It is also a family surname, apparently without kinship to the Hazlerigg family.

point of convergence, on the north side of Hazelrigg Beck, is an old site, now barely a ruin, called Hazelrig. It is rarely denoted on recent maps, and when it is (as on the map in Exhibit 2.1), the name is given as Hazel Rigg—perhaps reflecting loss of memory that there once was a settled place at that site, now naming literally a "hazel-growing ridge" (a small ridge is there indeed). Older maps record the name as "Hazelrig" and show habitation (e.g., the 1867 OS map of Cumberland; Exhibit 2.2).

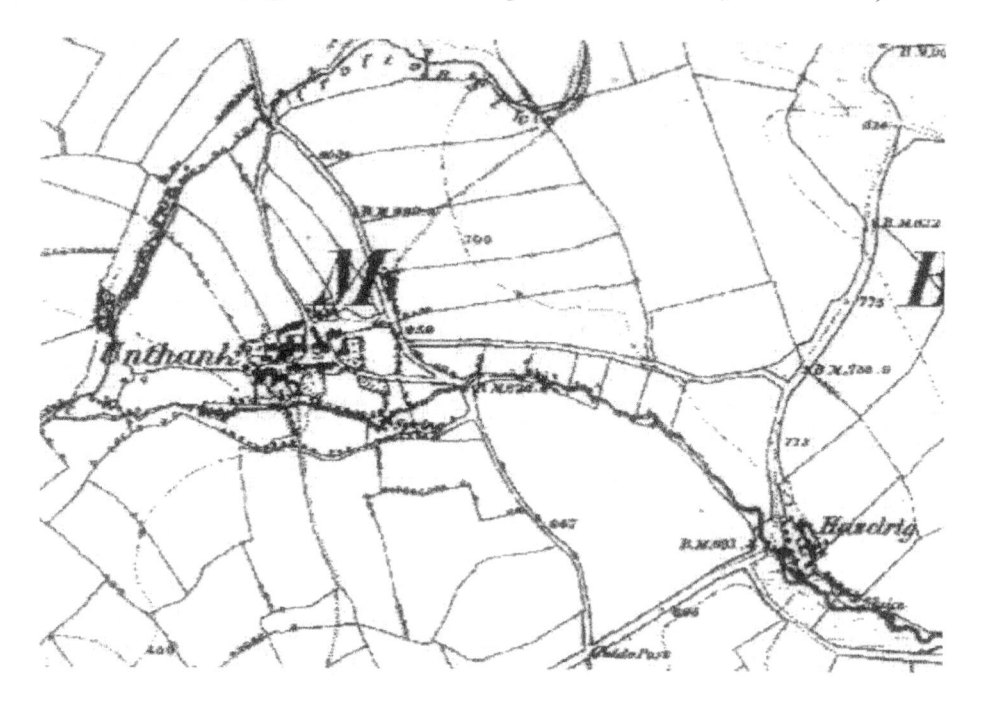

Exhibit 2.2. Hazelrig, near Unthank, Cumberland

A footpath beginning at the site of Hazelrig and extending up into the crags, past Hartside and on toward Twotop Hill, is locally known as Hazelrigg Footpath (see Exhibit 2.3).[7] By usual English standards of today, this counts as rough terrain even in fair weather. Some vistas are long (as in the photograph), sometimes rather bleak but sometimes, as when gorse is in bloom after spring's slow arrival becomes early summer, very lovely.

---

[7] Much of the footpath now looks more like a rough graveled lane. At last inspection, traffic was brisk enough on this and other local footpaths, as well as on the A686 road, to sustain a Hartside Cafe.

Exhibit 2.3. Hazelrigg Footpath near Unthank, Cumberland

Exhibit 2.4. Hazelrigg Cottage, Howscales, Cumberland

The third of the three sites in short compass is west-northwest of Unthank, about two miles overland but four by automobile, at a place called Howscales Cottages, on a lane between Kirkoswald and Renwick. (The lane parallels the south bank of Raven Beck, which runs behind the Howscales property.) Now a self-catering accommodations business consisting of cottages that were converted from old farm buildings, the site dates to its origin as a farmstead in the mid-1600s. One of the five cottages is named Hazelrigg, for reason now obscure, although one local informant believed that the farmstead had once been called Hazelrigg Farm (Exhibit 2.4). This naming would be consistent with two other Cumberland sites (yet to be described). Raven Beck is a tributary of the river Eden, which runs north-south near Kirkoswald. Named as "Church of Saint Oswald," this erstwhile market town lies about 18 miles south-southeast of Carlisle.

Nothing known of the foregoing sites indicates the presence of separate manorial estates. If ever part of a manor, it would have been Gamblesby manor or Glassonby manor, which was at one time held by the Neville family, then by the Dacre family, and then by the Musgrave family. The Hesilrige family was connected to the first two, the first by marriage; so that could account for the naming. If the sites have no connection with Roger de Heselrig, they could have been acquired later as reward for services to the crown. Although separated from the family's several Northumberland estates by the Pennine mountain chain, the physical distance from these sites in eastern Cumberland to the estates held by the family in southern Northumberland is today about 60 miles by most direct route and about 75 miles by a route that misses the mountainous track entirely. Given the dating of the farmstead at Howscales, together with its proximity to Carlisle, that property, probably younger than the settlement near Unthank, could have been due to Sir Arthur Hesilrige, the 2nd Bt.

There is a another Hazelrigg site, located well to the south at Old Town, which is on the B6254 northwest of Kirkby Lonsdale, in the old Mansergh parish, once part of Westmoreland (see Exhibit 2.5, lower right side). Between 1200 and 1226 William Marshall, then of Lancaster, gave as a grant in frankalmoigne to the canons of Cockersand Abbey "all his lands in Manzergh, namely one oxgang of land which John son of Bernard held of the lord Gilbert fitz Reinfred, and ten acres of land in Greenrigg, land called Heselrig, other land called Buth Swarther, ... [etc.,

etc.]."[8] Cockersand Abbey was at the edge of the Sands, southwest of Lancaster (see Exhibit 2.9, below). In 1501 one Thomas Middleton held land at Hesylryg, which has been identified as "Hazelrigg at Terry Bank."[9] Terry Bank was a farmstead located on the west side of the B6254, southwest of Old Town; the dwelling, still known as Hazelrigg, is shown in Exhibit 2.6. Was that land once part of a land grant to a family member? Possibly; but there is no evidence for it. The Middleton dating of 1501 indicates that the property predated the 2nd Bt. The surname spelling is one that appears in Northumberland and Nottingham records of that time and earlier (though orthography is at best very weak evidence of anything beyond itself). The man named Thomas Middleton was perhaps of the Northumberland family, which had connection to the Heselrigs of that shire, but again firm evidence is lacking.

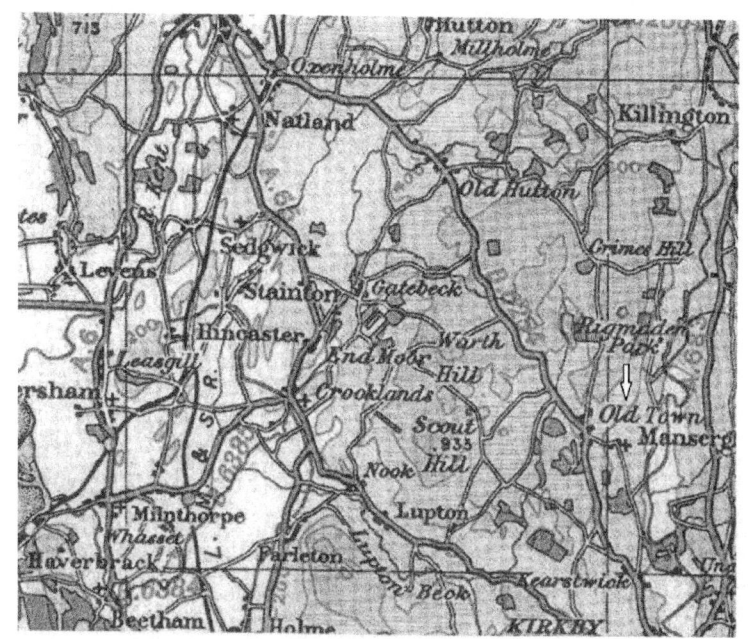

Exhibit 2.5. Old Town, Mansergh, Cumberland

---

[8] The quotation is from pages 1024-1026 of *The Chartulary of Cockersand Abbey of the Premonstratensian Order*, volume III, part II; which is volume 57 of *Remains Historical and Literary Connected with the Palatine Counties of Lancaster and Chester*, new series (Manchester: Chetham Society, 1905). The term "frankalmoigne" refers to a grant of land to an ecclesiastical body without obligation of service such as knightage. After 1290 such grants in England could be made only by the monarch.

[9] William Farrer and John F Curwen, editors, *Records relating to the Barony of Kendale*, volume 2 (Kendal: Cumberland and Westmorland Antiquarian and Archælogical Society, 1924), pages 374-397.

Exhibit 2.6. Hazelrigg at Terry Bank, Cumberland

    A fifth site, located near Newby Bridge, east of Ulverston, is locally known as Hazelrigg Farm, on the west side of Hazelrigg Lane (see Exhibits 2.7 and 2.8). County jurisdiction of this area has switched back and forth; it is now part of Cumberland again. Relevant records are very sparse. A citation dated 1651 for Lancashire refers to "Heslrygge in [Staveley, parish of] Cartmel." Staveley has been a township from at least 1451. An account in the Victoria History of Cumberland reports that Staveley had "no manor nor any noteworthy estate, the whole being held formerly by the customary tenants of the Cartmel canons." This latter reference is to the Cartmel Priory, which was chartered by William Marshall in 1189, on land he had been granted by Henry II a few years earlier.[10] A land reference from the late 1600s indicates that Cartmel included "tenements in Hazelrigg," which suggests the presence of a small vill. The fact that the two families, Heselrig and Marshall, were interconnected via marriages subsequent to William Marshall raises the possibility that the site was named after a member of the Hazlerigg family, but there is no known direct evidence for it. The coincidence of surnames for both this site and the site at Old Town is probably only that,

---

[10] Marshall, later styled "the flower of chivalry," wrote into the charter that Cartmel would only ever be a priory, subject to the Marshall family, never an abbey, which would have put it under the monarch's immediate authority.

coincidence. In any case, an inscription at the entrance to the stone farmhouse reads "Hazelrigg," a comparatively recent spelling of the surname.

Exhibit 2.7. Location of Hazelrigg Farm, near Ulverston

Yet another site identified as Hazlerigg Farm is located east of the site of Cockersand Abbey, near Ellel and Bailrigg. (See Exhibit 2.9: Hazlerigg is at the upper right corner of the map, while the Abbey is at lower left corner, marked by a hollow arrow.) Much of the farmland was sold last century to accommodate a national weather station, known as Hazelrigg Weather Station, as well as later expansion of the campus of the University of Lancaster. The remains consist of a few acres of land, an old barn, and a farmhouse of unknown vintage, on another lane named Hazelrigg (see Exhibit 2.10).

Exhibit 2.8. Main House, Hazelrigg Farm, near Ulverston

      Tracing land holdings is no easier in Lancashire than it is in shires to the north.[11] The earliest known relevant record indicates that the abbot of Leicester held land and tenements in Hazelrigg, among other places in this part of Lancashire, during the late 1200s. Hazelrigg was part of the vill of Scotforth in 1450. Thus, it appears that the place carried the name Hazelrigg (albeit surely by different spelling at that date) long before the 2nd Bt began accumulating landed estates far and wide. Was this site an extension of the Hazelrigg settlement to the north, near Ulverston? Not likely in geographic terms, because of distance. Could it have, in any case, been due to the same William Marshall? Yes, though again, these questions are suggestive; they cannot be answered by determined facts. Further research of relevant records might change that, however.

---

[11] This is an appropriate point at which to acknowledge the recent work of Martin and Jean Norgate, of Portsmouth University, who have greatly improved the organization and accessibility of historical geographies of Cumberland and many other parts of England. Their work has been very valuable, as have their replies to personal inquiries.

Exhibit 2.9. Hazlerigg Farm on Hazlerigg Lane, near Ellel, Lancashire

Exhibit 2.10. Farmhouse, Hazelrigg Farm, near Ellel, Lancashire

Northumberland: Known Estates, Early Records
Once again we begin from a point of ignorance: we do not know how early the family arrived in Northumberland or where in that shire the family maintained its first estate. The earliest known official record of an actual person of the family in all of England is in the *Magnus Rotulus Pipæ* for Northumberland: William de Heselrig is recorded for the year 1187.[12] Even that can be, has been, contested, for the transcriber wrote "Herselrig." The small difference is due almost surely to error by the transcriber from the original roll (many of which were in poor condition—faded, tattered, torn) or error by the original scribe. The fact that no surname "Herselrig" has otherwise been found in English or in Scottish records lends strength to the conjecture that this man was indeed William de Heselrig.

---

[12] John Hodgson, *History of Northumberland*, part 3, volume 3 (Newcastle on Tyne: John Blackwell and John Brunton Falconar, 1835), page 42

NOVA PLAC' 't NOVE CONVENT' p Arnisū de Nevill 't Malgꝰm (Withm*) le vavassur 't Rogm de Batuent de plac̄ foreste de Norhūbland . Gilbt° de Lavall redd comp̄ de x. m̄. q̄ injuste icarc̄avit Petrū 't Adā . In thro vj. m̄ . Et deḃ liij. m̄.—Id vic̄ redd comp̄ de j. m̄. de Sim̄ de Lucre p oblivic̄e placltoꝛ foreste . Et de j. m̄. de Witto de Framelintoñ p eod . Et de j. m̄. de Adū de Herweltoñ p eod . Et de j. m̄. de Gaufr̄ de Wudintoñ . Et de j. m̄. de Ric̄ de Havechille . Et de xx. s̄. de Witto de feugeris . Et de xx. s̄. de Witto de Herselrig p ijusta ip·sonatic̄e Petri 't Ade . Et de j. m̄. de villata de Suintere p nova p̄p̄st'u . Et de j. m̄. de villata de Benleia p wasto bosci . Et de j. m̄. de villata de Cheulingeha p eod . Et de j. m̄. de villata de Esseta . Et de vij. s̄. de fre Osbti de Calea de Fealtoñ p xiij. ac's aveñ . Et de viij. s̄. p xvj. ac's aveñ i villa de Aclinton . Et de j. m̄. de Robto de Forde p ijusta ip·soñ Ade 't Petri . S' ix. li. 't viij. s̄. 't liij. d. In thro libav̄ i xiiij. tatt . Et quiet° est.—Id vic̄ redd comp̄

Exhibit 2.11. Excerpt of Transcript of Pipe Roll, Northumberland, 1187

The relevant excerpt of this transcription appears as Exhibit 2.11. An interpretation will be useful, since the transcription, and the sheet from which it was made, contain a number of peculiarities. Most of the words are medieval Latin, which varied from place to place and from scribe to scribe, but English words (and occasionally words of other languages) were sprinkled in here and there.[13] Most of the Latin words were abbreviated, not always consistently even within the same passage. Some of the words are obscure. In general, the entries are sheriff's accounts of taxes and fines, naming the landholder responsible for the

---

[13] A prominent example is "forest," reflecting the new law of the forest introduced by the Norman kings. This law, apart from common law, set aside as royal domains certain forests (which did not necessarily contain dense woods) as hunting preserves, jealously guarded and a source of fees and fines into the royal treasury.

revenue and the amount, which is stated in marks and/or pounds, shillings, and pence. A mark was an accounting unit, not a coin. The other units were coinage and stated in usual abbreviated form: pound (i.e., *libre*, hence the letter l and later, for pound sterling, £), shilling (*solidi*, hence s), and pence (*denari*, hence d). Whereas the amount was always stated, the kind of tax—and there were many (cornage, socage, quayage, pannage, murage, lastage, scavage, and more)[14]—was often not specified. Most of the entries follow a rather standard format, repetitiously from entry to entry, as one would expect today of a book of accounts. (An example of part of one sheet, recall, was displayed as Exhibit 1.1.) In order to conserve print space, the transcriber generally strung the separate entry lines into a continuous line of type, the specific accounts separated by a long dash or a dot. In Exhibit 2.11 one can see an instance of the dash in line 5. That specific accounting reads: "The same sheriff rendered an account of one mark of Simon of Lucre for forgetting [i.e., disturbing] the calm of the forest." The next accounting, as with many others, includes an implied repetition of phrase, indicated by the word "And" (i.e., *Et*). Thus, this entry reads, with the implied phrase in brackets, "And [the same sheriff rendered an account of] one mark of William of Framelinton for the same." The next entry, likewise; and so on. Note that the accounts were typically grouped by a heading. Here the heading begins *Nova Plac*, the latter word an abbreviation of *Placita*, from the Latin *placēre*, "to please, to placate." Thus, "New Satisfactions" or "Placations." In other words, new revenues. Sometimes the phrase is translated as "New Pleas," but the entries were actually responses to levied taxes and fines, in satisfaction of the revenue claim.

Three of the entries are somewhat obscure, and one of these involves the man thought to be William de Heselrig. Let's begin with the first, on line 3: Gilbert de Lavall, a man of Norman descent "rendered an account of 10 marks because of improper carting of Peter and Adam; 6 marks were paid to the treasury; 4 marks are owed." It is the reason for the fine that is unclear. The word *injuste* surely meant "improper." The word *carcavit* meant a "hollow container used for transport" (i.e., a compound of *car*, from *carrum*, as in English words such as "carriage," "cart," and so forth; plus *cavit*, from *cavitās*). The Latin word appears in many tax accounts during this period, as in *carcavit in eadem di lastam*

---

[14] For excellent discussion with many illustrations, see Norman Scott Brien Gras' *The Early English Customs System* (Cambridge: Harvard University Press, 1918). Gras sifted through the many kinds of taxes (some of them obscure), how they were accounted, and with variations by place.

coriorum unde, which referred to an export tax ("lastage") on hides (*coria*).[15] This much seems straightforward. However, the citation of *Petrū 't Adē* ("Peter and Adam") is obscure. At best guess, the phrase was a euphemism for a behavior more often named as sodomy. The same odd citation appears in the entry, lines 10-11, for William de Herselrig. But here the phrase is introduced by, not *carcavit*, but a contraction of the word *personatus*. It appears, then, that the citation is of "properly disguised or masked Peter and Adam." Finally, the third entry is much like the one for William, except that here Robert de Ford was fined 1 mark, not 20 shillings as in William's case.

The obscurity may not have been correctly interpreted. Moreover, assuming the phrase "Peter and Adam" has been accurately interpreted, it is not clear that it was written by the scribe, rather than inserted by the transcriber for the sake of Victorian-era sensitivities. Further, it is not clear that any of the three named men were the principals of the cited behavior. As lords of their respective manors, each was responsible for the behaviors of those over whom he had lordship, and that would have included responsibility for payment of fines. Last but not least relevant, the behavior cited (assuming correct interpretation of an otherwise opaque phrase) was not the focus of such intense retribution as later developed (though never as strongly in England as in several other countries). This was late twelfth century England, and even the church offered a gentler, more tolerant hand. Core to that was the fact that words such as "sodomy" named a behavior, a social action, not an identity of person—and especially not the sort of all-absorptive identity that such words later exercised, like letters branded to the forehead.[16]

Back to the man assumed to have been mis-named by scribe or transcribe as William de Herselrig. While it cannot be proven that the name—place name or already familial surname—was actually Heselrig, the identification is probable, as is the assumption that the geographic site of the manor was in north-central Northumberland, between Wooler and Bedford, in Chatton parish (as it later came to be known). Remember, this was the year 1187. Even though far to the north, very near the river Tweed, Norman settlement had been in place for several decades. The

---

[15] Many examples can be seen in the compilations made by Gras, in *The Early English Customs System* (1918).

[16] For an exceptionally fine treatment of these matters within the context of time and place, see William Burgwinkle, *Sodomy, Masculinity and Law in Medieval Literature: France and England, 1050-1230* (Cambridge: Cambridge University Press, 2004).

barony of Wooler, held by the Muschamp family throughout the century, was created in 1107.[17]

In recent times the small area that was the site of Heselrig manor has featured at least four different place names (see Exhibit 2.12): Old Hazelrigg, which is probably the original site of the manor; North Hazelrigg and South Hazelrigg; and Hazelrigg Mill. The oldest known surviving structure was Hazelrigg Tower, as previously mentioned a watch tower that was still standing during the early 1700s but was later incorporated into a larger house, perhaps the only house now existing at Old Hazelrigg.[18] The general area is a broad valley, Hetton Burn feeding north-to-south into the river Till at Fowberry Tower. To the east the Kyloe Hills offer some protection against winter winds coming off the North Sea. It is today productive agricultural land, as it was during the twelfth century.

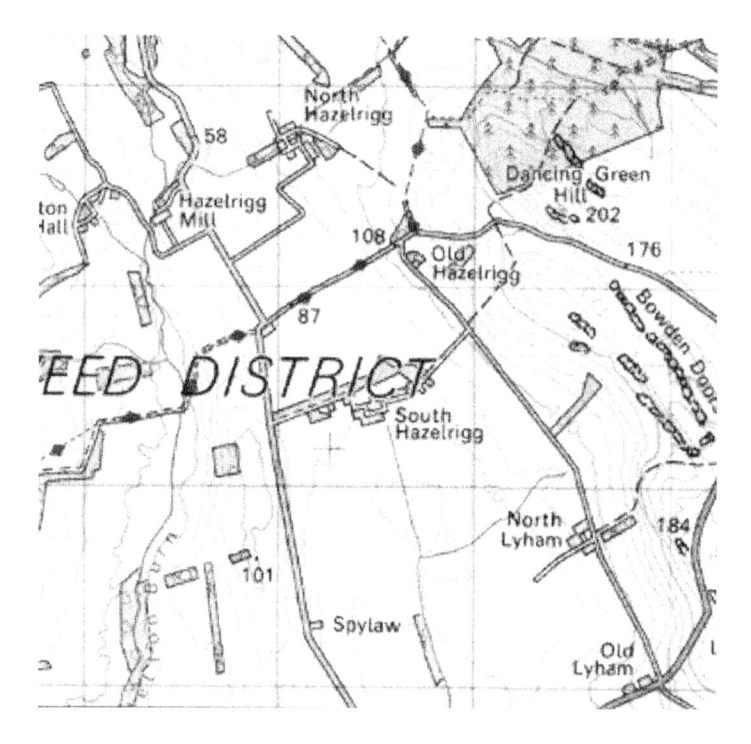

Exhibit 2.12. Heselrig Settlement, Chatton Parish, Northumberland

---

[17] Kenneth H Vickers, *A History of Northumberland*, volume 11 (Newcastle-upon-Tyne: A Reid, 1922), includes an account of the Wooler parish, among others in that area.
[18] Driving west from Belford, one passes on the western slope of Dancing Green Hill a structure that has at times been confused with Hazelrigg Tower. In fact, it is of twentieth-century vintage, a concrete pillbox erected against the threat of invasion.

Kapelle has argued that Norman settlement of Northumberland was impeded not only by local resistance and raids from the north but also by the Normans' strong preference for wheat as main staple, rather than oats and barley.[19] Whereas the latter grains produce well in cool damp climates, wheat does not. His research, based mainly on records of production in northern areas of Yorkshire, has indeed shown a north-south gradient to successes with wheat. However, he may have overstated the case, at least with regard to the area of those Heselrig settlements, for wheat has been very successfully grown there during recent decades. It is true, of course, that average temperatures have been somewhat warmer in recent decades, by comparison to averages that date to the nineteenth century for specific places, sometimes longer. But it is also true that northwestern Europe was experiencing warmer than usual weather during the twelfth century, a time known in retrospect as "The Warm Period." Even so, it is surely true also that wheat was a less reliable grain crop than oats or barley, though probably not so unreliable as to deter Norman settlement. Indeed, we do know from records (e.g., those of the barony of Wooler, cited above) that settlement had begun at least as early as the first decade of the twelfth century.

A few scenes of the area of Hazelrigg, Northumberland, as it was during the 1980s and 1990s, are presented in Exhibit 2.13. From top left are two views of the broad valley, the first looking westerly over meadowland, the second some area of wheat; from bottom left, a large structure that began as tenant housing at North Hazelrigg; and the house at Old Hazelrigg.[20]

Kapelle also noted what several earlier historians had found from their own inspections of records—namely, that Norman settlement of these areas occurred predominantly through the selection of "new men" by Henry I—in other words, men of "new families," families not already among the aristocracy. The Heselrig family was very likely among those. This is not a strike against the conjecture that Roger de Heselrig was a knight in duke William's army, nor should it be construed as evidence that the family had never held land granted by William and/or his son elsewhere in the realm. It is only a statement that the first land gained in

---

[19] Kapelle, *The Norman Conquest of the North* (1979), chapter 7.
[20] All of these lands are private property. They have not been among estates of the Hazlerigg family for centuries. The lane shown alongside the house at Old Hazelrigg is a public roadway, as are main roads leading to it; but some lanes are private, though generally may be traveled with due respect.

Northumberland by the family was probably this land in what became Chatton parish.

Exhibit 2.13. Four Scenes, Area of Hazelrigg, Northumberland

Recall from chapter 1 that William I began a chain of castles along the northwest coast of England, from what we know as Newcastle northward eventually to Bamburgh and Berwick at the river Tweed. Recall, too, that a chain of fees, landed estates with some fortification, was soon added, not only on the coastal plain but also inland, west of the first line of hills (e.g., Kyloe Hills). Wooler was among them. The map sketched in Exhibit 2.14 depicts a network of manors northward from Morpath to Wooler, most of which were associated with the Heselrig family in the twelfth century and after: from Morpeth itself, for instance, and Cambois on the coast, north to Old Swarland, Thrunton, Whittingham, Glanton, Eslington, Fowberry Tower, and Heselrig, or Old Hazelrigg. (Exhibit 2.15 shows the location of some family estates at sites from Newcastle to Morpeth.) These and other estates were accumulated rather rapidly by the family. Fletcher said that no one of the family name lived at the Heselrig manor in 1295, "though a William de

Heselrig then lived at Elwyke (*Lay Subs,* 158-1)"[21] Whatever evidence lay behind that negative claim, it was not reported. This is not to say that Fletcher had none, but only to remind that in general it is difficult to prove a negative. In any case, the implication is that *someone* was living at Hesilrig in 1295, but under a different surname. Nothing was said of that person's identity. If the claim is correct, it probably means that William had let the manor to another man, perhaps husband of a daughter or a brother of his wife, while he lived "at Elwyke." Records show that the manor was in Heselrig possession at a later date, so perhaps it had never left the family. As we saw in Exhibit 1.4, and as Fletcher stated (*ibid*.), in about 1350 Thomas de Hesilrige, second son of Simon, was "party to a deed with Thomas de Heselrigg, Lord of Heselrigg."

There is a connection between the fact that all of that new settlement implied many new construction projects and the fact that the Medieval Warm Period led to improved harvests even in Northumberland and the part of Scotland known as Lothian. Better harvests supported more and healthier people. And indeed the years from about 1000 to about 1250 or 1300 witnessed a population boom. Plentiful agricultural produce meant that fewer growers could support larger numbers of consumers, thus releasing labor for other uses. One such use was cathedral building, examples being the cathedrals of Exeter, Canterbury, and Lincoln, all built during that time. Another, if less grand, use of the surplus labor was a string of new, often fortified manor houses, including at least some of those built for the manors located in Exhibits 2.14 and 2.15. These maps will be useful points of reference for subsequent discussions of lineages and land holdings. Note that the hand-drawn map in Exhibit 2.14 is approximately to scale, and that the scale is different from that in the map shown in Exhibit 2.15 (which is from an Ordnance Survey).

---

[21] William George Dimock Fletcher, *Leicstershire Pedigrees and Royal Descents* (Leicester: Clarke and Hodgson, 1887), page 8. Elwyke (now Elwick Farm) is about seven mile east-northeast of Old Hesilrig, very near the coast. It was site of a pele tower at least as early as Edward III; see Hodgson, *History of Northumberland* (1835), part 3, volume 1, page 28, and part 3, volume 2, page 278. At last visit, Elwick Farm offered tourist cottages on weekly basis.

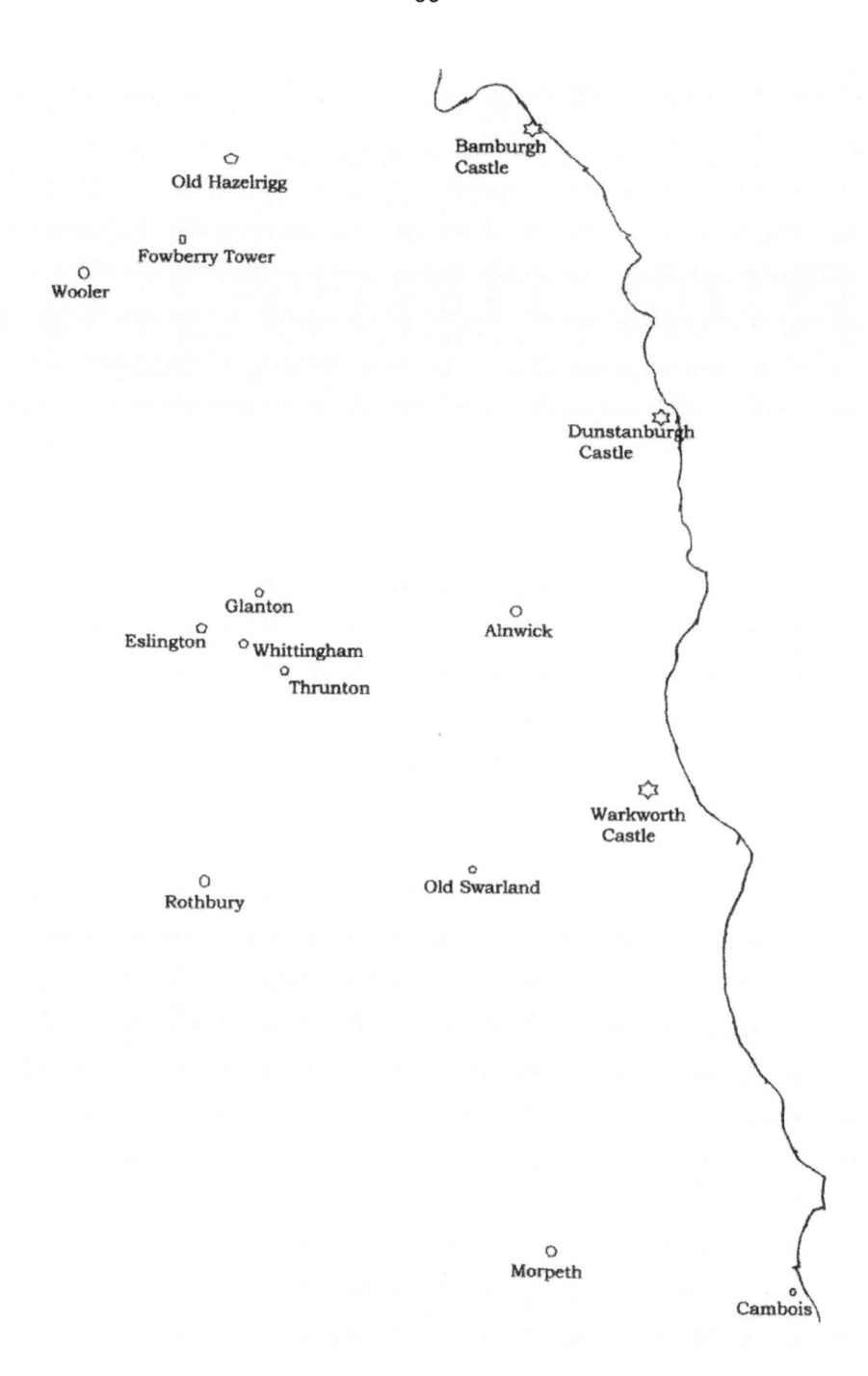

Exhibit 2.14. Some Northumberland Sites, Morpeth to Old Hazelrigg

Exhibit 2.15. Northumberland Sites near New Castle

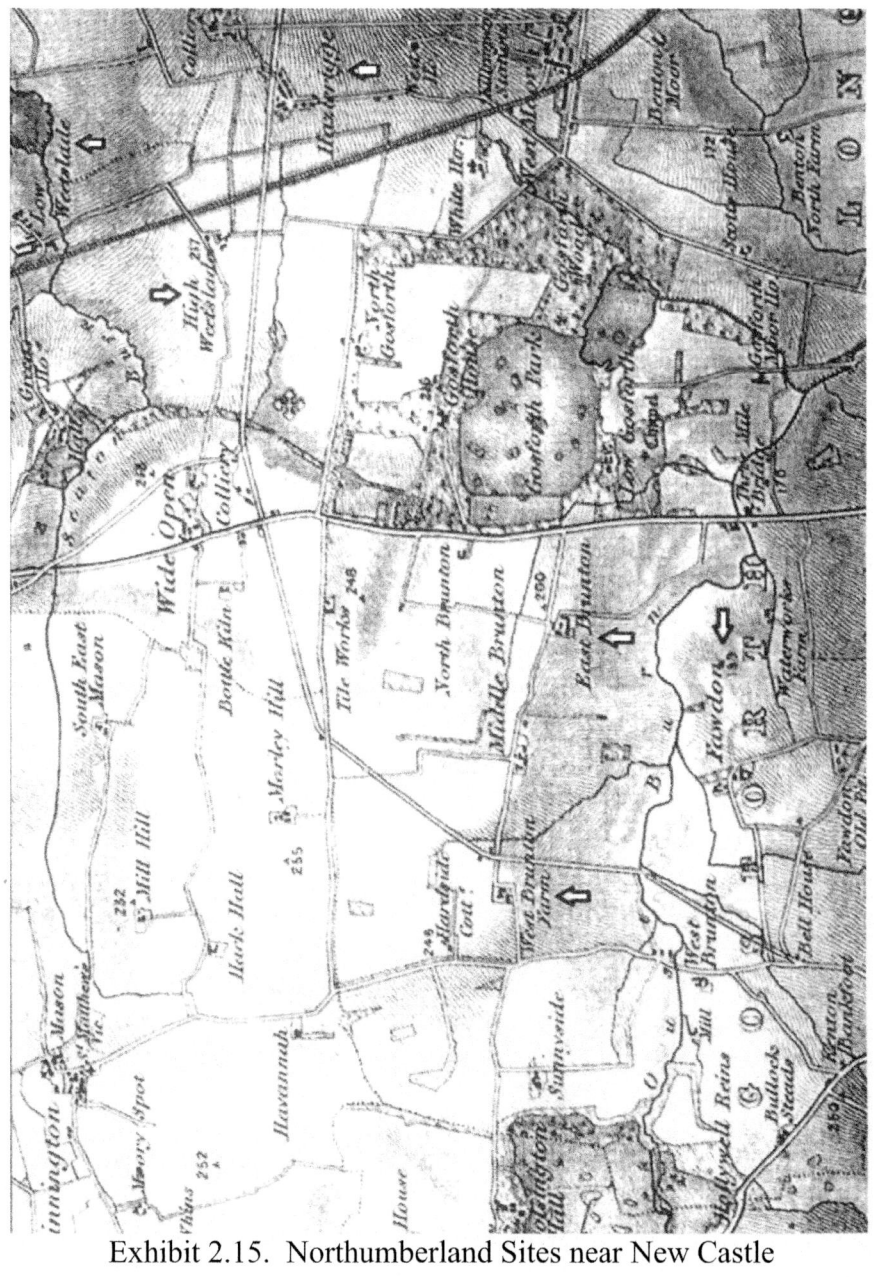

Early Lineages
The best we can do by public record—that is, by the best available documentation—is to begin with the William de Heselrig cited in the Northumberland Pipe Roll for 1187 (Exhibit 2.11) and relate it to Roger as best we can, thence to descendants. It is reasonable to suppose that Heselrig manor had been in existence for some time, but we lack means by which to estimate closely the foundation point. William was an adult, probably at least 25 years of age, perhaps as much as 50 or 60 years of age, which puts his birth year somewhere between c1125 and 1162. This range in turn implies that William was at least three, and possibly four generations removed from Roger (on the assumption that Roger arrived in 1066, then had a surviving son, and generational length of 30 years on average). Thus:

$$\text{Roger} > S_1 \text{ (b.c1070)} > S_2 \text{ (b. c1100)} > \text{William (b. c1130)}.$$

Estimating the number of missing generations is partly guesswork, of course, but there are some general facts that aid in the exercise—for instance, demographic facts about households. One can imagine that, lacking effective means of birth control the household of a typical couple, whether peasant, landed gentry, or aristocracy, was replete with children. Some were. However, the number of surviving children in medieval societies of northwest Europe ranged on average from four to six, depending on specific time and place (i.e., whether contagious disease was rampant or moderate, the vagaries of weather and hence crops, raids and warfare, and so forth). Of these four to six, one might expect that half were male: the proverbial "heir and spare," maybe plus one. But couples whose only surviving children were female were hardly rare. In a patrilineal, patrimonial society that meant no heir to continue the family name, at least in that particular lineage, unless a successful adoption and name change could be accomplished. Why only four to six surviving children, on average? Several factors led to that. For one, women were typically not as fecund in those days as they became in modern times, mainly because they did not have a chance to be: poor diet, poor sanitation, poor health practices all conspired against fecundity (a woman could be fertile but not all that successful in conceiving and carrying sufficiently to term a healthy baby). Age at first marriage for women was sometimes very young, by present-day standards. But age of puberty was typically higher (again, because of diet, etc.), and fecundity could be slow to develop. Further, as many as one-quarter (or more) of babies were still-born. Those who joined the outside world with a hearty cry faced very high risks of mortality from childhood disease and accident. Likewise, maternal death during or soon after childbirth was dreadfully high, one consequence of that being a high rate of serial marriage.

The sum total of what we know of the family's lineage during the late eleventh century and the entirety of the twelfth century is told at the start of this section: "hardly anything" is the correct summary. Before leaving the twelfth for the more informative records of the thirteenth and (more especially) fourteenth centuries, however, we should return once more to the chief alternative account of the family's early lineage. As previously described, Kapelle argued that Norman settlement of the Borders (i.e., the northern shires) did not occur until the reign of Henry I (i.e., 1106 to 1135). Further, he argued, Henry I

> brought to England a group of western Normans and Bretons who were willing to take lands on the other side [northern side] of the oat bread line, and he established these men in northwestern England and through Earl David [later, king David of Scotland] in Galloway. Their settlement shielded the East [i.e., Northumberland, northern Yorkshire] from the Galwegians and closed the routes through the hills [an example being the one shown in Exhibit 2.3]. Once this was done, Norman nobles pushed up the east coast plain from the Tyne to the Forth and even into Fife.[22]

Kapelle's evidence was not exactly plentiful or robust, but his argument cannot be dismissed. Recall that the barony of Wooler was established in 1107 and held by a Norman family, so it is certainly conceivable that the minor manor of Heselrig to the east of Wooler also existed by that time or soon thereafter.

Kapelle's point about wheat bread and the oat line was correct. In areas north of the Tyne the bulk of the diet for most people consisted of grains, and these were mainly oats, barley, and rye. Wheat could be grown, no doubt *was* grown, as far north as Teviotdale, but its produce was unreliable. Meat, especially fresh meat, was a luxury even for lords of small manors. Typical meals consisted of bread and porridge, each made of oats or barley, perhaps along with a scrap of salted meat now

---

[22] Kapelle, *The Norman Conquest of the North* (1979), page 234; also pages 205, 207, 216, 291 n. 142.

and then, accompanied by barley ale. Seasonal additions included vegetables such as beans, peas, and kale, fruits from wild flora, and some nuts.

Normans had arrived from warmer climates, by and large, and had been accustomed to wheat for their bread, porridge, and ale, generally disdaining the "crude" products of "lesser" grains. However, Kapelle also observed that western coastal areas of Normandy were cooler, wetter, and less fertile than inland areas, thus more reliant on oats and barley. It was from those western areas, he conjectured, that Henry I recruited his "new men." By that argument, it seems likely not only that William de Heselrig and his immediate ancestor(s) had not been residents of Northumberland (or Cumberland, etc.) prior to the twelfth century, but also that he, or they, could well have been among Henry's "new men," arrived from Normandy as part of the king's effort to create his "new man" aristocracy for the north, more reliably beholden to him as well as more tolerant of less "refined" cuisine and thus likelier to remain in place.

The foregoing, it must be emphasized, is speculative, with regard specifically to William and his ancestral lineage. Even if Kapelle's argument is wholly correct, it does not address specifically that lineage. While the account of our Roger as a knight accompanying the duke of Normandy is definitely apocryphal, lack of known authorship and supporting evidence does not mean necessarily that it is incorrect.

~ 3 ~
Building Patrimony

Available evidence, as described in the previous chapter, suggests that the earliest efforts of the family to build a patrimony large enough to be worth inheritance occurred during the twelfth century, in the far north of Northumberland. The scant record of successes extends well into the thirteenth century. In his transcription of the *Magnus Rotulus Pipæ* for Northumberland Hodgson found two members of the family among financial records for this century—namely, William de Heselbrigge (1248) and William de Herselrith (1272), in each case making his best guess of the scribe's spelling.[1] By now the "extra name" had become a family's name, not only the name of a manorial place; so we cannot be sure that either of these men, perhaps one and the same, were recorded of the Heselrig manor near Wooler or of one of the other estates which by now had been acquired by the family. Allen Mawer, previously cited as an authority on early Northumberland place names, observed from various records the existence of the Heselrig manor (or its residue) by that name across nearly four centuries (making five in all, given the record of its existence at least as early as 1187). Mawer reported the following spellings (with year and source):

    1288: Heselrig: Calendar of Inquisitions Post-Mortem
    1296: Hessilrig: Lay Subsidy Roll
    1428: Hesilrige: Inquisitions and Assessments, Feudal Aids
    1663: Heslerig: Rentals and Rents for Northumberland.[2]

Definitive proof is lacking, of course, but these are almost certainly four references to the same manor.

    A word of caution is in order here. Mawer's listing of four variant spellings of the family name in surviving records, plus the two cited in the prior paragraph ("Heselbrigge" and "Herselrith"), plus variants cited in previous chapters (e.g., "Herselrige"), could lead one to the erroneous conclusion that all known variants were within hair's breadth of a standard spelling. The error would be twofold. First, there really was no

---

[1] John Hodgson, *History of Northumberland*, part 3, volume 3 (Newcastle-upon-Tyne: John Blackwell and John Brunton Falconar, 1835), pages 217 and 296.
[2] Allen Mawer, *The Place-Names of Northumberland and Durham* (Cambridge: Cambridge University Press, 1920), page 107.

"standard spelling" for several centuries; even within the same (literate) household, variations occurred. Second, while most known variants were indeed similar to the ones noted above (plus, soon to be encountered, "Hysylryg"), at least one other could easily be overlooked unless the reader's ear as well as eye has been engaged: "Esselryke" (with or without an ending "s"). Craster extracted the 45 Northumbrian arms from the heraldic collection compiled c1580 by Robert Glover, herald to Elizabeth I, and among them is "Esselrykes: argent, three hazel-leaves vert. This coat was worn by Thomas Hasilrig of Fawdon."[3] This is not the only instance in which the family name was rendered in such an unusual spelling, and the fact of it suggests that still others might have gone unnoticed in records.

The main topic of this chapter is, as the chapter's title says, the family's record of accumulating heritable property rights, patrimony, concentrating on the thirteenth and fourteenth centuries. In conjunction with this focus, the process of reconstituting lineage will also continue. The twelfth century and the manor of Heselrig will figure in this chapter, too, primarily as point of departure. Main concern here is to identify and briefly describe as many acquisitions in Northumberland as are known, ending with brief mention of the fifteenth-century acquisition of the Noseley estate in Leicestershire, which marked the big jump in economic as well as geographic terms in the process of building patrimony. Some of the acquisitions during the thirteenth and fourteenth centuries were held such a short time or have left so little trace in records of evidence, or were otherwise of low significance, that their presence in this chapter will mark the end of coverage. Others, including Noseley, of course, will be treated in more detail later.

So far as can be said by evidence, the Heselrig manor of north-central Northumberland (i.e., Chatton parish) was the basis from which subsequent building of patrimony occurred. That basis consisted of economic resource, the fruit of hard work on difficult land tested by rugged weather, and often in the midst of surrounding conflicts. But economic resource as we think of it was by itself not enough. In that era at least as important was a rather less tangible resource known as "honor"—"social honor," as it would later be called—for this was, thanks to the Norman inheritance, an era of the feudalization of lands that

---

[3] H H E Craster, "A Northern Roll of Arms," *Archæological Æliana*, 3rd series, volume 2 (1906), pages 173-178, at page 175. Regarding the connection of "Thomas Hasilrig of Fawdon," Craster cited Joseph Foster, *Some Feudal Coats of Arms and Others* (Oxford: J Parker, 1902), page 106.

previously had been rather scattered ("decentralized," relative to what the Normans created) but now were organized in hierarchies of lordship by the manorial system. Honoring one's standing in that hierarchy, meeting one's obligation to one's overlord, was the fundamental condition and promise. Without that, an accumulation of landed estates, which generally occurred through marriages as well as by grants from above, could be no more than idle wish. The promise was of a self-perpetuating platform of stable resource, the patrimony, which could enable a family to endure the great uncertainties of medieval life.

The feudalization of landed relationships had been a remarkably effective means of organizing territory via networks of fealty extending from and to a central locus. A triad of instruments repeatedly served to expand the network into new territory: first, a castle; then a borough of loyal subjects around the castle; plus a religious house to align sacred and secular legitimacy within the network. When successfully deployed, the triad of instruments achieved materially and symbolically a convergence of lines of authority in the body of the monarch. However, feudalization was also built of a contradiction, which in time changed the system. The monarch sought to retain ultimate control of rights to all of the royal domain. Lands would be granted to this or that loyal subject for his (or, sometimes, her) use by favor of the monarch, in return for a share of what wealth the land generated, including fees of various kinds (e.g., a knight's fee of military service, work on bridges and roads, etc.). Understandably, a monarch was reluctant to grant rights of utility in perpetuity; for the sum of a royal domain was fixed but for conquest of territories held by another monarch. The interest of a family who had been recipient of a royal grant was, also understandably, to retain the bestowal as long as possible, and in the meantime to use it as means of expansion as well as maintenance. Thus, for the head of a family who had gained resource by royal favor, usually land, a principle of generational inheritance held growing importance, while for the monarch that same principle contained a degree of threat. Tensions and conflicts from that contradiction slowly resolved into modifications of the feudal system so as to accommodate some conditions of generational inheritance. Fitful as well as slow, that resolution is manifest in many events of the centuries here of main focus, including this family's successes in building patrimony.

For a family fortunate enough to have acquired an estate to pass on to an heir, household interest in satisfying the "heir and a spare" rule was understandably very high. The vagaries of basic demographic facts—birth, death, and, where it applied, migration—made satisfaction of the rule anything but automatic. Yet this rule was not the only strategic consideration, though of primary importance it was. The head of a manorial household, insofar as he was also head of the larger family, would have wanted to weigh in the balance the competing interests of his siblings (if any) and their households and heirs. It was in his interest, and those of the larger family, that siblings too should acquire and maintain landed estates, and the manor he headed could be used as a resource, political as well as economic, to that end. At the same time, it was incumbent on him to protect the rights of inheritance of his own heir and spare. But should an only-son heir die, or heir and spare when the latter had existed, he could look to a brother or a nephew as new inheritor. Strategic interests were, or ought to have been, familial in the larger sense whenever possible. The vital task of striking optimal balances among competing interests of the family's several lineages no doubt at times proved to be vexingly difficult in face of sibling rivalries, open or partly hidden jealousies of "minor" lineages toward the "main" lineage, and so on. The great "secret" of aristocracy, also followed by successful families of the landed gentry, was never to sacrifice the larger family's long-range interests for the sake of satisfying short-term interests. Sometimes, a mortgage against long-range interests seemed the only prudent choice. But it was a dangerous choice.

  To say that life was dangerous and otherwise difficult even under best of circumstances in twelfth and thirteenth-century England is hardly news except possibly as understatement. For us, that is. For inhabitants of that time, life was simply what it was: life. In fact, today one can see the possibility that for some of those inhabitants life could well have been judged as much improved. The comparison would have depended on how much historical perspective the inhabitant had, and few people then had more than the perspective of one or two generations. In most of their registers of life, change was slow. Again, that judgment is by our typical measures. But for them—though it simply was what it was—the temporal perspective needed in order to see very much difference in most persons' daily lives was quite beyond the usual length of one or two generations. Even so, a few observers surely noticed that "city life" was rebounding. With the collapse of the Roman Empire many centuries earlier, city life all but disappeared throughout Europe; and with it also disappeared long-distance trading, mercantilism, secular centers of inquiry, monumental construction and thus most forms of memorialism, various fine arts, and much more. Few people of thirteenth-century England knew about those events and the long shadow they cast. But word got around as, in fact, city life did begin to rebound and the means of supporting larger numbers of adults in endeavors other than daily provision of means of subsistence, endeavors of reading and writing and teaching and so forth, also recovered.[4] By the same token, thirteenth-century English men and women surely noticed that the wealth of the land had been growing. While their table fare might not have been witness to that, surges of monumental construction were difficult to miss, not only new castles, town centers, and the like, but more tellingly the conversion of cathedrals into the new, Gothic, style, beginning in the 1220s. Westminster was rebuilt during 1245-1269, for instance. But its new dressing had been preceded by similar conversions of others, including York Minster to the far north. The blessings and penalties associated with religious devotion being what they were, probably few people openly wondered about the expenditure of so much material wealth on matters of style. But surely there were some who did notice and held their tongues.

Another matter of historical context merits remark, lest there be misunderstanding by anachronism. Earlier in this section reference was made to "the fruit of hard work." While city life was reviving in England as elsewhere, most people worked the land, which was and would long remain the chief form and source of wealth. Virtually all of that work was done by hand, with or without the aid of a few simple tools and some animal power. Anyone today who has worked a plot of land with spade and hoe knows that physical strength and endurance, along with patience and a sense of cadence, are requisite to the task, and, with some reflection on that actual experience will know, too, how difficult it would be to supply one's household with all the necessities of a year's sustenance, to say nothing of the "extra" product needed to satisfy "tax" from above. It is easy to imagine that people of twelfth-century England and beyond thought of the activity as toil, drudgery, unpleasant, and indeed unsatisfying except by necessity. It might well have been thought to be as difficult as factory workers in the twentieth century thought theirs to be. And yet there is a difference: the latter must contend with a clock and oversight which the twelfth-century land worker did not know.

Productivity per worker has increased enormously during the past eight centuries. We typically say that this is due mainly to technology,

---

[4] The University of Oxford, founded probably before the twelfth century, enjoyed large growth during the latter decades of that century, and the University of Cambridge was founded in 1209. A third university was established by Henry III at Northampton in 1261, but he revoked its charter four years later at the behest of defenders of Oxford.

and the attribution is correct insofar as "technology" is meant to include not just things made but also the organization of work. Because of all the differences summed within that meaning, the average worker today, the average office worker as well as the average factory worker, endures greater toil and drudgery, more demanding work, than did the twelfth-century land worker. The difference shows in vocabulary and in attitude, along with actual activity and its associated maladies. Look at the Christian tradition, for example: the oldest accounts such as *Genesis* treat labor as unwelcome, something to be avoided so far as possible, even as punishment. The Garden of Eden story makes this very clear: only because of the sin of disobedience must humans engage in toil in order to survive. There is some distance between that world of the *Genesis* account and today's world of concerns about "workaholics" and "careerism."

The bias is older than Christianity, no doubt, inasmuch as *Genesis* was the first book of Moses. Further, the ancient Greeks held a similar bias against work, probably independently of the ancient Hebrews. This shows not only in the practice of slavery (not chattel slavery but a form of enforced labor enabling free citizens to engage in other pursuits). It was also present in their language. For example, at least since the time of Pindaros (522 - 443 BC), a Boeotian poet, to Thucydides (460 - 395 BC) and beyond, the common word for "engagement in business, occupation," and so forth, was *ascholia*, a word formed of two parts: the main part, *scholē* or *scholia*, meant "leisure" (and activities depending on leisure or "free time," such as "school"); plus the letter "*a*" (or alpha), in this function known as "the privative *a*," meaning negation of the word that follows it (thus, "no + leisure"). This word formation carried over into Latin: "leisure" = *otium*, and "business, commerce" = *negotium* (thence, "negotiation").

This negative attitude toward labor, work, and so forth, was still very much alive in early medieval England (and elsewhere). Peasants, especially landless peasants, were born poor and had no choice, given their station in life, but to toil. Toil, unwelcome as it was, was not a choice to be elected or not, just as being a member of the aristocracy was not a choice but a birthright, perfectly in keeping with the natural order of things as ordained by God.[5]

---

[5] One form of monasticism maintained a contrary tradition within Christianity, placing high value on *labor*, work in combination with prayer, sometimes with material charity to the local poor an added value. Some monasteries housed scribes who preserved (by copying) hallowed documents; some included figures who assayed and interpreted

Fortified Manors

Northumberland, Cumberland, Westmoreland, and southern parts of Scotland—the old Lothian region, the Clydesdale, other parts of Galloway—remained an area of contention between English and Scottish kings well into the fourteenth century, and occasionally even thereafter. When the respective kings were weak or otherwise preoccupied, the so-called Border Reivers (i.e., raiders) were a scourge on one side of the river Tweed or the other. Although sometimes abetted by a royal house, the reivers were usually in it for their own sake, collecting as much booty wherever it could be taken, with little or no attention to the "nationality" of victims. This fragility of any settled authority gave rise to some specific architectural forms in a primarily local response that could though did not necessarily signify allegiance to the crown in London. It had been a matter of survival to Anglo-Saxon barons, and it would be that still to the Normans who took their places. Among the forms, two in particular were deployed by Norman barons as outposts from the chain of castles begun by William I in 1080. One was the pele tower; the other, the bastle house. Both figured in the family's accumulation of estates.

Early pele towers ("pele," cognate with "pale" or enclosure) were usually three or four-storey towers of small footprint, thick stone walls, difficult entrance, narrow windows, and sometimes crenellated tops, with some sort of pot or basket at top for signal fires. The structure served as dwelling for the landholder's family, the larger ones being able to accommodate as well the attached tenants who normally lived in rustic quarters and needed protection during times of siege. Most of the towers have long since been pulled down, the stones used for other purposes. Hazelrigg Tower (as it is generally known in various records) was an early pele tower which later became the core of a larger house at what is today known as "Old Hazelrigg" (shown in Exhibit 2.13, lower right). Preston Tower, built in 1392, survives as a very fine example of the architecture—much finer, no doubt, than Hazelrigg Tower had ever been.

Bastle houses (from *bastille*, a fort or fortified dwelling) were built as farm houses fortified mainly against reivers (rather than invading forces). Typically two-storey rectangular structures, the ground floor was

---

scriptures, healing, salvation of souls, and possibilities of miracles; a few allowed the composition of musical scores and lyrics in celebration of religious festivals. In those and other activities one sees religious toleration of, even support for and encouragement of, practices which, with the recovery of city life, became occupational professions once again, the "free professions."

built with stone walls up to three feet thick and housed the most important livestock. The upper storey, usually also stone though not so thick and with narrow windows, housed the family. More elaborate bastle houses often had towers or turrets at two or more corners, connected by curtain walls. An example of a curtain wall can be seen in this wall of Swarland Old Hall (Exhibit 3.1), which, although built during the early 1600s, seems to have preserved its predecessor's crenellated curtain wall, with three blind Gothic windows.

Exhibit 3.1. Swarland Old Hall, Northumberland

Probably most if not all of the family's early manorial estates in Northumberland were fortified in some manner. But only guesses can be made, as records of actual construction are generally not available. The use of wood in earliest constructions, in typical motte-and-bailey style, is most likely, especially for the smaller estates.

An inventory of recorded estate acquisitions by the family follows in this section, arranged alphabetically by name of the estate (generally, its location), with brief description attached. For several of the estates these descriptions will suffice, either because the estate was small and did not attract much record keeping or because it was held by the family for a very short period of time (or, as was sometimes the case, because of both factors). A few of the estates will be mentioned in this inventory, only to be treated at some length later. Bounds of the inventory geographically are from Heselrig (now, Hazelrigg) in the north of Northumberland to an area just north of Newcastle-upon-Tyne, in particular an estate known as Weetslade (Weteslade, etc.). These geographic bounds also mark time to the latter part of the 1200s, although the inventory will encompass the following century as well. The period to the late 1200s is noteworthy in part because it clearly demonstrates already a determined effort to "move south"—to better land, better weather, better access to influence in the circles of royal largess, both directly and through strategic marriages. It was, after all, a time when estate acquisitions occurred not only by royal grant (the primary avenue early in the period) but also via manoeuvers that, the hope was, would end in advantageous junctures between landed families. Settling an estate, or some part of an estate, on a daughter at her marriage was not simply a "loss of wealth" but a major event in a family's strategic planning for its future patrimony. Being in a position to enter those marital negotiations required the possession of alienable estates, which, although still anything but firmly and systematically established, had become increasingly possible because of a series of reforms enacted from the time of the Magna Carta (1215) and subsequent Charter of the Forest (1217) to the Statute of Westminster II (1285) and other rulings during the reign of Edward I.

Before beginning the alphabetical portion of the inventory, some remarks about the two manorial estates that bound it in geography are in order. The older of the two, Heselrig, is presumed to have been the first, given identification with what became the family's surname. Surely it was acquired by royal grant, whether during the reign of Henry I or that of his father or brother. Very likely it had been an Anglo-Saxon estate, confiscated and then assigned as reward for participating in efforts to secure the northern border lands to Norman rule. The younger of the two bounding estates—actually a pair of them, Weetslade and West Brunton—located near the coast and the river Tyne, came into the family at some unknown date prior to 1281. We know that, because on 8 February of that year (which then counted as 1280, the new year still beginning in March) king Edward granted lands in Yethem Maynes and Yethem Corbet to Simon de Heselrig, who was already styled as the lord of Weteslade and West Brunton, two separate manorial estates. Both of these latter appear on John Speed's 1610 map of Northumberland, a section of which is printed as Exhibit 3.2.[6]

Exhibit 3.2. A Section of Speed's Map of Northumberland, 1610

    Weteslade was located on the northern bank of Seaton Burn, a stream emptying into the North Sea. West Brunton was to the southwest, named by Speed as "Bruntons," perhaps reflecting by 1610 a merger of what had been two. (Note that another estate soon to come into the family, Gosford, is also marked on the map, due east of the Bruntons.) Geoffrey of Weetslade held the manor by knight's fee to the barony of

---

[6] John Speed, *The Counties of Britain: A Tudor Atlas* (New York: Thames and Hudson, 1989), pages 138-139.

Merlay (which centered on Morpath) at least as early as 1240. As he was still there in 1256, it appears that Simon acquired Weetslade manor after that date, perhaps as late as the 1270s.

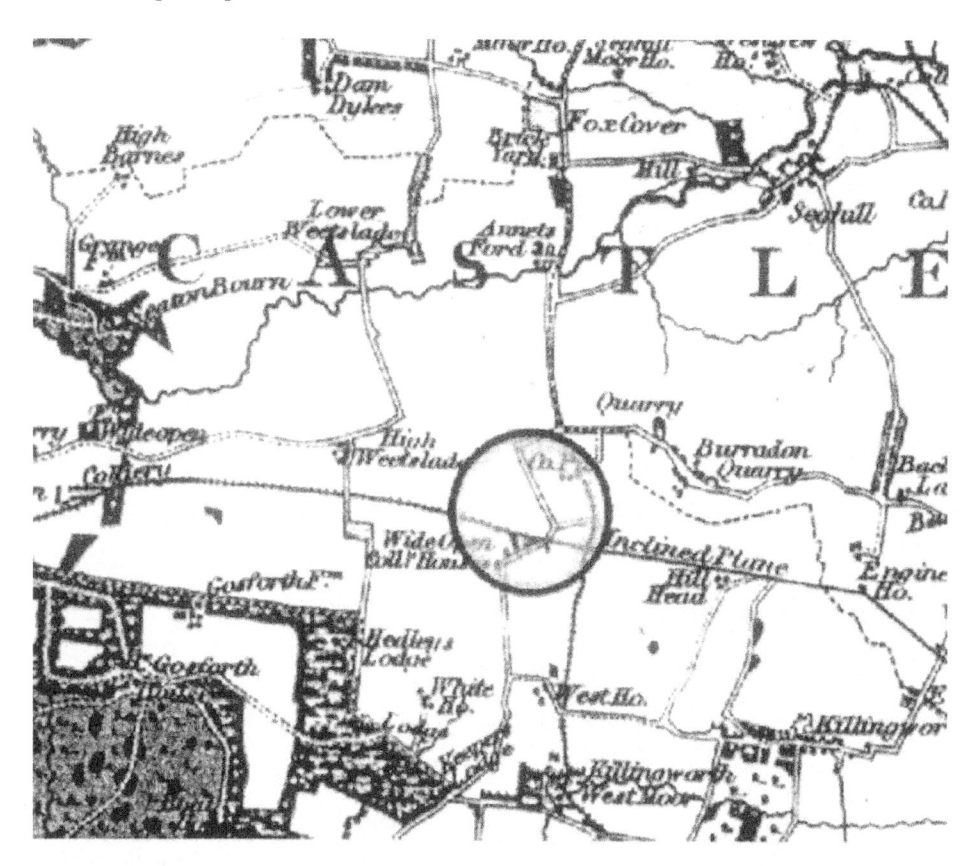

Exhibit 3.3. A Section of Greenwood's Map of Northumberland, 1828

Sometime before 1256 Weetslade manor was split into two: Low Weetslade, the original site, and, lying well south of Seaton Burn, High Weetslade (also known as South Weetslade).[7] The elevation referencing no doubt reflected the meaning of the place name, Weetslade, an Anglo-Saxon conjunction of "wet" and "landing," indicating swampy or boggy land as site of the original manor. Public works programs enacted later resulted in drainage of these low-lying areas (just as in the fens of the east coast of Norfolk), some effects of which can be seen in the map of that area by Greenwood in 1828 (e.g., dykes; see Exhibit 3.3). In showing

---

[7] See, e.g., page 95 in *Three Early Assize Rolls for the County of Northumberland sæc. XIII*, Publications of the Surtees Society, volume 88 (Durham: Andrews & Co., 1891).

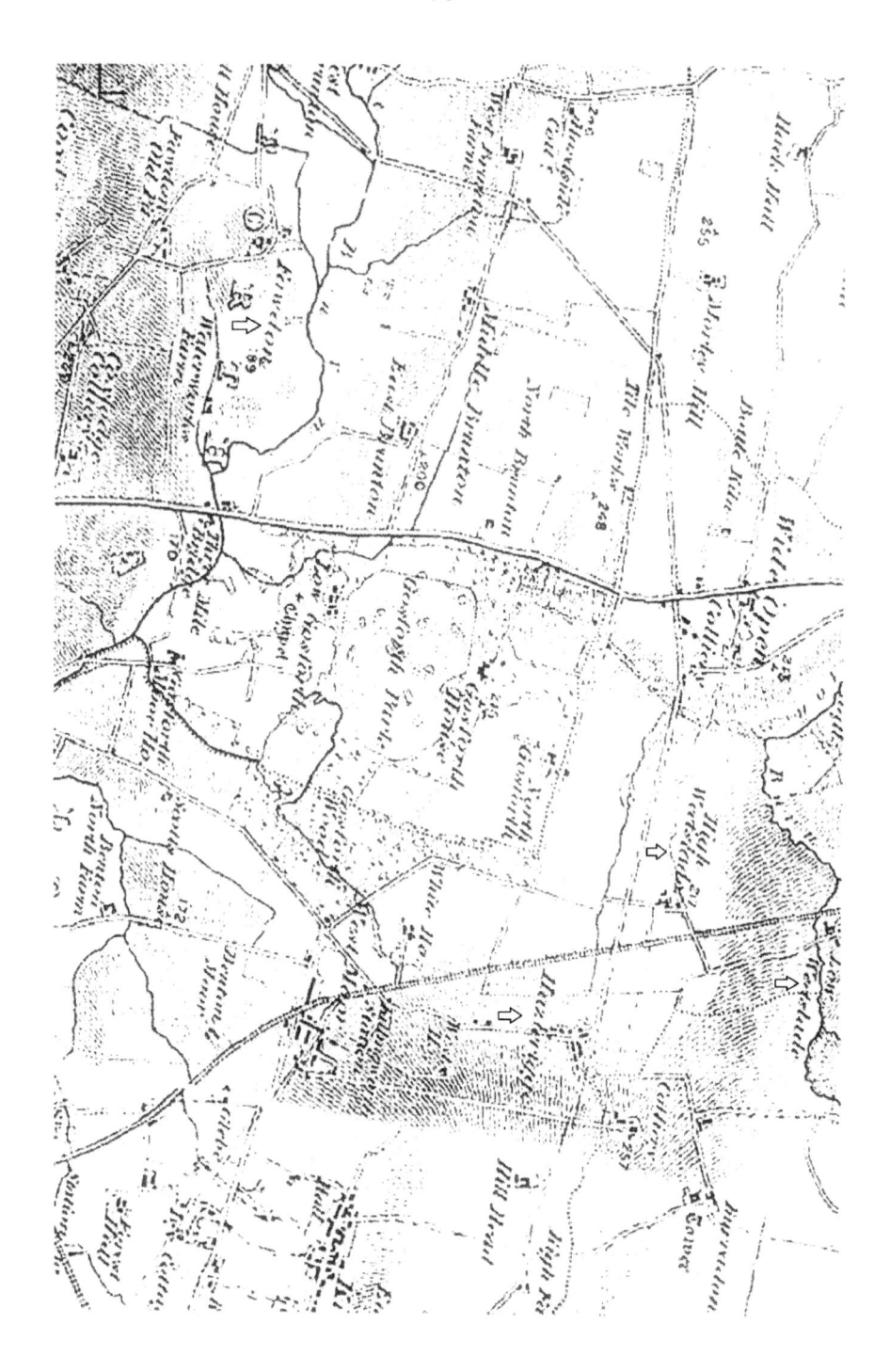

Exhibit 3.4. Area North of Newcastle-upon-Tyne, Late 1800s

relative locations of the two Weetslade manors, this map allows approximation of land size associated with the original manor.

Long before 1828 the southern of the two estates had become the dominant one. The Hazlerigg family maintained interest in High (or South) Weetslade until the mid-eighteenth century, when, upon the death Sir Arthur Hesilrige, 7th Bt, in 1763, his heirs sold the 539-acre estate to Charles Blanding. In the meantime, several members of the family had been identified with the estate in official records. For example, in 1360 William de Heslerigg was granted land that had been confiscated from a participant in Gilbert de Middleton's rebellion in 1317 (William was probably son of John de Hesilrigge, one of the soldiers who had captured Middleton at Mitford Castle).[8] Thomas Heslerigge held the Weetslade estate, by testimony at the inquest post-mortem (3 January 1429) for Roger Thornton. In the 1721 general election, Sir Robert Heslerigge was recorded as freeholder of the High Weetslade estate. And so forth.

As can be seen more clearly in Exhibit 3.4 (a small portion of an Ordnance Survey map), the general area of the Weetslade estates and the several Brunton estates (by this time not only East and West Brunton but also North and Middle) became centers of coal mining. In the northeast corner of the map, note Burradon, an old estate that developed into one of the largest collieries in the north of England. Note also, a short distance to the southwest of Burradon, a village then known as Hazlerigge (later renamed Camperdown): this had been part of South Weetslade township and for many years also featured a large mining operation, later merged with Burradon. Had the 7th Bt's heirs known what was in store for the South Weetslade estate, they surely would have rethought the idea of selling it to Blanding or anyone else.

Now to the alphabetical inventory of Northumberland estates. In some instances the estates will be described only or mainly here.

Akeld: a manorial center in Glendale (i.e., the valley of the river Glen), located about 8 miles west of Old Hazelrigg, near Wooler. The site is just west of the royal center, Ad Gefrin, of the old Anglian kingdoms of Bernecia and Northumbria, and east of the Stone Age site at Yeavering Bell. (Akeld, along with Coupland and Yever—i.e., Yeavering—appear on the maps in Exhibit 3.6, below.) William de Hesilrig received one-

---

[8] Sir Arthur E Middleton, *Gilbert de Middleton: And the Part He Took in the Rebellion in the North of England in 1317* (Newcastle-upon-Tyne: Mawson Swan and Morgan, 1918), page 52, and sources cited therein.

quarter of the manor of Akeld c1296, from overlord Nicholas Graham. It might have been held previously by a member of the Heselrig family.[9] Thomas Haggarston had held one-quarter c1291; he married Margaret Hesilrige, probably daughter of William.[10] William's son John held one-quarter of the manor as late as 1329, but by 1350 John was located at Sheepwash, which is on the river Blyth near the Cambois estate which his father had acquired (see entry on Cambois, below).

Barton: part of Whittingham parish (see entry on Whittingham, below); there is little information about Barton during the time it was part of the family's holdings (1300s), and the accounts always list it in conjunction with Thrunton, so Barton was probably not a manorial estate in itself but only a small vill or hamlet. By the 1800s it had been depopulated to the point of existing only as two farms, High Barton and Low Barton, and High Barton was gone by the end of the century. Today there are again two, Middle Barton and Low Barton, both located on the north side of the river Aln, east of Whittingham.

Blackden (aka Black-dene, Blacket, Blagdon): a very fine manor house was built there, the seat of the White family (later, and today, the White-Ridley family) during the early 1700s; that was after the Hesilrige family held the estate, which then included a house (and, some say, a pele tower, though there is no clear evidence of it); the Hesilrige family held it mainly as land. It was/is located in Seaton Burn parish, north of Low Weetslade (see Exhibit 3.2).

Brotherwick: a manor acquired during the 1360s by Donald de Heselrig of Eslington and Whittingham (which lie to the west of Alnwick; see the map in Exhibit 2.14) via his marriage to Johanna de Wauton. At one time a landed estate of 80 acres or more, on the river Coquet, Brotherwick was typical of manors "held directly from the Crown by sergeancy or the performance of specific services."[11] Additional account is given in the next chapter.

---

[9] William of Akeld, c1273, might have been a Heselrig son. John Hodgson, *A History of Northumberland*, part 3, volume 1 (Newcastle-upon-Tyne: printed for the author, 1820), page 211, records that William of Akeld held that manor, plus Coupland and Yever.

[10] Kenneth H Vickers, *A History of Northumberland*, volume 11 (Newcastle-upon-Tyne, 1922), pages 229-232. The Haggarston shield was quartered with Hesilrige.

[11] John Crawford Hodgson, *A History of Northumberland*, volume 5 (Newcastle-upon-Tyne: Andrew Reid & Co., 1899), pages 255-256.

Cambois: acquired by William de Hesilrig as a grant from the bishop of Durham, Richard Kellawe, of lands and tenements at Cambois in Bedlingtonshire, 25 Mar 1315, confirmed by Edward II at York on 16 Nov 1316. A small enclave wholly within Northumberland (until 1844), Bedlingtonshire, along with two other small districts in the north of Northumberland, Islandshire and Norhamshire (sometimes collectively known as "North Durham"), were legally part of the county palatinate of Durham, belonging to the prince bishops (since at least the tenth century). Cambois (pronounced "cammus") was a small settlement between the rivers Wansbeck and Blyth, along the coast ("Cammas" on Speed's map; Exhibit 3.2). Today the site is occupied by a large power station.

Dinnington: part of the barony of Mitford, the manor of Dinnington was acquired by the Heselrig family by the mid-1300s. In 1368 Thomas Heselrigg, "described as of Denington [Dinnington] took a lease of a rent charge or annuity charged to lands in Cleveland and Glantlees (about which, see below).[12] Robert Hesilrige reported rental income of 80£ in 1663.[13] The estate was sold to Matthew Bell in 1763. Now within the bounds of Newcastle, Dinnington was about six miles northwest of the town center, between Weteslade and Blackden.

East Brunton: since Simon was lord of Weteslade and West Brunton in 1281, it seems likely that the family acquired East Brunton soon thereafter, if not already. Robert Hesilrige reported rental income of £80 in 1663. Sir Arthur Hesilrige, 7th Bt, owned a farm there in 1731; perhaps it, too, was sold to Matthew Bell in 1763.

Eslington: part of Whittingham township (see below), this manorial estate and associated vill, with a defensive tower house—and today a hamlet about two miles west of Whittingham—came into the Hesilrigg family by 1360. Donald de Heselrig held it in 1362, in 1377, and at his death in 1385; his widow Joan held it entire at her death in 1400.[14] On 12 February 1433 Thomas Haselrigg of Eslington was recorded as party to a

---

[12] John Crawford Hodgson, *A History of Northumberland*, volume 7 (Newcastle-upon-Tyne: Andrew Reid & Co., 1904), page 412.

[13] Hodgson, *A History*, part 3, volume 1 (1820), page 321.

[14] Hodgson, *A History*, part 3, volume 1 (1820), pages 80-81, 88; J Crawford Hodgson, "On the Medieval and Later Owners of Eslington," *Archæologia Æliana*, 3rd series, volume 6 (Newcastle-upon Tyne: Andrew Reid, 1910), pages 1-33, at page 16.

deed, along with Nicholas Heselrigg of Swarland (about which, see entry for Swarland, below).[15] It later passed to the Collingwood family, though with some "back and forth" for a time. (See Hodgson's account). The estate was acquired by the Liddell family in 1715, and five years later they built the elegant Eslington House; the estate later became known as Eslington Park.

Fawdon: a manorial center, northwest of Newcastle, it was part of the barony of Whalton in 1242; acquired by William de Heselrig of Fawdon before 1346, it was held by his son, Thomas Heselrig of Fawdon (known as Thomas of Fawdon) c1400. Robert Hesilrige reported rental income of £100 from Fawdon in 1663.[16] It was sold to Matthew Bell in 1763.

Fowberry Tower: originally a pele tower on the south side of the river Till, upstream from the Old Hazelrigg manor (i.e., Heselrig), this estate might have been held by the Heselrig family for a short time during the mid-1200s; the inventory of baronies in the *Testa de Nevill*, which dates from c1326, says that William de Folebyr held the manors of Folebyr, Coldmorton, and Hessilrigg in 1273. He might have been a Heselrig. As surnames were adopted, landed men had a choice (e.g., an ancestral home or present home as identity). Fowberry (i.e., Folebyr) became a family name; the genealogical roots are unknown. We know by good evidence that Thomas of Fawdon was a Heselrig, and chose the latter rather than Fawdon as his surname. Likewise, William of Akeld. But in any given instance, one imagines, the choice could have gone in the other direction. In any case, "Thomas son of Thomas de Hesilrig held the vill of Hesilrig (in Chatton parish) and the vills of Fowberry and Coldmorton" in 1361.[17]

Glantlees: usually mentioned in conjunction with "the Greens," both in Felton parish, this hamlet was acquired about the same time as the manor of Swarland (see below), and its history "for the next three hundred years is similar to that of Swarland."[18]

Glanton: this village, located about two miles north of Whittingham, was probably never a manorial estate but either part of other nearby manors

---

[15] *Ex Cartis Heselrigg*, Landsdowne Manuscript 326, folio 101b; Hodgson, *A History*, volume 7 (1904), page 393, note 5.
[16] Hodgson, *A History*, part 3, volume 1 (1820), page 321.
[17] Hodgson, "On the Medieval and Later Owners" (1910), page 13, note 51.
[18] Hodgson, *A History*, volume 7 (1904), pages 412, 414.

(Whittingham itself perhaps) or held separately by manorial families. The Devil's Causeway runs along the eastern edge of today's Glanton village. Glanton was obtained by the Collingwood family. John Sykes added an interesting historical footnote (the year, 1716):

> As a mason was digging for stone, near Deer-street, beside Glanton Westfield, he discovered an empty stone chest, upwards of three feet long and two in breadth, with a stone cover. Some time afterwards, three more chests of a similar form, with covers, were discovered at the same place. There were two urns and some fine earth in each, with some charcoal and human bones, on which the marks of fire. Near these were two other urns, one large, and the other very small; they were of ordinary pottery, and on exposure to the air fell to pieces.[19]

Gosford (or Gosforth): South Gosford, a vill, was part of the barony of Whalton in 1166. One-third was acquired by the Heselrig family by 1296 (the remainder by deLisle family); Robert Hesilrige reported for the year 1663 a rental income of £230 from four holdings in Gosford parish and another £90 from a holding in nearby Longbenton parish.[20]

Heselrigg: perhaps the first manor held by the family—at least the first on clear record—this site has been described already and will be considered again in the next section of this chapter.

Kenton: little is known of this holding, which is in Gosforth parish, about three miles northwest of Newcastle-upon-Tyne; John de Kenton was high sheriff of Northumberland in 1313; in 1346 William de Heselrig held a sixth of Kenton, along with the vill of Fawdon, a third of Gosforth, and a moiety of Dinnington.[21] The township later passed to the Fenwick family. At some point, probably in more recent times, it was divided into two, East and West Kenton.[22]

---

[19] John Sykes, *Local Records* (Newcastle-upon-Tyne: Printed for John Sykes, 1824), pages 72-73.
[20] Hodgson, *A History*, part 3, volume 1 (1820), page 255.
[21] Hodgson, "On the Medieval and Later Owners" (1910), page 13.
[22] Samuel Lewis, editor, *A Topographical Dictionary of England*, 7th edition (London: S Lewis & Co., 1848).

Plessey: a manorial center, with hall and chapel, located about 40 miles south-southeast of South Hazelrigg and about seven miles north of the old Weetslade estate, came to the family pre-1350. Hodgson speculated that Thomas, son of William de Heselrige, was probably a relative of Roger de Widdrington, who acquired Plessey about 1350.[23] Perhaps Thomas' daughter married Roger. A new Plessey Hall, built c1680, is still standing (see Exhibit 3.5). Plessey Mill Farm is probably a remnant of the old manorial estate, which appears as "Plaβhē" on Speed's map of 1610 (Exhibit 3.2), due north of Weetslade.

Sheepwash: a small estate, held by John de Heselrig, son of William de Heselrig of Akeld and Cambois, probably only as farming land; it appears on Speed's map (Exhibit 3.2), on the south bank of the river Wansbeck; the hamlet has been absorbed by the town of Ashington.

Exhibit 3.5. Plessey Hall (from c1680)

Snook Bank: Much like Glantlees and the Greens, this estate was mostly farmland at the time it was held by the branch of the family seated at Swarland manor.

---

[23] Hodgson, "On the Medieval and Later Owners" (1910), page 14.

Swarland: a major manorial center in its day (as mentioned in regard to Exhibit 3.1), the curtain wall preserved from the original manor house is a good example of a crenellated fortified dwelling of that era. The manor was granted, from 1381, to John, son of William Heselrigg and Agnes his wife. Swarland was held by the Hesilrige family until 1741. Additional description is given in the next chapter.

Thrunton: Today's hamlet is a little more than a mile southeast of Whittingham, which seems rather close for it, too, to have been a manorial estate. A spring-fed mill is located nearby, but there is no indication that Thrunton Mill existed at the time the family held the lands. Joan, widow of Donald de Heselrig, held the vill at the time of her death in 1400.

Whittingham: this parish and township included a number of manors and vills held by the family—Eslington, Thrunton, Barton, Glanton (aka Glaunton)—as well as Whittingham manor itself. Whittingham village is on the banks of the river Aln, eight miles west of Alnwick, in the vale of Whittingham with sweeping vistas and rich soil. This location is about 25 miles south of the Old Hazelrigg settlement, if one traveled by the Devil's Causeway (and about 35 miles today by automobile). The village featured a strong defensive tower and the church of St. Bartholomew, which existed as an Anglo-Saxon church that after 1066 was reconstructed into a Norman style. Joan, widow of Donald, held the vills of Whittingham, Thrunton, and Barton, as well as the entirety of Eslingham, at her death in 1400.

Yetham Corbet and *Yetham Maynes*: On 8 Feb 1281 Edward I granted lands in Yetham Corbet and in Yetham Maynes to Simon de Heselrig, otherwise identified as lord of Weteslade and West Brunton, and as *valectus* (valet) to the king. Today the principal name is Yetholm, not Yetham, the latter a word that some have interpreted as meaning "gate to hamlet." These sites will be considered in the next section.

Therewith, the inventory. The only good reason for thinking that it is complete is that no other major estate holding has been seen in existing records pertaining to Northumberland. Thus, at least two good reasons for thinking that the inventory is *not* complete come to mind. One of them, failure of record, probably can never be remedied. The other, faulty inspection, if it be that, is still available for correction by another pair of eyes.

Nearly all of the Northumberland estates had passed from the family by the middle of the eighteenth century. A passage from a county history written a century later summarizes part of the story:

> East and West Brunton, Fawdon, Dinnington, Weetslade, and Wide Open [a small estate then at the edge of Newcastle], formed the manor and estate of the Hazlerigge family, and were sold in 1768, pursuant to an order of the High Court of Chancery, reserving only the coal-mines of Fawdon and Brunton, which were leased by a representative of John du Ponthieu, Esq.[24]

This particular volume of history, comparable to volumes written at the same time of towns and cities of the USA, and as such typically regarded as a movement of "city boosterism," was not entirely accurate (and for that reason, presumably, ignored by historians such as John Hodgson and John Crawford Hodgson). In fact, the family had held several manors as seats in Northumberland, as the preceding inventory indicates, and several of these had passed from the family well before the 1700s. But the sense of "a final chapter" conveyed by that passage is accurate: after 1768 only residual mineral rights in Northumberland remained. By his last will and testament, Robert Heselrigg, last to claim the seat of Swarland manor, passed that manor and associated estates to his cousin, Robert Heselrigg, 6th Bt, of Noseley in Leicestershire. His son, Arthur, 7th Bt, proceeded with liquidation of the remaining northern holdings, selling Glantlees, for example, to Joseph Cook of Newton-on-the-Moor, 27 September 1735. Following the death of Arthur, 7th Bt, family troubles had reached such proportions that posthumous settlements had to be achieved through the chancery process. This is a topic for a later chapter.

One of the King's Men

As noted earlier, England's northern border was not securely settled until the fourteenth century. While Henry I achieved important steps toward that goal, momentum was lost during the tumult of Stephen's reign and its aftermath, and intermittently thereafter. Contests between the claim of

---

[24] William Whellan & Co., *History, Topography, and Directory of Northumberland* (London: Whittaker & Co., 1855), page 451.

central authority by a monarch and sectional interests of landed barons often deflected energies away from consistent enforcement of policies and procedures toward Scotland's government and mutual interests in regulating territorial disputes. A prime example from the early thirteenth century is what became known as the First Barons' War, one of whose leaders, Simon de Montford, 6th earl of Leicestershire, would figure also in the Second Barons' War nearly a half-century later. The outcome of the first was disastrous for much of Northumberland. As historian John Hodgson later described it, early in 1216 king John, not the most adept of monarchs,

> marched against his rebellious barons in the north; many of whom had offended his irritable genius by doing homage to the king of Scotland at Felton. The Mailross Chronicle [Melrose Chronicle] is rather minute in its account of this fierce and desolating war, and says that the barons, to impede the king's progress, set fire to their villages and corn [grain]; and that the king himself in his progress destroyed the towns and villages that laid in his way with fire and sword, and especially in this frightful devastation, that Morpeth and Mitford were burnt by him on the 7th, Alnwick on the 9th, and Wark on the 11th of January. There is, however, perhaps some error in the dates of this account, for it is plain from the progresses of that monarch that he tested documents at Newcastle on the 9th of January, at Bedlington on the 9th and 10th, at Alnwick on the 11th, was at Berwick from the 14th to the 22nd, back to Mitford on the 24th and 26th, and again at Newcastle from the 26th to the 29th of that month.[25]

Although the latter part of the Melrose Chronicle is more accurate than the older parts, it is inconsistent both internally (as in this regard) and in relation to other sources. Nevertheless, its account of the devastation is not far off the mark. After all, the practices described therein were not invented by these barons and this king.

King John's grandson, Edward, ascended to the throne at the death of his father, Henry III, in 1272. Henry had enacted a number of reforms –for instance, election of two knights from each shire to the parliament in London beginning in 1254, the first inclusion of elected members—and

---

[25] John Hodgson, *A History of Northumberland*, part 2, volume 2 (Newcastle-upon-Tyne: printed for the author, 1832), page 481.

in due course Edward would extend reforms.[26] But first he was determined to secure the expanse of his domain, and initial attention in that respect was his campaign, 1277 to 1283, to annex the principality of Wales. As a result, most of Wales became part of the royal fiefdom, the heir to the throne thereafter styled the prince of Wales. Then, too, there was still the ever present threat of revolt by one or another faction of barons, and indeed late in his father's long reign Edward led the attack in the Second Barons' War (1264-1266), which resulted in the death of Simon de Montford, among others. Edward remembered his military skills when, early in his reign, he turned his attention to the securing of Wales. Among his next goals, securing the borderlands with Scotland was high on the list.

In fact, when Edward ascended the throne the influence of the English crown in the North was generally very limited. One measure of that can be seen in the Roll of Fines levied during the 55th year of his father's reign (i.e., 28 October 1270 to 27 October 1271).[27] More than 1600 entries are recorded on these sheets. Careful inspection of all the entries shows that only two dozen or so pertain to Westmoreland, Cumberland, and Northumberland, and Cumberland accounted for the majority of the levies.[28] Granted, those lands were sparsely settled. But people were hardly *that* thin on the ground; nor did they refrain from the behaviors that were likely to elicit fines.

It was Edward's concern to effect a reasonably permanent end to the cross-border raids and other incursions that very likely framed his decision to grant the Yethem lands to Simon de Heselrig, already lord of two manors near Newcastle, Weetslade and West Brunton, descendant of the old manor of Heselrig in the far north, and of a family that had long ties in Northumberland. Heselrig manor, held by the family at least as early as 1187 (33 Henry II), and probably much earlier, is located about 10 miles inland from Bamburgh Castle and about 50 miles north of Newcastle. In short, it was a small outpost of the chain of castles created under William I, probably one of the outposts created under Henry I (as discussed in the previous chapter). If one travels the valley of the river

---

[26] Michael Prestwich's *Edward I* (London: Methuen, 1988) is an excellent source.

[27] Henry III was the first of now five English monarchs whose reigns lasted longer than 50 years, in his case from 28 October 1216 to 16 November 1272, the beginning of his 57th year on the throne.

[28] Two dozen or so, an estimate (the reason being that my inspection was in search of names of family members, not a census by shire, and only after realising how rare the entries for the three shires did I begin a tally).

Till, which passes just west of the old manorial site, north-northwest about 18 miles, one comes to the river Tweed (which became the agreed boundary with southeast Scotland). Thus, Heselrig manor was one of a set of outposts in "the marches" from southeastern Scotland through valleys potentially all the way to north Yorkshire.[29] Another, even nearer the Tweed, was Etal manor, which also dates at least from the late 1100s. Another, between Etal and Heselrig, was Ford manor. Unlike its two northern neighbors, each of which received royal license to crenellate— to add various battlements to the manor house, usually parapets at top, on a wall, and the like—thus officially to become a castle, Heselrig did not obtain such license. Furthermore, whereas some barons crenellated without license, paying a negotiated fine when caught in violation of the crown's wish to control private (i.e., not royal) castles, there is no indication that the manor of Heselrig was crenellated at all. A pele tower, with garrison of up to twenty men, was erected. Its heavy stone construction was still largely intact at recently as the 1700s, when the family's shield could be seen over an entrance. Why no crenellation? Only speculative answers are possible, but one likely reason is the family's intent to move south, to better land, better weather, better access to Newcastle and hence sites of power and authority still further south.

The chain of movements south toward Newcastle was negotiated rather quickly, for by 1280, as we have seen, Simon de Heselrig was lord of two manors in that area. Simon was then *valectus* (valet) to Edward I, which means he had earned considerable trust by his behavior. It does not mean he was or ever had been in London (although that possibility cannot be ruled out of hand). When kings traveled, they took part of their court with them; but they also maintained officers of court in various parts of the realm, not only sheriffs and sergeants and justiciars but also personal attendants such as valets, and Simon was one such, available to service when the king was in Northumberland. To have such an office was an honor, of course, and it signified the likelihood of future favors. Favor was a coin of reciprocity. Simon had benefited, no doubt, from royal favor when he acquired Weteslade and West Brunton. When his king approached him with another favor, these grants of land close by the border with Scotland, Simon's proper response was the reciprocal favor

---

[29] They were "marches" by reference to marching an army from place to place. Late in the reign of Edward I an agreement was struck with Scotland that each crown would appoint a "Warden of the Marches," who would then have nearly supreme authority to police "the marches" each side of the border. Robert de Clifford was first warden of the Marches on the English side.

of reversing the family's momentum toward building patrimony more and more toward the south, and returning to the far north to build a defensive operation in service to his king.

The two sites known then as Yetham were in the county of Roxburgh, Scotland, barely north of the present-day border, repeatedly contested territory. Yetholm had been a vill in the old Anglian kingdom of Northumbria, and it probably was one that William I had left in Anglo-Saxon baronial hands. Had Simon previously lived in that locality? Very unlikely. Did he relocate to that area, having received his king's grant of land? Insofar as the grant came with a charge, which it probably did, Simon would have been expected to hold those lands *as if* he were continually in residence, if in fact not. The distance between Weetslade and Yetham was the better part of a two-day ride, which means that a distress call would have required about that length of time, followed by an equal or greater length of time for assistance to arrive. It is likely that Simon placed a son or sons in residence of one or both parcels in Yetham, each with a substantial garrison of soldiers and provisioners. There is no known record that establishes that conjecture as fact. However, we know from records of the king's itinerary that Edward I visited Yetham in August 1296, arriving on the 23rd, and that "William of Yetham swore fealty" to Edward during that two-day visit. Was this man a Heselrig? Perhaps. We also know that the king had appointed Sir William de Heselrig as sheriff of the Clydesdale, headquartered in Lanark, by 1297, probably the preceding summer. Was this the same William? Again, there is no record of relevance to the question. (This is Sir William, sheriff, who met his fate at the hands of William Wallace in 1297; about which, more below).

On today's map of the area Yetham remains as two distinct places, Town Yetholm and Kirk Yetholm, plus Yetholm Main, a farm (see top panel of Exhibit 3.6). The designation "Yetham Corbet" in Edward's grant in 1281 probably stems from the fact that David, Scotland's king and previously known as "prince of the Cumbrians," made Walter Corbet of Makerston the lord of Yetham during the 1100s. One of David's accomplishments during his reign (1124-1153) was to refashion the government of Scotland along Norman lines, and that included the system of land holdings. So Walter was no doubt expected to be a stalwart defender of the area of Yetham, against invasion from the south. The name "Yetham Corbet" probably refers to Walter's home estate, which, given Yetham's location and importance at the time, would surely have been organized as a manorial estate. Today's sites, Town Yetholm,

Kirk Yetholm, and Yetholm Mains farm, are probably remnants of that estate. The topography of the area suggests that "Yetham" referred to a passageway between hills, issuing into two or more roads leading to various other places. The two main sites known from today's geography, Town Yetholm and Kirk Yetholm, were totally demolished by Edward Seymour, 1st earl of Hertford, in 1545 during his great sweep of razings against Scottish strongholds, so there is nothing in the way of built structures to examine from the earlier centuries.

We have already seen "the marches" that run with the course of the river Till, down to the Heselrig manor and beyond. Now we can see from Exhibit 3.6 that the Cheviot Hills formed an obstruction to easy north-south movement to the west of Wooler, which is slightly west of the Till. The map in the bottom panel tells the story more clearly, by reporting elevations—for instance, Preston Hill, 526 meters; Yeavering Bell, 361 meters; Kilham Hill, 328 meters.[30] Coming from the north, one could pick passage from Yetholm by an arc above the hills to Wooler.[31] Or one could follow Bowmont Water, a stream running south to north along Yetholm, until coming to its confluence with College Burn which then forms the river Glen. In either case, it is clear, control of passage in the area of Yethem was important to English settlements to the south. Thus, the task assigned to Simon in that grant of land.

Let's turn now from one man, Simon, who served his king, to another, the man who had been knighted as Sir William and appointed as sheriff of the Clydesdale, with headquarters in the town of Lanark. This brings us to the famous episode of legend and myth, involving William Wallace and battles that have been styled in recent times as "the first war of Scottish independence." That phrase can be misleading. Context is important.

The modern system of independent nation-states did not exist in the thirteenth or fourteenth century. It dates from 1648 and the Treaty of Westphalia. In those earlier centuries, the feudal system was built of a principle of hierarchy that extended through a "country" into groups of (usually contiguous) "countries," with the result that monarchs competed

---

[30] This is a piece of Armstrong's map of Northumberland, 1769. Yeavering Bell, a twin-topped hill, was a Stone Age site of considerable importance; later, a walled fortification of dwellings, remnants of which can still be seen.

[31] Note that Akeld, Coupland, and Yever (i.e., Yeavering) follow the line of that arc. At least the first, perhaps all, of those three estates were held by the Heselrig family, c1296; how long before that date, and how long after, cannot be said. Was this William a son of Simon? Was he the same man who served Edward as sheriff in Lanark in 1297? The questions, important though their answers, remain open for future research.

among themselves for overlordship. At any given time, the strongest monarch in a region expected homage from other monarchs; the second

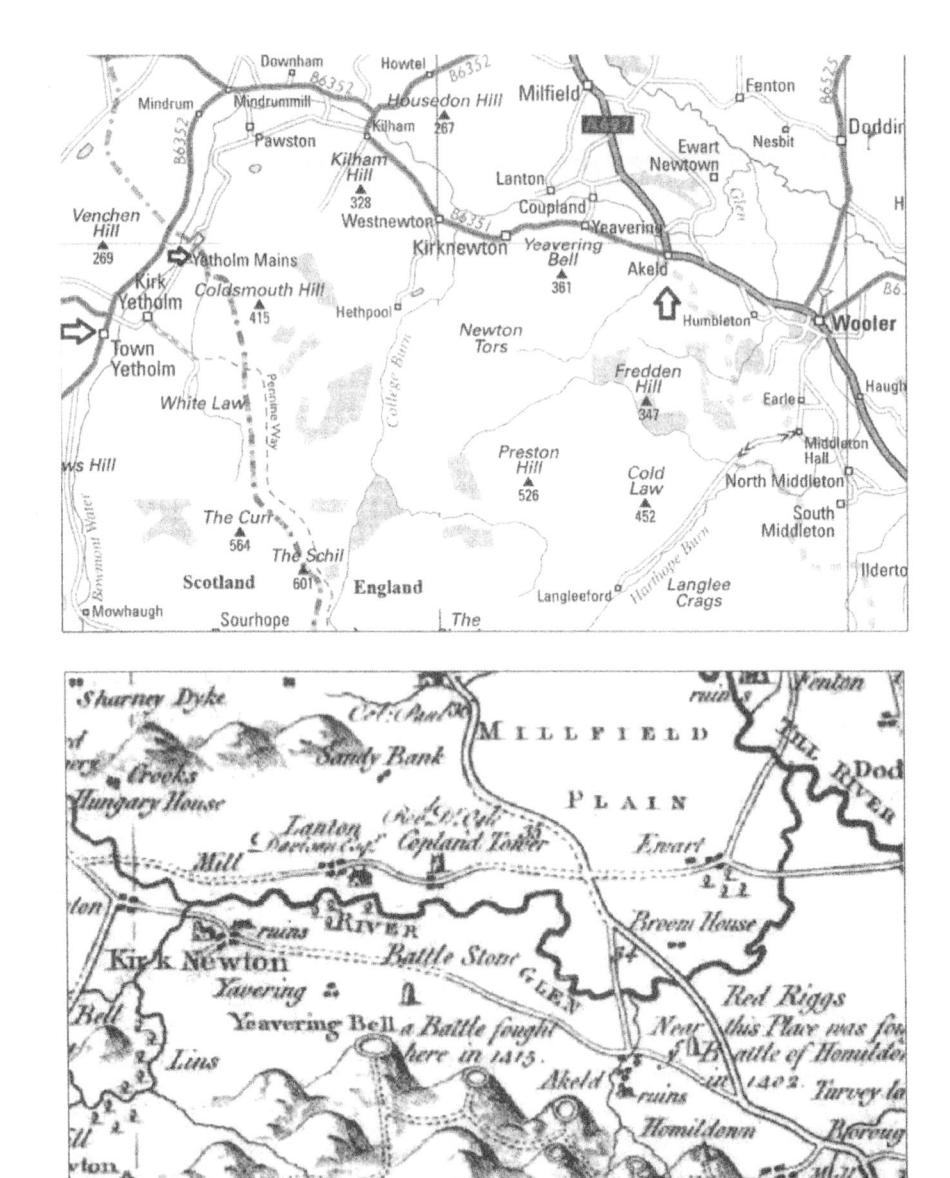

Exhibit 3.6. Maps of the Area between Wooler and Yetholm

strongest could expect homage from weaker monarchs; and so forth. The ranks typically depended on availability of resource by which to back threats of war, or by which to wage actual war, when existing settlements came undone. Resources were material, but equally vital was a monarch's ability to raise funds and troops from among his subjects, both sorts of "raising" coming at the expense of the nobility, aristocracy, and ultimately the land barons—in other words, lower ranks in that same chain of the feudal principle. Independence was relative.

Scotland was an independent realm of its own king. Until the crisis of succession to the Scottish throne beginning in 1286, relations between English and Scottish monarchs had been largely settled, with a quiet agreement that the English monarch was paramount. As the succession crisis evolved, the main disputants, Robert de Brus and John Balliol, were deadlocked in competing claims and supporters. Appeal was then made to England's Edward—not yet given the epithet "Hammer of the Scots"—to arbitrate the dispute. Edward agreed, and in November 1292 Balloil became John, king of Scotland. In the meantime, Edward had gained influence among Lowland Scottish barons, most of whom (like Balloil and de Brus) descended from Norman-French or Angevin-French forebears. Also in the meantime, Edward had been continuing to press claims against France. His expectation that Scotland would supply taxes and troops to that effort was repulsed, and to make the repulsion worse Scotland then allied with France. In retrospect one could easily say that the Scottish king's response would have been expected, in this chess game of feudal relations. But Edward was incensed. He mobilized a force against Berwick, which fell, then proceeded to do battle at Dunbar (April 1296) and won, confiscating Scotland's traditional coronation seat ("the Stone of Scone," only recently returned to Scotland by Elizabeth II), then captured the Scottish king John, transported him to London, and threw him into the Tower. Edward next installed Englishmen as governors in key posts. This enactment, in the summer of 1296, is almost surely the advent of Sir William Heselrig's appointment as sheriff of the Clydesdale, with central office in Lanark, about 75 miles west of the Yetham estates.

Thinking that he had regained subservience north of the Tweed, Edward again shifted main attention to France. He had been pressing his barons for more taxes and more troops; his barons were resisting; at one point relations became so strained that some feared another civil war. It was left to the Scots to change the subject once again, and they did. This led to events that have often been styled, somewhat anachronistically, "the First War of Scottish Independence."

As briefly described in chapter 1, Scotland had become a divided land because of invasions by Anglo-Saxons, Norse, Norman-French, and other ethnic groups, who increasingly pushed the predominantly Celtic population (a branch of Celts known as Gaels) into the very poor, rugged terrain of the Scottish Highlands. One of the Highland families had taken the family name "Wallace" (i.e., Wallis, Walles, etc.) probably signifying roots in Wales. The family's scion in 1296 was son William, a man now of great legend and myth. Very little that is said of him can be verified by independent record, and little attempt to sort demonstrable fact from the mythic parts of his legend will be made here.[32] The bare facts are that he succeeded in rallying Scottish forces to respond to Berwick, Dunbar, and other offenses by the English, and on 11 September 1297 he and Andrew de Moray (Murray) led a small force to victory over a larger English force in a battle known as Stirling Bridge. London was horrified. The effect was to unify English crown and nobility to common cause, which began with a large force defeating Wallace and his force in the Battle of Falkirk, on 22 July 1298. This was not the end of Wallace; he escaped and led ragtag forces in small forays, thereafter refusing frontal contact with the English army. In the end, he had been betrayed by a countryman, captured, taken to London, and beheaded.

Where, in that picture, does Sir William Heselrig, sheriff of the Clydesdale, fit? The known facts are few: sometime in May 1297 a small band of men led by Wallace gained entry to the sheriff's quarters and killed Heselrig, then escaped. One reasonably reliable source says that the sheriff's son was also killed. No doubt the sheriff's quarters had been in some manner fortified against attack, but there is no record of its size or its design. Nor do we know the ages of William Heselrig and his son (or the son's name). His appointment probably came with a grant of land in or near Lanark; but if so, there is no known record of it. Beyond that, we have legend. Hardly any physical features of the events remain, the only notable exception being a hill on which some sort of castle existed—if actually a castle, probably at later date (see Exhibit 3.7).

---

[32] Good sources are Pete Armstrong, *Stirling Bridge and Falkirk 1297-98* (Oxford: Osprey, 2003), Sir Thomas Gray, *Scalacronica* (edited by A King; London: Surtees Society, 2005), and George Vere Irving and Alexander Murray, *The Upper Ward of Lanarkshire* (Edinburgh: Thomas Murray, 1864), volume 1, pages 223-231. Irving and Murray did much to sort between parts of the legend that could be tested against other evidence and parts that could not, then identify the parts (e.g., the Bradfute parts) that lack support and are probably mostly confections of a romanticism.

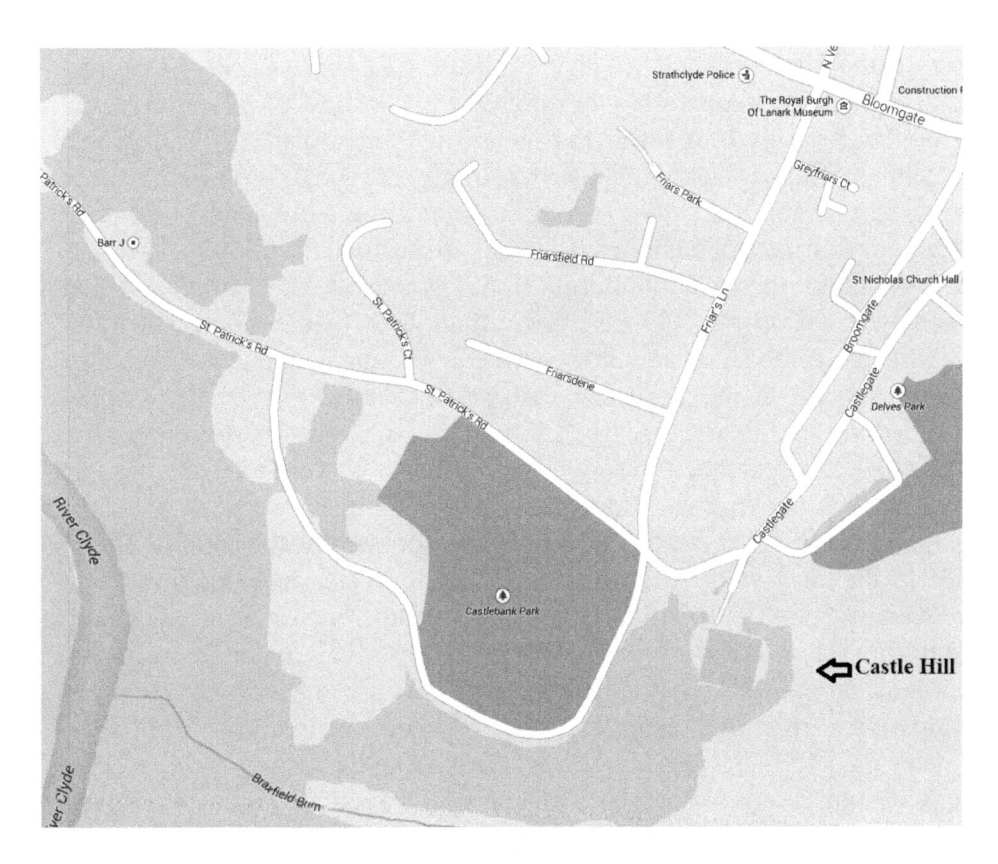

Exhibit 3.7. Map of Approximate Location of Lanark Castle

A key element of the mythic structure defines Wallace's killing of Heselrig as revenge—not revenge for the Scots' defeats at Berwick and Dunbar, nor for the capture and imprisonment of their king or for the English king's imposition of men such as Heselrig as their governors; but revenge in a very personal manner. [33] Supposedly, Wallace and a woman named Marian Bradfute were husband and wife, or betrothed, or at least sweethearts.[34] Supposedly, too, Wallace had been engaged in raids on English outposts, the behavior that had brought him to attention of the sheriff. The third part of the key element is that Heselrig captured or in some way used Bradfute as lure to the capture of Wallace. On this point

---

[33] Walter Scott rejuvenated the legend when, in his *Tales of a Grandfather*, he offered his extended account; see *The Prose Works of Sir Walter Scott* (Edinburgh: Cadell, 1836), volume 1, chapter 7, pages 80-81.

[34] The legend says further that she was heiress of a manorial estate; there is no evidence for it, nor do we have evidence that her family name was Bradfute.

different versions of the legend vary in details, some offering none and others elaborating with claims that Bradfute was abused and/or that she had been Heselrig's romantic interest and was now a focus of jealousy.

Today a town of fewer than 9,000 inhabitants, by the end of the thirteenth century Lanark (or "Lanrick," as many locals say) had been a "royal burgh" for more than a century since the Sottish king David's designation of that mercantile privilege was bestowed in 1140. Located about 30 miles west of Edinburgh, uphill from the eastern bank of the river Clyde, the market town served a wide area of the Clydesdale and had already gained considerable stature as a market center. What is remembered as "Lanark Castle" was probably a rather modest wooden fortification, built in typical motte-and-bailey style (judging by archaeological evidence). The motte (hillock or mound) remains as "Castle Hill," though one cannot say with confidence how much of it has changed since the late 1290s. In fact, it has not been well established that this was the location of sheriff's keep in 1297. In any case, judging from the existing "castle hill," this bailey (the palisade-encircled grounds and outbuildings) was a rather small oblong, all very likely made of wood, as was the keep atop the motte. The one odd fact about this fortification is its location: while the keep was raised by height of the motte, probably no more than 15 to 20 feet above the surrounding terrain, it surely did not occupy "high ground" within its area of location. Castlegate Road, shown in the map (Exhibit 3.7), rises considerably in elevation as one walks northward the 300 feet or so to its intersection with High Street and the A73. Observation of activities, counts of soldiers, and so forth, within the palisade would have been all too easy, and archers uphill would have had advantage.

The grant of the Yethem estate to Simon in 1281 is both the first and the last known record connecting that manor and its immediate area to the Hesilrige family. However, we know that the family's presence in the general area continued for at least another century. As mentioned in the inventory of estates, William de Heselrig held Akeld manor at least as late as 1306, probably until his death some time before 1319, and his son retained a quarter of the manor as late as 1329. Akeld manor, recall from Exhibit 3.6, lay between Wooler and the Yethem area. Also recall from those maps that between Akeld and the Yethem sites lay an area known as Newton, anchored by Kirk Newton and the town of West Newton. This is of interest here because on 29 September 1387, and again a month later, a charter granting one-half of the town of West Newton was drawn, dated, and signed by several witnesses at Newton. Among the witnesses were Sir Roger Heron, Sir John Manners, and John de Hesilrig.[35] We do not know the precise identity of this last-named man. William Heselrig of Akeld had a son named John; but since he was at Bannockburn in 1314 (with "horses and armor"; i.e., a warhorse plus, probably, a pack horse and a palfrey) he must have been at least in his mid-20s at that date, which implies that he would have been older than 90 in 1387—not impossible but unlikely, and still more unlikely that he would have been ambulatory for witnessing legal transactions. In any case, the fact of witness John de Hesilrig documents continuing presence of the family in the area near Yethem as the fourteenth century neared its end.

More Lineage
Between Roger, the legendary immigrant from the continent, and the first member of the Hesilrige family to appear in credible records, the William de Heselrig recorded in 1187, we face a gaping ignorance of 120 years. William was surely older than 20 years in 1187, however, since he was head of a manor (probably Heselrig manor near Wooler).[36] With that assumption the gap has been shortened to less than a century, perhaps less than three-quarters that. Assuming further that Roger's eventual heir did not arrive with him at Hastings, we could easily imagine that this William was great grandson of Roger—and at largest distance, probably, Roger's great great grandson. The missing three or four generations will undoubtedly remain beyond any hope of recovery. Absence of records is only partly the reason. There is also an inherent ambiguity within the early records that do exist, because we lack any means of dating the use of "de Heselrig" as a surname, a family name, rather than a designation of the manor to which a person was attached at the moment of record. We can be confident that a certain "Thomas of Fawdon" was a Heselrig man because of the existence of a record that named him "Thomas de Heselrig of Fawdon." Likewise, "John de Shepwash" was recorded also as "John de Heselrig of Shepwash." And so on. But these cases pertain to a time when use of a family name (surname) was generally well established in aristocratic families. In earlier times, when the practice was still new and irregular, the ambiguity of record is often unbreachable. If one comes to a midtwelfth-century record of a man named, say, "Simon de Cresswell" in the Glendale, and nothing more can be found that reliably ties him to a recorded *family* name, then or later, where in the ledger shall one place him? Further, what of the possibility of two brothers whose grandsons or

---

[35] See the *Calendar of the Laing Charters*, numbers 76 and 78.
[36] Hodgson, "On the Medieval and Later Owners" (1910), page 11, cites it as such.

great grandsons elect different family names because of divergent manors to which the cousins had been attached?

We can only note those and related possibilities and then leave them to the side.

Next we come to another William, listed in the Pipe Roll for 1248 and probably head of the manor at Heselrig. This gap of 61 years from 1187 could be filled by another two missing generations, if we assume that the prior William was born no later than, say, 1150 and issued his surviving heir in, say, 1180, who did likewise in another 30 years.

From that William of 1248 we come to a third William, named in 1256 as "Willelmi de Eselrig" in a record of assize. Henry II established in the Assize of Clarendon, 1166, trial by jury of twelve knights in land disputes, and these sessions ("assizes") of court, conducted by itinerant judges ("justiciars"), were held increasingly regularly as monarchal sway gained force in the north. One of the Northumberland cases in 1256 saw Thomas de Wetewude in the dock on the charge of having unjustly taken ("deseized") William Brun and his wife Emma of their tenement. Having said nothing to persuade the jurors of his innocence, he was fined one mark, which was pledged by William de Eselrig and Simon de Cresswell. Nothing further identifies either William or Simon (Thomas apparently was the same man who had made some repairs to Bamburgh castle some eighteen years earlier); nor do we know why William and Simon vouched for the fine (beyond the probable fact that Thomas could not then pay it and needed surety).[37]

Then we come to a fourth William, recorded in the Pipe Roll for the 55th year of the reign of Henry III, 1272. This man *could* have been the same as the William of 1248, as well as the William of 1256. If we assume the identity between 1272 and 1248, we are about six generations removed from Roger and Hastings. Even at five generations, the gap is substantial. To put it in personal perspective, the present writer is tenth generation from the Thomas Hesilrige who, in the 1630s or 1640s, migrated from England to the Virginia shores of British North America.

One last "unconnected" member of the family, before turning to the established pedigree: this one is Alan de Heselrig, recorded in the Assize Roll for 1282 (7 Edward I).[38] The land dispute is nearly the same as the dispute described above: in this case two brothers faced charges of having unjustly taken a tenement in "Holkshale" (i.e., Holthal, aka Hottal,

---

[37] *Three Early Assize Rolls for the County of Northumberland, sæc. XIII*. Publications of the Surtees Society, volume 88 (Durham: Andrews & Co., 1891), page 2.

[38] *Three Early Assize Rolls* (1891), pages 233, 387.

Holtalle, Holtehall, etc.), a village near Kirk Newton in Glendale. One of the brothers appeared in court. The other brother did not and "was arrested by William de Hopun and Alan de Hesilrig." No title was given for either of the latter men, but presumably they were acting as officers of the court. Nothing further is known reliably of this man, Alan. But nearly 37 years later, on 5 March 1319, several grants of land were made by individual holders to the Temple of North Ferriby (a village on the north bank of the Humber estuary, East Riding of Yorkshire), among them a grant "by William de Heselrig son of Alan of land in Alvesle" (or Elvelay).[39]

The official English pedigree begins with Simon de Heselrig, lord of Weteslade and West Brunton, *valectus* to Edward I; and so it must be here. Even thus, some relational discontinuities and uncertainties will be unavoidable in the period immediately after Simon, because of lack of evidence. In some instances suggestions of relationship will be made, but these must be held with due caution. Numeral superscripts will signify generational links, where they are known; by alphabetical notation within generation, probable order of birth. Lineage breaks will be marked in line by ʮ ʮ ʮ ʮ ʮ ʮ, though in some instances the break might not involve even one missing generation. More information for several of the individual persons will be supplied in later chapters. The segment of lineage presented below extends to the fifth generation of the pedigree, the break coming at approximately the move of the seat to Noseley in Leicestershire.

Simon[1] de Heselrig: lord of Wetislade and West Brunton; valectus to Edward I; granted land in Yetham (i.e., Yetholm Mains and Yetholm Corbet) in Roxburghshire, 8 Feb 1281

└-- **Simon**[2a] de Heselrig: fl. 1319-23; see below

└-- John[2b] de Heselrig: "son of Simon, acquired land [1258-1259] in Whittingham, Thrunton and Barton"[40] (nfi)

---

[39] *Calendar of Patent Rolls*, 12 Edward II. This "temple," a priory, later gained some attention as a supposed outpost of the order of the Knights Templar, but the attribution is surely in error; cf. Egerton Beck, "The Order of the Temple at North Ferriby," *English Historical Review* 26 (July), pages 498-501.

[40] John Crawford Hodgson, *A History* ..., (1904), page 462.

⋮⋮⋮⋮⋮⋮ (unknown relationship; probably no missing generation)

Alan de Heselrig: presumably officer of court, c1282; perhaps son or brother to Simon¹; perhaps resident of the Glendale area

⋮⋮⋮⋮⋮⋮ (unknown relationship; probably no missing generation)

Sir **William** de Heselrig: sheriff of the Clydesdale, appointed by Edward I; killed May 1297 by Wallace at Lanark; perhaps brother or son to Simon¹

└── Fnu de Heselrig: killed May 1297, probably in adolescence and probably without issue; might not have been only son

⋮⋮⋮⋮⋮⋮ (relationship unknown; perhaps not a generational break)

William Haselrigg: "a squire who sat for Northumberland; had fought at Halidon Hill in 1333 [19 July; near Berwick] when he was seventeen years old"[41]

⋮⋮⋮⋮⋮⋮ (relationship unknown; perhaps not a generational break)

Alan de Heselrig: named as father of a William de Heselrig who held land in Yorkshire's East Riding, 1319; perhaps same as Alan de Heselrig recorded c1282

└── **William** de Heselrig: held land in North Ferriby, Yorkshire, by 1319

⋮⋮⋮⋮⋮⋮ (perhaps not a generational break)

William de Hesilrig: acquired manor of Akeld in Glendale from Nicholas de Graham and Mary his wife, before 1306; grant from bishop of Durham, Richard Kellawe, of lands and tenements at Cambois in Bedlingtonshire, grant confirmed by Edward II at York 16 Nov 1316; apparently dead by 14 Mar 1319; perhaps same man as, or son of, the William de Heselrig recorded in 1272

---

[41] Jonathan Sumption, *The Hundred Years War*, volume 3: *Divided Houses* (London: Faber and Faber, 2009), page 256. The surname spelling is almost surely anachronistic, if not by Sumption then his source. If the implied birth year is correct (or at least nearly so), this man could not be any of the other known men named William.

∟-- **John** de Hesilrig (aka Hesilrygg):   b. <1290; present as one of the men at arms, in this case armored cavalry, at the battle of Bannockburn, 24 Jun 1314; held quarter part of manor of Akeld 1329; mentioned in a deed relating to Plessey, c1350, as John de Heselrigg of Sheepwash ("Shepwash")

ห ห ห ห ห ห (relationship unknown; perhaps not a generational break)

William de Hesilrig: knight of the shire for Northumberland in the Parliament of 1320 and 1321; perhaps brother to John de Hesilrig

ห ห ห ห ห ห (relationship uncertain)

Thomas de Heselrig: son of William de Heselrig; placed in remainder to the estate of Plessey which was acquired c1350 by Roger de Widdrington;[42] perhaps Thomas was brother to John (above) or son of the William immediately above

ห ห ห ห ห ห (relationship uncertain)

Thomas de Heselrig: same as Thomas immediately above?

∟-- **Thomas** de Hesilrig: lord of Hesilrig; held vill of Hesilrigg (Chatton parish) and vills of Fowberry and Coldmorton, c1346; mentioned in a deed relating to Plessey, c1350; described as son of Thomas de Hesilrig

ห ห ห ห ห ห (probably no missing generation)

Simon[2a] de Heselrig: son and heir of Simon[1] de Heselrig, lord of Weteslade and West Brunton,[43] he was among those charged by earl of Richmond, 15 Feb 1319, with having raided Aldborough and other

---

[42] Hodgson, "On the Medieval and Later Owners" (1910), page 13, suggested that Roger and William were kinsmen.

[43] The earliest known record of this relationship is William Camden, *The Visitation of the County of Leicester*. Publications of the Harleian Society, volume 2 (London: Taylor and Co., 1870), page 15. No independent evidence has come to light.

manors in Yorkshire; on list of Northumberland men at arms returned 7 July 1323 by Gilbert de Broughton, Sheriff[44]

  ᒪ-- **Donald**[3a] de Heselrig: b. c1320; m(1) c1361 Johanna de Wauton; m(2) c1377 Joan de Bredon, damsel of chamber of queen Philippa; appointed commissioner of array for North Riding, Yorkshire, 1 Jul 1377; knight of shire; d. Sunday after Easter (9 April) 1385, childless (according to inquisition p.m. of widow Joan, 7 Apr 1401); brother William[3b] is heir, at age 60

  ᒪ-- **William**[3b] de Heselrig: b. 1325, d. >1385, probably >1400; more below

  ᒪ-- Edmund[3c] de Heselrig: b. >1325, d. >1369, probably <1385 s.p.; held part of Eslington in trust for brother Donald and Johanna (*nee* de Wauton) his wife, from c1362; witness to Greenwell Deeds 1 Aug 1367 & 1 Aug 1369 Newcastle (see documents D/Gr 219 & D/Gr 222, Leicestershire Records Office)

  ᒪ-- Simon[3d] de Heselrig: b. >1325, d. >1367; witness to a Greenwell Deed 1 Aug 1367 Newcastle (see document D/Gr 219)

  ᒪ--Thomas[3e] de Heselrig: mentioned in deed c1350 relating to manor of Plessey; perhaps granted that manor that date

William[3b] Heselrig of Fawdon: (b. 1325, d. c1386; m. Agnes, daughter of Thomas Graper & Mary Stanhope; home seat, manor of Fawdon; in 1346 held the vill of Fawdon, third part of Gosforth, sixth part of Kenton, moiety of Dinnington; served in Scottish Wars of Edward III, granted lands in Wetislade South 20 Nov 1360, which in 1369 he settled upon his son William; witness to Greenwell Deeds 1 Aug 1367 & 1 Aug 1369 Newcastle (ref: D/Gr 219; D/Gr 222) and 20 May 1372 Denton (ref: D/Gr 230); knight of shire for Northumberland in 1375 and 1377; appointed commissioner of array for Northumberland, 1 Jul 1377; the manor of Fawdon plus lands in South Gosforth, Kenton, and Newcastle settled on son Thomas in 1386; manor of Swarland, inherited by wife Agnes, settled on son John[4e]

---

[44] John Hodgson, *A History of Northumberland*, part 1 (Newcastle-upon-Tyne: Thomas and James Pigg, 1858), page 303.

└-- Donald[4a] Hesilrige: b. <1342, d. by 12 Jul 1387; m. 1362 Joan, daughter of Nicholas Heron; named in settlement of 1386

└-- William[4b] Heselrig: b. c1350, d. <1400

└-- Thomas[4c] Heselrig of Fawdon: b. c1365 Fawdon, d. 15 Oct 1422 Eslington; seised of Eslington, recorded as owner of tower of Eslington 1415; seised of moieties of the vills of Whittingham, Thrunton, and Barton; m. 1395 at Noseley, Isabel (b. c1375, d. <1439), daughter and heir of Sir Roger Heron (b. 1330, d. c1397) and his wife Margaret (b. 1353, d. 7 Apr 1407 Noseley; daughter of Sir Ralph Hastings), which marriage brought the manor of Noseley; acquired manor of Gilmorton. Foster reported Thomas, with arms, in his inventory (see Exhibit 3.8, below).[45]

└--Thomas[5a] Hesilrige: b. 29 Sep 1407 Eslington, d. 21 Sep 1467; more later

└-- John[5b] Hesilrige: b. c1409 Noseley, d. 4 Jun 1432 Noseley; more later

└-- Robert[4d] Hesilrige: living 1392

└-- John[4e] Heselrig of Swarland: b. >1365; d. 1391; thus began the Swarland branch of the family (see next chapter)

---

[45] Joseph Foster, *Some Feudal Coats of Arms* (1902), page 106.

—COATS OF ARMS.

Ťľõ Haſilcrig   Ťp de Haſling

Harpden, Sir William de, of Oxon.—(E. II. Roll) bore, argent a mullet pierced gules, Parliamentary Roll; a Suffolk Knight of this surname bore (H. VI.) argent on a mullet gules, a bezant charged with a martlet sable; Arundel Roll.

Harpur(——) of Rushall, a plain cross—but bore the arms of Rushall, argent, a lyon rampant within a bordure engrailed sable.—Shirley.

Harsick, John de (E. III. Roll) bore, or, a chief indented per pale sable; Jenyns' Ordinary, also in Ashmole Roll. See Monumental Brass.

Hartford = Hertford.

Hartford, Robert (E. III. Roll) bore, argent, on a fess sable three harts' heads caboshed or; Jenyns' Ordinary.

Hartford, Thomas, of Badsworth (E. III. Roll) bore, argent, a lion purpure mascaly or; Jenyns' Ordinary.

Harthull, Sir Richard de, of co. Derby—(E. II. Roll) bore, argent two bars vert; Parliamentary Roll — also ascribed to JOHN HARTHULL, though tricked vair, in Jenyns' Ordinary.

Hartwell, —— (HARTWELL), an Essex? Knight (H. VI. Roll) bore, sable, a buck's head caboshed argent between the attires a cross patée or the last; Arundel Roll. F.

Haseley(——) a Suffolk Knight—(H. VI. Roll) bore, argent, a fess gules between three hazle nuts or, husks and stalks vert; Arundel Roll. F.

***Hasilrig, Thomas,** of Fawdon — bore, argent, a chevron between three hazel leaves slipped vert. Shirley. F.

Exhibit 3.8. Extract from Foster's *Some Feudal Coats of Arms*

~ 4 ~
From Swarland to Noseley

Success in building patrimony began with well-chosen acquisitions via grants, marital ties, and, when liquid capital allowed, purchases. But it did not end there. Success depended also on consolidating and securing what had been acquired, and that could be even more difficult to achieve.

A core strength of the feudal system of landholding was its hierarchical organization of economic, political, and social relations, chiefly loyalties and obligations, which in principle flowed both upward and downward, underlings responsible for duties toward and support, moral as well as material, for the overlord and overlords responsible for basic security and well-being of their underlings. However, that strength could also be, and often was, a weakness, inasmuch as it could magnify and ramify effects of uncertainty, doubt, and shifts in the virtually perpetual contests for advantage among land barons and between the barons, or factions of them, and their monarch. Estates acquired could slip from grasp even more quickly than gained, and the better an estate's quality the more slippery its possession. There was always a plentiful supply of others seeking a good manor, a prosperous vill, or even a particular messuage (dwelling house), tenement, or small parcel of meadowland. An overlord could be quick to seize on a perceived slight of loyalty in order to revoke a property "held in chief" to him, thus to have it in stock for rewarding another who could be a more beneficial underling. The threat of early mortality was ever present (and the middle of the fourteenth century, part of the period considered in this chapter, witnessed a huge onslaught of early deaths, known as the Black Death). A barren marriage could be addressed, but doing so could mean complications in property relations attached to the marriage agreement. Loss of all sons, through accident, battle, disease, homicide, ripped the future of a lineage from its roots, yet perhaps reparable via grafting of a nephew, a cousin, a drifting knight enlisted by a daughter. And for many English families during the fourteenth and fifteenth centuries, the bulk of the period covered in this chapter, monarchal contests over rights of succession to thrones on the continent as well as in Britain drained patrimonies of men (young and not so young) and materials (directly and via taxations—war levies, and so forth). These were the centuries of a

Hundred Years War, a War of the Roses, a great many lesser battles and skirmishes, famine, and plague.[1]

Despite all the obstacles to success, the Heselrig family managed to accumulate, consolidate, and secure a rather sizeable patrimony in Northumberland during those centuries, the chief focus of it being in an area between Morpeth and Newcastle, in particular the manor of Swarland. Evidence of acquisitions in Durham and in Yorkshire testify to an interest in migrating ever southward, to kinder weather, better soils, and nearer proximity to the great seat of power in London, for all the risk of opportunity, positive and negative, which that proximity entailed. By the end of the fifteenth century, the family was shifting its principal seat to Noseley manor, in Leicestershire, and with that change in location a different lineage gained predominance, as the lineage at Swarland (and associated sites) found itself without heir, at the beginning of the eighteenth century, and transferred most of their estates to the lineage ensconced at Noseley.

This chapter tells of that accumulation, that migration, that motion toward greater opportunity, all against a backdrop of enormous strife and suffering, as the fabric of "English society" was ripped apart by great loss of life to epidemic disease, by nearly incessant warfare in Britain and on the grounds of what had become for French kings English occupations of great swathes of territory from Normandy south to the Pyrenees and inland nearly to Paris itself, and by the huge destruction of wealth that England's barons had committed to their monarchs' repeated but ultimately futile efforts to win and then retain those continental holdings. Out of that destruction a new English society was created, one that marks the end of the medieval era and transition gradually to an early-modern era. The year 1485 is as good as any to mark the end of the old, in part because it was the end of the long reign (1154-1485) of the Plantagenet monarchs, fourteen of them in all. They began as the Angevins: Henry II of Anjou, then Richard I, John, Henry III, and the three Edwards, with lines of succession from Edward III contentious between two Plantagenet houses, the House of Lancaster, who prevailed first with Richard II and three Henrys (IV, V, and VI), and the House of York, with Edwards IV and V, followed by Richard III, who was defeated in battle on Bosworth Field in 1485 by the scion of an altogether different house, the son of Edmund Tudor, earl of Richmond. Although initially aligned with the House of Lancaster, this young man, who became Henry VII, established

---

[1] The subtitle to Barbara Tuchman's *A Distant Mirror* (New York: Knopf, 1978), "The Calamitous Fourteenth Century," is a fitting summary.

a new regime of state and, by his marriage to Elizabeth of York, declared the feud between those houses at end. Having won a national treasury (or the Exchequer) that was virtually empty, Henry VII made clear that he had no interest in the lost territories of the continent, made peace with the French monarchy, and turned his attentions to rebuilding the patrimony of England. What came to be called the Tudor style of administration of state, a prominent feature of which was bureaucratic centralization of authorities of revenue, militia, and intergovernmental relations, proved to be well suited to the aims of reconstruction. With Henry VII we are not yet in the presence of the modern nation-state, as it came to be during the late decades of the seventeenth century, for instance; but viewed from the vantage of 1648 and the Treaty of Westphalia, Henry's instruments of administration look like the grandparents of one's own children.

Famine, Black Death, and 150 Years of War along the Way
The broad-brush picture given above needs some detail, in order to gain a reasonably good impression of some basic conditions of life in England during the fourteenth and fifteenth centuries. Let's begin with the event remembered as the Black Death, which for England began in 1348. As background to that event, which by some estimates thinned England's population by about 50 percent, we need to consider some conditions *ex ante*. Recall from previous discussion the long period, ending c1300, known as the Medieval Warm Period. Agriculturally, times had been good. For the area of northwest Europe, including the British Isles, grain yields (oat, barley, wheat) had been increasing, which meant that cattle, sheep, swine, poultry, and wildlife animals were more plentiful, human bodies better nourished, better clothed, and longer lived, all populations blossoming as never before. Then, disaster: people of that day did not know the vocabulary, but it was climate change (though in that instance, short-lived). The years from 1310 to 1330 brought unusually severe winters, followed by cool, wet summers. Grain yields plummeted. In place of an average of seven grains for every one planted, the yield fell to as low as two to one. One for next year's planting left only one to eat. A consequence? Repeated famine. And that meant elevated mortality. Whereas life expectancy at birth in 1275 had been perhaps 35 years at best (judging from records of the English royal household), it dropped to about 30 during the first decade of the new century. Death by starvation, both direct and indirectly via stingy nourishment and weakened immunity, affected children most of all, then post-partum mothers, victims of injury or disease, the old and infirm. A thinning of population

so quickly on such large scale seemed to many to be unprecedented. Vocabularies of sin and salvation were repeated more often.

The worst of the famines in England held sway from 1315 until the end of that decade. By 1325 food stocks had recovered, relative to a reduced population, and human numbers began to grow again. But then in 1348 this terrible scourge hit England, moving rapidly from a Dorset port to nearly every part of Britain. Lacking any useful knowledge of the vectors of infectious disease, the people of England, like their European fellow beings, could only resort to available means of ignorance in reply. Because much of England's population lived in low-density villages, and because low density meant weaker vectors of transmission, and because some sturdy individuals who contracted, or seemed to have contracted, this terrible scourge did survive, patterns of infection, death, and survival often seemed to tell insights into cause and effect. Specific conditions or treatments that in fact had little or nothing to do with incidence rates of infection and/or survival became solutions, at least momentarily: blends of vinegar and rose water for washing the body, flagellation, lancing the ghastly sores, bleeding, placing a hen atop the swelling, any number of herbal concoctions, incantations of numerous sorts, and so forth. It was what today we know as a typical phenomenon of sampling on a small base, combined with the mistaken equation of correlation with causality. In fact, the human scourge disappeared (at least temporarily) once the weaker members of the human population of an area had been eliminated from the pool of potential victims. (Some actions of human sanitation also helped. If one tries anything and everything that comes to mind, one or another action might actually help, even as others hinder and most do nothing one way or the other. Improved sanitation helped.) The plague returned repeatedly over the next decades, though never again with the same enormous force of bodily and moral destruction as during that short interval from 1348.

City, town, and countryside were devastated. If life expectancy in 1275 had been as good as 35 years at birth, it was cut in half during the years from 1348. Part of that scythe cut immediately. But by far the larger part of the reduction in life expectancy was due to the chain of outcomes following the Black Death. At top of the list was an immediate massive and lasting labor shortage. Of course, there were fewer mouths to feed. But there were also many fewer hands and backs to till the soil, harvest the proceeds, and deliver them to markets. Fields lay fallow for years. Manors shifted production from grains to sheep, far less labor intensive but also more expensive as a foodstuff transported to towns and cities, where food prices soon rose by 200 to 300 percent. Manorial estates, desperate for workers even to tend the sheep and cattle, competed among themselves for the peasants roaming the countryside, who quickly learned how valuable their hands, backs, and knowledge of the arts of animal husbandry as well as grain production had become. To use a modern term anachronistically, their expected wage rates shot up. Best estimates indicate that, whereas agricultural wage rates had increased by about 14 percent in response to the labor shortage that resulted from the Great Famine of 1315-1317, they doubled during the period following the Black Death. After a slew of complaints from the land barons, London tried to impose wage and price controls. In the Statute of Labourers of 1351 provisions included a wage ceiling—no peasant could be paid more than the wages paid for comparable labor in 1346 (which, as it happened, had been a time of general economic depression)—and a stipulation that no peasant could leave the village to which he or she belonged.[2] There is some evidence of the intended consequence on wage rates, but historians by and large concur that the statute was mostly ignored.

All of the events and effects associated with the Black Death of 1348 occurred during the first part of the interrupted series of wars that historians have collected under one name, the Hundred Years War. The first part, often designated "Edwardian" because Edward III was chief instigator, extended from 1337 to 1360. It was followed by a truce which ended in 1369 with the start of twenty more years of warfare. Another, longer truce lasted until 1415, when the final sequence of wars brought an end to the whole in 1453. But two years later began the English civil war known as the War of the Roses, which was to a large extent an extension of the Hundred Years War. So in that sense, from the point of view of the people of England, the Hundred Years War was actually 150 years in duration (minus periods of truce), the War of the Roses ending in 1485 or, by some accounts, 1487.[3]

Among the great many changes that occurred during that interval, foremost surely was the reduction of England's royal domain to nearly the bounds of Britain. Close behind, however, was the end of feudalism as a system of organizing territory and population. The most prominent

---

[2] Data cited in the preceding paragraph come from a number of sources, including the recent careful investigation by Gregory Clark, "The Long March of History," *Economic History Review*, volume 60 (2007), pages 97-135. The text of the Statute of Labourers can be read at page 307 of the first volume of the compilation, *Statutes of the Realm*.
[3] There are many accounts of the Hundred Years War. A recent one, three volumes long with much detail, is Jonathan Sumption's *Hundreds Year War* (London: Faber and Faber, 1990, 1999, 2009).

sign of that change lay in the semi-professionalization of warfare: soldiers ceased to be levied through feudal chains of obligation, instead serving as paid combatants, according to rank and skill, from the national treasury.

The long period of strife began as a sort of family feud, an intense and extensive disagreement over rights of succession, sovereignty, and obligations of loyalty under the hierarchy of overlordship. In sum, more signs that the feudal system was breaking up from within, its strengths having become irreparable weaknesses, had generated perceptions of new opportunity but tinged with uncertainties and ambiguities of the link between "might" and "right." The old system of hierarchy was ordained and anchored from above by the supreme overlordship of Christianity's God, and none of the chief actors, even had he glimmers of doubt about that authority, could afford others' doubting him in his convictions, for they were one and the same. As it became more difficult to discern clear answer to the question, "What is the *right* thing to do?"—*here, now*, in *this* situation—answer to the corollary questions, "When and how to apply *might* of arms and destruction rightfully?" grew riskier on pain of mortal sin. Whereas the strength of belief of and in the old system offered a monarch protection against blasphemy when speaking "God's will," as that cloak of the old system faded, monarchs' risk of nudity, so to speak, increased. A relationship of mutual dependence between monarch and religious leader, such as the archbishop of Canterbury and through him the pope, gained greater vitality but also greater need of constant care from both sides, though mainly more careful diligence from the monarch's side of the bargain, to see that the new cloak remained whole and secure. With Edward III in England we are 132 years from the future Henry VIII—by conventional measure, at least four generations, yet in some ways not so far at all.

Because England's king William I had retained title to the duchy of Normandy, and because his successors beginning with Henry II were a family of Angevins who ruled territory stretching from Scotland to the Pyrenees mountains, English monarchs owed loyalty and homage to a sitting monarch of France. Indeed, for a brief time following the First Barons' War against England's king John, the French king, Louis VIII, was proclaimed in Saint Paul's (but never crowned) the king of England.[4]

---

[4] Because the Saint Paul's proclamation was disputed at the time, and later conceded by Louis as a non-event, most lists of England's (or Britain's) monarchs do not include him. The reign of Henry III began on 28 October 1216, nine days after the death of John. The claim of Louis VIII began at John's death but was abandoned the next year.

Sporadic contentions of rightful heirship were thereafter addressed and resolved rather quickly—until 1337, that is, when Edward III refused to pay homage to Philip VI. In Edward's view, Philip was usurper, since he, Edward, had been closest male heir to his uncle, Charles IV of France, when the latter died without direct male heir in 1328. But since the Paris court observed Salic law, which did not recognize legitimate heirship through a female descent (the basis of Edward's claim), Philip could, and did, rightfully reject the claim from London. Furthermore, in rebuke of Edward's act of disloyalty Philip confiscated the Aquitaine, the Angevins' large territory (previously known as Guyenne, which contained an older region known as Gascony), in southwestern France. Feud became overt war, with Edward exercising dominant hand. After destroying the French fleet, he launched a major invasion in July 1346, which led to defeats of the French forces (e.g., at the battle of Crécy) and capture of Calais, an enclave held by England until 1558. Battles raged for the better part of a quarter-century, with Edward's forces inflicting massive losses on the French armies and at one point on the verge of capturing Paris itself. Edward's son and heir, the Black Prince, invaded from his stronghold in Gascony, toward the broad mountain gap at Poitiers, connecting southern to northern basins in the heart of France, where he won a huge victory in 1356 (the battle of Poitiers), which included capture of the French king, the king's son, and many French nobles (some of whom, king and son among them, held for ransom). In the end, however, Edward III, despite so much destruction of French forces, countryside, and means of subsistence, along with so much of the English treasury, could not maintain control of such a vast territory, and in 1360, in the Treaty of Brétigny, he agreed to a truce. The terms of settlement included relinquishment of much of the territory that had been won. The Angevin lands of southwestern France were retained, but he renounced Normandy along with other claims, and he abandoned his claim to the French crown. It had been a costly quarter-century for both courts, their national treasuries, their nobles and landed gentry. Even aside from deaths due to the great plague of 1348-50, both sides, France more than England, counted large losses of young and mature men. One of the main lessons behind that cost was that while strategy and tactics are without doubt of great importance, logistics are determinative.

    The second part of the Hundred Years War is sometimes called the Caroline War or period (1369-89), in recognition of France's new and much more effective king, Charles V, who strove with great success to regain lost territories. At the same time, the Black Prince suffered ill health, returned to England, and in that event weakened Aquitaine's resistance to pressures from the north. Edward III was also in ill health, dying in 1377 soon after his son and heir. A child survived to become Richard II in difficult and precarious circumstances as much of England's landowning class were rapidly losing their holdings on the continent and, understandably, resented the loss of so much of their wealth in England, through taxation, only to lose their wealth across the Channel. By 1380 all of England's territory in France, excepting Calais, had been recovered by France's now smaller but more effective, more professionalized army.

At home Richard II had to contend with those resentments, with a major Peasants' Revolt in 1381 (against taxations), renewed conflicts at the Borders (1384-85), and two years later a revolt of the barons who wrested control of the central government in 1387. Richard took the reins again in 1389, struck peace with France, and exiled the leader of the barons' revolt, Henry Bolingbroke, son of John of Gaunt (who was third son of Edward III and first duke of Lancaster—thus founder of the House of Lancaster—and duke of Aquitaine).[5] Richard lacked sufficient support and thus sufficient force to forestall revenge by Henry and his fellow barons, however. Deposing Richard, Henry became king (Henry IV), with intent to rejoin battle on the continent and recover all of those lost lands. But a nearly empty treasury, troubles with uprisings in Wales and incursions in the Borders, and widespread fatigue with the burdens of tax stifled the king's intent. It was Henry V, son and heir of Henry IV, who resumed war with France, which in the meantime had become fractious and ineffective, ruled by a king who was often incapacitated by mental illness.

This third part of the Hundred Years War began with promise for England, as Henry V led his relatively small force, perhaps 8,000 strong, against a French army at least twice, perhaps four times that size, and the outcome was one of the most famous of victories in English history—in no small part due to Shakespeare's play, *Henry V*. This was the battle of Agincourt, 1415, which for England marked the beginning of the high point of this third part of the Hundreds Year War. In conjunction with the Treaty of Troyes, 1420, England regained Normandy and other land; Henry married the daughter of the French king, Catherine of Valois, thus uniting the two main lines of descent with claim to the French throne and positioning their heir to be king of both realms. Plans went awry when,

---

[5] Also, claimed by the profession of demography as a founder. By most accountings he was one of the wealthiest men in human history, having amassed holdings that, at peak, were worth in today's terms more than US$100 billion.

two years later, Henry V died, not yet 36 years of age. There was an heir; he became Henry VI; but he was an infant, the regency was weak, and other claims to the French throne were now emboldened. Young Henry was crowned king of England in 1429; king of France, two years later in ceremony at Notre-Dame, Paris. English forces struggled to endure for several more years, as they faced the usual problems of logistics within a context of geographic overreach. An even bigger obstacle, however, was popular sentiment. The French populace had long since fatigued of the repeated waves of razing, armies on the march and "living off the land," which meant confiscating local produce, and the huge losses of young and not so young men, all the while dealing with outbreaks of the plague, threats of famine, and other hardships to bear even when fighting had moved on to another locale.

But also a new force of popular sentiment had emerged. Whereas in the beginning the fight was mainly between different houses of royals and their claims of succession, gradually it also became a fight between native peoples, a fight between nations, between people who were born *here* rather than *there*. This democratization of the sentiments of warfare went hand in hand with the shift away from armies based on feudal principles of obligation and toward standing armies of professional soldiers. On French soil the first unmistakable outburst of this new sentiment of nationalism was embodied in an image far from that of a professional soldier, the image of a young woman who claimed to *be* France, rising against the invader. This "maid of Orléans," Jeanne d'Arc, rallied the populace to the cause of her nation, and to France's dauphin king, through succeeding battles until the English invaders burned her at the stake, age 19, creating a martyr who would continue to inspire the people of her country. At the battle of Castillon, 1453, in southwestern France, England saw the end, for all practical purposes, of its centuries-long ambition to be *the* power of the western European continent.

At home, Henry VI faced continued unrest and the anger of large landowners who were now stripped of their continental wealth, on top of depleted manorial treasuries at home. Henry VI was the third monarch of the House of Lancaster. He was soon challenged by the second branch of the Plantagenets, the House of York, and thus began the civil war usually called the War of Roses (red, for Lancaster; white, for York).

Until this latest sequence of civil-war battles, direct consequences of the century of warfare for English families had consisted mainly in the loss of men, the loss of wealth especially among the large landowners, a rise in sentiments of nationalism, more or less commensurate to the rise in France, and fatigue with continual calls for more revenue, especially as the revenues increasingly bought only losses. The material losses also created, however, new opportunities for families who were poised with potential for growth and expansion but with actual present wealth too low to attract the sorts of revenue siphoning that hovered over and around the wealthier families.

The extraordinary stresses and upheavals of famine, plague, war, and accelerated rates of loss of life were felt no doubt by most families in England, at least at times. As a result of the loss, an unknown number of families ceased to exist, in the sense that no one survived to carry on the family surname. Those families with the most to lose could be in the most precarious situations, of course, because of pressures to commit more of their wealth to the royal cause but also because of opportunities to enhance standing materially as well as in social honor; and both the pressures and the opportunities could ebb and flow rather quickly, during such times of rapid change in the social fabric. Alliances among families had always been potentially treacherous; during the tumult of these two centuries, the fourteenth and the fifteenth, they could be, and sometimes were, even more treacherous, more quickly.

A family could rise to moderate or greater height, then through one or another misstep plummet and lose all. Such was the experience of the Percy family, for example, beginning with Henry Percy (1341-1408), the 1st earl of Northumberland (for whom the ancient earldom was restored in 1377, one of several restorations of this earldom). For present purposes, a long and complicated story of intrigues and shifting loyalties may be reduced to simpler bounds: Henry Percy had been a supporter of Edward III and then of Richard II; but during the latter's troubles Percy switched support to Henry Bolingbroke's claim on the English throne. After Bolingbroke was crowned Henry IV, Percy and his son—the "Harry Hotspur" Percy of Shakespearean fame (*Henry IV, Part One*)— were assigned the task of subduing a Welsh rebellion led by Owain Glyndŵr. Their effort did not please the king, who believed that their pursuit of the quarry had lacked sufficient commitment. But the king, in the eyes of Percy father and son, had reneged on promises of proper compensation and had failed of proper support on other issues. Thus, father and son joined the forces of Percy Senior's brother-in-law, Sir Edmund Mortimer, who was claiming right to the throne as great grandson of Edward III. This rebellion failed in 1403, at the battle of Shrewsbury, which cost the Percys young Hotspur's life. Percy Senior then supported the Yorkshire rebellion of 1405, again lost, then fled to

Scotland, from which he returned with an invading force in 1408, only to die in the battle of Bramham Moor. And so it went for other earls of Northumberland. The 3rd earl got caught up in the early part of the War of the Roses, and lost his life in battle. The 4th earl, with his force on behalf of Richard III, survived the battle of Bosworth Field in 1485 (unlike the king), but came under suspicion of treason for having defended his king inadequately, and four years later participated in the rebellion of Yorkshire of 1489, losing his life in the process. The 8th earl, accused of various conspiracies, was thrice imprisoned in the Tower of London. The 9th earl, accused of involvement in the Gunpowder Plot of 1605, was imprisoned in the Tower until 1621. His son, the 10th earl, negotiated the civil wars of the 1640s rather more successfully, switching sides first in one direction, then another. Throughout the generations, of course, what one man lost a subsequent man regained, at least in part; for who better to rebuild a powerful barony in service to a monarch than the latest scion of a family who had achieved as much before, repeatedly.

By comparison with the Percys, members of the Hesilrige family were very small fish at best. Even so, becoming embroiled in shifting alliances would have been no less dangerous. Indeed, one could argue, *more* dangerous, precisely because the Hesilrige family at any given point during those centuries (as later) had accumulated far less material wealth, far less influence, and could have more easily suffered losses far beyond their ability to recover. One sign of recognition of the grave risk is the fact that throughout the period of the Hundred Years War only one Hesilrige man is known to have served his king as a knight, a position that was, as previously mentioned, one of the more expensive obligations of material wealth to put at risk in warfare. This was Donald de Heselrig, who served as knight in the standing force of Gascony under Edward, the prince of Wales (the Black Prince), in 1368 and 1369 (i.e., almost surely Donald[3a], who would have been in his 40s at the time).[6]

Donald was one of eight men named Heselrig (under this of other spelling) who appear in the muster rolls or related records of military service to England during the years 1369 to 1453. While we can assume that the facts of this list are reasonably accurate, we lack means of

---

[6] This and other facts of Heselrige men in military service during the Hundred Years War come from a data base assembled from surviving muster rolls and related records for the years 1369-1453. For a general account of the data base and studies of it, see Adrian R Bell, Anne Curry, Andy King, and David Simpkins, *The Soldier in Later Medieval England* (Oxford: Oxford University Press, 2013).

deciding completeness of the list. These eight were, in chronological order and with surname spelt as in the given record:

Donald de Heselrig, knight, the standing force of Gascony, 1368-1369, serving the Black Prince who was his captain and commander

Robert Heselrygg, man-at-arms, the garrison at St Sauveur, Lower Normandy, 1370-1371, serving Sir Alan de Buxhill who was his captain and commander

Robert Hesilrigg, man-at-arms, the force in the Scottish Marches, 1383, 1385, serving Walter Tailboys [Taillbois], his captain, and Henry Percy, 1st earl of Northumberland, his commander

Edmund Hesilrigg, rank unstated, an expedition to Scotland, 1400, captain and commander not stated

John de Hesylrygh, archer, an expedition to Scotland, 1400, Hugh Crese, his captain, and Henry IV, his commander

John Hesilrygg, archer, garrison at Berwick, 1403-1404, John of Lancaster his captain and commander

Nicholas Hesybryg, archer, expedition to France, 1415, John de Mowbray, earl of Norfolk, his captain, and Henry V, his commander

Donald Hessylryg, man-at-arms, foot, garrison at Louviers, Upper Normandy, 1415 or later, Sir Godfrey Hilton his captain, his commander not stated.

Of these eight named men, the two men named Robert could have been one and the same; the two named John probably were the same man; but the two named Donald were surely not the same man, *if* (as seems likely) the first of the list was indeed Donald[3a], who died in 1385. The man named Edmund was probably brother of Donald[3a] and probably a foot soldier or archer.[7] The other men in the list cannot be located within the family lineage, given what is known of their dates relative to dates of men identified in the lineage. They were very likely second-born or even third-born (or later) sons. As of the date of this writing (2014), these six, seven, or eight men were the only Hesilrige men identifiable as such in the (approximately) 220,000 entries of the data base.[8]

What more can be said of them? Obviously all of them survived the Great Famine (probably had not yet been born) and the Black Death (again, perhaps all but Sir Donald[3a] had not yet been born). Because the sources for all of the information are muster lists, we do not know with confidence that any of them, excepting Sir Donald[3a], survived service.

Depending on how we count the repeated name, John, three or four of the men were in service to the English cause in the Anglo-Scottish wars. Robert served during the major though brief war of 1384-85, in the Marches, under command of Henry Percy, 1st earl of Northumberland. This was just before dissatisfaction with the leadership of Richard II led to the barons' revolt in favor of Henry Bolingbroke. When Bolingbroke returned from exile and overthrew Richard, the brief period of turmoil emboldened the Scots to rise again, with the result being another English expedition, this one including Edmund Hesilrigg and John de Hesylrygh, no doubt both of them under command of Bolingbroke, Henry IV, and probably both of them archers. We do not know length of either man's service, but it may well have lasted until defeat of the Scots at the battle of Homildon, near Wooler, in 1402. It is likely that both men were of one of the family's estates in the area south of Wooler and cycled in and out of active service during the two years. Soon after that campaign against the Scots, and partly in consequence of it (from the Percys' point of view, failure by Henry IV to keep his bargain and pay expenses), the Percy rebellion against the king and alignment with Edmund Mortimer began (1403). This prompts an interesting question about the next entry in the list, John Hesilrygg, whether the same man as the foregoing or not. During his service in the garrison at Berwick, 1403-04, John's captain and commander was John of Lancaster, third surviving son of Henry IV, knighted in 1399 as Henry became king, appointed constable of England

---

[7] Perhaps the same Edmund Hesilrige received 5 July 1373 a letter patent of royal protection from Edward III for "royal service in company of Henry de Percy, knight," and for "all his men, lands and other possessions, which are to be protected against all attack and injury for one year" (Hazlerigg Collection, National Archives, DG21/250).
[8] Bell, *et al.*, *The Soldier* (2013) refer to an Edward Heselrig (page 237), but as this name has not been seen in the data base the reference was probably in fact to Edmund.

in 1403 and from that year to 1414 warden of the East March.[9] All of that is of considerable weight, no doubt, but the interesting question for present purposes derives from another fact: during the years 1403-05 John of Lancaster reaped major grants of land that his brother, the king, confiscated from the Percy family. This situated John Hesilrygg and his kin in the midst of the conflict between the earl of Northumberland (now former earl) and their king, whom the Percys had only recently supported in his conflict with Richard II. Had the Hesilrygg family, or at least that part of it, been taking sides in the chain of disputes, allied with the House of Lancaster all along, or had they been primarily "along for the ride," in the manner of feudalism's hierarchy of loyalties and obligations, when, in 1403, they found themselves in direct loyalty to the heart of the House of Lancaster? This question is partly about the dissolution of the feudal order in England's far north—probably more rapid, and from a less tightly bound base, there than in the south. If the family had somewhat greater "elbow room" in which to maneuver, the risks of getting caught between much larger forces were also greater.

The last two men in the list of Hesilrige combatants were on the continent during the third part of the Hundred Years War. Nicholas must have participated in the siege of Harfleur, begun by Henry V mid-August 1415. Being one of about 6,000 archers (by standard account), he had to have known that this siege was merely the first step in an expedition into the heart of France. Since there was relatively little combat at Harfleur (mostly an attack on the city by large guns, followed by typical tactics of isolating the city from outside help), Nicholas likely escaped death or injury by combat. Disease was always a threat, however, and dysentery was rampant at Harfleur. Many of the men in the king's force became ill; some died; others were sent home. Nicholas' captain, John de Mowbray, 5th earl of Norfolk and since 1413 the earl marshall of England, was one victim of dysentery; he survived; whether he remained with the garrison Henry V left at Harfleur or returned to England is unknown, but clearly he did not proceed with his king to Agincourt. Did Nicholas? There is no answer. He might have been in the small garrison. Assuming he was not among the victims of dysentery, however, the odds are that he stayed with the expedition to Agincourt. If he did fight in that battle, was he one of the few English fatalities? Again, we have no answer. Archers were

---

[9] In 1414 his brother, Henry V, created for him the earldoms of Kendal and Richmond and the duchy of Bedford. It was this man, now known simply as Bedford, who ordered the trial and execution of Joan d'Arc at Rouen, followed by coronation of young Henry VI at Notre-Dame in Paris.

usually killed rather than captured, there being no prospect of ransom for these combatants. On the other hand, relative numbers suggest that he would have been among the survivors, had outcomes been decided by a throw of dice.

Finally, the last in the list, Donald Hessylryg. Also party to the siege of Harfleur, he was at least initially one of 40 men-at-arms who, along with 120 archers, formed a unit led by Sir Godfrey Hilton. The one locational fact available to us puts Donald in Louviers, where Henry V left another garrison on his way to Agincourt. Louviers, about halfway between Harfleur and Paris, is south-southwest of Agincourt by nearly 120 miles. Thus, it is unlikely that he saw anything of Agincourt.

The fact that only one Hesilrige man in the data base held the rank of knight, Donald[3a] de Heselrig, earliest in the list, is consistent with the conclusion drawn generally by Bell and his colleagues from their study of the entire data base—namely, that fewer and fewer knights were agreeing to service during the period of the Hundred Years War. Whereas 15 to 20 percent of all men-at-arms in major English armies during the latter decades of the fourteenth century held the rank of knight, the proportion was only 5 to 6 percent when the expeditions to France began in 1415, and by the 1440s it dropped to half that or less.[10] An interaction of two factors was probably responsible for that change. On the one hand, from the time of Edward III on, English campaign strategy and tactics relied primarily on large numbers of longbow archers, and knights, though still deployed, were expected to dismount and fight on foot, an expectation that did not please them. On the other hand, knights were expensive tools of warfare, and manorial lords who supported them were decreasingly happy to offer those resources to a campaign so far from home and with such uncertain prospects. Exactly where the balance between those two factors lay—how much one, how much the other—cannot be determined. It likely shifted with time, but the "chicken and egg" question resists solution.

Descendants of the Norman families of 1066 and after were very prominent in the lists of knights for many generations, in part because they had a major headstart as recipients of confiscated baronial estates by William I and his successors. Indeed, these families flourished to a degree far out of proportion to their population size as immigrants during the late decades of the eleventh century. While many studies have shown that migrants are disproportionately successful mainly because migrants tend to be self-selected as among the more ambitious, energetic, risk-

---

[10] Bell, et al., *The Soldier ...* (2013), pages 56-58.

tolerant persons of their places of origin, a few studies have focused specifically on the Norman immigrants and their descendants in England. A recent study by Clark began with a sample of Norman surnames in the Domesday survey of 1086 and traced their descent lineages to recent times, concluding that the proportionate share of the Norman surnames in the total population of England's surnames probably doubled by the end of the nineteenth century.[11] A few of these surnames are now represented by 10,000 individuals, or more: for instance, Sinclair = St Clair (which derived from De Sancto Claro), Talbott = Tallboys (from Taillebois), and Mowbray (from De Molbrai). Others are represented by 100 or fewer persons: Berners (from De Berneres), Sackville (de Sackville), and Tourney = Tournay (from De Tournai). The Hazlerigg family—though its surname was very likely formed of Norse roots in northeastern England, not brought over from Normandy—is another example of the sparsely populated, probably never summing to more than 100 households at any given time throughout the whole of Great Britain.

Low population density did not necessarily mean low standing, however. Drawing on a sample of surnames that appeared in inquisitions post mortem during the period from 1236 to the end of that century, Clark found that the persistence of these surnames in the top one percent of the status distribution in England was very high even down to the beginning of the twenty-first century. Bear in mind that only the "propertied class" appeared in inquisitions post mortem (the purpose being to verify that the deceased person rightfully held land of the monarch's domain and that a claim of succession to that land was valid). These were, as Clark said, "members of the medieval upper classes." Their thirteenth-century status gave advantage not only to themselves but also, by and large, to their distant descendants. Imagine a population of 1,000 households in the year 1236, each with a different surname. If the distribution of status from generation to generation were a random lottery, each surname would have equal chance of being among the top ten in status during any later generation, assuming all surnames survived and reproduced in equal numbers. In fact, Clark found that the surnames from the inquisitions post mortem were 14 to 25 times more prevalent in a high-status category in the twenty-first century than they would have been had status been handed out by lottery.[12] The more prolific a family biologically, the better the chance that its surname would continue to be

---

[11] Gregory Clark, *The Son Also Rises* (Princeton: Princeton University Press, 2104), pages 81-83.
[12] Clark, *The Son Also Rises*, pages 78-80.

among the high-status group. But the tendency to persistence is strong enough, on average, that even a small family has been able to preserve its surname in positions of high status.

	absolute count	relative count*
John	30,785	.324
William	13,858	.146
Thomas	10,598	.112
Richard	7,244	.076
Robert	6,075	.064
Nicholas	1,952	.021
Roger	1,898	.020
Hugh	1,154	.012
Simon	545	.006
Edmund	442	.005
Edward	407	.004
Gilbert	254	.003
Alan	219	.002
Bartholomew	65	.0007
Bertram	19	.0002
Donald	10	.0001
Lancelot	3	.00003

*relative to base of 94,962 men in muster rolls

Exhibit 4.1. Selected Forename Counts

Before leaving this discussion of names, perhaps another point of some interest will be the frequency of *forenames* during the fourteenth and fifteenth centuries. The muster rolls referred to earlier enable one to make a good estimate of forename frequency based on the total of 94,962 entries for the period from 1369 to 1453. Attention here is focused on the forenames present within the Hesilrige family, three of them being also the most common in the muster rolls: John, William, and Thomas (see Exhibit 4.1). Lacking knowledge of the population of Hesilrige men at any given date, we cannot systematically address comparative frequencies of forenames. Three observations are possible, however. First, as already said, John, William, and Thomas were certainly among the most frequent forenames among Hesilrige men, as among the men in the muster rolls. Second, whereas only three of the nearly 95,000 men in the rolls were known as Lancelot (which, in that day, was considered a "pagan" name), at least that many Hesilrige men are known to have been so named (whether an allusion to the Arthurian legend or not). And third, given the context of the time, with a triplet of kings named Edward, plus a fourth, the Black Prince, renowned for his military prowess in France, who would have been king had he lived even another few years, it is surprising that this forename was so low in popularity: less than one-half of one percent in general, and no confirmed instance among men of the Hesilrige family during the eleventh through fifteenth centuries—all the more puzzling in view of prominent instances of service to the royal court, beginning with Edward I. Perhaps, by happenstance, sons named Edward failed to survive infancy or childhood.

More of the Lineage
It is time to resume attention to the lineage. Note that the beginning of the following account duplicates the latter part of the account given at the end of the prior chapter. Note also that this segment of the lineage, keyed mainly to the fourteenth, fifteenth, and sixteenth centuries, will be presented in two parts: first, the main lineage, immediately below; then, in a section later in this chapter, a cadet branch (as subsequently it was confirmed to be) centered on the manor of Swarland.

As before, several of the entries in the following segment report all or virtually all of the available facts pertaining to the given person. A few of the entries will be initially abbreviated, with further description postponed until later in this chapter.

Simon[2a] de Heselrig

L-- **Donald**[3a] de Heselrig: b. c1320, d. Sunday after Easter 1385 (9 April 1385), brother William[3b] heir at age 60; m(1) c1361 Johanna de Wauton; m(2) c1377 Joan de Bredon, damsel of chamber of queen Philippa; seised of moieties of vills of Whittingham, Thrunton, and

Barton; knight of shire; purchased manor of Eslington c1362 from Isabella (*nee* Eslington), widow of Robert de Bowes, then "conveyed the property to Sir Thomas Surtees, knight, Hugh Westwick, and Edmund Heselrigg, in trust for himself and his wife in conjunct fee, and for the heirs of Donald";[13] knight in arms to Edward, prince of Wales, Gascony, 1368-69; Johanna brought to marriage the manor of Brotherwick, of which she and Donald obtained licence 1370 "to enfeoff Edmund de Hesilrigg, Robert de Wycliff, clerk, and John de Feryby";[14] appointed commissioner of array for North Riding, Yorkshire, 1 Jul 1377; widow Joan held Eslington for life, along with moieties of vills of Whittingham, Thrunton, and Barton, as well as entitlements she had brought to the marriage; Joan d. 21 Dec 1400 at York; more in the next section

└-- **William**[3b] de Heselrig: b. 1325, d. >1385; more below

└-- Edmund[3c] de Heselrig: b. > 1325, d. >1373, probably <1385; held part of manor of Eslington in trust for brother Donald and his wife, from c1362; jointly enfeoffed of manor of Brotherwick 1370; witness to Greenwell Deeds (Ref: D/Gr 219 & D/Gr 222) 1 Aug 1367 and 1 Aug 1369 Newcastle; fined for fraud and collusion Mar 1373 (Calendar of Fine Rolls 47 Edward III; more in next section of this chapter)

└-- Simon[3d] de Heselrig: b>1325, d. >1367 probably <1385; witness to Greenwell Deed 1 Aug 1367 Newcastle (ref: D/Gr 219)

└-- Thomas[3e] de Heselrig: b. >1325, prob. d. >1350, probably <1385; mentioned in deed c1350 relating to manor of Plessey; perhaps granted that manor

William[3b] Heselrig of Fawdon: b. 1325, d. c1386; m. Agnes, daughter of Thomas and Mary (*nee* Stanhope) Graper; the manor of Fawdon, William's home seat; in 1346 held the vill of Fawdon, third part of Gosforth, sixth part of Kenton, moiety of Dinnington; 6 Oct 1356 Adam de Eggelston and his wife Constance acknowledged that the manor of East Brunton belonged to "William and his heirs, of the chief lords

---

[13] John Crawford Hodgson, "On the Medieval and Later Owners of Eslington," *Archæologia Æliana*, 3rd series, volume 6 (Newcastle-upon-Tyne: Andrew Reid & Co., 1910), page 14.

[14] John Crawford Hodgson, *A History of Northumberland*, volume 5 (Newcastle-upon-Tyne: Andrew Reid & Co., 1899), page 255.

forever," in exchange for 100 marks of silver (see Exhibit 4.2); served in Scottish Wars of Edward III, granted lands in Wetislade South 20 Nov 1360, which in 1369 he settled upon his son William; witness to Greenwood Deeds 1 Aug 1367 & 1 Aug 1369 Newcastle (ref: D/Gr 219 & D/Gr 222) and 20 May 1372 Denton (ref: D/Gr 230); knight of shire for Northumberland in 1375 and 1377; appointed commissioner of array for Northumberland 1 Jul 1377; the manor of Fawdon plus lands in South Gosforth, Kenton, and Newcastle settled on son Thomas in 1386; Agnes brought to marriage manor of Swarland, which she and William settled on son John. More discussion of William later in this section.

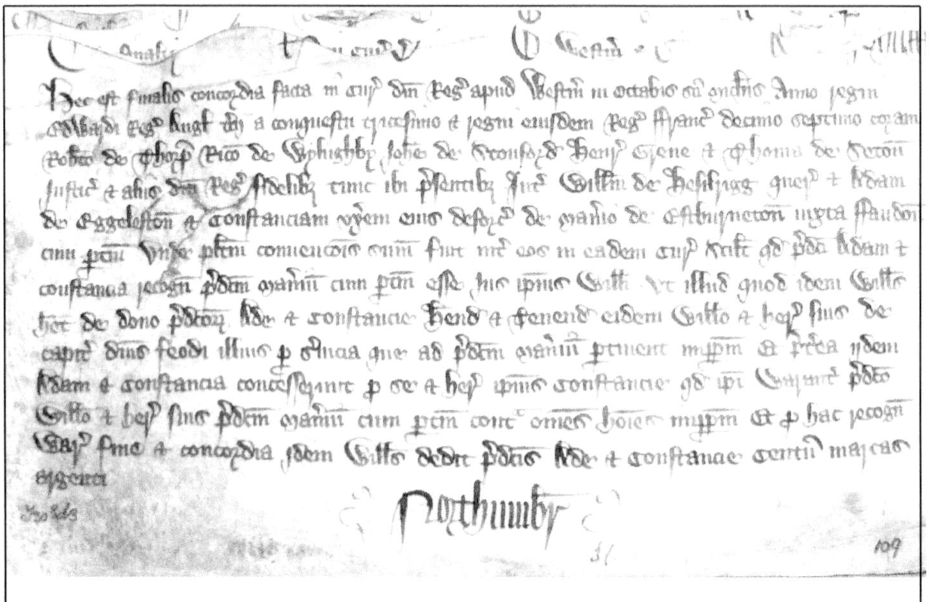

Exhibit 4.2. Image of Plea of Covenant, 6 October 1356

> The document says that Adam de Eggelston and Constance his wife have acknowledged that "the manor of East Brunton, by Fawdon," is "the right of William de Hesilrigg, as that which he has of their gift, to hold to William and his heirs, of the chief lords forever," in exchange of 100 marks silver.
>
> *source*: Chris Phillips' website, medievalgenealogy.org; image 0304, CP25/1/181/13, number 109; downloaded 16 June 2014

└── Donald[4a] Hesilrige: b. <1342, d. by 12 Jul 1387; named in settlement of 1386; m. 1362 Joan (b. 1341), daughter of Nicholas Heron

└── William[4b] Heselrig: b. >1342, d. >1369, probably <1387

└── **Thomas**[4c] Heselrig of Fawdon: b. c1365 Fawdon, d. 15 Oct 1422 Eslington; attested son & heir to William Heselrig of Fawdon, 10 Richard II (20 Oct 1386); seised of Eslington, recorded as owner of tower of Eslington 1415; seised of moieties of the vills of Whittingham, Thrunton, and Barton; m. 1395 at Noseley, Isabel (b. c1375, d. <1439), daughter and heir of Sir Roger Heron (b. 1330, d. c1397) and Margaret (b. 1353, d. 7 Apr 1407 Noseley), daughter of Sir Ralph Hastings, which marriage brought the manors of Noseley, Gilmorton (Gilden-Morton), and Newton Harcourt, all in Leicestershire; more below and next chapter

└── **Thomas**[5a] Hesilrige: b. 29 Sep 1407 Eslington, d. 21 Sep 1467; more below

└── **John**[5b] Hesilrige: b. c1409 Noseley, d. 4 Jun 1432 Noseley; more below

└── Elizabeth[5c] Hesilrig: b. c1400, d. >Sep 1431; m. John Fossour, Jr. (d. c1474; I.p.m. 23 Dec 1474 Durham), son & heir of John Fossour, Sr. (d. 1433); a Greenwell Deed says that Elizabeth Hesilrig and John Fossour both received charter, 5 Sep 1431, to two messuages and 140 acres of land in Kellowe [co. Durham], from John Fossour, Sr. (ref: D/Gr 294)[15]

└── Robert[4d] Hesilrig: b. c1367; living 1392; m. Christiana, daughter & heir of Nicholas de Eland; their daughter (heir of Christiana), Joan, m. 6 Henry IV (1406) John Mitford de Ponte Eland, from whom a Ponteland lineage

---

[15] See also the Calendar Rolls of Bishop Langley, in *Thirty-Third Annual Report of the Deputy Keeper of the Public Records*, volume 33 of *Parliamentary Papers, House of Commons and Command* (London: HMSO, 1872), pages 135, 137. Elizabeth's descent from this Thomas[4c] is not well attested: that the Thomas Hesilrig who appears in the sacrists' and feretrars' rolls of Durham Abbey, 1414 and again 1421, was Thomas[4c] has not been conclusively demonstrated; see *Extracts from the Account Rolls of the Abbey of Durham*, volume 2 (Durham: Andrews & Co., 1899), pages 405, 463. With respect to place names (e.g., Kellowe), recall the book by Allen Mawer on place names in Durham as well as Northumberland, cited at the beginning of chapter 3.

L-- Donald[5a] Hesilrig: b. >1388 Durham, d. >1456; by record of bishop Langley of Durham, 1456, "Donald, son and heir of Robert de Hesilrig and Christiana his wife, granted messuages and land in Estraynton [East Rainton, co. Durham] to John Bynchestre, chaplain"[16]

L-- John[4e] Heselrig of Swarland: b. >1365; d. 1391;   thus began the Swarland branch of the family, about which more in the next section of this chapter

Thomas[5a] Hesilrige: b. Michaelmas Day [29 Sep] 1407 Eslington, d. 21 Sep 1467 Noseley, Leicestershire; m. Elizabeth, daughter of Sir Thomas Broket, knight; more in next section of this chapter and in next chapter

L-- **William**[6a] Hesilrigge: b. c1437, d. 25 Feb 1474/5 Noseley; m. Elizabeth, daughter & coheir of Thomas Staunton, esq., of Sutton-on-Soar, Nottinghamshire (marriage settlement 13 Jul 1458); I.p.m. jurors, said William[6a] "had enfeoffed Robert Staunton, Thomas Staunton, John Gebley, clerk, and Edmund Hesylrigge of all his lands, to the intent that they should enfeoff his right heir thereof, when he should come to the full age of twenty one years" (Thomas[7a] then "aged twelve years and more"); more below[17]

L-- **Thomas**[7a] Hesylrigge: b. 1464, d. 24 May 1541 Leicestershire; more below

L-- Robert[7b] Hesilrigge of Castle Donington: b. >1464, d. 1554; m. Eleanor, daughter of Sir Ralph Shirley of Staunton Harold; more in next chapter, on Nottinghamshire

L-- John[7c] Hesilrigge: b. >1464, d. >1494; living Noseley 1494; married with issue:

L-- Robert[8a] Hesilrige:

---

[16] Calendar of Rolls of Bishop Langley, *op. cit.* (1872), page 170.
[17] Thomas Staunton was not of Staunton Harold and Castle Donington, "as Nichols states," but of Sutton-on-Soar. George Farnham and A Hamilton Thompson, "The Manor of Noseley," *Transactions of the Leicestershire Architectural Society*, volume 12 (1921-22), pages 214-271, at page 230. Having studied both sources at length, I believe Farnham and Thompson to be the more reliable.

└── Dorothy[8b] Hesilrige

└── Elizabeth[8c] Hesilrige

└── Katherine[7d] Hesilrigge: b. >1458 Noseley, Leics.; m. Thomas Ashby (b. 1442 Quenby, d. c1488 Quenby) of Quenby, Leics.

└── Ruth[7e] Hesilrigge: m. Richard Nele, second son of Sir Richard Nele of Prestwold

└── Edmund[6b] Hesylryge: b. >1437, d. >Dec 1476, at which time he was seated at manor of Rolston (Rolleston)

└── Margaret[6c] Hesilrige: b. >1437; m. a Villers man

└── Elizabeth[6d] Hesilrige: b. >1437; m. Sir William Turville, knight

John[5b] Hesilrige of Noseley: b. c1409 Noseley, d. 4 Jun 1432 Noseley; died seised of a moiety of the manor of Whittingham ("worth yearly, clear, £20"), the manor of Thrunton (£10), the manor of Barton (10 marks), a moiety of the manor of Glaunton (£10), and the manor of Eslington (£10);[18] John's heir, his son

└── Robert[6a] Hesilrige (b. 1426):

Thomas[7a] Hesylrigge: b. 1464, d. 24 May 1541 Leicestershire; home seat, manor of Noseley; m. Lucy (d. 8 Oct 1525 Noseley), daughter of Thomas Entwysill of Dalby on the Wolds (now "Old Dalby"), Leics., and Edith Bracebridge, daughter of Richard Bracebridge; Lucy bore at least 18 children, of whom only a dozen names are known; more in next chapter

└── **Bertine**[8a] (aka Bertram) Hesilrig: b. c1485, d. 25 Jul 1565; more in next chapter

└── John[8b] Hesilrig

---

[18] The valuations, all given as "worth yearly, clear," are from an inquisition taken 30 Sep 1442; see Hodgson, "On the Medieval and Later Owners ...," (1910), page 18n).

└── Robert[8c] Hesilrige: this man was probably the gentleman usher to Henry VIII; more in next chapter

└── William[8d] Hesilrige
└── Anthony[8e] Hesilrige
└── Walter[8f] Hesilrige
└── Daniel[8g] Hesilrige

└── Millicent[8h] Hesilrige: m(1) Walter Keble of Humberston, (2) Fnu Breame; issue by Keble: Francis (b. 1520), Lucia, Anne

└── Herald[8i] Hesilrige: m. David Williams of Abergavenny

└── Anne[8j] Hesilrige: m. Edward Catesby of Seaton, Rutland

└── Edith[8k] Hesilrige: m. John Thorney of Stamford

└── Elizabeth[8l] Hesilrige: m. Robert Collingwood

└── plus three other sons and three other daughters

It should be apparent from the just-viewed segment of lineage that more information was available for more persons during this period than during the period covered by the lineage segment in chapter 3. Indeed, for a few of the persons named above there is still more information to be reported, as it will be in the following section of this chapter. Before we turn to that, however, let us consider some additional observations about the foregoing segment.

Most obvious is the fact that daughters became more visible in the record. That is mainly because marriages were more often recorded and the resulting documents were more likely to survive. The daughters, now brides, still figured primarily as complementary nodes in marital alliances across families. But not only had they gained greater presence in record keeping; they usually were remembered by forename, and not merely as "daughter of Patriarch of Family Name," so to speak.

Also obvious is the fact that the number of children per household gradually if somewhat fitfully increased. Despite periodic drainage by famine, plague, and wars, there were times when some families witnessed improvements in the proportion of pregnancies issuing live births, in the proportion of live births surviving long enough to reproduce, and in the proportion of reproducing men and women who themselves survived long enough to support those children with material accumulations and security, so that at least a few of the children of any given household had some chance of seeing generational improvements of their family's conditions and prospects. The odds were still not good. But they did improve, and some families benefited during extended periods of time—some more than others, to be sure, as agrarian societies were typified by high rates of inequality, especially as agrarian technologies improved.

The opposite side of that coin is another fact, this one obvious by absence: the number of siblings per generational head in the foregoing segment varied from zero, in the case of Simon[2a], to seventeen, in the case of Bertine[8a]. Of course, there is a temporal dimension to it, as is signified by the generational number. Relatedly, female siblings show up in the records more often in later generations. Still, one wonders about missing siblings for Thomas[5a] and for William[6a]—in the latter only one brother and two sisters, in the other only one brother and no sisters. Is the fault with record keeping? Or was each of these men one of only two or four children (unlikely), or one of only two or three male children, or one of only two or three *surviving* male children? The last alternative is the likeliest, of course, even if only because of disease and injurious accident. What of war? It is unlikely to impossible that one or more of the unattributed men in the list of Hesilrige combatants in the Hundred Years War were siblings of Thomas[5a]; but there could have been other fatalities of that long sequence of conflicts. As for the generation of William[6a] and Edmund[6b], they may have come of age too late for the battles in France, but not for the War of the Roses, including the battle of Towton (29 March 1461), still remembered as the bloodiest battle ever fought on the island of Britain.[19]

Trials of Property Rights
As mentioned earlier, the centuries under view in this chapter witnessed dissolutions of the feudal system as a means of organizing territory and relations among its inhabitants. This meant that some other means of regulating land and its returns, across generations, was coming into use.

---

[19] Estimates of fatalities vary widely, with one implying a rate greater than 50 percent (i.e., 28,000 deaths of 50,000 combatants). Recent research of the grounds has indicated that Towton might have been the first land battle to use cannon with great effect.

An implication of that gradual process of replacement is that the feudal practice of "friendly court inquisitions"—a way of establishing an official record of who holds what where, with what entailments or rights of inheritance, and so forth—was losing effectiveness. The disadvantage of that "fictional" practice was its inconsistency with the feudal concept of entailment, which carried no inherent restriction on time. In principle, land "held in chief" (in capita) implied an "endless entail," because, or insofar as, there would always be a next incumbent of overlordship. But as the feudal system weakened, its descending principle of authority, with "top-down" enforcement of the dispositions of estates via familial ties of loyalty and obligation, no longer sufficed as a means of settling not just those fictional contests for purposes of record-making but, crucially, the *genuine* disagreements about inheritance. The often bloody contests over rightful claims of inheritance of royal thrones were increasingly playing out as well, though on smaller and usually less violent scale, in court proceedings between families and between generations within a given family. But, as Biancalana has documented with his study of legal innovations in England during the late 1400s, lawyers devised a number of new procedures and instruments in response to increasingly inefficient and often ineffective efforts at the regulation of disputes over rights of property and estate settlements.[20] One upshot was a regular process of entailment that enabled conveyance of an estate to a widow and children, cleanly and without endless tail.

When perusing abstracts of court proceedings conducted during the long period of transition from the old to the new, one must sometimes contend with the fact that it is not always obvious which proceeding was "friendly" (the fictional contest) and which was unfriendly, if not outright hostile. In preceding discussions we have seen a few instances of what were simply record-making transactions, and another will be seen when we come to the family's settlements in Nottinghamshire (regarding the manor of Sutton, c1515). Here we come to some proceedings that are more difficult to classify. One of them involves the charge of "fraud and collusion" mentioned above in the lineage (i.e., Donald[3a], William[3b], and Edmund[3c]). We return to that charge here.

In his report of the Heselrig pedigree as it was established during his 1615 heraldic visitation of Leicestershire, Richard St George included a manuscript record of a land grant that carries some interest. His report appears to be the first that draws specific attention to the family's

---

[20] Joseph Biancalana, *The Fee Tail and the Common Recovery in Medieval England, 1176-1502*. Cambridge: Cambridge University Press, 2001.

connection in this manuscript.[21] Due to its intrinsic interest but also because the report illustrates some of the caution that must be exercised, to the extent possible, when resourcing old records, some liberty will be taken to discuss the contents more than the bare intrinsic interest would otherwise warrant (Exhibit 4.3).

> Edwardus dux Ebore Comes Cantabrigiæ et d'ns manerij et libertatis de Warke in Tindale o'ibus ad quos presentes l're pervenerit Salutem licentia dedimus quantu' in nobis est dilecto nobis Will'mo de Heslerig licete possit feofare possit Johem de Wooderington filiu' et heredem Rogeri de Wooderington de Castro et Manerio de Halghton de villa de Homshagh quadam placea terræ in Thornton in Tindall vocat Staincrosse et de o'ibus alijs terr' etc. que Agnes que fuit vxor Rogeri tenet in dotem habend' et tenend' pred'co Johanni et heredibus masculis de corpore suo l'time procreat' etc. vna cu' reversione predict' remaneant Thome filio Willmi Heslerigg et heredibus masculis de corpore suo l'time exeuntibus portantibus Arma et cognomen pred'ci Rogeri de Wooderington tenend' etc. et si predict' Thomas obierit sine herede masculo de corpore suo procreat' quod pred' Castr' maner' terr' etc. remaneant Rogero filio Walteri Hero militis et heredibus masculis de corpore suo l'time procreat' portantibus arma et cognomen pred'ci Rogeri de Wooderington tenend' etc. et si Rogerus filius pred' Walteri obierit sine herede masculo de corpore suo procreat' l'time tunc Castr' et maner' etc. remaneant heredibus de corpore pred'ci Joh'is de Wooderington pro defectu talis exitus remaneant Christiano Montebouches et Alienore Buske filiabus pred' Rogeri de Wooderington. Teste Johanne de Mitford Custode sigilli n'ri apud Wark in Tyndall 20 die Octobris A° 10 Ri, 2.

Exhibit 4.3. Latin Text of a Land Transaction, 20 October 1386

That main interest can be stated quickly: William de Heslerig was given license to enfeoff John, son and heir of Roger de Widdrington, of "a plot of land in Thornton in Tindall called Staincrosse" (using in this quoted phrase the proper names as spelt in the manuscript as found in St George's report).[22] This was either William[4a] (as shown in the lineage segment above), father of William[5a], Edmund[5b], and Simon[5c], or the son William[5a]. Given the salutation of the document, which refers to "our beloved William" (a phrase likelier used for an elder), William[4a] was probably the man in question, even though at least one other record

---

[21] Richard St George, *Visitation of Leicestershire in 1615* (edited by George Marshall; London: Mitchell and Hughes, 1878), pages 19-20.
[22] The Latin text also appears in John Hodgson's *History of Northumberland*, part 2, volume 3 (Newcastle-upon-Tyne: printed for the author, 1840), pages 21-22.

suggests he was dead by the date of this transaction, 20 October 1386. In any case, the implication of the statement is that William de Heslerig had been in possession of the plot of land. The next statement adds to that "all the land, etc., which Agnes, who was wife of Roger, held in dowry." This probably means that Agnes had been second wife of Roger, who died in 1372 and whose first wife, Elizabeth (*nee* de Acton) had died by 1369. Further, it probably means also that Agnes was a daughter of this William de Heslerig.[23] Finally, the manuscript in general adds testimony to the previously noted southward migration of the Heselrig family during this period.

It is in regard to that testimony that the point about caution began. A search of old records for a place called Staincrosse quickly resulted in one candidate, a village (and wapentake) in the southeast corner of the West Riding of Yorkshire (now part of the borough of Barnsley in South Yorkshire). This fit with other evidence of migration into Yorkshire, but it also seemed to be evidence of a rather large "jump" southward (since Staincrosse is south of Leeds). It obviously did not, however, fit with "Thornton in Tindale"—not unless there was a duplicate naming (hardly an unheard-of event in the annals of place names). Other errors in the document suggested that lack of care, not duplicate naming, was the culprit. For example, the salutation and licencing of our William was authorized, according to the document as reproduced in St George's report, by "Edward duke of York, earl of Cambridge," etc. In 1386 those honors were held not by Edward but by his father, Edmund, who died in 1402.[24] The place name had been misread, or was otherwise transcribed incorrectly: what was written as "Staincross" in the St George document was in fact "Stanecroft," part of the old manor of Thornton. This name, Stanecroft, included reference to a Roman road, Stanegate, which ran east-west between Corbridge and Carlisle, just south of Hadrian's wall. The road was punctuated by small forts, one of which is in the church graveyard of present-day Newbrough, the site of the old manor.

That is not the sum of the lesson, however. The Calendar of Fines roll for the regnal year 47 Edward III (i.e., 1373-74) records on 26 March 1373, Westminster, an action that had taken place the prior April. The translated extract from membrane 23 of that roll reads as follows:

---

[23] Others, including John Hodgson, have speculated about kinship between the families; this was probably one, perhaps the only, instance of it.

[24] In fact, the manuscript, as it exists in the Harleian collection (Ms 1448, 22b), clearly says Edmund. Hodgson (page 21) reported it accordingly, only to misrepresent another (unrelated) aspect of the manuscript in a subsequent footnote (page 393).

Order to Alan de Strother, bailiff of the king's liberty of Tyndale,--pursuant to an inquisition made by him shewing that Roger de Woderyngton, by counsel of William de Heselriyg, Edmund de Heselrig and others of his council, on 3 April last enfeoffed Thomas Surtays, knight, Donald de Heselrig, knight, William de Heselrig and Edmund de Heselrig of the castle and manor of Halghton and the town of Hounshalgh, which are held of the king in chief as of his lordship of Werk in Tyndale, and of a parcel of land called Scaycroft in Thornton within the liberty of Tyndale, by fraud and collusion, in order to deprive the king of the profit of the wardship and marriage of John, son and heir of the said Roger,--to take the premises into the king's hand and keep them safely until further order, answering at the Exchequer for the issues thereof from the said 3 April.

The issue was the right of wardship, an element of the hierarchical principle of overlordship in feudal relations. Roger de Widdrington was anticipating death (it would come later in the year). His son and heir, John, was a minor, perhaps even younger and lacking standing as a legal subject of minority age. In any case, Roger, with the help of some confederates, was attempting to protect his son's inheritance from the potential uncertainties of wardship.

The right of wardship entitled an overlord to take control of a fief and a minor until the minor attained age of majority. Wardship also entitled an overlord to exercise approval of the minor's marital contract. The justification of wardship lay in the inability of a minor to satisfy obligations of an estate to the overlord. Chiefly in question was the obligation of military service, but an overlord could invoke wardship because of inadequate satisfaction of other obligations of service, such as socage or tax revenues from an estate's produce. The right of wardship could be invoked at any rank in the hierarchy of overlordship, ultimately ending in the monarch, in whom all rights of the realm were invested. The crown's interest in upward flows of revenue always prevailed, at least in principle, but monarchs typically left potential wardships involving small estates to overlords lower in the queue.

In time, as city life recovered and market organization became more extensive, new kinds of tradable goods and services circulated through market transactions. In England, by the fourteenth century, the right of wardship had become an item of commerce. This fact very likely had figured into the council undertaken by Roger with Donald[3a], William[3b], Edmund[3c], and others. It is noteworthy that the first-named person in the listing of principals of enfeoffment was Sir Thomas Surtees; he was high sheriff of Northumberland in 1373 (as Roger Widdrington had been eleven years earlier). It is impossible to know the motivation of Alan de Strother in conducting his inquiry; perhaps he genuinely believed fraud and collusion had been committed, but the possibility of interests by another party or parties cannot be ruled out. In any event, it is plain from subsequent records that John held his inheritance,[25] that the only enfeoffment that held fast for William[3b] Heselrig and his son and heir Thomas[4a] was the parcel of land at Stanecroft, and that William[3b] remained in good standing with their king. He was returned as knight of the shire in 1375 and in 1377.

The next case illustrates some of the extent to which a landholder had to engage in court actions, friendly or not, in an effort to maintain security of holdings. The principal actor is the same Donald[3a] discussed above. Recall from the lineage that he was born probably before 1330 and died 9 April 1385 in the East Riding of Yorkshire. His first known marriage, c1362, was to Johanna de Wauton, daughter of John de Wauton and sister and heir of Gilbert de Wauton, who had died shortly before 1362. With that marriage Donald[3a] acquired the manor of Brotherwyck. He married secondly, in 1377, Joan de Bredon, who had been a damsel of the chamber of queen Philippa of Hainault, wife of Edward III (which, as already noted with regard to other, similar appointments, meant not that she was at court in London but that she was part of the queen's traveling court and thus available to the queen whenever the latter was in the northeast). Queen Philippa had died in 1369 (Edward III died 1377), so Joan was free of those obligations as well as benefits.[26]

According to records cited by Hodgson,[27] Donald[3a] purchased the manor of Eslington from Isabella (*nee* Eslington), widow of Robert de Bowes, then "conveyed the property to Sir Thomas Surtees, knight, Hugh Westwick, an attorney, and Edmund[3c] Heselrigg, in trust for himself and

---

[25] As of 1415 Haughton castle was held by Sir John Widdrington. It was at roughly the date of the above-cited action that Haughton manor was additionally fortified and castellated, gaining the "castle" designation.

[26] John Crawford Hodgson, *A History ...*, volume 5 (1899), page 255. There has been some confusion about the surname of Donald's wife, the assumption having been only one woman named "Joan" (or "Johanna"). Inspection of the relevant documents, cited by Hodgson, shows that he got it right in 1899 but repeated the confusion later; see John Crawford Hodgson, "On the Medieval and Later Owners ...." (1910), page 14.

[27] John Crawford Hodgson, "On the Medieval and Later Owners ...." (1910), page 14.

his wife in conjunct fee, and for the heirs of Donald[3a]," and at about the same time was seised of moieties of vills of Whittingham, Thrunton, and Barton. One of the entries in the Inquisitions ad quod damnum for Northumberland says that "Donald de Heselrig to settle two-thirds of half the manors of Eslington, Whittingham, Thrunton, and Barton, with the reversion of the remaining third, now held for life by Elizabeth late the wife of Robert de Esselyngton, all acquired from Isabel daughter of the said Robert and late wife of Robert de Bowes, on himself and his heirs."
That clarifies the parceling of the estates. Documents of court hearings show that on 15 May 1360 "Isabel of Eslington" acknowledged that a moiety of the manors of Eslington and Whittingham were "the right of Donald," in exchange of £100 from Donald[3a]. It is not clear that this was the initial transaction involving either manorial estate, and in light of what follows one has reason to doubt that it was the first.[28] In any case, about a year later (7 May 1361) Donald[3a] was back in court, this time William de la Vale and his wife Christiana acknowledging Donald's[3a] right to a moiety of the manor of Eslington and a quarter of the manors of Whittingham, Thrunton and Barton, in exchange of 100 marks silver. It is not clear that this moiety was the same as, or the complement of, the moiety of Eslington acknowledged a year earlier. Likewise, the quarter of the other estates could have been an *additional* quarter, making three-quarters in all.[29]

But the following autumn (27 October 1361) Isabel, "who was wife of Robert de Bowes," acknowledged Donald's[3a] right to a moiety of the manors of Eslington, Whittingham, Thrunton, and Barton, in exchange of 200 marks silver. Recall that a "moiety" is one-half of a category (here, an estate). Thus, either we are faced with three halves of the same thing, or Donald[3a] had to defend his claim once again, and surely by now had right to the entirety of Eslington and to at least three quarters if not all of Whittingham, Thrunton, and Barton. (We do not know when Isabel's mother, Elizabeth, died.) It did not end there, however. Twice more, on 6 October 1362 and two years later, Donald[3a], now with wife Joan, had to seek judgment again, this time because "Elizabeth, wife of Robert de Eslington, knight," had "held in dower of the inheritance of Isabel" a third part of the moiety of the manors. In

---

[28] These documents can be inspected, along with transcribed extracts, on the website maintained by Chris Phillips (medievalgenealogy.org); ref. CP25/1/181/13 numbers 117, 120, 132, 133.

[29] Records for the de Bowes and the de la Vale families show intermarriages; although these are for a slightly later time, they might not have been the first.

other words, the dowry of Elizabeth (mother of Isabel) from her marriage to Robert de Eslington had included those manorial interests, and perhaps she had died by October 1362, which led to perceived need for juridical reaffirmation of Donald's[3a] rights vis-à-vis Isabel. So far as can be determined, these court actions were "friendly" undertakings.

There was still another action, this one in 1373. Although its relationship (if any) to the foregoing is obscure, it does suggest that Donald[3a], his brothers William[3b] and Edmund[3c], and Thomas Surtees had acquired an interest in an estate at Coldwell, now a village located about 25 miles south southwest of Whittingham. Dendy referred to this action in his extracts from plea rolls of the Court of Common Pleas for Northumberland: Robert de Umfreville, knight, and Alianora his wife, and Bertram Monboucher, knight, and Christiana, his wife, represented by Hugh de Westwyck (presumably the same attorney mentioned above), sought return of "the manor of Coldwell," and apparently prevailed (as there is no further indication of the estate as a family holding).[30] From other description of the place, the designation of Coldwell as a manor is very likely incorrect.[31] It was by all other known accounts a township of agricultural land.

As for his main interests, Donald[3a] prevailed. His widow, Joan, held Eslington for life, along with moieties of vills of Whittingham, Thrunton, and Barton, and entitlements she had brought to the marriage. In addition Richard II assured that she would have ample provision. On 2 July 1389 (13 Richard II) he remembered her service thusly: "Grant, for life, in consideration of her good service to the king's father and mother both before and after her marriage, to Joan, late the wife of Donald Hesilrygg, of 20 marks a year from issues of the county of York," among other sources. On 28 Nov 1390 the king added: "Grant, for four years, to Joan Haselryk of a tun of wine every year in the port of Hull."[32]

When Joan died, 21 Dec 1400 at York, the estates reverted to Donald's[3a] heir, his brother William[3b] (according to the inquisition post mortem of Joan, 7 April 1401, Donald[3a] had died childless). The court cases described above are but a single illustration of the difficulty of keeping track of rights to property in the midst of many different

---

[30] Frederick W Dendy, "Extracts from the De Banco Rolls Relating to Northumberland, 1308-1558," *Archæologia Æliana*, 3rd ser., volume 6 (1910), pages 41-88, at page 60.
[31] See, e.g., John Hodgson, *A History of Northumberland*, part 2, volume 1 (Newcastle, 1827), page 195; William Hutchinson, *A View of Northumberland*, volume 2 (Newcastle, 1778), page 325.
[32] *Calendar of Patent Rolls*, regnal years 13 & 14 Richard II, at Westminster.

claimants, none of them necessarily fraudulent. The person of an earldom seldom suffered this difficulty, of course. But for someone with the relative standing of Donald[3a] –which was not insubstantial, for he was a knight of the shire and later would be appointed a commissioner of the array[33]--the need to defend the security of holdings was ever present, and not without cost to one's purse. In absence of an independent and efficient "clearing house" (to use modern terms) that would investigate and establish clear titles to specific properties, opportunities for innocent confusions of claims through tangles of endowments, rights of inheritances, and so forth, to say nothing of opportunities for fraud and collusion, were a constant problem in the abstract, a constant source of headaches for many land holders, and a stream of income for lawyers.

> 231. Box B, No. 408. [July 9, 1489.] Letters exemplificatory of Henry VII recording that among the pleas enrolled at Westminster before Rob. Danby, Justice, 49 Hen. VI, the year of his recovery of royal power, in Hilary term Roll 94 is the following. *Leicestershire* ¶ Tho. Newton by Will. Halywell his attorney claimed against Rob. S[t]aunton, Will. Hoton, Edm. and Will. Hesilrig, a messuage and a virgate and a half in Norton by Galby (King's Norton) of which they unjustly disseised him. They could not deny, etc. In the same year and same term and same roll the same claims against the same two messuages and three virgates in the same place and they could not deny, etc.
> [Perfect seal of Court of Common Pleas ; as figured in the British Museum Catalogue of Seals No. 895.]

Exhibit 4.4. Contested Claims, King's Norton, 1489

Another case, abstracted in Exhibit 4.4, also involved a pair of brothers named William[6a] and Edmund[6b], although these from the borough of Leicester, and it illustrates a less than friendly litigation that, judging only from what the borough document says,[34] seems to have ended unhappily for the brothers.

---

[33] Recall that these commissions, introduced during the reign of Edward I, were a device for raising a military force during a time of emergency. A commissioner had royal authority, via a shire's government, to call trained soldiers to service in a royal cause. In the northeast of England these were usually occasions of combat against Scottish troops or reivers. Donald[3a] was appointed commissioner for the North Riding on 1 July 1377, again in 1384 and 1385, this last the year of his death.

[34] Records of the Borough of Leicester, Box B, No., 408.

Before addressing the core substance of that document, some comments on nomenclature might be useful. The calendar year for legal, scholastic, and other purposes was (and is) divided into four terms—Hilary, Easter, Trinity, and Michaelmas, with the Hilary term running from January to April. The regnal year 49 Henry VI ran from Aug 1470 to mid-April 1471 (i.e., the end of Henry's second period of kingship). So the claim registered in the Court of Common Pleas was an action between January and April of 1471. As noted in earlier discussion, a "messuage" was a dwelling house. A "virgate" was a unit of land, equal to two bovates or oxgangs, the amount of arable land that a team of two oxen could till in one ploughing season. (This varied from place to place, depending on the quality of the land.)

Now to the core of the case. Thomas Newton had claimed that William[6a] and Edmund[6b], together with Robert Staunton and William Hoton, had unjustly taken a messuage and the parcel of tillable land that had belonged to him in Norton by Galby (which today is known as King's Norton, a parish in Leicestershire centered on the village of Gaulby, about four miles northwest of Noseley). Was the case bound up in the great conflict between York and Lancaster? If it was, this would have been almost surely only in the sense that the added turmoil and confusion created opportunities for what today is called "judicial roulette." We do not know the date of the alleged disseisings by Edmund[6b], William[6a], and the two others, but it very likely would have been either toward the end of the first period of reign by Edward IV or during the first months of the second reign by Henry VI. According to the claim, the four defendants "could not deny" the charge. We do not know the immediate outcome of the court case. But we do know from the inquisition post mortem for William[6a] that he held those properties at death, that he also held the small manor of Humberstone (just outside Leicester), seised by his father in 1458, and that his son and heir Thomas[7a] inherited.

Before turning from this court case, one further point of possible interest is worth noting. Who exactly was the plaintiff, Thomas Newton? This is not an idle question mainly because, 35 miles to the northeast of Gaulby lay the village of Woolsthorpe-by-Colsterworth, Lincolnshire, which is the birth site of the future Isaac Newton. Was this Thomas Newton in the future Sir Isaac Newton's ancestral tree? William Stukeley reported in his manuscript, *Memoirs of Sir Isaac Newton's Life*, dated 1752, that Sir Isaac's paternal line had been traced back to his third great grandfather, John Newton, who died 1544 in Westby, Lincolnshire, a further 4 miles northeast of Woolsthorpe. Stukeley's account also said, however, that this John Newton, born perhaps in the late 1400s, had migrated from a place called Newton in Lancashire. We are in the dark as to date of migration. Perhaps it actually occurred during a prior generation. Or perhaps Thomas Newton—but then neither forename nor surname is exactly rare in England's history—had himself migrated from that place called Newton in Lancashire.

In the sequential presentation of the lineage segment, above, note was taken of a postponement of more discussion of the father of the two brothers recently considered, William[6a] and Edmund[6b] Hesilrige. It is time that we redeem that postponement and move back to the first half of the 1400s, to Thomas[5a] Hesilrige of Eslington, Northumberland, and add some threads of his life. We begin with his beginning, according to what we learn at his ending, his inquisition post mortem, dated 7 Henry VI: he "was born at Eslington on Michaelmas day [29th September], 1407, and the same day was baptised at Whittingham church with such pomp and circumstance as served him in good stead when he was called on to prove his age at an inquisition taken within the castle at Newcastle on the 22nd March, 1428 [i.e., 1429, by today's calendar]. Amongst the people assembled in the church for the ceremony, or who had good cause to remember the occasion, was James Buk, who that day, hunting the stag in the forest of Rothbury, was run by the quarry, and struck to the ground, his left arm being broken."[35]

As was mentioned in the lineage segment above, Thomas[5a] wed Elizabeth, daughter of Sir Thomas Broket, knight, probably about 1430. What was not mentioned was the circumstance of that marriage. Having observed the fifteenth anniversary of his birthday only two weeks earlier, Thomas[5a] found himself heir to a large estate left by his just deceased father; and he, that son and heir, was six years short of majority status. It was a circumstance, hardly rare, which sometimes resulted in contests for control, as we have seen in earlier discussions—control of estates through control of the minor heir via wardship. In this case that control went to Sir Thomas Broket. The record is silent as to specific reasons for that grant, and to the possibility of struggle leading up to it. Perhaps the grant had been arranged by the dying father himself. Likewise, only conjecture is available in answer to the question whether an arranged marriage was part of an agreement, or condition to uncontested conveyance of estate at age of majority. From what we do know, it appears that conveyance took place without controversy requiring additional court action.

---

[35] Hodgson, "On the Medieval and Later Owners ..." (1910), page 18.

Thomas[5a] died at the end of his sixth decade, in 1467, a longevity rather good for the times. The inquisition post mortem concluded that he

> was seised of the manor at Eschlyngton and of moieties of the vills of Whyttyngham, Thrownton, and Berton, and by charter, shewn to the jurors, dated 3rd March, 1455, granted the premises to John Collenwod and Robert Collenwod, son of the said John, in fee. John Collenwod has died and Robert now holds the premises with reversion to William Hasylryg, son and heir of Thomas.
>
> The said manor [Eslington] is held of the king in chief by service of six marks yearly payable to the sheriff, and 16*s* to Bamburgh castle for truncage ["truncage"—an obligation of timber carried to the castle]. It is worth yearly, clear, four marks and no more on account of the destruction by the Scotch.
>
> The said moieties are held of the king in chief by service of 3*s* 4*d* yearly, payable to the sheriff, and is worth yearly, five marks and no more, for the cause aforesaid.
>
> Thomas died 21st September last. William Hasylryg is his son and heir aged thirty years and more.

According to the Escheat roll of 1466, Thomas[5a] was seised also of the manor of Gilmorton (i.e., Gilden-Morton) in Leicestershire, which his father had acquired. In an action before the Court of Common Pleas, dated 3 Feb 1450, William Ingowe and Joan, his wife, acknowledged the manor of "Donington" (i.e., Dinnington, Northumberland) "to be the right of Thomas Hesilrygge," and "as that which the same Thomas, Nicholas [Girlington] and Thomas [Broket] have of their gift, and have remised and quitclaimed it." This account suggests that Thomas[5a] Hesilrygge and Thomas Broket not only were friends but perhaps had shared a marital tie prior to Elizabeth's marriage to Thomas[5a], although no record of it has been seen. It appears that neither the Broket nor the Girlington family records have been well researched, much less assembled; thus, a usual tactic of "triangulating" across family records is presently unavailable.

In the next chapter we will have opportunity to consider Thomas[5a] a bit further, in conjunction with a puzzle of sorting among several men named "Thomas." For the present, we must move to the manor of Swarland and its surrounds in east-central Northumberland. Swarland was for quite some time principal seat of the family.

Swarland and Vicinity
The process of building family patrimony was always open-ended in the dual sense that opportunities for new acquisitions could arise sometimes quite unexpectedly, but no acquisition was ever guaranteed to last either in one's holdings at all or as a source of sufficient satisfaction. This was a major focal point of the uncertainties of life: day-to-day uncertainties could easily rule personal imaginations, yet if skills in managing those uncertainties were to add up to one more year of life on a personal calendar (itself an unguaranteed good, of course) the "daily personal" had to be meshed with the "future familial." Even for monarchs, the goal was to convert the daily personal into a "dynastic continuity," simply a larger-scale version of any family's goal from generational survival to greater success of generation. The means of working out solutions to that goal typically involved competition between brothers, between cousins, between branches of a family; and although some adjustments had to be made, that intra-familial process of competition remained vital even as the feudal forms of organizing territory and relations among families and resources unravelled. A family, as a family, had to learn to regulate the internal competition in order to minimize its destructive tendencies and maximize the better outcomes. As with contests for royal succession, the regulation was easier to achieve when one member of a family dominated during any given period.

The junctures of succession carried greater risk of inadequately regulated competition when they occurred between heads of different branches ensconced in more or less equally important manors within a region. An example from the history of the Hesilrige family is centered on the branching between households that mainly migrated from the old manor of Heselrig southward to Eslington, Thrunton, Fawdon, and so on, and households that migrated from Heselrig mainly in an east-southeast direction, toward Warkworth castle and established a major presence at the manor of Swarland. From the perspective of today, because we know the comparative trajectories from that branching, it can seem in some sense inevitable that "the Swarland branch" of the family came to be the "cadet branch," in heraldic terms a branch of lower standing. But for a century or so from the early 1400s, an odds-maker might well have said differently.

The manor of Swarland did not come into the family until nearly the end of the 1300s. Probably the first presence in that general area was at a place called Sheepwash (or Shepwash)—a very small place, now virtually invisible but for the name of a road, on the river Wansbeck across from the town of Ashington (see Exhibit 3.2, page 74, upper right corner). Recall from chapter 3 that John de Hesilrigg, son of William de Heselrig of Akeld, was at one time (c1350) known as John de Hesilrigg of Sheepwash. This is the man who fought at the battle of Bannockburn, 24 June 1314. A recent study of that battle and its aftermath includes this passage:

> John Hesilrigg, a man-at-arms of Northumberland, informed the king [Edward II] that he had been made a prisoner during the "discomfiture" at Stirling, where he had lost horses and amour worth 200 marks. Hesilrigg's ransom had also been set at 200 marks and he evidently encountered problems in raising the necessary funds, remaining imprisoned by the Scots for two years and losing all the profits of his land in Northumberland for five years; he reckoned the total financial cost of his capture at a substantial 600 marks.[36]

The fact that he lost horses, in plural, worth 200 marks, armor included, indicates that he was old enough to have accumulated considerable property. Thus, he was surely at least in his late 20s in 1314, and very likely older.

While John had the king's attention (one could only hope), he reminded his king that he had been of service even more recently, as he had participated in the capture of Sir Gilbert de Middleton at Mitford Castle, 1317/8.[37] This addendum surely would have been of considerable interest to the king, for Middleton had been a leader in rebellion against him. Never one of the more adept of monarchs, Edward II had suffered a string of defeats and embarrassments during his first decade of reign. Determined at the outset to claw back what he thought had been unwise concessions made by his father to parliamentary standing, the new king proceeded to alienate most of his barons, lose battles with the Scots (e.g., at Bannockburn), and leave security of the northern shires to local enforcers. One such was Sir Gilbert de Middleton, who sought to reinforce the interests of his own family during this period of weakened

---

[36] David Cornell, *Bannockburn* (New Haven: Yale University Press, 2009), page 227. John's claim is recorded in the Wardrobe Accounts, 2 Edward II, *Archæologia London*, volume 26, page 330; his petition, in *Ancient Petitions*, Public Records Office, file 81, no. 4036. John appears in the early segment of lineage, at end of chapter 3, page 99.

[37] The date is somewhat ambiguous: capture might have occurred late in December 1317, but it could have come in January or February (1318, by our reckoning).

authority of London. Among his actions was gaining control of Mitford castle, c1315, as his base of operations. From there he engaged in kidnapping and brigandage. As if that had not been enough added embarrassment to the crown's claim of sovereignty, Middleton now, 1317, stood accused of having seized the bishop of Durham and of having robbed two cardinals at Acle (now Aycliffe, Durham), while they were on visit from Rome. Middleton was executed soon after capture.

John Hesilrigg was one of about nine men who were later acknowledged as having been principals in Middleton's capture. Among the others were four brothers, John, Peter, Roger, and William de Faudon (i.e., Fawdon).[38] John and William were recorded as holding land in Throphill and Mitford (both in Mitford parish); apparently nothing more was known of these four men. The date, c1317, is very near the time of William[3b] de Heselrig of Fawdon, who was born in 1325. Fawdon manor was, or became, his home seat, but we do not know when it was acquired by the Heselrig family. As previously mentioned, William[3b] and his son Thomas[4a] were referred to, at least on occasion, as William[3b] of Fawdon and Thomas[4a] of Fawdon, although both are well attested as men who carried the family name, Heselrig. (By this time, the early 1300s, the use of a heritable family name as "extra name" was well established among the aristocracy and was being adopted by commoners as well.) Were the four brothers who were cited as participants in the capture of Middleton—John, Peter, Roger, and William of Faudon—sons in the prior generation of the Heselrig family? No, almost surely not. Fawdon had circulated among several families during the latter half of the thirteenth century, the last being the Umfrevilles.

There is no indication that John's claim for reimbursement of loss succeeded. Nor is there any evidence that he benefited from involvement in the capture of Middleton. We know that he inherited a quarter of the parental manor at Akeld, a very small holding, and we know that about thirty years after the Middleton affair, he was recorded as witness to a legal transaction as John de Hesilrigg of Shepwash, also a small holding, near the coast of Northumberland, a place of frigid winter winds and dry chilly spring days. What was his life like? In 1350, when he was likely in his seventh decade, what was his view of life's fare?

---

[38] See the account by Sir Arthur E Middleton, *Sir Gilbert de Middleton* (Newcastle-upon-Tyne: Mawson Swan and Morgan, 1918), page 89. He combed all known records for information that would elucidate his ancestor's behavior. The results include an extensive list of the persons who relinquished land because of judgments of complicity (chapter 13) and lists of pardons, as well as of participants in the capture at Mitford.

Given what is known of John Hesilrig, it is easy to imagine him as a hapless man, someone who, like most of us, tried to follow more or less rational plans of action, tried to engage in opportunities in more or less the right way, observing customs and expectations, but who, despite all of that, found that the world of his surroundings failed to "answer to" his efforts with much reward. Following a modern tendency to mine the sense of social processes by "psychologizing" them, we might go so far as to "medicalize" signs of events when contemplating "what happened to John and why," and perhaps imagine a fourteenth-century version of post-traumatic stress disorder as the life-setting result of his experience at Bannockburn.

One overriding fact about historical accounts must be maintained foremost in mind, however: we are always working with what amounts to a sampling problem, whether recognized and utilized as such or not. It is inescapable. Think of the general problem this way: any past life was a trajectory of events and experiences, some good, some not; some were recorded, some were not; some records survived to future view, some did not. What a future "viewer of the record" does see, therefore, is simply a sample of all that happened, and the pieces comprising the sample do not come with tags that tell their relative proportions ("I was a rare event." "I was typical of his/her childhood." "I was the sort of event that happened for almost everyone when times were bad." And so forth.) In short, the viewer lacks means of answering with high confidence the key question of the sampling process: how well does it represent the sum of all that happened during and as that lifetime? The smattering of facts about John that have survived to our inspection could well have been the low point of an ascending trajectory. Or the typical. Or—one hesitates to imagine that life got worse for John—even the high point.

Other lives, as we have seen already, *were* better, some of them very much better. One such was the life of Sir Donald[3a] de Hesilrige, a man we have met repeatedly in his chapter. He illustrates, among other characteristics, what we could call the fourteenth-century entrepreneurial spirit of accumulating new holdings in (for the family) new areas by plots of carefully executed strategic actions. Correlated with that, of course, was a gratifying supply of good fortune, which remained in ample flow even into his fifth decade of life, during his foray as a knight fighting in the south of France for the cause of his king and his king's son and heir apparent, the Black Prince, who was known far and wide as a robustly active combatant. As we have seen, Donald[3a] acquired manorial estates not so much as personal abodes as investments for his household and his broader family. His record shows good evidence of intent to distribute holdings among separate households, while in some sense remaining in charge, and of intent to move the manorial center of the family as a whole southward. We have seen already that after his service in Gascony under Edward, prince of Wales, Donald[3a] established his main residence in Yorkshire (we return to that fact in the last section of this chapter). Here the focus is on a small manor in the east of Northumberland, near Warkworth castle, the manor of Brotherwick.

Brotherwick had been granted by Henry I to Henry de Hanvill, king's falconer, during the early 1100s, and it remained in that family's holding for some time, partly because small manors got less attention from distant London, leaving arrangements to local authorities. If, when Brotherwick came to Donald's[3a] hand by marriage to Johanna de Wauton, c1361, he was still subject to similar obligations as lord of the manor of Whittingham (if not yet also Eslington), as seems likely, he would have sought to avoid being overburdened, and Brotherwick was some distance away. Whatever the motivation, in 1370 Donald[3a] and Johanna obtained license to enfeoff his brother, Edmund[3c] de Heselrig, along with two other men, Robert de Wycliff and John de Feryby, with the Brotherwick manor, to be held in trust for Donald[3a] and Johanna. After Donald's[3a] death on Sunday, 9 April 1385, his second wife Joan (*nee* de Bredon) held Brotherwick until her death 21 December 1400 at York, after which it passed into the estate of Henry Percy, earl of Northumberland.[39] As a result of his part in rebellion against Henry IV, the earl forfeited his possessions. Brotherwick, along with Warkworth castle, was granted by Henry IV to his son John in 1405.

The inquisition post mortem for Donald[3a] confirmed that, having died childless, he left as heir in addition to his widow his brother William[3b], then aged 60 years, whose son and heir was Thomas[4a], then aged 30 years.[40] Notably, William[3b] had already been granted land at South Weteslade, on 20 Nov 1360, for his services in the wars against Scotland.[41]

---

[39] According to the inquisition post mortem, Donald[3a] died the Sunday after Easter,1385. The first full moon after spring equinox that year in England was 27th March; the next Sunday, 2nd April, was Easter.

[40] That Donald[3a] died without surviving child as heir is not doubted. That he had never sired children is a different question, to which the I.p.m. statement might not have been intended as answer. The basic issue of an inquisition post mortem was heirship, not total progeny (although the phrase, *obiit sine progenies*, "died without progeny," can be read as such).

[41] Hodgson, "On the Medieval and Later Owners ..." (1910), page 16.

When in 1615 Richard St George conducted his heraldic visitation of Northumberland, the only noted presence of the Hesilrige family in the entirety of the county was at the manor of Swarland. By that date, the chief seat of the family was at Noseley Hall, in Leicestershire, and the household at Swarland had become locus of the family's "cadet branch." But for several decades Swarland had fair claim to the status of principal seat of the Heselrig family. Failure in heirship, together with the family's intent to move southward, put paid to that claim.

For present purposes, the history of the Swarland manor begins, as St George reported it, with "Thome Karlioll Burgensi de novo Castro super Tinam"; or Thomas Karliol (Carlisle) who descended from a family in Cumbria, now a burgess of Newcastle-upon-Tyne.[42] Cecily, one of his daughters, married Peter Graper (d. before 25 April 1358), member of a wealthy merchant family of Newcastle. It appears that Cecily had gained complete control of the inheritance of Swarland by 25 April 1358, when she settled the manor of Swarland on son Thomas Graper. This man wed Mary, daughter of Richard Stanhope, burgess of Newcastle. They had two daughters, coheirs, Agnes and Isabel, on whom he settled the vill and manor of Swarland on All Saints day 1376. Agnes, the older, married by 1 May 1389 John, son of William de Heselrig. Isabel married William de Bishopdale, mayor of Newcastle. Dendy reported that in 1410 an heir of Thomas Karliol via Constancia, daughter of another of his five daughters, Alicia, made claim against Thomas Heselrig, son of John Heselrig and his wife Agnes, regarding rights to Swarland.[43] Apparently the claim failed, at what expense to Thomas Heselrig we do not know. Dendy also noticed some later complication when, following death of John Heselrig, his widow, Agnes, married William Bishopdale (presumably her sister, Isabel, also had died).[44] But the complication might well have been a confusion in the records, or in a reading of them.

In any case, Swarland was held by the family until, because of circumstances that will be described later, possession passed to Sir Arthur Hesilrige, 7th Bt., of Noseley, who sold the estate to Richard Grieve of Alnwick for £10,180, in what amounted to a lease purchase. Soon after the purchase was completed an assessment of the Swarland estate, in 1741, recorded that it included the manor and vill, seventeen farms, with

---

[42] Richard St George, *The Visitation of Northumberland in 1615* (edited by George W Marshall; London: Mitchell and Hughes, 1878), page 21.
[43] Dendy, "Extracts from the De Banco Rolls ..." (1910), page 69.
[44] Frederick Walter Dendy, "An Account of Jesmond," *Archaeologia Æliana* 3rd series, volume 1 (1904), p. 157.

Exhibit 4.5. Swarland Old Hall, c1904 & c2004

John Carr to build a new Swarland Hall and park in 1765. This new hall was demolished during the early 1930s, and in 1936 a village of 77 cottages was built on the site. Swarland Old Hall, still standing, was built during the 1600s by the Hesilrige family. It incorporates some of the older manor house. As was seen in Exhibit 3.1, a castellated full-height screen wall with three blind Gothic arches forms the east facade. The south front features four bays. Exhibit 4.5 features views of the front dated 1904 and 2004.[45] In recent times the hall has been operated by a private family as a charming bed-and-breakfast for tourists.

Swarland Lineage
A descent chart of the Swarland lineage is presented below, commencing with John, son of William^{3a} de Heselrig. In keeping with prior practice, superscript notation will continue as before, but (despite being a bit cumbersome) with addition of a prefix "S" to denote the Swarland branch. Added description of some of the entries will follow.

John^{S4e} Heselrig: b. <1365, d. 1391; m. <10 Oct 1381 Agnes, daughter & coheir of Thomas Graper of Newcastle and Swarland

   L-- **Thomas**^{S5a} Heselrig: b. c1381, d. > 1 Mar 1444/5; m. Agnes (maiden name unknown); more below

   L-- Nicholas^{S5b} Heselrig: party to deed 12 Feb 1432

Thomas^{S5a} Heselrig of Swarland: b. c1381; d. > 1 Mar 1444/5; wife Agnes party to a deed 8 Dec 1429

  L-- **John**^{S6a} Heselrig: b. >1420; confirmed father's grant 14 Mar 1454/5; wife unknown

    L-- Robert^{S7a} Heselrig: b. <1470, d. before father

    L-- **Henry**^{S7b} Heselrig: b. <1470; more below

---

[45] The older of the two images—apparently someone's sketch from memory, in light of its divergence from the recent photograph—is taken from John Crawford Hodgson's *A History ...*, volume 7 (1904), page 403. The lineage presented below relies heavily on Hodgson's work in his volume 7 (see especially pages 255, 390-400, 442, 444; several wills are included).

∟-- Alice[S7c] Heselrig: m. William Lewen

∟-- Margaret[S7d] Heselrig: m. Nicholas Crosier of Newbiggin, co. Durham

Henry[S7b] Heselrig of Swarland: b. <1470, d. <12 Sep 1516

∟-- **Lancelot**[S8a] Heselrig: b. c1490, d >c1525; m. c1517 Lucy, daughter of Sir William Lisle (marriage contract 12 Sep 1516)

∟-- **Lancelot**[S9a] Heselrig: b. c1525, d. 4 May 1565; m. 1561 Agnes, daughter of Thomas Lisle of Hazon (marriage settlement Michaelmas 1561)

∟-- **Robert**[S10a] Heselrig: b. 1563; more below

Robert[S10a] Heselrig: b. 1563, d. Jan 1638/9; m. Deborah, daughter of Tristram Fenwick of Brinkburn; (will 29 Dec 1638; inventory 15 Jan 1638/9; see Exhibit 4.6, below)[46]

∟-- **William**[S11a] Heselrig: b. 1601, d. c1661; more below

∟-- Margaret[S11b] Heselrig: b. c1601; m. Richard Heron of Bokenfield; she no issue, he died Sep 1665

∟-- George[S11c] Heselrig of Snook-bank: b. c1606, d. c1635; inventory 17 Mar 1635/6

∟-- **Robert**[S12a] Heselrig: b. c1633, d. 25 May 1700; apprenticed 1 June 1647 to Bertram Anderson of Newcastle, boothman; admitted 23 Aug 1658 to Merchants Company, as grain merchant

∟-- **Robert**[S13a] Heselrig: b. c1665; more below

---

[46] A manuscript entitled "Settlement by Roger Hesilrigg, of Swarland, of his Lands, etc., at Swarland and other places, to his own use, with remainder to his cousin, Michael Weldon," is inventoried in *A Catalogue of the Library belonging to the Society of Antiquaries of Newcastle* (Newcastle-upon-Tyne: William Dodd, 1863), page 80; but it has not been seen by this writer. The settlement is reportedly dated as 27 Elizabeth I (or c1585). No other evidence of this Roger Hesilrigg has been found. The forename could have been a misreading of "Robt"?

┗-- Sarah[S13b] Heselrig: b. c1665; m. 13 May 1694 Ralph Appleby

┗-- Alice[S13c] Heselrig: b. c1665; m. 24 Sep 1703 St Andrew, Newcastle, Edward Bulman; more below

┗-- Henry[S11d] Heselrig: will 20 Mar 1637/8, d. by 29 Dec 1638

┗-- John[S11e] Heselrig of Long Row, Longframlington parish: d. Apr 1654; will named "Katherine my wife and James my son"

┗-- Isabel[S11f] Heselrig: m. George Harbottle; issue: Henry, Robert

┗-- Agnes[S11g] (aka Ann) Heselrig: unmarried 29 Dec 1638

┗-- Jane[S11h] Heselrig: b. c1610; m. Robert Manners (bond 20 Oct 1633); issue: sons Robert (b. c1634) and Roger (b. >1636); Robert Sr., d. by 23 Aug 1649

┗-- Catherine[S11i] Heselrig: unmarried 29 Dec 1638

┗-- Dorothy[S11j] Heselrig: m. James Carr of Snook-bank; issue: Andrew, James, Elizabeth & Hester

┗-- Elizabeth[S11k] Heselrig: unmarried 29 Dec 1638

William[S11a] Heselrig: b. 1601, d. 9 Dec 1662; m. (1) >1615 Frances, daughter of Albany Featherstonehaugh, widow of Henry Crackenthorp (marriage bond 23 Oct 1615), no issue (?); m. (2) c1645 Isabel Carr; issue follow:[47]

┗-- **William**[S12a] Heselrig: b. c1645, d. 1670; m. (1) Jane Forster (bond 25 Jan 1664/5), m. (2) Nichola (*nee* unknown), she sole devisee in William's will, d. June 1699 Swarland; more below

---

[47] In his will, 10 May 1658, William Heselrigg of Swarland says that his second wife, Isabel, was mother of William Carr and wife of Robert Carr. This was Sir Robert Carr of Etal (the manor and castle) north of Heselrig (Chatton parish); William Carr was born 1634, attended Oxford and Gray's Inn, became a barrister; d. 1689. See, e.g., William Whellan & Co., *History, Topography and Directory of Northumberland* (London: Whittaker and Co., 1855), page 697.

└-- Robert[S12b] Heselrig: succeeded brother William; more below

└-- Gilbert[S12c] Heselrig: b. 1650, d. Apr 1662

└-- Arthur[S12d] Heselrig: b. 3 Dec 1654, d. 25 Dec 1662

Robert[S12b] Heselrig of Swarland: b. c1647, d. Dec 1716; succeeded his brother William 1681; high sheriff of Northumberland 1698; will 17 Aug 1714, named his cousin Robert Heselrig of South Shields as devisee

Robert[S13a] Heselrig: b. c1665 prob. Newcastle, d. 27 Mar 1728; m. Hannah (*nee* Eubank, widow of Matthew Curry of Bedlington)

And with that we have come to the end of the Hesilrige lineage of Swarland and vicinity. The descent lineage is far from complete, no doubt, but we can be happy to know the identity of the man previously described rather mysteriously, following Hodgson's account, as "cousin Robert." We can now be confident, thanks to Geoffrey Kendal's sharing of some wills (beginning with William[S11a]) that this cousin was none other than Robert[S13a] Heselrig. Our correction does not disparage the accomplishment of Hodgson, for one must consider what little he had as his point of departure, the 1615 visitation of Northumberland. Richard St. George had recorded 53 pedigrees from information supplied by those families. For most of those 53 families the relevant descent lineage consisted in a handful of generations, and the information included dates, sometimes place names, and sometimes names of wives and surviving children. The pedigree of the Heselrigg family, on the other hand, was twelve generations long, one of the longest. However, for all but the then current generation—namely, Robert[S10a], his wife Deborah (*nee* Fenwicke of Brinkburn), and their ten named children—the Heselrigg pedigree listed *only* names of *only* the main generational line of male heirs (no dates, no wives, only the heir among children). From that meagre series of names, one could only guess at identity of the referent who appeared as devisee in the will of Robert[S12b] Heselrigg as "cousin Robert Heselrigg of South Shields." One presumed, as Hodgson did, that the two men were agnatic cousins, but beyond that there was too little information to pinpoint a specific man.

It was clear from the will of Robert[S12b], dated 17 August 1714, that he had no surviving male heir. He thus assigned "to Sir Robert

Hesilrige, and his heirs, all those lands in the parish of Felton called Swarland, the Glantees and the Firth, being the ancient estate which belonged to Robert Heselrigg, esq., my late grandfather." He excepted "just debts" and a few legacies, several small ones to servants and two larger ones: to "my good friend Mrs Mary Ledgar of Swarland, and her heirs for ever, my lands of Overgrass, Overgrass Steed and mill"; and "to my cousin Robert Heselrig, late of South Shields, and Hannah his wife an annuity of £20 per annum charged to my estate."[48] Two years later, 20 December 1716, he had to append this codicil: "My cousin Mary Ledgar being now dead, I give that which I had intended for her to my cousin Robert Heselrigg of Sleighburn pans, in the parish of Bedlington, and his heirs for ever."

This latter referenced "cousin Robert" was surely Robert[S13a] Heselrig. At an earlier date he had been known as Robert of Blyth; next as Robert of South Shields; now (1716) as Robert of Sleighburn Panns (i.e., Sleekburn, "pans" being a flat area that is occasionally covered by water). Sleekburn is on the river Wansbeck, near Blyth, a few miles from Sheepwash. At one time, recall, the area of Bedlington was part of the Northumberland enclave of Durham. This historical confluence of places had suggested previously that "cousin Robert" might have descended through the John of Sheepwash, mentioned earlier in this section of the chapter. Some dates did not fit all that well, but as illustrated in the prior section recorded dates as well as place names were not always accurately recorded.

However, by his own testament "cousin Robert" must have been Robert[S13a] Heselrig. The direct evidence of identity is the fact that in his will, dated 5 May 1725 in Morpeth, he named Edward Bulman as his brother-in-law and Stephen Bulman as his nephew, both as annuitants. Edward had married Alice[S13c] Heselrig in 1703 in Newcastle (as recorded in the above lineage). Their son Stephen Bulman (b. c1705) sired sons Proctor (c1731) and Hesilrig (c1733) Bulman, the older of whom had a daughter Isabella, who married William Renshaw (b. c1764). Their son George (c1791) wed Mary Sellers, whose son, John Sellers Renshaw (c1817), sired by wife Elizabeth Sword a daughter, Mary Elizabeth Sellers Renshaw (b. c1840). This last-named woman wed Matthew George Kendal (b. c1837); they, in turn, were direct ancestors of the man who enabled this correction of lineage, Geoffrey Kendal.

In absence of well-attested public records, family records are a good point of departure especially when those records reflect effort to

---

[48] Hodgson, *A History ...*, volume 7 (1904), page 397.

sustain claims to landholdings (as in the 1615 visitation of Northumberland). But these, too, can be suspect, inasmuch as the success of a family's defense of claim would likely have depended on a negotiation. As noted above, for instance, the king's Norroy in the 1615 visitation, Richard St George, accepted many bare claims of succession in the Heselrigg pedigree as official, simply by his own written act of recording.

That record includes three men named Lancelot, in succession, absent any specifying information. While no evidence proves that the succession of three men, rather than two, of the same name was impossible (and proving a negative is usually impossible), there is room for doubt, based on implied evidence of the span of time accommodating that many successions. In any case, the known record is tenuous even for two of the three men. Let's begin with the older of these two men named Lancelot. (Nothing beyond name is known of the reported third Lancelot.)

It is well established that a Lancelot Hesylrigge was constable of the Warkworth castle in 1486, a date which means almost surely that he was born before 1466 and probably before 1456. An account in one of the Northumberland histories reads:[49]

> Early in the reign of Henry VII trees were felled at Shilbottle for the works of the castle. Lancelot Hesylrigge, the constable, paid by the lord's directions 10s. 8d. for making anew fourteen feet of glass in the windows where most required; 13d. was laid out in iron for the bands and 'les gelnewes' [very likely a mistranscription of "gemewes"—i.e., hingles]; the glazier provided 4 pounds of solder and 100 'glassenayle'. A tiler and his man repaired the stone roof [i.e., slate tiles] of the porter's lodge, and the roofs of the house over the well and of other houses in the castle. They covered 'the lord's stable within the castle,' and cleaned the gutters and leads of all the towers. A great cleaning of the hall and of the chambers of the lord and the lady, and other chambers and houses took place, in anticipation of the earl's arrival in August, 1486 [Hodgson's printer said 1480]. White straw was brought for the beds, and rushes for strewing in the hall and chambers.

Alarm at the appearance of Lambert Simnel [see below] and the expiry of the truce with Scotland perhaps caused the special

---

[49] John Crawford Hodgson, *A History ...*, volume 5 (1899), page 51.

allowance of 6s. 'for watching within the castle' made to Heselrigge as constable by the earl's orders; 6d. was expended on one great lock with a key for the door of a chamber within the castle called 'Crake ferguse'; 17s. 4d. was paid for carpenter's work, and building the walls of the 'slaughter howse' and roofing, and plastering it. In August, 1487, the earl was at Newcastle in attendance on Henry VII, who had come north himself to punish Simnel's adherents. Thirty salmon were supplied from Warkworth for the use of the earl's foreign household on this occasion.

The earl in question was Henry Percy, 4th earl of Northumberland, for whom Warkworth Castle was a home. Lambert Simnel was an imposter of Edward, 17th earl of Warwick, who as such claimed right by descent to the English throne. This claim, reported 24 May 1487, was very likely a ploy by the House of York. The ensuing rebellion was quickly defeated and Simnel, probably understood to be a dupe, was assigned permanently to duty in the king's kitchen.

Again, this Lancelot was too old to have been the Lancelot^{S8a} in the lineage. It is true that in his 1615 visitation St George reported three successive men with the forename "Lancelot."[50] But it would be difficult to shoehorn a third man between Henry^{S7a} and Lancelot^{S8a}, as the former's son and the latter's father, if that third man had been old enough to be constable at Warkworth in 1486.

There was still another man named Lancelot Heselrig, but the date for this man also does not fit what we know of the men named Lancelot in the lineage segment shown above. This man appears in the *Feodary's Book of Northumberland Freeholders* in 1568 as holding a number of estates, including those at Thrunton and Barton, land in Weteslade and Dinnington, and vills of Brountsel and Fawdon.[51] What is striking about that list is that the holdings are not associated with the Swarland Heselrig households but with the other branch descending from their common ancestor, Simon^{2a} Heselrig. The man to whom Robert^{S12b} of Swarland refers as "cousin Robert" was probably of the line of descent from Simon^{2a} to William^{3b} Heselrig of Fawdon to his son Thomas^{4c} (whose

---

[50] St George reported only the names, no particulars, for all three of his Lancelot men. Other, and more recent, histories of the area, including Hodgson's, have found evidence only of two, as reported in the lineage above.

[51] John Hodgson, *A History of Northumberland*, part 3, volume 3 (Newcastle-upon-Tyne: John Blackwell and John Brunton Falconar, 1835), page lxx. A feodary was a collector of revenues, in particular rents. The book in question has also been known as the *Escheats de Anno 10 Eliz. I*. The names in the list of estates are familiar—excepting the vill of "Brountsel," perhaps a confusion of Brunton.

brother begins the above segment of lineage as John[S4e]), and on eventually to Sir Robert Hesilrige of Noseley, 6th Bt.

Implicit in that chain of fact and conjecture is part of the reason for Robert[S12b] of Swarland's assignment to one "cousin Robert" and to yet another and even more distant cousin the extensive holdings which in his will he described with evident pride as "the ancient estate" that had belonged to his grandfather Robert[S10a] and wife Deborah (*nee* Fenwick). The other part of the reason is evident from the late entries in the lineage segment shown above: early mortality had removed nearer male relatives from the scene. Older brother William[S12a], whom he had succeeded in 1681, had no other male heir. Younger brothers Gilbert[S12c] (d. April 1662) and Arthur[S12d] (d. December 1662) apparently had succumbed to disease (perhaps another outbreak of plague) at ages too young to have sired progeny. Grandfather Robert[S10a] had produced three sons after William[S11a]: George[S11b] sired a son who was dead by 25 May 1700 and who had no known progeny; Henry[S11c] died very young; John[S11d] had one son, for whom there is no further record. Determined to keep the estates within the family, he devised to two distant but agnatic cousins.

Perched in their hall at Swarland and in surrounding abodes, this branch of the family watched the grand tapestry of English history unfold during the period from the second half of the 1300s to the mid-1700s. In broad scope, it was a time of transition from late-medieval society to early-modern society. In less broad scope, it was a time of continuing outbreaks of plague, on top of all the other hazards of disease and injury, and a time of repeated warfare, both across the Channel and at home. At Bosworth field in 1485 the successive struggles for control of the home throne was largely settled by what became the Tudor dynasty. But this gave way to another pair of civil wars during the middle third of the 1600s, although this struggle was more about ideologies, both religious and political, than about succession rights among different branches of royal lineage. In narrower scope, it was a time of competition for wealth, present and future, much as before but now with improving technical means of producing wealth and with better political and juridical means of defending holdings and regulating disputes between claimants.

The record is very sparse by which to make such judgments; but such as it is, one gains the impression that the Swarland branch, like their cousins to the west, generally sought to stay clear of the dynastic disputes between houses of Lancaster and York and the ideological conflicts of the 1600s. This is not to say, however, that they escaped being enmeshed in local conflicts. One likely scenario that stands out concerns marital ties of father and son named Lancelot who wed, respectively, Lucy Lisle c1517, and Agnes Lisle, 1561. Lucy was daughter of Sir William Lisle, a man who, in Hodgson's words, "inherited in fullest measure the active disposition and unruly temper" of his ancestors.[52] During the summer of 1527 he, his son Humphrey, and about 40 other men attacked the gaol of Newcastle, releasing nine prisoners. More brigandage followed, but soon Sir William was hanged, drawn, and quartered, his estates seized, within the year. Son Humphrey was pardoned. Was Lancelot[S8a] aware of the events prior to the execution? He must have been. But then, too, he must have been aware of the reputation of this branch of the Lisle family prior to his marriage. The fact that his son, Lancelot[S9a], also wed a daughter of the family, although of a different branch (Agnes, daughter of Thomas Lisle of Hazon), leads one to wonder if there had been some sympathy toward the Lisle family's actions.

Before leaving the Swarland story, two additional accountings are of interest. The first is an inventory of the estate of Robert[S10a] Heselrig of Swarland (Exhibit 4.6, below).[53] This inventory seems typical, as judged by comparison to inventoried household goods of other persons. As one example, Jane, widow of Robert Shafto, late of Newcastle, merchant and alderman, sold similar (though not as numerous) goods to a Mr Lyonnell Blagdon, 18 Sep 1671, for a total of £10.

> *Imprimis* ["In the first place"]: 17 oxen, £34; 2 longwaines [long wagons], 2 shortwaines [short wagons], 2 plows with the yoke, somes, bows, harrowes and other things belonging to them, £3; 14 stirkes [bullocks], £9 6s 8d; 33 sheep, £5 10s; 6 kine, 6 calves and one bull, £12; 6 mares, 4 foales and 2 fillies, £20; of wheat and rye in the stackyard, by estamacion, 30 bowles at 13s 4d the bowle, £20; of oates, by estamacion, 100 bowles at 5s the bowle, £25; of pease, by estimation, 4 bowles at 8s the bowle, £1 12s; of big, by estimation, 8 bowles, £4; of hardcorne sown in the fields, 13 bowles by estimation, £18; 2 hyves with the bees, 13s 4d; of hay, by estimation, £3 6s 8d; [illegible], 16s; *Goods within the house*: his purse and apparell, £6 13s 4d; one flaggon and one potle pot, 10s; one bason and an ewer

---

[52] John Crawford Hodgson, *A History ...*, volume 7 (1904), page 247. Hodgson cites a number of documents that recount accusations of theft, pillage, assault, and murder by Sir William Lisle and his father (who was dead by 1517).

[53] John Crawford Hodgson, *A History ...*, volume 7 (1904), pages 394-395. The date of inventory was 15 Jan 1638 by old calendar. Each instance of the "illegible" notation in square brackets was by the transcriber of the handwritten will. Other notations in square brackets are by the present writer. Spelling in the transcription has been retained.

[wash basin and water pitcher], 6s 8d; 4 candlesticks, 6s; 3 [illegible] and 9 doublers, 16s; 2 pyeplates, one [illegible] plate and a white lattin dripping pan, 4s; 2 chamberpots and 1 saltfat, 1s, 8d; 2 brasse pots, £1 10s; one caldron, £1; one pair of yron racks and 2 spitts, 6s 8d; 1 maskin tub [used in brewing], 1 single tub and 1 worte tub, 6s 8d; 2 barrells and 2 stannes, 2 roundlets [small barrel for wine] and 2 leaven tubs, 5 milk bowles and one churne and 2 pecks, 14s; 2 tables in the hall, 2 in the great chamber, one in Mr Heslrig's chamber, one in the parloure, £1; three cupboards, viz., one in the hall, one in the great chamber and one in the upper parloure, £1; 10 chaires, viz., 4 in the hall, 4 in the great chamber, one in the upper parlour and one in Mr Heslerig's chamber, £1; 11 buffet stooles and 2 formes, 6s 8d; 6 standing bedsteads, 3 trundle beds, £4; 3 fether beds, 1 bolster and 2 pillowes, £1; 6 happines, £1; 4 pairs of blankets, 10s; 3 coverings for tables, 10s; 4 pairs of linen sheetes, £1; one linnen table clothe and 6 table napkins, 6s, 8d; one rugge, couler grene, 10s; one gilt silver salte, £3 6s 8d; 2 silver bowles, one of them guilt, £3 6s 8d; 10 silver spounes, £3 6s 8d; 3 crookes, one payr of tongues, one payr of potclips and other implements in the house, 6s 8d. Total, £192 9s 8d.

Exhibit 4.6. Robert Heselrig Inventory, 15 Jan 1638/9

The second addition pertains most immediately to this Robert[S10a] Heselrig's grandson, William[S12a] Heselrig, who in 1650 was one of the commissioners presenting their report in Morpeth on certain aspects of the ecclesial institutions of Northumberland. The background, briefly, is this: the House of Commons, partly at behest of "Sir Arthur Heselrige, a considerable landed proprietor in Northumberland, and famous in the Annals of the Great Rebellion and the Commonwealth," authorized the conduct of an inquisition throughout the country, led in each county by local commissioners who could assess the financial and organizational health of local parishes, churches, chapels, and "preaching ministers."[54] One of the notable features of that legislative process is that members of the House of Commons insisted that the enabling legislation, instructions to the commissioners, and so forth, be written in English, not in Latin, so that all could freely read and understand.

---

[54] John Hodgson, *History of Northumberland*, part 3, volume 3 (1835), page xlix). A comment on the preceding page makes clear that Hodgson's sympathies did not lie with the "Great Rebellion." The above description and the image in Exhibit 4.7 are from Hodgson, pages xlix-xlx, which rely on journals of the House of Commons.

An early part of the report for Northumberland is shown below as Exhibit 4.7. One of the commissioners was William[S12a] Heselrigg.

ECCLESIASTICAL INQUESTS FOR NORTHUMBERLAND IN 1650.

(INDORSEMENT) To the Right Hono[ble] the Lords Commissioners of the Great Seale of England—In the High and Hon'ble Court of Chancerie att Westminster.

The RETORNE of a Commission for Enquireing of Eccl'icall livings within the County of Northumberland.

NORTHUMB'R.

An Inquisition taken at Morpeth in the said County of Northumberland the first day of June in the year of our Lord God One thousand six hundred and fifty Before William Fenwicke Raphe Delavale William Shaftou Henry Ogle *John Hall Luke* Killingworth Esquires and Henry Horsley Gent. By virtue of a Commission und' the Great Seal of England to them and others directed beareing *date* at Westminster the *sixth* day of Aprill in the aforesaid year of God One thousand six hundred and fiftie   Upon the oath of ⇨ William Heselrigg Esq' Ephra . . . . eld John Ilderton Christopher Ogle Roger . . . . age John Ridley Thomas Collingwood Cuthbert Collingwood William Arn . . . . . . Raphe . . . . George . . . . . . William Thom . . . . Raphe Bready John Lin . . . . y William Widdowes Hugh Arrowsmith Richard Wallis Thomas Salkeld Francis . . . . Gentlemen good and lawfull men of the said County impannelled and sworne to inquire of the severall articles in the said Commission w[th]in the . . . . of the said County   Whoe say upon their oathes as followeth . viz.

That the Parish of Rothbury in the said County is a p'sonage the late Bp'p of Carlisle Patron thereof Mr Ambrose Johnes a preaching minister the Incumbent and the value   T . . . hundred pounds   That the parish of Elsden is a p'sonage the Earle of Suffolke patron thereof Mr Thomas Pye . . . . of the . . thes worth p' ann. one hundred pounds That some part of the said parish being twelve miles distant . . . . And the Jury further p[e]sent that their are certaine small Tythes of the value of five pounds p' annu. w[th]holden . . . . Thirlewall and Mrs   Selby widdow Popish Recusants   That the parish of Allenton and Halliston . . . . Thirlewall Gent and Mrs   Selby patrons thereof Mr Starbucke incumbent p' tempore and the value of the said rectory . . . .

Exhibit 4.7. Northumberland Inquisition, 1 June 1650

Leaving Northumberland, Gradually

We have already seen evidence of the family's migration southward, both within Northumberland and beyond its southern border at the river Tyne.

The purpose of this last section of chapter 4 is to collect some of those threads, from which then to look to futures south of Tyneside.

One of the consequences of the Hundred Years War, surely a consequence intended by no one, was increased tolerance of, even expectation of, long-distance migration. The war experience in France involved large numbers of men who previously had never travelled such distances—for the times, vast distances. Nor had many, if any, of their recent ancestors travelled so far from home. The experience acquainted these men with the logistics of long-distance travel, and if they survived the combat they returned home with greater comfort of thought about undertaking journeys of hundreds of miles. Whereas in the thirteenth and early fourteen century relocating household rarely meant a move of more than a few dozen miles, by the end of the fifteenth century the thought of moving hundreds of miles was imagination not only of the possible, but increasingly often even of the probable.

If there was one family member who exemplified that conjunction of experiences and future orientation best of all, it was surely Donald[3a] de Heselrig, whose expedition in Gascony under Edward, prince of Wales, during 1368-69 must have offered abundant lessons in the relationship of logistics to tactics and strategy of commanding people and territory. He began in the household of his father, Simon[2a], somewhere in the southern part of Northumberland—perhaps Weteslade, perhaps Whittingham. We know his father had shown interest in northern Yorkshire manors at about the time of Donald's[3a] birth, but evidently only as resources to be raided, as noted in the previous chapter (page 99). Similar evidence of interests directed toward Yorkshire have already been mentioned in this chapter as well, and they have been connected with Donald[3a], by and large.

We have seen several instances of the north-to-south migration circuit during the fourteenth and fifteenth centuries, with an overall trend southward toward Newcastle. But it is important to recall that the circuit had already been completed by Simon[1] de Heselrig, who in 1281 carried what had become the family surname, in remembrance of the manorial home a few miles from the Scottish border, but who was now addressed in his king's writ as "Simon de Heselrig, lord of Weteslade and West Brunton," sites only a few miles north of Newcastle. Edward I made the new grant, lands in Yethem (Yetholm) as reward for Simon's services to his king. An implicit message in the grant was surely about future services to the king, however, which were wanted many miles north of Weteslade and West Brunton, in the Borders once again, in and near Yethem.

A half-century later the Borders were largely secure. Donald[3a], having served Edward III, was assigning some of his estates in southern Northumberland to relatives for safekeeping (e.g., part of the manor of Eslington and the manor of Brotherwick to brother Edmund[3c]), while he and second wife, Joan, were pursuing interests in Yorkshire. As noted in preceding sections, Donald[3a] was appointed a commissioner of array for the North Riding 1 July 1377, which suggests residence in that part of Yorkshire, and Joan's will designated bequests to "friends, chaplain, and servants" and the convent at Yarm (south bank of the river Tees, across from south Durham), which also suggests residence in that area. Further, Donald's[3a] inquisitions post mortem (20 Jan 1385 and again 4 June 1385) confirmed that his holdings included a moiety of the manor of Farburn and an interest in the manor of Killingholme.[55] Farburn is in Yorkshire, about a dozen miles southeast of Leeds. Killingholme, on the south bank of the Humber estuary, in Lincolnshire, about 50 miles east of Farburn, is 150 miles south southeast of Newcastle. One additional point may be noted. Recall that in Donald's[3a] enfeoffment of brother Edmund[3c] and others with the manor of Brotherwick, one of those others was a man called John de Feryby. Perhaps we are looking only at coincidence, nothing more; but on the north side of the Humber estuary, just a few miles from Killingholme, is North Ferriby.

These interests had been acquired before 1385, the year Donald[3a] died. Ten years later, the family gains a presence in Leicestershire, when his nephew, Thomas[4c] Heselrig of Fawdon, marries Isabel, daughter and heir of Sir Roger Heron, who brings to the union the manor of Noseley. A half-century later, William[6a], a grandson of Thomas[4c], gains interests in northern Leicestershire and its neighbor, Nottinghamshire, which leads to a branch of the family in and near the city of Nottingham. At about the same time, a case before the Court of Common Pleas in Middlesex, 1493, indicates that a Thomas Hasilrigge was a land holder in that county.[56] Middlesex is now the site of (part of) Greater London. Who was this man? Perhaps Thomas[7a] (1464-1541)?

Leaving Northumberland behind, reluctantly, these are people and places for the next chapters.

---

[55] The document of Donald's i.p.m. is posted on Chris Phillips' medieval genealogy website: CP25/1/181/13 number 133.
[56] The case record, CP52/251/11/8/1/1, is cited in Biancalana, *The Fee Tail ...* (2004), page 277 n.88.

~ 5 ~
Leicestershire, the Early Years

When scanning the calendar of migration events from Northumberland to Leicestershire, one can easily gain the impression that the move was undertaken with reluctance, as was suggested at the end of the preceding chapter. Reasons for reluctance are not far from imagination. During the course of three centuries and more, the Heselrig family had accumulated a sizeable patrimony of landed estates, and management of those assets from the distance of more than 200 miles during the fifteenth century could not have been free of various risks. Furthermore, there were some differences of regional culture between the northern shires and the Midlands. Would new arrivals from "the far North" have been embraced in Leicestershire gladly and warmly? Perhaps. But regional differences in customs, even in the sounds of spoken language, would have been noticed possibly to the extent of inducing subtle, or not so subtle, attitudes of cautiousness or suspicion toward, and a correlative self-consciousness in, the newcomer from the Borders.[1] Granted, Eslington, one of the home seats of the family in Northumberland, was quite some distance from the Scottish border. But from the perspective of someone born and raised in the Midlands, or farther south, the entire shire of Northumberland could easily be seen as "the Borders." Leicestershire was a community of long established networks of families and market relations, within a more densely settled population than found in Northumberland. Living in the Midlands meant being closer to the center of royal power and authority, but that brought serious risks as well as advantages. While "times had changed" throughout England, the Midlands were in several respects more "advanced" than the northern shires, wherein the combination of cold weather and mountainous terrain had impeded agricultural productivity, and domestic security had remained an everyday concern far longer than in shires south of the river Tyne.

Thus, as point of departure in this chapter, let's consider in as much detail as sources allow some circumstances of the arrival of Thomas[4b] and Isabel Heselrig in Leicestershire during the early 1400s. Following that, we will consider Leicestershire as a local community within its historical and regional context.

---

[1] With regard to differences of spoken language, recall from the preface to this book a discussion of "the Great Vowel Shift," which was well underway during this time and, because more advanced in the Midlands than in the Border shires, of stronger contrast than would have attended a migrant within the Midlands.

While the Heselrig family had been moving southward for some time, the move into Leicestershire occurred because of a marriage that took place in 1395, between children of two Northumberland families, one of whom had already moved into Leicestershire and acquired an estate in the east central part of the county, the manor of Noseley, which was the wedding venue. But let's back up a bit and begin with the grandfather of the bride, Sir Roger Heron, who was born in 1330 at Ford manor in Glendale, a few miles north of Heselrig, the family's early estate. Sir Roger married a daughter of Sir Ralph Hastings, Margaret, who was born in 1353 at Kirby, Leicestershire (she died 4 Apr 1407 at Noseley). Kirby was a manor with village (and later a castle) about five miles west of Leicester (later known as Kirby Muckelby, now Kirby Muxlee). The Hastings family were an established Leicestershire family, with a bit of history. Margaret's father, Sir Ralph Hastings (d. 1398), had served as one of John of Gaunt's main commanders. Her half-brother, Sir Ralph Hastings, heir to their father's estates, continued the family's tradition of loyalty to the Yorkist cause, which got him embroiled in the rebellion stoked by Richard Scrope, archbishop of York, just after the turn of the century. Designed to overthrow Henry IV, the rebellion failed, and conspirators were captured and executed, 1405, although there has been some doubt that Hastings was among them. His brothers, Richard and Leonard, inherited in sequence. Leonard's son, William (b. 1431), heir to the estates, became the first baron Hastings; but, caught up in the War of the Roses and accused of treason in 1483, he was executed on orders of Richard III.[2]

Margaret Hastings inherited Noseley through her mother, Isabel Saddington, whose family had held the estate through inheritance from the bishop of Salisbury, Roger Martival. Margaret brought the inheritance to Sir Roger Heron at marriage. They gained possession in 1398, at her father's death.

Apparently Margaret and Sir Roger Heron had only one surviving heir, a daughter Isabel (b. c1375), who arrived when her father was in his mid-40s. In 1395 Isabel married Thomas[4c] Heselrig of Fawdon (b. c1365 at Fawdon). Her father died about 1397, and her mother, Margaret, remarried, to Sir John Blaket, on whom she settled her manors for life. Thus, the Heselrig family did not gain possession of Noseley until 1434.[3]

---

[2] For some of the genealogy, see John Hodgson, *A History of Northumberland*, part 2, volume 1 (Newcastle-upon-Tyne, 1827), page 240.
[3] See the document DG21/27 in the Hazlerigg Collection in the Leicestershire Public Records Office; see also George Farnham and A. Hamilton Thompson, "The Manor of

This partly explains the delay in what eventually became the family's second seat, then primary seat. No known evidence addresses Margaret's motivation in delaying her daughter's inheritance. Indeed, her motivation might well have been directed entirely toward what was, for her, a positive outcome, with no implication of negative evaluation of her daughter or her marriage. Blaket was already a wealthy man, having acquired via two previous marriages estates in "the West Country" (an expression that usually refers to the combination of Cornwall, Devon, Dorset, and Somerset), and in Wiltshire and Cambridgeshire, from all of which his annual income was about £128. Perhaps Margaret believed that success in winning Blaket's agreement to marriage was contingent on the estates she could offer, which included not only Noseley but also the manors of Humberstone, Newton Harcourt, and Gilmorton, plus lands in Langton, Illston, Scraptoft, and Saddington.[4] In any case, he held those estates after Margaret's death in 1407, soon becoming a member of parliament for Leicestershire.

To repeat an earlier caution, it is important to maintain, as best one can, perspectives of the times. In the present instance, the relevant perspective is that of Thomas[4c] Heselrig, a 35-year-old man who, following the deaths of his two older brothers when he had barely attained majority age, had inherited all of the estates of one of the two main branches of the Northumberland family, both branches having been sired by William[3b] Heselrig of Fawdon, his father. His eldest paternal uncle, Donald[3a] (from whom his father, as an old man, had inherited the estates), had set the inclination to move south of the Tyne. Thomas[4c] showed some interest in following that inclination, when, at 30 years of age or so, he wed a daughter and only heir of a landed family in the middle of Leicestershire, about 190 miles south of the Tyne. Thomas[4c] had the company and support of at least a few men of the family in Northumberland. In Leicestershire there was none. He had the care and keeping of a substantial collection of estates within easy reach of Eslington. None was especially rich in proceeds, but he could see good reason to feel reasonably secure in them, such as they were. His family had gained some degree of prominence in Northumberland arenas of politics and market relations, and the alliances

---

Noseley," *Transactions of the Leicestershire Archaeological Society*, volume 12, part 2 (1921-22), pages 214-271, at page 228.

[4] There is an inconsistency in records: one says that Thomas[4c] Heselrig purchased the manor of Gilmorton, but another says that Margaret settled Gilmorton on Blaket as part of her inheritance. Perhaps Thomas[4c] bought the estate from Blaket. Note also that in 436 Margaret's surviving half-brother, Leonard Hastings, won claim to the manor of Newton Harcourt.

of families were well tested, reasonably predictable. Life in Leicestershire would be in many ways a process of beginning again, even though (or if) the estates in Northumberland could be entrusted to caretakers. In 1400 a journey of 200 miles and more counted as long and slow, never free of danger. From what one can imagine as a perspective something like that of Thomas[4c], a decision to move household, to move the principal seat of his lineage, all the way to Noseley would not have been easy, free of doubts. Now that his mother-in-law was dead and another man had sole control of a manorial estate that he had thought to be his new seat in Leicestershire, doubts and second guesses could have been plentiful.

Thomas[4b] and Isabel's first son, Thomas[5a], was born 29 September 1407 at Eslington, still their home estate. Their second son, John[5b], was born at Noseley a few years later, which suggests the possibility of an arrangement whereby Blaket's step-daughter, Isabel, and her husband would have residence at Noseley. In any case, there must have been days when Thomas[4b] wondered, who would die first? He or Sir John Blaket?

According to the record, Sir John Blaket died in 1434. Thomas[4c] had preceded him by a dozen years, dying at his Northumberland manor of Eslington after a quarter-century of marriage to Isabel. However, an agreement by John Blaket, dated 3 November 1403, affirmed that the manors of Noseley, Gilmorton, Newton Harcourt, and Humberstone, plus lands in Langton, Scraptoft, and Illston, remained to Isabel and her heirs, and the agreement held.[5] Their son, Thomas[5a], inherited the manor of Noseley. Henry VI affirmed, 27 June 1434, that "Thomas Hesilrigge, gent." held the manors of Noseley and so forth.[6] Thomas[4b] and Isabel's second son, John[5b], born at Noseley, died there as well, in 1432, ten years after death of his father. One presumes that the widowed Isabel was able to maintain residence at Noseley.

There were two inquisitions post mortem for Thomas[5a] Heselrig, one at Leicester, dated 16 October 1467; then a second one, dated 30 April 1468, at Alnwick, Northumberland. Between them, it is clear, Thomas[5a] died seised of the manor of Noseley, the manor of Gilmorton, with advowson of the church, the manor of Eslington, and a moiety of the towns of Whittingham, Thrunton and Barton. In 1458 he had settled the manor of Humberstone on his son and heir, William[6a], his wife Elizabeth, and on heirs of their bodies. In 1465 he had been recognized as lord of Noseley and rector of Noseley chapel. In 1466 he had endowed a chantry at Noseley, which he had expected to be his place of residence at death and

---

[5] See document DG21/24 in the Hazlerigg Collection, Leicestershire Records Office.
[6] See document DG21/27 in the Hazlerigg Collection, Leicestershire Records Office.

place of burial. A generation of new roots had grown well for this new seat in the community of Leicestershire, rather different from the one that had been home in Northumberland.

A Local Community in Context
As with any local history, the history of Leicestershire must be written with an eye to context of space as well as time; for while it might be that few if any events of the locality have consequences that extend beyond local borders, rarely if ever in late medieval times (and later) was a locality so isolated as to be immune to all impingement from without. In this section of the chapter we will attend to some matters of local history.[7] But various events and developments of the larger scene will be noticed, even though their specific implications for the local community of Leicestershire might be less than unique. While the main focus of this chapter is the Hesilrige family during the sixteenth century, we begin our consideration of local context with Eric Acheson's study of Leicestershire, *A Gentry Community*, even though he chose the battle of Bosworth and the advent of the Tudor regime as his terminus.[8]

Leicestershire is a land of rolling plains, with hills of only 200 to 500 feet elevation above sea level (excepting a few in the west) and rich soil containing boulder clay which acts as a moisture reservoir. Divided north-south by the river Soar, the county's eastern part is generally more fertile than the western part. For readers not familiar with the positional geography of Midland counties in relation to each other and to the north, Exhibit 5.1 offers some guidance. (Not all of the Midland counties are shown.)

Exhibit 5.2 continues past practice by depicting relative locations of some East Midland estates held by the Hesilrige family during the relevant period, from Nottingham ("2" in Exhibit 5.1) to just south of Northampton (not shown in "K" in Exhibit 5.1).

---

[7] Sources include John M Lee and Richard A McKinley, *A History of the County of Leicester, volume 5: Gartree Hundred* (Oxford: Oxford University Press, 1964), *passim* and pages 163-166 for Ilston-on-the-Hill, 264-270 for Noseley, and 312-321 for Theddingworth; John Burton's still useful *A Topographical History of the County of Leicester* (Ashby-de-la-Zouch: W. Hextall, 1831); Eric Acheson, *A Gentry Community* (Cambridge: Cambridge University Press, 1992); and, cited elsewhere in this chapter, works by George Farnham.

[8] Acheson's book is highly useful for its treatment of marital and other alliances, as well as its general survey of community life. Judging from the biographic data presented for the Hesilrige family in his appendix 3, however, there are numerous errors, especially of names and dates.

A: Northumberland
B: Durham
C: Yorkshire
D: Derbyshire
E: Nottinghamshire
F: Lincolnshire
G: Staffordshire
H: Leicestershire
I: Rutland
J: Warwickshire
K: Northamptonshire
L: Cambridgeshire

1: Derby
2: Nottingham
3: Leicester

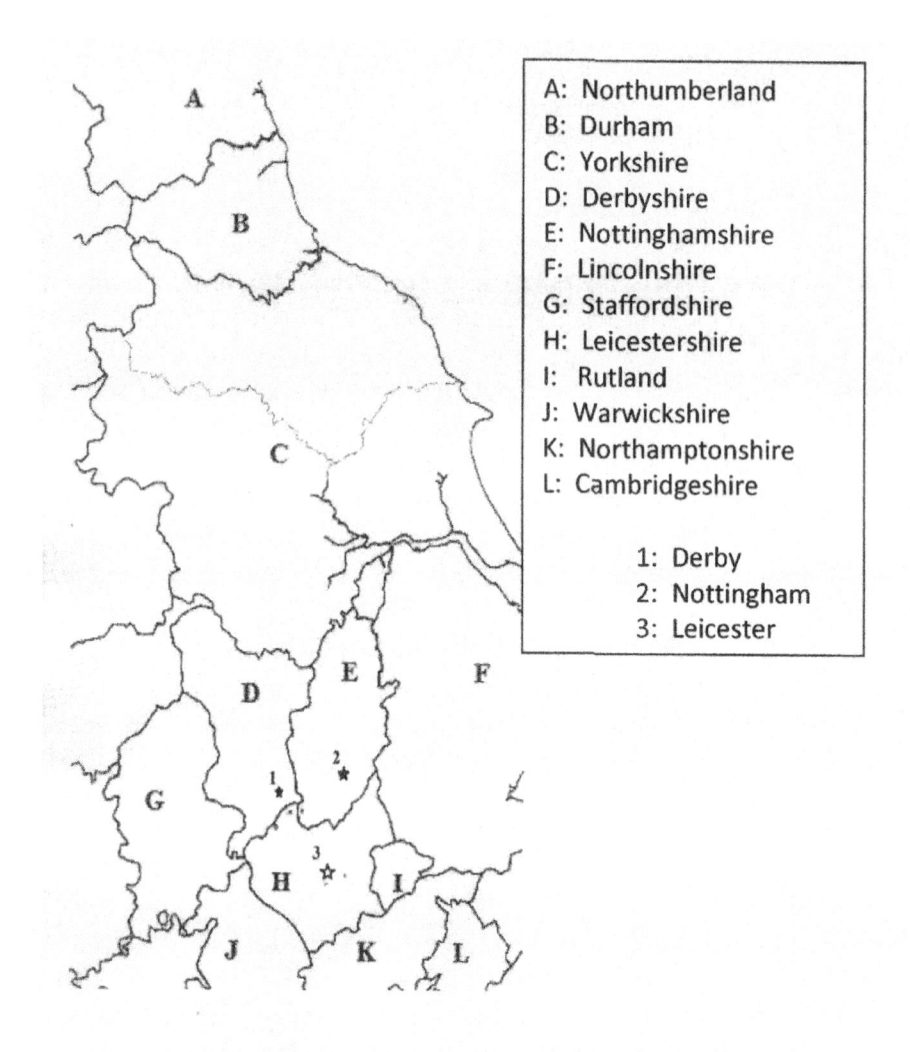

Exhibit 5.1. Some Northern and Midland Counties

With a population of about 51,000 people during the mid-1400s, Leicestershire was one of the most populous of the Midland counties. As a whole it was roughly median in wealth, the more prosperous eastern area thus considerably above median. Religious houses of the county were few and small, thus accounting for little of the wealth as compared to Somerset, for instance, with its Glastonbury Abbey. Wealth was still measured in amount and quality of land, and the income it could produce.

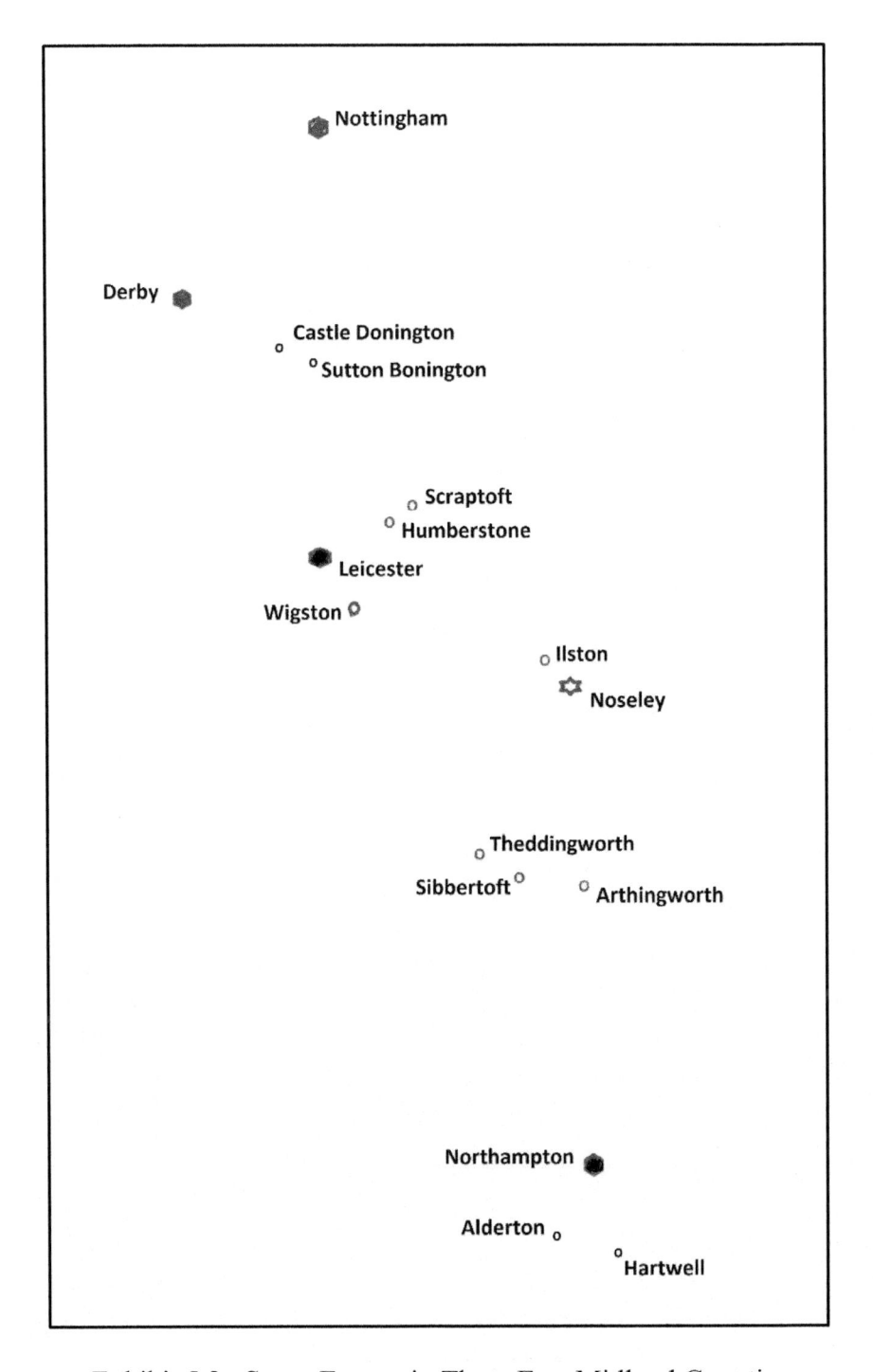

Exhibit 5.2. Some Estates in Three East Midland Counties

Politically, Leicestershire was especially distinctive during the period of Acheson's study for lacking a resident family of the nobility until the 1460s. This characteristic ramified throughout the county in important ways, the most general being that gentry families enjoyed greater latitude in roles of governance, allowing them to form their own alliances in both formal and informal means of community leadership. Relying on a variety of records (local family records, court records, income and tax records from the Exchequer), Acheson was able to reconstruct much of the fabric of those alliances—in office holding, marital ties, generational links, and estimates of wealth—during the larger part of the fifteenth century.

Acheson began his study with an inventory of "249 families of either gentry or potential gentry status." These were sorted into four main status groups: knights, family heads who were potential knights but had resisted even at penalty of a fine ("distrainees," they were called), esquires, and gentlemen. Of those 249 men, 76 were excluded primarily because their Leicestershire holdings were very small relative to their main estates in other counties or because too little information could be assayed. Of the remaining 173 families, 14 provided at least one knight during the period of study (1422-1485); 13 were "sufficiently wealthy for their heads to become knights had they wished to do so" (the distrainees); 46 were esquires; 14 were gentlemen; and 86 were "subgentry," men whose families were relatively well off and, in some cases, could have crossed the fuzzy boundary to "gentleman" status.[9]

A few more words in clarification of the "distrainee" category will be useful. As previously discussed, knighthood was an expensive dignity, and for that reason proportionately fewer men were volunteering. Acheson observed the same pattern in fifteenth-century Leicestershire: many men, "whose income would have supported knighthood, preferred to avoid the dignity, thereby escaping its onerous obligations," utilizing the resource instead in furtherance of the family patrimony. "The resulting decline in the number of knights prompted government attempts to stem the tide by issuing writs of distraint." These writs involved a fine, which was usually triggered by an annual income of £40 or more. (Thus, reported incomes display signs of strong tendency to conceal income.) Initially the fines saw use as general revenue. But as the wars in France required more and more soldiers, just as the feudal system of obligations was quickly decaying, it became necessary to pay soldiers for their wage-rate services from royal coffers. Distraint fines were applied in those payments. Military tactics

---

[9] Acheson, *A Gentry Community* (1992), pages, 38, 39.

and technology had been changing in the meantime, in favor of masses of longbow men, several of whom could be subsidized by the fine from one potential knight. Men wealthy enough to afford the fine year by year were in effect purchasing alternative military service by men of poorer means.[10]

An annual income of £40 was indeed a very substantial sum, enjoyed by very few. Gregory Clark (from whose work we benefited in chapter 4) has constructed a very long, year-by-year series of estimates of average annual earnings for the whole of England, both in terms of average *nominal* values and in terms of average annual *real* earnings (i.e., values adjusted to the worth of the pound in 2010, in an effort to nullify effects of inflation over time).[11] His estimates indicate that annual nominal earnings, averaged across the whole of England, amounted to a little more than £6 in 1550 (equivalent to about £1,827 in 2010 value). Nominal earnings slowly increased during the next 200 years, but in terms of "real value" average earnings first declined, by a quarter or more to 1625, then recovered to about £1740 in 1750. Not until the nineteenth century (i.e, the industrial revolution) did consistent growth in real earnings begin. It is more difficult, of course, to give comparable estimates for a smaller area such as Leicestershire as a whole. But judging from surviving reports of annual income (which is not exactly the same as "total earnings") for years in the mid-1500s, the average annual nominal value was probably about £8. Hoskins cited the rector of Galby's income, c1545, as "£18 2s 6d clear per annum," and reckoned that the "average Leicestershire living [was] worth only half this amount."[12] Thus, families who were assessed fines by writ of distraint during the mid-1400s were quite wealthy by incomes of at least £40 per year.

One of Acheson's 13 distrainee families was the Hasilrigge family, represented by four generations: Thomas[4c], who acquired manors in the county (and whose distraint fine in 1439 was £3 6s 8d); his son Thomas[5a]; grandsons William[6a] and Edmund[6b]; and great grandsons Thomas[7a] and Robert[7b]. Acheson's general account of these men and their households

---

[10] Acheson, *A Gentry Community* (1992), pages 33, 42.

[11] Clark uses several different bases for making the comparisons over time—e.g., by changes in the "retail price index" (which is based on a basket of typical goods, similar to the "consumer price index" used in the USA). Every basis has disadvantages; none is without a more or less distinctive bias. To see the complete series, using different bases of comparison, see Clark's website, measuringworth.com/ukearnrpi. The data are often updated, as new information comes to light.

[12] William George Hoskins, "A Short History of Galby & Frisby," *Transactions of the Leicestershire Archæological Society*, volume 22, part 3 (1943-44), pages 173-210, at page 198.

(in his appendix 3) emphasizes a number of main tendencies. First, it is clear that at least the main line (i.e., those men, after Thomas[4c], seated primarily at Noseley) enjoyed annual incomes sufficiently high that they could have supported the expense of knighthood but chose not to do so, at the cost of distraint fines. One would presume the motivation was to invest the resource in more directly familial, and probably more profitable, means of continued accumulation. Second, judging from government records (the Exchequer, etc.), the men were rather adept at concealing income. Official assessments that resulted in the distraint fines must have been based on an assessor's general observations of estate management, household goods, and the like, not on registers of actual income, which tend to be blank (see Acheson's appendix 1). Third, the men were shy of office holding in local government. While participants as witnesses, for example, in personal, relatively private agreements, they avoided taking on major roles in public governance until the generation of the great grandsons. Fourth, the men were active in building alliances, marital and otherwise, with other local families, and existing evidence suggests they were probably as strategic in their choices as any of their county peers (more about this below). Fifth, while we perhaps know more than Acheson learned from his search of public records about a family's holdings elsewhere in England, he was largely correct in concluding that the bulk of the men's estates lay within Leicestershire during that period. There is good evidence that the family continued to look toward London and surrounding counties when planning acquisitions, but fruition of that inclination mostly occurred later. Also, of course, the family maintained several estates in Northumberland, perhaps in Yorkshire as well, but these were less significant as income-bearing properties.

In general, one could easily conclude, the record reflects a family displaying a primarily cautious approach to the world during the fifteenth-century generations—not only Thomas[4c], for whom the necessary wait until recovery of inheritances of Noseley and other estates in Leicestershire was cut off by death, but also for his son Thomas[5a] and his grandsons William[6a] and Edmund[6b]. Perhaps they met with some resistance as "outsiders." Certainly internal migration within England had long been increasing, but judging from Acheson's accounts of the families who counted as knightly, distrainee, or esquire families of Leicestershire, most would not have been seen as "newcomers." In a related vein, perhaps a bias against inhabitants of the northern counties, the Borders, marked Thomas[4c] and his children as rustic or rough-hewn entrants into a better society. On the other hand, perhaps these early generations were simply cautious about being "too visible" in this county nearer the locus of royal power, a county which was also prime site of Lancastrian security in the East Midlands and therefore a site of contention with Yorkist supporters.

Judging from the pattern of marital ties, however, one gains a rather different picture. If bias against newcomers was a significant factor, its impact occurred only or at least mainly among the children of Thomas[4c] and Isabel. Of the three descendant generations, this is the one for which information is weakest, and there is one major reason to think that such bias was also not a notable factor of those children—namely, their mother was daughter of Sir Ralph Hastings, whose second and third sons, Sir Richard and then Sir Leonard, were gradually shifting the family's chief interests from Yorkshire to Leicestershire (and the latter's son, William, a court favorite by mid-century, became baron Hastings in 1461, thus ending formally the absence of a resident noble in the county). So the children of Thomas[4c] and Isabel should have had some coinage by virtue of maternal descent.

Acheson's genealogical charts (his appendix 2) show Hesilrige ties of marriage to three of the 72 other families in his register of the top three status groups (one family in each group: Shirley, Staunton of Sutton, and Entwysell). In fact, he did not have full benefit of family records, by which the count of direct marital ties is 13: four knightly families (Broket, Hastings, Neele, and Shirley), three distrainee families (Ashby, Brokeby, and Staunton of Sutton), and six families of esquire standing (Entwysell, Keble, Skeffington, Southill, Staunton of Donington, and Villers). Those 13 unions ramify outward, of course. By including marital ties through affinal parentage, the count increases rather quickly. As illustration of the point, consider that William[6a] married Elizabeth Staunton, whose sister Katherine married John Turville, who enlisted William[6a] and Elizabeth's son Thomas[7a] to be witness to his will. This Thomas[7a] wed an Entwysell sister, Lucy, whose sister Margaret wed William Wyville; and Robert[7b], brother of Thomas[7a], married Eleanor Shirley, whose second eldest sister Alice wed Robert Brokesby and whose third eldest sister Anne married John Danver. Taking just these few affines via sisters of wives into account, the list of alliances expands to 16 families, with the addition of one distrainee family (Wyville) and two of esquire standing (Danvers and Turville). And so it goes. Affinal connections were generally important even beyond the simple expansion of networks. Whereas there might be doubt about the trustworthiness of a particular consanguineous relative to subordinate his own individual self-interest to the interest of a given manorial lord's heirs, for example, affinal kin could be called upon as extra insurance.

All of those 16 marital ties, it bears repeating, were directly with families whose chief holdings were in Leicestershire. At the same time, the Hesilrige family, like others of the county, continued to seek ties to families in other counties (e.g., Northamptonshire, Warwickshire, and the historical county of Middlesex, now absorbed into London). London itself held considerable attraction, and not only because it was the seat of royal power and authority. English society was increasingly commercial, which entailed rapid growth in newer sorts of occupational activity and means of livelihood. Although not the only urban center of mercantile action, London was the beehive. By the mid-1500s London had roughly 60,000 inhabitants. This was only about two percent of England's 2.6 million people, but London had five times the population and ten times the wealth of England's next largest city. Moreover, the disparities had been increasing. In 1377, according to best estimates, London's population of 23,000 was about three times the population of the second largest, York. By 1662 London's population of 350,000 was at least ten times the size of Norwich, the second largest. Leicester was well behind Newcastle in all three years, seventeenth versus twelfth in rank in 1377, 29th versus fourth in 1523, and smaller than the 30th largest in 1662, versus Newcastle at fifth. It is much more difficult to achieve similar rankings of comparative wealth over time, but it is safe to say that as London's population grew at greater and greater rate, so did its wealth, though perhaps not on a per capita or per household basis. In any case, for many young men London was the place to be, if not in the royal household or in one of the liberal professions (law, clergy, teaching), then in merchandising, trade, and the like, or, failing to attain one of those stations, then in craft production.

The attractions of big cities were complemented by repulsions from rural areas, because of major changes in the organizational structure and regulation of agricultural production. These changes, which affected the Midland counties as much as elsewhere, and more, or more quickly, than in the north, had been underway since the fourteenth century. Villeinage was uncommon by the end of the century in Leicestershire, replaced by what amounted to wage labor.[13] Underlying factors had been greatly accelerated during the economic recession that followed the Great Plague and its smaller successors. Because of the labor shortage, wage rates went up, while prices for products that were labor-intensive fell. As demand by

---

[13] Rodney H Hilton, *The Economic Development of Some Leicestershire Estates in the 14th and 15th Centuries* (London: Oxford University Press, 1947), page 15.

labor declined, rents fell. Landlords had to compete for reduced supply of laborers, which lessened the income value of their croplands (grains, which are labor-intensive) and tenements. These cycles of effects were general to agricultural production; Leicestershire was not immune to them; and they extended well into the fifteenth-century.[14]

In shortest summary, those who had large estates withdrew their lands from labor-intensive productions, switching to pasturage and leasing of land and tenements to others who thus assumed the burdens and risks of achieving financial viability. A longer summary tells of a process of three interlinked components, enclosure, severance, and engrossing, which were pursued during the fifteenth, sixteenth, and early seventeenth centuries, generating major re-organizations of agricultural production, revolts by peasant populations especially in the Midlands, and governmental inquiry.

Enclosure (aka inclosure) consisted in the conversion of tillable land to pasture, usually for sheep or cattle grazing (fields were enclosed by hedges, the now-famous hedge rows). Severance consisted in separations of land from the buildings that had been part of it (i.e., becoming distinct legal entities of an estate, separably alienated). Engrossing consisted in the amalgamation of contingent farms. The sum of the three processes was agricultural consolidation and abandonment of small villages and hamlets. As farms were amalgamated, the buildings of the lesser farms were typically left to decay, and land that had been under tillage—for example, as a village commons—was often converted to grazing. During the 1400s engrossing, severance, and "the decaying of villages" accelerated in large part because of depopulation by the plague. As population growth rebounded late in the century, there was in some areas a scarcity of commons land. Needless to say, this quickly became a political issue, as peasants rioted and otherwise protested their circumstances. From 1488 the English government opposed engrossing and related practices, but the policy was not well enforced until 1536, when engrossing became an offense subject to prosecution by the crown.[15] An official "commission of inquiry" into the practices was charged with investigating complaints and issuing a report that would describe instances and name names, but the

---

[14] See Hilton's *Economic Development* ... (1947), *passim*, plus his essay "Medieval Agrarian History" in the Victoria County History of Leicestershire, volume 2, pages 145-198; and more generally, M M Postan's *The Medieval Economy and Society* (London: Weidenfeld and Nicolson, 1972).

[15] Penry Williams, *The Tudor Regime* (Oxford: Clarendon, 1979), page 181. See also Joan Thirsk, *The Rural Economy of England* (London: Hambledon, 1984) and her anthology, *The Agrarian History of England and Wales* (Cambridge: Cambridge University Press, 1985).

practices continued and grew more frequent nonetheless, especially in the Midlands, Leicestershire included. Four more commissions of inquiry were empanelled, the last of them in 1607 for the seven Midland counties that had been principal site of revolts against enclosure and engrossing.[16] Eventually, in Penry Williams' view, the parliamentary debates displayed "a considerable advance in economic understanding," with the result that efforts to prohibit the practices were abandoned either through the repeal of statutes or by the deliberate withdrawal of enforcement.[17]

The 1607 inquiry for Leicestershire is particularly interesting in a number of respects. First of all, one of the nine royal commissioners was "Thomas Hesilrige, Esquire" (that is, Thomas[11a]).[18] The commission's report did not list either Noseley or Alderton (the family's two principal estates at the time) as among the manors that had been accused of having engaged in engrossing, severance, and/or inclosure. While the process by which commissioners were chosen is not entirely clear, presumably care was taken not to select men who themselves had been publically defined as transgressors. Thomas[11a] then resided at Alderton, but his arrival was after changes at that manor, and Noseley would have been well beyond the controversy, since its village had been pulled down a century and a half earlier, during one of the large outbreaks of plague (as previously noted). Secondly, however, a third estate, the manor of Theddingworth, occupied by Edward[10b] Hasilrige, uncle to Thomas[11a], was included in the list. The commission determined that William Brocas, the owner of the estate in 1579, had "one howse of husbandry decayed and twentie acres of arable land converted from tillage into pasture"; because "the same is so continued by Edward Hasilrige," who had purchased the estate as it was, there was no culpability.[19]

Third, the commission concluded that "enclosure or severance had taken place in seventy-one villages or hamlets in the county between the years 1578 and 1607."[20] When severance had occurred, it was usually followed by enclosure; but enclosures also occurred independently of severance. While some of the activity might well have been landlords

---

[16] Isaac S Leadem collected returns of the inquiries of 1517-1518 in *The Domesday Inclosures*, 2 volumes (London: Longmans, Green, 1897. L A Parker did much the same for the 1607 inquiry; regarding Leicestershire see *The Depopulation Returns for Leicestershire in 1607* (London: W Thornley & Son, 1947).

[17] Williams, *The Tudor Regime* (1979), page 182.

[18] Parker, *The Depopulation Returns ...* (1947), page 4.

[19] Parker, *The Depopulation Returns ...* (1947), pages 55-56.

[20] Parker, *The Depopulation Returns ...* (1947), page 4.

stripping tenants of their access to tillage, it seems that most of it was motivated by interests of economy of scale. This stood in sharp contrast to the situation described in the inquisition of 1517, when tenants' rights were frequently transgressed.[21] In short, the "grandfathering" principle described just above was especially helpful to Leicestershire estates, in that most of the transgressions had occurred long before 1607.

Fourth, while depopulation was still occurring, the frequency was much reduced. The commission reported only two instances, one of them having just occurred (1601) at Scraptoft, a village then a few miles east of Leicester (and at one time held by the Hesilrige family): 400 acres of arable land had become pasture, following severance and decay of eight farm houses, with 40 people displaced.[22]

Fifth, it appears that most of the enclosures had involved 50 acres or less, although this estimate is badly troubled by the fact that different places used different areal standards of measurement. Often the areas were reported in "yardlands," but this measure varied from place to place, even between neighboring places, by as much as 100 percent. Parker noted, for instance, that independent assessments show that a yardland in the village of Wyfordby was sixteen acres but at Burton Lazars, its neighbor, twice that.[23]

As already mentioned, because of the long recession following the sharp and extended decline in population after the Great Plague, estate values declined markedly. Acheson compiled data for several cases of Leicestershire estates, from which two main conclusions can be drawn. On the one hand, some manors suffered declines of one-half or more during the period of five to six decades covered by his study, with some estates' messuages decayed so badly from lack of tenants and maintenance as to be worth nothing. But on the other hand, the gentry estates suffered decline at lower rate, on average, largely because greater shares of produce were consumed by the manorial household. This was true for the county gentry in general and for the Hesilrige family in particular. Like many of the upper-gentry families, the Hesilriges held several estates but distributed those apart from Noseley, and later Alderton, to other family members in subordinate assignments (e.g., Hallaton, part of the Langtons) or through marital alliances (e.g., Humberstone to Walter Keble via marriage to the eldest daughter of Thomas[7a] and Lucy, Millicent[8h] Hesilrige).

---

[21] See Williams, *The Tudor Regime* (1979), pages 183-84, and Leadem, *The Domesday Inclosures ...* (1897).

[22] Parker, *Depopulation Returns ...* (1947), pages 6, 13, 60.

[23] Parker, *Depopulation Returns ...* (1947), page 5.

Furthermore, Acheson argued, the more successful gentry families benefited from various innovative activities which could have a greater impact on the finances of smaller estates. Minerals such as lime, slate, and stone could be significant income-bearing sources, as timber had been for generations. Coal was available and occasionally mined, but no one had yet determined how it could be converted into an income-bearing resource. Some of the families encouraged younger sons to become adept in common legal matters, becoming local professionals with service for a fee on offer to neighbors. Successful gentry families were also benefiting financially from royal service (the Hesilrige family being one); likewise, from rewards of military service in France (by Acheson's count, 22 members of the Leicestershire gentry).[24] Despite hardships stemming from the long recession, some of the gentry families thrived, enlarging their holdings both within the county and beyond. The Hesilrige family were among those successes.

Intergenerational familial organization remained important during this period, but emphases were changing, shifting from collectivist to more individualist orientation. One of the central themes of Acheson's study is the rise among the gentry families of an individualism that looks very much like modern individualism. To some extent it can be seen as a culmination of a process that began centuries earlier, with major expression in historic events such as the Magna Carta. Many of the events that, in retrospect, can be nominated as markers in the decline of feudalism can also be said, if even more dependently on retrospection, to have been markers in the rise of individualism, as if one had been ground clearing for the other, or even as if the "later" had been inevitable outcome of the "earlier." The main issues, even some secondary or ancillary issues, have been matters of much contentiousness among professional historians from time to time, often differently at different times. There is no intent to wade into such matters here (and if there were such intent, no hope of any settlement). Suffice to say, regardless which bank is one's perch, the river was flowing in many streams of varying composition and pace, some with eddies but others not.

One of the main streams carried contentions of religious belief and practice, and some of those contentions can be, have been, read as contest between communalist and individualist preferences. From one bank the stream was seen mostly positively as a range of protests leading to a range of reforms of belief and practice, subordinating the pretense of papal voice across one unified world to sovereignty of state and its ruler among a larger community of states, each entitled to its own chosen ruler. From the other

---

[24] Acheson, *A Gentry Community* (1992), pages 59-60.

bank most events of that stream were seen mostly negatively as a range of attacks on godly authority leading to a range of reductions of belief and practice, subordinating the mysterious majesty of divine grace to everyday mundane interests of statecraft and commerce.

Henry VIII also brought the Protestant Reformation into official royal survey and partial legitimation. Disappointed that his queen had failed to provide him with male heir, he sought an annulment followed by approval of a new marriage, this time to Anne Boleyn. Church officials did not satisfy his expectations. In response, he embraced part of the reformation cause, bringing that part to his own royal cause, which was not only about his desire for a male heir but also encompassed an interest that a century later would became general to the ruling regimes of major European countries under a set of agreements that instituted the Peace of Westphalia. That interest favored a monarch's complete sovereignty of rulership, allowing no claim of superior or even equal authority from without the realm. The contribution due to Henry VIII began with an act of Parliament in 1533, known as the Act in Restraint of Appeals. Told in the vocabulary of the day and place, not that of a century later, this act basically set forth an early version of a theory of national sovereignty. A year later followed the First Act of Supremacy, which declared the king "the only supreme head on earth of the Church of England." Also in 1534 he began the process known as the dissolution of the monasteries, with visitations undertaken supposedly for assessments of quality but also, though surreptitiously, for assessments of valuation. Expropriations soon followed.

During March of the following year Henry VIII orchestrated his first Act of Succession to conclusion, the chief point of which was to invest the crown in his issue by Anne Boleyn, declaring princess Mary, his daughter by Katherine of Aragon, illegitimate. In process, however, the act was designed also to establish his reformation of the church. As recounted in the *Chronicles* attributed to Holinshed, an author observed of the events as follows:[25]

> The .xxx. day of March was the Parliament proroged, and there euerie Lorde, knight, and burges, and all other were sworne to the Acte of succession, and subscribed their handes to a parchment fixed to the same. The Parliament was proroged till the thirde of Novembre next.

---

[25] The *Chronicles of England, Scotland, and Ireland*, first published in 1577, is known generally as Holinshed's *Chronicles*, even though Raphael Holinshed was only one of the several authors. The passage quoted above is from the 1577 edition, volume 2, for March of the regnal year 25-26 Henry VIII. For valuable resources in recovering the importance of the *Chronicles*, see the website The Holinshed Project.

> After this were Commissioners sent into all parts of the realme, to take the othe of al men and women to the act of succession. Doctor Iohn Fisher, and sir Thomas Moore knight, and doctor Nicholas Wilson Parson of Saint Thomas Apostles in London, expressly denied at La(m)beth before the Archbishop of Canterb. to receyue that oth. The two first stood in their opinion as to the verie death (as after ye shall heare) but doctor Wilson was better aduised at length, & so dissembling the matter escaped out of further daunger.

The "oath of all men and women to the act of succession" included a short statement abjuring "any foreign potentate." The intended reference was of course to the pope; the oath required rejection of the doctrine of papal primacy. John Fisher, the chancellor of Cambridge University, and Sir Thomas More famously refused the oath. Each lost his head to the axe of the executioner the following year. Henry VIII prevailed and "the Church of *England*" was distinguished from "the Church of Rome," thereafter known as the *Roman* Catholic church.

The English king's interest might well have been conceived fully in terms of relatively narrow personal concerns—that is, the concerns of his royal person—but the underlying principle found favor among rulers of many other countries and resulted in a new institution, the sovereign nation-state, the sovereignty of a people in their *nativity*, under their own traditions and via their own "preferences" of rulership. Neither religious authority from Rome nor the imperial authority of a Holy Roman Empire should hold sway within any sovereign nation-state but by its internal consent and leave. There was no longer place for a single prevailing truth. If this was not an idea in the head of Henry VIII, and it almost surely was more expansive that anything he had in mind, it was an idea with roots in his more narrowly prescribed actions.

Indeed, by 1538 Henry VIII had become alarmed at the expansiveness of individual freedom that he had helped promote, and he began to squelch movements that he saw as threats to his own royal authority. As head of the established church of England, his rule of authenticity and propriety would be no less demanding and assiduously obeyed than had the pope's rule. An act of 1543 was promulgated "for the Advancement of True Religion"; among its provisions, Bible reading would henceforth be restricted to men and women of noble birth.

By 1547 Henry VIII was dead, and his only son and heir, Edward VI, renewed some of the more individualistic thrust of the movement of reform. But young Edward was dead six years later, and his half-sister, the princess Mary whom Henry VIII had wanted to remove from the line of succession, became queen. Being Catholic, like her mother Katherine, she restored ties with Rome and oversaw a campaign against Protestants. In turn, Mary I, reigning only five years, was succeeded by her half-sister, Elizabeth I, who cannily orchestrated a compromise among main factions, known as the Settlement. As one of the main consequences, the part of the movement that came to be called "Puritan" gained accommodation within the church of England. Although the more radical elements of this newly coalescing persuasion grew increasingly restive late in the century, most of the adherents of Puritanism held fast to the settlement.

How did the religious tumult affect life in Leicestershire? The answer comes in two large parts: before and after accession of the first king from the House of Stuart. That division of calendar pertains at least as much to the Hesilrige family as to life generally in Leicestershire, and indeed throughout the country. Discussion of life under the Stuarts will be deferred to the next chapter and after. Here attention to the question will be restricted mainly to the Tudor regime of Henry VIII and his children, with a modicum of foreshadowing of James I, first of the Stuart kings.

One venue in which to look for signs of religious strife in family life is the arrangement of marriages. For Leicestershire in general, it is worth noting that Acheson's chapter 6, devoted to marriage and kinship, among other features of household economy, is virtually silent about religion as a factor in social arrangements.[26] The silence tells not of the unimportance of religion; rather, for the period he covered, the fifteenth century until the advent of the Tudors (i.e., c1485), religion was not a major vector of civil strife. The Protestant Reformation began on the continent, with Luther and his *Ninety-Fives Theses on the Power and Efficacy of Indulgences* in 1517, and it was slow to develop into what today is mistakenly remembered as a unified movement. A Frenchman named Jehan Cauvin, renamed John Calvin in English, eight years old when Luther posted his complaint, did not become influential in England until late in the reign of Henry VIII, and then mainly through the British presence of two followers, John Knox and William Whittingham, from the late 1550s onward.

What of Hesilrige marriages during the latter half of the 1400s and the 1500s? Ten marriages of Hesilrige men, spanning the years from 1458 to about 1595, have been identified with enough information about brides' families to enable reasonable guesses. Five of the ten occurred before 1530 (roughly the beginning of the pressure by Henry VIII). There is no sign of controversy regarding religious confession. Of course, there was still one

---

[26] Acheson, *A Gentry Community* (1992), pages 135-173.

"common church" in England, even though tensions and some schismatic tendencies had been building. Information pertaining to those marriages is generally not detailed enough to capture "anti-popery" sentiments or overt discriminations. With the next marriage in chronological sequence, however, conditions were changing. The union itself, between Miles[9a] and Bridget, daughter of Sir Thomas Griffin, seems to have occurred without complication of confessional issues, and there is no evidence of it during the brief union (Miles[9a] died four years after the 1540 marriage). Bridget's older brother's daughter, Mary, born approximately the same year her uncle Miles[9a] died, became a recruiter for the Roman church. According to the entry on Mary's husband, Thomas Markham, in the *Oxford Dictionary of National Biography*, she persuaded her son to convert. The account suggests that her husband had been neither supportive nor obstructive of the conversion.[27] As for Bridget's father, Sir Thomas Griffin, all indications are that he tried to remain "above the fray" in regard to the religious controversies—much like his brother Edward, who served as attorney-general to Henry VIII and as solicitor-general to Edward VI, to Mary I, and then to Elizabeth I.

The next marriage in sequence was by Thomas[10a], who wed Ursula, daughter of Sir Thomas Andrew of Charwelton, Northamptonshire, in 1563. By this time many families were divided between allegiance to the church of England or to Protestantism in some form and allegiance to the church of Rome, the latter adherents known as "recuscents," from the Latin word meaning "refusal" (i.e., refusal to conform to dictates set forth by Henry VIII). Among these families, the Andrew family: Bridget and her parents were followers of the church of England. The bridal houses of the last three marriages in the sequence—Thomas Nicholls of Pitchley and Sir William Gorges of Alderton, both Northamptonshire, and William Brocas of Theddingworth, Leicestershire—were clearly protestant in some form, in some instances (e.g., Thomas Nicholls' son Sir Augustine) quite strongly.

The 1560s were still a time of relative peace among religious tribes in England. As MacCulloch recently summarized it, under Elizabeth I "the government was not eager to offend traditionalist noblemen with particular local spheres of influence," while on the other side, "[r]eceiving little leadership from Catholic clergy, English conservatives did not cause large-scale trouble." But the relative peace dissolved during the 1570s, as each

---

[27] See also *The Epigrams of Sir John Harington*, edited by Gerard Kilroy (Farnham, Surrey: Ashgate, 2009), page 7. Harington is reported to have said of Mary that she was "a great persuader of weak women to popery."

side became much less tolerant and much more energetic.[28] Yet another long slog of human butchery in the name of religion was underway. Here we have only glanced through some windows of it. A more sustained gaze will come in the next chapter.

The movements collectively known as the Protestant Reformation (which, by expansion, could include the co-optive thrusts of the Counter-Reformation) were enormous in reach and lasting in consequences. Both characteristics can be attributed in large part to the fact that the movements were themselves effects of more general and more profound changes in the social fabric of everyday life as it transpired in minds and in outward acts. If a single word need be chosen in description of the changes, probably the usual term, "individualism," is as good as any. But the crux of the gradual developments, long before Martin Luther, John Calvin, and the like, had been greater variation in public thinking and, with that, challenges to what had been accepted, central authority. During the High Latin Middle Ages of Europe, the strongest institutional form of that authority was the church (the church of Rome, the Greek Orthodox church, etc.), and the disputes of that authority most obviously took the form of what the church sought to brand, usually successfully, as heresy. To be sure, "heretical thought" was nothing new. But it was appearing more often, and it was confounding relations between the church's central authority and increasingly powerful and numerous monarchies of state authority. Meister Eckhart was a case in point, late thirteenth and early fourteenth century. Nicholas of Cusa was another (1401-1464). Copernicus, still another (1473-1543). Then, during Nicholas' adult lifetime, an accelerator came along: Johannes Gutenberg developed mechanical movable type, and the modern printing press was born. (It arrived in England in 1475.) More and more books flowed from presses. By the end of the 1500s as many as 200 million volumes had been printed, many of them in vernacular languages. The causes and responses that made "household names" of Copernicus, Giordano Bruno, Galileo, and Kepler (among many others) spread throughout populations of readers remarkably fast, even as those populations grew remarkably fast. Literacy was moving out of privileged quarters of the Latinate and into vernacular minds of tens and hundreds of thousands of men and, increasingly, women. The bounds of audacity, of ingenuity, of innovation, shifted accordingly.

We know very little of the libraries of fifteenth-century families of Leicestershire. For most, perhaps all, of them "the" Christian Bible held prime if not sole location, and it was in English for any who preferred that reading. English dictionaries and grammar books did not appear until the

---

[28] Diarmaid MacCulloch, *The Reformation* (New York: Viking, 2003), page 322.

early 1600s. The printing press itself created demand for such manuals, as it furthered the standardization of the English language, thus increasing the utility and efficiency of a standard dictionary and grammar book. But books accelerated the circulation of ideas by word of mouth as well, as the weakly or non-literate listened to others expound of what they had read. It was in "literature," to be sure—Chaucer's *Canterbury Tales*, William Baldwin's *Beware the Cat*—but it was also in various matters practical, and these included designs of one or another contraption.

One such contraption was the windmill. Far from an invention of this era, it was the focus of considerable efforts of improved mechanics of gearing and blades and of architectural design. Leicestershire was a major site of those efforts, owing probably to the fact that it rivers were too slow to offer enough energy to watermills. Langdon's inventory of 445 windmills in fourteenth-century England numbered 130 in East Midland counties, second only to 132 in East Anglia, in each area exceeding the count of watermills by about 30 percent.[29] Within Leicestershire the area of Wigston was one prominent site of experimentation in harnessing the wind, and had been since the twelfth century. Kealey cited "a veritable explosion of windmill construction in Leicestershire" from those early beginnings.[30] Much of that construction consisted in cooperative ventures in "harvesting the air," which was seen as a free resource (although rules were soon passed to limit the building of windmills). The ventures were an outlet of entrepreneurial spirit. With a small plot of land at the right elevation and a small fund of capital for parts of construction, a small band of investors could erect a milling operation which generated considerable income. Land barons took note, of course, and aside from trying to prevent such constructions they often erected their own. We do not know the date of construction at Noseley, but we know that Bertine[8a] was proud owner of a windmill as of February 1544/5 (as testified by his son's will).[31]

Officers of the Exchequer were always on watch for new revenues that could be taxed, windmills not excepted. But tax directly on income was difficult to administer and, as previously mentioned, usually avoided in favor of taxes more directly on land and its products. Even so, probably most manorial lords were careful to avoid "conspicuous consumption" (as it is termed today), for lessons of the possible consequence of too much

---

[29] John Langdon, "Lordship and Peasant Consumerism in the Milling Industry of Early Fourteenth-Century England," *Past and Present*, no. 145 (1994), pages 3-46.
[30] Edward J Kealey, *Harvesting the Air* (Berkeley: University of California Press, 1987), page 81.
[31] Farnham and Thompson, "The Manor of Noseley" (1921-22), page 231.

display of income were all too conspicuous. The story of how Henry VIII acquired Hampton Court, a sumptuous palace newly built by the king's chief minister and court favorite, Thomas Wolsey, then archbishop of York (later a cardinal), is too well known to need repeating. Other manorial lords were, if less careful to conserve image, far less fortunate in outcome.

Hoskins referred to the reign of Henry VIII as "the age of plunder." This is not so much an inaccurate as an incomplete description, inasmuch as the plunder had begun with his father, Henry VII, and that, too, was anything but unprecedented in the royal annals of England.[32] After defeating Richard III at the battle of Bosworth in 1485 to become the first Tudor king, Henry VII gained the throne of a monarchy that was for all practical purposes fiscally bankrupt. Aided by relatively peaceful external relations, the new king set about restoring the national treasury by exercising the taxation whip. In 1497 John Morton was appointed lord chancellor, whose primary responsibility was the collection of taxes. It is not for nothing that the expression "Morton's Fork" gained its name and exemplar from him. (The expression means "damned if you do, damned if you don't.") A common practice among barons was to feign hard times whenever the tax collection came calling. Morton's response was indifferent. Anyone who appeared to be doing very well could obviously afford a high tax. Anyone whose circumstances were modest were obviously frugal and probably had substantial saving; so they, too, could afford a high tax. In addition, Henry VII sought successfully to raise the stature of the commons land as a commercial resource and a barrier against the power of the barons.

It was this Henry who began devising what became the famous Tudor mode of centralizing governance. Whereas prior monarchs such as Edward I (reigned 1272-1307), Edward III (1327-1377), Henry VI (1422-1461), and Edward IV (1461-1483) had been strong, unifying forces, they depended vitally on their ties with powerful barons. Henry VII (1485-1509) was comparatively successful in centralizing political authority and power under the emblem of the crown and in a growing bureaucracy of the court.

When Henry VII died in 1509, he left a healthy treasury and a reformed currency to his heir, Henry VIII, who proved to be even more aggressive about revenues than his father had been. Not only did he press taxes; after his famous conflict with pope Clement VII, he also confiscated properties of the religious orders, which he then sold to various loyalists.

---

[32] William George Hoskins, *The Age of Plunder: the England of Henry VIII, 1500-1547* (London: Longmans, 1976).

Despite those many reapings, however, Henry VIII was so profligate in his personal habits and in his management of the realm's fiscal policies that he unraveled much of what his father had achieved. Constantly battling for more resources from powerful barons, by the 1540s he had become so desperate for added revenues that he devalued the currency, with the effect of increasing taxes yet again on his subjects. At the end of his 37-year reign, he left a shambles to his frail 9-year-old son, Edward VI.

If wars were to be fought, whether in advance of territorial claims on the continent or in defense of a king's own island nation, capital had to be accumulated; and as the feudal system of ascending tithes broke down, general taxations were the next lucrative avenues of "revenue enhancement." Although attempts at implementing a tax on general income had been made at various times, the principal base of tax revenues was, under the Tudors as it had always been, land, "real estate," which was assessed through rentals on the land. Names and details of the policy changed from time to time—it was a General Subsidy during the 1500s, a Commonwealth Monthly Assessment a century later—but the basic practice was largely the same. New details of rate and base imposition were soon met by new, and increasingly successful, efforts of tax avoidance. Cycles of behavior that look very much like evolutionary sequences of pressures, adaptations, and selections are evident in the record. "Of a general income tax," Seligman concluded from his study, "we find no trace at all" before the 1800s.[33] There had been *selective* applications of an income tax from time to time. Parliament granted a graduated income tax in 1436, in support of the war in France. The rates were 2s 6d for annual incomes of £5, plus 6d for each pound beyond £5 to £100; 8d per pound between £100 and £400; and those with incomes greater than £400, the rate was 2s per pound of total income.[34] It was very unpopular, and much was hidden from inspection. Seligman cited another effort, this one during the 1600s: "any person exercising any publick office or employment for profit" was subject to a tax rate of four shillings for every pound of salary. But the high rate (33 percent) was intended to deter such profit-making, more than to raise revenue, and returns were "scarce."

Despite the hazards of royal disfavor during the time of Henry VIII, the gentry families of Leicestershire generally prospered and expanded, often into counties nearer London. The Hesilrige family was among them. Indeed, by the generation of Thomas[4c] and Isabel's great grandsons, one

---

[33] Edwin R A Seligman, *The Income Tax* (London: Macmillan, 1914), pages 48, 49.
[34] Taxable income included income from freehold land, annuities, and fees. Acheson, *A Gentry Community* (1992), pages 36-37.

member of the family was literally within arm's reach of Henry VIII and managed the eddying, sometimes torrential currents that flowed from and around the monarch well enough to survive, prosper, and pass fruits of the experience to descendants. Having gained such advantages, however, the family pulled back from court during the tumult of Henry's successors, Edward IV and Mary I, even from the more stable period of Elizabeth I. Not until the first Stuart king, ironically, did the family re-engage, when Thomas[11a] Hesilrige thought it prudent not to continue the habit of paying the distraint fine and accepted knighthood in 1608.

It is time to resume attention to the main lineage once again.

Another Segment of the Lineage
In keeping with past practice, this lineage segment repeats the latter part of the segment shown in chapter 4, as reminder. Also as before, further details, when known, will be added immediately following this segment.

Thomas[4c] Heselrig of Fawdon: b. c1365 Fawdon manor, Northumberland, d. 15 Oct 1422 Eslington manor, Northumberland; seised of Eslington, recorded as owner of tower of Eslington 1415; seised of moieties of the vills of Whittingham, Thrunton, and Barton; m. 1395 at Noseley manor, Leicestershire, Isabel (b. c1375, d. <1439), daughter and heir of Sir Roger Heron (b. 1330, d. c1397) and Margaret (b. 1353, d. 7 Apr 1407 Noseley), daughter and heir of Sir Ralph Hastings, which marriage brought the manors of Noseley, Gilmorton (Gilden-Morton), and Newton Harcourt, all in Leicestershire.

└── **Thomas**[5a] Hesilrige: b. 29 Sep 1407 at manor of Eslington, Northumberland, d. 21 Sep 1467; more below

└── **John**[5b] Hesilrige: b. c1409 Noseley, d. 4 Jun 1432 Noseley; more below

└── **Elizabeth**[5c] Hesilrig: b. c1400, d. >Sep 1431; more in lineage segment reported in chapter 4

Thomas[5a] Hesilrige: b. 29 Sep 1407 Eslington, d. 21 Sep 1467 Noseley; m. (1) Elizabeth (or Mabilla?), daughter of Sir Thomas Broket, knight;[35]

---

[35] Camden's 1619 visitation of Leicestershire records the Broket daughter's forename as Mabilla (or Mable); possible reason for confusion is discussed below (footnote 46).

m. (2)? 1429 Elizabeth, daughter of Thomas Frowycke of Old Fold, Middlesex; endowed a chantry at Noseley, 1466; more above, following the lineage segment in chapter 4, and below

    L-- **William**[6a] Hesilrigge: b. c1437, d. 25 Feb 1474/5 Noseley; m. Elizabeth, daughter & coheir of Thomas Staunton, esq., of Sutton-on-Soar, Nottinghamshire (marriage settlement 13 Jul 1458); more above, following lineage segment in chapter 4, and below

        L-- **Thomas**[7a] Hesylrigge: b. 1464, d. 24 May 1541 Leicestershire; more below

        L-- **Robert**[7b] Hesilrigge of Castle Donington: b. >1464, d. 26 Mar 1536; more below

        L-- John[7c] Hesilrigge: b. >1464, d. > 1494

        L-- Katherine[7d] Hesilrigge: b. >1458 Noseley; m. Thomas Ashby (b. 1442, d. c1488) of Quenby, Leicestershire

        L-- Ruth[7e] Hesilrigge: m. Richard Nele (i.e., Neele; b. c1470), second son of Sir Richard Nele of Prestwold, Leicestershire; more below

    L-- Edmund[6b] Hesylryge: b. >1437, d. > Dec 1476, at which time he was seated at manor of Rolston (Rolleston), Leicestershire

    L-- Margaret[6c] Hesilrige: b. c1437; m. "a Villers man"; probably the Villers family of Brooksby, Leicestershire; more below

    L-- Elizabeth[6d] Hesilrige: b. c1437; m. Sir William Turville, knight

John[5b] Hesilrige of Noseley: b. c1409 Noseley, d. 4 Jun 1432 Noseley; d. seised of a moiety of manor of Whittingham ("worth yearly, clear, £20"), the manor of Thrunton ("worth yearly, clear, £10"), the manor of Barton ("worth yearly, clear, 10 marks"), a moiety of the manor of Glaunton ("worth yearly, clear, £10"), and the manor of Eslington ("worth yearly, clear, £10"; these valuations are from an inquisition taken 30 Sep 1442;[36] John's heir, his son

    L-- Robert[6a] Hesilrige: b. 1426 (nfi)

Thomas[7a] Hesylrigge: b. 1464, d. 24 May 1541 Leicestershire; home seat manor of Noseley; m. Lucy (d. 8 Oct 1525 Noseley), daughter of Thomas Entwysill (Entwystle) of Dalby on the Wolds, Leicestershire, and Edith, daughter of Richard Bracebridge of Kingsbury, Warwickshire (Richard d. 1501); esquire of the body to Henry VIII; more below

    L-- **Bertine** [8a] (aka Bartram, Batholomew) Haslerigg: b. c1485, d. 25 Jul 1565; more below[37]

    L-- John[8b] Haslerigg: b. >1485
    L-- Robert[8c] Haslerigg
    L-- William[8d] Haslerigg
    L-- Anthony[8e] Haslerigg

    L-- Walter[8f] Haslerigg: b. c1599; BA Oxford 1516; "secular deacon"

    L-- Daniel[8g] Haslerigg

    L-- Millicent[8h] Haslerigg: m. (1) Walter Keble of Humberstone, Leicestershire, serjeant-at-law; m.(2) Fnu Breame; issue by Keble: Francis (b. 1520), Lucia, Anne

    L-- Herald[8i] Haslerigg: m. David Williams of Abergavenny, Wales

---

[36] See page 18n of John Crawford Hodgson's "On the Medieval and Later Owners of Eslington," *Archæologia Æliana*, 3rd series volume 6 (Newcastle-upon-Tyne: Andrew Reid & Co., 1910), pages 1-33.

[37] The order of children of Thomas[7a] and Lucy follows the order given in William G D Fletcher's *Leicestershire Pedigrees and Royal Descents* (Leicester: Clarke and Hodgson, 1887), page 11. William Camden's *The Visitation of Leicestershire in the Year 1619* (London, 1870), page 15, curiously shows only six children of Thomas[7a], of whom only one son, Bartram. Camden's accuracy leaves something to be desired, here as in other respects as well, but we do owe to him more information about daughters than was typical for that era.

∟--Anne[8j] Haslerigg: m. Edward Catesby of Seaton, Rutland (b. c1476 Whiston, Northamptonshire); issue: Michael Catesby (b. c1496 Seaton, Rutland)

∟-- Edith[8k] Haslerigg: b. <1495, d. >1515; m. John Thorneff (aka Thorney; b. <1495, d. 11 Mar 1521) of Stamford, Lincolnshire; issue: Christopher Thorneff (b. >1515), Francis (b. c1515, d. >1563) who was MP for Stamford

∟-- Elizabeth[8l] Haslerigg: m. Robert Collingwood

∟-- plus three other sons and three other daughters, names of whom (assuming they *were* named) have been lost

Robert[7b] Hesilrigge of Castle Donington: b. >1464, d. 26 Mar 1536; m. Eleanor (b. c1475), daughter of John Shirley of Staunton Harold, Leicestershire; more below, in next section of this chapter

∟-- Hugh[8a] Hesilrige of Sutton-Bonington: b. c1495, d. <1566; m. c1519 Joan, daughter and coheir of Thomas Harvey of Elmesthorpe, Leicestershire; Joan (d. <1566) brought to marriage one-quarter of the manor of Fleckney, Leicestershire

∟-- Francis[9a] Hesilrige: b. c1520, d. c1566 Hertfordshire; without issue

∟-- Michael[9b] Hesilrige: b. >1520, d. >1579; m. 17 Nov 1572 Isabel, daughter of Robert Bainbridge of Lockington, Leicestershire

∟-- Anne Hesilrige: b. >1540, d>1575; m. 6 July 1575 Richard Hedge at St Michael's Church, Sutton Bonington, Nottinghamshire

∟-- Catherine[9c] Hesilrige:
∟-- John[9d] Hesilrige: b. >1520, d. <1579

∟-- Rachel[8b] Hesilrige: b. c1510, d. >1535; m. c1535 Thomas Skeffington, captain of the Castle of Nottingham (b. c1509, d. >1548); issue: John Skeffington of Tunbridge (i.e., Tonbridge), Kent

Bertine[8a] Haslerigg: b. c1485, d. 25 Jul 1565: aka Bertinus, Bartram, Bartholomew; m. c1509 Anne, daughter of John Southill of Stockerston (aka Stock Faston), Leicestershire; more below

└── **Miles**[9a] Hesilrige: b. c1510, d. 18 Nov 1544 Arthingworth manor, Northamptonshire; m. June 1540 Bridget (b. c1519, d. 1577), daughter of Sir Thomas Griffin, knight, of Braybrooke, Northamptonshire

└── **Thomas**[10a] Haslerigge: b. 1541, d. 31 May 1600 Noseley; more below

└── **Edward**[10b] Heslerigge: b. c1543, d. >1618; m. Anne, daughter of Thomas Nichols of Pitchley, Northamptonshire; more below

└── Mary[10c] Heslerigge: b.>Feb 1544/5; m. Edward Rouse

Thomas[10a] Heslerigge: b. 1541, d. 31 May 1600; m. 12 June 1563 Ursula (b. c1544 Charwelton, d. >1600), daughter of Sir Thomas Andrew of Charwhelton and Wynwicke, Northamptonshire, and his wife Katherine, daughter and coheir of Edward Cave, esq.; more below

└── **Thomas**[11a] Hesilrige: b. 1563, d. 11 Jan 1629/30 Alderton; m. Frances, daughter of Sir William Gorges of Alderton, Northamptonshire; known as Thomas Hesilrige of Hartwell, Northamptonshire, when (1599) Thomas[10a] purchased land for him in Illston-on-the-Hill, Leicestershire; knighted 19 June 1608, raised to baronetcy 21 Aug 1622; more below

└── **Mary**[11b] Hesilrige: b. c1565, d. >1580; m. William Stafford of Blatherwick, Northamptonshire

└── **Joan**[11c] Hesilrige: b. >1565, d. > 1580; m. Anthony Forest of Mabourne, co. Huntingdon

└── **Bridget**[11d] Hesilrige: b. >1565; d. without issue

Edward[10b] Heslerigge: b. c1543, d. >1618; m. Anne, daughter of Thomas Nicholls of Pitchley, Northamptonshire (Thomas, b. 1530, purchased a third of the manor of Hardwick, Northamptonshire 7 May 1567; he died 29 Jun 1568); Edward[10b] inherited manor of Arthingworth, Northhants.

∟ Edward[11a] Hesilrige of Arthingworth: b. >1560, d. October 1604 (shot on Fleet Street, London); m. Frances, daughter of William Brocas of Theddingworth, Leicestershire, esq. (d. 1601); Edward[11a] member of Middle Temple; acquired manor of Theddingworth

∟ Bertine[12a] Hesilrige of Theddingworth, Leicestershire: b. >1580, d. 4 May 1634 London (monument inscription St Clement Danes Church, Westminster, Middlesex)

∟ Frances[12b] Hesilrige: b. <1605, d. >1670; inherited Theddingworth after her brother's death; m. (1) 2 July 1632 Sir Walter Chetwynd of Grendon, Warwickshire; issue: Walter Chetwynd of Ingestre (b. 1632; fellow, Royal Society, 1678, an antiquarian, historian; portrait in 17th century folder); m. (2) 1 Sep 1670, at Swebston, Wolstan Dixie, esq. (b. 1602, d. 13 Feb 1682; created baronet 14 Jul 1660), no issue

∟ Francis[11b] Hesilrige: b. >1570 (probably the investor, 1607 and after, in the Virginia Company of London)

∟ Thomas[11c] Hesilrige: b. >1570, d. Dec 1646; m. 7 November 1633 Sarah (d. by 1654), daughter of Oliver Dixon, at St Andrew, Holborn, Camden borough, London
    ∟ Sarah[12a] Hesilrige: b. Feb 1634, d. 15 Mar 1649
    ∟ Arthur[12b] Hesilrige: d. in infancy
    ∟ Ann[12c] Hesilrige: d. in infancy
    ∟ Donald[12d] Hesilrige: b. by 1647, d. <April 1672
    ∟ Thomas[12e] Hesilrige: b. by 1647, d. 1679; m. 17 June 1679 St Leonard's Shoreditch, London, Frances Unknown

∟ Austrius[11d] Hesilrige: b>1570; d. >1617 London[38]

∟ Bridget[11e] Hesilrige: b. c1558; m. Thomas, son of John Alicock of Sibbertoft, Northamptonshire; issue: John (b. c1583), Thomas; more below

∟ Elizabeth[11f] Hesilrige: m. Fnu Forster of Northamptonshire

∟ Mary[11g] Hesilrige: b. >1560; m. Henry Newdigate of Ashtead,

---

[38] In his will, dated 1617, he named his brother Thomas[11c] as heir.

Surrey (he died without issue)[39]

    └- Susanna[11h] Hesilrige: nfi

    └- Anna[11i] Heslerig: b. >1560, d. June 1634; m. 1607 Thomas Hunt of Lindon (Lyndon; b. 1563), Rutland; issue: Edward Hunt, Thomas Hunt, John Hunt

    One trend apparent from a scan of that segment of lineage is the increasing prominence of daughters. That is, of course, a feature of the record-keeping; daughters surely did not account for a smaller fraction of births in the early 1400s than in the early 1500s or early 1600s. Yet in another sense they *had* become prominent, as testified by the fact that their names were recorded, and sometimes more. Of the eighteen children of Thomas[7a] and Lucy (Entwysill) Hesilrige born between c1485 and 1525, ten were boys, and we know the names of seven (though little more for most of these seven). We know not only the names but also the husbands' names of five of the eight girls. Contrast that record with corresponding information for the generation of Thomas[5a] Heselrig, born early in the 1400s: we do know the name of one sister, Elizabeth[5c], and indeed the name of her husband (as discussed in chapter 4), both relatively rare facts for the times. But nothing beyond her. Perhaps she had no sisters, or none surviving childhood. Yet we do know of the existence of at least one other Hesilrige daughter of that time, though we do not know her name or her place in the lineage. We know from the history of the Lowell family that Raffe (Ralph) Lowle, born c1400, married a Hesilrige daughter by c1430, the approximate date of first son's birth. Their fifth-great grandson was Percival Lowell (1571-1664), a prosperous merchant in Somerset, who in c1639, seeing his future in the New World of Massachusetts, uprooted his mature household and migrated to Newbury, becoming the first or second known descendent of Roger de Heselrig to complete the westward trek from the continent of Europe to the continent of North America.[40]

    Whereas we have too little information to fund even speculation in the case of the Hesilrige daughter who married Raffe Lowle during the early 1400s, the information base improves a bit even during that century. For example, Margaret[6c], sister of William[6a] Hesilrige, is recorded as having married "a Villers man." On the assumption of physical proximity,

---

[39] W Harry Rylands, editor, *The Visitation of the County of Warwick, 1682 and 1683* (London, 1911), page 33.

[40] This story of migration will be continued in later chapters.

the likeliest candidates are men of the Villers family of Brokesby (i.e., Brooksby). Of these, three stand out as possibilities: William (b. 1408) and his two known sons, John (b. c1433) and Bartholomew (b. c1435). All three have known wives: Joan Bellers (m. c1428), Elizabeth Southill of Stockerston (m. c1463), and Margaret, daughter and heir of Francis Clarke of Whissendine, Rutland. Perhaps Margaret[6c] Hesilrige was a second wife to one of these men. By contrast, when Margaret's[6a] nieces, Katherine[7d] and Ruth[7e], marry later in the century, recordings have become sufficiently detailed that we have full names and locations of the grooms: Thomas Ashby of Quenby, Leicestershire, and Richard Neele of Prestwold, also in Leicestershire. For the latter man, indeed, information enables us to locate him within a lineage. He was son of Sir Richard Neele, knight, and his first wife, Isabel (*nee* Riddings), and his descent lineage leads to a great grandson, George Neele, who married Winifred, sister of Sir Edward Coke, from 1613 the lord chief justice of England.[41]

There is a pair of concordant records for another daughter, known only as "Lucy Hasilrige of Noseley." Judging from what little more of her we know, she might well have been one of the three unnamed daughters of Thomas[7a] and Lucy. According to her will, dated 1558, she would have been of the right age. The other record tells us that she had been awarded on 20 Dec 1539 a pension of 45s (which was in addition to a previously awarded pension of 8s; source unsaid), for her service as a canoness of Nuneaton Priory, a monastic double house (monks and nuns), located in Warwickshire. The nunnery was dissolved in 1539; thus, Lucy's return to Noseley. She never married.[42]

Turning again to the male portion of the lineage, some details can be added to the brief accounts given above, in selected cases. It has been said, for instance, that Thomas[5a] Heselrig was the first to be buried at Noseley. There is one reason to doubt the accuracy of that claim—namely, that his brother John[5b] died at Noseley in 1432, long before Thomas[5a] had intimation of his own demise (which must have occurred in 1466, when he endowed a chantry at Noseley). Perhaps what we have in that claim is the shining of the klieg lights of genealogy, which illuminate mainly the center of the stage, where the principal cast of inheritances played their scenes.

---

[41] Showing compelling evidence, Farnham corrected Nichols' account (which lists Isabel as daughter of the Butlers of Warrington); George Farnham, "Prestwold and Its Hamlets in Medieval Times," *Transactions of the Leicestershire Archæological and Historical Society*, volume 17, part 1 (1931-32), pages 1-84, at pages 6, 43.

[42] *Calendars of Wills and Administrations relating to the County of Leicester* (London: British Record Society, 1902), page 37.

Of course, being center stage in the bright light of the mid-1400s did not necessarily mean that much detail of a life, male or female, would be recorded, and this was true of Thomas[5a] (as of others) to such an extent that we cannot always be confident that a given record pertains to him rather than to a son or a cousin. Certainly it is better to know *of* an existence even dimly than not at all. Yet sorting the existences into proper slots of a genealogy can depend on information we do not have. A case in point, multiple men named Thomas Hesilrige (under one or another spelling), follows.

No. 2.—Calendar of French Rolls : Henry VI.—*continued*.

1445–6.   MEMBRANES 8, 7, 6.

Jan. 3.   Confirmation of the prorogation of the truce with France until
Windsor.   April 1, 1447, dated London, December 19.

MEMBRANE 5.

Nov. 12.   Power for the marquis of Suffolk, Adam Moleyns, bishop elect of
Westm.   Chichester, keeper of the privy seal, John viscount of Beaumont,
                constable of England, and Ralph Botiller, lord de Sudeley,
                treasurer, to treat with the French ambassadors.

Feb. 11.   Custody of Marke and Oye, in the marches of Calais, entrusted to
do.   Humphrey Stafford, lieutenant of Calais.

Mar. 10.   Safe-conduct for Jas. Fane, of Bruges, coming to England to trade.
do.

Mar. 12.   Same for Martin Ochea and Ochea Perys, merchants, of Spain.
do.

May—July.   Protection to John White, of London, in the retinue of Rob.
do.   Whityngham, knight; Wm. Lemenden in the retinue of lord de
                Bourgchier; [letters of attorney to Thos. Rempston, knight];
                John Tyrell and Thos. Hasylrygge in the retinue of Rich.
                Vernon, knight; and Thos. Kymberle, of Colchester, in the
                retinue of lord de Bourgchier.

Exhibit 5.3. Extract from the Calendar of French Rolls, 1445-1446

The administrations of Henry V and Henry VI maintained a series of records known as the French Rolls, reporting such matters as royal appointments and commissions in France, licences to merchants to export goods to the continent, letters of protection and safe-conduct to foreign legations and to persons of the English realm traveling to France or to the

Low Countries.[43] Examples are shown in Exhibit 5.3, an extract from a sequence of four "membranes" for the years 1445-1446. (Recall that "membranes" were the sheets that, sewn together, formed rolls, the so-called pipe rolls.) Three of these membranes had to do with the truce negotiated between England and France. Membrane 5, the first of the four, included authorization of some English officials "to treat with the French ambassadors," an instruction concerning Calais, England's coastal enclave, and some letters of protection and safe conduct.

The last of the entries on this Membrane 5 records some letters of protection authorized by Henry VI at Westminster palace during May to July. One of the recipients was a Thomas Hasylrygge. Who was this man? We cannot be sure, but he was probably Thomas[5a] Heselrig, once and still of Eslington but now also of Noseley. What was his business in France? Letters of protection and safe-conduct were typically given to soldiers, merchants, diplomats, and pilgrims. These mens' missions in France were not recorded, but they probably had to do with mercantile or diplomatic interests.

Thomas was in the retinue of a knight, Sir Richard Vernon (1390-1451), a prominent person who had served as member of parliament from Derbyshire and Staffordshire, as speaker of the House of Commons, and in other capacities. Given that Vernon would be treasurer of Calais in 1450-51 (perhaps earlier as well), one could guess that business in Calais had prompted the letters of protection.

Thomas' companion in the Vernon retinue, John Tyrell, was probably a son or nephew of Sir John Tyrell (c1382-1437), who had been speaker of the House of Commons, then treasurer of the royal household. There might well have been a marital tie between Tyrell and the Hesilrige family; or, if not already a tie, one might have lain in store, for Thomas[7a] Hesilrige was benefactor of a grant of land to a John Tyrell near Leicester some forty years later.

Note that another pair of letters of royal protection, issued about the same time, went to men of the retinue of lord de Bourgchier—that is, Henry de Bourchier, baron of Eu and (elevated in 1446) the viscount de Bourchier. This man was matrilineal great-grandson of Edward III; he had served Henry VI as treasurer; his wife's nephew would soon ascend to the throne as Edward IV. These missions, whatever their particular aims may have been, clearly rested with some well-connected people. The Hundred Years War was all but over, England having lost all of its continental

---

[43] DeLloyd J Guth compiled an excellent inventory of records for the period, in *Late-Medieval England, 1377-1485* (Cambridge: Cambridge University Press, 1976).

territories except the pale of Calais. The years 1445 and 1446 saw peace talks with France, the English crown represented by Humphrey Stafford, 1st duke of Buckingham, who had been serving also as the king's lieutenant of Calais, as can be seen in the second entry on this membrane. Perhaps the missions led by lord de Bourchier and Vernon had connection with that activity. But Calais was now England's principal port to the continent for mercantile purposes (especially the export of sheep products, a major source of revenue for England), and this function was the more likely reason for the summer passage of Thomas Hasylrygge over the Channel.

A third man named Thomas Haselrigge shall be brought into the play at this point. According to a number of sources,[44] including the Frowick family history, Thomas Hasilrigg (b. 1405 Noseley) married in 1429 in South Mimms, Hertfordshire., Elizabeth Frowick (b. 1408 South Mimms), daughter of Thomas de Frowick (b. 1378 Old Fold, Middlesex, d. 1448 South Mimms) and Elizabeth Ashe (b. 1385 Shenley, Hertfordshire, d. 1455 South Mimms). Elizabeth had one brother, Henry (b. 1410, d. 1484). The Frowick (aka Frowyk) family were a prosperous family of London goldsmiths, merchants, and lawyers since at least c1275, when they bought the manor of Old Fold, near the northern-most peak of Middlesex as it was before it disappeared into London. (The peak was bounded on three sides by Hertfordshire, of which it was once a part. When the boundary changed, South Mimms found itself in Middlesex.)

So who was *this* Thomas Hasilrigg? The proximity of the cited birth year to that of Thomas[5c] Hesilrige (1407 vis-à-vis 1405) is suggestive, as is the fact that the groom was named as "Thomas Hasilrigg, Esq., of Noseley," which is consistent with the evidence that Thomas[5a] persistently resisted knighthood (but of course most men were not knights, so that latter point says little). Cass reproduced the will of Elizabeth's father, which was signed 2 October 1439 and extended on 20 March 1441; it named "Thomas Hasilrigg, Armiger" (i.e., "armiger" = "esquire") as his son-in-law and co-executor.[45] Thomas[5a] was one of three sons-in-law (the others, Thomas Raynes of Bedfordshire, who married Alice, and Thomas Hutford, who married Anne or Agnes). That Thomas[5a] was co-executor suggests not only that Elizabeth was the eldest of the daughters but also that he was very

---

[44] Frederick Charles Cass' history, *South Mimms* (Westminster: Nicholls and Sons, 1877), pages 85, 86-88; George Armytage's compilation, *Middlesex Pedigrees* (London: Harleian Society, 1914), page 90; Walter Goodwin Davis, *The Ancestry of Mary Isaac* (Portland, ME: Anthuensen Press, 1955), page 233; William J Loftie, *A History of London*, 2 volumes (London: Edward Stanford, 1883)

[45] Cass, *South Mimms*, pages 85, 86, 88.

likely resident in Middlesex. This was near the time, the second quarter of 1446, that letters of protection were granted by Henry VI to "John Tyrell and Thomas Hasylrygge in the retinue of Richard Vernon, knight."

    Note, by the way, that while it could have been literally true to say of Elizabeth Frowyk's groom in 1429 that he was "Thomas Hasilrigg, Esq.," by the 1440s that would have been an accurate designation only in the sense of an honorific. Recall that in the feudal hierarchy an "armiger" or "esquire" was one who served a knight as bearer of armor (among other duties). Service typically began at age 14 and continued for seven years, after which the young man was age-eligible for candidacy to knighthood. Those who were not dubbed "knight" after the passage of some years moved on to other occupation (and lower standing; "gentleman," or lower). With continued decay of feudal tradition, the designation "esquire" was continued as an honorific for men who were lords of smaller manors. But in 1429, recall, Thomas[5c] Hesilrige was not yet lord of Noseley (as he was cited in the Frowick record, and in 1447, though he was now the lord of Noseley (among other manors in Leicestershire and Northumberland), he probably would not have styled himself "esquire"—both despite and, in a sense, because of the fact that he had been resisting knighthood. It is notable that in the letter of protection granted by Henry VI, Thomas Hasylrygge was cited without any title. It is unlikely that, if this man was in fact Thomas[5c], he would have been a 40-year-old servant to Sir Richard Vernon; not in the 1440s.

    In any case, we are no closer to certain identification of the man who married the Frowick daughter, and how he relates to the other men named "Thomas Hasilrigg." There is another clue that will help the quest for answers, but prior to its introduction a review of generational sequence with as much attention to chronology of specific events as available information allows will be useful. Let's begin with Thomas[4c], who died 15 October 1422 when his son and heir, Thomas[5a], was barely 15 years old. Sir Thomas Broket, knight (b. c1363, d. 1435), became protector of the inheritance rights of young Thomas[5a], who married Broket's daughter, Elizabeth (although she is named Mabilla, daughter of John Broket, in Camden's 1619 visitation). The date of that marriage is unknown. Often, in those "arranged marriages," the legal union took place during the teen years, or even earlier. In any case, given the circumstances, one would assume that this was first marriage for Thomas[5a], very likely occurring before he attained majority age in October 1428. If in fact Thomas[5a] was the man who married Elizabeth Frowyk in 1429 in South Mimms, then his first wife, the daughter of Thomas (or John) Broket, must have died by that date—hardly inconceivable, given maternal mortality rates of that era.[46] This would also mean that William[6a], son and heir of Thomas[5c], was born to Elizabeth Frowyk, not to Elizabeth (or Mabilla) Broket, since we know that he was "30 years and more" at the date of his father's inquisition post mortem (30 Apr 1468), which puts his birth date sometime between May 1437 and 30 April 1438.

William[6a] married when he was about 21, in 1458, to another Elizabeth, this one daughter and coheir of Thomas Staunton, esq., of Sutton (Sutton-on-Soar), Nottinghamshire. Not as fortunate in longevity as his father, William[6a] died before his 40th birthday anniversary, leaving as heir his sole son (or sole surviving son), Thomas[7a], who was said to be 12 years old at the date of his father's inquisition post mortem (14 Dec 1476). As previously noted, William[6a] had sufficient notice of impending death that, following past practice, he sought to protect his young son's interests by enfeoffing "Robert Staunton, Thomas Staunton, John Gebly, clerk, and Edmund Hesylrigge of all of his lands, to the intent that they should enfeoff his right heir thereof, when he should come to the full age of twenty one years."[47] However, the inquisition jurors concluded that "enfeoffment was made through fraud and collusion in order that the king might be excluded from the wardship of the heir." (Bear in mind that the War of the Roses was still underway, that the Yorkist king, Edward IV, had only recently regained the throne from Henry VI, a Lancastrian who had many friends and supporters in Leicestershire, and who had been king until 1461, when insanity rendered him helpless, and the duke of York became Edward IV.)

So it seems clear that William's[6a] widow, Elizabeth (*nee* Staunton), took matters into hand and married Thomas Entwysell (his second marriage), who thus became protector of the inheritance due Thomas[7a] Hesilrige. Thomas Entwysell of Dalby-on-the-Wolds and his previous wife had at least two daughters. Margaret married William Wyville of Stonton Wyville, who died in May 1494 (after which Margaret's father was briefly styled "Thomas Entwysell of Stonton Wyville"). And Lucy Entwysell married Thomas[7a] Hesilrige by virtue of the grant of 1478 which gave Thomas Entwysell custody not only of the inherited estates of Thomas[7a] but also his marital rights. Entwysell's son, also named Thomas, wed Katherine Warde, niece and heir of William Wyville, and assumed the

---

[46] If Camden's informant was correct and the Broket daughter's forename was Mabilla, a confusion by backfill from the second marriage could account for remembrance of her name as "Elizabeth." ("Mabilla," "Mabillia," etc., are Latin equivalents of "Mable.")

[47] This and the following continuation are from J C Hodgson's "On the Medieval and Later Owners …" (1910), page 19.

"of Stonton Wyville" designator. Thomas Entwysell senior died in 1507; Thomas junior soon thereafter, without heir.

Now let's introduce the additional clue mentioned above. It comes from a quitclaim deed dated 25 April 1488, by which "Thomas Entwysyll of Noseley, esq.," conceded to "Thomas Hesulryg of Gloreston [Glooston], esq., all of his rights and claims to the lands and tenements which he holds by lease and grant from [Thomas Hesulryg], and which are occupied by John Fynour and William Boteler [i.e., Butler]," in South Mimms, Middlesex.[48] From this we can draw several conclusions with some confidence. First, bear in mind (1) that this Hesilrige man is Thomas[7a], son of William[6a]; (2) that William[6a] died in 1475 when his son Thomas[7a] was not yet a dozen years old; and (3) that Thomas Entwysell, new husband of William's[6a] widow, became legal agent of young Thomas[7a], exercising authority over his inheritance and marriage. We now see that Entwysell had assumed residence of the manor of Noseley and that in 1488, at a time when Thomas[7a] was well into his own majority, Entwysell was still at Noseley, Thomas[7a] residing at the small manor of Glooston. It would appear that Entwysell had been in no hurry to relinquish his position, having gained advantage from daughter Lucy's marriage to Thomas[7a], as from daughter Margaret's marriage to William Wyville of Stonton Wyville. (Both Glooston and Stonton Wyville are neighbors of Noseley, a brisk walk to the north).[49] Secondly, the fact that Entwysell released possession of the land in Middlesex before giving up Noseley could be indication that young Thomas[7a] had shown inclination to move south. As noted in the previous chapter, there is in the records of the Court of Common Pleas, for the year 1493, a case which indicates that a Thomas Haselrigge was a landowner in Middlesex.[50] As this could not have been Thomas[5a], we may conclude, thirdly, that the land was held in 1493 by Thomas[7a] (1464-1541). When was it acquired? There is no known record of that transaction, but it could have been due to Thomas[5a] earlier in the century, either in conjunction with or subsequent to his marriage to Elizabeth Frowyk. It is worth noting that her brother, Henry Frowyk, had been a highly placed and influential figure in the political and juridical life of London, and even though Henry was now dead (1410-1484) the family

---

[48] See document DG21/31 in the Hazlerigg Collection, Leicestershire Records Office.
[49] See Lee and McKinley, *A History* ... (1964), pages 112-115.
[50] The case record is CP52/251/11/8/1/1. It is cited in Joseph Biancalana, *The Fee Tail and the Common Recovery in Medieval England, 1176-1502* (Cambridge: Cambridge University Press, 2004), page 277 note 88.

connection could have had some lodestone quality to young Thomas[7a], especially if he was in fact Elizabeth's grandson.

Summing across the bare facts, we could conclude that we have one and the same Thomas Hesilrige. But definitive evidence remains elusive. Not only is there no *definitive* evidence that Elizabeth Frowyk's groom was Thomas[5c] Hesilrige; even if we assume that we have the right man, we do not know when she died (or where), and thus can only conjecture that she was mother of William[6a], heir of Thomas[5c] and father of Thomas[7a], who had rights to land in Middlesex in 1488 and who likely was the same man who was recorded as a Middlesex landowner in 1493.

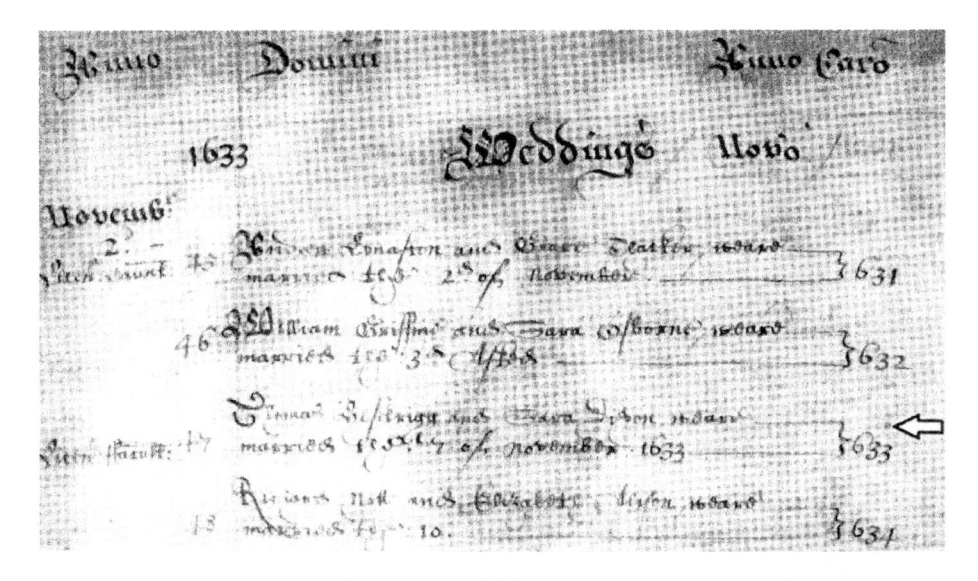

Exhibit 5.4. Thomas Heselrigg Weds Sarah Dixon, 1633

We do know also that various members of the family had major interests in the London area (Thomas[7a] among them, as will be discussed shortly), and those interests expanded during the sixteenth and seventeenth centuries. We have seen some evidence of that, even if the several pieces cannot be fitted into one continuous fabric. In addition (as recorded in the lineage segment above), Francis[11b] Hesilrige, born during the latter part of the 1500s, was an investor in the Virginia Company of London in 1607 and later. Thomas[11c] Heselrigg, also of the later 1500s, wed Sarah Dixon on 7 November 1633 at St Andrew in Holborn parish, London (see the image of part of a page of the parish register in Exhibit 5.4).[51] Nearby, in the city of Westminster, Bertine[12a] died and was buried at St Clement Danes, where a monument with arms and a Latin inscription—"Bartinus Heselrigg armiger capetaneus militae Leicestrensis hic sepultus qui obit 4 Maii 1634"—was erected in the church (though the church was demolished in 1680 and then rebuilt to design by Sir Christopher Wren in 1682).[52] And according to a Middlesex record of marriages, a Thomas Hesilrige of St Andrew, probably son of Thomas[11c] and Sarah (Dixon) Heselrigg, wed at reported age 30 a woman named only as Frances, age 24, at St Leonard's, Shoreditch, on 17 June 1679. This man was born before 1649, however, if he was son of Thomas[11c] (who died in 1646). And the younger Thomas died a few months after his wedding.

But we are getting ahead of ourselves; the foregoing are in part events and relations to be considered later. For the moment, however, one might note that the move of the Hesilrige family to Noseley, which was completed during the fourth decade of the fifteenth century, also brought the family to the vicinity of London before that century had finished, and long before the notoriety of events that came to be associated, in the minds of some definitively, with the family's London heritage.

Let's return to Thomas[7a] Hesilrige. Born shortly after the mid-point of the fifteenth century, probably at the manor of Noseley, his death more than seventy years later, probably also at Noseley, placed him high in the list of male longevities for that era. Only 12 years of age at his father's death in February 1474/5, Thomas[7a] attained majority under protection of kin, as had become the custom with the waning of feudal order. One of the first legal actions in which he participated occurred when he was about 26 years of age. William Ferrers of Wykingeston (Wigston) and Agnes, his wife, acknowledged on 18 November 1488 the rights of Thomas[7a] Hesilrig, esq., Ralph Shirley, knt. (whose sister Eleanor married Robert[7b], next eldest brother of Thomas[7a]), Thomas Kebell, sergeant-at-law (whose son Walter would wed Millicent[8l], daughter of Thomas[7a]), Thomas Entwysell, esq. (father-in-law to Thomas[7a]), and Thomas Ashby, gentleman (who, as noted above, had or would wed Katherine[7c], sister of Thomas[7a]), to give to John Tyrell, esq., one messuage, 26 acres of land and

---

[51] According to widow Sarah's will (1654), Thomas held estates in Bishops Middleham, Durham, and in Lincolnshire. Sir Arthur Hesilrige, 2nd Bt, was executor. Information in document DG21/189, Hazlerigg Collection, makes the conjectured parentage of this man probably correct.

[52] The inscription (which says that he was "head of the Leicestershire militia," that he is "here buried," and that he "died 4 May 1634") is recorded in J C Hodgson, "On the Medieval and later Owners ..." (1910), page 29.

eight acres of meadow in Wigston. This was at a time when Wigston was one of the main sites of experimentation and innovation with windmills. As mentioned above, Bertine's[8a] windmill was thought valuable enough to be separately treated in his son's will.

Thomas Entwysell, father of Lucy who married Thomas[7a], was of a Lancashire family, once centered in an area a few miles northwest of Manchester, an area that included a village named Entwistle which, along with Bolton and Turton, comprised the family's early locus.[53] According to one account in the family history, their surname was after the village, which lay at a fork in a river (probably the Edgewater and one of its feeder streams). By this account the name is an Old English conjunction of two words, "ened" and "twisla," which translate as "river fork populated by ducks." Perhaps that explains one of the easiest known spellings of the name, "Hennetwisel."

Hodgson summarized a number of records of Thomas[7a] with the following remarks (after a reminder of grandfather and father):[54]

> William Hesylrigge, son of Thomas Hesylrigge, esquire, married Elizabeth Staunton, daughter of Thomas Staunton, esquire, the marriage settlement being dated Thursday, 13th July, 1458 [Inq. post mortem, 14 Edw IV, No. 25].
>
> Thomas Heselrig [their son] was born circa 1464, and became an esquire of the body to king Henry VIII. No record has been found of visits to his Northumbrian estates and, very probably, when not on duty at the court, he resided at his Leicestershire home at Noseley. In the list of Northumbrian holds, drawn up in 1509, it is stated that Eslington, belonging to [Thomas] and inhabited by Robert Collingwood, was suitable for a garrison of twenty horsemen; and when Leland visited Northumberland about 1538, he wrote in his note-book that Hasilrig of Northamptonshire (corrected, in the margin of the MS., but in another hand, to Leicestershire) held in the county, lands worth

---

[53] There is today a street in Bolton named Entwistle; and in Turton, Entwistle Reservoir. But the village of Entwistle has apparently disappeared.

[54] Hodgson, "On the Medieval and Later Owners ...." (1910), page 20. Farnham and Thompson, "The Manor of Noseley" (1921-22), page 230, point out that "Elizabeth, widow of William Hasylrigge, became second wife of Thomas Entwysell," thus "stepmother to her own daughter-in-law."

50/. [£50] per annum, and that at Eslington he had a 'pratie pile,' in which one of the Collingwoods dwelt, who had the oversight of the said Mr. Hasilrig's lands. In Bowes and Ellerker's well-known 'View of the Castles, etc., in the East and Middle Marches,' drawn up in 1541, it is stated that 'at Elslyngton ys a toure [tower] with a barmekyn [i.e., barmekin or barmkin, a Middle English & Scots word, naming a defensive enclosure around a small castle, tower house, pele tower, or bastle house, in the north of England and in Scotland] of the inherytaunce of one ... Heslerygge, esquier, and in the tenor and occupaco'n of Robt. Collingewood, esquire, who kepeth the same in good repac'ons.' In the following year, 1542, Bertinus Haslerigg, with the consent of his son Miles Haslerigg, sold his property of Eslington, Whittingham, Thrunton, and Barton, to his tenant (and brother-in-law) Robert Collingwood.

That passage captures a number of interesting points, of which two will be mentioned. First, note the sequence of spellings of the family surname: it illustrates well the shift that occurred in conjunction with the "Great Vowel Shift" (as it was denoted in the preface). Nearly all of the variation in orthography during the early centuries came after the letters "He" of the surname; but by the 1500s documents often recorded the surname with an initial "Ha," whether it be "Hasilrig" or "Haslerigg" or a similar spelling. In the first half of the 1600s we will see (among other and usually related contests) a difference between "Hesilrige," the preference displayed by Sir Arthur Hesilrige in his own hand, and "Haselrig" or "Haslerig," printed on covers of his own writings.

The second notable point is the fact that Thomas[7a] held the office of "esquire of the body" to Henry VIII. The initial appointment was apparently made in 1515. He was serving in that position in 1520, when Henry VIII was treating with the king of France in London. We do not know how often Thomas[7a] was called to service in that capacity, but Hodgson speculated that he probably remained at court rather than riding back and forth between Noseley and London. It appears he continued to serve in that position until 1535. Thomas[7a] had held other offices prior to this appointment and, one presumes, had demonstrated his sensitivity and probity, as well as loyalty, to the king's satisfaction. We know he was sheriff of Leicestershire in 1501 and that during the first year of reign by Henry VIII he was appointed to a Commission on Gaol Delivery at Leicester castle (8 October 1509) and to the Commission of the Peace—

that is, as a Justice of the Peace (12 November 1509).[55] In May 1511 he, along with three other men, was granted licence to found a charity of one chaplain. In other ways, too, no doubt, he was concerned to promote and conserve family interests at Noseley and elsewhere. By 1515 he was in personal service to his king; and as Hodgson suggested, that would have taken priority. To recall the position's full title (as defined in the *Liber Niger*, the manual of all positions of the royal court during the time of Henry VIII), an Esquire in Ordinary of the King's Body was a privileged office in several senses, perhaps the most personal being that "no man else" was allowed "to set hands on the king." Duties were open-ended: to be "attendant upon the king's person, to array and unray him, and to watch day and night" to answer the king's need.[56] It was without doubt a position of great honor and trust. To foreshadow later discussion, Thomas[7a] could have used that trust to obtain a position in royal chambers for his one of his sons, Robert (see below). To foreshadow a still later discussion, following restoration of monarchy, after events of the civil wars in which a great-great grandson of Thomas[7a], Sir Arthur Hesilrige, 2nd Bt, played such a prominent part, it would have been utterly astonishing to see ever again any member of the Hazlerigg family engaged in any personal office to a reigning monarch, much less one that allowed touch of the monarch's body.

But back to the 1500s.

Consideration of the eldest son and heir of Thomas[7a] and Lucy, Bertine[8a], will be postponed in order to address, first, a case of fratricide that, by reasonable conjecture, involved two sons of Thomas[7a] and that prompted Henry VIII to issue a pardon; then, second, a man known as Robert Haselrig who served at the court of Henry VIII and who might have been, as mentioned above, a son of Thomas[7a] and Lucy.

Among the grants made by Henry VIII, dated 27 Henry VIII (i.e., 17 Feb 1536) at Westminster, there is this cryptic entry—in fact, no more cryptic than other entries, except that this entry leaves a rather large and

---

[55] See the compilation in James Gairdner, *Letters and Papers, Foreign and Domestic, Henry VIII*, volume 10: January-June 1536 (London: Longmans, 1887). The phrase, "gaol delivery" referred to a provision in English law which was designed to ensure trial of the accused without undue delay. The monarch issued a letter patent appointing a person to this judicial position with responsibility to deliver prisoners to trial.

[56] See e.g., Herbert Norris, *Costume and Fashion, Volume Three: The Tudors* (London: J M Dent & Sons, 1938). A useful post-Restoration guide is *Officials of the Royal Household 1660-1837*, compiled by Sir John Sainty, KCB, and Robert Bucholz, 2 volumes (London: Institute of Historical Research, 1997-98), together with a Database of Court Officers.

dramatic mystery: who were these brothers, and why did one of them kill the other? The text of the entry is reproduced as Exhibit 5.5, below.[57] Because the original script is quite small and does not reproduce well in magnification, a repetition of the key part of the text (with abbreviations expanded) will be offered first: "Brian Haselrigge of Halloughton, Leicestershire. Pardon for the murder of Walter Haselrigge, clerk, brother of the said Brian." This was tenth in a series of petitions granted by the king under privy seal at Westminster on that day, 17 February 1536.

> 1536.
> Feb.
>
> GRANTS.
>
> 10. Brian Haselrigge of Halloughton, Leic. Pardon for the murder of Walter Haselrigge, clk., brother of the said Brian. Westm., 17 Feb. 27 Hen. VIII. Del. 5 Feb. "anno subscripto" (sic).—P.S. Pat. p. 2, m. 27.

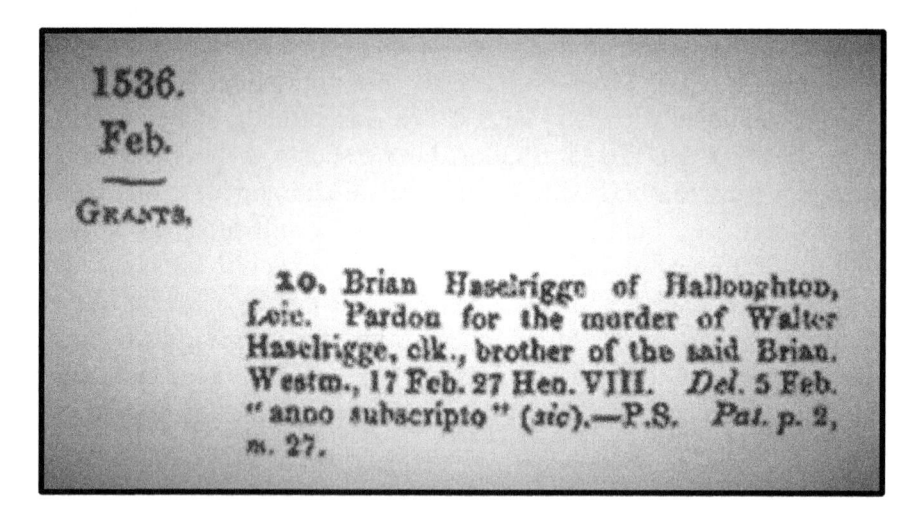

Exhibit 5.5. A Pardon for Murder, 1536

No other pertinent evidence has come to light. We do not know the circumstances of the murder. Nor do we know the ages of the brothers, their location in the lineage, or their residences at the time of the murder. With regard to the lineage question, however, a few facts lead to a suggestion, though no more than that. The relevance of these facts is contingent on the assumption that the place called "Halloughton" in 1536 is the same place later called "Hallaton." Circumstantial evidence supports that assumption, but a definitive linkage has escaped attention.[58] The first fact is that a William Heselrige was recorded as having written a will,

---

[57] This record is in the compilation by James Gairdner, *Letters and Papers, ...* (1887), volume 10, page 157.
[58] A passing comment in Farnham and Thompson's "The Manor of Noseley" (1921-22), page 220, supports the assumption.

1543, in Hallaton, Leicestershire.[59] Perhaps William was father to or a brother to Brian and Walter. An inspection of the known lineage for that period in Leicestershire raises a possibility of fraternity. Among the ten known sons of Thomas[7a] and Lucy (Entwysill) Hasilrige are one named William[8c] and another named Walter[8f]—dates unknown for both, except that by tradition William[8c] has been named third in order and Walter[8f] sixth in order, which could mean that the former was born at least four years, and Walter[8f] at least ten years, after Bertine[8a] (b. c1485). Names are unknown for three of the ten sons; perhaps one of them was Brian.

The second fact has relevance partly in connection with the designation of Walter as a "clerk," which would still have carried the significance of a religious office, especially for a place as small as Hallaton (where, unlike London, there were no counting houses or other organizations in which the newly secularized meaning of "clerical" as an occupational term was occurring). The church of Hallaton, a very old (and still well-kept) church, properly known as St Michael and All Angels, was from at least 1367 subject to a split advowson, which gave the person or persons who held the advowson the right to nominate someone to be the parish priest (with bishopric approval). In that year one-half of the advowson was held by the chantry college of Noseley. The other half was held by Roger Martival, bishop of Salisbury, from whom it passed to Isabel de Saddington, thence to her husband, Sir Ralph Hastings, thence to their daughter Margaret, thence to her husband and widower, Sir John Blaket. The college half passed to the Hazlerigg family at unknown date. The other half might have redounded to the Hazlerigg family as well, if it was part of the agreement when Isabel, daughter and heir of Margaret Hastings and Sir Roger Heron, married Thomas[4b] in 1395. The college of Noseley also held some land in the area of Hallaton until 1549. Advowsons offered a family a secure placement for a son who had attained majority without having become heir (or spare) to the family's manorial estate. Assuming the advowson had remained in the family to the time of Thomas[7a] and Lucy (Entwistle) Hasilrige, the heir, Bertine[8a], was apparently in robust health, and Walter[8c], apparently "second spare" at best, could have been the "clerk" nominated by his father.[60]

---

[59] The fact of the will is recorded in *Calendars of Wills and Administrations Relating to the County of Leicestershire* (London: British Record Society, 1902), but the will itself apparently no longer exists.

[60] The account of the advowson relies on Lee and McKinley's *A History ... Gartree Hundred* (1964), pages 121-133. Notably, William Greville Hazlerigg (1847-1898), son of Sir Arthur Grey Hazlerigg, 12th Bt, was rector of Hallaton.

Nothing more is known of the brothers Brian and Walter. Indeed, that they were brothers of Bertine[8a] can only be conjecture, in absence of more definitive information.

Now to another man who was in service to Henry VIII, at about the same time as Thomas[7a] Haselrig. The court record is clear that a man named Robert Hasilrige (or some usual or, in one instance, unusual variant of the family name) held several offices in the chambers of Henry VIII. To itemize these appointments, more or less chronologically:[61]

> Robert Hasilrige: "To be, during pleasure, yeoman of the standing wardrobe in the Tower of London"; 18 May 1509
> Robert Hesulrygge: a groom of the Chamber; May 1509
> Robert Hasilrig: "yeoman usher with the Queen Katherine of Aragon"; coronation 24 June 1509
> Robert Hasilrig: "To be, during pleasure, keeper of the wardrobe in Westminster Palace"; 23 Nov 1509
> Robert Hasilrygge: "yeoman usher of the Queen's chamber. To be, Keeper, during pleasure, of the King's garden in the Tower of London"; 8 Oct 1511
> Robert Hasilrige: gentleman usher to the King

Note that the first four of those appointments were all made during the first year of the king's reign (which began in April 1509). This suggests that Robert had been known to someone within the royal circle, someone who acted as his sponsor. Further, he must have gained favorable attention in his initial appointments, for he moved up quickly, from a yeoman servant in the Tower of London to a yeoman usher to the queen in June 1509, attending her during coronation, thence, two years later, yeoman usher of the Queen's chamber.

Who was his sponsor? The question cannot be answered with high confidence. Once again, the key piece of evidence has been elusive. While that condition has hardly been unusual for this undertaking of family history, there is considerable irony in this conjunction of a relatively common condition and the rather uncommon position of the family member under consideration. One would think there would have been very clear memory, within the family, of exactly *which* Robert had been an attendant of Henry VIII.

---

[61] John S Brewer, *Letters and Papers, Foreign and Domestic, Henry VIII*, volume 1: 1509-1514 (London: Longmans, 1862).

In fact, by traditional account of the branch of the Hesilrige family who established at Castle Donington and then in southern Nottinghamshire and Nottingham city itself, this man was Robert[7b] Hesilrige of Castle Donington (of whom, more in the next section). The attribution is almost certainly incorrect, in part because Robert[7b] was much too busy attending matters public and private in Nottinghamshire to have been able to maintain service to the royal court with such regularity and satisfaction. According to the account of Robert[7b] in the history of members of parliament (the author of which also strongly doubts the traditional attribution), the Robert Hasilrige who was gentleman usher to Henry VIII was a member of the royal chambers for "nearly 30 years." That account says that he died in 1534. Since his first appointment to the court of Henry VIII as king could have come no earlier than 1509, the "nearly 30 years," in conjunction with the 1534 year of death suggests that he had been in service to the *future* king as well. It is possible that he began as a boy servant, an adolescent boy. If we assume that, say, 28 is "nearly 30," the implied birth year could be as late as the 1490s.

If this Robert was in fact not Robert[7b] of Castle Donington, later mayor of Nottingham and similarly active in the political and commercial life of Nottingham and surrounds—and, to repeat, the equation of the two men is implausible—then the likeliest alternative is that he was nephew to Robert[7b], and son of Thomas[7a], as suggested earlier. According to Fletcher, the birth order of the eldest sons of Thomas[7a] and Lucy commences with Bertine[8a], then to John[8b], and then to Robert[8c] as third son.[62] Given the best estimate of Bertine's[8a] birth year as c1485, and assuming no daughters among the next two births, a birth year of 1489 to 1491 is plausible for Robert[8c], which fits with the foregoing assumption rather well. Even with an intervening pregnancy the numbers fit well enough. Of course, it must be emphasized that this exercise is only conjectural. We end as we began, lacking firm evidence of the man's identity.

Now to Bertine[8a] himself. One puzzle is his forename. Judging from some documents, it appears that he was born "Bartholomew."[63] Perhaps he was then addressed as "Bertie" and later in life, preferring the sound of that to "Bartholomew," he expanded it to "Bertine," although he was known as "Bartram" as well. The later practice of assigning multiple "forenames," still generations away, can be ruled out. On the other hand, forenames had become more standardized by the 1500s, largely due to the

---

[62] Fletcher, *Leicestershire Pedigrees* ... (1887), page 11.
[63] See, e.g., Hodgson, "On the Medieval and Later Owners ..." (1910), page 21.

printing press. So it appears that the alternative naming for this man was idiosyncratic.

As noted above, Bertine[8a] married Anne, daughter of John Southill (then spelled Sothill; John died 2 June 1493) and his wife, Elizabeth (*nee* Plumpton; d. 21 September 1506). At John's death the family resided at a village in Leicestershire near the border with Rutland, Stock Faston (now known as Stockerston). In her will Elizabeth stipulated a small bequest to daughter Anne and her husband, Bertine[8a] (whom Elizabeth addressed only as "my brother"). Her heirs were infant twin daughters of her recently deceased son, Henry Sothill, a lawyer in London, and his wife Joan, daughter of "the notorious Sir Richard Empson."[64] And why was Sir Richard "notorious"? He served Henry VII as a principal minister and, in that capacity along with Sir Edmund Dudley, was responsible for administering (and some say partly inventing) the king's notoriously arbitrary and injurious practice of taxation. At accession of this king's son, Henry VIII, both Empson and Dudley were arrested, charged with treason, and executed on Tower Hill in 1510. One wonders if Bertine[8a] used his "family connections" to gain a bit of advantage with the tax collector—prior to 1510, that is.

An inquisition post mortem for Bertine[8a] was held on 13 November 1565, a little more than three months after his death. Such matters were now proceeding more briskly than had been true for his Northumberland ancestors. The inquisition found that he, "Bartholomew, and

> Miles, his son and heir apparent, were seised for life of lands in Fawdoun, Keynton, East Brunton, West Brunton, Dunyngtoun, Weiteslade, and Blackeden, [all in] county Northumberland, of the yearly value of £28 with reversion in fee simple to Miles.
>
> Miles died 18th November, 1544, and Bartholomew remained seised of the premises for life with reversion to Thomas Heslerigge, son and heir of Miles.
>
> Bartholomew died 30th July last, and the premises remained to said Thomas, who is now seised thereof, and is aged 24 years and more.
>
> The premises in Kynton, Fawdoun and Brunton East are held of Lionard Dacre, esquire, as of his manor of Whalton by service of socage and 12*d* rent.

---

[64] *Testamenta Eboracensia*, compiled by James Raine (London: Surtees Society, 1869), page 169.

The premises of Weitslade and Blackden are held of Thomas Lord Dacre, as of his manor of Morpethe by service of socage and rent of 6*d*.

The premises of Dunyngton are held of Thomas Earl of Northumberland, as of his manor of Metford, by service of socage and 4*d* rent.

The premises in Brunton West are held of Henry Earl of Westmoreland, as of his manor of Bywell, by service of socage and 7*d* rent.[65]

The inventory seems straightforward and unexceptional. But there is another puzzle. As noted in chapter 4 (pages 151-52), there is a record reported by Hodgson which says that in 1568 a Launcelot Heselrige held estates at Thrunton and Barton, Fawdon, Weteslade, and Dinnington.[66] An identification of this Launcelot is as elusive now as it was in chapter 4, so we have nothing more to help us sort too few pieces of the puzzle. Miles[9a] was dead by 1565, but as his son and heir Thomas[10a] was well into majority status by that date (he was born in 1541), it would not have been a matter of protective enfeoffment. Might Launcelot have been one of the brothers of Bertine[8a] whose forenames we do not know? Perhaps. But in absence of any other shred of evidence, that "perhaps" struggles to advance beyond the great realm of idle speculation. Note, however, a discrepancy between the list of estates in the inquisition for Bertine[8a] and the list of estates cited for Launcelot: Fawdon, Weteslade, and Dinnington appear in both lists, but Kenton, the two Brunton estates, and Blackeden (i.e., Blagdon) appear only in the list for Bertine[8a] and his heirs, while Thrunton and Barton appear only in the list for Launcelot. Whittingham, with which Thrunton and Barton were usually associated, appears in neither list. (Likewise, of course, Eslington, which Bertine[8a] had sold, with consent of Miles[9a], to his

---

[65] This was mid-sixteenth century and feudalism was all but dead. But that did not mean absence of a land tenure system. It did mean that "personal service" tenures (serjeanty, etc.) were mostly defunct forms. What took their place was a generalization of socage, a land-tenure form that typically involved only the payment of rent. Notably, the estates addressed in this i.p.m. were still "held in chief"—that is, of an overlord—but the rents were small. A yearly income of £28, while hardly a fortune, was substantial income nonetheless.

[66] John Hodgson, *History of Northumberland*, part 3, volume 3 (Newcastle-upon-Tyne: John Blackwell and John Brunton Falconar, 1835), page lxx. Hodgson was reporting from the feodary book for 10 Elizabeth (i.e., 1568—although the printer goofed on this page and set the year as *1658*). As noted before, Hodgson's work was generally very accurate.

brother-in-law, Robert Collingwood.)[67] Note further that Bertine's[8a] inquisition refers only to "lands in" the several places, no manors. Likewise, the list of estates associated with Launcelot—except that the latter also includes a citation of "the vill of Brounset and Fawdon." Perhaps "Brounset" was a confusion (by scribe or transcriber) of "Brunton"; otherwise the place is unknown. In any case, there seems to be no reason to alter, but nor is there reason to improve upon, the conjecture in chapter 4 that this Launcelot was a descendant of the "western branch" of the Northumberland Heselrigs who stayed behind when William's[3b] descendants moved south of the Tyne.

Little more is known of Bertine's[8a] son and heir, Miles[9a], largely due to the fact that his adult life was so short. Judging from the marriage settlement dated June 1540, he married at about age 30, to Bridget, daughter of Sir Thomas Griffin and his wife Jane (daughter and coheir of Richard Newton, esq., of Weke, Somerset). Four years later he was dead; cause unknown. Unlike his father, who was one of eighteen children, Miles[9a] was apparently an only child. But despite the short tenure of his marriage, he managed to sire at least three children. His seat was the manor of Arthingworth, Northamptonshire (see Exhibit 5.2), which was directed by his will to his second son Edward[10b], presumably because first son Thomas[10a] would be abundantly endowed with Leicestershire estates. The will also provided a bequest of 200 marks for any posthumous child, who in fact arrived as Mary[10c] after her father's death.

Indeed, younger son Edward[10b] did well for himself and his heirs, despite the potential double disadvantage of being second son and losing his father when only a year old. After Miles[9a] died, Bridget wed William Lane of Cottesbrooke (which is about seven miles south-southwest of Arthingworth). Presumably her children remained with her. In any case, Bertine[8a] survived long enough to protect his grandsons' inheritances until they had reached majority. Edward[10b] married Anne Nicholls, whose father, Thomas, purchased a third of the manor of Hardwick, in south Northamptonshire, about a year before he died, and it appears that this interest then came to Edward[10b] and Anne. They had several children, of whom the eldest son, Edward[11a], was killed by gunshot in Fleet Street, London, in 1604, circumstances unknown. Prior to that misfortune he had married Frances, daughter and coheir (with three sisters) of William Brocas of Theddingworth. Edward[11a] then purchased the shares of two of Frances' sisters, making the manor of Theddingworth their home seat.

---

[67] However, as mentioned above, Hodgson reported that Bertine[8a] had sold Whittingham and Thrunton and Barton, as well as Eslington, to Robert Collingwood.

Offspring of Edward[11a] and Frances included a son Bertine[12a], who inherited the main interest in Theddingworth, and a daughter Frances[12b], who inherited after her brother's death in 1630.[68] Frances[12b] married first Sir Walter Chetwynd of Grindon, Warwickshire. Their son, Walter Chetwynd of Ingestre (b. 1632) distinguished himself as an antiquarian (that day's version of "historian") and, after 1678, as fellow of the Royal Society. In 1632 Frances[12b] sold the Theddingworth estate to John Newdigate of Arbury, Warwickshire.[69]

The second son of Edward[10b] and Anne (Nicholls) Hesilrige was probably the Francis[11a] Haselrig who was recorded in account books of the Virginia Company of London as an investor in that joint-stock company as early as 1607 and at least twice thereafter, the last about 1622, just before James I assumed control of the company (which was financially failing), making it a property of the crown.[70]

A third son, Thomas[11c] Haselrig, at one time thought to be prime candidate as the Thomas Haselrig who emigrated permanently to Virginia during the 1630s, is now known to have remained in England throughout his lifetime. His record of marriage and children in England confutes the logistics of that one-way trans-Atlantic migration under any conceivable circumstances.

Of the five known daughters of Edward[10b] and Ann (*nee* Nichols), the eldest was probably Bridget[11e]. She married Thomas, son of John Alicock of Sibbertoft, Northamptonshire, and their issue included at least two sons, John (b. c1583) and Thomas. Were they also parents of a Jeremy Alicock of Sibbertoft? No known evidence says that they were, but the dating fits: Jeremy was born in 1578 or 1579. This we know from the records of the first settlers of James Fort, who included on arrival (14 May 1607) Jeremy Alicock of Sibbertoft, age 28. The young man probably was

---

[68] In his history of *The Family of Brocas of Beaurepaire and Roche court* (London: Longmans, Green, 1886), pages 205-206, Montagu Burrows named the son Edward, not Bertine, and said that he was killed in a duel in London. Perhaps there is a confusion of events, son vis-à-vis father; but whether here or in Burrows is not clear. One might note, by the way, that the eldest Brocas daughter, Elizabeth, married Sir Robert Cotton, well-known antiquarian and an inspiration to young Walter Chetwynd, son of Frances[12b] (*nee* Hasilrige) Chetwynd.

[69] It appears that Edward[10b] Haslerigg had some sort of interest in the manor of Isham of Harrowden, Rutland, as of 1610, but the nature of that interest has not been determined.

[70] Francis Haselrig is also recorded as an "adventurer" (the term then used as "investor") in the Virginia Company. A record in the family history archives maintained in Salt Lake City by the Latter Day Saints can be read as implying that Francis was present at Jamestown. That reading is almost certainly false (the "almost" leaving room for the very unlikely possibility that he visited Jamestown briefly in 1607).

among those who believed on arrival that the hazardous part of the journey now lay behind them. Far from it: the fatality rate at James Fort surely stirred memories, historical accounts, of outbreaks of the plague. Jeremy died three months after going ashore. Edward Maria Wingfield, one of the grantees of the Virginia charter of 1606 and elected first president of the council at James Fort, remembered Jeremy as one of the young men he had recruited.[71]

Thomas[10a] Hesilrige, born 1541, died during the last year of the sixteenth century. Thirty-seven years earlier, on 12 June 1563, he married Ursula Andrew at her parental home, Charwelton, Northamptonshire. Her family name has been given variously as "Andrews" and "Andrewes" as well as "Andrew."[72] Her father, Thomas, who died the year after she wed, had been sheriff of Northamptonshire, following in the footsteps of his grandfather. As noted earlier in the discussion of religion and marriages, the Andrew family seems to have been one of those families who were rent by the religious divisions of the era, one branch electing the faith of Calvinism, while another branch remained in the church that now had to be distinguished officially as Roman Catholic vis-à-vis the established church of England. Ursula's parental family were of the Calvinist persuasion. Her husband's preference favored a protestant or reformational orientation, but its specific flavor is unknown. Their son Thomas[11a] (b. 1564, d. 1629) has been remembered as Calvinist, though we lack evidence by his own words. Thomas[11a] can be viewed as a hinge between centuries—from the sixteenth to the seventeenth century—and not merely because of his vital dates. He will be treated accordingly, at greater length, in the next chapter.

The other known children of Thomas[10a] and Ursula were daughters. Of these, the eldest, Mary[11b], married William Stafford (d. 1637). There is some confusion as to which Stafford branch, however. By one account he was second son of Hervey Bagot, 5th baron of Stafford, who changed his family name to Stafford. By another account he was son of a William Stafford. A third account has placed him in descent from the Humphrey Stafford who was 1st duke of Buckingham (mentioned earlier). Judging

---

[71] Wingfield was ancestor of a lineage in British North America, one of his descendants, Edward Wingfield (b. 22 October 1766 Albemarle County, Virginia), marrying in that county on 27 December 1790 Nancy (b. 1768 Albemarle County), daughter of Abel and Mary (*nee* Thurmond) Haslerig of that county.

[72] The surname is spelled "Andrew" in Walter Medcalfe's compilation, *The Visitations of Northamptonshire, 1564 and 1618-19* (London: Mitchell and Hughes, 1887), page 64, and given the proximity of dates, that spelling will be followed here.

from the history of members of parliament, he was probably the man who, on second marriage (to Elizabeth Treadway of Beckley, Oxfordshire), was father to the William Stafford of Blatherwick (1627-1665) who served his constituency of Stamford during the 1660s.

Further discussion of the children of Thomas[10a] and Ursula (*nee* Andrew) Hesilrige—in particular, their son Thomas[11a]—will be deferred to the last section of this chapter, thence to chapter 6. In the meantime, we will pick up the thread of another line of descent from William[6a] Hesilrige.

Castle Donington, Sutton Bonington

The Hesilrige family's long connection with Nottinghamshire apparently began when in 1458 William[6a] Hesilrige (1437-1475) married Elizabeth, daughter and coheir of Thomas Staunton of Staunton of the Soar (river) and Castle Donington. Their first child (or perhaps first surviving child), Thomas[7a], was not yet 10 years of age when it became evident that his father, William[6a], probably had only months, perhaps a few years, of life ahead of him. Recall that in order to protect his young son's rights of inheritance, William[6a] enfeoffed his brother Edmund[6b] Hesilrige, along with his father-in-law and his wife's brother, Robert Staunton, with an estate to be conveyed to Thomas[7a] when the latter attained majority.[73] The effort was successful, and Thomas[7a] was ensconced at the manor of Noseley, as was discussed above.

William[6a] and Elizabeth had a second son, Robert[7b], who, after his father's death, was probably reared by his mother in the midst of Staunton households in and around Castle Donington, until she married secondly Thomas Entwysell. It is this son, Robert[7b], who by tradition has been accorded the status of progenitor of the Nottinghamshire branch of the family, mainly in and around the manor of Sutton as well as in Castle Donington.

Before proceeding with an account of this lineage, some clarity of geographic location will be gained by thumbing back to the map shown as Exhibit 5.1 (page 164). Note that the shape of Leicestershire features a pair of triangular projections at northern border, a smaller one to the west

---

[73] That Robert and Elizabeth were siblings is inferred from the inscription on memorial brasses in the church of St. Edward, King and Martyr, in Castle Donington, whereon he is identified as a son of Thomas Staunton. This church, named like its older counterpart in Cambridge after King Edward the Martyr (975-978), has been known in recent times simply as the church of Castle Donington. Regarding the enfeoffment, see George F Farnham and A Hamilton Thompson, "The Castle and Manor of Castle Donington," *Transactions of the Leicestershire Archæological Society*, volume 14 (1925-26), pages 32-88, at page 82.

and a larger one to the east. Attention should be directed to the smaller of those triangles. Any reader already alert to the political geography of England will know that Castle Donington is in Leicestershire, roughly at the location of a small dot in that triangle, near the Derbyshire line. So, too, just south of that dot, is Staunton Harold and the manor of Staunton Harold, home seat of the Shirley family one of whose daughters, Eleanor, married Robert[7b] at the end of the fifteenth century. Notice another small dot, on the Nottinghamshire side of the line of that same triangle. This is roughly the location of Sutton Bonington—a merger of two towns, one of which, Sutton, had been associated with the manor of Sutton-on-Soar, home of Thomas Staunton (as discussed earlier). Both Castle Donington and Staunton Harold are so near the county line that they have been at times treated as if they lay within a neighboring county for purposes of administrative services. Indeed, at present Castle Donington has a postal code as if in Derbyshire. Sutton Bonington has likewise had considerable traffic with Leicestershire.

Of course, Nottingham itself is seat of its own county, but despite all the attention due to the Robin Hood legend, Nottingham has seemingly suffered enough neglect that it has sometimes sported the face (in a sort of "reverse psychology") of "the town no one remembers." In any case, it was in this town of perhaps 3,500 inhabitants that Robert[7b] Hesilrige made his way to some degree of wealth and influence. Often styled Robert[7b] Hesilrigge of Castle Donington, he ended his political career as member of the House of Commons for the city of Nottingham, elected in March 1553. He began nearly forty years earlier as sheriff, elected for the 1517-18 term and again for the 1523-24 term. In 1525 he was elected to his first term as mayor of the city, with returns for 1532-33 and 1539-40 (and perhaps other years). Prior to that political career, Robert[7b] had acquired substantial holdings. For the year 1514-1515, according to the borough records of the city of Nottingham, he was paying rents to the duchy of Lancaster of £10 a year, plus £5 a year "for pannage and herbage of the park." Among his holdings were "3 messuages and 2 yard land" and "2 messuages and 2 yard land," plus several plots of land, some of it pasture, some meadow, and some moor.[74] One of the buildings was a commercial firm known as The Falcon—probably a tavern and inn, the name recalled in today's Falcon Inn—located on High Pavement, one of the first streets of Nottingham. In addition, he held a horse-powered mill for which he paid rent of 20s 8d in

---

[74] By English custom, agricultural meadow was grassland that was grown for cutting of hay during and at end of summer, whereas pasture was grassland grazed throughout summer.

1514, and four years later he was granted a forty-year lease on the entire complex of mills (mostly water mills) known as "the King's Mills." These had begun as individual mills, but by the late 1400s a small community known as Milne Thorpe had grown up around the mills. His lease included two corn mills (i.e., grain mills; wheat and barley, unlikely maize), two fulling mills, the fishing assets of the complex, and flood gates.

Reference was made earlier to the claim, repeated often enough to become accepted fact, that Robert[7b] was the Robert Hasilrige who served the court of Henry VIII for nearly three decades. There is every reason to dispute that claim. The record of office holding in Nottingham, recounted above, is alone enough to indicate that a confusion of Hesilrige men named "Robert" has been at play (as clarified in the previous discussion).

Exhibit 5.6. Robert and Eleanor Hasylryg Tomb

Robert's[7b] mother, Elizabeth, was of a family prominent in south Nottinghamshire and northern Leicestershire for at least a century prior to his arrival on the scene, and the two families were interlinked in several ways besides that marriage. As noted above, his brother Thomas[7a] and Harold Staunton were "granted a licence to found a chantry in the church [at Castle Donington] for one priest" in 1509.[75] Already they had jointly

---

[75] Farnham and Thompson, "The Castle and Manor ..." (1925-26), page 45.

founded a school house in the area, and the chantry (i.e., a trust fund for the maintenance of the priest) was intended for priestly instruction at the school as well as for the traditional underwriting of masses for the dead. This was the church of St Edward, King and Martyr, probably the site of Robert's[7b] wedding to Eleanor, youngest or second youngest daughter of John Shirley of Staunton Harold, and it was there that Robert[7b] directed construction of a beautiful alabaster table tomb for Eleanor and himself (see Exhibit 5.6).[76] The inscription gives the surname as Hasylryg: since he oversaw the work, one presumes that "Hasylryg" was Robert's[7b] own choice. A window on the north facade of the church shows embedded arms of Hesilrige, of Shirley, and "Hesilrige impaling Shirley" (i.e., signifying a Hesilrige man uniting with a Shirley woman).

Farnham and Thompson reported some notes by a Mr Routh and Mr Philip B Chatwin on the tomb and effigies. These bear repetition, mainly for their extensive descriptions of Robert's[7b] armory and Eleanor's attire. First, Rouse's description of Robert's[7b] effigy:

> The fine monument of Robert Hazelrig and his wife, Eleanor (Shirley) shows considerable development in defensive armour since the Staunton brass was made.
>
> Robert is shown lying with his wife on his left; his head rests on his tilting helmet with mantling, but with the crest broken away. On the front of the helmet is the buckle by means of which it was attached to the breastplate, and on the back is shown the ring which secured it by a chain to the cuirass, in the event of it becoming dislodged in any way from the knight's head.
>
> He wears a cuirass; but the joint between the back and breastplate is not shown, and under his hands, which are raised in the attitude of prayer, is seen the coiled-up strap, fitting the buckle on the helmet, before mentioned.
>
> The upper arms and shoulders are protected by pauldrons with large neck-guards, secured to the breastplate by buckles; that on the right shoulder being larger than that on the left, and cut away below the arm-pits at back and front to receive the lance, the lance-rest being securely fixed to the right side of the breastplate, where it can be seen in the photograph [see page 216], with the collar of SS passing over it.

---

[76] Farnham and Thompson, "The Castle and Manor ..." (1925-26), pages 85-86; Alice Dryden, editor, *Memorials of Old Leicestershire* (London: George Allen & Sons, 1911), page 236.

Below the breastplate is a skirt of five or more taces, the lower one being hidden by two pairs of large fan-shaped tuiles suspended from the fourth tace by means of straps and buckles—three of which are visible in the plate [page 216]—and below the tuiles, the fall of mail extends almost to the knees.

His legs are encased in plate: both cuissarts and grevières being reinforced by lams above and below the knees, while the knee-caps are rather large. On his feet, which rest upon a dog wearing a collar of Tudor roses (head broken off), are square-toed laminated sabatons.

The left foot is broken, as also are his hands, from which he had removed his gauntlets, which he has hung on one of the quillons of his sword by means of a looped cord. This unusual feature is, however, hidden in the photograph by the figure of Eleanor.

The sword, which is broken, has the pommel worked into a Tudor rose, as is also the pendant of the collar of SS.

From a narrow cingulum around the waist is suspended by a looped cord his dagger; and, as usual at this period, the sheath is made double, in order that one or more knives may be carried in a second compartment.

Next, Chatwin's description of the effigy of Eleanor:

She wears a pedimented head-dress formed of several folds of some ornamental or embroidered cloth; her hair is braided on her forehead. A mantle hangs from her shoulders, secured by a cord across the breast. Her coat is cut low and square at the neck; it is tight fitting to the hips, from which it hangs in wavy folds.

A loose girdle lifts the front edge of the skirt almost to the knees, showing the kirtle beneath. The sleeves of her coat are pleated, and are fastened along the lower side leaving openings, through which are seen the inner sleeves of lawn or some other soft material, ending towards the wrists in puffs.

She wears a sash with a single bow which is upright.

Round her throat are three chains, and on her feet are broad-toed shoes, but they are nearly hidden by the folds of the kirtle. A little dog bites the hem of the kirtle.

Exhibit 5.7. Robert and Eleanor Hasylryg in Effigy

There was also at one time a tomb for Thomas Staunton and his wife Millicent (although it is not clear that this tomb survived recent restoration work). The inscription reads (or read): Hic jacent Thom. Staunton & Milisenta uxor ejus filia Willhelmi Mering militis ("Here lies Thomas Staunton and Millicent his wife, daughter of William Mering, soldier.")

As usual, marital alliances formed networks of families who then supported, but also competed with, one another. Sir Ralph Shirley, son and heir of John and Eleanor (*nee* Willoughby) Shirley, already enjoyed very considerable standing in the community (and the family soon would be elevated considerably more). Interlinked with them and the Hasylryg family as well as the Staunton family were three others. Thomas Harvey of Elmesthorpe, Leicestershire, was sire of one daughter, Joan, who wed Robert[7b] and Eleanor's son and heir, Hugh[8a]; and another daughter, Lucy, married Thomas Cotton, whose family included a member of parliament for Huntingdon (1558)—home seat of Robert Cromwell and his soon-to-be-born (1599) son Oliver—and John Cotton (born 1585 in Derbyshire) who, after sustaining pressures against clergy who were considered, in polite phrase, "non-conforming," abandoned his position at St Botolph's in Boston, Lincolnshire, for the future of another Boston, this one in the colony of Massachusetts. William Brocas' daughter, Elizabeth, married a Cotton man, Sir Robert, soon elevated to the baronetage, while daughter Frances married Edward[11a] Hesilrige of Arthingworth and London, whose brother Francis[11b] was (as said before) very likely the "Francis Haselrig, adventurer," as investors were called, in the Virginia Company of London early in the new (seventeenth) century.

Robert[7b] and Eleanor had at least two children, a son Hugh[8a] and a daughter Rachel[8b]. (The possibility of two other children will be discussed below.) Records in Thoroton's history of Nottinghamshire tell of Robert[7b], together with Ralph Shirley and Thomas Entwysill (among others), establishing claim to the manor of Sutton and its appurtenances, plus "a third part of 15 messuages, three tofts, one mill, 200 acres of land, sixty of meadow, sixty of pasture, two of wood, one hundred of moor, with the appurtenances, in Sutton Bonington, Kinston, and Normanton."[77] Some part of those substantial holdings were assigned to Hugh[8a], who became known as Hugh[8a] of Sutton Bonington and sometimes accorded the status of founder of the Sutton Bonington line of the family. The known record of that line becomes very thin very quickly, unfortunately.

According to the entry on Fleckney in the *Victoria History of the County of Leicestershire*, Joan (*nee* Harvey) Hesilrige died before 1566 (and after her husband, Hugh[8a]); for the small manor of Fleckney, situated a few miles southeast of Leicester, was inherited that year by their eldest son, Francis[9a]. But then he must have died shortly thereafter, and without surviving issue, for in 1568 the quarter share was inherited by Michael[9b], second son of Hugh[8a] and Joan. An implication is that third son, John[9d],

---

[77]John Throsby, editor, *Thoroton's History of Nottinghamshire*, 3 volumes (Nottingham, 1790, 1797), volume 1, pages 16-17.

had died before Michael[9b], because the quarter share of the manor passed to another, older line of inheritance after Michael's[9b] death.[78]

Michael[9b] died after 1579. According to a record cited by Fletcher as well as the Bainbridge family, he married Isabel, daughter of Robert Baynbrigg (Bainbridge), esq., of Lockington, Leicestershire (a village on the outskirts of Castle Donington), on 17 November 1572.[79] That seems to be the extent of the record. Was this a second (or later) marriage, or was Michael[9b] slow to marry? We do not know. He had at least one child, a daughter Anne, who married Richard Hedge on 6 July 1575 at St Michael's church in Sutton Bonington, so if the date of marriage to Isabel Baynbrigg is correct the conclusion is that Anne was daughter by a previous union.

A curious feature pertaining to Michael[9b] is worth a brief mention. The bell tower of St Michael's church in Sutton Bonington has five bells, of which the fourth, tenor, is inscribed with the names of five donors, "Michael Haselrig Gen. HMVTSY, 1579" among them. The year must refer to the foundry date. According to an account written during the 1920s, the string of capital letters was added probably only "to fill vacant spaces."[80] While it would seem unlikely that a cutter would expend labor time for such purpose, in fact the inscriptions were not cut into the metal but added as individual wax letters during the moulding process.[81] There is another string of six letters, this for a second donor: "Fostin Fielding Esq. MVXWFI." Perhaps it was happenstance that of the five donors only these two were accorded honors (gentleman and esquire) *and* seemingly empty strings of capital letters.

Rachel[8b] must have encountered her future husband during civic ceremonies in town and at the Castle of Nottingham at various times. As captain of the castle guard, Thomas Skeffington would surely have cut a striking figure. Times at the castle were now peaceful, in comparison to the era of Rachel's[8b] fourth great grandfather Hesilrige, for it was at this castle that William[3b] Hesilrige's contemporary decided it was time that he assume personal authority of rulership as Edward III and, on 19 Oct 1330, not yet 18 years of age, orchestrated his coup against his mother and her

---

[78] J M Lee and R A McKinley, *A History of the County of Leicestershire, volume 5: Gartree Hundred* (London: 1964), pages 84-90. The relevant parts of the entry on Fleckney rely on Farnham's notes on Leicestershire. The implications and inferences in the above account are based on reported dates of inheritances of the Fleckney estate.

[79] William G D Fletcher, *The Early History of the Family of Hesilrige, of Noseley* (Leicester: Clarke and Hodgson, 1892), page 12.

[80] W E Buckland, "Notes and Jottings about Sutton Bonington," *Transactions of the Thoroton Society*, volume 29 (1925), pages 133-169.

[81] Thanks to George A Dawson and Andy Nicholson for their assistance.

consort (and would-be king), Edmund Mortimer. Remnants of that coup are visible yet today, although the castle proper was pulled down in 1649. Perhaps, one might imagine, Captain Skeffington took Rachel[8b] on a personal tour of the secret passageways, cellars, and tunnel that a young king used to great advantage.

From time to time notice has been given in these pages of major inconsistencies across records. One such was implicated without remark in discussions above. A number of accounts of the Hesilrige family have reported (erroneously) that Robert's[7b] wife Eleanor was daughter of Sir Ralph Shirley, not his sister.[82] She has also been named as "Elizabeth, sister to Robert Shirley, knt," which is doubly erroneous. Various other records, including extensive papers of the Shirley family (housed in the Records Office) leave no doubt as to her parentage or her forename, and they offer a good estimate of her birth year, c1475. One of at least thirteen children (fourth or fifth of five daughters), Eleanor was named after her mother, Eleanor Willoughby, whose family heritage was doubtless behind the choice of forename for Robert[7b] and Eleanor's son, Hugh[8a].

Some accounts have attributed to Robert[7b] and Eleanor another daughter, Eleanor, and by implication another son, John (the implication due to the fact that this Eleanor had a younger brother named John). The only known evidence in support of this attribution is the shared forename, hardly compelling. Let's first consider what is known of this Eleanor and her brother.

Since more is known of John, let's begin with him, bearing in mind that by all indications he was considerably younger than Eleanor. Since he served as member of parliament for the constituency of Haslemere, then a small borough in Surrey, in 1588-89, John must have been born prior to 1568. Living in Clapham, Surrey, and a neighbor of Bartholomew Clerke, master of requests and his sister Eleanor's second husband, John's election to the seat has been attributed to the influence of his brother-in-law, to whom he had been a servant.[83] Despite having lived in Clapham for some time, he was known as "John Haselrigge of Noseley," suggesting that that had been his place of birth, although the attribution could have derived more from the fact that late in life (c1606) he returned to Leicestershire and added to his investments (an inn, the Angel, and the swine market). He also acquired two messuages in Bedford and three acres of land in Harrowden, Northamptonshire. His will, proved soon after his death on

---

[82] For instance, Fletcher, *Leicestershire Pedigrees* ... (1887), page 11.
[83] *The History of Parliament: The House of Commons 1558-1603*, edited by P W Hasler (London: Boydell and Brewer, 1981).

15 August 1612, showed that he also held two inns in London, the King's Head and, in a lease from the dean and chapter of St Paul's, Paul's Head, plus an estate in Dunsford, Surrey, which he had inherited from his sister at her death in 1594, who had inherited it from her first husband, Thomas Smith (or Smyth).[84] In 1595 John Haselrygge acquired a portion of the barony and castle of Lewes, together with portions of the manors of Hounden, Kymer, Haldleigh, and Cookefield, all in eastern Sussex.[85] (The town of Lewes is a few miles northeast of Brighton.) This is probably the same man, but we cannot be certain. John's will says nothing of those Sussex properties; either he had already disposed of them, or there was another John Haselrygge.

We also know from his will that John had two young daughters, Eleanor and Anne, each under age four at his death. His wife's name was Margaret; she married secondly Anthony Faunt. From that and from the record of John Haselrigge (of Mitcham, Surrey, gentleman, dated 3 July 1606) attesting consent of marriage of his wife's niece, Elizabeth Cage, age 20, to Charles Hutchins, age 26, we know that Margaret was born Margaret Travers (whose sister Elizabeth married Thomas Cage).

One additional item should be mentioned, for it seems to confirm that John was indeed "of Noseley." A "revocation of settlements," dated 7 June 1592, included as principal signatories the following men (in order): Thomas Hesilrige of Noseley, Esq., Thomas Andrewe of Wynwicke, Northamptonshire, Esq., Edward Hesilrigee of Arthingworth, gentleman, and John Hesilrigge of London, gentleman.[86] Judging from the details presented in the preceding paragraph, together with the fact that no other candidate appears in the known lineage, the likely conclusion is that we have one and the same "John Hesilrigge of London."

Now to Eleanor. Given what we know of her younger brother, as well as estimated vital dates of her children and other relevant dates, she must have been born no later than 1542. She married first Thomas Smith, by whom she had several children, according to parish records of Saints

---

[84] *Calendars of Wills and Administrations* ... (1902), page 100. The manor of Dunsford was developed from lands held by Merton Priory in Wandsworth parish. At dissolution of monasteries it passed through the hands of Thomas Cromwell (1539) and Robert Dudley, before purchase by Thomas Smith. See records in ACC/1730, of the London Metropolitan Archives, City of London.

[85] See the records abstracted by Edwin H W Dunkin in the first volume of his *Sussex Manors, Advowsons, Etc.* which is volume 19 of *Sussex Record Society* (London, 1914), at page 272.

[86] See document DG21/46 in the Hazlerigg Collection, Leicestershire Records Office. The document was signed and sealed.

Peter and Paul in Mitcham, Surrey.[87] Smith died in January 1575/6; son and heir George was born in 1561, apparently preceded by two daughters, Elinor and Mary. This suggests that Eleanor Haselrigge was born no later than 1542. (If daughter of Robert, she would have been born about five years earlier than that, since he died 26 March 1536.) Smith's inquisition post mortem reports several properties, including the manor of Dunsford. Eleanor next married, 21 February 1575/6, Bartholomew Clerke (Clarke), born c1537, a prominent official. With him she had two children, son and heir Francis (b. c1577, d. >1623), and daughter Cecily (b. c1581, d. 1629). After Bartholomew died, 12 March 1589/90, Eleanor enlisted brother John as overseer of all the properties and trustee of her young children. It is in connection with one of the properties, very likely, that the map of Clapham in south London today shows a Haselrigg Road (see Exhibit 5.8).

Eleanor died before 23 July 1594, her son George Smith acting as executor of her will and estate. She had borne at least one other son by Thomas Smith, Edward, who was baptized on 17 August 1564. The brief account of her union with Smith reported in the 1623 visitation of Surrey lists several other children, in addition to the four mentioned (which seem to be reasonably well attested), but in that regard the report is not free of reason to doubt its accuracy.

Where do Eleanor and John fit in the known lineage? The short answer is: "unknown." The record is strong on several points, including that they were indeed siblings. That they were children of Robert$^{/b}$ is thus unlikely, given that John was several years younger than Eleanor, which would put his birth date probably much more than nine months after the death of Robert^{7a}. While siblings were referred to as "of Noseley," that reference *could* have merely reflected the fact that Noseley was known as the principal seat of the family in Leicestershire. However, given that Robert^{7b} had been member of parliament for Nottinghamshire, and given his rather high visibility in the business and political communities of Nottingham, he would surely have been remembered firstly for those county associations, his children likewise.

---

[87] Robert Garraway Rice, "On the Parish Registers of SS Peter and Paul, Mitcham, Surrey," *The Reliquary*, volume 18 (London: Bemrose & Sons, 1887-88), at pages 141, 142-43, a most valuable resource; Owen Manning and William Bray, *The History and Antiquities of the County of Surrey*, 3 volumes (London, 1804), volume 3, page 365n. There is also *The Visitations of the County of Surrey, 1530, 1572, and 1623*, edited by W Bruce Bannerman (London: The Harleian Society, 1899), pages 98-9, 148; but the record is sparse and less than completely reliable.

The conundrum remains: if not Robert[7b], who? At best guess Eleanor was of the generation of Thomas[10]; but his father, Miles[9a], lived hardly long enough to father five children rather than the three on record.

Exhibit 5.8. Haselrigg Road, Clapham, London

Noseley

As discussed above, Noseley came to the Hazlerigg family during the early 1400s by marriage of Thomas[4c] Hesilrige to Isabel Heron, who had inherited the estate from her mother, Margaret (*nee* Hastings) Heron. Margaret Hastings had, in turn, inherited Noseley from her mother, Isabel, who was daughter of Sir Robert de Sadington and his wife, Joyce, who was sister to Roger de Martival.[88] At the end of his life in 1329, he was lord of Noseley. It had been a very rich life for Roger. He was archdeacon of Huntingdon in 1286-1295, during which time he also served for a year (1293-1294) as chancellor of Oxford University. From 1295 to 1310 he was archdeacon of Leicester. In 1310 he became dean of Lincoln, which position he held until 1315. In that year Roger was elected bishop of Salisbury, his final post until death on 14 March 1329/30. He was buried in a fine table tomb in Salisbury Cathedral.

Noseley parish occupied an area of a little more than 1300 acres. The Domesday enumeration in 1086 recorded a population of 28 persons. Three hundred years later the population stood at 44, despite the losses due to outbreaks of bubonic plague. A period of depopulation followed, not so much because of disease as because of enclosure and engrossing. While the old village of Noseley had been pulled down soon after the Great Plague of the mid-1300s—the old village had been located to the northwest of Noseley Hall (see the map in Exhibit 5.9)—some small "croft and toft" operations remained during the next century or so, until the early 1500s when cultivation supposedly ceased throughout the parish. This was at a time when Thomas[7a] Hesilrige was being accused of unlawful enclosures and depopulations. Disputing the accusations, he nonetheless sought and received a royal pardon in 1530. By 1670 Noseley Hall was apparently the only dwelling in the entire parish (although the fact that a total of "20 communicants" was reported in the ecclesiastical survey of 1676 suggests that at least a few dependent houses remained populated).[89]

Noseley Hall and its park (i.e., immediate grounds, mostly to the south of the hall and chapel) claimed about 75 of those acres, plus another 100 acres of woodland. Hundreds more acres were held in attached farms

---

[88] The account of Noseley manor and parish draws mainly on Farnham and Thompson, "The Manor of Noseley" (1921-22) and on Lee and McKinley's account of Gartree Hundred in their volume 5 of the Victoria History of Leicestershire (1964). Only a few details from those extensive treatments are included here.

[89] Anne Whiteman, with Mary Clapinson, *The Compton Census of 1676: A Critical Edition* (London: The British Academy and Oxford University Press, 1986), page 334. The 20 were 13 men and 7 women; all were described as "conformist," not a single "nonconformist" among them. This was, after all, very soon after restoration.

(e.g., Cotton's Field Farm, with more than 300 acres, Three Gates Farm, South Field), as well as the Home Farm.

The parish had its own church, of course, not far from the old village which it served. After years of decay, it was pulled down during the mid-1500s. A memory of it could still be seen in the recent times, in a small area known as Church Field.

The map in Exhibit 5.9 (dating from 1835) features Noseley Hall at center and to its northwest the site of the medieval village of Noseley. (Ignore the straight lines intersecting as right angle; an effect of original splicing.) North of Noseley is the manor of Rolleston, to the east the manor of Goadby, and to the northwest, Illston-on-the-Hill. As the latter name says, the area is rolling, the undulations resulting in different exposures to winter weather. Whereas Noseley is a sheltered site, Illston, Goadby, Carlton, and Galby (including its now-extinct dependent hamlet, Frisby) are more exposed to cold winds. Snow is not unusual on the landscape of the area, but it is seldom heavy. In all seasons precipitation generally comes in small but frequent amounts. The loam soil with an underbed of clayish soil conserves moisture quite well, resulting in normal lush growth of vegetation.

Note at top center of the map in Exhibit 5.9 an old coaching inn, known as Hazlerigg Arms (now, New Inn Farm). Built during the 1600s, and made of ironstone with a brick wing added later, the inn, now farmhouse, is flanked at rear by a set of brick coach houses and stables which were added in the early 1800s. A description of the Hazlerigg Arms in the Victoria History of Leicestershire reports that at "the south gable-end a large chimney is flanked on the first floor [i.e., "second floor" to readers in the USA] by so-called 'hiding places', accessible only from the loft [attic] above. These walled-in embrasures appear to be fairly common in the district, particularly where the flues were originally largely one of timber and plaster construction."

Note also in the map, at left center, the designation "Three Gates." This designates a junction of "three roads," no doubt a recall of the Old Norse word *gata*, meaning "road," but in not too distant times when traffic was slower and infrequent on small lanes through the countryside it was not uncommon to find a roadway gated. Here, the B6047, a main secondary road running north-south, intersects with two lanes, Three Gates Lane (which runs to The Avenue, at Noseley) and a lane running southwest toward Kibworth.[90]

---

[90] The map also features examples of a "spinney," a wooded area with undergrowth.

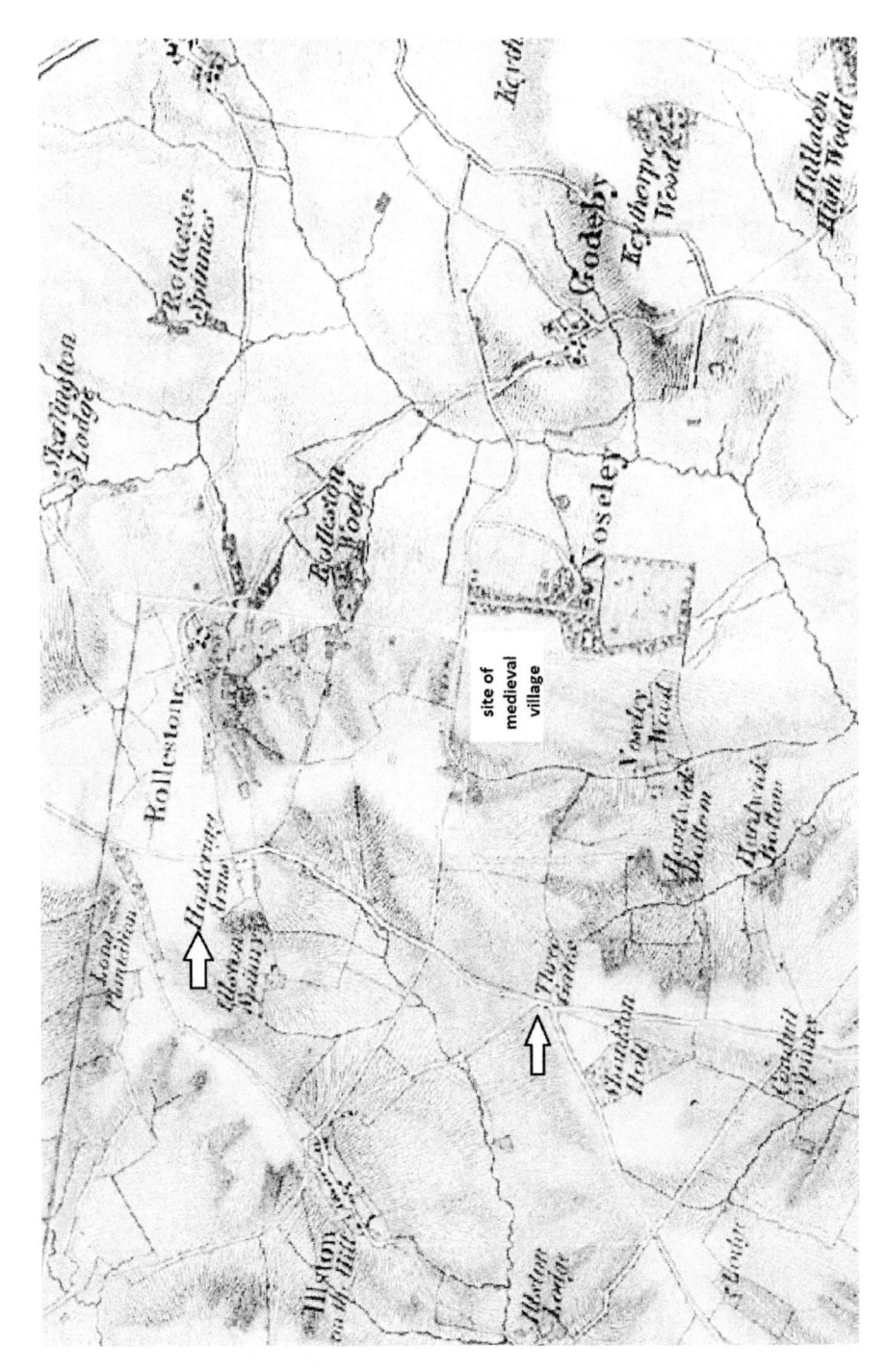

Exhibit 5.9. Some Sites to the West of Noseley Hall

Exhibit 5.10. Two Views of Noseley Hall and Chapel, 1700s

    Later chapters will offer photographs of Noseley Hall and Chapel as they have appeared in recent times. Here, in Exhibit 5.10, we see two of the earliest known depictions of the hall and chapel. The sketch at top dates from about 1735. The similar view at bottom is a painting that was made several years later. The foregrounded pond (which still exists) and horses reflect a time when there was new and growing interest in horse breeding for purposes of racing and related sport. This was the advent of the Thoroughbred, a breed of horse developed in England from native mares and Arabian (among other) stallions. Later we will have occasion to meet one famous offspring, Ringtail, whose accomplishments lived on in Noseley Hall, centuries after she enjoyed her last pasture.

One can see in the top panel of Exhibit 5.10 a depiction of Noseley chapel, surely the greatest gem of all of Noseley manor. It was begun late in the thirteenth century, probably by Anketil Martival (d. 1274), father of Roger, who finished the construction. It has been restored, refitted, and revitalized a number of times (major instances being by the 7th Bt, again in 1894 by the 13th Bt, and in recent decades by the 2nd and 3rd barons).[91] It is apparent from the picture that some major changes have been made. At one time, for instance, a tower with belfry was attached to the north side at east end. Subsidence had weakened its integrity by 1797, and it along with two antechambers connecting it to the rest of the chapel had to be pulled down.

Despite such changes, the building plan still shows to full effect the chapel's beginnings as a collegiate chapel. For example, stalls paralleling north and south (long) walls offered seating to the college's canons and fellows, who thus faced inward toward opposite stall holders, not toward the altar at east end.

A collegiate chapel or church was a secular (i.e., non-monastic) community of clergy who maintained the daily office of worship as a self-governing college of canons. It was self-supporting typically by virtue of an endowment of sufficient land (as with a monastery). Often support came also by chantry endowments (will legacies to underwrite chanted song-prayers for the repose of souls of testators and their families). A few collegiate churches and chapels successfully resisted dissolution following the 1547 action of Edward VI. Among these were (are) some famous sites: the colleges of Oxford and Cambridge universities, no doubt the most well-known. Noseley chapel was another that remained active, although mainly by oversight of the dissolution commissioners. (We will return for the rest of this story in the next chapter.)

---

[91] Restoring slate roofs of chapel and hall costs well over £1 million. That is because the materials are expensive and costly to install. (But when installed correctly, slate lasts a long time.) There is another factor in cost, however, not insignificant. To use an illustration familiar to a US audience, imagine you, a young person, have just inherited your parents' low-mileage high-end Cadillac: you are thrilled. Then one day you learn that maintenance is very substantially greater than it would have been had you bought a new Chevrolet sedan. Automotive parts and services for both Cadillac and Chevrolet come from the same sources; indeed, they are mostly interchangeable. "Yes, but," the shop owner says, "if you can afford to drive a Cadillac, you can afford premium parts and services"—that is to say, the *premium* for Cadillac parts and services.

Exhibit 5.11. Part of Floor of Chancel, Noseley Chapel

The photograph in Exhibit 5.11 shows part of the floor of the area of the chapel known as the chancel (i.e., the area near the altar). Several stone slabs are incised with memorials, the oldest being to Margaret Heron (d. 1406). Nichols reported an inventory of these memorials toward the end of the eighteenth century—among them, three children of Thomas[11c] and his wife Sarah (*nee* Dixon), Sarah (d. 1649/50), Arthur, and Ann; Thomas[10a] Hesilrige (d. 1600), Bertine[9a] Hesilrige (d. 1565), and, the slab centered in Exhibit 5.11, an armored figure of Thomas[5a] Hesilrige (d. 1467) and his wife Elizabeth (*nee* Broket).[92] Some inscriptions are no longer completely legible. For example, the inscription for Thomas[7a] and his wife Lucy (*nee* Entwisell), on a slab showing arms of Martival and Entwisell, reads:

> Hic jacent Thomas Haselrige, armiger pro corpore
> excellentissimi Domini Henrici Octavi, and Lucia uxor ejus; que
> quodem Lucia obiit octavo die mensis Octobris anno millesimo

---

[92] John Nichols, *History and Antiquities of the County of Leicester* (London, 1798), pages 754-755. Some of his recording was inaccurate. The engraving in Exhibit 5.12, below, is his Plate 74.

cccccxxvi° et dictus Thomas obit ... die ... quorum animabus
propitietur Deus. Amen

      (Here lie Thomas Haselrige, esquire to the body of
the most excellent Lord Henry VIII, and Lucy his wife;
Lucy who died the eighth of the month of October in the
year one thousand five hundred twenty-six and the aforesaid
Thomas died .... commend their souls to a merciful God.
Amen)

Similarly, an alabaster monument with two figures and the arms of Martival, Staunton, and Staunton impaling Hesilrige, for William[6a] and his wife Elizabeth (*nee* Staunton) carries this incomplete wording:

Hic jacent Will'o Hesilrige armiger et Elizabeth uxor ejus
... quondam dominus de Nowesley, Qui Willielmus obiit
die Sancti Mathei, litera Domenicali .... m°ccccxxiii
quorum animabus propitietur Deus. Amen

    The name Staunton raises an interesting question with regard to one of the charming peculiarities of the chapel's furnishings, the elegant fifteenth-century oak stalls and desks. As one authority has described it, each desk-end features "an elaborate poppy-head" and a very prominent "carved wooden cock on each of the ledges formed by the inward curve of the sides." Speculation is that the cock is from the Staunton family's crest.[93]

    The arms of many families (as well as countries, counties, towns, etc.) have been displayed in the chapel over the centuries, most of them no longer present except by representation. An inventory conducted in 1613 recorded the following (in addition to Hesilrige as well as others mentioned above: England, France (ancient), Castile, and Leon; Leicester, Cornwall, and the see of Durham; the earl of Lancaster; and the families Lacy, Clare, Beauchamp, Percy, Verdon, Tiptoft, Clifford, Ros, Wake, Bardolf, St John, and Seagrave.

    Several large wall tablets in memorial to family members adorn the walls of the chapel, and of course there are the two very large table tombs, one for Thomas[11a], the 1st Bt, and his wife Frances, and a second one for Arthur[12b], the 2nd Bt, and his wives Frances and Dorothy. More will be seen and said of these monuments in later chapters. Here, one last Exhibit from Nichols' fine engravings has been included. It depicts the two table

---

[93] Lee and McKinley, *A History of ... Leicestershire, volume 5* (1964), page 268.

tombs, along with other features from the chapel. To the left, the 1st Bt; to the right, the 2nd; between, the intricately carved font with wooden cover; above it, one dominant version of the coat of arms; the 2nd Bt's penant, also at top, along with arms showing his first and second wives; and arrayed at bottom several other arms.

Exhibit 5.12. Table Tomb Illustrations from Nichols

Other Leicestershire Estates

Recall that Thomas[11a] did not succeed to his father's estates until the 100th year of the sixteenth century, the year Thomas[10a] died. During the prior year, 36th for Thomas[11a], his father purchased some land for him in Illston-on-the-Hill, just down the road from Noseley (DG21/49 of the Hazlerig Collection). The document records him at that date as Thomas of Hartwell, which is in Northamptonshire and presumably was his seat. There had been a manor of Hartwell, but after creation of the honor of Grafton in 1542 most of the township of Hartwell, manor included, was held by the crown. By the time of Elizabeth I (in contrast to preferences by Henry VIII) the manor might have been among the properties available for long-term leasing. But more likely by 1599 home for Thomas[11a] was Hartwell End, a farming estate, which definitely was available for leasing.

As we have seen in this chapter, interest in moving south did not cease with acquisition of Noseley. If anything, the motivation grew more concerted. However, one should not conclude that the family lost interest in adding to the estate within Leicestershire itself. To the contrary: several other manorial estates in the vicinity of Noseley, held by the family at one time or another, have been mentioned in preceding discussions as well as in the lineage segment above. In this last, short section of the chapter, additional description will be made of a few of them.

Fleckney: an old manor, dating from before 1086 (when its population totaled 3), it is located about 7 miles southwest of Noseley. The present-day manor house dates from the 1700s. Held by the Hastings family for several generations, it passed to Thomas Harvey (d. 1544) whose wife Elizabeth inherited, and at her death to their four daughters; of whom the second, Joan, married Hugh[8a] Hesilrige, and their two sons, Francis[9a] and Michael[9b], inherited equally the quarter. The manor reverted to Harvey descendants; and in 1815, via marriage, to lord Byron.

Gilmorton (originally Gilden-Morton): a manorial center located about 14 miles southwest of Noseley, it was once the site of a Norman timber castle (only earthworks remain, at edge of the village). Gilmorton came to the family, along with Noseley and other manors, with the marriage of Thomas[4c] Hesilrige and Isabel Heron.

Goadby: another old manor, dating to pre-Conquest times, Goadby was held by the Preston family in the thirteenth century, with the Martival family of Noseley, its near neighbor to the west, holding some land. This seems to have been the usual pattern for Goadby (as with many other manorial estates), the manor belonging to one family and various parcels of land belonging to or leased by others. Thomas[7a] Hesilrige leased three farms of Goadby from Edward Catesby in 1511. Although Goadby was contiguous with Noseley, the Hesilrige family apparently did not acquire the manor until purchase by the 12th Bt in the mid-1800s. He restored Goadby's early thirteenth-century chapel in 1848 and erected a National school building in 1857. Goadby then passed to his second son, Major-General Thomas Maynard Hazlerigg (1840-1903), who probably used it as a residence after his return from the Afghan wars. Goadby next passed to Lt.-Col. Thomas Hazlerigg (1877-1935), who, following the Great War, retired to the manor's Holme Lodge, built on the site of the old glebe house.[94] There is a mural tablet to the latter man in Goadby's chapel.

Exhibit 5.13. Hesilrige Manor, Humberstone

Hesilrige Manor, Humberstone: An old manor at Humberstone, then a few miles northeast of Leicester, was divided into two at some unknown date.[95] One became Hotoft's manor, present as early as 1316, and the other eventually became Hesilrige's manor after it was acquired by Thomas[4c] via his marriage to Isabel Heron. This latter manor was settled on Walter Keble in 1519 when he wed Millicent[8h], daughter of Thomas[7a] Hesilrige and Lucy Entwysill. Now sometimes known as the Martival-Hesilrige manor (and sometimes simply as Humberstone manor), the old manor house (though obviously not the original one; see the Exhibit above) and much of the farmland remain to view within the eastern bounds of the city of Leicester. Until recent times a footpath named Hesilrige Walk extended

---

[94] A "glebe" was a property dedicated as benefice to support, via rents, etc., a parish priest or vicar. It could contain one or more houses, a farm or farms, tenements, etc.
[95] George E Kendall, *Humberstone, a brief History of the Church and Manors* (Leicester: Johnson, Wykes & Paine, 1916).

probably from the site of the old Hotoft manor, near Hungarton Boulevard, to Humberstone's Main Street, which runs westerly toward Martival-Hesilrige manor. Judging from John Speed's map of 1610, the latter manor was then about five miles east of Leicester's Humberstone Gate, and Hungarton was another few miles further east. The two manors carried the names, Hotoft and Hesilrige,

Illston-on-the-Hill (earlier, Illveston):[96] located on a hill of some 550 feet near Noseley, Illston was initially a dependent chapelry, not becoming an independent parish until about 1700. Most of the land was held by an abbey until 1507, when, all abbey members having died from an epidemic disease, the property reverted to the crown. Soon after it was granted as Illston manor to Christ College, Cambridge. The abbey farmer, Thomas Entwhistle, remained with the farm. The existing manor house, dating only to the late 1600s, was held by the Needham family (a tablet over the main doorway carries their arms). Sir Arthur Hesilrige, 7th Bt, acquired land within Illston parish, the last purchase in 1755, and his successors continued that interest. While apparently never acquiring the manor proper, by 1928 the 13th Bt had acquired most of the lands of Illston.

Theddingworth: perhaps as many as three separate manors during the 1200s, even the 1300s, most of the land was monastic property until 1540 (dissolution of the monasteries), after which one chief manor remained. The Catesby family were an early presence, followed by the Wigston family toward the end of the fifteenth century. In 1576 William Brocas of Horton Hall purchased some of the land of Theddingworth; then in the following year he acquired further interest via his marriage to Elizabeth, daughter and heir of Thomas Dexter (d. 1574). Brocas established his residence there, farming the extensive land holdings. Brocas (d. 1601) left four daughters as equal heirs. Edward[11a] Hesilrige of Arthingworth married the third daughter, Frances, then purchased the shares belonging to the second and fourth daughters. (The eldest daughter married Sir Robert Cotton.) Edward[11a] was succeeded first by son Bertine[12a]; secondly by daughter Frances[12b], who in 1632 wed Walter Chetwynd. Frances[12b] sold her part of Theddingworth manor to John Newdigate of Arbury, Warwickshire, in 1632.

---

[96] Rosaland M T Hill, editor, *The Rolls and Registers of Bishop Oliver Sutton 1280-1299*, 2 volumes (Hereford: The Lincoln Record Society, 1950), volume 2, pages 1-2; also see DG21/35n in The Hazlerigg Collection.

Exhibit 5.14. Recent Aerial View of Noseley Hall and Chapel

~ 6 ~
The Road to Civil Wars, 1601-1641

Nomenclatures are cultural. That is to say, a nomenclature is a feature of a particular culture. So it is with processes, relations, and events that are topics of this book. So it is, inescapably, for the book itself.

Other words could have been substituted in the title of this chapter. In place of "civil wars," the title might have read "revolution." Or, with an eye first to 1660, "revolution failed"; or, rather, 1688, "revolution postponed." But this is England, not its sister country across that body of water known to the French not as "the channel" but as "the sleeve" (*La Manche*). Even nomenclatures, words, can be contentious, and that will characterize this chapter perhaps more than any of its companions.

To say that the three decades from 1630 in England were a time of protests is both to speak accurately in an obvious sort of way and to engage in question begging. One of the begged questions would be, "And which third of a century in England did not witness protests?" But that counts as among the most obvious of the begged questions. One less obvious would have to do with the way in which the word "protest" got affixed primarily to one set of participants in a dispute, and about one set of issues which have been rendered under one general heading, religion. Part of that latter assignment is due, admittedly, to the fact that England was only one venue, and not exactly typical of the whole, for the struggles of conscience that were experienced, and have been remembered, as "religious," and for which "Protestant Reformation" became historians' banner headline. But within England, too, only some factions were regarded as "protesting," and it was mainly these factions whose actions were understood as being "religious" with a peculiar fervor, an out-of-the-ordinary insistence on knowledge of "*the* godly way," and at times an unhinged will to serve that way, supplying salvation by homicide. It is in such cauldrons that one can see brews simultaneously religious and political, simultaneously other-worldly and this-worldly—at once sacred where profane because profane where sacred, and vice versa.

After Henry VIII declared sovereignty over *all* of his realm, the full array of its religious obedience included, England's population emerged with a diversity not previously experienced. All believers—or all believers who had mattered—had been Christian, of course. Jews had been expelled in 1290, an expulsion not lifted until the 1650s.[1] Muslims were dimly available to consciousness; likewise, Hindus and Buddhists and all other "exotic" peoples. England was and had ever been—at least since Saints George, Andrew, Patrick in nationalist mythologies—a Christian nation. Now, however, there were true and proper Christians suffering these foreign Christians, "the papists." Henry VIII did not invent the animosity; it had been simmering for some time, as part of the spreading interests in full national sovereignty. But it was his insistence organizationally of a church sovereign in *England* that lent official recognition and centralized form to the long-present emotional energies of identity and difference. At first, the main residuum of the king's motions, believers increasingly styled as *Roman* Catholic, sought sanctuary in quiet observances and secret relationships. But they, too, protested. As the king's first regnant daughter attempted to regain papal dominance, protests from both sides sometimes turned vicious and bloody. The blood for which "Bloody Queen Mary" was renown came from both sides, even as her followers restarted the orgy of burning living bodies at the stake.

As discussed in the previous chapter, attitudes of individualism in the gentry culture that had grown much more prominent in England had been well established by the end of fifteenth century. That movement was furthered by actions of Henry VIII—whatever his aims might have been—to an extent that soon alarmed the king himself and his supporters. Among these supporters were men who, as one should have expected, had gained for themselves high status and perquisites in the hierarchical structure of this newly established church of England. England's monarch would be head of the church—no need of a foreign potentate—while an episcopacy would continue much as before, with the office of the archbishop of Canterbury serving as a sitting monarch's first administration of all things religious. Not only did Rome's catholic church in England see that arrangement differently. Rising voices of protest were being heard also from other Christians, confessors who chafed against what they believed to be impositions by a hierarchy of bishops into matters so intensely personal and private as the conscience of an individual person in daily confession to his or her God. These protestors came to be called, by the royal court and its official church, "Nonconformists."

How should one understand those conflicts and underlying stresses in England's social order? Were they precursors of revolutionary forces, or of unravelings that separate factions into civil war? Were their decisive

---

[1] Robin R Mundill, *England's Jewish Solution* (Cambridge: Cambridge University Press, 1998).

events "turning points" that made war inevitable, the death of a king no less inevitable? If there were such events, which were they? How did they line up in a sequence, "one event leading to a next, and then a next and a next"? Such questions have enlivened debates among historians for many years, and continue to generate disagreements as first one revision and then another demands attention.

For events so momentous as those of England's 1640s and 1650s, however, one might be surprised in learning that the historians' quarrels over those events are no older than they are, dating for the most part from the mid-nineteenth century and after. If the events collectively assembled as "the French Revolution" sparked contending assessments so soon after those barricades came down, why did English writers become so quiet in wake of the 1650s? In fact they were not quiet. But with a few partial exceptions (e.g., Thomas Hobbes' *Leviathan*), what they wrote looked little like work of the modern historian's craft. A century later, however, the written discourse was changing in England, with figures such as Henry St John, the 1st viscount Bolingbroke, Richard Price, and Edmund Burke engaging in what was for the time different perspectives in historiography.

One of the most noticeable features of that engagement is that so little was said directly of the 1640s and 1650s. Rather, it was England's "Glorious Revolution" of 1688 that stood forward as a lighthouse for disagreements about later events such as the colonial struggle for independence in British North America and the French Revolution. Recency was one reason for that preference. Another was that events of 1688 could be celebrated as having achieved peacefully some part of what earlier had been in contention, but without mentioning those earlier times and their unspeakable features.

What was it about events of the 1640s and 1650s that made attention to them so unseemly? Not only was this far from the first time that England had seen civil war: what should one call the contest that had been settled on Bosworth Field a century and a half earlier (aside, of course, from "The War of the Roses"; a question of nomenclature again)? But it was also not the first instance of regicide. Perhaps the principal difference was in how regicide occurred—not in a battle between claimants to the throne, as on that Bosworth terrain, nor in secretive administrations of strangulation or poisonous potions, as had been rumored on several occasions, but as a result of the form of a trial by peers, so audacious the presumption of that.

During the nineteenth century historians (as we know them) began to address the issues less tremulously, one result being disagreements about what happened and why. That result came about in large part due to an expectation that understanding such momentous events required the use of a master narrative, a single storyline with all the major episodes tucked neatly into the fold. One historian argued, for example, that the main story was unwillingness of the landed gentry to continue funding the debts of an increasingly decaying feudal aristocracy. Another argued that the wars were England's "bourgeois revolution," an early version of 1789. (But few of his colleagues were comfortable with his "Marxist" orientation.) As another historian saw it, the master narrative centered on a religious (i.e., Puritan) revolution, a revolt of the godly against the ungodly. For still another, all events followed from parliament's assertion of constitutional authority against royalist claims (late that they were) of absolute authority by divine right. According to another historian, the chief storyline was class resentment—not of the landed gentry but of those who had been left out of distribution of the pie, especially the lower orders of gentlemen from parts of the country that had lost wealth relative to London.[2] A twentieth-century view saw no revolutionary movement of intersecting and increasingly mutually reinforcing lines of conflict rushing into overt warfare but only normal courtly politics at work, until a tone-deaf king tried to impose his will against the religious preferences of some sectarians not in England but in Scotland, and then bumbled his way from one disaster to another. Even then, by this account, few people in England had interest in joining battle over disputes that were seen as ordinary temporary flares that had no consequence for them.

No effort will be made in these pages to adjudicate among the many contending views. This is not a history of the civil wars but of members of one family who participated in one degree or another in those wars and in events that could be, have been, addressed as in some sense precursors. Needless to say, of course, the line between what these pages "are not" and what they "are" is anything but bright. By intent, the present narrative has abjured a "view of history" that features a master storyline, any single factor of explanation, any simple chain of cause-and-effect connections from event to event, actor to actor, and the like. By intent, the following narrative will be an effort to extract as much as possible documented acts of known actors, Hesilrige and other, drawing on works of minimally narrativist chronology, such as Samuel R Gardiner's monumental effort, on works of participants who made no effort to conceal their views of who

---

[2] Indeed, London *had* grown enormously during the century to 1650, and its relative advantage would expand even more by 1750 (when, e.g., its 675,000 inhabitants would dwarf the 45,000 of the next largest city, Bristol).

was in the right and who was not, such as Edward Hyde's history, and on works of recent historical scholarship that have assayed others' narrative interpretations while offering their own, such as John Adamson's study specifically of the overthrow of Charles I.[3] Too many volumes have been consulted for it to be convenient to list all of them. Because one member of the Hesilrige family was principally involved in the main events to 1660, the extractions referred to above are centrally about him, in an effort to know what *he* did, when, with whom, for what apparent aim, with what consequences, and so forth. The total number of main actors during those events was quite small. One recent historian has said of "the establishment of Jacobean England" that it was "as small as a village" and cited the estimate of Thomas Cecil, 2nd baron Burghley, that during the early 1600s only "about 100 people were politically significant."[4] That number had grown by the 1650s, but not by much. Sir Arthur Hesilrige, 2nd Bt, was one of the significant actors, though his significance varied in time and by venue. Perhaps because he was one of the staunchest of republicans throughout the period, but especially during the latter half of the 1650s, his part in the events was oddly neglected until recent times, and even now the volume of material in description of his part is rather small. Little effort will be made in this chapter to ascertain his motivations beyond what seem to lie at the surface of his acts, or to assess matters of general character and habit. These will be pursued in the next two chapters, to the extent that available information allows even speculation and conjecture.

We begin, however, with his father, Thomas[11a] Hesilrige, who can be seen as a transitional figure, one who maintained attention to preserving and extending family fortune while also evincing willingness to engage more closely affairs of the royal court. Following a short introduction to his engagement, we will then step back to consider first a segment of the lineage leading from him to his grandchildren, then, second, an effort to discern the beginnings of Puritanism within the family. After that, we will return to Thomas[11a] and various matters of context, before moving into the

---

[3] Gardiner's *History of England from the Accession of James I to the Outbreak of the Civil War, 1603-1642* (1891), *History of the Great Civil War, 1642-1649* (1901), and *The Fall of the Monarchy of Charles I, 1637-1649* ((1882), all published by Longmans, Green of London; Edward Hyde, *The History of the Rebellion and Civil Wars in England*, 8 volumes (Oxford: Clarendon Press, 1826); and John Adamson, *Noble Revolt* (London: Weidenfeld & Nicolson, 2007). And regarding debates among historians, consult the excellent study by Roger C Richardson, *The Debate on the English Revolution*, 3rd edition (Manchester: Manchester University Press, 1998).

[4] Adam Nicolson, *God's Secretaries* (New York: HarperCollins, 2003), pages 46, 112. Cecil, an official in the government of Elizabeth I, was then elevated to 1st earl Essex.

times of tensions and disputes that became civil war (chapter 7). The war itself is divided into two, the first and the second civil war, even a third, though with some continuity from one to the next. Finally, attention moves to the 1650s, the Cromwellian protectorate, the brief period of republican government that followed, and the resumption of monarchy in 1660. There had been civil wars before, there had been regicides before, but the quarter century from 1635 was unlike any that had gone before, for England as a whole and for the Hesilrige family (among others) in particular.

Accepting Knighthood, Rewarded with Baronetcy
As previously observed, the family had been, since the time of Donald[3a] (mid-1300s), diligently but carefully resistant to calls to accept the honor (and expense) of knighthood, even at the cost of incurring fines. Pressures to accept the honors had lessened greatly during the reign of Elizabeth I (1558-1603), but her successor, James VI of Scotland who, on the Act of Union of the Crowns in 1603 became James I of the United Kingdoms, resumed past uses of honors as a means of cementing loyalties and funding an army.[5] The new king was well experienced in such matters, having been king of Scotland since his first birthday anniversary, having negotiated bickering factions both within and between Lowlanders and Highlanders, and having dealt with animosities of religious doctrine and custom between those who not long ago had been simply "the Church" and the new movements of reform. By one tabulation, "[m]ore than 900 gentlemen were knighted during the first four months of James' reign."[6] By long practice a conciliator, James I knew the advantages to be won by turning on the taps that his predecessor had pinched to a trickle, letting the backlog of thirst rush through.

Thomas[11a] Haselrigge accepted knighthood while in his mid-40s, probably having resisted indirect overtures about as long as he felt prudent. During four nights of August 1605 James I visited Grafton manor, his queen, Anne, spending her time nearby as a guest of the Hesilrige family at Alderton. Three years later James I himself visited Alderton, choosing the occasion to dub Thomas[11a] as Sir Thomas, knight. No doubt the arrangement had been made well in advance, perhaps as early as 1605. That is how matters stood for the next fourteen years, until Thomas[11a] was

---

[5] As Elizabeth died without heir, James laid claim to the throne as great-grandson of Margaret Tudor, older sister of Henry VIII. His claim was weak, since preference was for agnatic succession (i.e., through male lineage), but he had assiduously cultivated Elizabeth, among others, and the fact that his lineage claim was not agnatic was ignored.
[6] Nicholson, *God's Secretaries*, page 14.

created a baronet.[7] Although the baronet title had been bestowed as early as the 1300s, it was James I who created England's hereditary Order of Baronetage on 22 May 1611, as a revenue device. To be a candidate a man had to be of a family in good standing and have an income of at least £1,000 per year.[8] Thomas[11a] was the 43rd recipient, of the total of 200 such honors bestowed by James I during his reign. The hereditary honor of baronetcy stands between knighthood and barony. A baronet is not automatically or necessarily a knight: one can be a baronet but not a knight, and one can be a knight but not a baronet. Thus, some men were twice honored, as was Thomas[11a]: knighted on 19 June 1608, then elevated to baronet on 21 July 1622, and styled Sir Thomas Hesilrige, knight and baronet. To say that the baronetage was a "revenue device" is to say not only that a recipient was expected, in effect, to purchase the honor but also to assist in subsequent quests for financial flows to the royal court. These extra-parliamentary avenues had become increasingly important as parliament had learned to be more effective in regulating official revenues.

The portrait of Thomas[11a] shown in Exhibit 6.1 probably dates from soon after the time of his grant of knighthood but before his elevation to the baronetcy. This judgment is made wholly from inspection of the face, which is not particularly revealing. One gathers that the artist intended to give a pleasing likeness without obvious flattery. The attire is basically conventional for the time: a doublet (short-waisted padded jacket) topped by a ruff. Here, both items are "plain style," as preferred by most people who were of Calvinist or Puritan persuasion. The doublet is somber brown without embroidery or other ornamentation. The ruff appears to be single layer, undyed cotton cloth with a fringe of lacework, probably starched.

Before proceeding to the lineage segment, comment will be made once again on variant spellings of the surname. In many of the records of the day, as during the reign of Elizabeth I, the surname is given as "Hesilrigge" (sometimes without the doubled letter "g"). In a record of the knighthood it is given as "Haselrigge." As best one can judge the family preference, the "e" prevailed over "a" as first vowel; but in London circles the opposite choice prevailed in many documents. Whereas, for instance, Sir Arthur[12b] Hesilrige, 2nd Bt, signed the surname as just spelled, it was

---

[7] William Betham, *The Baronetage of England* (London: William Miller, 1801), volume 1, pages 260-264.

[8] Using purchasing power (i.e., relative standard of living) as criterion, that minimal sum would be equal to more than £175,000 in 2014. Using as criterion the relative influence that the amount of income would give one with respect to the size of the total economy (a measure of one's economic power), the equivalent would be nearly £40,000,000.

altered to "Haselrig" (or similar) on printed copies of articles that he wrote in his own hand for publication (as will be seen later).

Exhibit 6.1. Sir Thomas Hesilrige, Knight & 1st Baronet

It is not always clear that a document was written by or at close direction from a family member. We do see signatures on documents, but that does not always add discernable preference. While men of the family could and did sign their own names to legal documents, penmanship suffered lack of practice. As illustration of the point, consult the five signatures in Exhibit 6.2. They are by, respectively top to bottom, Thomas[10a], Edward[10b], John (the John whom, in the previous chapter, we failed to locate in the lineage), Robert (which man is unclear) and Sir Arthur[12b] Hesilrige; the dates range from 1592 (the first three) to about 1642 in the case of Sir Arthur's[12b] signature.

Of the three signatures recorded in June of 1592, the third, by John, seems to manifest greater practice of penmanship. Notably, John's name was given as "of London," which suggests greater activity in endeavors of law or commerce. If this was the John who was brother to Eleanor, thus brother-in-law to Bartholomew Clerke (Clarke)—as discussed in the prior chapter—he probably had numerous occasions on which to practice his signature for clarity and uniformity as well as style. By contrast, if one did not know from the document on which it appears (as on several other documents) that the top signature names Thomas[10a] Hesilrigge, one would be mostly at a loss. (The prefatory marks are probably "Dno," Latin abbreviation for "Lord," as in "lord of manor.")

Thomas Hesilrigge

Edward Hesilrigge

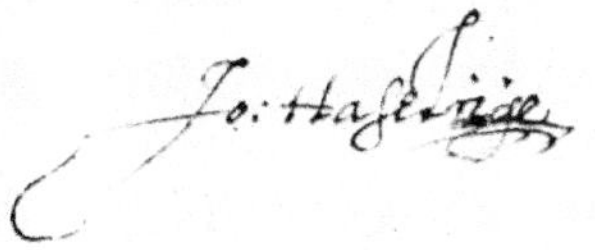

John Hasilrigge

Robert Hesilrige

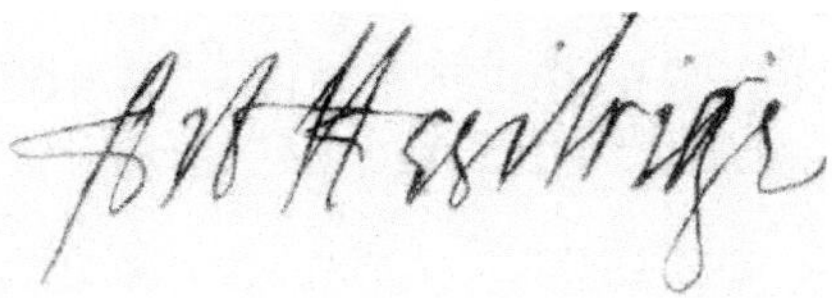

Sir Arthur Hesilrige

Exhibit 6.2. Five Signatures, 1592 to 1642

A Seventeenth-Century Segment of Lineage
Most of the discussion of family members in this chapter will focus on two men, Thomas[11a] and Arthur[12b]. In order to place them within context of lineage, and in so doing introduce other members of the generations, another short segment of lineage will next appear. In covering all known descendants of Thomas[11a] through the generation of Arthur's[12b] children, it also covers the larger part of the seventeenth century.

Thomas[11a] Hesilrige, 1st Bt.: b. 1563, d. 11 January 1629/30 Alderton; m. Frances (b. c1575, d. 1668), daughter of William Gorges (d. 2 June 1589 Alderton) and Cecilia Sparchford; Thomas[11a] knighted 19 June 1608, raised to baronetcy 21 July 1622; more below

   L-- Donald[12a] Hesilrige: b. c1592, d. September 1623 Theddingworth, Leicestershire, without issue; matriculated 3 June 1608 Brasenose College, Oxford; admitted March 1622 Gray's Inn

   L-- **Arthur**[12b] Hesilrige, 2nd Bt.: b. July 1601 Alderton, d. 7 January 1660/1 Tower of London; more below

   L-- Anthony[12c] Hesilrige: b. >1601
   L-- Thomas[12d] Hesilrige: b. c1603, d. 1608

   L-- John[12e] Hesilrige of Alderton: b. 1603, d. 22 July 1655; m. c1628 Elizabeth (*nee* Unknown)

      L-- Thomas[13a] Hesilrige: b. >1628
      L-- Francis[13b] Hesilrige: b. > 1629
      L-- Anthony[13c] Hesilrige: b. >1630

      L-- Arthur[13d] Hesilrige: b. c1635, d. 1670; m. c1668 (?) Mary[14c], daughter of Thomas[13a] Hesilrige and Elizabeth Fenwick; see below

   L-- Thomas[12f] Hesilrige of St Martin's, Ludgate: b. c1610, d. October 1651 London, buried 30 October 1651 Westminster Abbey; m. 6 September 1632 St Luke's, Chelsea, Middlesex, Rebecca (b. 1610 Welford, Buckinghamshire), daughter of Thomas Scheaffe and Maria Wilson; more below

└-- Rebecka[13a] Hesilrige: b. c1635
└-- Dorothy[13b] Hesilrige: b. c1638; m. John Grimstone
└-- Frances[13c] Hesilrige: b. c1642

└-- Thomas[13d] Hesilrige: b. 1646, christened 19 July 1646 Humberstone, Leicestershire, d. June 1652 St Martin's, Ludgate

└-- Robert[12g] Hesilrige: b. >1609
└-- William[12h] Hesilrige: b. >1610, d. >1658

└-- Mary[12i] Hesilrige: b. May 1595 Alderton, Northamptonshire, d. 19 August 1659 Allesley, Warwickshire; m.(1) 1621 John Plumbe of Marston, m.(2) Fnu Flint, m.(3) Francis Blythe of Allesley, Warwickshire

└-- Anne[12j] Hesilrige: b. c1610, d. >1625; m. Thomas Waite of London

└-- Frances[12k] Hesilrige: b. 1613, d. >1633; m. c1633 Eslington, Northumberland (?), Edward Wood

└-- Jane[12l] Hesilrige: b. c1615, d. >1640; m. c1635 John Wedgwood, esq. (b. 1604), of Harkeles, Staffordshire, son of John Wedgwood and Margaret Ford; issue: Frances (b. c1631), William (b. c1633), Margaret (b. c1635), John (b. 1639 Leek, Staffordshire, d. 1694), Arthur (b. >1640), Anne (b. >1640), Egerton (b. >1640)

└-- Judith[12m] Hesilrige: b. c1617
└-- Elizabeth[12n] Hesilrige: b. c1619

Arthur[12b] Hesilrige, 2nd Bt.: b. Jul 1601 Alderton, d. 7 January 1660/1 Tower of London; m.(1) 24 May 1624 Frances (b. May 1606, d. 1632 Noseley), daughter of Thomas Elmes and Christiana Hickling; m.(2) 21 February 1634/5 Dorothy (b. 1605, d. 28 Jan 1650/1 Noseley), daughter of Fulke Greville and Mary Margaret Copley, and sister of Robert Greville, 2nd baron Brooke of Beauchamps Court, Warwickshire

└-- **Thomas**[13a] Hesilrige, 3rd Bt.: b. c1625, d. 24 February 1680; m. c1659 Elizabeth (b. <1640, d. 30 May 1673), elder daughter and coheir of George Fenwick of Brunton Hall, Northumberland, and Alice Boteler (*nee* Apsley); more below

└── **Thomas**[14a] Hesilrige, 4th Bt.: b. 1664, d. 11 July1700; never married, died without issue

└── Arabella[14b] Hesilrige: b. c1660, d. <1716; m. Rawson Hart, esq., of Grantham, Lincolnshire (his will dated 24 May 1716); issue: Mary Hart (b. c1695)

└── Mary[14c] Hesilrige: b. >1660, d. <1699; m.(1) c1668 (?) Arthur[13d] Hesilrige (son of John[12e] of Alderton), m.(2) Sir Samuel Rolle, knight, Heanton, Devon; see below

└── Diane[14d] Hesilrige: b >1661, d. <June 1673
└── Elizabeth[14e] Hesilrige: b.>1664, d. <June 1673

└── Dorothy[14f] Hesilrige: b>1665, d. >1735; m. Robert Shafto, esq. (b. Apr 1634, d. 1714) of Benwell Tower, Northumberland; issue: Robert (b. >1690, d. 3 November 1735), Dorothy (d. >1734)

└── [Second Son]: b. c1628, d. <1632
└── [First Daughter]
└── [Second Daughter]

└── Catherine[13b] Hesilrige: b. November 1635 Brooke House, London, d. 28 August 1670 Harnham House, Northumberland; m.(1) 1652 George Fenwick (b. c1603 Brinkburn, Northumberland, d. March 1657 Berwick-on-Tweed, Northumberland); m.(2) <1660 Philip Babington (b. c1632 Northumberland, d. 1690 Ireland); more below

└── Arthur[13c] Hesilrige: b. 1637, baptized 29 April 1637 Fawsley, Northamptonshire, d. 1649

└── Robert[13d] Hesilrige of Ilveston (Illston), 5th Bt: b. Jul 1639 Noseley, baptized 2 August 1639 Fawsley, Northamptonshire, d. 22 May 1713; m. 3 May 1664 St Mary's, Islington, Middlesex, Bridget (b. 1642), daughter of Sir Samuel Rolle, knight, Heanton, Devon

┗-- Dorothy[13e] Hesilrige: b. c1642, d. 29 June 1705; m. John Doucett, esq.; buried Knoll, Warwickshire

┗-- Frances[13f] Hesilrige: b. c1648, d. <1696; m. c1668 Sir William Humble, 1st Bt (b. c1640, d. 1705) of Kensington, Middlesex; no issue

┗-- Mary[13g] Hesilrige: b. c1645; m. 8 June 1679 St Katherine by the Tower, Middlesex, Richard Chamberlain (b. c1640)

┗-- plus two more, names unknown

Most of the information in that lineage segment is straightforward enough. Some of it will be augmented later in the chapter. One curiosity must be addressed here, in proximity to other information in the segment. In his *History and Antiquities of Northamptonshire*, John Bridges noted that Mary[14c], daughter of Thomas[13a], 3rd Bt, and his wife Elizabeth (*nee* Fenwick), married twice: first, to her cousin Arthur[13d] (son of John[12e] of Alderton); second, to Sir Samuel Rolle (whose daughter Bridget later married Robert[13d], 5th Bt).[9] The claim was repeated and, presumably, attested in the recent addition of a fifth volume to the Victoria History of Northamptonshire.[10] There is no independent base of evidence by which to disprove the claim, but it is difficult to reconcile dates, given what can be said even as approximation from other, and attested, information. One suspects a confusion of persons has been at work.

And the First Puritan Hesilrige Was …?
Sir Arthur[12b] Hesilrige, 2nd Bt, declared to his fellow parliamentarians in Commons session on 8 March 1658/9 that "I was bred a Puritan and am for public liberty."[11] This declaration would have been superfluous for his

---

[9] Bridges, 2 volumes (Oxford: Clarendon, 1791), volume 1, page 281. Some accounts have given the latter surname as Rolles rather than Rolle, and at least one family tree has assimilated Samuel Rolle to Samuel Rolt. But Rolle seems likeliest.

[10] Philip Riden and Charles Insley, *A History of the County of Northampton, volume 5: The Hundred of Cleley* (London: Boydell and Brewer, 2002), pages 39-58. Bridges is cited as source.

[11] Recorded in the *Diary of Thomas Burton*, 4 volumes, edited by John T Rutt (London: H Colburn, 1828), volume 4, page 77. A member from Westmoreland in the parliaments of 1656 to 1659, Thomas Burton maintained a diary of proceedings session by session. Note, by the way, that throughout his diary Burton gave Sir Arthur's[12b] surname as Haslerigge.

colleagues, given his prior pronouncements and actions. That he felt the need to repeat the claim to identity is a measure of how central it was to his public posture. The words imply that he had been raised a Puritan by Puritan parents. That, too, fits what we know of Thomas[11a], as the portrait shown above indicates by example and as testified by known facts of his household, such as his wife's apparel made from cloth of her own making: a "plain style," which many Puritans favored. While we cannot be certain of the *specific* religious sympathies of Thomas[11a] and Frances, we have reason to be think that their sympathies lay with the Protestant movement in general, probably with emphasis that would have won them the label, "Nonconformist."

Who was the first Puritan Hesilrige? That person might not have been of a household in the titled lineage, in which case the likelihood of coming to his or her unique identity would be vanishingly small. Even if a person of the titled lineage, his or her identity could be approached only in speculative mode, since for any promising candidate one would almost surely be left with the question of his or her parents. So it is here. But the speculation proves to be interesting. In his valuable study of "the Great Puritan Families of Early Stuart England," Cliffe identified the Hesilrige family as one of 123 such families, spread across 35 counties.[12] All but one of the entries pertained to the 2nd Bt, and the exception, to his father, was subsidiary.

Let's proceed by working backwards from that father, Thomas[11a], the 1st Bt. While we can be confident that he was in some measure and degree a "protestant" against restrictions imposed on his religious liberty, we cannot be as confident that his protesting attitude (to say nothing of his behavior) was as strenuously presented or as uncompromising as that of his heir, the 2nd Bt. The epitaph on his memorial in Noseley chapel recalls him as "trusted with the places of greatest honour and power in the county," and as "prudent and of impartial justice, of great temperance and sobriety." This last phrase was veritable motto of the Puritan character.

We do not know his religious sentiments in youth. One interesting fact in that regard is his matriculation in 1582 at University College, one of the three oldest colleges of Oxford University. This college had a long heritage of being open only to fellows studying theology. The restriction had recently been relaxed, but in many ways the heritage lived on for some time. Indeed, the component colleges of both Oxford and Cambridge place much weight on distinctive traditions, each college having its own. Would Thomas[11a] have chosen this college, one of 16 at Oxford, knowing that his

---

[12] John T Cliffe, *The Puritan Gentry* (London: Routledge & Kegan Paul, 1984).

studies would carry much flavor of theology—necessarily the theology of the official church? In fact, the coincidence is not as telling as one might imagine, because in 1582 the Elizabethan settlement was holding rather well, and while the church did have an episcopal organization, its doctrine was becoming Calvinist in flavor.[13] So it remained until the 1620s. This latter fact provides context as well for the choice of college when it came time for Donald[12a], first-born son and presumed heir of Thomas[11a], to matriculate in 1608: Brasenose College at Oxford, a new college (1509) and one that was known for sympathies toward Roman Catholics. From the 1620s on, it predominantly favored the royalist cause. But that was a very different time.

Those facts of biography, one could conclude, indicate a less than ardent conviction in Protestantism. Perhaps what one is seeing, however, is evidence of the same pragmatic flexibility that Thomas[11a] later displayed when it seemed to him that the time had come to accept knighthood. Interests of family patrimony would, as with his ancestors, prevail.

What then of Thomas[10a], father of Thomas[11a]? Was he a Puritan? Here the evidence is even more circumstantial, less firm; but the case that can be made offers some interest nonetheless.

First of all, his vital dates (1541-1600) tell us that Thomas[10a] came on the scene after the hullabaloo over king Henry's marital and heirship woes were of recent history; after the accession of another boy king, Edward VI (1547); and after the issuance of Cranmer's second, more radical, prayer book (1552). A year later, the twelfth year of life for Thomas[10a], Edward VI was dead, and his half-sister was on the throne as queen Mary, her realm's first queen regnant (i.e., ruling on her own). But under Mary the authority of the Roman papacy regained high standing, and religious Protestants in England were often persecuted, dozens burned at the stake. Remembered as Bloody Mary, she was dead before the end of 1558, and her half-sister, soon known as Good Queen Bess, replaced her as Elizabeth I. Thomas[10a], now within striking distance of his majority age, would have benefited from the greater tolerance, as well as improved political sense, that came with Good Queen Bess' orchestration of a settlement among the major contestants for religious, and politico-

---

[13] C M Dent, *Protestant Reformers in Elizabeth Oxford* (Oxford: Oxford University Press, 1983). In his *Predestination, Policy and Polemic* (Cambridge: Cambridge University Press, 2002), Peter White cited data showing that college libraries at Oxford and Cambridge did not acquire works by Calvin (among others) until the 1580s (pages 83-84). Partly from such data he argued that "doctrinal Reformation generally made much slower progress in the Elizabethan church" than earlier historians had realized.

religious, loyalty. Not that Protestants of Puritan persuasion were always welcomed. Whereas one archbishop of Canterbury, Edmund Grindal, began his tenure in 1575 with warm greetings to Puritans, his queen was not pleased, and at his death eight years later she replaced him with John Whitgift, who rather than welcome nonconformists persecuted them. But there was more elbow room than had been true of the worst of queen Mary's regime.

When Thomas[10a] was 22 he married Ursula, daughter of Thomas Andrew of Winwick and Charwelton, Northamptonshire. The import of that fact for present purposes is that the Andrew family was one that had been rent by religious confession, with some maintaining allegiance to Rome, others conforming to the England's official church, while still others rejected both in favor of a Protestant sect. Moreover, Ursula's paternal grandfather was son of the eldest daughter of Richard Knightley, esq., of Fawsley, Northamptonshire. The Knightley family would be, by the date of Ursula's marriage to Thomas[10a], prominent in the Puritan movement centered on Northampton. Sir Richard Knightley of Fawsley (1533-1615), a relatively quiet Puritan and a member of parliament (returned five times, 1584 to 1601), quietly sheltered a printing press from which came Puritan pamphlets written pseudonymously in 1588 and 1589 by Martin Marprelate (to great controversy). After Charles I dissolved what therefore became known as "the Short Parliament" (1640), a number of stalwart leaders of the Puritan cause (e.g., John Pym, probably Sir Arthur Hesilrige) traveled to Fawsley, then seat of Sir Richard Knightley (1617-1661), to discuss their next moves. Sir Richard's wife Elizabeth, by the way, was daughter of John Hampden, another prominent Puritan. It had become a fairly tight circle of leaders, and events began to move quickly. In Thomas[10a] and Ursula's day, by contrast, successfully regulating the religious tensions was often less fraught partly because nonconformists, whatever their more specific stripe, were mostly content to practice their beliefs privately and quietly in small gatherings, were usually allowed to do so, and in many parishes could count on sympathy from vicars and rectors.[14] By comparison to their children and grandchildren, they were generally successful in achieving accommodations within the established church, not always happily but suitably enough to benefit from mutual tolerance and cooperation.

That is not to say, however, that all refrained from overt displays of what was increasingly seen by many Protestants as a personal right of

---

[14] See, e.g., Patrick Collinson, *Godly People* (London: Hambledon, 1983), pages 213-244, and his *The Elizabethan Puritan Movement* (Bristol: J W Arrowsmith, 1967).

liberty of religious belief and practice. Nor more especially did they all refrain from resisting what they regarded as unacceptable constraints on that liberty. In the previous chapter we took notice of an event that surely did reflect resistance by Thomas[10a] to a constraint against his liberty with respect to Noseley chapel. To what extent he saw the issue as involving a contest specifically over religious liberty we cannot say. At such remove in time and place it is difficult in general to draw a line between what was a matter of religious freedom and what was one of political freedom. For a particular person who was not so thoughtful as to leave a detailed essay for our scrutiny, we simply lack means of knowing how he or she saw the difference.

Recall that in June of 1592 Thomas[10a] revoked a family settlement of his estate, replacing it the same day with a companion document that established his sole claim to his entire estate in England.[15] In the latter document he stipulated that the entirely of his estate, excepting lands in Noseley that were to be settled on the future wife of Thomas[11a], son and heir, would be held by him for life; then by his wife Ursula for life (she did survive him); then by son and heir Thomas[11a] and his heirs male; then of other sons and their heirs male.[16] In perusing the background to those two documents we might see evidence not simply that Thomas[10a] had challenged the crown's claim against the liberty of Noseley chapel—and challenge it he did—but also that the basis was religious liberty.

Prior to 1547 the warden of Noseley chapel was also rector of Noseley parish. In that year, by act of parliament under aegis of Henry VIII, chantry colleges were dissolved, Noseley included. Henceforth, the chapel became a private chapel held by the Hesilrige family, who as patrons supplied the living (donative) of a rector whom they appointed and presented to congregants. This procedure, begun by Bertin[8a] in 1547, was continued through Miles[9a] to Thomas[10a] Hesilrige. However, the person who was presented in 1577 refused his oath, as a result of which his institution was canceled. The controversy sparked an investigation, which concluded at inquisition in 1584 that the right of presentation had in fact

---

[15] These documents are, respectively, DG21/46 and DG21/47 in the Hazlerigg collection, housed in the Leicestershire Records Office.

[16] This last reference—other sons and their heirs male—is puzzling. The known lineage shows only one son (Thomas[11a]), who did in fact inherit, and the fact that no "other sons" were named suggests either that they were unborn or that he was allowing the possibility or one or more illegitimate sons. Of the latter nothing is known or even suspected. Of the former, perhaps he had good reason to think that Ursula, then about 48 years of age, was still fecund. Perhaps more generally, however, he was simply being very cautiously protective of his estate.

passed to the crown at dissolution in 1547. In consequence, the crown granted the chapel as of 1583 to one of queen Elizabeth's favorite pensioners, John Farnham of Quorndon, Leicestershire, and assessed the sitting lord of Noseley, Thomas[10a], all arrears of tithes for the years from 1547 to 1584. In lieu of payment, the crown leased the manor of Noseley for 90 years to Thomas Andrew of Winwick and Edward[10b] Hesilrige of Arthingworth, described in later accounts as father-in-law and brother of Thomas[10a] Hesilrige. That Edward[10b] and Thomas[10a] were brothers is undoubted. Because lineage records in the Andrew family indicate that Ursula's father died in 1568, it seems more likely that the cited Thomas Andrew was in fact Ursula's brother Thomas, who was heir to the father.

The foregoing account, confirmed by surviving documents, has been interpreted by some writers as evidence that Bertine[8a] and his heirs deliberately, knowingly, cheated the crown by failing to relinquish what rightfully became the crown's holding at the dissolution of chantry chapels—namely, all rights to the land, buildings, and accoutrements of the chapel.[17] Reversion had no doubt been intended by Henry VIII and his advisors when he began the more general process of dissolving all monasteries and other religious houses in England—the intent being both a continuation of feudal rights of overlordship and a means of generating more revenue to the crown via grants or sales of land and buildings. It is likely that Bertine[8a] did know what he was doing: he was protecting his inheritance and the inheritance of his heirs, against claims of a then-dying feudal system of land control and taxation. Thirty years later his grandson would have been doing the same—except that now, after those many years, it would have been an established practice, as what was left of the feudal system amounted to frayed remnants. Was the contest that Thomas[10a] thus waged with the crown simply a political struggle over land and its revenue-bearing properties? It might have been only that, or mainly that. It might have been instead, however, or also, a struggle over the liberty of a chapel and a family to freely worship within it as it had been doing for more than a century.

The upshot is (in quick compass) that the same two men, Thomas Andrew of Winwick and Edward[10b] Hesilrige of Arthingworth purchased the chapel of Noseley, along with a moiety of the tithes of neighboring

---

[17] See, e.g., George F Farnham and A Hamilton Thompson, "The Manor of Noseley," *Transactions of the Leicestershire Archæological Society*, volume 12, part 2 (1921-22), pages 214-271, at pages 257-263. See also documents DG21/37 to 45 (as well as 46 and 47) in the Hazlerigg Collection.

Illston, for £1500 on 3 February 1590/91.[18] Once again the free chapel was in the possession of the Hesilrige family. Thomas[10a], Puritan or not, regained the whole of his estate the following year.

Thomas, the 1st Bt, and King James I

Returning to Thomas[11a]—son of the Thomas[10a] considered just above and father of Arthur[12b]—let's rely once more on John Crawford Hodgson for a quick summary of some basic facts of biography. Thomas[11a], he said:[19]

> was educated at University College, Oxford, at which he matriculated in 1582 at the age of 17. He was knighted by king James I on the 19th of June, 1608, was high sheriff of Leicestershire in 1612, was created a baronet on the 21st August, 1622, and represented his county as knight of the shire in the parliaments of 1614 and 1624. He died at the age of sixty-six on the 11th January, 1629 [i.e., 1630], and was buried at Noseley under a magnificent tomb, rich in heraldry, and with full length effigies of his wife and of himself. The epitaph records that he was 'trusted with the places of the greatest honor and power in the county,' whilst his wife 'adorn'd her family with fine cloth of her owne spining.'

Indeed, the fact that his wife, Frances (*nee* Gorges) Hesilrige, did her own spinning was probably not only a matter of personal pleasure or sense of craft skill but a reflection of a religious attitude toward self-sufficiency and independence—an attitude not unique to Puritans but much prized by them.

The inquisition post mortem for Thomas[11a] conducted at the castle of Newcastle-upon-Tyne, 21 August 1632, declared that he

> was seised of the manors, townships and vills of Fawden, Dunington, East Burneton, West Burneton and Weytslade, a fourth part of the vill of West Bruneton, a moiety of the manor of Thronton, two husbandlands in Blackden and certain lands within the vill of Kinton. [These were in addition to estates in the Midlands. A "husbandland" usually referred to arable land

---

[18] See the document DG21/40 in the Hazlerigg Collection.
[19] John Crawford Hodgson, "On the Medieval and Later Owners of Eslington," *Archæologia Æliana*, 3rd series, volume 6 (Newcastle-upon-Tyne: Andrew Reid & Co., 1910), pages 1-33, at pages 21-22.

held by a tenant farm, as distinguished from the demense; the area was typically two bovates, an area tillable by two oxen.]

In consideration of a marriage to be had between Arthur Hessellrigg, then son and heir apparent of the said Thomas, and Frances Elmes, one of the daughters of Thomas Elmes of Greenes Norton, co. Northampton, esq., for 3,000£, marriage portion of Frances, by fine in Easter term 22 James I and by indenture to limit the uses of the fine dated 10th April, 1621, between the said Thomas Hessellrigg and the said Thomas Elmes, Arthur Hessellrigg and Frances Elmes, and Thomas Dacre, knight, and William Elmes, esq., Thomas [Hesilrige] conveyed the premises to Thomas Dacre and William Elmes in trust to the uses specified; as to the premises in Northumberland to his own use for life, and then to the said Arthur Hessellrigg, and his heirs male, and on failure of such issue to his [Thomas'] own right heirs.

By now well ensconced at Noseley and other manors of the Midlands, the family nonetheless could see no advantage in selling the Northumberland estates, for they were reasonably good income-bearing properties. As we will see later, Sir Arthur Hesilrige, 2nd Bt, displayed a number of features of the entrepreneurial spirit, of which in general subsequent commentators such as David Hume and Adam Smith were praise-singers. Of course, as with Thomas[11a], so with Arthur[12b], much of the household income came from practices of an older, *rentier* spirit. That remained the character of a gentry (agrarian) economy. However, entrepreneurial endeavors typified the large commercially oriented cities, which had ramifications for gentry families interested in improvements of agricultural production. Moreover, the endeavors importantly included investments in transport and trade. Arthur[12b], perhaps Thomas[11a] before him, assembled a small private fleet of merchant ships, from which he gained a substantial fortune.

Thomas[11a] was born into a Leicestershire political community that had changed a great deal from the fifteenth-century gentry community we visited in the previous chapter, partly via Acheson's study. One of the most important differences ramified from the fact that whereas then the gentry families were free of immediate overlordship, there being no seat of aristocracy within the county, and thus could more easily experiment with processes of self-governance, now in 1565 (approximate birth year of Thomas[11a]), as during the preceding one hundred years, Leicestershire was domain of the Hastings family. At first a baronial family seated in the county (since the 1460s), the Hastings were elevated in 1529 when the earldom of Huntingdon was resurrected for the seventh time, this time by Henry VIII, who granted the earldom to George, 3rd baron Hastings, as reward for military service. Thomas[11a] succeeded to the Hesilrige family's estates in 1600, and four years later Henry Hastings (1586-1643) succeeded his grandfather as 5th earl of Huntingdon. Thomas[11a] accepted the earl's tutelage, a prerequisite to advancement in Leicestershire's political offices. Thomas[11a] began promoting his son and heir, Donald[12a], in 1620, with the earl's approval. After Donald's[12a] death, c1623, it was second son Arthur's[12b] turn.

In the meantime, Thomas[11a] held a variety of shire positions, a few of them noted above (via Hodgson's account). In addition to serving as a commissioner on depopulation in Leicestershire in 1607 and then on the subsidy in 1608 and again in 1621-22 and 1624, he served as sheriff 1612-13 and as justice of the peace 1611 to 1626. Appointed by the earl of Huntingdon in 1616 to command the Leicestershire cavalry, he was promoted in 1618 to be one of the earl's deputy lieutenants of the shire. In 1614 he was returned for Leicestershire as member of parliament, no doubt with the earl's blessing. This, the second of the four parliaments of James I (the first having sat from 1604 to 1611), gained as sobriquet, "the Addled Parliament," because from at least one point of view it managed to accomplish nothing. The king dissolved it after two months. From another point of view, however, the Commons accomplished its duty to uphold its standing as protector of the people's interests, sending to the king the message that they would not vote for funding unless the king could show sufficient cause for it, whereas the funds he had sought were mostly for courtly extravagances. For more than a decade James ruled without calling a new parliament. When he did issue a call, in 1621, the result again was conflict over finances and parliamentary rights, and soon this third parliament was dissolved. The last of the parliaments of James I was called in 1624, and Thomas[11a] was again returned for Leicestershire. During this time Thomas[11a] settled most of his estate on Arthur[12b], moving his seat permanently from Noseley Hall back to the manor of Alderton, Northamptonshire, where he and Frances had begun married life. From 1628 until death he served as justice of the peace in Northamptonshire.

Surely he had wearied of the tumultuous days of parliamentary sessions and the attendant life of London. Those days were not his first extended experience with life in the big city; yet times were very different now, partly because his own situation was different. In 1584, after years at University College, Oxford, Thomas[11a] had been admitted to the Middle

Temple in London, one of the four Inns of Court, which at that time were the principal law schools of England.[20] He was still there in 1591, when his name entered into legal documents as "Thomas Haselrigge, Middle Temple, London, gent." Had he by that date become a barrister? Probably not. More likely he had apprenticed as a solicitor and then worked in that capacity for an established firm. In any case, the following year, 1592, he married Frances Gorges, heir of the manor of Alderton; and as her father, William Gorges, esq., who had been lord of the manor, died about the time of the marriage, Thomas[11a] assumed Alderton as his residence. We know that Thomas[11a] had gained attention of the royal court, perhaps via his Middle Temple associates or courtesy of the earl of Huntingdon, for it was at Alderton that he hosted first the queen and then the king. But there is no evidence that he sought employments in London after landing at Alderton.

The son of Mary, Queen of Scots, and Henry Stuart, duke of Albany, and grandson of Matthew Stuart, 4th earl of Lennox, and great grandson of Margaret Tudor, elder sister of Henry VIII, James had been Scotland's king for 36 years when queen Elizabeth died. The first several years of his reign, as James VI of Scotland, were as a boy king under regency. He had learned considerable skill in the exercise of power and intrigue and had developed his own personal thesis of "divine right of kings," which he set forth in a book published in Edinburgh in 1598, *The True Law of Free Monarchies; or, The Reciprocal and Mutual Duty Betwixt a Free King and His Natural Subjects*. Knowing that England's parliament had moved increasingly to a contractarian view of the relation of monarchy—that the tie, represented by and through parliament, was one of free contractual agreement—James was judicious in promoting his view that the relation was actually one of apostolic hierarchy. He also knew that more immediate practical matters needed attention, especially those of the royal purse. While in general a popular king in England, he clashed with parliament, soon and repeatedly, as parliament insisted on control of the purse and tax proposals. Embroiled as well in the religious controversies due to his background (the House of Lennox was leading champion of the Catholic cause in Scotland, although James himself had converted to Protestantism years before his accession to the English throne), James proved rather adept in maneuvering through the thickets, often ignoring parliament when it suited his interests. Like some of his predecessors, he recruited his own supporters by bestowing new honors on members of the landed gentry and aristocracy. Favors for favors.

---

[20] Middle Inn Hall, an elegant Elizabethan building, is now mostly barristers' chambers.

An exemplary case study of the king's skill in human management begins with complaints being voiced by Puritans as he was settling into the royal scene in London. Puritan members of the established church had been voicing objections to various features of the two official translations of the Christian Bible, one authorized by Henry VIII in 1535 (commonly known as "the Great Bible") and its successor since 1568, the Bishops' Bible. Some of their objections focused on specific passages which they argued were corruptions in one degree or another of the Greek original (in the New Testament) and the Hebrew or Aramaic (in the Old). They also disliked that an episcopal organization was assumed as incontrovertible necessity, allowing no alternatives. James saw an opportunity to defuse and coopt. Accordingly, he convened a conference at Hampton Court for the purpose of producing a new translation, involving the participation of all quarters of the established church, Puritan as well as those of the center. It was an enormous undertaking. It would have been that even without the controversies that had stimulated the convention. But now the task was to create a translation that would bind divisions by gaining agreement in the meanings of words and phrases that were written millennia ago in tongues and contexts hardly anyone in England understood. The venture consumed the better part of seven years, 1604-11, and the resulting product, known usually as the Authorized Version or as the King James Bible, was in many ways a remarkable success. James had insisted at the beginning that the matter of episcopacy would never be in doubt. Thus, Puritan members who agreed to participate would do so on that assumption. This had the effect of sorting between Puritan members in the beginning, those seen by James and the church hierarchy as "too radical" pushed away. The Puritan participants would thus be allowed free voice to negotiate compromises on issues of translation—a safe arrangement since they would never be even close to a majority of the conference membership. James' assumption that the radicals would be cast as renegades, as unreasonably severe, stubborn, unsportsman-like, was sufficiently proven as to buy respite for remaining years of his reign.[21]

Unfortunately, we have no direct evidence of how the Puritan Hesilriges perceived the workings of the conference or its outcome. One can imagine that Thomas[11a] saw increments of progress, a willingness to accommodate diversity of belief and practice. William Tyndale's work during the 1530s, resulting in the first English translation of books of the

---

[21] The story of the Hampton Court conference has been well-told by Nicolson in *God's Secretaries* (2003). See also Benson Bobrick, *Wide as the Waters* (New York: Simon and Schuster, 2001).

Bible and the one which Hampton Court eminences took as point of departure, rendered the Greek *ekklesia* as "congregation," not as "church," and that memory did not vanish. England's official church had never succeeded in regaining for London and the territory of Britain the monopoly over that rarest of goods, salvation, which the church of Rome had exercised over much of the world. Dissenters from the official church were no longer burned at the stake, as they had been under queen Mary. Not all Puritans were sanguine, but James' strategy had accomplished much of what he had wanted.

London's New Urban World
It has been estimated that on any ordinary day in 1600 London had about 140,000 inhabitants who were joined by another 100,000 people who had come for the day to work at various jobs; to bring vegetables, fish, animal carcasses, grains, wool, pelts and hides, wood, herbal agents, and various other commodities, to local markets and to wharves for transport beyond the Thames estuary; to study at a school; to petition the court; to serve a militia; even simply to behold a place so thick with human beings. Being so thick with people, it was also thick with pollution—poor sanitation left excrement in the streets to mingle with mounds of horse manure; soot from wood-burning fireplaces hung in the air before settling to ground, water, foodstuffs, clothes, and lungs. Infectious disease vectors thickened from this surfeit of networked nodes. Magnitudes led to interactions. Thus, for instance, thicker disease vectors resulted in more dead bodies to dispose as quickly as possible, which was not quickly at all when large outbreaks of death occurred (such as the plague outbreaks of 1623, 1625, 1630, 1636 and 1642).[22] The short taste of climate change known as the "little ice age" meant that Londoners could celebrate winter festival by skating the Thames, frozen solid by late January; but it also increased consumption of firewood, not only in longer winters but also in chilly summers.

This urban world was being built from, by, and for the expanding wealth and power of a mercantile class of long-distance traders, bankers, merchants, and counting houses. The expansion was horizontal—that is, geographic and territorial—as well as vertically organizational on the home front. New markets were being created in faraway places such as islands of the Caribbean and coastal areas of North America. London had gained practice in "planting," or the uses of a "plantation economy of

---

[22] Paul Slack, *The Impact of Plague in Tudor and Stuart England* (Oxford: Oxford University Press, 1991) and Leeds Barroll, *Politics, Plague and Shakespeare's Theatre* (Ithaca: Cornell University Press, 1995) are excellent sources.

markets," closer to home, on an island to the west of Britain. While "the Pale of Ireland" had begun as a residuum of Norman-Anglo lordship over the Celtic cultures of Ireland, by the late 1500s it served as an enclave of economic and political dominance of markets, especially insofar as those markets had interest in trade beyond the island. With the advent of a new politics under Henry VIII, joining offices of religion and offices of royal court under the English sovereign, religious issues permeated that enclave, soon remarking it as contested ground between the church of Roman Catholicism and the church of England. But maintenance of "the Pale" (see Exhibit 6.3) never lost its economic significance.

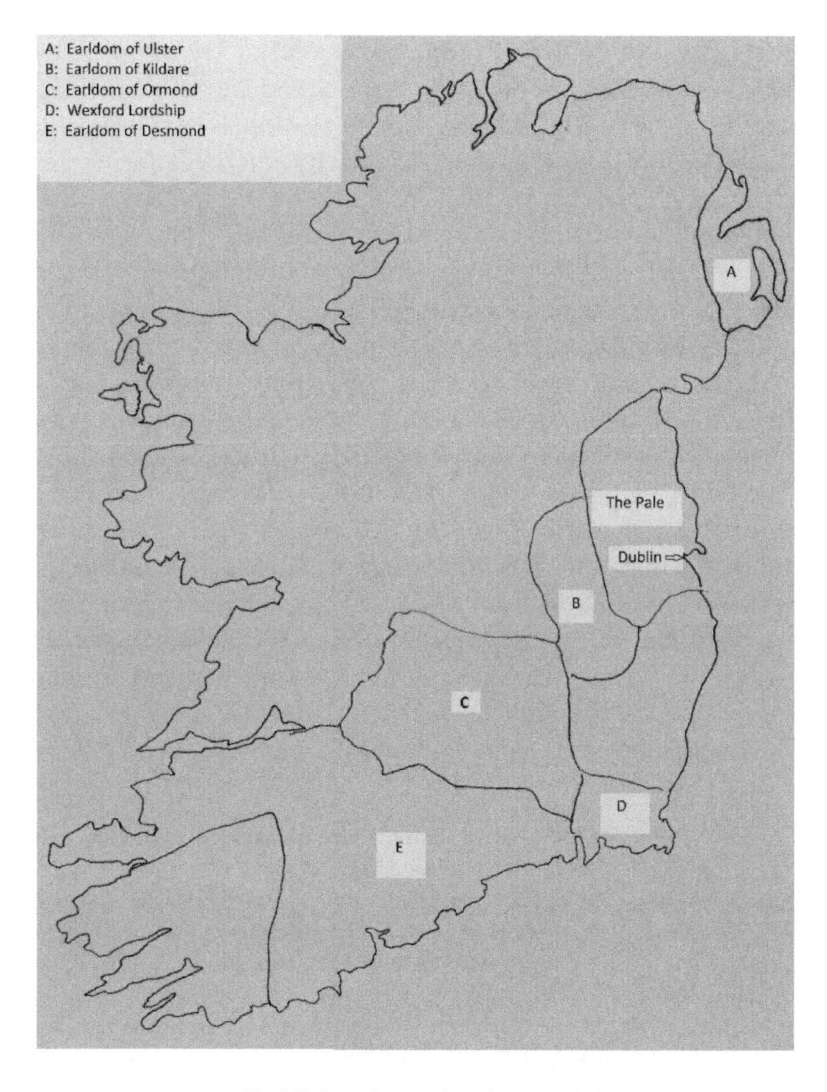

Exhibit 6.3. Ireland, c1450

The map in Exhibit 6.3 depicts both the Pale, focused on Dublin and its fine harbor, and four earldoms—Ulster, Kildare, Ormond, and Desmond—plus the lordship of Wexford, all of which held much of the best land of Ireland in the hands of English families.

The beginnings of Britain's far-flung empire were taking shape during the years of king James' reign. Several investors formed an ambitious private venture along the coast of North America, the Virginia Company of London. As mentioned earlier, at least one member of the Hesilrige family, Francis[11b], son of Edward[10b], was an early (1607) and repeating investor. The initial geographic claim of the company extended along the coast from some point south of the present state of North Carolina to the coast of the state of Maine. Soon the territory was divided into Northern Virginia and Southern Virginia. Part of Northern Virginia became New England, with migrations from Boston, Lincolnshire, to an area that included the future Boston, Massachusetts. So far as can be determined, Francis[11b] never visited the new rough territory, north or south. His cousin Sir Arthur[12b] would later make plans, never executed, to migrate to a colony he and fellow Puritans had staked out in New England (Saybrooke). There is some evidence that Sir Arthur[12b] developed interests in the Providence Island Company as well, perhaps also in the Somers Isles Company, and, judging from a letter by Roger Williams, at least tangentially in the Rhode-Island colony.[23] As stated above, Sir Arthur[12b] maintained a small merchant fleet, engaged in long-distance transport (possibly including the slave trade). His brother Thomas[12f], a mercer by trade in the cordwainer ward of the City of London, assisted Sir Arthur[12b] by maintaining the books.[24] It is clear from the entry for Thomas[12f] in the 1633-34 visitation of London (see Exhibit 6.4) that he felt fraternal loyalty and pride toward his oldest surviving brother. We do not know where Arthur[12b] was living at that time; he does not have independent presence in the visitation record.[25] Probably he was maintaining principal residence at Noseley, but with periodic visits in London, perhaps staying with his

---

[23] These "colonial" ventures will be discussed in the next chapter, in connection with the interest in migration, briefly considered during the mid-1630s.

[24] While previously designating mainly a merchant in luxurious fabrics, by this time the word "mercer" referred to a merchant of any number of different goods. Cordwainer ward got its name from the presence of many shoemakers, a most profitable of trades, but by now (1630s) various merchants and craftsmen were present.

[25] The contents of Exhibit 6.4 are from Henry St George and Richard St George, *The Visitations of London, 1633, 1634, and 1635*, 2 volumes (London: Publications of the Harleian Society, 1880), volume 1, page 380. The alphabetical notations within the shield and crest denote colors (e.g., A = argent, g = gules) and profile.

brother, for purposes of the shipping business. Given that Frances, his first wife and mother of his son and heir, had recently died (1632), he might have been spending time also at Brooke House in Holborn (about 2.5 miles northwest of cordwainer ward), the London residence of his future brother-in-law Robert Greville, 2nd baron of Beauchamps Court.

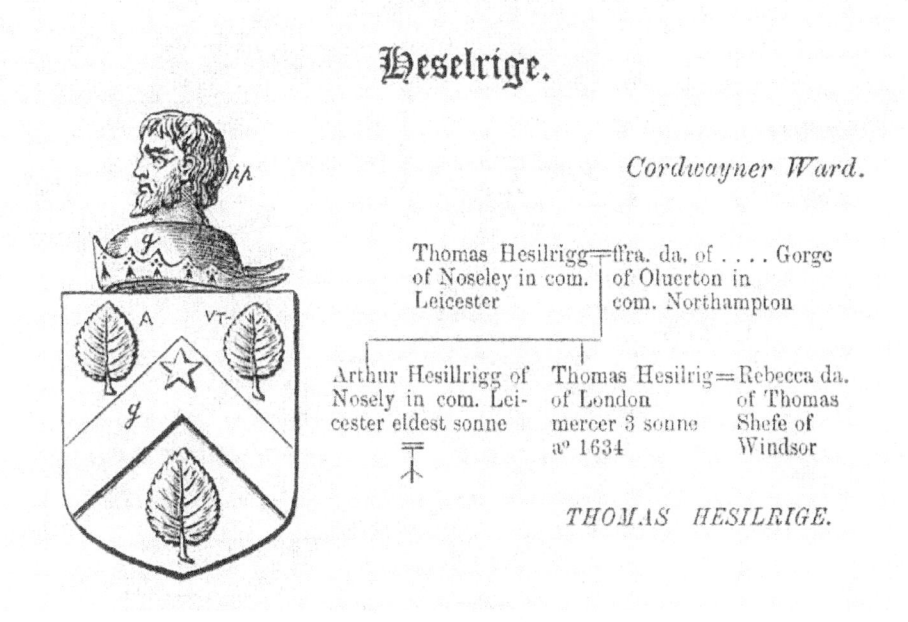

Exhibit 6.4. Record of Thomas Hesilrige, London, 1634

The several topics of mercantilism, colonialism, and emigration will be considered again in this and in later chapters. For the moment, it is time to change generation—most particularly, from Thomas[11a] to his son and heir Arthur[12b] and from king James to his son and heir king Charles. They surely could not have known when their respective fathers died that their destinies would be so intertwined.

Arthur, the 2nd Bt, and King Charles I

To repeat some biographic data already noted, Arthur[12b] Hesilrige was born during the first year of the seventeenth century. He died before his sixtieth birthday anniversary, in the damp cold of the Tower of London. Between those dates he lived a most eventful life. More of his personal private life will be addressed in chapter 8. Here and in the next chapter the main focus is on his public life. Second-born son (and third- or fourth-born child), his horizon was limited by the rule of primogeniture until he was in his early twenties, when his older brother Donald[12a] died. Prior to that date in September 1623, Arthur[12b] had matriculated first at the Royal College of St Peter in Westminster (commonly known as Westminster School) and then at Cambridge University's Magdalene College, Easter term 1617.[26] We do not know his plans or intents. Perhaps in anticipation of his brother's death, he pursued legal training, with admission to Gray's Inn, one of London's four main Inns of Court 29 January 1623. As we have seen, knowledge and skills of the law of the land had become vital to continued success in managing the patrimony of a landed estate in England. While the employment of lawyers for transactions had been established practice for some time, abilities of self-reliance offered prudential surety in any family, and for a family of Puritan inclination they were well-nigh essential goods, highly prized.[27] One also became skilled in the arts of debate, a skill very useful for presence in a parliament.

In 1624 Arthur[12b] married Frances, daughter of Thomas Elmes and Christiana (*nee* Hickling) of Greens Norton, Northamptonshire.[28] One of Frances' elder sisters, Martha, married (1609) Sir Thomas Dacre, knight (1587-1668), of Hertfordshire, who, along with Sir John Boteler, was elected a member of parliament for Hertfordshire in 1626 and again in 1641, and a strong supporter of the parliamentary side during the civil wars. No doubt he and Arthur[12b] shared sympathies and interests during Dacre's years in the 1626 parliament, which king Charles dissolved in 1629 after mounting frustrations with his opponents (about which, more below).

Frances bore Arthur[12b] four children, only one of whom, the first, Thomas[13a], survived. The three others presumably died at very young ages (we do not know even their forenames, if any they were given). Noseley chapel, being a private or extra-liberty chapel (i.e., outside the established church), and its incumbents being Puritan, did not participate in the official parish-registry system. Frances died in 1632. Two years later Arthur[12b]

---

[26] Magdalene, pronounced Maud'-lin, is after the Biblical character, Mary Magdalene.
[27] There have been many brief accounts of the 2nd Bt, almost all of them in terms of the civil wars. Over time they have become more measured and more detailed, though still often written from a monarchist point of view. Charles H Firth's biography of the 2nd Bt for the 1885-1900 edition of the *Dictionary of National Biography* conveys both the more detailed and measured, yet monarchist flavor of, account. Barry Denton's *Only in Heaven* (Sheffield: Sheffield Academic Press, 1997), is a valiant effort to write a book-length biography on the basis of such a sparse record. Denton's title comes from the 2nd Bt's favorite advice, "Hope only in heaven."
[28] Some accounts make Thomas Elmes of Lilford, Northamptonshire, but that is a later branch of the Elmes family.

married secondly Dorothea (or Dorothy), daughter of Fulke Greville and Mary Margaret (*nee* Copley), and sister to Robert Greville, 2nd baron Brooke of Beauchamps Court. In the meantime, Arthur[12b] had succeeded to his father's estate and dignity as 2nd baronet, remaining at Noseley as his seat. By this time (1630) he had also gained interests in mercantile trade, maintaining a fleet of ships (perhaps inherited from his father), and was pursuing activities that brought him into association with other men engaged in mercantile trade and shipping. Now with his marital tie to lord Brooke, he was embedded even more into a network of families with dissenting or Puritan background and strong support for the claims of parliament to be at least co-equal, if not superior, institution of governance with the monarch. This network included the Rich family of Essex (e.g., Sir Nathaniel Rich) and Warwick (Robert Rich, 2nd earl Warwick), the Fiennes family of Warwickshire (William Fiennes, 8th baron and 1st viscount Saye and Sele), and the Knightley family of Northamptonshire, among others, some of whom (e.g., Nathaniel Rich) had interests in the colonization projects of the New World.

Exhibit 6.5. Sir Arthur Hesirige, 2nd Baronet

Arthur[12b] began moving into the leadership of Leicestershire soon after the death of his older brother. In 1624, for instance, with the backing of Henry Hastings, 5th earl of Huntingdon, he was made captain of horse in the Leicestershire Trained Bands (county militia). Soon thereafter—the timing and circumstances are murky—he incurred the earl's displeasure, and when in 1625 he stood for election to parliament he found opposition by the earl's brother, Sir George Hastings, insurmountable. One suspects that his future reputation for rash behavior was on display. In any case, the earl's displeasure quickly expired, and Arthur[12b] resumed a promising course. During this time he learned by family lesson something of the cost of defending both patrimony and the interests of parliamentary authority. In 1621 and again in 1627 his father rejected what he and many others saw as unlawful imposition of taxes, taxes not authorized by parliamentary act, under the guise of loans from the county. Huntingdon, also of Puritan persuasion, carefully advised effective responses to the imposition so as to minimize penalties. But short of capitulation, costs could not always be avoided.

Some parallels between father-and-son pairs are worth noting. As previously mentioned, James I was reasonably adept in the appearance of flexibility and compromise. The imposition of "county loans" in 1621 was by his authority, and although rarely if ever welcomed its reception was still mostly cautious protest within the bounds of civil practice. His son and heir, Charles I, lacked the same abilities of finesse. Where sire did believe in divinity of kingship but promoted that belief with pragmatic caution, scion usually acted as if his rule, because by divine right, must never be questioned. A similar generational contrast is evident between Thomas[11a] and Arthur[12b] Hesilrige, the father more cautious and pragmatic in pursuit of goals, the son quicker to anger, take offense, reply impulsively to perceived threat. Born within a year of one another, neither son stood as heir until past childhood: Charles was 12 when his older brother, prince Henry, died of typhoid; Arthur[12a] was a decade older when his brother died. Charles was 25 at accession; Arthur[12b], 29 when he succeeded his father in 1630. Both men were reportedly of short height. Charles had been a weak child, perhaps had suffered rickets, and sought to hide his underdeveloped legs. From all accounts, Arthur[12b] had been a robust child; but he might have been sensitive about height, perhaps finding an "equalization" in his horse, especially on the battle field.

Even though these comparisons involve contiguous generations, father to son, much was changing during the time from father's thirtieth birthday anniversary and son's thirtieth year. The pace of change had been accelerating, and that trend had only begun. As observers, our view is still of the era of mercantilism, not yet of the era of modern capitalism; but we are catching glimpses of what would be important elements of the later era.

For instance, while land and what can be extracted from it are still the basis of wealth, fortunes are being made through trade, through buying and selling goods (and services, such as legal skill) that were produced perhaps far away and may have already passed through other intermediary hands. Accordingly, markets have expanded in depth, in reach, and in complexity of relations, putting ever greater emphasis on media of exchange (money, contracts, etc.) that are standardized, enforceable anywhere, articulating actors unknown to each other, in distant transactions of mutual trust. Localism is weakening rapidly, as locality becomes mainly a node in a larger and larger network of trading points. Accordingly, the sense of individuality is changing: individual identity is no longer tied to a concrete place (e.g., a manor and its villages, or a market town and its local hierarchy of people, or to a parish and its vicar or rector or relation to a single, uniform ecclesiastical hierarchy—or even to a tradition of family and its standing in the local hierarchy of aristocracy, gentry, and so forth. A new individualism, one that enfolded individual identity into a comfort of dependency on relations among anonymous actors while maintaining a strong sense of personal security and capability, is coming together within a new economics, a new politics, and a new religiosity. What could be called "the contents of mind" are changing accordingly. Literacy, both depending on and furthered by the printing press, is spreading to all walks of life, both male and female, and new forms of reading, new forms of literature, are developing. A rationalization of spiritual and intellectual as well as material life is underway, seeds of which had been sprouting even before the advent of Calvinist and related ideas. A new, experimentalist science is taking root, already bringing into question traditional ideas about the hierarchical organization of authority. Its main advertisement says that anyone with means of experimentation can test claims of truth and arrive at judgments based on those tests, without asking permission from another.

At the same time that new fortunes were being made—fortunes now sometimes identified with a particular individual first and foremost, secondarily perhaps with a family—inequality was increasing, and it was nowhere more conspicuous than under the magnifying glass of London. During the early 1600s an annual income of £75 was unusually good even for London. But for a small number of men in London that was a pittance, sometimes acquired within the course of a day. Some of these men could be seen profiting from public office. There was another crucial difference at work: such inequality, and the corrupt means by which it sometimes began and/or grew, had a new audience, not rural peasants who had mostly accepted inequality between lord and villein but urban workers (many of them born to rural peasantry), whose literacy was improving, whose social networks were thickening much more easily in the density of London, and whose consciousness of fair play had been ripening in the fervor of protesting sectarian groups—Presbyterians, congregationalists of various stripe, including Puritan—groups who spoke both for individual liberty of conscience and for equal standing in law and justice. It was no secret that in place of the surplus that Elizabeth I had left behind in the national treasury, James I had, in a few short years, amassed a royal deficit of £600,000, a princely sum in any capital city. This stark fact, along with the culture that had grown up around the court of James and his ample favors of access and wealth to those who gave him loyalty, provided much material for the biting account of circuits of credit and debt, honor and dishonor, written by Shakespeare c1608 in *Timon of Athens*. The same stark fact provided a new backdrop to appeals for funding from the royal court of James' heir, Charles I. Seemingly the same fact: but so much else had changed that it had a much different significance when uttered by Charles.

Soon after accession the new king realized he needed more funds by which to press his case in the Thirty Years War. Actually a series of wars, all on the continent (and hugely destructive), it began as a chiefly "religious war" between predominantly Protestant and predominantly Catholic countries but soon became a war of the Hapsburg empire and its enemies. Few in England beyond the royal house had much interest in it, a fact which Charles knew but considered irrelevant. Already in 1625 we see the first display of his conviction that, ruling by divine right, his call must be obeyed, and his parliament sits only at his pleasure. Parliament did not heed his call for more money. He then followed his father's practice and obtained what came to be known as "forced loans"—for all practical purposes, taxations without parliamentary agreement—and he dissolved this parliament (which thereafter was known by the label he and his courtiers affixed, "the Useless Parliament").

The initial loans were mostly arranged with wealthy men who saw opportunity to ingratiate and/or who believed prudence dictated complicity at least in the short run. Finding these sources insufficient, Charles called a new parliament (the Second Parliament of Charles I) in 1626. This time he demanded in effect the right of direct taxation. Parliament refused. He proceeded anyway, expanding the use of forced loans. As many of his subjects refused to pay, the king's policy shifted to intimidation through arrests of those who disobeyed their king's order, with some of those who were arrested imprisoned for short periods. Arthur[12b] Hesilrige was one of the offenders, imprisoned briefly in the Tower of London.

Having dissolved his second parliament but realizing his new tactic had been gaining too little in extra funding, he called his third parliament in 1628. By now, popular anger against the king had swelled enough to embolden this parliament to take action against what many of its members perceived to be offences by the crown: illegal revenue, forced billeting of soldiers in private homes, illegal imprisonment, and the king's declaration of martial law without agreement by parliament. This began a movement to reaffirm a document agreed by king and a council of barons on the plains of Runnymede more than four hundred years earlier, the Magna Carta, many principles of which were being violated by Charles. The result was a Petition of Right, led by Sir Edward Coke and passed by the houses of parliament 7 June 1628, and finally accepted by the king (though he later ignored it).[29] Strong echoes of the Petition of Right can be read in the Bill of Rights of the Constitution of the United States of America.

All of the foregoing amounted to a conflictual preamble to the eventual arrival of Sir Arthur[12b] Hesilrige to a seat in parliament (1640). King Charles, sorely frustrated, dissolved his Third Parliament in 1629 and declared Personal Rule. By the time Arthur[12b] had won his seat in what quickly became known as the Short Parliament, Charles had eroded his standing with parliamentary interests to such an extent that he would have needed extraordinary sociopolitical skills to recover. And those he lacked.

Monarchs had long since been "trained" to the notion that the sun rose and set to royal schedule. After all, official business, and therefore much besides, was designated primarily by year of the sitting monarch's reign—for instance, 13 Henry VIII, 9 Charles ("the First" was then superfluous as there had been no other Charles, king of England)—then secondarily by the quarter of the religious-legal calendar (which began with Easter, then Trinity, Michaelmas, and Hilary).[30] For many years barons had been increasingly successful in modifying monarchy into an evolving oligarchy, the monarch being assigned liberal status as "first among equals," and some monarchs had learned to adapt, adjust, and maintain regal standing with shared authority. Some of them had learned reluctantly, even grudgingly, and unevenly the necessary political lessons

---

[29] Coke's sister Winifred, it may be recalled, married a great grandson of Richard and Ruth[7e] (*nee* Hesilrige) Neele.

[30] That is, until courts re-arranged the order to fit the calendar of the legal academy (i.e., Michaelmas, Hilary, Easter, and Trinity), although even so the terms were still regulated by counts of Sundays relative to the feast day of St Hilary.

appropriate to time and circumstance (e.g., Henry VIII). Others had learned adeptly, with cunning, even creating new lessons for others (e.g., Elizabeth I). Still others learned but applied the lessons less skillfully (e.g., James I vis-à-vis Elizabeth I). Charles I learned far too little to be able to survive tests that several of his recent predecessors would surely have finessed quite handily.

Arthur[12b], too, needed instruction, as we have already seen, lessons especially in how best to harness his passionate interests. One teacher who had offered some stiff instruction well before Arthur[12b] gained his seat in Commons was Henry Hastings, 5th earl of Huntingdon. A leader of the Puritan cause but with moderation (e.g., he was a supporter of theatrical arts, anathema to some Puritans), Huntingdon, although only sixteen years older than Arthur[12b], seemingly acted as something of a stern uncle, a role that might have been reinforced shortly after Thomas[11a] died, when his aunt Catherine Hastings married Sir Walter Chetwynd of Ingestre, whose first son by his first wife (Mary, daughter of John Mullins, archdeacon of London) was Sir Walter Chetwynd of Grendon, Warwickshire, who in 1632 wed Arthur's[12b] cousin Frances[12b], daughter of Edward[11a] Hesilrige of Arthingworth, Northamptonshire. Unlike Charles I, who labored under the disadvantage of being a king who believes he has no bounds other than those given as divine right, Arthur[12b] labored under, sometimes against, the bounds of a community of like-minded men and women who both urged individual liberty and levied sometimes harsh penalties against lapses from godliness. The community of Puritans had been growing in size, but it remained in most areas a tightly interdependent network of friends and relatives which itself entailed constraint as well as enablement.

Escape to the New World?
During the eleven years of "Personal Rule" by Charles I, conditions for that community of Puritans, and other Dissenters, were neither satisfying in the moment nor propitious of future times. The king's churchly offices continued to repress, oppress, and persecute, all in the name of religious duty and obedience to the crown. For its part, offices of the crown also continued to repress, oppress, and persecute, all in the name of divine right and the need for funds. Not surprisingly, given events on the other side of the Atlantic Ocean, some people spied what they imagined to be improved prospects only a (dangerous) ship ride away. For one brief period perhaps Sir Arthur[12b] Hesilrige was among them. This we will consider in the present section. Because his name will appear so often in this and in the

next section, a convenience of referring to him as "AH" will be used, in order to reduce redundancy and to conserve space.

The actions of men whom Games called "English cosmopolitans" –adventurers, merchants, soldiers, and of course "renegade clerics" and their followers—demonstrated that their world of the seventeenth century was shrinking along and across the Atlantic Ocean, and in the process they were also showing others how to adapt to different environments, in part so as to adapt those environments to English ways.[31] The process had begun during the prior century, although not successfully for England. It was the Virginia Company of London, a joint-stock adventure in which Francis[11b] Hesilrige was early investor, that put the first permanent English stamp on the North American continent. Francis[11b] was probably the first member of the family to be involved in that nascent "web of empire," although he himself very likely never set foot on the continent. Soon after 1607 and James' Fort (later, Jamestown), however, the pace of British settlement accelerated, spurred by stories not of El Dorado or cities of gold but of Biblical cities on a hill.

Puritans and members of other dissenting, nonconformist groups were prominent among the movements to establish plantations, "godly communities," in the New World, either as investors who provided the initial funds or as emigrants or as both. The colony at Jamestown, which began as a more general venture, had been a marginal effort often on the verge of collapse. By 1624 it had become more secure in demographic development. But in that year the private company's charter was revoked by James I, who assumed the settlement as a crown colony. That could have ended any attraction Jamestown might have had for Puritans and kindred men and women, except that as of the mid-1620s they were mostly still ambitious of reforming the established church from within. However, the ambition soon changed, once the court of Charles I and the church of archbishop William Laud moved with persecutory intent and action against dissent and nonconformity.

Already by 1620, of course, Plymouth Colony was established far to the north of Jamestown, as a ship, the Mayflower, sought refuge from storms in an arm-crook of land later named Provincetown Harbor. Once the storms subsided, the ship made permanent landfall across the large bay, at a place named after the ship's port, Plymouth, Devon. Of the ship's 101 passengers, 41 were fleeing religious persecution. They called themselves "Saints" and the 60 other passengers—adventurers, tradesmen, servants— "Strangers." This colony succeeded quite well, but it would be another ten

---

[31] Alison Games, *The Web of Empires* (Oxford: Oxford University Press, 2008).

years before it gained a neighbor in the Massachusetts Bay Colony, to the west. There is no indication that AH had direct involvement in either of these plantations, though he surely noted their existence and progress.

One of AH's relatives—whether either was aware of the kinship is not known—did have direct involvement, however. About nine years after the founding of the Massachusetts Bay Colony, Percival Lowell, whose fifth-great-grandparents were Raffe Lowle and a Hesilrige daughter (as discussed previously), uprooted his household and their prosperous merchandising firm in Somerset and migrated to Newbury, Massachusetts.[32] This event, along with the migration of Thomas Hesilrige to Virginia during the 1630s, are exemplary cases of early emigration to British North America by members of the Hesilrige family. A bit farther afield in marital linkages is another case, Thomas Dudley. Born 12 October 1576 in Yardley Hastings, a small village near Northampton, he became a clerk to Sir Augustine Nicholls, a justice of the court of common pleas and a kinsman of his mother. (The exact kinship is unknown; they might have been siblings.) Nicholls was a son of Thomas Nicholls of Pitchley, Northamptonshire, whose daughter Anne married, about 1563, Edward[10b] Hesilrige of Theddingworth, Leicestershire. Dudley soon became a principal in the founding of the Massachusetts Bay Colony and in 1630 migrated to that colony, which he served in various capacities including the governorship. He married Anne Bradstreet, often remembered as the first poet of British North America. He died 31 July 1653 in Roxbury, Massachusetts.[33]

Of course, Puritans were hardly the only investors or settlers in the distant colonies, and here as in other realms of activity a given family could find itself divided by religious preferences. One case in point is the Gorges family. AH's mother, recall, was Frances Gorges. Her great grandfather was Sir Edward Gorges of Wraxall, Wiltshire (via his second wife). One of his second-great-grandsons, via his first wife, was Sir Fernando Gorges, knight (b. c1565, d. 1647), who led an interesting life in one part of which he was granted the province of Maine in British North America. As the editor of the journal of John Winthrop, Jr, observed, "in 1639 Gorges was confirmed as lord-palatine of Maine, and taking the royal side, vexed to

---

[32] The locution "fifth-great-grandparents" (and similar others) is abbreviation of the otherwise long string, "great-great-great-great-great-grandparents."

[33] Among the several sources, see William Richard Cutter, *Genealogical and Family History of New York*, volume 1 (New York: Lewis Historical Publishing Co., 1910), page 226.

his life's end his Puritan neighbors."[34] From all accounts he never left England. AH almost surely knew of (perhaps knew) Sir Fernando. Did he know of the kinship through his mother?

AH probably had no investment in either the Maine adventure or one of the Massachusetts colonies, and he surely had not thought of migrating to any of them. Both conditions—the investment and the thought of migration—would soon change, however, the target being a colony at the south end of the Connecticut river, known as Saybrooke. Before turning to that adventure, another consideration of the situation in New England must be made, for it might shed a glimmer of light on his attitude toward the colonial experience at a later date.

The Massachusetts Bay Colony proved to be internally contentious on a number of issues, mainly having to do with issues of what should count as "godly" (or as each contestant was prone to see it, what counted as "godly" in God's eyes—which of course any given contestant was unusually privileged to know). One result was a strong tendency to fissiparity. Roger Williams, for example, fled Massachusetts, to found Providence Plantation in 1636 in the Narragansett Bay. Anne Hutchinson was banished a year later. In wake of the latter event, William Coddington freely left and began a settlement on Rhode Island. In 1643 Roger Williams went to London in order to gain a new charter, one that would sanction unification of four settlements on Narragansett Bay, including his and Coddington's. Apparently he had not consulted other members of these communities, much less obtained their approval, but he nonetheless secured the charter. Coddington and others ignored it until matters became difficult, at which time Coddington went to London to gain relief. Henry Vane, who had lived in the Massachusetts Bay Colony before returning permanently to England, and thus knew from first-hand experience the rancor of religious politics in the colonies, had been a supporter of Williams but now agreed in the decision of England's Council of State to annul the Williams charter and grant Coddington a commission to break free of the union. No sooner had Coddington returned to reclaim the independence of his colony than Roger Williams and two of his supporters, Dr John Clarke and William Dyer, scooted to London, accused Coddington of having aided the Dutch, and won revocation of his commission (after which Coddington retired from public life for several years). What is here

---

[34] John Winthrop, Jr, *Winthrop's Journal: "History of New England,"* edited by James Kendall Hosmer (New York: Charles Scribner's Sons, 1908), volume 1, page 29n. To be "lord palatine" meant that within his realm Gorges could exercise certain powers on behalf of the king.

of particular interest in this contest is a letter that Roger Williams wrote to his fellow colonists while he was still in London, not yet successful in his endeavor. The following excerpt of the letter (dated 1 April 1653) contains Williams' main point in writing.[35]

> I hope it may have pleased the most high Lord of son [sun] and land to bring Capt. Ch-rst-n's [Christian's] ship and dear Mr Dyre [William Dyer] unto you, and with him the counsels letters [Council of State letters], which answer the petition Sir Henry Vane and myself drew up [presumably the petition of 1643], and the council by Sir Henry's mediation granted us, for the confirmation of the charter, until the determination of the controversy. This determination you may please to understand is hindered by two main obstructions. The first is the might war with the Dutch, which makes England and Holland and the nations tremble: This hath made the parliament sit Sir Henry Vane and two or three more as commissioners to manage the war, which they have done [etc., etc.]. Our second obstruction is the opposition of our adversaries, Sir Arther [sic] Haselrig and Colonel Fenwicke, who hath married his daughter; Mr Winslow and Mr Hopkins, both in great place; and all the friends they can make in the parliament and council and all the priests both Presbyterian and independent; so that we stand as two armies ready to engage, observing the motions and postures each of other, and yet shy each of other.

Why was AH an adversary? If there were a Puritan leader of any of the colonies whose basic views were more aligned with AH's great emphasis on individual liberty than were the views of Roger Williams, his existence has been lost to history. Just as AH's views were often dismissed as rash, impractical, too radical, and the like, so, too, were the views of Williams. It was in his colonies that laws were passed to abolish imprisonment for debts, trials for witchcraft, capital punishment (with a few exceptions), and chattel slavery (of Africans as well as others). It was Williams who had insisted on purchasing land from the native inhabitants ("Indians") rather

---

[35] The date suggests an "April Fools" joke, and that custom in England was popular (at least since Chaucer's *Canterbury Tales*). But Williams' letter was entirely serious in intent and execution. It was reprinted as "Memoirs of Rhode Island, 1653" on 22 May 1833 in the *Rhode-Island Republican*, a Newport weekly that became *The Rhode Islander*.

than taking it by force. And it was Williams who had stressed that the state may regulate only relations between members of a political community, to the exclusion of relations between any individual person and God, which exclusion, he insisted, meant that the first four of the ten Mosaic laws or commandments lay beyond the jurisdiction of any government, civil or religious. Likewise, Williams rejected "forced worship." As Gardiner saw the matter, "If the full doctrine of liberty was a natural result of extreme exclusiveness and singularity, where was it more likely to be found than in the mouth of Roger Williams?"[36]

Again the question, Why was AH considered by Williams to be his adversary? The answer, very likely, is that Williams' positions on some issues were a step, or two or three, too far for AH. Gardiner underscored the basic evaluation, when he said that "Between all these seekers after liberty there were points of contact, but there were also points of variance." Another relevant observation by Gardiner contains a sting of irony, though he did not draw it to attention: "doctrines which exalted human reason above faith and revelation" were both a threat to the latter and, by the same token, a vulnerability of the former by which accusation and conviction of being insufficiently godly loomed ever ready.[37] In Williams' mind, all of his positions were staunch by faith and revelation. His critics, AH among them no doubt, were also quick to invoke faith, if not always revelation, but their criticisms stemmed in large measure from reasoning that no civil community would hold fast in itself *as* a community when individual liberty was taken too far. It was the same sort of inconsistency at the boundary between faith and reason that led believers in predestination to seek reasoned confirmation, to still their nagging pangs of doubt, that they were indeed among the elect. All too often faith was not sufficient; yet reason could easily come unbound, to the detriment of faith. Liberty of conscience could lead to dangerous loosening of "proper bounds," could it not? But where lie those "proper bounds"? Where exactly is the line of liberty "too far"? Who is to say? And for whom?

The foregoing answer to the question of Williams' perception of AH is very general, of course, and it could well neglect pertinent particular

---

[36] Samuel R Gardiner, *History of the Great Civil War, 1642-1649*, new edition, 4 volumes (London: Longmans, Green, 1894), volume 1, page 287.

[37] Gardiner, *Civil War ...* (1894), volume 1, pages 289, 284. It is worth adding that soon after Williams' book, *The Bloody Tenant [Tenet] of Persecution for Cause of Conscience* was published in 1644, parliament, now largely controlled by anti-Laudian members, ordered the burning of all copies, on grounds that it was too radical and, in effect, anarchistic. Edward Underhill, in his introduction to the 1848 edition, said that Williams' position was "too unlimited" even for the Independents (page xxxv).

factors of which we have no direct evidence in the relationship. We do know, for instance, that both men could be very judgmental and unyielding, and that AH at least could be quick to take personal offense. Perhaps this sort of personal factor was present, honing more general disagreements (these latter, after all, would have pertained to other members of the Council of State, though Williams did allow that others might hold the same obstructionist views). But to repeat the general element of the answer as it pertains to AH, we have probably seen evidence of limits to his championship of individual liberty. Other limits will become apparent as we move along.

Now to the Saybrooke venture. The collection of Puritans who had centered on the Fawsley manor of the Knightley family for some of their meetings included Robert Rich, 2nd earl of Warwick, William Fiennes, 8th baron Saye and Sele (succeeded 1616) and created the 1st viscount Saye and Sele in 1624, Robert Greville, 2nd baron Brooke, Greville's father-in-law, Francis Russell, 4th earl of Bedford, Oliver St John, John Pym, Sir Richard Saltonstall and Richard Knightley.[38] All were by the late 1620s becoming involved as investors in North American settlements. By 1633 they gained a patent to establish a colony in Connecticut, at the estuary of the Connecticut river into Long Island Sound. John Winthrop, junior, was appointed to lead an expedition, with a commission signed on behalf of all of the company shareholders by AH and George Fenwick, who were charged with administering from London first stages of the venture. From 1635 Fenwick served as agent for the patentees, and then governor of a fort that was constructed near the coastline. In 1639 he and his wife settled at Saybrooke (as previously mentioned). After his wife died, and in the midst of quarrels with other colonies, Fenwick returned to London, where he again joined forces with AH.[39]

Fenwick was not the only investor to contemplate emigration to Saybrooke. Conditions at home had steadily deteriorated for Puritans and other Dissenters, because of Laud's efforts to force everyone to conform to "his" church. At the same time, the king's policies on a variety of issues in addition to religious conformity had been biting deeper. The issue of ship money grew more contentious. A decision by a corrupted judiciary

---

[38] Hexter referred to this group as the "Bedford Western Gentry connection," seeing the earl of Bedford (Russell) as leader of the whole. Jack H Hexter, *The Reign of King Pym* (Cambridge: Harvard University Press, 1941), page 78.
[39] *Winthrop's Journal* (1908), volume 1, page 308; also Denton, *Only in Heaven* (1997), page 28. The settlement survived. Today the site is Old Saybrook, one borough of which is named Fenwick.

in November 1638 added to the contest by fueling the flames of divine right: the king was held to be above all human law; if he said "danger," there must be danger; his ship levy was perfectly correct because he said it was correct.[40]

Already in 1637 viscount Saye and Sele had provoked a fight when he refused to pay the ship money; but the king's men chose to attack men of lower rank instead (e.g., John Hampden). Others followed suit. Indeed, that contest had been going on for some time, with many men refusing to countenance such policies as "forced loans" as early as the mid-1620s (e.g., the earl of Warwick, Robert Rich). By the mid-1630s AH was in the thick of it, though not always with the same wily finesse that Rich, Fiennes, and others brought to the contests. An episode recited by Denton illustrates the point:

> Sir Arthur Haslerig and Sir William Faunt having been sent for on a complaint made by the Earl of Huntingdon Lord Lieutenant of co. Leicestershire, that they refused to pay the levies made for the Muster-Master, on the 23rd inst. [23 November 1632], made their appearance and the same time were present Sir Henry Skipwith and Sir John Skeffington, two of the Deputy Lieutenants of that county. When the case had been heard and an order made to refer the examination thereof to a committee, Sir Arthur urged these words to Sir John Skeffington: "If such gentlemen as you shall be suffered to shark the country of their money, it will be a very pretty thing." When Sir John complained to the Lords, Sir Arthur replied softly, "I do not say to the Lords, but only to you in private." Sir Arthur was thereupon committed, but returning into the chamber on his knees he humbly craved pardon.[41]

The year 1635 was particularly troublesome for AH, as he was in one contest after another with the Court of the High Commission and on one occasion was briefly imprisoned.[42] Having refused opportunities of

---

[40] See the discussion in Geoffrey Robertson's *The Tyrannicide Brief* (New York: Pantheon, 2005), pages 48-49.

[41] *Only in Heaven* (1997), pages 26-27. This John Skeffington, by the way, was likely of the same family as the Thomas Skeffington whom Rachel[7b] Hesilrige married c1535.

[42] Hugh R Engstrom, Jr, "Sir Arthur Hesilrige and the Saybrook Colony," *Albion*, volume 5 (Autumn 1973), pages 157-168, at page 164; Denton, *Only in Heaven* (1997), pages 28-29. The Court of the High Commission was an ecclesiastical commission that

knighthood, he was repeatedly subject to fine. By 1637, according to one story that gained wide circulation and repetition over time, he not only contemplated emigration; he went so far as to begin negotiations to buy the house of the one of the founders of the Massachusetts colony, John Endicott, but then changed his mind on realizing that the house was very heavily mortgaged. According to the most common version of the story, AH was one of several who attempted to leave but, as Cotton Mather later reported in his *Magnalia* (1st edition, 1702, page 23), were "forcibly detained" before their ships could leave the Thames estuary. Adding to the credibility, Oliver Cromwell was quoted as having said in 1641 that had a certain bill (the "Grand Remonstrance"; see below) not passed in parliament, "he would have sold all that he had the next morning and never have seen England more."[43]

The supposed embarkation occurred in 1637. This date fits nicely with the fact that a royal proclamation dated 30 April 1637 announced to all that a license would thereafter be required for emigration, in order to "restrain the disorderly Transporting of his Majesty's Subjects" to any of the colonies. Curiously, however, there is no contemporaneous record of ships having been blocked from leaving the Thames estuary during that time or of the forcible detention of persons of such standing and public reputation. Given that standing and reputation, it seems highly probable that notice would have been taken. A review of the reports of the alleged emigrations, beginning with what appears to have been the earliest report (by George Bates, physician in turn to Charles I, to Cromwell, and to Charles II), undertaken 150 years ago casts serious doubt on the claim.[44] It was probably a concoction invented by royalist sympathizers, possibly by Dr Bates himself, a quarter-century or more after the purported event.

Saybrooke was probably not the only colonial adventure in which AH participated, whether as shareholder or as shipper (or both). Both the settlement at Jamestown and its offshoot, the Somers Isles Company (est. 1615) had been established too early for him. In the one case, conversion to a crown colony in 1624 would have precluded any interest, and the

---

was used as a general instrument of governance; see Leo Solt, *Church and State in Early Modern England, 1509-1640* (Oxford: Oxford University Press, 1990).

[43] Thomas Goddard Wright, *Literary Culture in Early New England, 1620-1730* (New Haven: Yale University Press, 1920), page 68. The quotations are of Wright's words, which capture the flavor of the sources. (With regard to Cromwell, he cited Clarendon's *Rebellion*, book 4, §52.)

[44] John Ward Dean, *The Story of the Embarkation of Cromwell and his Friends for New England* (Boston: D Clapp & Son, 1866).

Somers Isles colony, because it was a consistent success so quickly, had fewer investment opportunities to offer by 1630 (when AH succeeded to the family estates).[45] Another, more likely opportunity would have been the Providence Island Company, set on an island about 120 miles east of the Nicaraguan coast. Proposed during a meeting at Brooke House in Holborn, London, in 1629, the early members were of the same group as previously listed—chief among them, Robert Rich, 2nd earl of Warwick, William Fiennes, 1st viscount Saye and Sele, Robert Greville, 2nd baron Brooke of Beauchamps Court. The colony quickly developed sugarcane plantations, using enslaved Africans brought in for that purpose. While there is no record of AH's involvement, his ships might have been used to transport people from England and enslaved Africans. This colony as well as its offspring on Tortuga (aka Association Island, off the coast of Hispaniola) were destroyed by Spain in 1641.

During shareholder meetings in 1638, however, William Fiennes and Robert Greville, perhaps others, declared their intention to move to Providence Island. One wonders how much they actually knew of their supposed destination, and whether their declarations were really only a discharge of frustrations with affairs in England. In any case, they soon changed their minds, having learned that a National Covenant had been signed in Edinburgh, as Covenanters began approaching them to make common cause against the king.[46]

Denton was almost surely correct when he concluded from the available evidence that, whatever actual plans AH might have formulated to migrate to Saybrooke, he had set them aside by 1637, when he shifted his financial investments from the support of new colonial ventures and toward furtherance of his landed estate in England.[47] It was also by that time that he, along with others in the Puritan movement, had determined to fight against what they saw as tyrannical actions by the church of Laud and the royal court of Charles I and his personal rule. Of the several events that contributed to that resolve was the king's change in policy, in 1635, to raise money in support of a royal navy not only from the coastal counties but also from inland counties. As a matter of abstract rationality the change made perfect sense. After all, every part of England derived much benefit from unimpeded trade on the high seas, so all should share equally in the support of naval assurance of free navigation. In the abstract, one can well imagine, AH would have agreed. But the politics of the decision left far

---

[45] The Somers Isles, sometimes called the Summer Isles, later became Bermuda.
[46] Cliffe, *The Puritan Gentry* (1984), pages 203-206.
[47] Denton, *Only in Heaven* (1997), page 29.

too much unaccounted, simply because this was another imposition by the crown. Whereas it ought to have been a freely deliberated decision by parliament, it was instead another imposition by the king's personal rule. Puritan grandees were not the only people to protest, but they were heavily involved in organizing and leading resistance to that levy. The principle behind their resistance could have been, soon would be, summarized in four words: no taxation without representation.

When examining the record of AH's participation during the 1630s in that resistance, one could gain the impression that his fight was mainly about the politics of governance and less about religious tolerance of the preferences of Puritans in worship. That impression reflects the way we tend to divide events and processes. For many, probably most Puritans, as for many other Dissenters, the basic issue was one of individual liberty. For William Laud, archbishop of Canterbury, and Charles Stuart, king of England, governance, necessary to the maintenance of personal liberty in a commonwealth, was inseparably religious and political, because their rule was by divine right, directly for the king, indirectly via the king for the archbishop. AH and many others were struggling with that instance of inseparability. Was it, could it ever be, compatible with individual liberty, liberty of conscience? The king and his archbishop said, in effect, not simply that it is and can be compatible; rather, it *must* be compatible. But it *can* be compatible only insofar as each of the king's subjects shall agree in the king's divine right to rule. A loyal subject will accede to that right freely. Others will accede forcibly.

Seeds of a New Civil War
It is unlikely that civil war was on anyone's mind during the 1630s, and certainly not during the time that Thomas[11a] was titular head of family. When Thomas[11a] was appointed to the commission on depopulation in Leicestershire in 1607, he surely understood the circumstances involved, for Noseley had been one of the many sites of popular discontent, and he understood the gravity of the issue both in its own immediate terms and as a continuing threat to peace of the realm. The food riots that had been spreading throughout the Midlands—probably a part of Shakespeare's foil in the play, *Coriolanus* (c1608)—brought alarm to the royal court as well as (and because) fueling a sense of common cause among the growing numbers of impoverished people in London. Just as the rioters in ancient Rome had become incensed by evidence that some well-placed people were hoarding food, so, too, their English counterparts centuries later had been charging foul against producers, traders, and merchants who withheld

food in order to drive up its price. The entrepreneurial spirit of the seventeenth-century had not invented such instruments of supply and demand; nor the idea of accumulation for its own sake; nor manipulations of balance between having and being.[48] But gaps had widened greatly, stores of wealth had grown greatly, balances had shifted greatly; and the lens of an urban mass such as London magnified all of it to ever greater proportion. Differences of degree can eventually add to a sum that equals the condition of a difference in kind—kind of situation, kind of perception, kind of behavior. Whether tensions and civil unrest during the early 1600s were or became great enough to stoke civil war is doubtful; they could have been addressed more effectively than they were. But the question is not one that will be decided here.

As emphasized at the beginning of this chapter, present intent is not to address, much less try to settle such questions of cause and effect, or distant cause, proximate cause, immediate cause, and the like. While not unimportant, they are beyond the scope of this book. The view here is a simpler one, a sequence of events with enough connective tissue to achieve minimal coherence, with as little interpretation of motives, plans, and relative weights as possible while maintaining coherence. The chief focus is on events in which Sir Arthur[12b] Hesilrige was involved. That is, chief focus is on a single person in context of events, with little attention to that person's psychic constitution beyond the main outlines of a personal preference for doctrines that are (and largely were) considered Puritan, republican, in favor of individual liberty but within limits, doctrines that put him in opposition to his king, the established church, and many of their supporters. The fervor of AH's opposition might have been about as high during the 1630s as it clearly was during the early 1640s. But he was not only not alone in that fervor; his role in events was sporadic and relatively small (with few exceptions) during the 1640s. It was during the 1650s, especially as he opposed some of the policies and actions of Oliver Cromwell and then after the Cromwellian Protectorate ended, that his influence became great and relatively steady.

The sequence that is described below has five phases, aligned to the main activities of the 2nd Bt: first, a period of parliamentary activity; second, a period of military activity, as he commands regiments in the first civil war; third, again a period of parliamentary activity as he obeys a Self-

---

[48] Katharine Eisaman Maus, in her *Being and Having in Shakespeare* (Oxford: Oxford University Press, 2013), has explored much of this, and does so against the backdrop of a line in Act I of Shakespeare's *Richard II* (1595) that says because "felony" is defined as an offense *against* the sovereign, it cannot be a crime committed *by* a sovereign.

Denying Ordinance (to be military or civilian, not both); fourth, a brief return to military activity mainly in the north; fifth, parliamentary activity with occasional reminders by him and others that military force could be brought into play. This fifth period is in many respects the most complex and the most difficult to parse even in terms of an event history.

One last preliminary: a set of maps—actually, panoramas built as maps—follow as aids to the reader who does not have a mental image of places and geographic relationships of London during the early 1600s. Portions of a panorama produced by Claes van Visscher, a Dutch engraver and printer, in 1616, are used. Because of its size (length) and in the interest of legibility, the image (public domain) has been divided into three sections, with overlap, which are displayed on successive pages. A few remarks will add some locational information.

In the first (left) panel the main landmarks on the north side of the Thames are Whitehall Palace (at left) and Old St Paul's Church on Ludgate hill (at right). (The church, which lost its tall spire by fire in 1561, was destroyed in the Great Fire of 1666 and was replaced, on site, by the new St Paul's, designed by Christopher Wren.) On the south bank, Lambeth's marsh was being drained, with many buildings filling in the space. Two structures of note are (left to right), the Swan, a theater or play house, and the Bear Garden, which featured bear-baiting, bull-baiting, and the like. Puritans regarded both activities, perhaps animal-baiting more than theatrics, as reprehensible, although some Puritans were not only tolerant of play acting but offered support (e.g., the earl of Huntingdon).

In the second (center) panel the main landmarks north of the river are (again) St Paul's and the area of London Bridge. On the south side we see (from left to right) the Globe, Shakespeare's theater, Winchester House, and St Mary Overies (now Southwark Cathedral). The appellation "Overies" was a contraction or corruption of "over the water," a designation to distinguish this from other churches in London named St Mary's.

In the third (right) panel we see (again) the Bridge and then, on the north bank, the Tower of London and to the right of that compound St Katherine's at the Tower. The main interest on the south bank is the south gate of the Bridge, atop which the artist depicted the rows of heads on long pikes, a usual scene in those days.

The three panoramic panels are then supplemented by a map of the city of Westminster.

Exhibit 6.6, parts a,b,c, and d, follow, on four successive pages..

Old St Paul's Church
THAMESIS
The Bear Garden
The Swan
Whitehall

Old St Paul's Church
The Globe
AMESIS
FLUVIUS
Winchester House
South
Warke
St Mary Overies Church

Tower of London

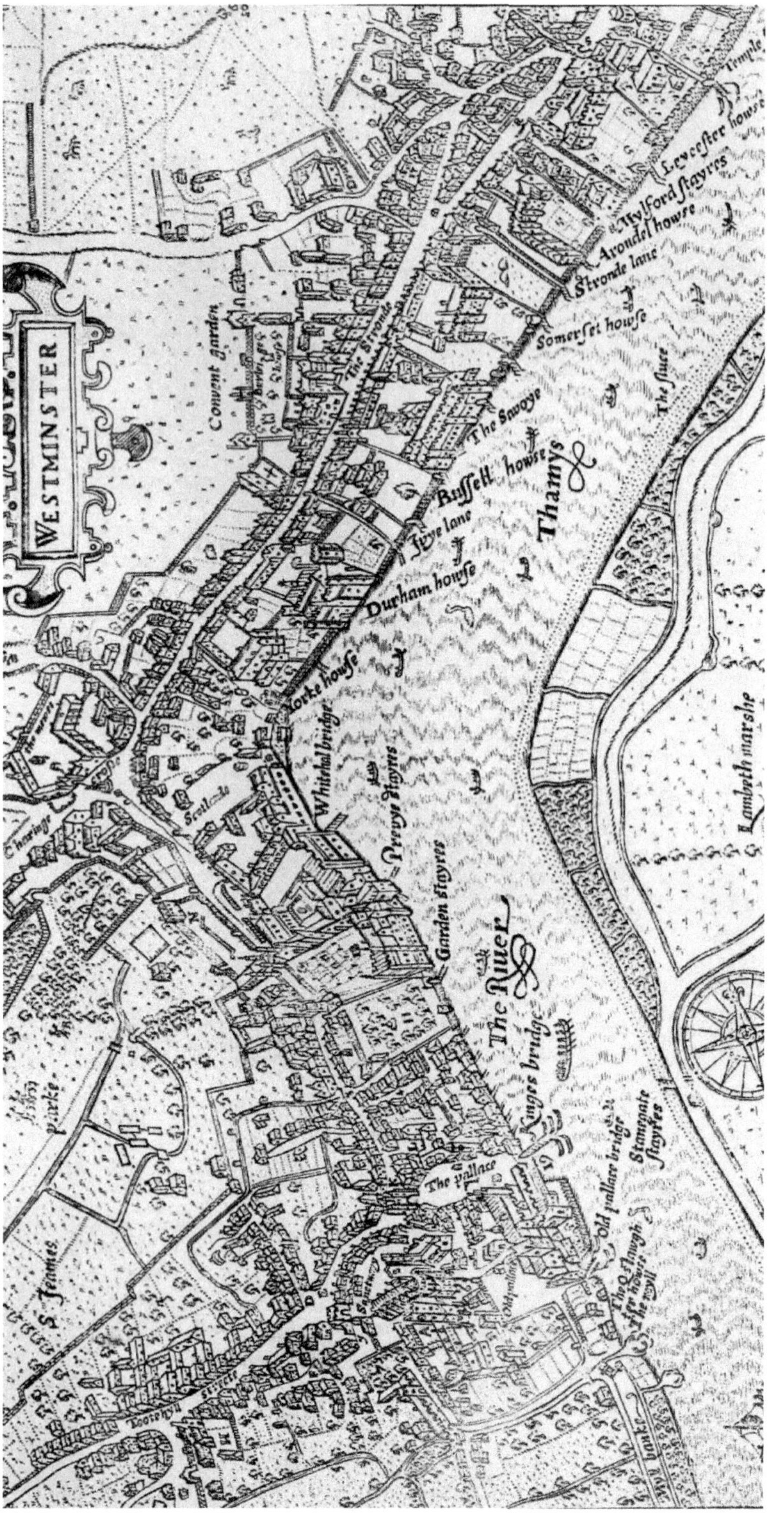
WESTMINSTER
Convent garden
The Stronde
Temple
Leycester howse
Wylford stayres
Arondel howse
Stronde lane
Somerset howse
The Sawoye
Russell howse
Ivye lane
Durham howse
Yorke howse
Whitehal bridge
Scotland
Chearinge
Pryvye stayres
Garden stayres
The Ryuer
Thamys
Kinges bridge
The pallace
Old pallace bridge
Stanngate stayres
The sluce
Lambeth marshe
S. Iames
parke
St. Iames

The panorama produced by van Visscher extends up-river only to the area of Whitehall. Further upstream lay the old Westminster palace, which housed parliamentary offices and, in the great hall, the sessions. A depiction by John Norden of the city of Westminster in 1593 is shown in the fourth of the four maps. Until the early 1500s this city was separated from the city of London (to the east) by open fields and a few dwellings. Some landmarks may be noted. First, while the old palace lay parallel to the river, Westminster abbey was (is) perpendicular, its front facing the river. At the front (east) end of the palace ready access to the river could be gained by stairs along King's Bridge and by a boat dock. At the rear, access to the river could be gained by stairs at the Old Slaughter House. (These features will be pertinent to later discussion.) Finally, even though it has no relevance to this chapter, note at the very top center of the image the name of Charing road. Follow that road southeast to a tower in the middle of an intersection. That is one of the crosses erected by Edward I in memory of his queen, Eleanor (one of a series of crosses throughout the country). Hence, Charing Cross road, still today a landmark street of Greater London.[49]

The following accounts of events are necessarily abbreviated and general, excepting relevant focus on the parts played (relative to others) by Sir Arthur[12b] Hesilrige (AH). At times his part was primarily political (i.e., parliamentary); at other times, primarily military. No effort is made here to engage in the game of the armchair general or that of the political strategist or tactician. Accounts by others will be the primary and main fare. For the civil wars and political struggles of the 1640s and 1650s we are fortunate to have several records, some of them extensive. This is not to say, obviously, that any of them were written from a neutral point of view. None was, although some of them are more balanced than others. Even the more unbalanced records can be very useful, since it is usually not only possible to recognize the general direction of bias but also to make specific adjustments accordingly. For example, as mentioned early in this chapter, one of the more extensive accounts was written by a man who was in the thick of it, Edward Hyde, the 1st earl of Clarendon (an account usually cited as "Clarendon's History"). Hyde, a royalist, an advisor to Charles I and a member of parliament, made no effort in his *History* to

---

[49] Another incidental note: from the Eleanor cross look straight down to a large open area. That was the old Scotland Yard—i.e., the yard of Scotland House (probably the building depicted at top of the "S"), which was residence in London for visiting officials of Scotland. Initial headquarters of the Metropolitan Police were at 4 Whitehall Place, at the end of Whitehall palace, and bordered the yard of Scotland House.

disguise those personal facts, and was rather free with his penalties as well as with his accolades. Needless to say, he did not think kindly of AH, sometimes going out of his way to record that sentiment. He could be a deft writer, and he often used that skill to good effect ("good," from his point of view). A significant early example is a bit of stage-setting finesse he composed in Book 1. Referring to the period from 1628 to 1640, the years of Charles' "Personal Rule," he said matter-of-factly that during those years the kingdom of England had "enjoyed the greatest calm, and the fullest measure of felicity, that any people in any age, for so long a time together, have been blessed with; to the wonder and envy of all the other parts of Christendom."[50] If one accepts Hyde's description, one has rendered irrelevant, even obliterated, the very large volume of objections urged by many people, Puritans among them, to the king's rule as if the institution of parliament had really been merely cosmetic. One need not believe that anyone in 1640 believed civil war to be either imminent or impossible, in order to think, as Hyde supposedly did, that those objections were not seriously held, much less that they were irrelevant or nonexistent.

Where shall we begin in the great chain of causes, effects, and chance? A typical starting point in past accounts is the effort of Charles I to impose his will on Scotland, in 1639, in the form of English episcopacy and the Book of Common Prayer. This was not an effort without a history behind it, of course; but needing a convenient starting point we shall begin with that one.

By 1639 the main religious perspective and practice in Scotland was Presbyterian, which rejected the episcopal structure and England's Book of Common Prayer with it. The general consequence of Charles' arrogance was uproar in Scotland and a sympathetic ear among Dissenters in England. Charles prepared for war against the Scots. He put Thomas Wentworth, newly created the earl of Strafford, in charge of the war effort (which became known as the Bishops War). But he needed money in order to recruit soldiers. One must bear in mind that England had no standing army, the nearest thing to it being the possibility of a collection of the several county militias. If a king or queen wanted their services, wages had to be offered. Thus, after eleven years of personal rule, the king saw no choice, if he insisted on forcing his will on Scotland, but to call a parliament into session. This he did in April of 1640. Rather than approve the money, however, members of this new parliament proceeded to raise questions about various of the king's policies during the preceding years and called for cessation of the ship levy and reform of the ecclesiastical

---

[50] Edward Hyde, *History* ... (1826), volume 1, page 131.

regime. John Pym, John Hampden, and Oliver St John were among the prominent questioners.[51] Such manners being an affront to a king who believed himself to be beyond question, Charles dissolved what would ever after be known as the Short Parliament. It had sat only three weeks.

In 1640 the Bishops War came to an end with defeat of the king's forces, as the Scots overran Northumberland and Durham, holding them hostage. Charles went to Scotland the following year, acceded to Scottish rights to challenge his ministers and to their right to decide church structure as they deemed appropriate. The concessions were duly noted by English MPs at Westminster palace, site of the English parliament.

Soon the king realized that, distasteful though it was, he had no choice but to call another parliament into session, because bills were due for payment of war debts, among others. Thus, on 3 November 1640 what became known as the Long Parliament began, with AH returned as MP for Leicestershire. The name was due to the fact that the MPs passed an act, accepted by the king, that dissolution could occur only with agreement by the members, and they did not agree to dissolution until 16 March 1660, although (as we will see below) there were interruptions.

About a month after the first session began, several MPs, AH among them, began efforts to abolish episcopacy in England, thus to free congregations of centralized authority and restrictions on their liberties of worship. As said earlier, from the time of John Whitgift's appointment as archbishop of Canterbury in 1583, official church policy countenanced and even encouraged persecutions of people who were judged to be nonconformist. Persecutions were thereafter uneven in frequency and in severity, but they remained a major abrasion upon various believers in Calvinist doctrines, Puritans included. During the eleven years of the king's personal rule, the situation did not improve for dissenters. Men such as William Laud, an increasingly prominent bishop of the church, were disinclined to compromise. To the contrary. Laud himself had been a champion of enforcing uniformity of ritual across all segments of the church's presence, and that enforcement became all the more vigorous with his appointment by Charles as archbishop of Canterbury in 1633. One year later the ship Griffin set sail for North America, carrying Anne Hutchinson and other dissenters. It had become clear to them that there were no prospects of any future in England that would not require great caution against oppressions by the church. One of the first actions by the Long Parliament was to voice stern objections to "Laudism"—its covert

---

[51] Oliver Cromwell, MP for Cambridge, and Sir Arthur[12b] Hesilrige, for Leicestershire, both new to parliament, were relatively quiet.

encouragement of Roman Catholic doctrine, its severe censorship, its increased violence against dissenters such as William Prynne who had his ears cropped and his forehead branded. Laud had become even more of an autocrat than Charles during the period of the king's personal rule. As one recent historian described him, Laud was "the greatest calamity ever visited upon the English Church."[52]

In December 1640 a committee of Commons, known as the Grand Committee for Religion, undertook the charge to investigate corruption and decay in the established church. The bulk of the committee members were Puritan—among them, John Hampden, Sir Arthur Hesilrige, Sir Robert Harley, Sir John Dryden (not the poet, his uncle), and Sir John Wray. On the 18th of the month Denzil Holles moved impeachment of Laud, and the archbishop was detained. Eventually he came to trial in the House of Lords, was attainted and convicted—in a manner rather like the typical proceedings of the royal court's Star Chamber—and remanded to the Tower of London. Laud was executed 10 January 1644/5. Before the end, Laud declared that the king he had so loyally served had not been a strong enough leader, Laud's destination being patent proof of his claim.

A few weeks later a document known as the Root and Branch Petition, signed by about 15,000 Londoners, was presented to Commons as a call for the removal of all bishops' parliamentary seats, indeed removal of bishops from civil government entirely, root and branch.[53] The petition was assigned to committee in Feb 1640/1, but many Commoners were shy of the proposal. Oliver St John drafted a bill which was formally presented by Henry Vane the younger and Oliver Cromwell. The bill was defeated in August. However, parliament passed the Bishops Exclusion Act the following year, as a result of which bishops lost their seats in Lords. Five years later parliament passed legislation that was similar to acts under Henry VIII: whereas those acts had abolished the jurisdiction of the papacy in England, dissolved the monasteries, and confiscated monastic properties, this act abolished the jurisdiction of archbishops and bishops in England and settled their lands and possessions on trustees for the use of the commonwealth. But this was October 1646; we are getting ahead of the story.

---

[52] Patrick Collinson, *The Religion of Protestants* (Oxford: Oxford University Press, 1984), page 90.
[53] The text of the petition is collected in Henry Gee and William J Hardy, editors, *Documents Illustrative of English Church History* (London: Macmillan, 1914), pages 537-545.

In March 1640/1 the focus of much the same set of MPs shifted to Thomas Wentworth, earl of Strafford and one of Charles' closest advisors. Born in 1593 and an MP for Yorkshire from 1614 on, Wentworth began as a critic of the regime of Charles I. His second wife was sister to another critic, Denzil Holles, and, like John Hampden and other MPs, Wentworth refused to pay for the king's forced loans, as a result of which he was sent to prison in 1627. Soon thereafter, however, he declared himself totally loyal to the king, and his fortunes changed. Put in charge of Ireland, he soon gained a reputation for harsh actions. Importing Protestants planters to replace native landlords, he then, in alliance with Laud, harassed them into conformity. From the point of view of the royal court, he proved himself to be an effective and efficient administrator. In reward he was brought back to London and elevated to the dignity of 1st earl of Strafford.

In the meantime, Wentworth had become a large symbol of what critics saw as the corruption and capriciousness of the king's regime. There was substantial evidence that Wentworth had enriched himself in land and money by his public office and that many of his decisions were biased against members of the gentry who had friends among members of parliament. Indeed, he had done little to hide either "offense" precisely because in the mind of his patron, the king, neither behavior *was* an offense. None of the evidence could reach standard of proof for a charge of treason, simply because the only basis for a conviction of treason was proof that the king had been damaged, and it was up to the king and the king alone to decide whether he had been injured. As all of this reasoning became increasingly clear, Wentworth's opponents decided on a different approach.

On 13 April 1641 AH brought forth a bill of attainder, which, if passed, would convict Wentworth of crime *ipso facto*. Perfectly legal at the time, attainder was later judged to be contrary to sound legal principles (e.g., a law should be directed at a category of behavior, not at a specific person; also, separation of powers). But, vicious though it was, attainder had been used many times before as an efficient weapon to remove an obstacle from someone's path. Did AH write this bill? Very likely not. Authorship is in fact unknown, but the likeliest candidate would be John Pym or Oliver St John, or both. At this point, AH was still a pupil under training by Pym, among others, in the ways of parliamentary procedure. When later critics said that AH had been a pawn of Pym, this was the sort of action that they had in mind.[54]

---

[54] Hyde, *History* ... (1826), volume 1, page 397.

While the bill of attainder did ultimately prove to have been a shrewd move, at the time it probably looked a good deal less imposing. While passage by the House of Commons was expected, few thought it had much of a chance in Lords. And if it did manage to pass Lords, it then had to be ratified by Charles; and who could imagine that the king would attaint his own man Strafford? Unexpectedly, after some delay the bill gained majority vote in the House of Lords. Charles gave assurances that he would never approve the bill. However, even more unexpectedly, after listening to advisors urging him to see that the majority of his subjects who cared one way or the other favored conviction (hence, execution), Charles relented and, as a sign that their king understood his subjects and their grievances against corruption of the public till, signed the bill. The earl of Stafford was executed. What neither the king nor his advisors recognized, apparently, was that by signing the bill the king had authorized extension of the grounds for conviction of treason—or so it could be argued—such that political attacks on the king's *realm*, by subverting laws, abusing delegated powers, and the like, would henceforth count as evidence in favor of conviction. Conceivably, this opened the door to the possibility that, as Robertson put it, "treason might be committed by a king who attacked another sovereign institution"—namely, parliament.[55]

Was that sequence of events entirely happenstance? It is easy to think otherwise. Begin not with the outcome, unlikely that it is, but with a question: What did Pym and others imagine that they might achieve by introducing the bill? Presumably they made the introduction only after having concluded that the trial would end in acquittal. So was the bill merely an emotional outburst, a missive of frustration? This would have been the one condition that could have pointed to AH as author, since his reputation for distemper was secure. Had he actually written the bill and brought in onto the floor in surprise of others? Possibly, but unlikely. It seems more likely that he was given the privilege of introducing the bill for the same reason, however, though in reverse: if it failed, the failure could be ascribed to his rashness. AH, still relatively new to such judicial proceedings as parliament could, and often did, conduct, might not have understood the slim chance of a treason charge being made good. But Pym and St John, among others, must have known that the chances of winning a treason charge against Wentworth were poor—and for the very reasons that they *were* poor. So was the point in bringing the charge only to harass Wentworth, perchance embarrass Charles, and augment popular support in the streets of London?

---

[55] Robertson, *The Tyrannicide Brief* (2005), page 57.

That could have been the sum of it. After all, one never knows in advance what hidden embarrassments might emerge by a little pressure. And if none, well, in the meantime Charles' court will have been put on the defensive. And yet: presumably in that time as now, a good lawyer knew not to ask a question unless he/she had high confidence about the answer.[56] Embarrassment is one thing, delicious though it might be for the king's critics. But if they should embarrass the court only to lose the case, what then? Courtly repercussions could be expected, possibly severe ones.

Instead of motivation from a frustration-aggression syndrome, perhaps some cunning of reason was present. Perhaps the sequence had been planned in the beginning: first open trial, arousing public interest and indignation, the indignation increasing as it becomes clear that the earl will be acquitted despite the display of evidence of corruption and abuse of office; then, as pressure both inside parliament and on the streets has risen, bring the bill of attainder, on the chance that it will pass and Charles will make exactly the "mistake" that he did make. If the first step, the trial, was worth taking at all, it was worth taking mostly as a prelude to the second step. If AH was lacking in subtlety of thought, as some of his critics asserted, he had as mentor an expert in Mr Pym.

Now back on his heels, the king quickly learned that his troubles had not ended with the sacrifice of the earl of Strafford. For one thing, while the earl surely had enemies within the royal court—anyone with his power was bound to have them—even those courtiers must have been a bit shocked that the king abandoned one of his favorites seemingly so easily. For another, the king's critics in parliament were unrelenting. Next on the agenda was an act that affirmed the right of anyone imprisoned by the king to file a writ of habeas corpus. This was July 1641, barely two months past the execution of Strafford on Tower Hill. That great source of grievances, the Star Chamber, was abolished. And the crusade against episcopacy continued, with an ordinance introduced in October for the abolition of archbishops and bishops in England and Wales, and for settling their lands into a trust for the common good. November brought rebellion in Ireland, with a major slaughter of Protestants—sure to arouse more anger against "popish conspiracies." Next, the Bishops Exclusion Act was introduced in December, declaring that officials of the church had no temporal authority and would be excluded from the House of Lords.

In the meantime, several members of Commons had concluded that a systematic protest to the king over several grievances needed to be made.

---

[56] Hexter, *Reign of Pym* (1941), page 32, argued that Pym refrained from pushing a bill unless he was confident of success.

The result was a document known as the Grand Remonstrance, which, in a notable mixture of cautious and incautious wording, listed grievances against current and past governmental regimes. It was approved by the Long Parliament on 22 November 1641 and sent to the king on the first of December. On the one hand, the authors avoided naming any persons as targets either in specific or in example. On the other hand, by naming its targets in highly general terms of Roman Catholic conspiracy and the persecution of nonconformists, it left itself open to ambiguity of intent and future specification of responsible persons. Few could doubt who the actual targets were, but few could be confident how widely the net might be cast. Response from the king not coming quickly enough, leaders of Commons had the document published and widely circulated, in effect inviting the formation of a popular constituency. The king's eventual response did not include any offer of continued discussion but declared that he could not reconcile the document's perceptions of reality with his own. Opportunity to defuse and divide, if ever considered, was rejected.[57]

Led by Pym, several members of Commons were consulted in the contentious debates that led to the Grand Remonstrance, AH among them. One of the most important immediate effects of those debates was clarity in alignments of the members of Commons. It was here, for instance, that Edward Hyde, later to be made 1st earl of Clarendon, subordinated his own prior criticisms of the king and his court, refusing to support the document.

While Charles was deliberating his response to the Remonstrance, another debate was unfolding that no doubt sealed the conviction of Hyde and other MPs that the path on which Commons was headed would lead to great strife. This debate was whether to deny the monarch sovereignty of sword. Ostensibly the debate began and proceeded for a time as concern that parliament needed its own protective force, that it should not have to rely on the royal court for its own security in such troubled times. As one recent scholar summarized the concern that "erupted in the fall of 1641," it was a "response to a series of events—rumors of plots involving the king, the presence in London of disbanded soldiers who had returned from the war with Scotland, the 'Incident' in Scotland, and above all the rebellion in Ireland which required the levying of an army to subdue those rebels."[58]

---

[57] Robertson, *The Tyrannicide Brief* (2005), page 61 and note 3.
[58] Lois G Schwoerer, "'The Fittest Subject for a King's Quarrel': An Essay on the Militia Controversy 1641-1642," *Journal of British Studies*, volume 11 (November 1971), pages 45-76, at page 45. The "Incident" she mentioned was an alleged royalist plot in October 1641 to kidnap several prominent Scottish Covenanters who had been highly critical of Charles—some of the fall-out of his unsuccessful Bishops War.

The alarms were genuine, the fear of conspiracy and plots was genuine, whatever the actual substance of those plots and conspiracy might have been. Especially concerned that the king would turn the army used in Ireland against the House of Commons, "members of the Long Parliament appointed their own guard to protect the Parliament." Then, "after evident reluctance," AH introduced on the floor of Commons a "Militia Bill" that gave authority to call county militias into national service henceforth to an an office of lord general, who would be appointed by parliament on behalf of the monarch. This introduction occurred on 7 December. Aside from a small number of members of Commons, interest in the bill was "desultory" (as Schwoerer assessed the record) until, less than a month later, Charles "attempted to arrest five leaders of the opposition in the House of Commons," thus demonstrating palpable cause for all the prior alarm and concern. "The reaction to that episode led directly to the Militia Ordinance, which was issued by both Houses without royal assent." Hyde observed that whereas few MPs were in favor of the militia bill prior to that event in January, afterward it became for the majority "a very necessary provision." And after Hyde, most observers have agreed with Ollard: control of the militia would thereafter remain "the point on which all attempts at compromise [between king and parliament] broke down."[59]

The turning point occurred within the House of Commons on 4 January 1641/2, when five members of Commons would be linked ever after as "The Five Members." The linkage had been in formation for some time, even though the names and number of links changed now and then. As Gardiner (among others) pointed out, plots were seen brewing on both sides of the divide that was separating parliament from king. No sooner had Charles grown more concerned about activities of "the radicals" in Commons, than he was alerted that members led by Pym "had resolved to impeach [queen Henrietta Maria] as having conspired against the public liberties, and as having held intelligence with the Irish rebels."[60] Gardiner cited correspondence to that effect, observed that evidence in support of the charges could indeed have been presented, and then offered this:

---

[59] Schwoerer, "'Fittest Subject' ..." (1971), pages 46-47; Hyde, *History* (1826), volume 1, page 522, also page 486; Richard Ollard, *This War without an Enemy* (New York: Atheneum, 1976), page 53.

[60] See Gardiner, *Fall* ..., volume 2, page 382; for the remainder of the paragraph, pages 382-84; for the "Five Members" episode generally, pages 380-408. According to Hyde, Charles had initially composed a list of 16 members to be charged with high treason, of whom five were in the House of Lords. Exactly when and why that list was pruned to five is unknown. See Hyde, *History* ... (1826), volume 3, page 618, and volume 2, pages 124-161, 258.

Five members of the House of Commons—Pym, Hampden, Holles, Hazlerigg, and Strode—were selected as the main offenders. There can be no doubt, that if by the fundamental laws of England was meant that constitutional arrangement which had prevailed in the days of Elizabeth, they were guilty of treason at least as much as Strafford had been guilty. If he had done his best to reduce Parliaments to a cipher, they had done their best to reduce the Royal authority to a cipher. The true defence of both Strafford and Pym was, that the old Constitution had broken down and needed reconstruction; but, so far as Pym was concerned, this was not an argument likely to find favor with Charles.

Gardiner's evaluation was well measured, for the most part. The constitution (unwritten) that had prevailed within (and beyond) the Elizabethan settlement had indeed broken down. It had worked during the conditions of the late 1500s, and because of her deft hand in balancing interests. But conditions had changed, and a major part of that change was due to the anachronism of Charles Stuart's insistence on a concept of kingship that had been coming apart even before the reign of Henry VIII. Absolutism of royal authority, whether decorated in the costume of "divine right" or asserted plainly, was no longer tolerable to a great many people: members of the landed gentry, the aristocracy, and the growing population of urban merchants, lawyers, teachers, and craftsmen.

Some commentators have speculated that Charles was misled by his advisors.[61] That surely was a factor, but how large a factor is open to question. If even approaching the level of decisiveness, it could only have been because Charles was extraordinarily ignorant of his country's history since 1215 and the present mood of his people or because he so intensely, blindly believed *in* (that is, within and through) the "divine right" mentality that he could not understand how insensible it had become to so many people. Probably both dimensions, one secular and the other (in his mind) sacred, were at play. As for his advisors, Laud had surely been a poor one to follow—as the king reportedly later acknowledged—but in the moment of action the two men were most likely a mutually self-reinforcing duality. Other advisors were, no doubt, all too often chiefly concerned with their

---

[61] Ollard, in *This War* ... (1976), page 55, saw George Digby, 2nd earl of Bristol, whose typical advice consisted in "miraculous cures for the nation's troubles," as chief author of the king's invasion of Commons. Surely it would not have been Hyde. But perhaps Charles' queen was the main prod.

own continued standing and fortune, thus too unwilling, perhaps in a sense even unable, to tell their king what they knew he did not want to hear, and might have been unable to understand. In retrospect it is easy to see much evidence of a self-delusion fueled by a combination of ignorance and an egomania of religious conviction that, ironically, aspired to the same sort of "saintliness" that impelled some of his opponents toward a "revolution of the saints."[62]

In any case, Charles instructed his attorney general to present the charges of treason to the House of Lords and to "ask for a secret committee to examine evidence." He was to object if certain men were named to the committee—among them, Essex, Warwick, Saye, Brooke, and Mandeville, all known for sympathies to Puritanism—for "the King intended to call them as witnesses."[63] Soon thereafter the viscount Mandeville's name was shifted from this list to the list of men accused of treason. Reason for this change is unknown; but as Gardiner pointed out, it was a tactical error inasmuch as it asked the Peers to "sacrifice a member of their own House."[64] The viscount Mandeville, Edward Montagu (after succeeding his father he became the 2nd earl of Manchester), was a very popular member of the House of Lords (to which he was seated in 1626, the year he married Anne, daughter of Robert Rich, 2nd earl of Warwick). Moderately in favor of the parliamentary side of the struggle, he opposed the trial of Charles and withdrew from public life. Why the king would have thought it wise to add his name to the list of purported traitors is a mystery.

On the afternoon of Tuesday, 4 January 1641/2, Charles set out by coach from Whitehall to Westminster with a contingent of armed men. The exact number is unknown—Gardiner said "three or four hundred"—large enough that it raised alarm in the streets.[65] Lord Saye and Sele, William Fiennes, was reportedly at Whitehall at the time, understood what might be happening, and hurried back to his colleagues at Westminster. Whether he arrived ahead of the king is not known. But never mind: warning had arrived well before Charles, and the targets of his attack were safely gone.

---

[62] Michael Walzer, *The Revolution of the Saints* (Cambridge: Harvard University Press, 1982; David Zaret, *Heavenly Contract* (Chicago: University of Chicago Press, 1985.
[63] According to Hyde, all but Saye were in the initial list of sixteen.
[64] Gardiner, *Fall* ..., volume 2, page 384.
[65] Gardiner, *Fall* ..., volume 2, pages 392-93; Hyde, *History* ... (1826), volume 2, pages 124, 634; Ludlow, *Memoirs* (1894), volume 1, pages 24-25; Robertson, *Tyrannicide Brief* (2005), page 62.

For many years commentators speculated about the identity of this agent of alarm. Purkiss, referring to suggestions made by unspecified contemporary accounts, concluded that the warning was delivered by Lucy Hay, countess of Carlisle, and daughter of Henry Percy, 9th earl of Northumberland.[66] Lucy had married James Hay, 1st earl of Carlisle and typically described as one of king James' favorites. As countess of Carlisle, she became one of queen Henrietta's courtiers, thus obviously well-placed to be a conduit of information from within the royal court. There is little doubt that she was indeed the source if not the immediate bearer of the warning. It appears that she herself later confessed to the king that she had undone his plan, and that he responded with kind understanding.[67] What is more, in his speech to Commons on 7 Feb 1658/9 AH clearly identified her as his (and his colleagues') benefactor.[68] One wonders: had later writers not read, or at least not remembered, his speech; or did they think he had been speaking falsely? On the other hand, it is curious, to say the least, that AH spoke of her in such unalloyed terms, no apparent reservations at all; for when all the evidence is considered, one can only conclude that Lucy Hay had been duplicitous all around—in twentieth-century jargon, a double agent.

Having been forewarned, the five members of Commons fled by boat to the City of London, downstream. As one can see from the panoramic maps shown above, in Exhibit 6.6, alternative stairs and docks were available, boats typically in waiting for whatever traffic might come. Some accounts have suggested rather precise knowledge of timing, in particular that one or another of the five was slow to leave the chamber and had to be forcibly encouraged to flee. Strumming the usual chord of impetuosity, some commentators have named AH as the laggard. These various claims appeal to greater accuracy of detailed knowledge than would likely have been at hand. As we know today from repeated experiments, eyewitness testimony especially under stressful conditions generally lacks accuracy and reliability.

There is one related report, however, that intriguingly invites further research. Hyde reported, without citing evidence, that it "was very well known where the accused persons were, all together in one house in Coleman-street."[69] A short street that ran (and still does run) south from London Wall, Coleman was the main roadway of an area in the City known

---

[66] Diane Purkiss, *The English Civil War* (New York: Basic Books, 2006), pages 123-24.
[67] Gardiner, *Fall* ..., volume 2, page 407, cites a memoir that reports the confession.
[68] This speech is reproduced in entirety as Exhibit 8.10 (chapter 8).
[69] Hyde, *History* ... (1826), volume 2, page 135.

as a Puritan stronghold. Its anchor was a church, St Stephen's, of which John Davenport was vicar until, under royal pressure, he resigned and soon thereafter led a contingent of refugees to Boston (North America) by way of Holland.[70] The church (lost by fire, rebuilt, then lost by bombs during World War II) was located about one-half mile northeast of St Paul's. Judging from later maps of the area, there were not many houses on Coleman Street in 1642. The house in question very likely did not survive the Great Fire of 1666. But there might have been parish records which might have survived and which might offer some insight into occupants.

Foiled in his pursuit of his enemies, the king retreated. His return to Whitehall was reportedly a raucous journey, as first people of parliament, then trades people and others on the streets, shouted various words at him, some supportive but most oppositional and even threatening. One of the most quoted of shouts was "Privilege of Parliament," a reference to the fact that Charles had violated a long-held tradition, that a monarch was welcome into the House of Commons only by invitation. To this day, that privilege and the event of its violation more than 370 years ago are commemorated at each State Opening of Parliament by the reigning monarch. She or he, sitting on the throne in the House of Lords, instructs her or his personal attendant in Lords, known as the Gentleman Usher of the Black Rod, to summon members of Commons. Black Rod reaches the doors to Commons chamber; the doors are slammed in his face. He bangs sharply with his rod three times; the doors then open to him. In sum, Commons declares that its chambers will never again be entered by force by a monarch or a monarch's servant when Commons is sitting.

The next day, the king sought his quarry in the City, to no avail. What he did find was an increased hostility from his subjects, and this was so alarming that he was prompted to collect his family and leave London, fearing for their safety. It is difficult to assay how much or how little he did understand of what had been happening in this, the capital city of his realm. Writing of his forced entry into the chambers of the House of Commons, Gardiner opined that as the king "stepped through the door which none of his predecessors had ever passed, he was, little as he thought it, formally acknowledging that power had passed into new hands."[71] Very likely he did not think that, for it failed to conform to his view of himself and the authority he rightfully held as king. But he surely must have known of the loss he had incurred. As Gardiner observed of the London

---

[70] See, e.g., Isabel MacBeath Calder, *The New Haven Colony* (New Haven: Yale University Press, 1934).

[71] Gardiner, *From James I ...* (1891), volume 10, pages 138-39.

scene when morning broke on Monday, the 10th of January, "All the constituted authorities were now against Charles. The popular current ran in the same direction." Later than day he fled London, not to return until his life was near end. The next day, the already famous quintuplet of Commons men returned to their chambers, by boat, at one o'clock in the afternoon, "surrounded by a multitude of gaily dressed boats, firing volleys as they passed along." [72] In retrospect it is very clear that a page had been turned, from one chapter to a next. It could not have been so clear to those five men, or to their celebrants. Charles was still king. He still had support among members of parliament. The powers on which he could call were formidable. Had his world, the world as he saw it, been less anachronistic, he could have kept his crown as well as his head, perhaps to become a subsequently celebrated monarch who inaugurated what would in fact transpire less than half a century later. But he simply did not understand how anachronistic he and his world were, and had been from the start.

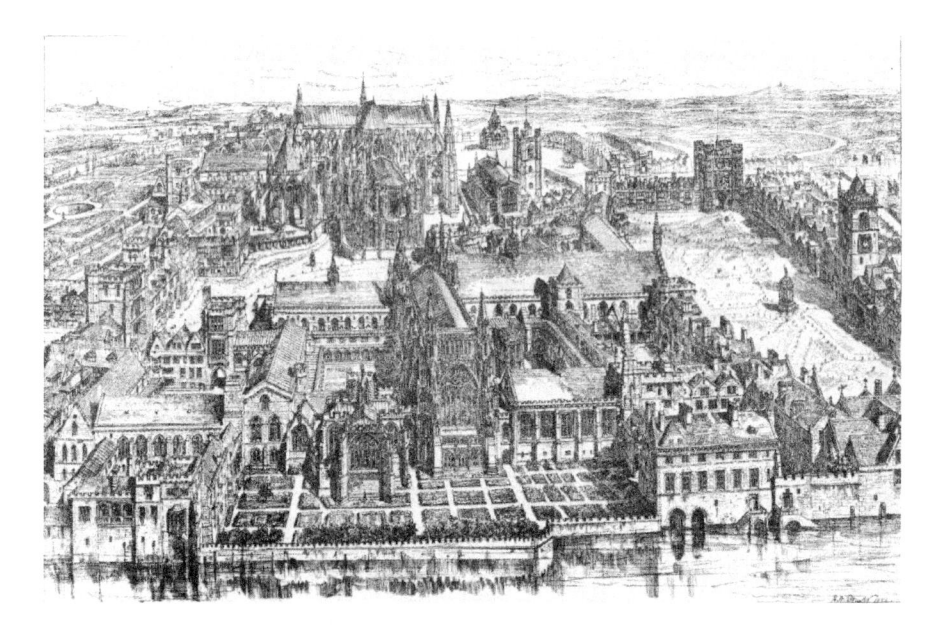

Exhibit 6.7. Westminster Palace (foreground) and Abbey (behind), St Margaret's Church (right of abbey)

---

[72] Gardiner, *Fall* ..., volume 2, pages 405, 408.

~ 7 ~
War, Revolution, Republic, 1642-1660

War or peace? As of the first of June 1642, the coin had not yet come to ground. In May both houses of the Long Parliament formulated a list of nineteen propositions which they sent to king Charles, who was in York. This document, known to history as The Nineteen Propositions, presented an enumerated list of changes mainly for a greater parliamentary role in governance, especially in the conduct of foreign policy and defence of the nation, and in making the king's ministers accountable to parliament.

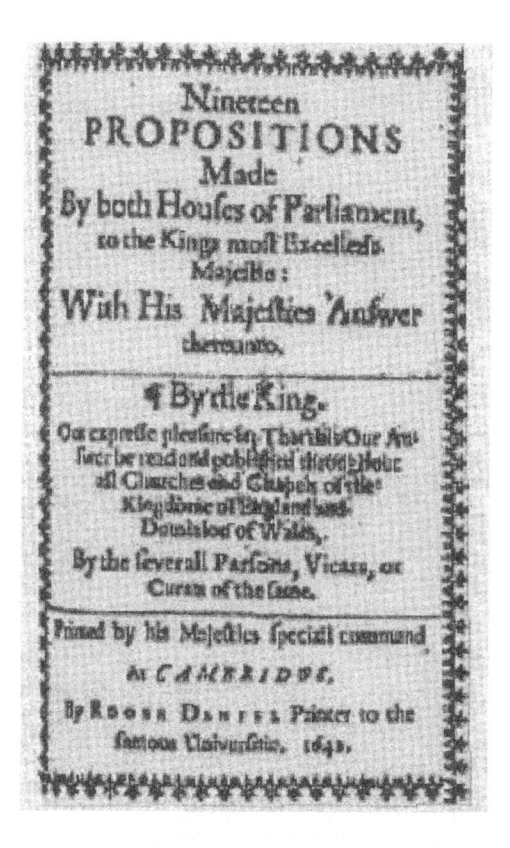

Exhibit 7.1 Cover of Booklet, *Nineteen Propositions*

The propositions could have been read as outright demands or as points for negotiation. Limited insight into the thinking of Charles and his circle of advisors suggests that negotiation was never entertained, and his response, coming later in June, confirmed that there would be nothing to negotiate. The king simply rejected all points, asserting that change of the present regime of governance was unnecessary and unwanted. Had the coin finally come to rest?

There were weeks of uncertainty, confusion, deliberations to and fro among parliamentarians. For his part, the king seemed emboldened by the exchange, and by his special command a booklet containing the nineteenth propositions and his response was published. Printing presses were instruments of mass persuasion, or at least of furtherance of conflict and confrontation. Did the king believe his brief explanation of refusal would stimulate a groundswell of support? Did he still believe, after the fiasco in London, being chased from his own capital city, that his subjects would rally to his absolutism? It would appear that he did. Or perhaps his own conviction in absolutism was so severe that his subjects' opinions did not matter to him, not in the final analysis. But then, why publish?

Uncertainty and confusion were resolved when, on 22 August, the king raised his standard at Nottingham castle. The coin had landed, and it said war there would be. The king had declared war on his own parliament. Except that, in his mind, the parliament in London was illegitimate. Having fled London he blessed a new parliament in Oxford, and this parliament always endorsed his decisions. War there would be.

The First Civil War
Accounts of the military battles of the first civil war of the 1640s have been offered by many others, some of whom give the impression of having been an eyewitness who combined acute observation of intents as well as movements with sagacity of military strategy and tactics as they existed in seventeenth-century England. No attempt to duplicate any of that will be read in these pages. Accounts will be brief in general and focused particularly on the actions of AH, so far as these can be determined from available sources.[1] As mentioned previously in similar contexts, accounts even by biased reporters can be useful, if the bias is reasonably evident; and it usually is. As Firth observed during his entry on AH in the Dictionary of National Biography (1885-1900 edition), Denzil Holles—one of AH's persistent critics even though they were largely on the same side of the divide between king and parliament—was a critic "who always

---

[1] Richard Ollard's *This War without an Enemy* (New York: Atheneum, 1976) presents good, compact accounts of the main battles and in the process noted relevant divisions and conflicts within particular families. Barry Denton's *Only in Heaven* (Sheffield: Sheffield Academic Press, 1997) presents accounts of AH's roles in various battles.

accuses his enemies of cowardice [and who] relates a story of Hesilrige's misconduct at Cheriton, which has obtained more credit than it deserves. His [AH's] fault throughout his life was overboldness rather than want of courage. Parliament showed appreciation of his services by stipulating in the Uxbridge treaty that he should be made a baron, and given lands worth 2,000*l.* a year (*Commons' Journals*, iv. 360).[2]

More particularly, Holles, a Presbyterian, tended to favor negotiation with Charles I, preferring a settlement that would make the established church hospitable to, if not entirely controlled by, Presbyterians. AH, in contrast, wanted no established church of any stripe, no government presence at all in religious life.

As it became apparent that war was likely, AH raised a troop of horse in the area of London. Regiments were identified in the field by pinons or banners, the design usually left to the regimental command. AH chose the design shown in Exhibit 7.2: an Anchor in Heaven, the motto an abbreviation of one of his favorite expressions, "Hope Only in Heaven."

Exhibit 7.2

Banner of the Regiment of Horse commanded by Sir Arthur Hesilrige

---

[2] The "story" to which Firth referred is given in Denzil Holles, *Memoirs of Denzil Lord Holles* (London: T Goodwin, 1699), pages 27-28: that AH had been caught "crying under a hedge" at the battle of Cheriton.

His first engagement, under Sir William Balfour, was fought at the battle of Edgehill (Warwickshire), 23 October 1642, the first major battle of the first civil war. A bloody draw, with about 3,000 casualties, Edgehill was a precursor of what lay in store. Estimates of war casualties have always been tenuous, and so it was with these civil wars. However, a reasonable guess is that more than 60,000 adult men were killed in the fighting, with another 100,000 "lost from collateral damage and war-borne disease."[3] It has often been said that a "higher proportion of the British population" was killed during the civil wars of the 1640s "than in any war before or since."[4]

Little is known of AH's action at Edgehill. A pamphleteer, John Vicars (whom Denton rightly described as a one-man fan club of AH), said of him that he was a "most pious patriot of his country, a most worthie member of the House of Commons and a most valiant and courageous commander in the famous battle at Keinton" (the battle was fought in the area between two villages, Kineton and Edgehill).[5] For an amateur leader of a troop of horse, engaged in such a bloody confrontation as took place that October day, he no doubt knew the conflictively vehement passions of fear and courage in the immediate experience of lethal combat. He was very likely certain that God's side would win the contest. But could he have been as certain that God's side was his?

Not every engagement was as bloody as Edgehill. But there were many engagements, and several of them resulted in extensive casualties on one side or the other, often on both sides. AH's regiments—and as will become clear, he had more than one, in sequence—were involved in nearly twenty engagements from Edgehill until April 1645, when he stood down from military service under orders of legislation called the Self-Denying Ordinance (about which, more below). Later, finding that military service was needed again, he raised another regiment. But that is a topic for the second civil war (below). His military service during the first civil war included, in sequence, the following engagements:

1642	October	battle of Edgehill
	November	storming of Farnham castle
	December	battle of Winchester
	December	siege of Chichester
1643	March	storming of Malmesbury

---

[3] Geoffrey Robertson, *The Tyrannicide Brief* (New York: Pantheon, 2005), page 90.
[4] For example, Adam Nicolson, *God's Secretaries* (New York: HarperCollins, 2003), page 62.
[5] Denton, *Only in Heaven* (1997), page 50.

	March	battle of Highnam
	April	skirmish at Little Dean
	July	battle of Lansdown
	July	siege of Devizes
	July	battle of Roundway Down
	November	siege of Basing House
	November	skirmish at Farnham
	December	storming of Alton church
	December	siege of Arundel
1644	March	battle of Cheriton
	April	first battle of Newbury
	June	battle of Copredy Bridge
	August	siege of Wareham
	October	second battle of Newbury

And in April 1645, in compliance with the Self-Denying Ordinance, AH handed his regiment of horse to Colonel John Butler. He had survived some very fierce fighting—though just, having sustained several wounds and on one occasion reportedly near-fatal wounds.

In the following paragraphs some detail will be added to a few of those military engagements. Interspersed will be descriptions of political events involving AH in one capacity or another, for during these years he often wore two hats, military commander and member of parliament, in his public life, while remaining husband, father, titular head of the family, and manager of the family estates (duties partly shared with his brothers).

About a month after Edgehill, Sir William Waller, now Colonel Waller, fresh from his successful siege of Portsmouth, captured Farnham castle, Surrey, with its huge store of money, plate, weapons, gunpowder, and provisions. Waller subsequently used the castle as his headquarters when in the area. At this stage of the war, the parliamentary forces were loosely organized, inexperienced, and often poorly led. The overall field commander, Robert Devereux, 3rd earl of Essex, compared unfavorably to field commanders of the royalist forces, and the difference showed all too often. Waller, on the rebels' side, had acquired experience in battlefields of the Thirty Years War (among others) and had a better strategic as well as tactical sense of field maneuvers and coordination of forces. AH, while a good horseman, was lacking in experience of actual combat and benefited greatly from coming into association with Waller, who could temper some of the tendency to rash behavior and provide useful direction. By and large AH acceded to the direction; but there were lapses, as will be noted.

After taking Farnham castle, Waller's forces, including AH and his regiment of horse, relieved Marlborough in Hampshire (early December 1642), then defeated royalist forces at Winchester. Several days later their siege of Chichester succeeded, with the city's surrender. Soldiers engaged in plunder in both cities, cathedrals included. Some of AH's critics liked to hold him personally, almost uniquely responsible for the plundering. According to one account, for instance, he "enthusiastically supported" his troops' "sacking and desecrating" Chichester cathedral. "Sacking," to be sure. "Desecrating"? That depended on point of view as to what rightfully had "sacred character": Puritans, among others, disagreed with the established church about that. To put it all in context, bear in mind that "All over England people were trying to seize the plate and horses of known sympathizers with the opposite party, to secure strong forts and castles, to make sure of magazines belonging to the militia or trained bands."[6] As the king and his entourage passed through Birmingham on 17 October 1642, locals hijacked the royal carriages, confiscated the royal plate and furniture, and sent them to Warwick castle for safekeeping. Plate was one of the most fungible stores of value that could be plundered, and thus readily useful for the vital purposes of paying one's soldiers. The royalist side was especially short of funding, since it was parliament that the king's subjects had come to accept as keeper of the purse strings, but the parliamentary army as well needed more funding. In a letter to Commons dated 6 January, in wake of Chichester, Waller, AH, and William Cawley reported that "The value of the plate is about one thousand pounds."[7] Whether the army of Waller's Western Association in 1643-44 or the New Model Army under the Presbyterian-controlled parliament of 1646-47 or the northern regiment of AH at Newcastle in 1648, the payment of soldiers was typically if intermittently in arrears.[8]

Usual military practice was to seek shelter and respite in "winter quarters" beginning in December. Waller was an exception, as we have seen above, but he, too, took shelter in January. Those field commanders who were also members of parliament, as Waller and AH were, could then return to their seats at Westminster for the second session. Thus, during February 1642/3 a committee of the Long Parliament was formed for the

---

[6] Richard Ollard, *This War without an Enemy* (New York: Atheneum, 1976), page 61.
[7] Reproduced in an appendix to John Webb, *Military Memoir of Colonel John Birch*, edited by Thomas W Webb (London: Camden Society, 1873), pages 202-03.
[8] Denton, *Only in Heaven* (1997), page 149. Waller's "Western Association" refers to the fact that his army was an amalgamation of militias, those of Gloustershire, Wiltshire, Somerset, Worcestershire, Shropshire, and Bristol, at this early stage of fighting.

purpose of exercising certain executive functions on behalf of parliament, chiefly execution of the war and negotiations about settlement, which some MPs, especially a Presbyterian faction known as "moderates," constantly sought. Known as the Committee of the Two Kingdoms, its membership initially included the earls of Essex (Robert Devereux), Warwick (Robert Rich), Manchester (Edward Montagu), and Northumberland (Algernon Percy), the viscount Saye and Sele (William Fiennes), Sir William Waller, Oliver St John, Oliver Cromwell, AH, and the two Henry Vanes, elder and younger, plus Scottish members of whom Sir Archibald Johnston of Warriston was one. Gardiner ascribed three important qualities to it: its "influence on the conduct of the war"; it was "the first germ of a political union between England and Scotland"; and it was "the first germ of the modern Cabinet system."[9] Dissolved by parliament in February 1648/9, it was replaced by the Council of State, a stronger executive body.

The Spring 1642/3 campaign began with successes on the field but with a fatality that struck home for AH. Having won Stratford-upon-Avon in February, Robert Greville, 2nd baron Brooke, and brother-in-law to AH, proceeded with his troops to a siege of Lichfield, during which he was killed allegedly by a sniper.[10] Greville (b. 1607) had authored several tracts on philosophy and religion, one of which, entitled *A Discourse Opening the Nature of that Episcopacie*, had startled many readers by the extent of his advocacy of freedom of expression: "Heresies must come," he declared (page 86), his point being that no person could judge what God would consider "heretical" and what not. The difference is God's, and it must remain a matter solely between any individual and his or her God. Greville and his brother-in-law must have shared discussions of this and related points, as AH enjoyed accommodations in Greville's Brooke House in Holborn, London.

The field battles continued. Next was on 13 April 1643 at Ripple Field between Glouster and Worcester: AH led a cavalry attack intended to stall an advancing attack by prince Maurice's forces and thus rally other units of Waller's army. But he failed, losing much of his regiment. He thus returned to London, to raise a new regiment of horse, and this time he outfitted his troops, at his own expense, with cuirassiers, a heavier armor which had a peaked breastplate (as can be seen in Exhibit 7.4). Thus was born "the London Lobsters" regiment.

---

[9] Samuel R Gardiner, *History of the Great Civil War*, 4 volumes (London: Longmans, Green & Co., 1886-1901), volume 1, page 360.

[10] Gardiner, *Civil War ...* (1886), volume 1, page 113.

Exhibit 7.3. Robert Greville, 2nd baron Brooke

According to one estimate, the cost of a cuirassier was about four and a half pounds in 1629, more than three times the cost of the light, more common armor.[11] Judgments of its utility varied, for the added weight slowed the average horse and weakened long-term stamina. It is evident from the date of the portrait in Exhibit 7.4, however, that AH had been familiar with the armor at least since 1640 and had concluded from that experience that the trade-off was acceptable. Sir Ralph Hopton, a royalist commander with whom Waller and AH would engage, recalled in his memoir that "there came to his [Waller's] assistance Sir Arthur Haselridge with a verie strong Regiment of extraordinarily arm'd horse (by the Royalists surnamed the Lobsters because of the bright iron-shell with which they are all covered)." He then quoted this item from the (13th to 20th) June, 1643, issue of the *Weekly Intelligencer*: "Six gallant troops of horse went to him [Waller] from London the last week under the command

---

[11] Philip Haythornthwaite, *The English Civil War 1642-1651: An Illustrated Military History* (Poole: Blandford Press, 1983), pages 45, 49.

of Sir Arthur Hazlerigg."[12] By Hyde's estimate, his regiment of horse numbered 500 men, so it was a very expensive proposition to outfit all of them in the ironwork.[13]

Exhibit 7.4. Sir Arthur Hesilrige in "Lobster" Armor, 1640

---

[12]Ralph Hopton, *Bellum Civile: Hopton's Narrative of his Campaign in the West (1642-1644) and Other Papers*, edited by Charles E H Chadwyck Healey (London: Harrison and Sons, 1902), page 51.
[13] Edward Hyde, *History of the Rebellion and Civil War*, 8 volumes (Oxford: Clarendon Press), volume 4, page 120.

Early July brought a series of skirmishes between Waller's army, AH's Lobster regiment included, and royalist forces including Hopton's regiment. These were mostly fought to draws. But overall they could be summed as a victory for the royalists, since their advance toward London was not stymied. However, their cost in casualties was very heavy. AH's regiment acquitted themselves quite well: the Lobsters, as some royalist opponents assessed them, "had shown themselves to be possessed of better military qualities than was found in the cavalry of Essex' army" (i.e., the eastern army under command of the earl of Essex).[14] AH was wounded in battle, how seriously is unknown. Vicars reported that he was wounded in a thigh by the "push of a pike" and then in an "arm; but not mortal or dangerous."[15] Apparently he was able to recover for the siege of Devises, in Wiltshire, a few days later. Since this operation saw little action, however, he would have had additional time for recovery. Complete recovery would have proved fortunate, because on the 13th of the month came a major battle on Roundway Down in Wiltshire. It was a rout for the king's cause. Waller's army disintegrated, in part because AH's regiment failed to hold. Accounts vary, of course, depending on loyalty of witness. The account given by Gardiner suggests a major tactical blunder at the outset, as Waller's army was poorly positioned on slick, hilly terrain of the downs, and rather than withdraw in order to regroup on more favorable terrain they engaged. In any case, said Gardiner, "Hazlerigg impetuously charged up the hill, but on the steep slippery down the courage of the Lobsters was executed in vain." They were repulsed, and that "repulse

> struck terror into the western horsemen, the relics of Stamford's horse, who formed the weakest part of Waller's army. The whole of the Parliamentary cavalry rushed madly down the hillside, 'where never horses went down or up before.' Waller joined in the flight, and his infantry, abandoned by their comrades and their general, knew their case to be hopeless.[16]

Hyde summarized part of the disaster by saying that "after a sharp conflict, in which Sir Arthur Haslerig received many wounds, that impenetrable regiment [the Lobsters] was routed." In the rout it was "every man shifting for himself with greater danger by the precipices of that hill" than from the

---

[14] Gardiner, *Civil War* ... (1886), volume 1, pages 199-202.
[15] Denton, *Only in Heaven* (1997), page 75.
[16] Gardiner, *Civil War* ... (1886), volume 1, pages 203-204.

regiment's pursuers, who also had to contend with the slippery terrain.[17] By at least one account, AH nearly died from his wounds. In absence of reliable evidence of the wound(s), we can only surmise, from subsequent behavior, that the initial wound carried rather low threat of mortality but that infection, perhaps combined with initial loss of blood and/or blunt-force trauma, raised the likelihood of death. Physicians did the best they could with what they knew, but they knew hardly anything, and some of what they thought they knew was more harmful than helpful. The germ theory of disease had been proposed a century earlier, and microscopic examinations as well as other evidence rapidly accumulated to support it. But little effective use of it in combating infection was yet possible, for lack of technical application. Infected wounds that by present-day means would be minor then often proved fatal.

A captain of prince Maurice's horse at Roundway Down, Richard Atkins, later, while writing his memoir, *Vindication of Richard Atkyns* (published in 1669), remembered his engagement with AH. An extract of that memoir, featuring his account of his participation in the first civil war, has been edited and published as part of a series of military memoirs.[18] All of Atkyns' service including at Roundway Down took place in 1643, so this part of his *Vindication* is based on a memory of events 25 years old. As editor Young said in his introductory remarks, Atkyns sought to present himself "in the best possible light," and with regard to his military adventure "he certainly succeeds."[19]

> 'Twas my fortune in a direct line to charge their general of horse [AH], which I supposed to be so by his place; he dis-charged his carbine first, but at a distance not to hurt us, and afterwards one of his pistols, before I came up to him, and missed with both: I then immediately struck into him, and touched him before I discharged mine; and I'm sure I hit him, for he staggered, and presently wheeled off from his party and ran.
>
> Here I must desire the readers to be very particular in this relation, because twenty several persons have entitled them-selves to this action and a Knight that shall be nameless, that is dead (speaking of his great services and small rewards to me) told

---

[17] Edward Hyde, *History* ..., (1826), volume 4, page 134.
[18] Richard Atkyns, *Vindication of Richard Atkyns*, edited by Peter Young (London: Longmans, Green, 1967). It is published together with a memoir by John Gwyn.
[19] Atkyns, *Vindication* (1967), page 4. The following quotation is from pages 23-25. The interpolations (other than square brackets) are by the editor, Peter Young.

me the very ensuing story himself, all but that he could not give so good reason as I could, why it was Sir Arthur Haslerigge. When he wheeled off, I pursued him, and had not gone twenty yards after him, but I heard a voice saying, ''Tis Sir Arthur Haslerigge follow him'; but from which party the voice came I knew not they being joined, nor never did know till about seven years since, but follow him I did, and in six score yards I came up to him, and discharged the other pistol at him, and I'm sure I hit his head, for I touched it before I gave fire, and it amazed him at that present, but he was too well armed all over for a pistol bullet to do him any hurt, having a coat of mail all over his arms and a headpiece (I am confident) musket proof, his sword had two edges and a ridge in the middle, and mine [was] a strong tuck [a long, straight, heavy cavalry sword]; after I had slackened by pace a little, he was gone twenty yards from me, riding three-quarters speed, and down the side of a hill, his posture was waving his sword right and left hand of his horse, not looking back [to see] whether he were pursued or not, (as I conceive) to daunt any horse that should come up to him; [in] about six score more I came up to him again (having a very swift horse that Cornet Washnage gave me) and stuck by him a good while, and tried him from head to the saddle, and could not penetrate him, nor do him any hurt; but in his attempt he cut my horse's nose, that you might put your finger in the wound, and gave me such a blow on the inside of my arm amongst the veins that I could hardly hold my sword; he went on as before, and I slackened my pace again, and found my horse drop blood, and not so bold as before; but about eight score more I got up to him again, thinking to have pulled him off his horse; but he having now found the way, struck my horse upon the cheek, and cut off half the headstall of my bridle, but falling off from him, I ran his horse into the body and resolved to attempt nothing further than to kill his horse; all this time we were together hand to fist.

In the nick of time up came Mr Holmes [Atkyns' cornet] to my assistance (who never failed me in time of danger) and went up to him with a great resolution, and felt him before he discharged his pistol, and though I saw him hit him, 'twas but a flea-biting to him; whilst he charged him, I employed myself in killing his horse, and ran him into several places, and upon the faltering of his horse his headpiece opened behind, and I gave him a prick in the neck, and I had run him through the head if my horse had not stumbled at the same place; then came in Captain Buck [presumably a reformado officer] a gentleman of my troop, and discharged his pistol upon him also, but with the same success as before, and being a very strong man, and charging with a mighty hanger [a kind of cutlass], stormed him and amazed him, but fell off again; by this time his horse began to faint with bleeding, and fell off from his rate, at which said Sir Arthur, 'What good will it do you to kill a poor man?' said I 'Take quarter then', with that he stopped his horse, and I came up to him, and bid him deliver his sword, which he was loathe to do; and being tied twice about his wrist, he was fumbling a great while before he would part with it; but before he delivered it, there was a runaway troop of theirs that had espied him in hold; says one of them 'My Lord General is taken prisoner'; says another, 'Sir Arthur Haslerigge is taken prisoner, face about and charge', with that they rallied and charged us, and rescued him; wherein I received a shot with a pistol, which only took off the skin upon the blade bone of my shoulder.

Atkins' memoir was written while he was in prison for debts and published soon after his release. A copy of the first edition of the complete memoir is in the British Museum. The subsequent literature of commentary (on AH, mainly) contains a somewhat abbreviated version that differs in a few particulars, but these are inconsequential.[20]

The reliability of Atkins' account is open to question. There are some internal reasons for doubting its accuracy, perhaps its veracity. For one, the account is remarkably detailed for a memory that was 25 years distant from the events of that afternoon on Roundway Down. At the least, it is strongly suggestive of the common tendency to intersperse among the fragments of memory connective tissue of "what must have happened" in order for the whole to seem coherent. This is a characteristic of memory in general, not Atkyns' memory alone. Virtually all memories are fabrics of indeliberately reconstructed pieces, and the reconstructions themselves are fluid, changing with time and circumstance. While each of us likes to think that one's own memories are different, are complete and immutable and perfect or nearly perfect exactitudes of "what really happened," they virtually never are.

---

[20] See, e.g., the account cited in Denton, *Only in Heaven* (1997), page 79.

Then, too, sometimes memories are more or less deliberately altered, altered in ways that make the person remembering look better in some fashion, more honest or braver or less embarrassing, and so on. One suspects that memories of combat—that is, those memories that a person *wants* to keep and to share—are among the most malleable in predictable directions. Atkins' account could well be an example. His subsequent years lend substance to that possibility. As the entry for him in the 1904 (corrected) edition of the *Dictionary of National Biography* indicates, prior to writing his *Vindication* while in prison for debts Atkins had attempted to claim credit for discovery of an old manuscript that was later shown to be a hoax. Whether he was author of the hoax or a dupe, he had clearly sought to profit from it, both financially and in influence with the royal court. Neither benefit occurred. The vindication he chiefly sought in his memoir was in relation to that scandal, his indebtedness, and his time in prison. His account of the contest with AH was as a character reference, so to speak. But it proved to be one that some of AH's critics endorsed with gusto, having reversed the target of the reference so that it would be presented as proof of cowardice.

Next came the siege of Basing House (Basingstoke, Hampshire), a royalist stronghold on the west road leading to London. Because details of this siege are murky, we can only guess as to the participants at any given date, but it is unlikely that AH was there, or even in the vicinity; more likely he was in London, nursing his wounds. The siege began in July and continued until November, when Waller, after sustaining major losses to his army elsewhere, withdrew his forces, leaving the field to the king's forces. The war in the west was not going well for parliament's army, and some of the more radical Independents had begun calling for more aggressive leadership in the field. Waller was on the defensive in London as well as in the western field. He relied upon AH to quiet the tempers in Commons. AH had raised a regiment of foot in London and, on 2 September 1643, assigned it to the command of John Birch, as a newly appointed lieutenant colonel. He had never shown much interest in foot soldiering, in any case, but at the moment his skills were needed for an essentially political task. Waller assigned him, as head of council, the task of examining "the merits of every man that should stand to bear any office in the army, with power to cross all such out of the list as should be judged unfit or unworthy."[21]

---

[21] John Adair, *Roundhead General: A Military Biography of Sir William Waller* (London: Macdonald, 1969), page 107; Denton, *Only in Heaven* (1997), page 86.

Soon word arrived that the earl of Essex, Robert Devereux, had won a victory at Newbury in Berkshire, which, like Basingstoke, lay about 60 miles to the west of London. A few days later the Long Parliament, in wake of earlier negotiations initiated by John Pym, ratified an agreement with the Scottish Covenanters to make common cause, thus bringing the Scots into the war and opening another front to the north.

Early in October, the earl of Manchester, Edward Montagu, along with others of the Eastern Association including a "slowly emerging cavalry commander, Oliver Cromwell, whose name was just becoming known outside his own East Anglia," won a victory at Winceby, bringing Lincolnshire into the Eastern Association.[22] With this strategic victory in hand, the parliamentary forces were once again looking more like a major offensive threat to the royalists, lessening the impact of Waller's retreat from his siege of Basing House. The change of momentum appeared to be confirmed in November, as the remains of Waller's army of the Western Association, now including AH's regiment of foot under John Birch, set out from Farnham to engage Ralph Hopton's forces in the southwest. In early December AH's horse was involved in a successful skirmish at Alton in Hampshire, but AH himself was probably in London. Perhaps he was still recovering from his battle wounds, possibly psychological as well as physical (there is some suggestion that he had lost his zest for battle after Roundway Down). But political matters had also kept him at Westminster duties, for adjustments had been needed. One sort of needed adjustment was described above, motions to placate the most radical members of the Independent faction of MPs, who, by Hyde's telling (among others), had counted AH as one of the leading members. But since December 8th still another adjustment was needed, for on that day John Pym had died. It was not an unexpected death; he had suffered pains of stomach cancer during the months of autumn, and physicians had nothing to match tumors. Even so, the loss of Pym's presence was heavily felt.

Once again, the armies took winter quarters. But this year, winter quarters ended early, briefly, for a crucial battle in Cheshire, the battle of Nantwich. At the time, Nantwich was the only town in the area still held by forces on the side of rebellion, and it had come under siege by a royalist force led by John, 1st baron Byron.[23] On 25 January 1643/4, as the town was about to succumb, a force led by Sir Thomas Fairfax rode to rescue of a failing parliamentary army, defeated the siege, saved Nantwich, and in

---

[22] Denton, *Only in Heaven* (1997), page 87.
[23] A descendant of his brother became the 6th baron Byron, George Gordon Byron, better known as lord Byron, romanticist poet.

the process captured a royalist general, George Monck, who would sit out the remainder of the first civil war in the Tower of London. Fairfax went on to play an important role in the remainder of the first civil war; Monck, later in the second and its aftermath.

The next major battle was another in Hampshire, this one on site between two villages, Cheriton and Alresford, on 29 March 1644. Simply from the list of engagements in Hampshire alone, it is easy to see why some critics of the parliamentary military forces had become agitated. After 17 months of fighting since Edgehill, this would be the fifth battle within a radius of 20 miles, none of which seemingly had led to permanent advantage in the county. The battle of Cheriton, won by the rebels after a three-hour standstill, would leave the critics in no better mood, for soon there would be another siege of Basing House, 18 miles away, another battle of Newbury, 32 miles away.

One difference at Cheriton, by comparison to Alton and other recent engagements, was AH's presence in combat again, leading his horse to victory. After hours of parrying with no discernable change, he "at last ... spied a gap between the enemy's horse and foot. Thrusting his troopers into the unoccupied space, he gained a position which decided the battle."[24] Gardiner pointed out that whereas Hyde had apparently sought to lessen implications of the royalist defeat by saying that their horse troops had not fought well, this was accurate only of a unit of French troops (who, after all, had less at stake). Gardiner quoted a royalist who said, "I am confident our horse did perform more gallant charges that day than hath been known in any one [other] battle this war." AH's report to Commons concurred: "their horse, being very good, gave many charges, and maintained their charges on both sides three hours." Hopton, the royalist commander, said of the key event that, AH, having brought his troops into the gap, "in view of our whole Army (much to our discouragement) kills and takes every man."[25]

At one point during the battle at Cheriton, an interesting bit of banter occurred between AH and Col. John Birch, according to the latter's memoir.[26] Their forces having just sustained something of a (temporary)

---

[24] Gardiner, *Civil War* ... (1886), volume 1, pages 383-84; and for the next passages, page 383n.

[25] Hopton, *Bellum Civile* (1902), page 102.

[26] John Webb, *Birch Memoir* ... (1873), pages 9-10. This memoir, recall, only 37 pages in length, was recorded by a man known only by his last name, Roe, who served Birch in the field as something of an adjutant and secretary. He recorded Birch's events and accounts in the second person. Here, the personal pronouns "you" and "your" have been replaced with Birch's name.

setback, AH, "seeing our men put to soe shamefull a route, turned to [Birch,] saying, 'Now, Colonel, have you Fighting enough?' [Birch's] answer instantly given was, 'Sir, this is but a rub; wee shall yet winn the cast.'" To which the editor of the memoir added his own footnote: "The cheerful allusion to bowls tells us that Roundheads as well as Cavaliers amused themselves with this favourite game." The anecdote suggests that AH had acquired a more mature perspective on combat, in comparison to his initial attitude, but also that he had regained a robustness of confidence, if in fact it had been depleted because of Roundway Down. Speculation is all that available evidence allows, however. Denton, in considering the same anecdote, did not see in it a comradely jibe but only a boastful claim by Birch's adjutant-secretary about his commander.[27] In fact, Denton was seemingly unsure that AH (as opposed to "Hesilrige's horse") had even been engaged in the battle of Cheriton, although Denton did address Denzil Holles' claim that AH had been observed "crying under a hedge" (as noted at the beginning of this chapter).

The record does show, however, that AH travelled back and forth between London and Waller's army of the Western Association following Cheriton.[28] Much of his time in London was devoted to meetings of the Committee of Both Kingdoms (aka "of the Two Kingdoms"), principally a matter of coordinating military activities of the Scottish forces in the far north and the armies of the south. It has been speculated that during these meetings AH and Oliver Cromwell became good friends. Both men were active on the committee, and it is clear that they worked cooperatively with one another. Whether an actual friendship developed is not so clear. While several letters from Cromwell to AH exist, some of them giving personal regard, correspondence in the other direction is nearly nonexistent. For a man who spent his adult years in such momentous affairs, political, social, and military, and who, the evidence shows (as partly reproduced in the next chapter), did write extensively, very little of his correspondence survived, whether in Cromwell's estate or in other repositories.

The month of June (1644) saw the start of another siege of Basing House (this one, not involving AH, continuing into October). AH had returned to Waller's army and soon, with Waller, addressed the Committee with a proposal to stop the dithering, bring the two armies—Devereux' (Essex) and Waller's—into a unified force, which would exceed Charles' army at Oxford, and proceed to "separate the king from his army." This

---

[27] Denton, *Only in Heaven* (1997), pages 92-93.
[28] *Calendar of State Papers, Domestic (1644)*, pages 117-18, 121-22; Denton, *Only in Heaven* (1997), page 95.

was, as Denton said, a "revolutionary" idea, proposed in their letter of the 7th of June to the Committee of Both Kingdoms: to capture the king, thus ending the war, and taking him to London.[29] It was not an idea that many in the Long Parliament were prepared to entertain. Because the initial term of the Committee had expired, and because the House of Lords was slow to agree a new membership, coordination among parliamentary factions had taken a holiday. But more generally, it is clear at least in retrospect, that few MPs had extended their serious planning to the consequence, however likely or unlikely they might have thought it, of a captured king. What would they do with him? Perhaps the unstated assumption had been that, as in the War of the Roses, and Richard III at Bosworth Field, the king would be killed in battle, his body sent to earthly repose and forgotten under a later century's layer of asphalt.

No answer from the Long Parliament would counter the next passel of bad news: the month was not yet over, and Waller's army suffered a devastating defeat at Cropredy Bridge in Oxfordshire. Jealousy between the two field generals, Devereux and Waller (by some accounts, more the former toward the latter), indecisiveness in the Long Parliament, and the long grind on soldiers who often struggled with fatigue, poor conditions in the field, and intermittent pay, had been exacting heavy costs since the early months of the year, when it seemed that entry of the Scottish forces in the north was aiding the cause by drawing royalist forces northward.

In fact, the aid of Scotland's Army of the Covenanters was proving crucial, although that might not have been so clear until early July and the battle of Marston Moor in the North Riding of Yorkshire. The Scottish army was commanded by Alexander Leslie, 1st earl of Leven, who had an extensive background in military training and experience in Sweden and elsewhere. Leslie had been made supreme commander of the Army of Both Kingdoms, which included from the English side Edward Montagu's (earl of Manchester) army and Sir Thomas Fairfax' army.[30] In surely the largest battle ever fought on English soil, Leslie's force met the royalist army commanded by the king's nephew, prince Rupert of the Rhine, on the evening of 2 July. Initially holding its own, the royalist force was then quickly overwhelmed, with at least 4,000 dead and 1,500 captured, while Leslie's forces sustained losses in the low hundreds. The defeat was so severe that Charles' presence in the northern counties effectively came to an end, cutting him off from supply lines through the northeastern ports to the continent as well as from resources of loyalists in the northern part of

---

[29] Denton, *Only in Heaven* (1997), page 100.
[30] Ollard, *This War* ... (1976), pages 105-21.

his own kingdom. He had been more or less isolated to the counties around his base at Oxford.

One would think that a decisive turn in the war, now two years old, had occurred at last. And yet, a few months after Marston Moor, at the second battle of Newbury the king's army met the combined armies of Waller, Devereux (Essex), and Montagu (Manchester). Devereux, fighting a cold, had retired to a house in Reading, leaving his army to be divided between the two other commanders. AH was present, leading a cavalry regiment under Lieutenant-General Sir William Balfour. The outcome has been called by some commentators a tactical victory for the rebel armies, but strategically it was at best a draw on that late October day, with heavy casualties on both sides. Considering that the royalist force numbered fewer than half their opponents, there was much cause for relief among the former and dissatisfaction among the latter. As the royalist army retreated, some leaders of the parliamentary army urged pursuit and, at the moment of advantage, re-engagement. Because others expressed doubt, a council of war was held in the field on 10 November. Commanders in attendance included Montagu, the over-all commander, Waller, Balfour, Cromwell, and AH. The main point of contention was whether to pursue the retreating Charles and his army or to end the campaign for the winter. Concern about the state of the parliamentary army was expressed: battlefield losses had mounted; their ranks were thinning also by desertions, as many soldiers were peeling off to forage for food in the nearby towns; fatigue had long been apparent, horses and foot soldiers alike. But underlying all of that concern, a simmering suspicion had been magnified by dissatisfaction with the army's performance at Newbury. Was Montagu really in this war, or was he mostly watching from the sidelines? He himself lent new credence to that doubt when he uttered his famous "gambling" scenario:

> Gentlemen, I beseech you, let's consider what we do. The king need not care how oft he fights, but it concerns us to be wary for in fighting we venture all to nothing. If we fight 100 times and beat him 99 he will be king still, but if he beats us once, or the last time, we shall be hanged, we shall lose our estates, and our posterities be undone.[31]

---

[31] *Calendar of State Papers,* Domestic (1644-45), pages 150-51. In his *Civil War* (1886) volume 1, pages 508-18, Gardiner gave a different account, apparently having misread the record. See also Denton, *Only in Heaven* (1997), pages 114-15, for a similar discussion of the account in context.

AH had already expressed his impatience with the dithering, to which Montagu retorted, "Thou art a Bloody Fellow."[32] But now, having heard Montagu's explanation of caution, Cromwell erupted in anger, accusing Montagu of having, by his own account, wasted so many lives for nothing.

Denton has offered a commendable account of some of the details of the ensuing controversy, including AH's testimony before a committee of the Long Parliament on the 8th and again on the 28th of December.[33] The committee had been formed to consider Cromwell's charges of Montagu's ineptitude, and AH sided with Cromwell. Rather than reproduce all of that, interesting though it is, let's cut to the conclusion. Cromwell won the contest. Having served as first officer to the highly experienced and skilled Thomas Fairfax in the north, and having seen the success of the combined forces of Alexander Leslie in Yorkshire, Cromwell knew better than any of his southern comrades—Waller, Montagu, Devereux, Balfour, or AH—what a professional army looked like, and what it could do. Parliament needed a standing army of professional soldiers. But to achieve that goal, powerful resistance in the House of Lords (Montagu, recall, was the earl of Manchester; Devereux, the earl of Essex; and so forth), and in some of the counties for which local militias had served virtually as private armies of local lords, had to be overcome. Presbyterian members of parliament, believing that with the Scottish Covenanters now involved they were on the way to becoming the established church of England as well as Scotland, resisted change. And many Puritans, AH included, were suspicious of too much centralization of power and authority.

The sometimes heated competition between Presbyterians and the faction of Independents in Commons, plus the partly parallel competition between the Presbyterian powers in the Long Parliament and the radical "junto" of merchants, traders, and nascent capitalists who ruled London's local government, had to be negotiated, subordinated to the extent possible, if Cromwell's proposal was to succeed. Presbyterians, holding the balance of power in Commons, could be persuaded by the example of the army of the Covenanters. But what that could mean to the Puritans, especially the more radical faction of them, might be gauged by the example of a recently published booklet by John Milton, the eventually famous *Areopagitica*, hot off the press on 23 November 1644. Toward the end of his plea, Milton said "It is

---

[32] Cecil E Lucas-Phillips, *Cromwell's Captains* (London: Heinemann, 1938), page 125; Denton, *Only in Heaven* (1997), pages 114, 118.
[33] Denton, *Only in Heaven* (1997), pages 114-18. See also *Calendar of State Papers, Domestic* (1644-45), pages 151, 156-57.

liberty which is the nurse of all great wits. This is that which hath rarify'd and enlighten'd our spirits like the influence of heav'n; this is that which hath enfranchis'd, enlarg'd and lifted up our apprehensions degrees above themselves....

... Give me the liberty to know, to utter, and to argue freely according to conscience, above all liberties.

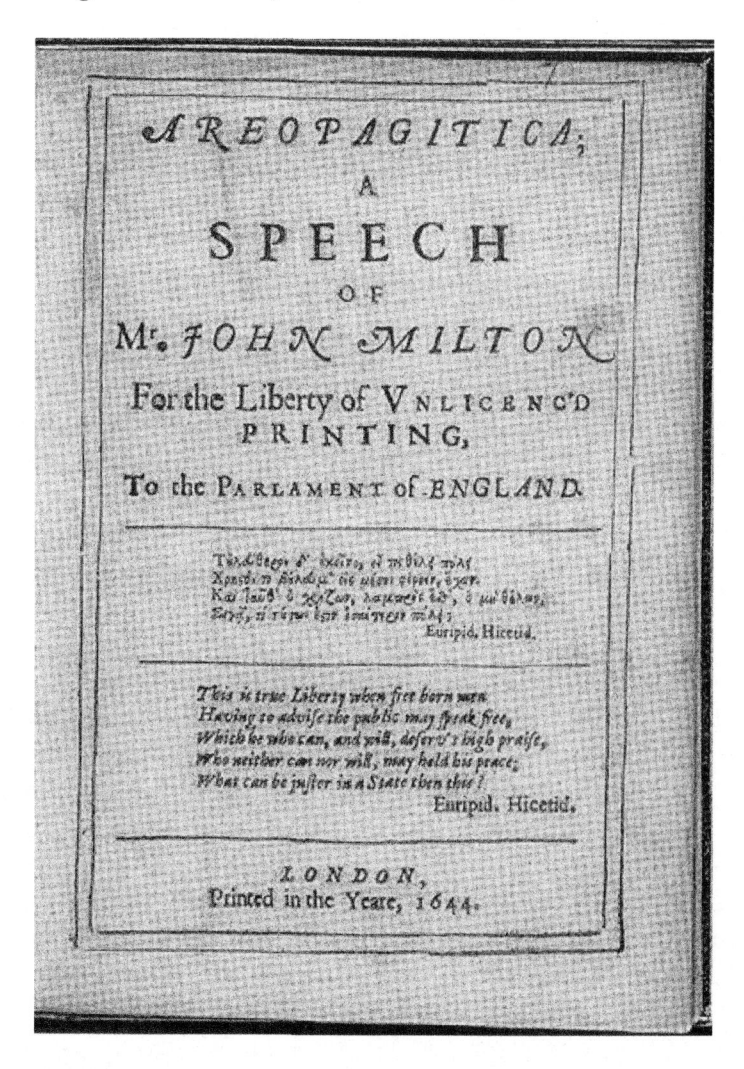

Exhibit 7.5. Cover of John Milton's *Areopagitica*, 1644

His appeal was against acts of censorship which had been enacted by the Presbyterian-dominated MPs, under the usual guise of requiring a licence to print, in order to impose their own beliefs on the nation as a whole. This terrible "war without an enemy," as it was named by Waller to his friend Hopton, commanders of opposing armies, was being fought by the rebels as an act against one regime's denial of liberty of conscience for the sake of an absolutism and concentration of power. Was the aim simply to install a wall of censorship around a different set of beliefs? Was the aim merely to exchange one concentration of power and authority for another, now under the name of a "professional army"? But could the initial cause of liberty ever be achieved by agglomerations of so many local "trained bands" under the command of mutually jealous local lords who thought of their engagements as a game for aristocratic men born to titular gallantry?

Again, winter recess gave pause and respite. On the political front, the most notable overt act occurred on 10 January 1644/5 when the Long Parliament finally resolved to execute the former archbishop Laud, who had languished in prison months upon end. But behind the scenes changes were underway, as the Committee of Both Kingdoms was considering "the Frame or Model of the whole Militia" (i.e., the parliamentary army). This was the beginning of what was then called the "new-modelled" army, later to be known as "the New Model Army." Authorization was separate from but closely associated with an act, the Self-Denying Ordinance, which passed Commons on 19 December 1644 and eventually, on 3 April 1645, the House of Lords. Declaring that no member of parliament could hold office in the parliamentary army, this ordinance, probably composed by Henry Vane the younger and Oliver St John, had the clear intent to remove leadership and administration of the army from the jealousies and localist loyalties of men such as the earl of Manchester (Montague) and the earl of Essex (Devereux). What was presented as a free choice—resign one's seat in parliament or resign one's military commission—was in fact no choice at all for Peers, since they could not resign their seats in Lords without abandoning their standings in the peerage. The ordinance was written so as not to affect Alexander Leslie, commander of the Scottish Covenanters, since his earldom was Scottish, not English. An ad hoc exception was granted Cromwell at the request of Thomas Fairfax, who was appointed as first commander-in-chief of the army. One must bear in mind that at this point Cromwell was known almost entirely as a military person. While having been in Commons as long as AH, for example, he had gained very little presence as a parliamentarian.[34]

---

[34] Gardiner, *Civil War ...* (1886), volume 1, page 186; Robertson, *Tyrannicide Brief*, (2005), page 66.

Once the new army took the field, the fortunes of war changed markedly. Fairfax moved westward to Oxford, laying siege to the town. Part of the king's army countered by taking Leicester. Fairfax then moved toward Leicester and engaged the royalist force in battle near the village of Naseby in Northamptonshire (about 16 miles south of Noseley). The king's force was destroyed, the king himself barely rescued by his nephew, Prince Rupert. Fairfax next destroyed the remainder of the royalist army, then took all of the royalist fortresses in the west and south of England. Naseby was, as Ollard has said, "the last great set-piece battle of the civil war to be fought on English soil." Fairfax' subsequent operation had been made the easier, because at Naseby the king's "foot and guns were all captured, as were such of his cavalry as were not killed," excepting the few who directly attended the king. Yet, as "if anything could be worse, the victors captured and published all of the king's secret correspondence," having found it in his mobile cabinets. This publication, *The King's Cabinet Opened*, "proved to anyone whose mind was still ajar to evidence that Charles could not be trusted."[35]

King Charles and a small retinue surrendered to a Scottish force at Southwell, Nottinghamshire, on 5 May 1646. Some royalist forces here and there remained active, but they were easily defeated. At last the civil war was over. Or so it seemed.

Revolutionary Politics
AH had been almost entirely at politics since the battle of Cheriton; mostly, even before. His tasks on the Committee of Both Kingdoms included acts of diplomacy designed to smooth jealousies and controversies among commanders of the field, persuasive messages to other members of the committee, and to MPs more generally, to accelerate overdue pay to troops in the field, and, increasingly after Newbury, to seek possible agreements that could move the war forward to desired conclusion. No sooner had the king surrendered than he found himself in the middle of a struggle between the New Model Army and leading lights of both houses of parliament. If, as a famous military theorist of the nineteenth century said, war is simply a continuation of politics by other means, the settlement in wake of a just-ended war sometimes contains unrecognized seeds, even means, of a next war. So it was here, in part because the victors were sharply disparate with regard to some elements of a settlement, thus signaling strategic possibility for a king who would not relent. Charles knew he still had royalist support throughout England; he knew the Long Parliament was divided between

---

[35] Ollard, *This War* ... (1976), pages 133, 136.

two main factions, Presbyterians and Independents; and he knew that the Scots were both fractious and suspicious that Westminster had not been wholly content with the alliance because of disagreements about religion. Perhaps he could recruit an Irish army. Perhaps he could recruit support in France. Many possibilities were in the offing.

Charles was being held at Newcastle-upon-Tyne by a Scottish contingent who treated him lightly. Little more than a month passed since his surrender and he received from the Long Parliament a set of proposals as basis for a treaty. Known as the Newcastle Propositions, they included abolition of episcopacy, reform of the established church along the lines of Presbyterianism, parliamentary control of the army and militias for twenty years, and parliamentary nomination of leading officials and judges. The king did not intend to accept any of them, but he knew that delay would allow fissures to form and grow. So he delayed his response. In this he misjudged his captors' interests. In February they surrendered Charles to Westminster in return for a £4,000,000 indemnity, and the Scottish Army of Covenanters went home. In May 1647 Charles offered a modified basis for entreaty, carefully designed to promote a coalition of Scots with the Presbyterian faction and royalists in England. In the meantime, he pursued possibilities of an Irish army and inquiries in France.

The king's strategy of "divide and conquer" showed some signs of eventual success, as the Presbyterian faction, the majority parliamentary faction, expressed interest in his proposal. At this point the Independents seemed weakly organized across their disparate (informal) membership, uncertain about a next course of action mainly because they were uncertain what they wanted to accomplish. In another fifteen months or so, Cromwell will have declared in effect for the Independents. But the evidence supports Ollard's thesis that throughout 1647 and at least most of 1648 Cromwell remained largely uncommitted in the conflict between Independent and Presbyterian factions. If anything, he seemed more sympathetic to the latter faction in Commons, although that could have been an effect of their majority status.[36] Cromwell's tendency when faced with strategic, sometimes even tactical choices, was to wait for a balance of "signs," a tendency that continued well into his later status as "lord protector." From present-day perspective one could think he tended to wait "to see which way the cookie crumbled"; and in a sense that description does fit—except that in his mind the "cookie crumbled" by God's hand. Certainly there is an important psychological dimension to that process that remains unanswered: how did he know, by what internal

---

[36] Ollard, *This War* ... (1976), page 161.

scale, when the line had been drawn under "signs" such that he was confident of their summation? When did he cease interpretation with a conclusive message of God's word? In any case, the record of events suggests that on this debate he did not hear a conclusion until after the Putney debates (see below) and perhaps not with finality of conclusion until well into the resumption of civil war in 1648.

For his part, AH seemingly remained rather quiet during the latter part of 1647. We know that during the period from 1645 to 1648, perhaps beyond, he was residing in a house in Islington (today a borough of London nearly due north of St Peter's Cathedral, then a "suburban" or "satellite" village).[37] Whether it was accommodation just for him or for his wife and children as well we do not know. But the household record suggests that new children had been, perhaps were being, added. The ride from London to Noseley required the better part of three days each way; banditry along the roads was an ever present risk; so it seems unlikely that AH would have made that journey a routine part of his usual course of life, especially not after all the riding he had just recently endured between Westminster and various army encampments. All in all, one suspects he was engaged in the roles of husband and father far more than he had been in many months. That would have continued until December 1647, when he was appointed governor of Newcastle. Was this at his request or with his consent? Again, we do not know. Surely he consented, but that he had requested the move seems unlikely though possible. Bear in mind that the Presbyterian faction was in ascendancy in Parliament. Perhaps he did not see near-term change in that fact and sought some distance from the on-going intrigue and unrest in London. Or perhaps the Presbyterian faction wanted to put him at greater distance for their own purposes. In either case, he was back at Westminster by the middle of January 1647/8, as will be seen below.

Controversy and unrest had increased in London mainly because of all the disruptions that ensued from the civil war, the absence of the royal court, and the efforts to create replacement institutions of governance. Add to that the fact that many soldiers and officers of the New Model Army were dissatisfied with their treatment, especially but not exclusively because of the wage arrears, and one can well imagine the bubbling cauldron. At the end of April 1647 the army had elected a delegation ("the Agitators," they were sometimes called) to present grievances to the Long Parliament. Less than six weeks later a contingent of troops "relieved" a

---

[37] J Richards, "The Greys of Bradgate in the English Civil War," *Transactions of the Leicestershire Archæological and Historical Society*, volume 62 (1988), pages 32-52, at pages 35, 44.

small parliamentary commission of their loose custody of the king and put him under control of the army. A few days prior to that action the army's general council had agreed a document entitled *Solemn Engagement*, an assertion of the army's refusal to disband and its interest, especially in light of willingness to compromise with the king, to reach a final settlement that would not mock the sacrifices that had been made. This document went to Parliament on 8 June 1647. Needless to say, it alarmed the Presbyterian faction, who soon began a campaign to mobilize Londoners against the army. The army had singled out, as MPs who were plotting against the army and for return of the king, eleven members, among them Denzil Holles and Sir William Waller. All of the men, known thereafter as "the Eleven Members," were conceivably involved in efforts to achieve a negotiated settlement that would bring back the king into a somewhat reduced role, but it is unlikely that Waller (among some others, probably excluding Holles) was opposed to the army's interests in wage payments and general respect. In any case, on 26 July 1647 supporters of the Presbyterian faction, who had gained control of the London Militia Committee, rioted in the streets, threatened the Long Parliament because it had not called for the king's return, and demanded several changes in governance. As a result, many Independent MPs, plus the speaker of each house, fled Westminster and sought shelter by the army. On 6 August General Thomas Fairfax marched contingents of the New Model Army into London and restored the Independent MPs to their seats. It became clear that much of the army, including officers, had lost patience with the dithering and the various intrigues on behalf of the king, and were ready to take action. Most of the Eleven Members fled to the continent, Holles and Waller among them. A year later, in the midst of renewed civil war, the ten surviving members were allowed to return to their seats.[38]

The army remained dissatisfied. Internal divisions had long been apparent, and had become all the more thorny with the recent actions. This stimulated a series of proposals and debates, beginning in late August with a document offered by the army's general council, the Heads of Proposals (i.e., proposals for a negotiated settlement), which exacerbated already simmering anger among army radicals who were suspicious of some of their officers, Cromwell included. This cemented a bifurcation between the radicals, often called "Levellers," and the moderate-to-conservative faction, the "Grandees." By early October the radicals had formulated a contrary document, "An Agreement of the People for a firm and present

---

[38] Austin Woolrych, *Soldiers and Statesmen* (Oxford: Clarendon, 1987) offers a good account of the army debates of 1647-48.

peace upon grounds of common right."[39] Its main principles were freedom of religion, frequent election of new parliaments, equality of all under the law, and a later addition of universal suffrage among male property holders at national and local levels. The contrasting documents led to a sequence of debates, beginning late October, in a Surrey town that thereafter gave the event its name, the Putney Debates.

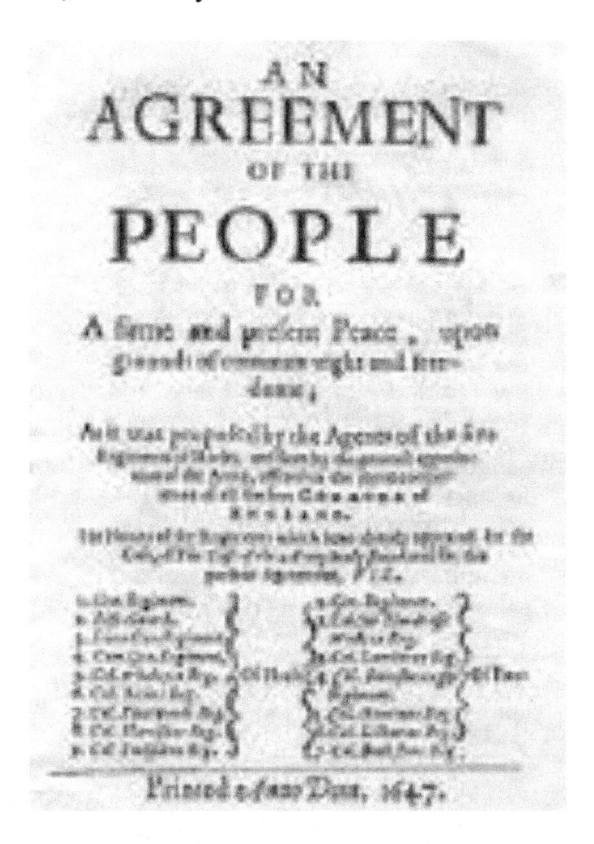

Exhibit 7.6. Cover of Agreement of the People, 1647

Until 2 November the debates were recorded in a shorthand. The reconstituted manuscript was published long after.[40] It is remarkable, well worth reading today. Cromwell, as Fairfax' Lieutenant General, served as chairperson of the meeting. His son-in-law, Henry Ireton, was the leading spokesman for the Grandees. Col. Thomas Rainsborough was the leading spokesman for the army radicals, who had mostly endorsed the Levellers'

---

[39] The document was later revised, at least twice.
[40] Arthur S P Woodhouse, editor, *Puritanism and Liberty* (Chicago: University of Chicago Press, 1951.

"Agreement of the People." Much of the recorded debate centered on the franchise: radicals argued that, as it was fundamental to all other rights, it should be universal to all men; the Grandees opposed by using the long-tested specter of anarchy (at least as old as ancient Athens). Reading the transcript for the 28th and 29th, one cannot but be struck by the effort of Cromwell, at first via his son-in-law but then directly, to refuse recognition of the "one man, one vote" principle, urging Rainsborough (and others) not to insist on it. Rainsborough would have none of this. While trying to avoid confrontation, he persistently rejected Cromwell's guidance.[41]

At least one historian of the period has argued that at the start of the debates Cromwell "wanted to see Charles I removed from the throne, preferably by abdication, but ... did not want to abolish monarchy." The king, "believing rightly that Cromwell did not want Regicide but abdication, gambled on [Cromwell's] unwillingness to resort to the former if he refused to abdicate under the threat of trial and execution. Charles called his bluff and lost."[42] Morrill's argument is that whereas Cromwell began the Putney debates defending the principle of monarchy and arguing for a negotiated settlement, by the end of 1648 he had decided that regicide would be the only workable solution; and that this shift in his view could have begun during the last part of the debates, for which no transcript exists. That last claim, about the unrecorded sessions of the debates, is an interesting speculation, dubious but finally undecidable. That Cromwell had swung in favor of regicide by the end of 1648 is highly probable, if not certain. He would not have been the last—but nearer the last than the first.

We are again ahead of the story. On 8 November 1647 the council was suspended. Cromwell ordered troops back to their regiments, and a new committee, composed of officers only, was installed. Needless to say, many of the troops were less than content with those actions. To make matters worse, they soon learned that the king has escaped custody (on 11 November); regardless actual circumstances, contrivance or at least agreement by those sympathetic to the king seemed indisputable. Four days later a large protest by troops, considered a "near mutiny" by record, erupted at Corkbush Field, just north of London in Hertfordshire. It was forcibly put down by Cromwell and Fairfax. No doubt heartened by news of that episode, the king was heartened even more to win agreement from

---

[41] Rainsborough was killed the next October, as a royalist band attempted capture. At the time, and yet today, there is suspicion that his death was actually assassination, a plot involving enemies in the army and/or parliament.

[42] John Morrill, "Rewriting Cromwell," *Canadian Journal of History*, volume 38 (December 2003), pages 553-578, at pages 559, 568-72.

a faction in Scotland to support his return to England with military force in exchange with his assent to abolish episcopacy and adopt Presbyterian doctrine as England's establish church. Agreed in December 1647, this "Engagement with the Scots" held no genuine commitment by Charles, for he, once restored, could simply reject any unwanted provisions as tactical necessities agreed under a kingly privilege of mental reservation.

The Second Civil War
At Westminster in early January 1647/8 AH introduced a bill calling for an end to all negotiations with the king. Commons approved this "Vote of No Addresses" on the 3rd but the Lords balked. On the 11th the army council of officers at Windsor declared in favor of the bill. Cromwell's interest in a negotiated settlement had all but evaporated, due mainly to the interception of one of Charles' letters to his queen, in which he openly discussed his intrigues and deceptions. Two regiments of troops were sent to London, as protection of the offices of parliament but also as a signal of intent. The Peers who had been resistant gave way, and the bill became law. In support of the legislation, the final declaration listed all of the grievances against the king, including the evidence of his duplicitous and untrustworthy behavior during negotiations. This brought to an end the Committee for Both Kingdoms and, for all practical purposes, the start of the second civil war. It did not last long.

Skirmishes, rebellions, seizures, and mutinies for the king occurred during the spring months, the royalist forces seemingly gaining momentum in the north (capturing Carlisle and Berwick), in the west (e.g., Wales), and in the south (e.g., uprisings in Kent). While the Scottish army, led by James, 1st duke of Hamilton, was slow to cross the border, the king's son, the prince of Wales, optimistically sailed from Holland with the royalist fleet on 17 July. The tide had already turned against them, however, as General Fairfax subdued royalist forces first one place, then another, and Cromwell defeated the royalist forces in Wales. Then on 17 August the Scottish army led by Hamilton was destroyed at the battle of Preston; ten days later Fairfax ordered the execution of royalist commanders after the siege of Colchester; and four days after that Charles, prince of Wales, fled to Holland.

In the meantime, most of the Presbyterian "Eleven Members" who a year earlier had tried to mobilize Londoners to force Commons to accept negotiated settlement with the king had returned to their seats, and at the end of the fighting they led Commons in another attempt, this the so-called Treaty of Newport, named after the place on the Isle of Wight where the king had been held.[43] As a first step, Commons repealed the Vote of No Addresses. Second, a parliamentary commission of nine Peers and six of Commons (including Denzil Holles and Sir Henry Vane) were appointed to conduct the negotiations. Adamantly against compromise on some matters, Charles offered concessions on others, although there was reason to doubt that he was being any less duplicitous than he himself had said of his earlier negotiations. After weeks of slow movement toward conclusion of the talks, Cromwell's son-in-law, General Henry Ireton, convinced the council of officers, including General Fairfax, that once again they and their interests were being sacrificed. The result was adoption of the army's *Remonstrance* against the king and a demand that negotiations cease. The king was moved to secure quarters in Hurst castle, on the south coast of Hampshire, the intent clearly being that the king would be held to account one way or the other. Thus began the process that led to trial of the king. The next step in that process was an army purge of the Long Parliament.

Frustrated and angered that so many of the Presbyterian members of the Long Parliament had been willing to ignore what they thought were the king's obvious ploys and deceits, radical members of the New Model Army resolved to take matters into their own hands. Some, Henry Ireton among them, had concluded to dissolve the Long Parliament altogether. Others were unwilling or uncertain to go that far, concerned about the implications of what in today's vocabulary would be called a military coup. On the 5th of December a meeting of officers led by Ireton with Independent members of Commons discussed the options and finally settled on a purge. The next morning a regiment of foot led by Col. Thomas Pride and a regiment of horse led by Col. Nathaniel Rich, plus other forces on the perimeter, took up positions in Palace Yard and at entrances to Westminster Hall. Pride had a list of MPs to be "secluded" (refused entry). His seconds, Thomas, lord Grey of Groby, Leicestershire, and Sir Hardress Waller, identified the prohibited members as they approached.[44] Pride held the list, ordered the exclusions, and therefore gained fame for "Pride's Purge." About 180 names were on the list. Most of those who appeared the morning of the 6th were simply turned away.

---

[43] The island is 30 to 35 miles off the south coast of England; Newport is in the middle of the island; Charles was held in Carisbrooke castle, southwestern edge of the town.

[44] Lord Grey was son of Henry Grey, earl of Stamford, who, as will be seen in the next chapter, was a sometimes violent critic of AH (among others). Here is another prime instance of civil war dividing a family: father was eventually royalist, although for a time he fought against the king, while son was persistently anti-royalist. Sir Hardress Waller was cousin to Sir William Waller.

But several had been named as "too extreme" or "dangerous" and were arrested, then imprisoned for a time. Among them, Sir William Waller and John Birch, neither happy with the decision. Denzil Holles became aware of the event in time to flee.

Cromwell had been engaged in a "mopping up" operation in the field of battle and arrived the day after the purge. Given the relationship between him and Ireton, it is highly unlikely that he had not known of the plan (as Thomas Fairfax had not). Arriving on the scene, he pronounced his approval (whereas Fairfax protested, to no avail). The purge complete, the Long Parliament was reduced to "the Rump Parliament." The door to trial of the king was now open. On 6 January 1648/9 the Rump Parliament declared itself with full legislative powers. Two weeks later a High Court of Justice opened the trial of Charles, king of England. In another seven days the trial had ended and a warrant for execution of the king had been signed. On the morning of the 30th the Rump passed legislation against the proclamation of any person as "King of England or Ireland, or Dominions thereof." Early in the afternoon of that day Charles Stuart was beheaded.[45] England no longer lived under monarchy. The question now was, under what form of government *would* it live? But for many the question was still about kingship, now regicide. Two years later Thomas Hobbes issued his indictment in *Leviathan* (1651): a civilized society can endure only in the grand bargain of a noble sovereign and his subjects. It seemed so unprecedented, that a king should be killed other than in the glory of some great battle, as Harold had been nearly six hundred years earlier. Thus, a present-day scholar has observed of the contest between parliament and king, as it had developed through the second civil war, "There is no way out of this contradiction, except by regicide, which is damned."[46] Another has said, replying in part to Hobbes' indictment, "Tyrannicide was in the air as soon as medieval Europeans learned to conjugate *occīdêre*."[47] What is the difference if a king is "cut down" by trial of judges, rather than in battle? One is "damned," the other not? Is a king to be, as Charles insisted, above all human law but his own?

The proposal to put the king on trial had been opposed by many who had been his strongest critics—among them, the chief justices, Oliver

---

[45] For an exceptionally detailed account of the trial and execution, see Charles Spencer, *Killers of the King* (London: Bloomsbury, 2014).

[46] Rebecca Bushnell, *Tragedies of Tyrants: Political Thought and Theatre in the English Renaissance* (Ithaca: Cornell University Press, 1990), page 166.

[47] Christian Thorne, *The Dialectic of Counter-Enlightenment* (Cambridge: Harvard University Press, 2010), page 188.

St John, and Henry Vane, Jr. In large part their opposition was on legal grounds: authority and procedures simply did not exist in statutory law or in the unwritten constitution. But for some of them the thought of trying and perhaps killing their king, regardless the legality or illegality of it, came with a shudder. Be that as it may, the committee of Commons nominated 135 men to serve on a new High Court of Justice, a tribunal created specifically for the task. Because the Lords had not approved the bill authorizing the court and trial, no English lords were named. But the names of a Scottish lord, an Irish lord, some scions of lords, and several baronets were among the nominees. AH was on the list. However, he, like some nominated army officers, had assignment elsewhere and did not attend. Wedgwood's recent accounting betrayed her exasperation no less than her sympathy: "that active Parliament man, Sir Arthur Haslerig ... was busy persecuting Royalist delinquents and quarrelling with John Lilburne in Durham."[48] Whether he would have agreed to serve had he been available can be answered only in speculative mood, to little or no point. Years later Thomas Burton recorded him as voicing approval of the trial and execution.[49] Agreement in abstraction is hardly equivalent to agreement in the concrete event, however.

Of the 135 nominees, 47 never attended court at any time, so far as can be determined by the record.[50] It appears that as few as 67 of the remaining 88 attended on any given day. We know from the document itself that 59 of the 88 signed the death warrant. One of the 59 whose signatures appear on the warrant was Thomas Horton. At one time he was described as AH's falconer, which he may have been at some earlier date; but research has shown that Horton was an independent figure of considerable standing well before the trial, and there is no reason to think he was acting as agent for AH.

AH remained away from London all through the purge, the trial, the execution. We know that in December 1647 there was much anxiety about invasion from Scotland. In addition, AH among others had grown a bit frustrated with Cromwell's vacillation or inconsistency of view with regard to a negotiated settlement. One piece of evidence is the celebrated

---

[48] Cicely Veronica Wedgwood, *The Trial of Charles I* (London: Collins, 1964), page 109. Did Wedgwood know that she was related to the husband of AH's sister Jane[121], John Wedgwood of Harkeles, Staffordshire?

[49] Burton, *Diary of Thomas Burton, esq.*, edited by John T Rutt (London: H Colburn, 1828), volume 3, pages 96, 99.

[50] The record is an "alphabetical catalogue" appended to John Nalson's *A True Copy of the Journal of the High Court of Justice for the Tryal of King Charles I* (London: Thomas Dring, 1684).

outburst by AH toward Cromwell: "If you prove not an honest man, I will never trust a fellow with a great nose for your sake!" Some (among them Denton) have wanted to see in that a humorously barbed exchange between two good friends. Perhaps. More likely, it was AH's temper, stimulated by frustration.[51] What seemed to some observers Cromwell's vacillation was for him (among others) a sort of "decision tree" that he believed to be divinely guided. Reports of the process by which regiments were chosen for duty in Ireland—Cromwell's effort to subordinate that land to Protestant belief and practice—indicate that casting of lots was used not merely as a sortation device (as in "fair selection by chance") but as a cleromancy, a divination of signs. Whereas Christians today generally refuse the practice as a subordination of "the word of God" as expressed in the Christian Bible, seventeenth-century Protestants frequently invoked the casting of lots as a divination, based on accounts in the Old Testament. Thus, when the army's general council met at Whitehall that April day, they began with prayer to God, then cast lots in order to see which regiments were chosen for the mission to Ireland.[52] So began what was for the Irish of Drogheda and Wexford (as elsewhere) the terrible "storming" that Cromwell unleashed late summer, 1649.

  We know that on 29 December 1647 General Fairfax appointed AH as governor of Newcastle. It is easy to see a logic in Fairfax' choice: as Denton put it, AH was "an experienced administrator" and "someone trusted by the army." Furthermore, his Northumberland connections of family and friendship would have given him useful contacts and a basis for raising local forces. On the other hand, the record indicates that Fairfax had had little direct experience with him, which raises the possibility that another had recommended him to the post. Cromwell and/or Ireton come quickly to mind. All of the positive factors just outlined are not contrary to the possibility that Cromwell had wanted to put AH at a distance from London, if he saw him as too inclined to side with the Independents. In any case, while AH was back at Westminster in January 1647/8 for the session in which he introduced the No Addresses bill, he was back in Newcastle no later than the end of March, when he and George Fenwick were ordered by the Long Parliament to take seats on all committees of

---

[51] Gardiner, *Civil War* ... (1886), volume 4, page 48; according to whom, the reporter of that remark added, "It's very like him; he is very downright usually according to his principles." Denton, *Only in Heaven* (1997), page 135, suggests the "jesting" account.

[52] Denis Murphy, *Cromwell in Ireland* (Dublin: M H Gill & Son, 1897), pages 55-56.

sequestrations in the four northern counties. On 18 May he wrote to the speaker of Commons from Newcastle urging that more members be added to the committee of sequestration in Durham.[53]

During the summer months of 1648 AH was either in Newcastle or perhaps on campaign in Scotland with Cromwell (the records regarding the latter are not entirely clear). In August he recaptured the castle at Tynemouth from forces led by Henry Lilburne, who had switched to the royalist cause. No doubt AH remained at Newcastle for some time, given the unrest in the area, the incursions by Scottish bands, uncertainties about reprisals from Scotland because of defeats at Dunbar and Preston on their own soil, expeditions in which AH may have participated.[54] Was that the sum of it, or did AH labor under uncertainties of his own about the right course of action at Westminster? We know that he had been named to the list of Commissioners of the High Court of Justice, "but at no time did he sit"—a "mystery," in Denton's mind.[55] He still had his seat in Commons, now of the Rump Parliament, but he remained in Newcastle during the purge, the trial, and the execution. He returned to Westminster the second week of February, resuming his seat and active in Commons. When the Committee of Both Kingdoms was abolished, AH was named to the Council of State which replaced it in February 1648/9, now the executive branch of government. By the same token, his connection with the northeast remained in general awareness; for on the 24th of February he was ordered by the Council of State to ensure that no horses (now in very short supply) leave England by the northern border. And at some date—we do not know exactly—when the formerly royal palace of Whitehall was appropriated for use as offices and residences of government leaders, a grand act of political theatre, AH assumed residence there.[56]

What, finally, can we make of the distance between Newcastle and London, for AH in particular, during the months from the end of the second civil war to early February 1648/9? Had he been deliberately sidelined, or had he stayed away so as to avoid the hard decisions of trial and aftermath? Had he himself deliberated some sense of the "damnation" that would attend regicide? It is worth noting, in that regard, the opinion of an

---

[53] Denton, *Only in Heaven* (1997), page 137; Gardiner, *Civil War ...* (1886), volume 4, chapter 58; Robertson, *Tyrannicide Brief* (2005), page 111.
[54] See, e.g., DG21/275d, h, j, and l, Hazlerigg Collection.
[55] Denton, *Only in Heaven* (1997), page 158.
[56] Charles H Firth, *The Memoirs of Edmund Ludlow, 1625-1672*, 2 volumes (Oxford: Clarendon, 1894), volume 2, page 204 note 1; Sean Kelsey, *Inventing a Republic* (Stanford: Stanford University Press, 1997), page 54.

anonymous reviewer of Diane Purkiss' book, *The English Civil War*: the execution "helped to preserve the monarchy into its present age of unassailable irrelevance—a 350-year apology from loyal subjects for having been so beastly."[57] Does that capture something of an uncertainty of thought by AH? Probably not; but one cannot be sure. On the other hand, was he engaged in some sort of thinking, even planning, for a post-monarchal England? If we are to believe Edward Hyde, earl of Clarendon, AH was not capable of more than "weak understanding." But then Hyde viewed everything and everyone via a lens that saw anarchy as the only alternative to monarchy—preferably a monarchy benignly intelligent and wise, but monarchy nonetheless. There were others—for instance, James Harrington—who *were* contemplating alternative forms of governance.[58] AH might well have been among them ("weak" or not). Great political thinkers are not always to be had, when practicalities of life press upon people various claims of change; and sometimes when they *are* available, they are as conservative as a dead king, looking for ways to restore the past, with all its alleged certainties and securities (e.g., Thomas Hobbes).

Struggles for a Republic
When did serious thoughts of an English republic begin? The best we can do in effort to answer to that question is to examine the written record; and according to one analyst of the surviving record, "As late as December 1648, the idea of an English republic had no intellectual progenitor and no contemporary political advocate."[59] That verdict might seem strange to us: where were the memories, the considerations, of ancient Greek and Roman discourses on forms of governance—Plato's *Republic*, for instance, and Aristotle's *On Politics*? Surely there had been recorded discussions of how one might adapt lessons from those cultures to a rapidly changing England in the late sixteenth, early seventeenth century? What of the Englishman's schooling in the classics? In fact, there was little of it. Instruction in the classical languages was limited, not well regarded, and usually quickly forgotten. Literacy had indeed been spreading, down the social scale as well as geographically, but few people who did read read beyond the Bible and the increasingly popular "newsbooks" and pamphlets. Shakespeare's

---

[57] Purkiss, *The English Civil War* (New York: Basic Books, 2006); *The Economist* volume 380 (22 July 2006), page 81.
[58] James Harrington, *The Common-Wealth of Oceana* (London: Livewell Chapman, 1656). This man was cousin to the Sir James Harrington, 3rd Bt of Ridlington, who sat in Commons, was a judge in the trial of Charles, and so on.
[59] Robertson, *Tyrannicide Brief* (2005), page 125.

plays were attractive far more for their ribaldry, clever jibes, and memorials of British history than for the large volume of reference to Greek and Roman mythology, history, and literary survivals. These latter citations and allusions, intelligible to very few theater-goers other than as verbal emblems or slogans that make a twentieth-century guide such as Benét's *Reader's Encyclopedia* seem almost pedantically detailed, could be ignored with pleasure, and generally were.

As for politics and forms of governance, AH, like others grouped as the "party" of Independents, opposed hereditary monarchy mainly (if not only) because they had opposed Charles and what he represented as and for the principle of monarchy. There is no evidence that they had gone so far as to propose a republic as successor to Charles, either leaving open the question of an alternative form or perhaps vaguely thinking of a parliamentary monarchy, as had many of the Presbyterian faction. And yet, even if mostly ignorant of discourses of ancient Athens or the Roman Republic, surely some of them were aware of the successes of the Dutch Republic—that is, from 1581 after independence from Spain, the Republic of the Seven United Netherlands—one of the richest countries in the world, master of a large and growing colonial empire, sailing the largest merchant fleet, demonstrating the value of a successful stock exchange at home, and living via a self-governance without collapsing into that much-vaunted spectre, anarchy.[60]

Whatever his thoughts of such matters may have been, AH, along with other "Rumpers," was busy with legislation. On 17 March the office of king was abolished. Two days later they abolished the House of Lords. On 19 May 1649 they declared England a commonwealth—in effect, a republic, with sovereignty resting in the people of the commonwealth and governance vested in parliament and in the council of state. Clearly, some minds had been at work.

Fighting had not ceased with death of the king or with declaration of a commonwealth. Close to London, a series of uprisings or mutinies among the soldiers had to be quelled. The issues were an amalgam of the longstanding concerns about arrears and the more narrowly based wishes of the faction known as Levellers. It is difficult to impossible to sort out that mixture in any given uprising—at Bishopsgate, for example, or later at Banbury. The large majority of soldiers had grown angry about loss of wages, rightly so. A smaller proportion, probably never a majority, of the

---

[60] Granted, the Dutch Republic succumbed to internal monarchism in 1672, having been weakened by wars with Britain (especially the Third Anglo-Dutch War) and with France largely due to competitions for colonial possessions.

soldiers favored a republic founded on universal male franchise—that is, no regard to property ownership—and as the loss of wages continued this smaller faction no doubt grew proportionately. The mutinies were put down with increasing furor, and by the end of May 1649 Cromwell's fury had sealed the message.

Away from London sporadic fighting by royalist forces continued, resulting in a sequence of skirmishes and battles that recent historians have begun to designate "the Third Civil War." There is no evidence that AH was ever a combatant during these years. However, in August 1650 he raised a regiment in the north, apparently under a nominal colonelcy. His regiment was garrisoned the following month at Linlithgow in Scotland, then participated in skirmishes at Stirling and Dumbarton. In June 1651 the regiment was assigned to the colonelcy of James Berry, with whom it remained until October 1659.[61]

While no longer a combatant as horseman, AH was anything but free of controversy and conflict as a landlord. There can be no doubt that his memory during an extended retrospective address in 1659 (treated in the next chapter) was perfectly accurate, when he declared that he had been neither a Leveller nor a sympathizer of their cause. Among the stores of evidence, some of the most abundant resulted from a long-running dispute by John Lilburne. The details have been well told by others, including AH's biographer Barry Denton (who, among other elements, offers initial publication of a document that seals the case against Lilburne, if any further evidence had been needed).[62] In a nutshell, Lilburne had repeatedly pressed a claim that AH had cheated the Lilburne family of property and thus impoverished them. The first part of the claim is defensible only in the sense that AH was quicker to accumulate sequestered estates than his competitors, including members of the Lilburne family. The second part of the claim is patently false, as much evidence demonstrates. Actions of local courts and eventually of the House of Commons repeatedly rejected John Lilburne's claims, the last part occurring in his trial during 24 to 26 October 1649, the result being that his long effort to ruin AH resulted in his own ruin. Of greater interest here, however, is John Lilburne as sharp exemplar of a position in a debate that AH had himself almost certainly engaged with himself privately, and perhaps with others. The core point was addressed earlier. The choice in wake of regicide had been between a resumption of obedience to tradition, to the "old, safe ground of established

---

[61] A history of AH's regiment is given in Charles Firth and Godfrey Davies' *The Regimental History of Cromwell's Army* (Oxford: Clarendon Press, 1940).
[62] Denton, *Only in Heaven* (1997), pages 162-73.

practices," some sort of modified monarchy perhaps, or some sort of new arrangement of social agreements as fluid as the conditions supporting them. Lilburne's position, once stripped of his personalistic animus, was a variety of the latter choice. So, too, to a degree, was AH's position. The chief difference was about property, and in the context still of the 1600s the property that counted most, land. John Lilburne was, as he was often called, "free-born," a spirit free of such restrictions—unlike other members of the family who were major landowners, just as was AH. In that sense, the "old order," the "old game," was continuing, whether under monarchy or under republican rule. Movement toward greater political democracy was one thing; toward economic democracy, quite another, and well-nigh unthinkable.

The decade of the 1650s proved to be one of trial and error, high anxiety, desperate interventions, hopeful innovation, and final exhaustion. Because the civil wars, like wars generally, were disruptive of what had been traditional alliances and settlements, anxieties about public order spread through the population, probably more especially in the southern counties. These anxieties were exacerbated during the 1650s as the often conflicting multiple lines of influence impeded the formation of new alliances and settlements. Part of it unfolded in and from disagreements over the meaning, means, and implementation of "godly rule." Diversity is often a problem for people who have been unsettled and feel threatened by uncertainties of horizon, and the 1650s quickly proved to be a hotbed of diversities and consequent perceptions of threat. Venues ranged from parties and constituencies with parliaments to local communities in many of which vicars and rectors, facing increased assertiveness along with diversity of view from parishioners, struggled to maintain the traditional function of moulding inhabitants into a unified community of believers who respect central authority, whether the center be manifested as pulpit, as sheriff's or lord lieutenant's office, as judicial bar, ultimately as royal throne. Traditionally, the several ranks were simply links in a hierarchy, a chain that united apex and root as identical in essence, living testimony, for a monarch who assumed rule by divine right as plainly obvious, that his or her rule was automatically godly rule. Now the order of apex and root was being turned upside down, by proponents of republicanism and religious doctrines such as Puritanism, with those who had been royal subjects, now reconceived as free individuals, elevated to apex in the collectivity named "the people," because they were the root of sovereignty. Those proponents were, in varying degree and recipe, struggling to reconceive the ground and the form of godly rule.

One of the curious features of that struggle was the great extent of concern about sexual behavior. One of the first acts passed by the Rump Parliament, in May 1650, was the Act against Adulterers and Fornicators, which came three months before passage of the Blasphemy Act. Attacks against alehouses, swearing and lewd language, and failure to observe the Sabbath also increased, though seemingly without the urgency of efforts to penalize sexual behaviors. One might think that the people of England had been, or had suddenly become, a singularly debauched people. Yet records of judicial proceedings during prior years show no indication of that; and, as a recent writer noted, "Several historians have observed that though quarter sessions benches in the Republic were unprecedentedly active, they still saw only a trickle of morals cases."[63] Perhaps many MPs thought the legislation urgent because of generalized worry about loosened fetters in wake of civil war and now, with efforts to fashion new offices of authority, in the midst of so much change and uncertainty.

Other legislative activities included an ordinance of 26 November 1650 for maintenance of the army. Revenues had to be raised county by county, and the usual procedure called for a list of commissioners in each county having the responsibility to see that its contribution was met. AH was on the commission of each of four counties: Leicestershire, along with his son Thomas; Northumberland, along with George Fenwick; Durham, with both his son Thomas and George Fenwick; Cumberland; and, with George Fenwick again, separately for the city of Newcastle.[64]

In addition, there was much activity concerned with modifying existing institutions to republican frameworks and inventing new ones as circumstances seemingly required. Much of this, as Kelsey has recently described, had to do with the ceremonial and imaginal character of offices of governance.[65] While such matters can be little more than cosmetic—and, if so, eventually undermining of the better intents—when properly constructed and utilized they offer assurances of familiarity, continuity, and common attention. A large part, and most of the majestic part, of royal authority rests in mystery, traditionally cultivated in the doctrine of "the two bodies of kingship": the ordinary human personage of a monarch, who

---

[63] Derek Hirst, "The Failure of Godly Rule," *Past and Present*, number 132 (August 1991), pages 33-66, at page 52. See James A Sharpe, *Crime in Seventeenth-Century England* (Cambridge: Cambridge University Press, 1983) for an intensive study of one county.

[64] Charles H Firth and Robert S Rait, editors, *Acts and Ordinances of the Interregnum, 1642-1660* (London: HMSO, 1911), pages 456-490.

[65] Kelsey, *Inventing a Republic* (1997).

bled like any other human being; but behind that surface, the mystery of a being whose authority descends "from above," whether the "above" be a Heaven of God and Saints or a Tradition of Founders and Heroic Knights. Republicanism was opposed to that sort of mystery. Its very name said as much: governance should be a thoroughly "public thing," an agreement of the people. But that in itself can have elements that are rather mysterious—that is, how a diverse people pursuing diverse interests can nonetheless come together in and for something as large, as complex, as productive, as a unified body politic. A pageantry of politics advertises and celebrates that fact, when it is a fact. The very difficult task is to create from the debris of revolution a pageantry in which "the people"—who are not yet "*a* people"—can believe, and through that belief celebrate their unity.

Issuing new coinage, new memorial medals, and a new "great seal of England" were all part of the pageantry, as were new banquets, honours, and carefully staged spectacles. John Lambert's "well-attested dandyism" was part of the spectacle; so, too, AH's "coach-and-six, attended by page boys with silver buckles on their shoes."[66] Whether this coach display was a matter of personal self-flattery or a deliberated act of political theatre cannot be decided, but in either case potential for satire was no doubt often realized in the streets of London at the time, and later. Kelsey has given a fine assessment of matters that have too often been depreciated as without serious value: "Commonwealth politics navigated a sophisticated political landscape whose major failing was its polymorphous complexity," which could only translate into a complexity of governmental processes, if government was to be effective in meeting the needs of a diverse people. The republican constitution, a work in process, "was what made the free state a living, breathing political organism; its political culture media were what made that organism such a vivid, rare bird, and 'the republican' a species of infinite variety"—as various as the people themselves, for the over-riding simplification that had long been the rule, "king and subjects," was now defunct, or on the way to being defunct. At least that was the hope.[67]

Self-governance requires abilities of compromise and cooperation among and across divergent interests of divergent people. The notion that sufficient guidance and glue would be provided by "godly people" for a "godly rule" was far too inarticulate to achieve effective orchestration of all the plurality of perspectives and interests, even if one left to the side the

---

[66] Kelsey, *Inventing a Republic* (1997), page 54; Maurice Ashley, *Cromwell's Generals* (London: Jonathan Cape, 1954), page 105.

[67] Kelsey, *Inventing a Republic* (1997), page 217.

ever-hopeful royalist factions. The militarism that had removed obstacles to the possibility of a republic was inclined to look at political relations of the commonwealth and see excessive diversity, scarcity of discipline. The resulting difficulties were anything but alleviated by the tendency of the commonwealth leaders themselves to ask the army to solve problems of governance that they found too complicated or resistant to solve by their own supposedly preferred means. Pride's purge was the most conspicuous instance of that tendency—prior, that is, to Cromwell's usurpation of the commonwealth authority as its militaristic protector.

AH continued throughout the first years of the commonwealth to engage in activities designed to build and strengthen the institutions and practices of republican government. Having appointed Alexander Pearson to be his secretary for affairs in the four northern counties (Pearson was also steward of copyholds court at Durham), AH could devote attention to affairs at Westminster for extended periods, dealing with law reforms, giving administrative support to Cromwell's campaigns against Scots at Dunbar and his defeat of forces allied with Charles II, the declared king of Scotland, handling other activities as a member of the council of state, and taking his turn as head of the council. Even so, he maintained enough presence in the north to purchase at bargain rates many of the bishops' estates that had been sequestered in Durham, a fact that gained him notoriety at the time, and especially later, for exercising "unfair advantage" and even theft, as was seen in the case with John Lilburne (more about the acquisitions in the next chapter).

All in all, the years to early 1653 must have been satisfying, by and large, to those who, with AH, firmly advocated republican government and had set about building one. Even Trevor-Roper, a historian who offered little sympathy for AH and others he considered (anachronistically though it was) "too Whiggish," declared that the "Rump Parliament, which governed England from 1649 to 1653, may have been justly hated as a corrupt oligarchy, but it governed effectively, preserved the revolution, made and financed victorious war [the First Anglo-Dutch War], and carried out a consistent policy of aggressive mercantile imperialism." It was "the most systematic government of the Interregnum."[68]

Dissatisfied with what he considered weak discipline and worried about anarchy, Cromwell proposed in early 1653 to replace parliament with a "government of godly men," similar to the organization of which he had reaped many successes, the New Model Army, staffed by carefully

---

[68] Hugh Trevor-Roper, *The Crisis of the Seventeenth Century*, revised edition (London: Secker and Warburg, 1984), page 328.

chosen "godly officers." AH openly opposed Cromwell's call. Tensions between the two men had been increasingly noticeable, but now a fissure opened too wide to be camouflaged by usual words of courtesy. AH's open opposition was probably the proximate cause of Cromwell's enforced expulsion of the Rump, 20 April 1653. Cromwell the same day dismissed the council of state. On the 29th, with support of the army's council of officers, a new council of state was appointed, consisting of thirteen members of whom nine were army officers. It was then perhaps not apparent to military officers that the discipline that can be obtained by military organization—which always has expulsion or death as last resort when expected discipline is lost—cannot be achieved for any length of time in society at large. This was less true of medieval society, no doubt, but England was well past that age. The modern society that was coming to life more and more rapidly sported the new diversity and abundance of modern urban society with admiration, sometimes gleeful expectation, and frequent bouts of confusion and nostalgia for "a simpler life." Militaristic opportunists could rely on that nostalgia as support only so long. Unless they were willing to try to convert all of civilian society into a militaristic organization, with death camps, forced labor, and the paranoia generated by a "secret police," they had limited future. Fortunately, Britain was far removed from that kind of tolerance.

Cromwell began his reign, his "Protectorate," by calling for a parliament on his terms, officially known as the Nominated Parliament but popularly named and remembered as the Barebones Parliament. This assemblage began with 140 nominated members (AH not among them) on 4 July 1653. It was from the beginning a flounder. Five months later it resigned its authority to Cromwell. Again, AH voiced his opposition, but he now had little or no audience of consequence. Cromwell remodeled the council of state into his own privy council (i.e., private council), and called new elections. AH was returned as MP for Leicestershire.

The First Protectorate Parliament, which sat from 3 September 1654 to 22 January 1654/5, was an unprecedented institution in the annals of English government in several respects. First of all, it was based on the first-ever redistribution of parliamentary seats, which had been urged by the new Instrument of Government, a document drafted the previous year by Major General Lambert who relied partly on a document written in 1647 as basis of a new constitution. Although the Instrument had not yet been validated by a parliament, it was accepted informally as a redesign of institutions of government. The Instrument stipulated a total of 400 seats for England and Wales (later expanded to 436 with the addition of seats for Scotland and Ireland—another first) and stipulated distribution of those seats by county and by boroughs within county. Second, the county of Durham gained membership for the first time; so, too, the boroughs of Leeds and Manchester. Third, distributions by county and borough were brought more into alignment with demographic weight. Fourth, the extant rotten boroughs were effectively abolished. The overall result was a parliamentary distribution that would not be matched until the early nineteenth century, with the Reform Act of 1832. These were progressive developments, to be sure.

Writing of that apparatus, Trevor-Roper opined that "even under the new franchise the experienced republicans had contrived to re-enter parliament." He was referring explicitly to AH and Thomas Scot, whom he had named "an inseparable and effective parliamentary combine" who were the "principal champions of sound republican doctrine" (citing words of Edmund Ludlow) even though one of "mercantile aggression" (Trevor-Roper's words). They had "contrived to re-enter parliament" by being elected by their constituents—Leicester and Newcastle, in the one case, Wycombe (Buckinghamshire), Canterbury (Kent), and three counties in Ireland in the case of Scot. (It was, had not been, unusual for an MP to be returned by more than one constituency.) "Once in," Trevor-Roper continued, the pair "moved with effortless rapidity into the vacuum created by the Protector's virtuous but misguided refusal to form a party. The speed with which they operated is astonishing: one is forced to conclude either that Hesilrige and Scot were really brilliant tacticians (a conclusion which the recorded evidence hardly warrants), or that Cromwell had no vestige of an organization to resist them."[69]

In fact, Cromwell's first protectorate Commons passed not a single bill, and he dissolved it as soon as he could do and remain in accord with terms of the Instrument of Government. Why the inactivity? Various accounts in answer to that question have been offered during the past three and one-half centuries. Trevor-Roper would have us believe that two MPs, AH and Thomas Scot, even though not "master tacticians" (and they were not), were responsible, with help from their friends: "From 1653 onwards, when the 'Whig' policy which they had grafted on to the revolution had been repudiated, Hesilrige and Scot and their friends were simply obstructionists." As already noted, the term "Whig" was a bit anachronistic in that setting. Prior to its use in the later debate over the legitimacy of succession by James II, younger brother of Charles II

---

[69] Trevor-Roper, *Crisis* (1984), pages 329, 344; Firth, *Ludlow Memoirs* (1894), volume 1, pages 388, 391.

("Whigs" were opposed; "Tories" favored it), the term had generally been used to designate nonconformity and rebellion—both of which AH and Scot were, but so had been the Presbyterians of earlier parliaments. Later it named a party whose members were heavily aristocratic and landowning. Apparently for Trevor-Roper it meant mainly support for mercantile and imperial policies (i.e., colonization, control of the sea lanes for trade, etc.). In any case, his better answer for the failure of this parliament of Cromwell was the one he gave for the failure of his Nominated Parliament: "believing that forms of government were indifferent," Cromwell's nominees "counted simply on working with the existing institutions," even though the institutions of government—"first monarchy, then republic—had been destroyed" by the sequence of purges and dissolutions which he himself had endorsed when not ordered.[70]

The first Anglo-Dutch War having concluded to England's favor in 1654, Cromwell embarked on his Anglo-Spanish War, which consisted in a regiment of his New Army sent to the Caribbean island of Hispaniola, where it failed, and then to Jamaica, where it won a better return. At home, governance had unraveled rather quickly, a fact which prompted Cromwell to appoint his choice of major-generals to rule the counties. These appointments were made in September 1655, and in the short run they achieved some improved stability. During this time, having been sidelined by opposition to Cromwell's protectorate, AH attended his estate acquisitions in Durham, his home seat at Noseley, and his young household now motherless since the death of Dorothy (Greville) Hesilrige in late January 1650/1 (about which, more in the next chapter).

Cromwell summoned his Second Protectorate Parliament 10 July 1656, perhaps thinking that AH's apparent quiescence was acquiescence in Cromwell's form of governance and that he would not stand for election. In fact, he did stand and was returned by the borough of Leicester. When the first session was assembled in September he was barred entry.[71] Very likely he was not surprised, for the prior month Edmund Ludlow, William Bradshaw, and Henry Vane had been "called on the carpet," so to speak, by the council of state for opposing the protectorate.

A group of MPs led by Oliver St John, Edward Montagu, and Roger Boyle, 1st baron of Broghill, Ireland, proposed, 23 February 1656/7, a document known as the Humble Petition and Advice, the main provisions of which were two: to reinstall an upper house of parliament (only ever officially referred to as "the other house"; to invite Cromwell to assume

---

[70] Trevor-Roper, *Crisis* (1984), pages 354, 333.

[71] Firth, *Ludlow Memoirs* (1894), volume 2, page 18.

the office and the title of king. The intent of the latter provision, not wholly evident, was to bind Cromwell into the existing legal tradition of kingship and in that way create some constraints on his behavior. Whether the intent was evident to Cromwell is itself a question without clearly evident answer either way, but he deliberated the petition during the next several weeks, before declining the crown in April. The MPs returned with a new version of the document, having removed terminology of kingship and offering Cromwell the protectorship for life, with right to choose his own successor. This Cromwell accepted, and on 26th of June he was installed in lifetime protectorship with a ceremony that in some respects was nothing less than a royal coronation (which AH attended).[72] The matter of designing new institutions and ceremony of a republic had been reduced to revising the institutions and ceremonies of monarchy in all but name. For sharply differing reasons, the army faction led by General John Lambert and the republicans of whom AH among others had been leaders strongly opposed the agreement. But to no avail.

Among the next tasks undertaken by Cromwell, probably the most time-consuming and most frustrating was his effort to fill "that which was called the Other House," as Ludlow put it. One part of his effort revealed how little he understood of his erstwhile friend, Sir Arthur Hesilrige. In a move obviously intended to mollify and at the same time marginalize AH from his "republican constituency," Cromwell nominated him to a seat in this new house that was not, at least in name, to be a House of Lords. AH did not reveal his answer, despite not so subtle efforts to prod it from him, until it was time for the second session of this parliament. Then, on that day, 20 January 1657/8, he took his seat in Commons, remarking in one of his better remembered statements (2 February 1657/8): "I will not take the Bishop's seat because I know not how long after I shall keep the Bishop's lands," a reference to his controversial purchases of lands formerly held by the church, mainly in Durham.[73] Two weeks later Cromwell dissolved his second parliament.

Who knows where his navigations would next have taken him. He was now at loggerheads between his frustration with resistances to his will, which he believed to be divinely guided, and his tendency to await divinely inspired signs as to next steps. Perhaps this stress, at age 58, had prompted a reportedly sudden recurrence of his malarial infection. In any case, while ill with that outbreak he once again developed a urinary infection, which

---

[72] Denton, *Only in Heaven* (1997), page 200.
[73] Firth, *Ludlow Memoirs* (1894), volume 2, pages 31-33; Burton, *Diary* (1828), volume 2, pages 346, 423-24; Trevor-Roper, *Crisis* (1984), page 352.

probably became septicemic, and he died 3 September 1658. His seat and crown-that-was-not-a-crown now passed to his son Richard, who had neither the loyal constituency of his father nor the self-assuredness of will. Richard called his first and only, the Third Protectorate Parliament, which sat for three months beginning 27 January 1658/9 and accomplished only its own dissolution via another military coup.

At this point it will be useful to break momentarily the sequence of "event accounts" in order to consider some interpretive work by a British historian during the 1960s, William Lamont. In a book entitled *Godly Rule* Lamont presented (among other offerings) a good antidote to the image of uniformity among people called "the Puritans" and, as one consequence of that sensitivity, an astute diagnosis of what could be called "the problem of order" that developed during the interregnum.[74]

Just as the 1650s were very different from the 1630s, and still again from early years of the century, so Puritanism varied across those decades. In addition, however, at any given time there was considerable variation among those who described themselves as proponents of the Puritan cause. These differences grew during the 1640s and 1650s. An example previously mentioned was disagreement as to the fate of the king: some self-defined Puritans favored execution; others did not. A second example is the fact that Oliver Cromwell ordered a state funeral and burial in Westminster Abbey for an archbishop of the official church (James Ussher), though clearly one who had professed beliefs that were counted as Calvinist and sympathies for Puritans, even while remaining loyal to his king, Charles I.

Lamont's discussion is especially good in showing that the basic differences stemmed in part from a contradiction and instability at the heart of the Puritan movement. The instability could be traced in part to ambiguities and inconsistencies in statements of doctrine, but the greater instability, ultimately the contradiction, lay in the quest for "godly rule," a quest shared at least in name across most Puritans and with members of other sectarian movements (e.g., Presbyterian) and "even" with members of the established church.[75]

One of the signal features of the rebellion against the established church—whether it be the church that remained after Henry VIII or that of Elizabeth or that of James—was the development and spread of values of individual liberty. This engendered a centrifugal fluidity which made

---

[74] Lamont, *Godly Rule: Politics and Religion, 1603-60* (London: Macmillan, 1969).

[75] Also, one could argue, with members of the Roman Catholic church; but by now they were not welcome to the conversation.

collective agreement in belief and action more difficult than it had been, and at the same time raised alarms about preservation of public order. The conjunction became glaringly problematic during the interregnum, Lamont argued, in part because the unifying force of a common enemy, in the persons of William Laud and Charles I, along with their many apologists, had disappeared. Whereas the civil wars had "left a vacuum at the centre" as a happenstance of wartime disruptions, under Cromwell the vacuum at the center was deliberate, and increasingly seen as such, in part because of his refusal to use his authority "to impose doctrine" even as "he *did* use his authority to prevent others imposing *their* doctrines."[76] Thus, Presbyterians were frustrated in their efforts to impose doctrine on the whole of England, or at least the whole of the established church; and likewise, the Erastians and other sectarian groups as well as the Anglican core (as they thought of themselves) of the established church.

Lamont described in some detail the "back and forth" of ensuing contests and the effects of that competition on both the several sectarian doctrines and on public order. The upshot for present purposes is a grasp of the dynamic of the contradictory character of the several efforts to establish godly rule.

First of all, bear in mind that there was general, although mostly implicit, agreement that godly rule was singular, not multiple, and firmly uniform across all segments of the population. God was one and unitary; godly rule in this world could only be singular and uniform. Second, it was agreed that a vital task in support of, and as a consequence of, godly rule was to bring up, protect, and promote godly people. Here, one could see more clearly, at the time, fissures in purported uniformity. Different groups had different descriptions of what counted, in particulars, as being a godly person (indeed also in the particulars of God). Contests to prevail in that arena tended to be very serious affairs among "true believers" who could not agree on all particulars of "the truth." In consequence, efforts to create a "godly people" often had the effect of undermining the ideal of a godly rule. Even those (such as Sir Arthur Hesilrige) who formed the loosely knit group, Independents, while generally most sympathetic to Cromwell's refusal to impose a religious doctrine, disagreed among themselves about which goals were most important, which means should be used, and how diversities of doctrines and rituals should be handled. If the core value was each and every individual person's right to decide, what should be the response to those who decided to leave matters to a bishop? If the nest of individual freedom was in the freely chosen membership of

---

[76] Lamont, *Godly Rule* (1969), page 143; and below, pages 166-169.

a congregation, what should be the response of public order to a congregation of believers in "Roman idolatry"? If godly rule is singular and uniform, how can it ever reconcile among divergent sects without impositions? If a congregation are a godly people in their own way, freely exercised, why should they not feel in the right when pressing others to give up their blasphemies and join in the one true light? And so it goes.

The problem has been present all along. It can be addressed in the terms of "reading signs." For example, if one is comforted by perceptions of parallel lives, a true believer such as Charles could find contentment in the thought that his pain and martyrdom were a validating sampling of the pain and martyrdom of his Christ figure, and the contentment could last to the point of being at rest, doing nothing more. Conversely, Oliver Cromwell's God was a more austere, vindictive presence, so the signs he sought were affirmations by vanquishing the enemy in combat. But there would always be another combat lying ahead, if not military then political, another test of godliness. We know that Cromwell was not particularly intellectual, that he read little beyond his Bible, that he listened to others debate issues as a forum within which to decide his own mind this way or that. Letting others venture forth with, even *as*, test cases, he then read the signs from their successes or failures and proceeded accordingly, having determined what his God was telling him to do. Thus, his tendency to retire to Whitehall in Olympian detachment (as Trevor-Roper put it), leaving to Commons the task of working out the next set of problems.

Having redefined the problem of order so as to accord with a notion of "a godly people" engaged in "godly rule," the Puritan factions led most crucially by Oliver Cromwell had faced the inherent contradictions and had failed to resolve them in any manner other than by the direct force of will and example exercised by Cromwell at the center, and that resolution was inherently unstable, ripe for explosive failure. Cromwell had mostly accomplished the destruction of the institutional promises of governance by republican principles during the pre-protectorate commonwealth. In wake of collapse of the Cromwellian protectorate, there was virtually no surviving institutional means of governance by which to address and quell the by-now rampant loss of public authority. That message was broadly advertised by the failure of son Richard's parliament: by the time Richard had no choice but to dissolve it, three months after its start, it had passed not one act. The MPs who had been attempting to rebuild some semblance of republican government were conclusively blocked. One indication of that is told by the fact that they were defeated on every vote. AH had been the teller (i.e., reporting votes on his side) ten times, and he lost every time.

So, too, Henry Nevil (teller on seven votes, all of them lost); Henry Vane (twice, both lost); Thomas Scot (once, lost). Likewise, John Lambert: not quite a republican (at least not of a civilian republic), though at times allied with them, he had been teller on five votes, all of them lost.[77] And yet no other proposal of governance had gained sufficient support as alternative to the Commonwealth's promising beginning. Royalists, however, could believe again in their day.

AH's emphasis had long been on a strong parliament that would nonetheless remain sensitive to the grass-roots electorate. This is evident in a variety of ways. For one, Sir Archibald Johnston of Warriston (now a northern suburb of Edinburgh) recorded in his diary AH saying that he was

> for a successive Parliament and they to choose a Counsel as they do now, and the elections to be by one of ten out of every parish, and this to meet in country [county] elections for choosing Commissioners to Parliament, and this in Parliament to sit perpetually, but that every year one 3rd part to go out another 3rd part to come in, and so in the Council.[78]

This was said late in AH's tenure and represented some refinements of his thinking, no doubt, by comparison to his views in, say, 1650. But the basic thrust was much the same. There is no reason to think that he had changed his mind at any time during 1659. There *is* reason, however, increasingly abundant as the year wore on, to think that he knew it would not be so, not during his lifetime.

The End Game
Richard Cromwell summoned the Third Protectorate Parliament on 9 December 1658. It assembled on 27 January 1658/9, and AH took his seat in Commons.

During a meeting of Commons on Monday, 7 February 1658/9, AH addressed his fellow MPs with regard to the issue at hand, "An Act of Recognition of His Highness' right and title to be Protector ..." (etc.). His aim was to persuade them of a simple but crucial assertion: "The business we are about is the setting up a power over this nation." In other words,

---

[77] The tabulations were made by Gilbert Farthing, in his master's thesis, *The Country-City "Alliance" of Cromwellian England 1658-1660* (Vancouver: University of British Columbia, 1962), page 98, a still-valuable study.
[78] *Diary of Sir Archibald Johnston of Wariston, 1655-1660*, edited by James D Ogilvie (Edinburgh: Scottish History Society, 1940), volume 3, page 124.

they should understand that the task before them was not some simple routine of recognizing an assumed continuity—not merely another routine act of recognizing "what is"—but an act of establishing "what will be." He then proceeded with a review of "what we have been," in order that they understand clearly their present situation and their opportunities for future days. Toward the end of his recitation of that history, he concluded:

> We see what a confusion we are in. We have not prospered. Our army at Jamaica prospered not. The trade and glory of the nation are much diminished. The council have been exceedingly bewildered. The government you see twice set up, presently pulled down. The strange oppression by making Acts of Parliament without a Parliament; raising monies; denying *habeas corpus*; sending learned long robe gentlemen to the Tower, for asserting *Magna Charta*, such as all the Kings of England never did; all this because we knew not the good mind of God. We were in darkness. It is God's mercy that we are here to declare ourselves in this place. [79]

All of his references in that passage were to policies and practices that had held sway under Oliver Cromwell. Now, he asked in so many words, are we willing to agree to continuation of that record? He professed that his concern was not about the person of Richard Cromwell. It was, as he said at the beginning, about the kind of "power over this nation" that they would endorse.

The next major issue was Oliver Cromwell's "other house": the choice was to work with it as it was and thus affirm it legitimacy or to replace it with a restored House of Lords, recalling the old Lords. AH made clear in his address to the issue in Commons on Tuesday, 8 March 1658/9, that he was against this "other house."[80] It did not fill any good function, since its members had been appointed by Cromwell mainly from people in the military, the legal professions, and trades, men who had demonstrated loyalty to him personally. They lacked standing in the various regions of the country. They lacked an independence of wealth. As Burton stated it, "They have not interest, not the forty-thousandth part of England."[81] AH began by reminding listeners of his credentials: "I was bred a Puritan, and am for public liberty." He also reminded them that he

---

[79] Burton, *Diary* (1828), volume 4, pages 85-118, esp. page 89.
[80] Burton, *Diary* (1828), volume 4, pages 76-77.
[81] Burton, *Diary* (1828), volume 2, page 390.

had not been involved in Pride's Purge, having been "in the North" at that time. Then, this: "I had rather, with all my soul, those noble Lords were in [i.e., the old Lords], to all intents and purposes, than those persons that have two swords, two strings to their bows; persons that have torn Parliaments out, and pulled your Speaker out of the chair." This last was clearly a reference to Oliver Cromwell, who at one point had ordered the Speaker of Commons pulled from his chair. By "those noble Lords," AH was referring to men such as Algernon Percy, earl of Northumberland, and William Fiennes, the viscount Saye and Sele. He referred explicitly to a distinction between "country lords" and "court lords," regarding the former as honorable and, by neglect, saying otherwise of the latter.

Having read the whole of his address of 7 February, one could conclude that he had not given up the fight to establish a working republican government, at least equivalent to what that of the former commonwealth had been, at least as a starting point. For that to happen, it is clear, the first step was to deny Richard Cromwell his inheritance as lord protector. Once again, unfortunately, the army was instrument of that denial, as it dissolved the protectorate parliament in April, and Cromwell had little choice but to resign, which he did the following month. Next, the Rump Parliament was reconvened, and even though it faced financial problems left by the protectorate government, and even though its ad hoc reconvening opened again the question of the purged members of the Long Parliament, there is some evidence of positive activity by AH during that summer to think that indeed he had regained some optimism about what he could achieve. As late as 15 August 1659, he was writing from Whitehall, as president of the council of state, to inform General Monck in Edinburgh that Monck was authorized to negotiate with the responsible parties of Edinburgh to adjust assessments in a way that would be fair to that city.[82]

The cool weather of October brought reason for discouragement, however. AH had detected the makings of a military coup led by General John Lambert. In response, Lambert's commission was voided, as a new set of commissioners of the army were appointed. Thomas Hobbes, in the fourth dialogue of his *Behemoth*, described the events of and leading from the 12 October 1659 this way: Commons voted that "the army should be governed by a commission to Fleetwood, Monk, Hazlerig, Walton, Morley, and Overton"—he omitted Ludlow, third of the three, with

---

[82] *The Clarke Papers*, edited by Charles H Firth (London: Longmans, Green, and Co., 1901), volume 4, pages 42-43.

Fleetwood and Monk, who were army officers. This act voided the commission of John Lambert.

> And to make this good against the force they expected from Lambert, they ordered Hazlerig and Morley to issue warrants to such officers as they could trust, to bring their soldiers next morning in Westminster; which was done somewhat too late. For Lambert has first brought his soldiers thither, and beset the House, and turned back the Speaker, [who] was then coming to it; Hazlerig's forces marching about St James' park-wall [see Exhibit 7.7], came into St Margaret's churchyard; and so both parties looked all day one upon another, like enemies, but offered not to fight: whereby the Rump was put out of possession of the House.[83]

Governance was now by an army-staffed council of safety.

Various indications are that AH had been feeling fatigue, perhaps due in part to his battle injuries, perhaps due in part to chronic disease and age (he was 58), and surely due to the unending stress of upholding the cause of republican government with diminishing support of others. John Pym was long gone; so, too John Hampden, William Strode and his father-in-law Robert Greville. Gone also was Oliver Cromwell, who, for all their disagreement, had been a stanchion against which AH could wield a moral authority that gave him persuasive voice. Oliver St John and Henry Vane were still active, but AH had never been that close to either man, both of whom saw him as too insistently radical. In addition, of course, Dorothy was gone. It is easy to imagine that he was feeling isolated as well as tired. In fact, of course, we cannot know his exact state of mind. But it is worth noting that on the occasion of the wedding of his son and heir, Thomas, to Elizabeth, daughter of George Fenwick, AH settled his home estates on Thomas, 22 October 1659. Given AH's wealth, it is clear that a marriage settlement could have been arranged in any number of other, substantially favorable ways, without yet assigning the home estates. That AH chose this specific arrangement at this date could have been acknowledgment that the tide had turned, in political if not yet in biological terms.

---

[83] Thomas Hobbes, *Behemoth*, edited by F Tönnies (London: Simpkin, Marshall, and Co., 1889), pages 197-98; Firth, *Ludlow Memoirs* (1894), volume 2, page 137; *Clarke Papers*, (1901), volume 4, pages 60, 70-71.

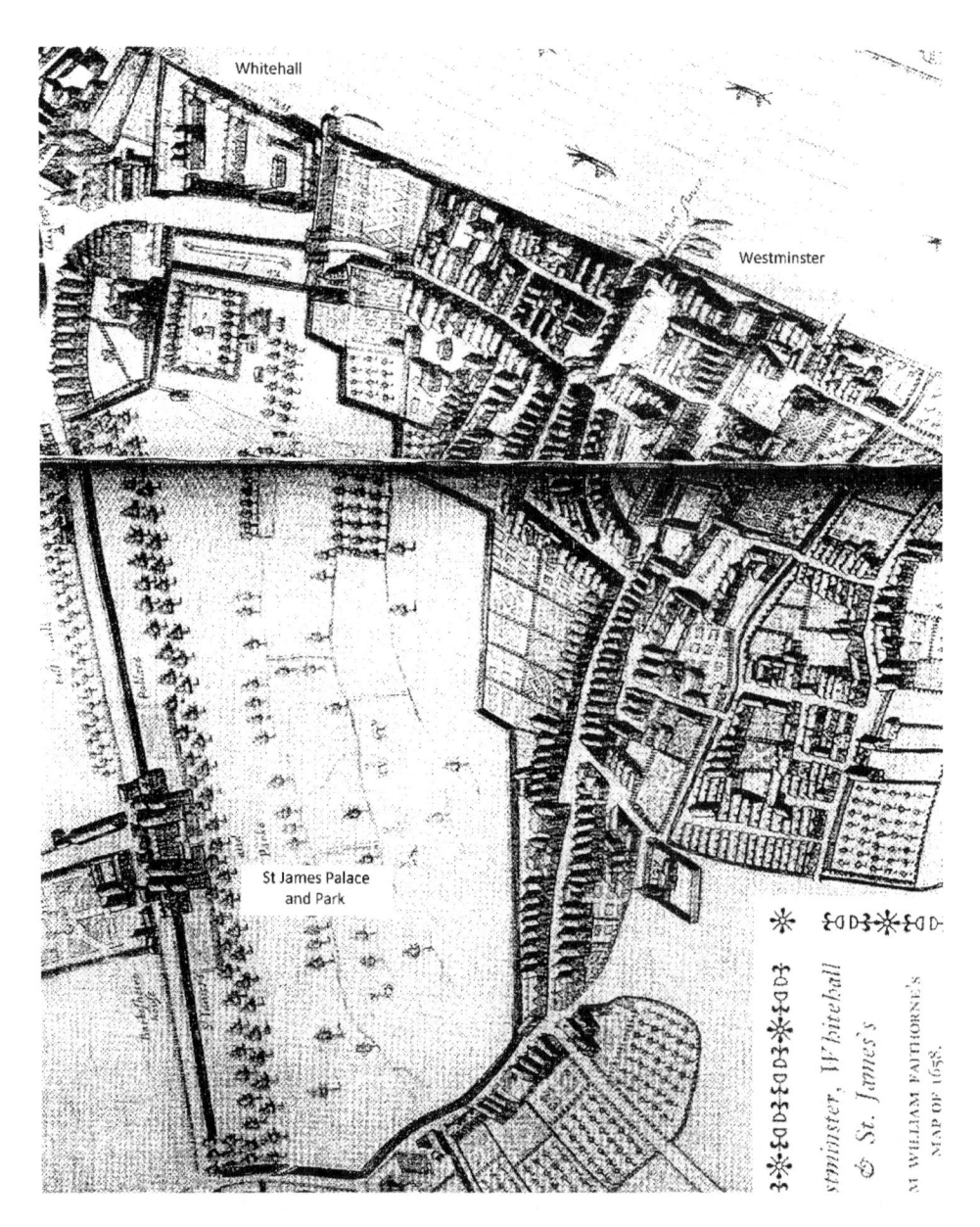

Exhibit 7.7. Part of Faithorne's Map, 1658

AH had at least one more fight in him, however. He rode to Portsmouth and its naval forces, the command of which (along with the city government) had remained on parliament's side, and raised a force of "about fifteen troops of horse and a regiment of foot." On learning of this, the London mood shifted from worry to satisfaction. The December 13th issue of a London newsletter had reported that the "face of affaires never looks worse in this place than at this time," for the general populace expect any day "to be in ears with the soldiery." Eleven days later, the report said that "We are near an end of our troubles; all parts are up for Parliament," and "Sir Arthur Haslerigge has 3000 horse and foot at Portsmouth, and this day hath produced" a resurgence of support of forces in "London and the Tower." In the meantime, AH had written to Monck, asking for his support of the parliamentary cause. Monck purged his army of sympathizers for the Lambert faction and declared for Parliament. AH and Morley marched their troops to London. Lambert backed away.[84] The Rump was restored. However, the inherent instability of the situation remained.

Seeing much evidence of that remaining instability, and knowing of no effective governmental response, General Monck designed a return to monarchy. He began moving his army south into England on 1 January 1659/60. Did AH know what was a foot? Clearly he suspected as much, for he sought assurances from Monck that his concern was misguided. He received those assurances, though one suspects he half-believed them at best. Monck later acknowledged his deception and explained it in a letter to Sir Edward Turnor (speaker of Commons from 8 May 1661):

> no man was so capable to obstruct my designs as Sir Arthur Hesilrige, who had in his immediate command the government of Berwick, Carlisle, Newcastle, and Tynemouth, with a regiment of foot and one of the best regiments of horse in the Army, and had an influence upon all the rest of the regiments in England.

Monck knew, moreover, the volume of loyalty that AH could command in the north even aside from those regiments. That loyalty had been remarked before. For example, writing from Ravensworth castle on 3 August 1654 to his brother Sir Henry, William Vane reported with some amazement that "Sir Arthur has been in these parts a fortnight, and seems to have been chosen [as MP] both in Leicestershire and Newcastle against his will." It was this loyalty both of regiment and of general populace that had said to Monck that his better course of action would be to deceive AH until no option remained, and he could, as he said to the Turner, convince AH to

---

[84] *Clarke Papers* (1901), volume 4, pages 164-66, 169-71, 187, 219-20; Hyde, *History* ... (1826, volume 7, pages 366-75, 390-91. Denton, *Only in Heaven* (1997), page 226, said that Col. Herbert Morley was son-in-law to AH. This is doubtful; known marriages of AH's daughters, together with Morley's 1648 marriage to Mary, daughter of Sir John Trevor, by whom she had four children as of c1656, argue against the claim.

retire from the scene to a quiet life in return for Monck's support on behalf of his life and estate. This latter point might have been the occasion of Monck's letter to Turnor, dated 4 July 1660. There had been considerable discussion and disagreement between Commons and Lords about disposition of AH's case—whether he would be excepted from the bill to "forgive and forget," and if so, whether the exception would include his life as well as his "pain, penalty, and forfeitures." Monck's persistent intercession was critical. Even so, it was a close call, finally put to rest with AH's death. The "Act of Free and General Pardon, Indemnity, and Oblivion," shepherded by Edward Hyde into law on 29 August 1660, was a remarkably generous agreement in giving pardon to all persons excepting those who had officiated at the execution of Charles I. Crown lands and lands of the established church were immediately restored, but others were subject to negotiation. Seven persons were initially on the list of exceptions. But as scores were to be settled, names were added and names were subtracted during the ensuing months. [85]

Prior to that Act by the new parliament, the Convention Parliament, conditions had become dangerous for AH, among others. By the end of January 1659/60, he had agreed to remove his regiment of horse from London, ostensibly to make room for Monck's force. But the real change was evident to most, and without the loyalty of his own regiment behind him, AH surely felt vulnerable. After meeting with Monck in the city, Londoners began celebrating a "Roasting of the Rump," and AH was no longer comfortable on the streets. It was then that a young diarist named Samuel Pepys, having recently begun his later-famous diary, added entries for days of February (especially the 11th, the 12th, and the 19th) that indicated AH's signs of increasing distress.[86] Monck had become the center of attention. Could he be trusted to keep his agreement with AH? And even if he could, would events henceforth remain enough in Monck's grasp to enable his verbal agreement to mean anything? Before the end of the month those surviving MPs of the Long Parliament who had been purged were restored to their seats, putting the Presbyterian faction back in power. AH capitulated.[87] In March the Long Parliament stepped aside

---

[85] *Clarke Papers* (1901), volume 4, pages 302-303; *Calendar of State Papers, Domestic* (1654), page 286; *Commons Journal*, volume 8 (25 August 1660), pages 135-37; Denton, *Only in Heaven* (1997), pages 192, 197.

[86] Pepys' entry for the 19th included a report that AH "was afraid to have the candle carried before him, for fear that the people seeing him, would do him hurt."

[87] Firth, *Ludlow Memoirs* (1894), volume 2, pages 211, 219; Robertson, *Tyrannicide Brief* (2005), pages, 271-72; Denton, *Only in Heaven* (1997), pages 229-31.

to make way for the Convention Parliament. Captain Thomas Hesilrige, son and heir of AH, surrendered his troop on 22 April and was arrested briefly. No doubt increasingly apprehensive, AH thought a reminder to General Monck might be timely, so on the 30th he wrote this letter:[88]

> My Lord,
> I beseech your Lordship to let the Council understand that I have neither directly nor indirectly done anything in opposition to the present authority settled by the Parliament in the Council of State. Neither was I knowing in the least degree of the disturbance made by Lambert. I have always acted with the authority of Parliament, and never against it, and hold it my duty to submit to the authority of the Nation and not to oppose it, and have hazarded my all to bring the military power under the civil authority. I forgot to give you the two pence, it is here enclosed, and, being secured by your Lordship's promise, I hope to end the remainder of my days in peace and quiet.
> Arthur Hasilrige
> 30 April, 1660

None of this information would have been new to Monck. The point was his reminder of the agreement. The "tuppence" had been Monck's barbed request of value for value, so to speak, and AH's reminder was his sign of submission.

On 8 May Charles II of Scotland was proclaimed king of England and Wales as well. Soon thereafter, AH was sent to the Tower of London. This was not his first visit. It would be his last. He died of "fever" on the 7th day of January 1660/1.

Edward Hyde, the earl of Clarendon (having regained his favor in royal court), offered something of a tribute toward the end of his *History*, writing of events of 1659-60:

> Haslerig was, as to the state, perfectly republican; and as to religion, perfectly Presbyterian: and so he might be sure never to be troubled with a king or bishop was indifferent to other things; only he believed the parliament to be the only government that would infallibly keep those two out.

---

[88] *Clarke Papers* (1901), volume 4, page 268.

To which Hyde then added:

> A model of such a government, as the people must acquiesce in, and submit to, would require very much agitation, and very long time; which the present conjuncture would not bear.[89]

That Hyde thought AH a Presbyterian is curious, probably simply a lapse in attention as he was composing his enormous work. Surely he had been more carefully observant as the long chain of actual events unfolded in their partly coordinated lives. However that may be, his testimony to, and about, Sir Arthur Hesilrige was toward the end mostly accurate. For all his criticism of AH as an opponent and as a person, he could recognize and appreciate integrity of cause, even though he thought the cause was at best premature.

Restoration, 1660

While the coronation of Charles II was viewed by some as proof of the utter futility and thus needless destruction of "the Great Rebellion," in fact it proved to be another accommodation, eventually between monarch and parliament, but immediately between the centralizing assertion of power in London, for a time represented most centrally in the royal court, and the power of the several counties. A recent historian put it this way: "the events of 1660 were a compromise between the power of [the world of counties, each centered on its gentry] and the power of the nation-state. Or rather they were an agreement to differ, an *entente*, a recognition that each world needed the other in order to survive."[90]

The restoration of monarchy in 1660 came with the hope of many for a restoration of peace, unity, and prosperity. While that hope was eventually realized, the early years were dominated by two enormous disasters. The first was the Great Plague of London (1665-66), which, at peak voracity, wiped out a thousand lives each day. This disaster was shortened by a second, the Great Fire of London (1666), which devastated the larger part of the physical edifice of London's center. Charles II thus began his reign not only as the heir of a national debt of about £2 million but also as the leader of a greatly diminished and demoralized population

---

[89] Hyde, *History* ... (1826), volume 7, pages 373-74.
[90] Alan M Everitt, *Change in the Provinces* (Leicester: Leicester University, 1969), page 48; see also Roger C Richardson's *The Debate on the English Revolution* (London: Routledge, 1998), page 171, and Phil Withington, *The Politics of Commonwealth* (Cambridge: Cambridge University Press, 2005).

and principal city. But for the survivors, no matter: they had peace. If the new king seemed dissolute by contrast to his father, no matter: there was peace. If some of the surviving members of his father's royalist party felt they had been depreciated by an Act of Oblivion (forgetfulness) that required them to fight for the return of lands that had once been in the family, no matter: peace was on the land. A great many people were truly relieved.

Restoration of the Hesilrige family had begun even before the last days of Sir Arthur Hesilrige in January 1660/1. General Monck, now the duke of Albemarle, played some part in this, just as his intercession had spared Sir Arthur a trip to the executioner's block. Another part no doubt was served, perhaps also with Monck's aid, by a petition submitted to Charles II by Sir Arthur during the summer of 1660. It is written in a bold hand, whether by a paid scribe or by Arthur himself is not known in fact; but unless his health would not support the effort, one suspects he held the pen.[91]

As Denton observed, the document is accurate in all stated details, and there are many. That it omitted some details is perhaps not surprising, although the important ones had long been known, and doubtless many record keepers awaited favor of the royal court. What is remarkable is that Arthur did not bend his principle of faith in either his God or his republican ideal. At one key juncture he said,

> And the God almighty having by wonderfull dispensation restored your Majesty to your Kingdome in peace, your petitioner doth rejoyce in the good hand of God in bringing it about without the effusion of blood.

Acknowledging that he had been cause of provocations, he would not feign sorrowfulness but would promise "exemplary obedience and faithfulness to redeem his former miscarriages." He would bend his knee, and did; but not his principles.

---

[91] See DG21/253 & 254 for the manuscript. A complete transcript is in Denton, *Only in Heaven* (1997), pages 232-34.

~ 8 ~
A Portrait of Arthur Hesilrige

The events of the 1640s were not unprecedented. The outcome certainly was. A century earlier Henry VIII had been temporarily shaken when a large group of citizens, centered mainly in Lincolnshire and Yorkshire, rose up in protest of his policies on religion and his taxes. That they were able to field an army of some 30,000 men, which, led by some prominent members of the aristocracy, was about to rout the king's forces in the area, took Henry by surprise, and he quickly proceeded with negotiations that bought him time until he could gain the upper hand—at which point he dispatched the rebels with severe prejudice. Daughter Elizabeth well understood that lesson of the rebellion of 1536-37. Charles, of a different family and in a different time, apparently could not believe that such lessons pertained to him at all.

Arthur[12b] Hesilrige's life was ever after remembered because of his role in political actions that led to civil war, his military actions during the wars, and his political actions during and after the last of the wars had come to an end. No doubt a major part of that memory is due to the fact that the king was tried and, even more momentously, executed—and for doing no more than what he thought was his divinely ordained right as king. There is considerable truth to Gardiner's summation in his *History of the Great Civil War*: "Charles was always honestly desirous of putting an end to the war, if only he was not expected to abandon any of his claims."[1] To the mind of Arthur[12b], as to the minds of many other English men and women, the time for that prejudice was long gone. The king's "claim" clearly *was* prejudicial—that is, prejudging situations of government during the early 1600s—because the claim was so far out of tune with the times. But just as there was more to Charles than the main events of his reign incline us to remember and recite, so it was with Arthur[12b], too.

The chief focus of this chapter will be on Arthur[12b], more fully on the man as a person in the round, to the extent that this is possible within the bounds of available records and reasonable speculation. Scrutiny will include a reprise of some of his participation in the wars, protectorate, and post-protectorate periods, but from a somewhat different angle. Effort will center on insights into "contents of mind." Accordingly, we will look again at his upbringing, his education, his formative years, and his adult

---

[1] Samuel R Gardiner, *History* ... (London: Longmans, Green, 18nn), volume 1, page 361. From the king's point of view, of course, there was a flaw in Gardiner's summary: his were not mere "claims"; they were rights, and rights not merely human but divine.

character as it seemed to evolve during the course of events that were so momentous for him as for so very many others. This journey will take us into his published writings as well as others' accounts of his behavior and character.

Nothing like this chapter has been written for any other member of the family, before or since. For recent members something like this one could have been written but was not, for reasons of privacy. Why this one, for the 2nd Bt? Mainly because we know so much about him, at least with respect to events, and quite a lot has been written in context of those events, much of it rather negative in tenor. Considering all of that together, it seemed appropriate to venture into a modality of portraiture, in an effort to gain a more rounded appreciation of the person, the man, both within and behind the historical personage.

Note that as in the previous chapter Arthur[12b] Hesilrige will again be cited as "AH"; further, because so few other family members will figure in the discussion, the superscripting of names will give way to ordinary kinship terms.

A Puritan Household
Why would a person become a Puritan? It is such an austere doctrinal belief centered on a highly individualistic relation between the believer and the believer's God. The term itself denoted a "purified" form of an already austere doctrine, Calvinism, with its emphasis on predestination or the predetermined membership of "the Elect," the select few destined for an afterlife in Heaven.[2] In context of late sixteenth and early seventeenth-century England, the word "Puritan" was often intended as a term of abuse, applied to someone who was seen as "too radical" or "demented." But as we have seen in previous chapters, AH embraced the designation, saying as a matter of dignity that he was "bred a Puritan." Part of the answer to the question, "Why Puritan?" is of course necessarily a social component. The radical individualism centered on the privileged linkage of believer and God necessarily holds some implications for a believer's conception of the relationship between his or her connection to God and his or her connection to other persons. The core implication is individual liberty: each person must be free to worship God as he or she believes proper, and thus must allow equivalent liberty to others. This can lead to a level of tolerance that in the eyes of some is "excessive." And in any case, the

---

[2] As had often been noted, followers of Calvinism tended to be more stringent than was Calvin himself, a typical pattern of "conversion" psychology. See William Bouwsma's biographic study, *John Calvin* (New York: Oxford University Press, 1988).

insistence of individual liberty of conscience and practice easily poses grievous threat to an established authority that depends on obedience to its own founding agreement.

By the same token, while the radical individualism of belief and practice would in principle leave the social organization of a congregation of like believers in secondary status, interests of local community, along with interests in supporting one another against external suspicions and hostilities, lent the congregational form "as church," rather than as a scattering of individual believers, considerable attraction. But the place of a cleric, a minister or preacher, in that churchly form was precarious, an insecure dispensability. Clerics responded by offering a mirror, for the most part, commiserating with pains and sorrows, arguing in league with the safety of sins. That could be a bit tricky, however. Consider the twin problems of drunkenness and fornication, seemingly everyone's top-of-list concerns about health of the world. These were concerns not for social reasons, however, not because they contributed to the "excess population" of vagabonds, beggars, orphans, prostitutes, and such, but for religious reasons. One of the favored explanations from the pulpit held that these acts "stank in the nostrils" of God.[3] But this was merely projection. Why did clerics, why did anyone, believe that such "stench" existed and that it offended God? What forces drove that projective behavior by individuals, and to such uniform extent that it perversely celebrated certain sorts of social relationship as camouflage for the plain fact that the problem of "excess population" was due mainly to practices of forced enclosure and engrossment?[4]

The issues of sociality for a religion so individualistic go beyond that, however, for the simple reason that one typically became a Puritan not in isolation but in a family, in that most inertial of age-graded arrangements of authority, a household. Arthur became a Puritan in an already Puritan household.[5] The matter of individual liberty typically comes with blinders, so to speak. A child can renounce a parent's authority of belief; and some children of Puritan households did. But either way, the options of "free choice" are always already suffused with context, a social context, which is virtually never neutral in all of its various dimensions.

---

[3] William Hunt, *The Puritan Moment* (Cambridge: Harvard University Press, 1983), pages 404, 408; Jonathan Bate, *Soul of the Age* (New York: Random House, 2009), page 203.
[4] Joan Thirsk, *The Rural Economy of England* (London: Hambledon, 1984).
[5] On the general point see, e.g., Nancy Armstrong and Leonard Tennenhouse, *The Imaginary Puritan* (Berkeley: University of California Press, 1992).

This makes convincing answers to the question with which this section of the chapter began rather scarce. We must begin with Arthur's childhood, his parents' household, even though we know very little of it. And that ever-present regressive question, "Who taught the teacher?" can only be acknowledged as always open.

We know hardly anything of the "inner life" of Thomas Hesilrige, and less still for his wife, Frances (*nee* Gorges). The canvas has slightly more paint to show for their eldest son, Donald, and that pertains mainly to his education. A picture forms when we come to second son and eventual heir, Arthur. But even here, excepting what can be gleaned from his published writings and from others' responses to and comments about Arthur, all pertaining to his adult years during the conflict, we are left grasping after straws in a very noisy wind.

A little support is offered by a recent study of *Kinds of Christianity in Post-Reformation England* during the years from 1570 to the beginning of the civil wars. The author, Christopher Haigh, surveyed a number of writings published during that period in England, books that might be called "practical manuals for the proper Christian soul," with due consideration to the main variations of what then counted as "proper Christian."[6] For the earlier years of that period a prime example was a small book, *Country Divinity*, published in 1581 by George Gifford, who was later described by Benjamin Brook in his *Lives of the Puritans* as "a great and diligent preacher." Gifford's public voice resulted in a trial and conviction on charges of nonconformity—surely not a difficult charge to prove, given the wording of the charges and the underlying law—and he was imprisoned. Perhaps the most popular book among Puritans was Arthur Dent's *The Plain Man's Pathway to Heaven*, which remained in print after Dent's death in 1607 and by 1640 had reached its 25th edition. Another popular homiletic, this one also written in plain style, was Lewis Bayley's *The Practice of Piety*, published in 1611. A fourth popular manual considered by Haigh, George Herbert's *The Country Parson*, came at the end of the period, and presented a point of view different from the Puritan.

There is no evidence that Thomas read Gifford's book. But given its popularity and controversy it is likely that he did read it or at least was familiar with its contents. Was it in the household library, and perhaps available as a study in character to Thomas' children? That, too, seems

---

[6] The main title of Haigh's book (the one shown above is his subtitle) was *The Plain Man's Pathway to Heaven* (Oxford University Press, 2009), a repeat of one of the most popular of the early seventeenth-century books, Dent's, considered below.

likely, in part because the presence of books was considered a mark of advancement in late sixteenth-century households. Even more likely was the presence of Dent's book, published the year of AH's birth. Puritans were far from uniform in their beliefs and practices. But the message of Dent's book appealed to a great many, and its longevity in print tells us that Dent and then his literary heirs managed the book's fit to the broad middle ground of his readership as that middle ground evolved over the course of three increasingly unsettled decades. Unless the Hesilrige men, father and son, stood at an extreme in the range of Puritan sentiments—and there is no evidence that either of them did—it seems reasonable to assume that Dent's book reflected their own views rather well. Of course, that tells us more of their views of general matters of Puritan doctrine—individual conscience, salvation, personal responsibility—than about any inner doubts, conflicts, or elations that either of them felt in religious life. But these latter experiences lie beyond the reach of our evidence.

However, particular features of Puritan doctrine do afford insight into *some* probable characteristics of Thomas and Arthur. First of all, it is important to bear in mind that *concerted* opposition to the established church did not develop until the 1620s and the advent of Laudian reform combined with the king's tone-deaf insistence on authority by divine right. There is, in that regard, one passage in Dent's book that gives us insight into the probable origin and grounds of young Arthur's fierce conviction and self-confidence in destiny—his conviction that he must take charge of his own individual destiny, and his confidence that he was correct in bringing that same conviction to his country as a whole—in both characteristics probably more stringently determined than his father, Thomas, who even into the early 1620s was, like other Puritans, showing signs of working a compromise of mutual tolerance with his king, James. The passage refers to the Calvinist doctrine of assurance—that is, the notion that the Elect know with perfect certainty that they *are* the Elect— a belief which many Christians found simply *un*believable. Of the four characters Dent presented as representative of popular points of view, one, "Asunetus, an ignorant man," doubts the doctrine, while another, "Theologus, a divine," defends it, saying:

> We may not venture our salvation upon uncertain hopes, as if a man should hope it would be a fair day tomorrow; but he cannot certainly tell. No, no. We must in this case, being of such infinite importance as it is, grow to some certainty and full resolution. ... [Otherwise,] what comfort can [a person] have in anything?

> Besides this, the persuasion of God's love and cheerfull obedience towards him. For therefore we love him and obey him, because we know he hath loved us first, and written out names in the book of life. But on the contrary, the doctrine of the Papists, which would have men always doubt and fear in a servile sort, is most hellish and uncomfortable. For so long as a man holds that, what encouragement can he have to serve God? What love to his Majesty? What hope in the promises? What comfort in trouble? What patience in adversity?[7]

What we would call the Puritan psychology was extremely austere in offering a stark choice, certainty in one's belief in God *and* in being among God's Elect or everlasting utter despair from lack of confidence in one's God and thus in oneself. Moreover, assurance could come not from another, not from a priest or a father or a king, not from any written or spoken word, not from a hope or a display of piety or any harvest of successes. It could come only from *within*. This was a most radical individualism, leaving each person ultimately to bear total responsibility and destiny for himself or herself (though gender bias put women in a less succinctly described position).

    One had to believe in oneself. But there were different ways of doing that, different kinds and sources of believing in oneself. A cooper could rightfully believe in his ability to craft as fine a barrel as ever seen, and his conviction in that belief could remain unshaken in face of any and all competitors' severest criticisms. There was a product for all to see, however, and to judge, and to try to better, in regard to the conviction and the self-confidence. For the Puritan believer there was no possibility of such feedback, no point of comparison, not in *this* life. A weak believer who was successful in some endeavor could point to that success as a sign. But although a common course, this was actually a *failure* of belief, as judged by the doctrine of assurance. From a different point of view, nothing could be more doubtful than one's destiny as ordained by one's God. From that point of view *within* a religion, to claim that one actually knew God's mind, choices made by God, was highly reductive, a kind of blasphemy—as if a mere mortal could be capable of knowing the mind of God. But from the point of view of Puritanism's doctrine of assurance, it was not a matter of knowing God's mind, not even a single one of God's thoughts or decisions. Rather, it was a matter of having such confidence

---

[7] Arthur Dent, *The Plain Man's Pathways to Heaven*, 50th edition (Belfast: North of Ireland Book and Tract Depository, 1859), pages 189-190, 196.

of conviction in a belief that one did *not* doubt what was, for someone lacking that confidence, eminently doubtable.

That sort of conviction and confidence was well apparent in AH's decisions and actions in the political realm of Caroline England from the early 1640s. It continued after the execution of the king. It became even stronger after Cromwell's turn to more dictatorial practices. Cromwell's strength acted as a bulwark against Arthur's convictions, for good or ill. With succession by a weak Richard Cromwell in 1658, Arthur no longer had to contend against that well of strength. One consequence, it can be argued, was that Arthur's personal conviction in republicanism, and his self-certainty in that conviction of belief, blinded him to the possibility—or, with the aid of hindsight, the near certainty—that civic institutions of public order were too anemic to support the moral load of a republic, a *res publica* or "public thing." This could account for the fact that George Monck, previously an ally of Arthur and staunch defender of Parliament, deceived Arthur in order to have him disband his Lobsters regiment, thus to arrange return of the dead king's son as Charles II. Monck had been generally known as a straightforward leader. Why did he not attempt to persuade Arthur to his view that the people of England were simply not ready for the responsibilities of a republic? Perhaps he did make the attempt and found it futile. More likely he did not make the attempt, for the same reason that Arthur himself had shown no inclination toward that view: absence of doubt that his view, not Monck's, was the correct view.

Arthur's biographer, Barry Denton, believed that the Hesilrige family did not become Puritan until the 1630s, until the influence of John Pym, Robert Greville, and others.[8] He did not argue his case so much as assume it, but the conclusion cannot be dismissed out of hand. Relevant evidence is meagre; much depends on how one draws the list of qualities defining "Puritan." However, the argument made in chapter 6, based on available evidence, seems more persuasive than any counter-argument. The influence of Pym and others no doubt did mould AH into a more effective debater, perhaps also a more effective Puritan politician, in part by urging him to control better his rashness (as some observers described him) and make more effective use of parliamentary procedures. These observers, it should be noted, were writing of a man late in life, and in some instances after his death. Thus, it would indeed be rash to rely on their views for evidence of AH as a young man. But thin though it is, the record of that young man offers some insight into his character, and that insight, held in conjunction with what is known of his parents, lends

---

[8] Barry Denton, *Only in Heaven* (Sheffield: Sheffield Academic Press, 1997), page 19.

support to the conclusion that he grew to early maturity in a household of Puritan sympathies, if not strongly doctrinaire, and professed them as his own. This is not to say that he began adult life as a separatist—one who was determined to separate from the official church, much less one who sought to overthrow that church's hierarchy and abolish the episcopacy. Hirst was probably correct when he said that "Separatists were few in number compared to those who still sought to establish the proper form of a national church"—or to reform the established church.[9] He was referring to London in 1641, however, and by that time AH was surely among those few.

That was 1641. Let's back up, to 1615, a time four hundred years ago, when AH was a teenager (though he would not have recognized that twentieth-century neologism). In his own mind he was on the verge of adulthood. With an older brother, Donald, in front of him, thoughts of that adulthood were probably troubled by uncertainties, mainly due to the rule of primogeniture. He had survived the uncertainties of early childhood, the years when death's scythe cut many boys and girls to the ground. Now some uncertainties of his impending future years had to be entertained and resolved in advance, as best he could. His prospects did not include inheritance of his father's title (now knighthood; the baronetcy was still several years ahead and probably not anticipated), nor was his father's favored estate, Alderton, in store for him. Donald was soon to enter legal majority, and he would inherit Alderton, perhaps Noseley as well. Or perhaps Arthur could expect Noseley? Perhaps a career in military service or in the clergy was better suited to his ambitions and character? Or did his thoughts turn to "urban life" in burgeoning London? After all, he had several cousins who were making their way in that life rather well, and his younger brothers John and Thomas could have been engaged in encouraging talk of life in the big city. How much did he actually know of the urban world of London? How did he weigh his prospects of life there, given what he did know, or thought he knew? Answers surely depend to some extent on his self-understanding within and relative to the religious contests that suffused public life and many (but not all) private lives. Judging from what (little) we know of his parents, including our imaginations drawn from the one extant portrait of Thomas (date unknown but probably after 1600), Arthur had been raised within a Calvinist setting of values and expectations. This reading is reinforced by the line from the only surviving memory of his mother, Frances (*nee* Gorges), as recorded

---

[9] Derek Hirst, "The Failure of Godly Rule in the English Republic," *Past and Present*, number 132 (August 1991), pages 33-66, at page 35.

in the epitaph to her tomb (and cited in the preceding chapter): she "adorn'd her family with fine cloth of her owne spining." The implication is that she made the cloth from which then she cut and sewed apparel. The implication further is that this was done not from economic necessity—after all, many wives and daughters spun wool into fabric from which clothes were then cut and sewn—but as an action of purity and grace, an expression of basic values within her household. Expeditions of Puritans to the New World were still a few years ahead, probably not yet topics of serious conversation, and reports from the settlement at Jamestown were not exactly encouraging. So Arthur probably contemplated a life in England, though not as titular head of the family.

Being "spare to the heir" still entailed some attention to matters of primogeniture. But while there were almost always prospects of conflict with one or another continental power, there was little prospect of a major confrontation that might carry brother Donald off to the dangers of combat. He had matriculated at Brasenose College, Oxford, in 1608, at age 16 or thereabout, the typical age for college in that era, and by the time Arthur was in his teen years Donald was occupied with matters of family estate management. Risks of deadly injury by animal, death from the plague or other disease, the foolishness of dueling, and an ever-present threat of being accosted by highwaymen, all meant that a "spare" needed to be able and ready. But by 1615 or so, Donald was well past the thickest part of the early curve of mortality risk, so Arthur was very likely contemplating a life different from those of elder brother and father. He had been a pupil at the Royal College of St Peter in Westminster, which gave him access to attractions of city life and in close proximity to parliament and the Inns of Court. He matriculated at Magdalene College, Cambridge, Easter term of 1617, and following those years he was admitted to Gray's Inn for legal training. The profession of law was a rapidly growing one, in numbers and in importance to the world of landed estates as well as politics. It is easy to think that Arthur saw his future in some part of that world of law.

During the Elizabethan period Calvinist inclinations were present at both of the main universities, Oxford and Cambridge, and as we saw in a previous chapter Thomas Hesilrige chose Oxford for his eldest son and heir apparent, Donald, though Brasnose, not Magdalene College, the latter having been "the most important centre of Puritanism in the university of Oxford" during the time of Elizabeth. This emphasis on Puritan doctrine and practice continued though lessened during the reign of James I. With the election of "a disciple of Laud as President of Magdalen College in 1626," however, that tradition ended, and "the final curtain came down on the long history of the college as a Puritan academy" at Oxford.[10] Indeed, Laud became chancellor of the university in 1629, and from that date forward the colleges grew more and more inhospitable to all non-conformists. The fact that Thomas chose Magdalen College at Cambridge for young Arthur might have been due at least in part to his perception of change even before Laud's arrival.

Very little is known of Arthur's time at Cambridge. This is not an unusual circumstance. Samuel Pepys, later to gain fame as a diarist, also matriculated at Magdalene College, Cambridge, a generation after Arthur, and we know hardly anything of his experience.[11] Judging from the brief mentions of Arthur's time at Magdalene, there is good reason to believe that he found the experience a positive one in general and good education in the humanities in particular, but he had nothing specifically to say about his studies or even his extracurricular activities. College attendance increased markedly during the sixteenth and seventeenth centuries, by as much as a factor of four (versus a factor of two for England's population as a whole). During the early part of that period of growth, the typical sequence of study would have been something similar to a "general studies" sequence in recent times. Attention to modern sciences was increasing, as these new disciplines such as geology, physics, chemistry, anatomy, and physiology began to flourish. Oxford showed quicker grasp of the potential than did Cambridge, however, one indication of the difference being that whereas the number of positions for teaching science at Oxford more than doubled (from three to seven) between 1600 and 1640, at Cambridge the number remained constant at two.[12] One can search in vain for references in AH's surviving writings to any of the new insights achieved by William Harvey in anatomy and physiology or by Robert Boyle in chemistry (although the latter began toward the end of AH's life). To the extent that his writing has traces of his time at Magdalene, these are mainly in the art of written composition, with occasional reference to a classical text (as well as to the Bible, knowledge of which he had gained well before college).

---

[10] John T Cliffe, *The Puritan Gentry* (London: Routledge & Kegan Paul, 1984), pages 85, 87.

[11] Samuel Pepys, *The Diary*, complete transcription, edited by Robert Latham and William Matthews, 11 volumes (London: Bell & Hyman, 1970-83). The brief entry for 26 February 1660 is typical.

[12] Robert G Frank, Jr, *Harvey and the Oxford Physiologists* (Berkeley: University of California Press, 1980), pages 45-46. Both universities soon lagged behind universities across the Channel, however, and after the late 1600s enrollments declined sharply as reputations of both Oxford and Cambridge suffered by comparison.

Contents of Mind
The 1600s were a time of rapid change, including the invention of ideas, relationships, and things. The century has often been nominated as the start of "modern society." Such choices always contain some element of arbitrariness, but the 1600s are nonetheless a reasonable choice. For purposes here, it is important to recognize that the changing times formed AH's context and conditions, even as he became a participant in the changes, both attempted and actual. If we are to grasp anything of the likely contents of his mind, we must begin with matters of context and condition. Much of the contextual and conditional scope of AH's world has been addressed at least briefly in the previous two chapters and will not be repeated here. Rather, emphasis here will be on ideas, concepts, relationships, perspectives, and the like, that offer furnishings of a mind, whether by deliberations undertaken by the person in question or by indeliberate, unnoticed, even incidental seepings from the external world into that great inner world of thoughts, emotions, perceptions. We must operate by indirection and conjecture, for the most part, lacking direct access, as we do, to his thoughts and (as previously lamented more than once) even the indirect access of the personal diary the existence of which we can infer from habits of Puritans in general.

Judging mainly from records of his actions, AH's motivations in adulthood were organized around three main preoccupations: patrimony, always a concern; religion, at first almost solely private but then shifting to a national arena, because of restrictions on freedom of worship; and politics, initially local but then again transferring to national arena, owing only in part to those same restrictions on liberty. At times, politics slid into warfare, and during the early part of those times AH indulged himself in a youthful exuberance of cavalry charges. But an unexpected introduction to his own death brought recognition that the glories of a gallant horseman in combat decay even more rapidly than the body lucky enough to feel some of that glory, and he realized there could be greater, potentially more lasting accomplishments awaiting his attentions.

All of that motivation, even the most intense of it, existed not in a vacuum but in a welter of other stimulations imposing themselves on a busy consciousness. Some of those stimulations were calls of tradition—the tradition of family and patrimony, for one, a tradition that for AH included an already established familial tradition of Calvinist thought and rejection of a state-established church. But other of the stimulations were new, and some of these were upsetting of one or another tradition. That meant disturbance and conflict, but it often also meant excitements of new possibilities.

Invention tends to be sensitive to environment. The act itself is not necessarily impeded by tumultuous conditions; in fact, the tumult of challenge to existing conditions, to hallowed tradition, and the like, can actually stimulate the creativity of designing something new, radically new. But a tumultuous environment can stall development and spread of the newly invented, especially if it is, or is seen to be, very different from the customary.

A textbook illustration is provided by the life of William Petty (1623-1687). Notably intelligent, ambitious, and courageous, the young Hampshire lad made his way to London, engaging in political discourse on the side of the republican cause. He had already studied medicine in Amsterdam and Paris, in the latter city working as a secretary to Thomas Hobbes, in which capacity he became acquainted with the philosopher and mathematician, René Descartes. These influences strengthened his conviction in the importance of assembling data in systematic ways that could provide the basis on which to draw new insights, a process of statistical analysis in which he became highly skilled. Now in London from 1646, Petty threw in his lot with the rebellion against Charles I. Acquainted with Samuel Pepys and AH, among others, he rose quite rapidly in intellectual as well as political circles, all the while improving his empirical skills and furthering his speculations about economic conditions and processes. During 1654-1656, for example, he was in charge of the Down survey, an economic charting of all of Ireland. One of the tasks he set for himself was to determine how to estimate the value of estates, his own included. This he achieved, in the process inventing a system of national accounts based on the notion of "present discounted value" (the centerpiece of modern finance). He also devised a "quantity theory of money," the core of monetary economics. He proposed that long periods of unemployment would degrade workers' skill levels and attitudes; therefore, that during times of economic decline public works should be organized both to the immediate benefit of the public good and to the longer-range benefit of keeping workers engaged. During a severe outbreak of plague in London in the 1660s, Petty calculated the costs and benefits of moving people out of London until the plague had subsided, concluding that the net return on that investment would average about 84 pounds as the rate of survival increased. In other words, he demonstrated how to calculate the net monetary benefit of a healthy surviving worker, relative to that same worker dead. This was another radical notion for the time. Because of his standing among contemporaries, Petty survived the restoration in 1660 with only some loss of estate in Ireland. He was a founding member of the Royal Society in 1662, for example, signaling approval by Charles II as well as by others. For all his inventiveness, however, Petty was soon largely lost to the annals of economics and the social sciences generally. Hardly any of his work was maintained and developed during the next hundred years or so, after which first one and then another of his notions were invented again (e.g., David Hume on the quantity theory of money in 1752).[13]

AH was of the first generation of readers who could have had, and many did have, personal copies of collected editions of Chaucer, Spenser, Jonson, and Shakespeare, among others. In 1611, for example, a Scottish poet, William Drummond of Hawthornden, catalogued his library at 522 books (copies of the aforementioned authors among them).[14] AH surely had been exposed to many of the authors in Drummond's collection, and may have had copies in his own library. The Puritan interest in religious liberty had been both prod to and product of the conversion of discourses to vernacular languages, which had the effect of pulling proportionately more people into conversations that traded in "new and strange" ideas as well as old traditions. Vernacular literacy also furthered expectations and practices of mental agility. In the oral tradition, memory, especially the accuracy of detail in memory, carried great weight. Habits formed within that tradition carried over to cultures of writing and reading, which in turn placed new and heavier demands on capabilities of the human brain. (Learning to read was, and is, the single most taxing demand, resulting in huge growth of neural complexity.) Memory in oral tradition involved making a "knowledge that" and a "knowledge how" integral to one's being. Rote exercises were the road to that integration. Writing/reading extended that by creating a range of prosthetic devices that store details of knowledge, to which one can return repeatedly for refreshments of knowledge. Brain functions were being externalized in rapidly growing forms, books being one such. This was occurring at the very time that a great sustained explosion of detail-in-the-world was underway. AH was early in that process.

---

[13] Ted McCormick's *William Petty and the Ambitions of Political Arithmetic* (Oxford: Oxford University Press, 2010) is an excellent general source on Petty.

[14] Jonathan Bate, *Soul of the Age* (New York: Random House, 2009), page 134. As an interesting snippet of the "small world" phenomenon, note that this William Drummond was ancestral to a nineteenth-century Margaret Walker-Drummond, who wed Thomas Maynard Hazlerigg (more in chapter 11).

The list of innovations and developments issuing from the process included such exotic events as a new interiorization of the body (William Harvey's anatomy of the circulatory system, for instance, on analogy to the mechanics of a pump-and-piping system); a new geology of the planet (one which integrated fossils as records of life-forms into the age-grading of sedimentary layers); a microscopic world of otherwise invisible animals (with evidence that some of those animals lived within the human body); a telescopic world of other planets and other suns (which had entailed not only a "de-centering" of Earth but also a strong suspicion that God's universe was vastly older than archbishop James Ussher's pronouncement in the 1650s of an exact dating of creation, the night prior to Sunday, 23 October 4004BC (Julian calendar); Johannes Kepler's equations defining the orbital motions of planets (which led to Isaac Newton's generalized system of mechanics); the list goes on and on. AH was no doubt aware of most if not all of such events as occurred prior to 1660, though at times his attention was likely consumed mostly by affairs of state.

While much of that record of innovation and development took place after AH was dead, as already mentioned, drawing fast lines can be misleading. As illustration, consider Robert Hooke's *Micrographia*, published in 1665. A "best seller" for that day, its publication date was after AH's last years. But demand for a book, then as now, assumed a readership who were prepared for it, a sufficiently large number of people who understood what the book was about, found that interesting, and wanted to learn more. This assumption of readership describes the cumulative results of a process that does not happen quickly. AH's generation would have been at the leading edge of those cumulative results. While we have no way of knowing that AH would have read the book had he lived another half-dozen years in requisite health or, more realistically, if the book had appeared seven or eight years earlier, we do know from some events of his biography—his interest in colonizing North America, his effort to adapt an older style of armour to new cavalry tactics—that he had an inquisitive mind. The attention that these new technologies of vision, the microscope and telescope, had been attracting since the days of Zacharias Jansen (c1590) and Galileo Galilei (c1609) filtered into London largely on the wings of religious controversy, as perspectives being offered by developments of a new (i.e., modern) science disturbed old settlements of authority. Galileo's *Il Saggiatore* ("The Assayer"), a book published in Rome in 1623, would wait centuries before appearing in an English edition. But its main argument circulated among English minds that would eventually coalesce to found The Royal Society, an organization known at one time by the longer name, the Royal Society of London for Improving Natural Knowledge—in short, something of a sanctuary for new thinking. The date was 28 November 1660, about six weeks before the death of AH. Robert Hooke was its first Curator of Experiments. His *Micrographia* was the Society's second publication. The book featured not only drawings of extraordinary views (e.g., magnified images of the eye of a fly, the body of a louse, distant planets), demonstrating that there are levels or depths of reality of the world around us that our unaided senses cannot perceive; it also presented a wave theory of light and argued that fossils are of organic origin from distant times. The Society adopted as its motto *Nullius Verba*, "Take nobody's word for it": in the circumstances of seventeenth-century England, a very radical idea; indeed, a very radical idea still today. Would AH have endorsed the motto? Probably. But like virtually everyone else who has endorsed it, he would have thought of limits.

That notice of limits must bring us back to AH and religion—to his late-in-life declaration that he had been bred a Puritan, and to uncertainty, our uncertainty, as to what that meant for the contents of his mind. In many respects the intense inwardness of Puritan conscience, together with the severity of the doctrine of predestination, conduced to an individualized isolation that would leave this world as it is. The only utopist impulse has already been written in an otherworldliness to which only a select few, The Elect, have entry tickets. Why bother with efforts to improve this world? What would the point be? And yet AH did struggle, ultimately desperately, to improve the world as it was during the 1650s in England. But conflicted: he was concerned about "overpopulation" as a problem, for example, as were many, and the rising numbers of poor people congregated in cities; but he also opposed "remedial" efforts that would compound the problem by enabling the poor to survive however pitifully and bear more children who in turn would have poor chances, and so on—or so the thinking was, well before Thomas Malthus.

By the same token, many Puritans stressed a "plain style" of living, which could include rejection of traditional festivities in the name of a religion—for instance, Christmas, a serious occasion to be celebrated in quiet reverence and meditation with one's God. While we lack evidence of how AH regarded Christmas celebration, we have abundant evidence of his elaborate carriage and livery for travel from his Whitehall apartment to Westminster, or elsewhere, an extravagance that might well have been intended as part of the inventions of ceremonial grandeur for a republic but which made him the butt of some scorching satire. Then, too, there was the business of theatrical production, seen by some Puritans as anathema to right living. Lack of evidence again prevents judgment of AH's view of, say, Shakespearean theatrics at The Globe, although absence of allusion to the bard's work in AH's written record is reason for mild surprise. After all, by 1623 a first-folio publication of 36 plays in about 900 pages, printed both sides, had a press run of about 800 copies (known officially as "the First Folio" edition), and since printing was gauged by expected sales we can assume that most of the copies were sold (at a price of £1 per unbound copy, an extra pound or two required to bind the sewn quires into a leather cover).[15] However, being a Puritan did not necessarily preclude one from partaking either of the book(s) or of the live stage. Recall that AH's early mentor, Henry Hastings, Leicestershire's 5th earl of Huntingdon, a Puritan of some renown and influence, was a very active supporter of theatre in London.

Previous discussions of "context and conditions" in sixteenth and seventeenth-century England have put considerable emphasis on the rise of individualism as a social force. Let's examine that movement in more personal terms, in particular changes in experiences at personal level, such as AH might have noticed. A major manifestation of such changes during the late sixteenth and seventeen centuries that remains available to us is pictorial art, and this could be viewed as a realm in which a Puritan stress on "plain style" would have been apparent. Yet judging from the surviving full-length portrait of AH, c1640, painted in oil on a canvas measuring 50 inches high by 40 inches wide (see Exhibit 7.4, page 307), he was not averse to following current style in portraiture.[16]

To put that in context, consider paintings of persons during, say, Europe's fourteenth century and earlier. First of all, they tend to be of religious themes. Second, faces were not rendered with much, or even any, individual variation, and they are generally smooth, nearly featureless visages. In those instances in which a known person was being portrayed (known, that is, other than as Biblical figure), whether singly or in some group arrangement or landscape, the face is without blemish—no wens or warts, no broken noses or crooked teeth (in fact, rarely a smile). The

---

[15] The equivalent bound-book price in 2005 would have been about US$210, judging from comparisons to books of approximately that size and kind published c2005. This judgment is informed by research that was conducted in conjunction with a Sotheby auction of a First Folio copy in 2006. Of course, the auction price for such a rare book was considerably greater (US$2.5 million). It was leather-bound and complete. Fewer than 240 copies of the First Folio edition are known to exist; of these, 40 are complete.
[16] The original of this painting (NPG6440) is in the National Portrait Gallery, London.

person being portrayed—usually a duke or king or cardinal or such, if an actual, historical person—is rendered as he (rarely she) would want to appear. Gradations of status among persons in the scene were given by placement in the visual field—center versus periphery, foreground versus background, large versus small—and by apparel or related finery. Station in life was all, and faces as such said nothing of that.

Next, as contrast, consider the portraiture works of a seventeenth-century artist who became an iconic figure/name as *artist*, Rembrandt. A significant portion of his work consisted in portraits of known persons, self-portraits included. In these works, one notices, faces are both highly individualized and (to use a word mainly in its naïve sense) realistic. That is, the sitter got his (rarely her) face "as it really was," warts, wrinkles, scars, and all. Now, Rembrandt did not initiate that difference. It began centuries earlier, with painters such as Ghirlandaio (whose tempera painting, *Old Man and His Grandson*, c1490, has become emblematic of the transition). Rembrandt only continued that trajectory. His innovation was a use of color and light in a way that said, "The face is all." Context is heavily shadowed, given in somber colors with highlights that are so subtle, muted, one must seek them out. This typically includes apparel as well as any notion of backdrop, drapery, furniture, and the like—all of which, we are being told, is secondary, one might even say incidental, to the face, except that it heightens the effect. The face gives out light—reflected beams, we know, yet with some quality of an inner source as well. Rembrandt's self-portraits invite us to consider the double play of a dialectic of "subject and object" with a dialectic of "internal and external." If that seems obscure, go to a mirror; fill it with your image. On the one hand, you are observing an object that has the same standing as the blouse or shirt you are wearing, the section of wall or cabinetry visible in the background, and so forth. On the other hand, you are observing yourself, your *self*, who just a few moments ago came to this mirror, now looks back, and in another few moments will leave. This is the identity of *you*, subject *and* object all at once, and it is an identity that exists for you (the one who looks, who perceives), precisely because you *can* see two parts in that one, the subjective part and the objective part. Now, one more step: imagine you are artist, looking in the mirror in order to paint what you see. And what *do* you see? As artists learned to paint not merely some stylized, almost featureless human face, as if copying from a standard template, but a face with blemishes and all, they learned to paint an *individual* being as she or he "really is." And that phrase encompassed not simply the external terrain of a face, and perhaps entire front of body, but also an internal terrain of "character," a terrain of the meaningful experience of being *me*. Character portrayal also was not initiated by Rembrandt. Those earlier painters of dukes and kings and the like also sought to render some sense of character—typically flattering and, in that, usually rather stylized by elements of bearing, posture, accoutrements, and so forth. Rembrandt (though not he alone) rendered character through a sense of illumination from within: it is the sense of a person's inner quality being externalized. When an artist succeeds in that rendering, he or she has presented an external visage that, so the viewer is told, reveals the person's character, inner being. But what of a self-portrait? Is the external visage a report of who the artist "really is," or a report of who the artist *wants* the viewer to see?

  We have no way of knowing whether AH ever saw any of Rembrandt's self-portraits, much less took the time to reflect on any of those dimensions and their history. There is no doubt that his work was known in England, or at least in London. Rembrandt was obviously entrepreneurial in spirit, of his workshop as of the market in art. Charles I had collected at least one of Rembrandt's self-portraits, apparently through a third party, and of course he as well as his father had sat for portraits by a number of Dutch artists: Daniel Mytens, Gerhard van Honthorst, and Arnold Bronckorst, as well as by the Flemish painter Anthony van Dyke.[17] Several members of the aristocracy had engaged in collection of art, though not on the scale it would become a hundred years later. Not that many, if any, persons outside the circles of the king, Thomas Howard, the earl of Arundel, George Villiers, the duke of Buckingham, and the like, had actually viewed the great collections. While a few commentators have suggested that the expense of Charles' collection (which was great) fueled resentment among the general population of London, there is little if any evidence for it, and the claim is doubtful simply because the general public did not know. Only after his death, when much of the collection was put to auction in order to pay down some of his enormous debts, did the paintings gain outside attention, with some of the smaller pieces purchased for display in homes by people of modest means (e.g., other painters, glaziers, clothiers).[18]

---

[17] Svetlana Alpers reports Charles' Rembrandt painting, in her *Rembrandt's Enterprise* (Chicago: University of Chicago Press, 1988), page 62 and n.7. See also H Perry Chapman, *Rembrandt's Self-Portraits: A Study in Seventeenth-Century Identity* (Princeton: Princeton University Press, 1990).

[18] Francis Haskell's *The King's Pictures* (New Haven: Yale University Press, 2013) is a superb account of the accumulation and then dispersion of Charles' collection.

The point is not, however, that AH did or did not actually see Rembrandt's self-portrait (or any other of his paintings). The point is that the attitude, the self-conception, the very idea of selfhood as conveyed in Rembrandt's portraits, was a major new development in how persons had been learning to see themselves as individuals. The same dynamic was at work in the upsurge of diary keeping—opening one's interiority to one's own inspection in the presence of God, a process of caring for the self. Rembrandt was apparently the first to show this development in such a strikingly visible way. But neither the development nor this general understanding of it (as distinguished from its artistic presentation) was unique to him. To what extent it had entered AH's thinking we cannot say. We do know that he saw a number of portraits—his father's, perhaps his mother's (which no longer exists if ever it did), his wife Dorothy's (and perhaps that of his first wife, Frances), his daughter Dorothea's, and of course his own—and these we can view for ourselves (see Exhibit 8.2 for wife and daughter; Exhibit 6.4 for father; and Exhibit 7.4 for self).

While Puritanism emphasized simplicity of dress and furnishings, which can be seen more clearly in the portrait of Thomas[11a] than in the others, it did not necessarily frown upon the notion of painting in general or of portraiture in particular. Haskell noted that while a few Puritans, when viewing the king's painting for auction, thought some of them to be objectionable and argued that they be destroyed, there is no indication that such wish ever became action. A case could be made that the Puritan emphasis on self-examination (as in diary keeping) was reasonably well extended to the modest presence of mirrors and self-portraits. Puritans' displeasure with idols generally did not extend to the idea that a self-image, whether in polished metal, silvered glass, or painted canvas, imprisoned or violated or supplanted the human soul. Their iconoclasm focused on religious figurations that were treated as objects of worship, interrupting the direct relation of believer to his or her God. Their iconoclasm was by intent literally that, a breaking of icons.

To repeat the precaution with which we began, ultimately we lack means of knowing specifically the contents of AH's mind. Ultimately, that determination is difficult enough when attempted with a living person who consents to direct interrogation. But we do know something of the general consciousness of life during AH's time and place, and surely he, like any other specific person, was a person, a self-identity, a complexity of thought and emotion, *of* his time and place. His republican sentiments and hopes, certainly unusual for his time and place though not unprecedented, linked mostly consistently with his puritan sentiments and hopes, and that linkage was consistent with the growing development of individualist formations of social, political, and economic processes, including the innovative force of a new kind of knowledge-seeking, modern science with its emphasis on experimentation and technical application. In many respects, AH, like all other prominent actors of his time and place, was caught in a quickening swirl of processes which he tried to harness to particular purposes, even as surely, at least at times, he realized that he, along with friends and foes, were being swept along in currents stronger than his (and their) strokes. One wishes that his putative diary had survived. And yet, chances are, it would be hardly more revealing, probably no more enlightening, no less general and superficial as analysis, than the foregoing account of contexts and conditions. Then again ….

Family Man
As we saw above, circumstances for Arthur changed rapidly after his father was raised to baronetcy in July 1622. Arthur himself entered law school at Gray's Inn the following Easter term. Still a bachelor and seemingly with no serious interests in marriage (at least in part, no doubt, because his own economic future remained uncertain), he had the large panorama of life in London before him. Judging retrospectively from later behaviors, his response to that panorama was probably cautiousness of all the ways a young man could go wrong. Besides, if indeed some part of the blooming legal profession enticed him as future endeavor, he probably conserved his time and energy for studies. But that autumn, with the death of Donald, he became heir—the burden of "spareship" now passing to John (seemingly, the next eldest son)—and patrimonial requirements loomed much larger. Foremost of those requirements was a good marriage. We do not know how Arthur and young Frances Elmes, at most only a handful of years younger than he, came to know one another. But they had been at least acquaintances for some sufficient period of time that both were amenable to marriage. They wed in May 1624. Frances was second eldest daughter and fifth child of Thomas and Christian (nee Hickling) Elmes of Greens Norton, Northamptonshire. A short segment of the Elmes family tree is reproduced below.

Thomas Elmes: b. 1549 Lilford, Northamptonshire, d. September 1632 Greens Norton, Northamptonshire.
 + Christian Hickling: b. 1560 Greens Norton, m. 1602 Greens Norton, d. May 1635 Greens Norton
　└-- Mary Elmes: b. c1581 Greens Norton

└-- William Elmes: b. 1584 Greens Norton, d. 1641
└-- Thomas Elmes: b. 1586 Greens Norton
└-- Anthony Elmes: b. >1587, d. <May 1646
   + Grace Bevel: b. <1607, d. <May 1646
      └-- Thomas Elmes: b. c1624 Greens Norton, d. 1690
            Lilford, Northamptonshire; attended
            Christ's College from 9 Sep 1641
         + Margaret Verney: b. 30 Sep 1623, m. 1646,
            d. 1667
└-- Frances Elmes: b. 1602 or 1606 Greens Norton, d. 1632
         Noseley, Leicestershire
   + Arthur Hesilrige: b. 1601, m. May 1624

Within this short segment one can note the success that Elmes men had with strategic marriages. Christian Hickling brought the Greens Norton estate to her marriage with Thomas the elder. An old manor, village, and parish long in possession of the Green family (e.g., Sir Thomas Green, grandfather of Katherine Parr, queen consort to Henry VIII), this estate was located about 35 miles south of Noseley. Then, grandson Thomas wed Margaret Verney, who was sister to Sir Ralph Verney, 1st Bt (1613-1696), of Middle Claydon, Buckinghamshire, and Mary (1616-1650), daughter of John Blacknall of Abingdon, Berkshire (now in Oxfordshire). The Blacknall family were a wealthy merchant family at that time. Sir Ralph Verney, a moderate Puritan and supporter of the parliamentary side during the civil wars, was, despite those sympathies, pushed into exile because of his family's royalist ties—his father, Sir Edmund, having been a courtier to Charles I, and most of Ralph's siblings being of royalist inclination. Margaret was ninth of twelve children.[19]

Frances Elmes had been reared in a pious household and seemingly maintained a quietly pious demeanor throughout her adult years. That fact might have been the main trait of selection, intended as counterbalance to AH's youthful tendency to zealous, sometimes ill-mannered behavior. It is easy to imagine that she often prayed for guidance and fortitude.

---

[19] Accounts of the union (and separation) of Thomas Elmes and Margaret Verney, along with much more detail of the Verney family, can be found in Margaret M Verney's *Memoirs of the Verney Family*, 4 volumes (London: Longmans, Green, 1899), volume 4, pages 89-95 *et passim*; also see Adrian Tinniswood's more succinct overview, *The Verneys* (New York: Riverhead, 2007).

First son and heir Thomas (b. c1625) was the only survivor of AH's children by Frances Elmes. Of the three who did not survive, we know not even their forenames (and not because AH was the spare at the time, for Robert had died in Sept 1623). They departed at young ages, no doubt. But to the extent that we can judge accurately from the memorial to AH's ten known children in Noseley chapel (see Exhibit 8.1), it would appear that none of the three was an infant, though probably all were younger than seven, traditionally the advent of legal status as a minor. (Note the children holding skulls, the sign of death in childhood.) This evidence suggests that at least two of the non-surviving children had been given forenames, but no record of the naming, no record of baptism or christening, survived. Further, it appears that the first-born was a girl, followed by son and heir Thomas. Relative sizes of the statues give no obvious indication of twinning, which suggests that the four children appeared at two-year intervals. Also, the fourth child appears to have been old enough that we can rule out maternal death due to birthing, although complications of the fourth birth could have resulted in slow postpartum decline.

Before leaving this image, note the disproportionate size of the statue of AH's first son, Arthur, by his second wife—physical proof of other evidence indicating that this son was favored in the revised household, probably something of an irritant to son and heir Thomas.

Exhibit 8.1. Memorial to Children of Sir Arthur Hesilrige, 2nd Bt

AH married secondly Dorothea, daughter of Fulke Greville and sister of Robert Greville, baron of Beauchamps Court, Warwickshire. She was about 30 years of age, relatively old and by custom of the day denoted a "spinster." The two probably had met as AH attended the meetings of leading Puritans at Fawsley manor in Northamptonshire, and perhaps by this date at the residence of Robert Greville (lord Brooke), Brooke House, in Holborn, then a distinct area at the western gate to London city. AH was about 33 years old when he agreed the marriage settlement 24 June 1634, in the presence of lord Brooke and three witnesses: Sir Thomas Dacres of Cheshunt, Hertfordshire, knight; Richard Knightley of Preston, Northamptonshire, esq.; and William Elmes of Lilford, also Northamptonshire, esq. The last named man was probably brother to AH's first wife, Frances: William Elmes of Lilford (b. 1584 Greens Norton, d. 1641), probably then head of family in that Elmes lineage, and as such present to affirm that any residual interest of the Elmes family had been satisfied. For reason unknown, the marriage did not occur until February 1634/5.

Exhibit 8.2. Portraits of Dorothea, Wife (left), and Daughters Dorothy and Mary (right) of Sir Arthur Hesilrige, 2nd Bt

In the settlement, AH covenanted to "stand seised of the manor of Noseley and his lands there to his use and then to the use of his heirs male; and of the manors of Dinnington, Fawden, East and West Brunton, Kenton, Blackdale [Blagdon] and Weetslade, Northumberland, and his lands in Illston and Goadby, to his use, then to the use of Dorothy, then of their heirs, with remainder to his heirs." He also covenanted "to stand seised of the same uses of the manors of Eslington, Whittingham, Barton, and Thrunton, Northumberland," if he should recover them "in a lawsuit now pending" (which he did recover); otherwise, he agreed to purchase other lands to the value of £200 per annum to be settled similarly. The settlement was in consideration of "a marriage portion of £5,000."[20]

First child, Catherine, was born in 1635 at Brooke House, Holborn, followed two years later by Arthur (b. 1637), probably also born at Brooke House. Note that both of these children arrived around the time that AH, along with his brother-in-law and other frustrated Puritan families, were seriously thinking of emigration to the New World, the Saybrooke colony in particular. It was soon after birth of second son, Arthur, that AH's plans changed, and he concentrated energy and attention to building patrimony in England, with renewed interest in his seat at Noseley. Thus, his third son, Robert, was born at Noseley in 1639. Then followed three daughters, Dorothy (b. c1641), Frances (b. c1645), and Mary (b. c1648), all of whom were born during the upheavals of parliamentary politics and civil war.[21] It may be noted that the family record shows a total of eight children, two of them unnamed and presumably either still-born or early fatalities. In view of the sequence of birth years for the six named children, it seems likely that at least one of the unnamed children was also born during the tumult of the 1640s. Denton speculated, based on a comment in one of Oliver Cromwell's letters to AH, dated 4 September 1650, that Dorothea was well into another pregnancy.[22] Denton enumerated it as her ninth, which it may have been, but it could instead have been the eighth of eight. If his reading of Cromwell's "postscripted" message to AH is correct, and there is good reason to think it is, the pregnancy could have been proximate cause or at least contributing factor in Dorothea's death on 25 January 1650/1. In any case, her death came during her mid-forties, and during the so-called third civil war, a time when AH was again on duty at Newcastle and indeed had been visiting Cromwell in Edinburgh when news arrived at headquarters in Newcastle that his wife was gravely ill.

When Dorothy died, AH was left with a household of mature, near-mature, and very young children. Thomas, eldest son and heir apparent, unmarried, was about twenty-five. Catherine was fifteen. Arthur had died

---

[20] This document is DG21/55, Hazlerigg Collection. Note may be taken of an ambiguity in the spelling of Dorothea Greville's forename. Some records say "Dorothy."

[21] Second oldest daughter Dorothy is depicted in a painting (dated 1680) in Exhibit 8.2, along with daughter Mary; none of middle daughter Frances has been located. Nichols said that AH sired by Dorothy "Arthur, and two other sons, though only one, Sir Robert, … survived him; and five daughters, Catherine …, Dorothy, … Mary, Frances …, and Mary," which indicates that youngest daughter Mary was second effort to have a girl so named. John Nichols, *The History and Antiquities of the County of Leicester*, 4 volumes (London, 1795-1815), volume 2, part 2, page 748.

[22] Denton, *Only in Heaven* (1997), page 185.

at age twelve, shortly before his mother (cause unknown). Robert, now the spare, was eleven. The three youngest daughters ranged in age from eight or nine years to about two years. Their main domicile had probably been Noseley, although much of the time, we know, Thomas was away, serving as captain of a cavalry unit. We know that during the mid-1640s AH had a residence in Islington, a town on the northern edge of London, giving him quick access to affairs at Westminster, and sometime after 1649, probably after 1650, he took quarters in Whitehall palace, in one of the smaller apartments. It is unlikely he would have been comfortable having his young children living in London; he would have thought them more secure living at Noseley. His brother, William, was probably still close at hand to Noseley, ready to lend guidance and assistance. But Catherine probably became female head of household after her mother died. No doubt she had abundant staff for assistance. But even so, the responsibility probably contributed to her later reputation as a redoubtable presence. When she married in 1652, it was to her father's friend and associate, George Fenwick, leading member of an old and well-respected Northumberland family, and thirty years her senior. She would have been "mature for her years," yet secure in the company of an older man, trusted by her father.

If we may entertain another question impossible to answer, what sort of father was Sir Arthur? Denton concluded that daughters Catherine and Dorothy "were always devoted" to him and that "his second son Robert also loved his father. But with the Restoration, Thomas, the son and heir to the title and estate, turned from him, denouncing his actions and like Pilate washing his hands of his family's involvement with the Commonwealth." Denton then suggested the "turn" could have been strategic: "perhaps such action was necessary to keep the great estates."[23] (Or at least was *thought* necessary; one could not be certain, given relevant circumstances, but a little insurance would not hurt.) Denton was silent about the younger daughters, except to repeat a tale that one of them became notorious in London for her allegedly dissolute behavior.

Can we learn anything by trying to see AH through the eyes of his eldest son and eventual successor? Given what we know of the public view of AH during his adult years, one wonders about the childhood lives of his children, especially Thomas, the first-born and surviving-heir son. Even men who were sympathetic to AH's activities and apparent missions drew pictures of him that were, while more balanced than others' accounts, still at least partly unflattering, and overall one can only wonder what sort

---

[23] Denton, *Only in Heaven* (1997), pages 235, 236.

of husband, what sort of father, he must have been. Caution is in order, however. A man most vile and vicious in his adult life with other men can yet be tenderly loving and supportive of his own children; and AH was far short of "vile and vicious" in portraits left to us by even his harshest critics. The fact is, of course, we have virtually no direct evidence testifying to his performances as either husband or father, and the indirect evidence is sparse. But we can piece together some relevant facts about the son who viewed his father over the course of some exceedingly difficult years and then, for whatever reason, turned away.

By the date of his eighth birthday anniversary Thomas has seen his only siblings, three of them, die; so, too, his mother, in 1632. Causes are unknown to us, but contagious disease was the likeliest culprit, perhaps excepting his mother. His father had recently inherited the family estates, which meant greater household income (not that they had been living in poverty) but which also entailed greater responsibility in managing the patrimony. In addition, his father had been occupied in important positions of power and influence in Leicester, had shown interest in becoming a member of the House of Commons, and soon after his wife's death (if not before) became involved in a circle of well-placed Puritans who gravitated between London (e.g., Holborn, about 95 miles southeast of Noseley) and Warwickshire (e.g., Beauchamps Court, near Alcester, about 60 miles southwest of Noseley). Who cared for young Thomas during the years immediately after his mother's death? Perhaps the Elmes family? Or did AH hire a nanny and governess, keeping his son at home at Noseley?

When Thomas was about nine years old his father married a woman he had met during his visits in Holborn and/or at Beauchamps Court, Dorothea. Gaining a step-mother was hardly an unusual event, but Thomas might have noticed some differences between this woman and his birth mother, given the general difference in social, economic, and political standing between the Elmes and the Greville families. His father had by now become tightly integrated into the so-called West Bedford network of dissenters, mainly Puritan, and was spending more time in Warwickshire and in London. Then, in November 1635 at age ten (more or less) Thomas gained a half-sister, Catherine (his first sibling who would survive far into adulthood). She was born at Brooke House, Holborn, her maternal granduncle's home, where Thomas' father and step-mother lived part of the time. Two years later he gained a half-brother, Arthur. From Thomas' point of view this lad was naturally a rival, at least in the way that an heir tends to see the spare. But in addition, young Arthur was considered to be unusually bright, quickly skillful in several languages, reading literatures in those languages, and perhaps more. Clearly this rival had soon become "favorite child," even though Thomas was still around and therefore the heir apparent. By the time Thomas reached majority age, his half-brother was being touted as consummate scholar. Something of the relative visions can be seen in the memorials (Exhibit 8.1) in Noseley chapel. There is the difference in relative sizes, to be sure, as previously remarked. But also, whereas Thomas is presented with the bearing of an adult lord of the manor, Arthur's statue gives more the impression of a sturdy monk or college don. (Neither of them, note, carries a sword. That was left to third son, Robert.)

Young Arthur did not survive the 1640s, however. In the meantime, Thomas had gained a second half-brother, Robert, who was apparently regarded as less exceptional than young Arthur. That, plus the age difference—Thomas was about fourteen when Robert was born—gave reason for assurance.

As several historians have said, religion was considered to be an essential determinant in Puritan households when making arrangements for the education of one's children.[24] A number of well-worn manuals had retained popularity into AH's adult years and were probably available, along with the Bible, at Noseley. AH had retained his own personal choice of chaplain at Noseley, a Puritan man who offered instruction and counsel, and no doubt was involved in the education of AH's children. Some of the instructional manuals that would have been approved for use included (some of them mentioned earlier) Arthur Dent's *The Plaine Man's Pathway to Heaven* as well as his *The Ruine of Rome*, Richard Rogers' *Seven Treatises*, which was in its seventh edition by 1630, and George Gifford's *Country Divinity*, or his *Sermons upon the Whole Book of the Revelation*, or one of his collections of "Sermons preached at Maldon" (Essex). When Thomas was about 15 his step-mother's uncle, Robert Greville, published his own treatise, *The Nature of Truth and Its Union and Unity with the Soul* (1640).[25] Surely it would have been on the expected reading list, for father as for sons and daughters.

Denton followed Nichols in reporting a break of Thomas with his father.[26] Neither source offers details. Nichols, in describing Thomas's recovery of estates, said it was "the mediation of the duke of Albemarle [George Monck], and his [Thomas'] own dislike to his father's conduct,"

---

[24] See, e.g., Cliffe, *The Puritan Gentry* (1984), pages 77-82.
[25] Douglas Bush, *English Literature in the Earlier Seventeenth Century* (Oxford: Clarendon, 1959), chapter 10 in general, and page 540 on Robert Greville.
[26] Nichols, *History and Antiquities* ... (1795-1815), volume 2, part 2, page 748.

that "occasioned him to be restored to all those lands which Sir Arthur enjoyed that did not belong to the church" (a statement that was not entirely correct, as will be seen in the next chapter). Perhaps a culmination of some emotions of resentment stemming from childhood, emotions of having had little choice as a young man but to abide by his father's expectations about politics and military service, and conviction to be seen as an independent actor in pursuit of his own adult interests, all of that orchestrated by a need to behave strategically for the sake of the family patrimony, that created very persuasively an impression of son rejecting his now defeated father.

As has been remarked in previous chapters, fissures within a family were not uncommon during the contests of the 1630s, 40s, and 50s. We noted within the discussion of emigrations in chapter 6 that AH's mother, Frances *(nee* Gorges) was cousin to a prominent royalist, Sir Fernando Gorges, who at one time had royal claim to the whole of (an unknown extent of) Maine in North America. In the chapter before that we saw that one of AH's father's cousins, Frances[12b], daughter of Edward[11a] Hesilrige, married secondly an ardent royalist, Sir Wolstan Dixie (1602-1682), albeit in 1670. Was she sympathetic, or was her attitude basically one of apolitical advantage? One could conclude that she had turned her back against her famous/infamous cousin, Sir Arthur. But that would attribute motive for an action solely from an outward face of the action.

Exhibit 8.3. Probably Thomas Hesilrige, 1652

During the late 1650s, we know, Thomas fought in support of the commonwealth and his father's republican project. Whether this was an act of genuine personal preference cannot be said. Certainly as heir to the family estate he would have felt some obligations; and for all the advances of individualism in English society, filial piety was still expected of adult children, most especially heirs and spares. The portrait shown in Exhibit 8.3 is probably Thomas Hesilrige, future 3rd Bt. A watercolor on vellum, the work is apparently by John Hoskins, son and successor of the better known John Hoskins the Elder, well regarded for his miniatures. The work is inscribed with a monogram identified with Hoskins the younger and is dated 1652. Thomas would have been about twenty-seven years of age at that date, by which time the second civil war was over. The young man's armour appears to be well-fitted but without obvious marks of combat. It could well have been a ceremonial suit or a newly fitted suit for a young man still developing upper-body musculature. Proof that this depiction is of the 2nd Bt's son and heir, Thomas, has escaped attention of art experts, if it exists. Unfortunately, the painting's record of provenance is broken. The most that can be said is that expert opinion has settled on Thomas as the likeliest candidate.

One last piece of evidence relevant to the question of Thomas' act toward his father is an indenture between father and son, dated 22 October 1659. A transcription of this document is given immediately below.

THIS INDENTURE made the two and twentieth day of October in the year of our Lord god one thousand six hundred fifty and nine between Sir Arthur Hesilrige of Noseley in the county of Leicester, Baronet, on the one part and Thomas Hesilrige of Noseley in the said county, esq., son and heir apparent of the said Sir Arthur on the other part, Witness that the said Sir Arthur Hesilrige for and in consideration of a marriage already had and solemnized between the said Thomas Hesilrige and Elizabeth Hesilrige his wife, one of the daughters and coheirs of George Fenwick of Brenkburne in the county of Northumberland, esq., deceased, And for and in consideration of the sum of four thousand pounds of lawful English money paid unto the said Sir Arthur Hesilrige by the said Elizabeth Hesilrige which he acknowledged to have received, And for the settling of a competent jointure for the said Elizabeth, and for and in consideration of the payment of four score pounds per annum a piece for the maintenance of Dorothy Hesilrige, Frances Hesilrige, and Mary Hesilrige, daughters of the said Sir Arthur Hesilrige respectively until they shall have respectively attained their several and respective ages of eighteen years, and also for and in consideration of the payment of five hundred pounds per annum during the natural life of the Earl of Anglesey, and four score pounds yearly to Major George Sedascue and Mary Sedascue his wife during their lives and the longer liver of them, and for and in consideration of the great debts which the said Thomas Hesilrige stands engaged for and with the said Sir Arthur Hesilrige by bond and otherwise, and for divers other good causes and considerations him the said Sir Arthur Hesilrige thereunto moving, HATH granted and by these presents doth grant bargain sell and demise unto the said Thomas Hesilrige his executors and administrators all that the Manor and Lordship of Noseley in the county of Leicester with its rights members and appurtenances, And all that the Manor or Lordship of Hardwick with the appurtenances, And the lands, farms and grounds called or known by the name of Hardwick in the parish of Shankton in the said county of Leicester, And all those his lands and hereditaments in Ilston, alias Ilveston, in the county of Leicester, And all other his Manors and lands tenements and hereditaments within the hundred of Gartree in the said county, And all other his lands and hereditaments whatsoever within the said county of Leicester, TO HAVE and to hold the said Manors, Lordships, Lands, Tenements, hereditaments and premises above mentioned with their and every of their rights members and appurtenances unto the said Thomas Hesilrige, his executors, administrators, and assignees from the day before the date of these presents unto the end and for and during the time and term of ninety and nine years from thence next ensuing and fully to be complete and ended without impeachment of waste if it shall happen that the said Sir Arthur Hesilrige shall so long live, And to the further intent and purpose that the said Elizabeth Hesilrige wife of the said Thomas Hesilrige shall and may from and immediately after the death of her said husband have and take out of the said Manor and premises of Noseley aforesaid the yearly rent of or sum of six hundred pounds of like lawful money of England upon the five and twentieth day of March and nine and twentieth day of September yearly by even and equal portions for and during all the term of her natural life for her jointure and in lieu of her dower, the first payment thereof to be made at such of the said days as shall first and next happen after the decease of the said Thomas Hesilrige, And to the intent and purpose that if it shall happen the said yearly rent of six hundred pounds to be behind and unpaid in part or in all in any of the days or times aforesaid during the time the that said rent is to continue payable as aforesaid by the true intent and meaning of these presents That then and from henceforth upon any default of payment, And so oft and from time to time as the said annual rent or any part thereof shall happen to be arrear and unpaid at any of the said days or times whereat the same ought to be paid as aforesaid, it shall and may be lawful to and for the said Elizabeth Hesilrige wife of the said Thomas Hesilrige and her assignees to whom such rent shall be so arrear into the said Manor or Lordship and premises and into every and any part thereof to enter and distrain, And the distress or distresses then and there found and taken to lead, drive, chase, carry away, impound, detain and keep until the said yearly rent so paid, And all arrearages thereof if any shall happen to be shall be truly satisfied and paid according to the intent and meaning of these presents,

IN WITNESS whereof the said parties to these presents their hands and seals interchangeably have set the day and year first above written.

[signature]

    Signed sealed and delivered in the presence of
        William Hesilrige
        Tho. Norcott
        Bartell Byner
        Robert Hutchin

From all appearances, AH was not only arranging a marriage settlement between his son and his new daughter-in-law. He was also arranging his son's succession to the family patrimony in Leicestershire. The document reads much like a last will and testament. There was some reason for that. We do not know the condition of AH's physical health that autumn. He had made passing reference, at times, to feelings of fatigue, and that surely is understandable, given what he had gone through, and was still in the midst of experiencing. But more than that, even though this was 1659, not 1660, he had had many occasions during which his battle for a republic, the great cause, seemed to be spent; and he knew, as he had acknowledged in public addresses, that he and his lands would be in grave danger, should the cause be lost. But as a last will and testament, the indenture would have much chance of succeeding only if Thomas could convincingly turn his back. That it was in fact a strategic action seems likely. That it was an action easier to take than it would have been had Thomas not felt a store of slights and frustrations is nonetheless also possible, without exclusion.

    Before leaving this document of indenture, a few specific features should be noted. First, AH made specific bequests to his three minor daughters, Dorothy, Frances, and Mary, maintenance of each until she attained her eighteenth birth anniversary. Second, he included a bequest to Major George Sedascue and his wife Mary (*nee* Bosville). Sedascue, born Jan Georg Sadowski of an aristocratic Polish family, served in the New Model Army, although at one time he lost his commission (reason unknown). Uprisings in Poland against Swedish domination involved a war of predominantly Catholic Poles against predominantly Protestant Swedes, which, in 1656, led to the final destruction of the Sadowski

(Protestant) estates in Poland. It was probably because of that misfortune that AH left financial support to the major and his wife.[27]

Finally, a fifth, and much larger, bequest was left to the earl of Anglesley. Here, too, we can rely only on conjecture of reason. At that date the 2nd earl of Anglesey was Charles Villiers, who was born probably late 1620s. In 1655 he fought a duel with Col. Charles Dillon, eldest son of Thomas, 4th viscount Dillon, and received two wounds which were not thought at the time to be lethal.[28] However, he died 4 February 1660/1. Perhaps he had been having serious medical problems and lacked income. It is also possible that he was a relative by marriage, though the only known link was more than two centuries earlier—Margaret[6c] Hesilrige (b. c1437) wed "a Villers man" (by conjecture one of the Villiers men of Brokesby; see the lineage segment in chapter 5)—which seems rather distant even for an era in which family ties were highly important. Perhaps this Villiers man and AH were simply good friends, possibly the junior man having been under the senior man's cavalry command at one time. Denton gave a scattering of AH's known episodes of generosity; this might have been one such, and nothing more.

Images of Character
One of the most often repeated comments about AH is by Edward Hyde, the 1st earl of Clarendon. He described "sir Arthur Haslerig, (brother-in-law of the lord Brooke)," as "an absurd, bold man, brought up by Mr Pym, and so employed by that party to make any attempt."[29] Offered in book 3 of his *History*, Clarendon's assessment was made as preface to his report of the bill of attainder against the earl of Strafford on charges of high treason. While Hyde was an occasional, mostly mild critic of the king's regime early in the contests, he switched to the royalist cause and evinced an open loathing of several of the leaders in parliament, John Pym most especially.

Granted that Hyde had no affection for AH, was his assessment simply animus by political opposition? In at least one respect, it rings of some truth: anyone who saw fit to challenge a sitting monarch and all of

---

[27] Robert K G Temple, "The Original Officer List of the New Model Army," *Historical Research*, volume 59 (May 1986), pages 50-77.
[28] *The Nicholas Papers: Correspondence of Sir Edward Nicholas, Secretary of State*, edited by George F Warner (London: The Camden Society, 1892), volume 2, page 256.
[29] Edward Hyde, *The History of the Rebellion and Civil Wars in England*, 8 volumes (Oxford: Clarendon Press, 1826), volume 1, page 397. This edition was presented as faithful to the original manuscript, with "all the suppressed passages" restored.

his court so boldly as AH did could well be called "rash" (as some critics did) and as "rashly bold," even "absurdly bold." One is reminded of Perry Miller's words of perplexity years ago when contemplating the Puritan character: were the Puritans "really dauntless souls or only foolhardy eccentrics"; "shrewd or merely incredibly naïve"; "so resolute as they often give the impression of being, or ... simply borne up by an indestructible self-righteousness"?[30]

But had the 1650s ended as AH had sought, and then been followed by a decade of strong, unified leadership that restored public confidence in governance, thus promoting a broader understanding of and allegiance to republicanism, the adjectives of choice by which AH and other proponents of republican governance would have been described in the history books would have read "boldly innovative" (or "revolutionary") rather than "absurdly bold." One lesson from the *actual* ending of the 1650s was that AH *was*—in the event, the proof being in the pudding—absurdly bold, at least in the sense of a leader who does not, perhaps could not, recognize that he was getting too far in front of his followers, actual and potential. His boldness would have been literally *absurd*—that is, without ground. That flaw, a flaw in how one sees oneself vis-à-vis friends, enemies, and bystanders, is often fatal.

Because the record is so thin, it is difficult to make judgments about his character development or change even over the course of his adult years when, especially the 1640s and 1650s, more was said of him in records that survived. With that limitation in mind, however, one can still see what appears to be evidence that in his leadership of troops he operated with greater precaution and preparation. One can understand good reason for that: training and experience of military leadership gave much weight not only to coordination down the chain of command but also to communication *up* from (as well as down to) the ranks. A field commander needed to know that his troops felt confident in themselves, in each other, and in the officers above, including more especially the commander himself. Even then the "fog of war" was sufficient to devastate a well-conceived strategy and make the execution of field tactics much less effective than anticipated, leaving an army mainly dependent on quality of logistics, of field officers' ability to regroup repeatedly, and of troops' confidence in their own abilities to take the initiative, rally each other, and fill in the gaps. These are lessons that AH had learned and applied when leading troops for Balfour and then Waller.

---

[30] Perry Miller, Review of Calder's *New Haven Colony*, *The New England Quarterly*, volume 8 (December 1935), pages 582-83, at page 582.

The political arena was rather different. Civil wars as military operations had been fought before, even though not by these combatants, and many of the lessons from earlier instances carried over to the 1640s. Once war had been settled, however, the task of negotiating a transition from monarchic to some sort of oligarchic-democratic parliamentarian regime lay ahead, and that was a new, very large undertaking for which usable lessons were scattered, inconsistent, and fraught with tensions that could easily spark into dreaded anarchy, new civil war, or both, perhaps thus inviting invasion by France, by Spain, by the Dutch Republic, or even by some rump army of the Holy Roman Empire.

AH's efforts, given their failure by 1659/60, could hardly have been better formulated as material for the arts of satire, and the timing was impeccable. Literary scholars tend to agree that the great age of English satire began about 1660, in an outpouring that urges the question, "Why now? What changed?" Marshall has inventoried and studied more than 3,000 distinct works of satire for the period she called "the long eighteenth century," 1658 to 1770.[31] Of course, satire in its various forms did not arise in 1660 or 1658, even though it could be seen as comparatively rare when one views from the vantage point of 1770. There was undeniably a thickening and spreading of the genre after the restoration of Charles II, and he himself had something to do with that in the beginning, as some of his behaviors especially in the realm of sexuality contrasted so sharply, so stupendously mockingly, against the grain of his continued claim of divine rights and its accoutrements, as well as against the staid image of his father. Satire and its performances of irony, ridicule, and burlesque could hardly have wanted better soil in which to grow, than in the broadly furrowed inconsistencies of England's public culture during the 1660s, 70s, and 80s. As one recent scholar of that scene has observed, tragicomedy gave record to "the uneven process of generic and cultural differentiation," including "the attempt to pull together an uneasily integrated culture."[32] Why tragicomedy? For the time, it was the form that gave more latitude, thus subtlety, to moods of irony and satire, and for the actions of what the ancient Greeks called *peripeteia*. Playwrights sought "to gloss over post-regicide inconsistencies," a seemingly necessary precondition to their efforts to redefine "society" for their present and future age, "by fabricating pious, backward-looking, and repetitious myths of monarchy." Satire,

---

[31] Ashley Marshall, *The Practice of Satire in England, 1658-1770* (Baltimore: Johns Hopkins University Press, 2013).
[32] Nancy Klein Maguire, *Regicide and Restoration* (Cambridge: Cambridge University Press, 1992), page 217; and for the following quote, page 218.

once launched during the three decades from 1658 to 1688, became enshrined as a staple of the cultivated consciousness and conscience, allowing multiply inconsistent views to be held at once.

AH had the honour of being target of numerous efforts satirical, some ragged, lacking in complexity or depth but some strikingly good as examples of the fine art. One, a ribald lampoon written to the tune of a folk ditty, was a typical example of the very old art by which "the lower orders" sought their revenge against "their betters." It was intended to bite, and no doubt it did, if not to AH himself (date of composition is unknown) then to surviving family and friends (see Exhibit 8.4).

A large number of items, many of them barely satirical beyond the rudiments in envy and resentment, attended the political events of the war years and the 1650s. A collection of these was published in two volumes in 1662 under the title, *Rump: Or, an Collection of the Choycest Poems and Songs Relating to the Late Times, ... 1639 to 1661*, assembled and printed in London for Henry Brome and Henry Marsh.[33] As one should do with any collection, questions about sampling must be entertained. But here the assemblers are openly royalist and accommodating of Charles II.

AH was a frequent target, but the frequency varied over time, in correlation with visibility of target. In the early years he was usually mentioned as one of "the Five Members," sometimes joined by a list of lords (especially the earls of Essex and Warwick, as well as lord Kimbolton, i.e., Edward Montagu). As the 1640s grew old, lamentations for the king became more frequent, AH's name less frequent. Oliver Cromwell was prime target during the 1650s, with little mention of AH until the late years of the decade, usually in context of mockeries of the Rump, followed by salutations of General Monck. If there is surprise in regard to tenor of the entries, it is that they were less caustic than one might have expected. Whether this was an effect of sampling by Brome and Marsh, deliberate or not, cannot be determined.

An example from the early part of Brome and Marsh's collection, shown as Exhibit 8.5, pertains to the notoriety of "the Five Members." It will be noted that the name of Denzil Holles, one of the five, is present only by suggestion. This omission, which occurred in other poems that referred to the five, was due no doubt to the fact that Holles was alive (he

---

[33] Brome and Marsh were busy publishers of royalist works during this period. Their one greatest commercial success was the work entitled *Eikon Basilike* (rendered usually as "King's Image" or "King's Portrait"), a pathos of martyrdom received at publication on the day of Charles' burial (8 February 1649) as due to Charles' own hand but later claimed by others as a tribute to the king.

♪   Sir Arthur and Charming Mollee   ♪

As noble Sir Arthur one morning did ride,
With his hounds at his feet, his sword by his side,
He saw a fair maid sitting under a tree,
He asked her her name, she said 'tis Mollee.

Oh, charming Mollee, you my butler shall be,
To draw the red wine for yourself and for me!
I'll make you a lady so high in degree,
If you will but love me, my charming Mollee!

I'll give you fine ribbons, I'll give you fine rings,
I'll give you fine jewels, and many fine things;
I'll give you a petticoat flounced to the knee,
If you will but love me, my charming Mollee!

I'll have none of your ribbon, none of your rings,
None of your jewels, and many fine things;
And I've got a petticoat suits my degree,
And I'll ne'er love a married man till his wife dee.

Oh, charming Mollee, lend me then your penknife,
And I will go home, and I'll kill my own wife;
I'll kill my own wife, and my bairnies three,
If you will but love me, my charming Mollee!

Oh, noble Sir Arthur, it must not be so,
Go home to your wife, and let nobody know;
For seven long years I will wait upon thee,
But I'll ne'er love a married man till his wife dee.

Now seven long years are gone and past,
The old woman went to her long home at last;
The old woman died, and Sir Arthur was free,
And he soon came a-courtin to charming Mollee.

Now charming Mollee in her carriage doth ride,
With her hounds at her feet, her lord by her side;
Now all ye fair maids take a warning by me,
And ne'er love a married man till his wife dee.

Exhibit 8.4. Lampooning Sir Arthur Hesilrige, 2nd Bt

> 22   *Rump Songs.*   Part I.
>
> *To the five Principal Members of the Honourable House of Commons.*
>
> *The Humble Petition of the* POETS.
>
> After so many Concurring Petitions
> From all Ages and Sexes, and all conditions,
> We come in the Rear to present our Follies
> To *Pym, Stroude, Haslerig, Hampden,* and ──
> And we hope for our labour we shall not be shent,
> For this comes from *Christendom,* & not from *Kent;*
> Though set form of *Prayers* be an *Abomination,*
> Set forms of *Petitions* find great Approbation :
> Therefore, as others from th' bottom of their souls,
> So wee from the depth and bottom of our *Bowles,*
> According unto the blessed form taught us,
> We thank you first for the *Ills* you have brought us,
> For the *Good* we receive we thank him that gave it,
> And you for the Confidence only to crave it.
> Next in course, we Complain of the great *violation*
> Of *Privilege* (like the rest of our Nation)
> But 'tis none of yours of which we have spoken
> Which never had being, untill they were broken :
> But our is a *Privilege* Antient and Native,
> Hangs not on *Ordinance,* or power *Legislative.*
> And first, 'tis to speak whatever we please
> Without fear of a *Prison,* or *Pursuivants* fees.
> Next, that we only may *lye* by Authority,
> But in that also you have got the Priority.
> Next, an old Custom, our Fathers did name it
> *Poetical license,* and alwayes did claim it.

Exhibit 8.5. An Early Selection from *Rump Songs*, 1662

died in February 1679/80), remembered in part for his abilities as a fierce opponent, had been successful in gaining favor with Charles II (indeed, had in effect led an advance team as the restored king returned to England),

and in April 1661 was rewarded by elevation to 1st baron Holles of Ifield, Sussex. Brome and Marsh were wisely cautious in printing the surname as if it were the dimly hinted underlayer of a palimpsest.

Another example, this one from 1659 or 1660, is the second of a two-part song, "Saint George for England," which was composed to be sung to "the tune of 'To drive the cold Winter away'" (aka "In Praise of Christmas"), a popular song of the very early 1600s and perhaps earlier. The lyrics of the second stanza are:

> Scot, Nevil, and Vane,
> With the rest of that train,
> Are in *Oceana* fled,
> Sir Arthur the brave,
> That's as arrant a knave,
> Has Harrington's Rota in's Head,
> But he's now full of cares
> For his Foals and his Mares,
> As when he was routed before:
> But I think he despairs,
> By his Armes, or his Prayers,
> To set up the Rump any more.[34]

The citation of James Harrington's book, *The Commonwealth of Oceana*, is obvious: a utopist treatise proposing means and regulations of a republican government, and largely neglected after its publication in 1656. The citation of "Rota" is more obscure. This was the Rota Club, founded by Harrington in November 1659, with frequent meetings in a coffeehouse in the Palace Yard, devoted to discussion and debate regarding republican principles and practices, and more generally part of the new popular scene of coffeehouse sociality in London.[35] Harrington's valiant effort was late in the larger game, however, and the club disbanded in February 1659/60. Attendants had included a protégé of John Milton (Cyriak Skinner), but Milton himself (along with many others) regarded Harrington's proposals as quite unrealistic for the current political situation. The name "Rota" derived from Harrington's principle of "rotation" among officeholders, a

---

[34] *Rump* (1662), volume 2, pages 159-160. The poem shown in Exhibit 8.5 is from volume 1, page 22.
[35] For a general view of the phenomenon, see Brian W Cowan, *Social Life of Coffee* (New Haven: Yale University Press, 2005).

principle which, recall, AH had included in his conception of republican governance.[36]

Lest one conclude from this brief survey that the voice of royalism had the auditorium to itself, it will be noted that the restored monarchy and its supporters did not stop revolutionary thinking and acting by dissenters.[37] This included the uses of publication. One of the most famous instances was John Milton's retort to the royalist paen, *Eikon Basilike*, the title ready for enactment: *Eikonoklastes* ("Icon-Breaking"). Commissioned to be the official response of the Long Parliament, it was published in October 1649, eight months after *Eikon Basilike*. Soon after the monarchy was restored, Milton's book joined the list of publications condemned to fire, but it lived on in that day's version of an underground circulation.

By far the larger volume of satirical remembrance lay against the republican cause, however, and some of it gained a modicum of fame beyond the bounds of England's seventeenth century. One such instance is Samuel Butler's mock heroic poem, *Hudibras*, its first complete edition appearing in 1684. While this Samuel Butler is not so well remembered today as the Victorian-era iconoclast who wrote the utopian-satirical novel, *Erewhon*, his poem remained highly popular long after his death. A relevant passage from part 3, canto 2 (lines 1535-1542), of *Hudibras* reads as follows:

> That worthy Patriot, once the bellows,
> And tinder-box, of all his fellows,
> The Activ'st member of the Five,
> As well as most primitive;
> Who, for his faithful service then,
> Is chosen for a Fifth agen;
> For, since the State has made a Quint
> Of Generals, he's listed in't.

The subject was, of course, Sir Arthur Hesilrige. The "Fifth agen" referred to his presence on the late list of commissioners of the army.

---

[36] See the statement cited in *Diary of Sir Archibald Johnston of Wariston, 1655-1660*, edited by James D Ogilvie (Edinburgh: Scottish Historical Society, 1940), volume 3, page 124.

[37] See, e.g., Richard L Greaves, *Enemies under his Feet* (Stanford: Stanford University Press, 1990).

Estate Acquisitions

As previously mentioned, an interest in furthering the cause of republicanism was (and is) consistent with a personal preference for individual liberty in the pursuit of religious-ideological values such as were prominent in the Puritan movement. So it was for the 2nd Bt. An interest in republicanism was an interest in self-rule, in the authority of democracy as represented in a national parliament as in local councils. That did not mean, however, that AH was any more inclined than most of his royalist contemporaries to champion an *economic* democracy. His sympathies lay not with the Levellers, nor was he any more inclined in his fifties than he had been in his thirties to relinquish title and standing of aristocracy. Ultimately we cannot know his mind when he looked out on the streets of London and saw daily evidence of mayhem: was it different in kind from the mayhem of London's streets during the 1630s, when the king was still in charge? Was it different even in prevalence? And most to the point, did he see in it evidence that "the people" were incapable of self-rule, that good order, peace, and security required the strong hand of a monarch in lead of any parliament? Or, put differently, was he more confident in the capability of "the people" to learn rules of order under self-rule than, say, George Monck was by the end of the 1650s; or was he only more reluctant to admit that his efforts, the efforts of like-minded others, in the cause of republicanism, had been a failure? We do not know his mind regarding such questions.

We do know, however, that his interest in individual liberty of religious conscience and in republican self-rule had not translated into an interest in economic democracy. As a matter of concept, of principle, in fact, such notion perhaps never occurred to him. What we do know by his behavior, however, is that the regulative interest of his motivations as an economic actor consisted primarily and mainly, probably even wholly, in his understanding of the principle of aristocracy—a principle neither unique to him nor restricted to the heights of aristocratic families. This was, as repeatedly said before, a principle of patrimony that united into one organization across time the dead, the living, and the still-unborn members of a family, all to the preeminent cause of building, defending, securing, and always trying to further that family's standing in society. Standing was foremost a matter of social honor and dignity. But its necessary support was economic wealth and the power this provided. Sir Arthur pursued that cause before the civil wars began, he pursued it during the wars, as time and opportunity permitted, and he pursued it after the wars were ended, during the period that proved to be an interregnum. He was sometimes vilified for it—as if *he*, of all people, ought to have translated his principles of republicanism as a form of political democratization into commensurate principles of an economic democratization.

The vilification is understandable, of course. But the selective perspective on which it stood must be acknowledged. Families had been competitively acquiring estates by any allowable means for generations. It had traditionally been via royal grants and arranged marriages, although outright purchases had become more frequent. What was different about AH's mode of acquisition? Mostly he purchased the estates. Granted, the purchases were often at "fire sale" prices, but that advantage was surely not novel either in conception or in execution. The practice seemed vile to some because the estates mostly had been held by the established church. Again, objection rested on selective memory. The Russell family, to take but one recent example, had acquired "massive wealth, most of it derived from ex-monastic lands" which they had gained during the reign of Henry VIII. Francis Russell, the family's titular head as the 4th earl of Bedford, and a "Puritan Grandee" during the 1640s, had an annual income of more than £15,000. Stupendous wealth, indeed.[38]

Acquisitions of estates by AH and his son and heir, Thomas, in Durham and in Northumberland have been attested repeatedly.[39] AH purchased three major estates in what had been the see of Durham (in 1647 simply the county of Durham): Bishop's Auckland manor for £6102 8s 11d on 8 March 1647; Easing Wood borough for £5833 9s 9d on 5 April 1650; and Wolsingham manor for £6764 14s 4d on 1 June 1650. Thomas bought Middleham manor in Northumberland for £3306 6s 6d on 9 November 1649. Those were substantial sums of money. Converting the value of £5,000 in 1650 to equivalent value in 2010 results in a range from one-half million pounds, if one uses a simple purchasing-power criterion, to £22 million, if one assumes that the sum was invested in an income-bearing commodity.

In this opinion of this writer, however, that account is only partly accurate as to names of estates. Bishop's Auckland is correctly given; so, too, is Wolsingham manor (aka Chapel Walls), a manor and deer park, then 10 miles northwest of Bishop's Auckland. "Easing Wood borough" was, I believe, a confusion for Evenwood borough. The former was then a very

---

[38] John Adamson, *The Noble Revolt* (London: Weidenfeld & Nicolson, 2007), pages 139, 141. In 2010 valuation by relative standard of living, that income is roughly equal to £2 million; by relative economic power, about £443 million.

[39] E.g., Thomas Wooton, *The Baronetage of England* (London, 1741), vol. 1, page 522; and subsequent similar compilations—which admittedly, however, tend to be repetitive.

small market town, not a borough, in the North Riding, Yorkshire, whereas Evenwood was indeed a borough and located at Bishop's Auckland. The latter identification is consistent with AH's motivation to acquire land of the bishops, as "assurance" that they would not regain it. Similarly, the "Middleham manor, Northumberland," supposedly purchased by Thomas, was in fact Bishop Middleham, which was about 9 miles southwest of Durham city. (No "Middleham manor" has been found in Northumberland records.) Bishop Middleham was a residence of the bishop of Durham until c1400, when it was acquired by the Eure family of Witton castle. Today only earthworks remain. Note that to the southwest of Bishop Middleham is Aycliffe, which, in the old part now known as School Aycliffe, includes Haselrigg Close (a short street, dead-end, off High Barn Road), once part of a farm perhaps known as Haselrig farm. Next street to the north is Lord Greville Drive.

Finally, one addition to the list of four estates may be noted. In 1410 Sir Ralph Eure gained permission to crenellate his manor house, thus making it Witton castle. Sir William Darcy, a royalist, held the castle at the start of the civil war but lost it. AH acquired it, whether by purchase or by appropriation is not known. Darcy regained the castle after 1660.

Note that AH's son and heir, Thomas, appears in some records as lord of the manor Cornforth in county Durham. Cornforth was part of the Bishop Middleham estate which he bought in 1649.

In sum, all of the acquired estates were in close proximity one to another, and all had been associated with the bishop of Durham, held by Thomas Morton between 1632 and 1659. In 1646 the episcopate was abolished, and Morton retired. Presumably all of these estates reverted to the crown and church in 1660 in fact, not just in expectation. According to the Mickelton and Spearmans manuscripts housed in the Durham University library (manuscript 25, f41r through f44r), after restoration the bishop of Durham, John Cosin, petitioned Charles II for assistance in repair, then for return, of what had been the bishop's residence. On 18 April 1662 the king granted to Cosin "the forfeited estates of Sir Arthur Haselrig which he held on 25 March 1646." As of that date, AH had purchased only Bishop Auckland manor.

Moving westward to Cumberland and Lancashire, recall discussion in chapter 2 of several places in those counties that carried (and in some instances still carry) the name "Hazlerigg," under some version of spelling. Note was there made of the possibility that for at least some of those places the naming might have been a consequence of the family having held a manor or an estate in land at or near the place in question. The "places" include farmsteads and erstwhile hamlets or vills but also a beck, a footpath, and country lanes, these latter all located in proximity to one or another of the hamlets and/or farmsteads. The logic of that "naming" thesis is straightforward: one or another member of a family named "H" held a particular parcel of land of human habitation long enough and with sufficient attentiveness that the parcel, in whole or in part, became known as a "place"—an estate, farm, hamlet, mill, or whatever--named "H." Straightforward though the logic, however, the testimony of known facts suggests that most, if not all, of those cited places in the two counties, Cumberland and Lancashire, probably acquired their names as a botanic-topographic description of place, just as did the small manor of Heselrig in the Chatton area of Northumberland: an area of ridges, with hazel trees or shrubs. The facts are far too short for this to be a definite conclusion, of course; they are at best suggestive. But as a matter not just of possibility but of probability, all of the known relevant facts point toward the botanic-topographic; few if any point also to the possibility of a family naming; on balance, then, the latter alternative is deemed unlikely.

Consider, for instance, the place named Hazelrigg on Hazelrigg Lane near the river Conder in Ellel Township of Lancashire. Now a mere remnant of a once large farmstead (most of the land having been sold for siting of Hazelrigg Meteorological Station and for expansion of Lancaster University), it was apparently always only pasture or meadowland, never a hamlet or vill, much less a manor. The known record of charters, grants, and the like, is comparatively rich in detail, and nothing of it offers so much as a hint of connection to the Hesilrige family. The list of local families includes only one with a surname, Ford, that suggests a connection to the Hesilrige family (Ford having been a small manor north of Heselrig in Northumberland), but the record indicates their presence in north Lancashire dated from about 1740, long after the naming of the farm estate.

Similarly, in the vill of Scotforth, south of Ellel, another acreage known as Hazelrigg (plus apparently a second, smaller one known as Little Hazelrigg) has had that name at least since the early 1200s, judging from *The Chartulary of Cockersand Abbey*, as cited by Ekwall.[40] Should one wish to speculate that this dating is consistent with the claim, vaguely held at times within the Hazlerigg family, that some early grants of land by William I to the family were in Cumberland, and with the fact that part of the area in question has at times been within the jurisdiction of Cumberland, one must contend with a major obstacle: soon after 1066 this

---

[40] Eilert Ekwall, *The Place-Names of Lancashire* (Manchester: The University Press, 1922), page 174.

area (and much more) was in the hands of count Roger of Poitou, from whom it passed to the Lancaster family with whom it remained for quite some time.[41]

Finally, to consider one more instance, there is the question of yet another Hazelrigg Farm, this one in the township of Staveley in Cartmel parish, which is east and north of Ellel (all once in Lancashire, but now Staveley is in the South Lake district of Cumbria). Due to two factors in intersection, this site could be considered still at issue as to its naming. The first factor is that the evidence from the Cockersand Abbey's charter does not itself extend to Cartmel parish, which means that while Ekwall's citation of namings as early as 1250 as having been generated by botanic and topographic considerations is almost certainly correct, it does not necessarily imply that *every* site named "Hazelrigg" in north Lancashire or in south Cumbria became a proper noun due to that same reasoning. The second factor has to do with the possibility, perhaps even likelihood, of a connection between two families, one represented by a Leicestershire man named Staveley and the other represented by Sir Arthur Hesilrige.

The discussion of some places collectively called "the Langtons," in Gartree Hundred, in the Victoria History of Leicestershire, mentions a Thomas Staveley. There is suggestion, nothing more definitive, that this man knew Sir Thomas Hesilrige, 1st Bt, and his son Sir Arthur, 2nd Bt. He christened his son Arthur. He was active in Leicestershire governance during the interregnum. The Hesilrige family had been involved in that part of the county, Church Langton in particular, at least since the 1500s. For example, Farnham reproduced a court record, dated 1501, that says "Thomas Hasylryg, of Church Langton, esq.," was party to a land dispute with Christopher Neel over 100 acres in Keythorp (which the Neel family had gained via Christopher's first marriage, to Margery, daughter and heir of Joan, wife of Thomas Rokes and one of two daughters and co-heirs of Thomas Palmer of Holt.)[42] Note also that Christopher's brother, Richard (b. c1470), married Ruth[7e], daughter of William[6a] Hesilrige.

Did Thomas Staveley descend from a Staveley family—that is, a family of the place, Staveley in Cartmel parish, near Ulverston? And if he did, was there a family connection, one that accounts for the Hazelrigg

---

[41] Born in Normandy at about the time of Hastings, this Roger was son of Roger de Montgomery, 1st earl of Shrewsbury. He acquired the "de Poitou" appellation by reason of marriage to an heiress from Poitou.

[42] George Farnham, "Prestwold and Its Hamlets in Medieval Times," *Transactions of the Leicestershire Archæological and Historical Society*, volume 17, part 1 (1931-32), pages 1-84, at pages 46-47.

farm in Staveley township, perhaps a union between a Staveley man and a Hesilrige daughter?

Those questions pertain to the possibility that the farm came to the family via purchase by the 2nd Bt (or by his father). However, while the possibility cannot be ruled out of hand, it does fail, in view of some known records, to rise to the status of probable fact. The key document derives from records of a longstanding local family, the Townley family, now housed in the Lancashire Records Office. A deed (DDTY 1/2/2), dated 22 November 1651, tells us of "James Brockbanck of Heslrigge in Cartmel, yeoman—a messuage and tenement at Haslrig and a mesuage and tenement at Cannyhill in Heslrigge, with appurtenances." We can draw from that statement two points, one of them bearing directly on the issue of naming, the other slightly askance to it. Taking the latter point first, the reference to "Cannyhill in Heslrigge," distinguished from the first-mentioned messuage "at Haslrig," indicates that an area larger than a single farm was covered by the "Heslrigge" place name. At least judging by the geography of today, the place of Canny Hill (now mainly site of a "caravan park") is about one mile from the farmhouse which has presented itself as "Hazelrigg" (see Exhibit 8.6, as well as Exhibit 2.8) and which reportedly dates from the 1600s.[43] Inference to that conclusion can be made also from other citations of the Hazelrigg (in Staveley) place name.

Along with other records, this can put to rest the notion that the place called "Heslrigge" was so named because acquired by the 2nd Bt; for it had carried that name well before the period of his acquisitions. Of course, that conclusion leaves open the possibility that the "causal order" was the other way around—that he acquired the "Heslrigge" property *because* it carried that name. Lying as it does at the southern end of the famous Lake Windermere, it is a very pretty landscape of long meadows and pastures in a valley trailing into the lake. But the idea that AH's acquisitions were motivated in any significant degree by a romanticist aestheticism seems a bit fanciful.

We know that AH had considerable interest in Cumberland, one of the four northern counties over which he exercised authority for the sequestration process, among others. This authority extended to clergy lands, as it did in Durham. But Durham was exceptional, in that large estates had been accumulated by the bishopry. Nothing like that had

---

[43] Both photographs date from the 1990s. Today that landscape looks rather different, as Hazelrigg Lane (and surrounding area) has become dotted with new constructions, some of them designed for holiday visitors of Windermere, the southern tip of which is only a brisk walk away.

occurred in the three other northern counties since the dissolution of the monastic system under Henry VIII. AH's actions were typified by the case of Aikton rectory (which included Gamelsby, Biglands, and Burgh upon the Sands). In 1650 the sitting rector was ejected. AH appointed Rowland Nichols as replacement.[44] Nichols served until 1660, conformed and continued serving until 1694. A similar ejection and replacement under AH's authority occurred at about the same time in Graystock parish, Leeth ward, Cumberland. So far as can be determined, no land transaction was involved in either case. Typically, there was little land held by these small rectories and vicarages.

Exhibit 8.6. Hazelrigg Farmhouse, Hazelrigg Lane, near Ulverston

---

[44] William Hutchison, *The History and Antiquities of Cumberland*, 2 volumes (Carlisle: F. Jollie, 1794), volume 2, page 481; Joseph Nicholson and Richard Burn, *The History and Antiquities of the Counties of Westmoreland and Cumberland*, 2 volumes (London: W Strahan and T Cadel, 1777), volume 2, page 201.

A Sample of Sir Arthur's Published Words

As the volume of printed works increased during the sixteenth century, authorities royal and ecclesial became more concerned about consequences. On one side of the ledger, public edicts were never so easily distributed in large numbers of uniform copies as could now be achieved. But on the other side, the same presses could spread rumors and evidences of challenge to established authority to equally large numbers of readers, albeit with less ease since the cost and the size of presses made them still rather scarce and difficult to conceal. These concerns continued into the 1600s. Efforts of censorship—for instance, that royal licence was needed of printed works—mingled with other controversies of the extent of royal authority. As was noted chapter 6, a concealed printing press had become a valuable weapon in the battle for "popular opinion" throughout England, though mainly in cities and towns.

Aside from Bibles, legal case books, and the like, most of the product of presses, especially product that counted in the on-going political debates, consisted of short works—pamphlets or booklets, we would call them. So it is with most of the published writing of AH. He had the advantage of being able to call on the official printers of parliamentary business, and he was not shy of using that advantage to further his own cause. He provided the handwritten copy, or in some instances had a scribe or (as with Thomas Burton, MP, for instance) a diarist sitting in Commons take dictation and then render it in continuous hand, which could be given to a printer.

Printers took pride in their work, of course, and they often developed different styles, which could be displayed to greatest effect on covers or title pages. Roger Chartier has helpfully given comparisons of these and other differences both in time and from place to place. How was the space distributed? What information was supplied, and where was it put? How were size and style of typeface arrayed?

Using as one example the title page of Cervantes' famous novel, *Don Quixote*, the first part of which was published in 1605, he pointed out that the title was printed in large letters at top of page, followed by the statement of authorship, roughly similar to the style we see still today. Next came "the dedicatee with his titles in full" (see Exhibit 8.7). The dedication typically signified patronage, and proper gratitude thereto, but also a degree of protection for the author: "The upper third of the title page is thus given over to the fundamental relationship that dominated literary activity until the mid-eighteenth century: the connecting of an author (already constituted as such) to a protector from whom he expected support and gratifications." The bottom part of the title page included the date, the printer and printer's mark, and the licensing to publish—that is, "the proper indications to satisfy the requirements of the book trade: mention of the privileges, the mark of royal authority, the place of publication and the name of the printer and, at the very bottom under a solid horizontal line, the address at which the eventual buyer could buy the work."[45]

Exhibit 8.7. Title Page of Cervantes' *Don Quixote*, 1605

The publications of AH follow a similar pattern, although some differences can be seen especially in his earliest publications. For instance, in the 1641 publication of his speech in Commons about the proper place of the clergy (not shown here) the title page shows first the author's name in large type, followed by the title of the work; these consume the top *half*

---

[45] Roger Chartier, *The Order of Books*, translated by Lydia G Cochrane (Cambridge: Polity Press, 1994), page 44.

and more of the title page. Next comes the date of the speech—the original date of publication, as it were—and beneath that is the printer's mark, followed by place of publication, printer's name, and year of publication.[46] The space that would earlier have been devoted to a dedicatee and to the declaration of license/approval to publish was now given over to larger type for the author and title of work. This distribution of space was not unusual for that time. A similar distribution was seen in the title page of *Nineteen Propositions* (Exhibit 7.1) and that of John Milton's *Areopagitica* (Exhibit 7.5). Note that the former of these was adorned with printer's artwork, as were some of AH's works (see below). Ink was expensive, so one assumes that decisions about embellishment were by purse's owner, although the choice of design might have been left to the printer.

The printed works represented below are a small sample of the total.[47] The present selection has been governed by two main factors: length of document and legibility. One of the documents, AH's address to the House of Commons on 7 February 1658/9, has been transcribed from the *Journal* of the House.

Note for future reference that several documents of the era were composed by critics of AH and then passed off as if by his own hand. The fakery is usually so blatant that no one today, if then, would be deceived.

---

[46] Although exceptions did occur, general convention held that statement of year alone was sufficient for date of publication, mainly because the process of printing often took place over weeks, even months.

[47] Many of the works were included in the collection, Early English Books. Most of that collection is now available at a website, EarlyEnglishBooksOnline.

Sir Arthur Haslerigg

his Speech in Parliament,

the fifth of January last.

Whereby he cleareth himselfe of the Articles of high Treason, exhibited against himselfe, the Lord *Kimbolton*, Mr. *I. Pym*, Mr. *Hampden*, Mr. *Stroud*, and M. *Hollis*, by his Majesty on tuesday 4. of Ianu. 1641.

Whereunto is added

Master PIM his SPEECH

In PARLIAMENT, Concerning the Vote of the House of Commons, for his Discharge upon the Accusation of High Treason, exhibited against himself, and others.

London, Printed for *F. C.* and *T. B.* 1641.

Exhibit 8.8. Defense against Treason, 5 January 1641/2

Sir *Arthur Haslerigg* his Speech in PARLIMENT.

Mr. Speaker.

THis misfortune of mine seemes to mee at the first exceeding strange, not onely in respect of the Crimes laid to my charge, but most of all having thereby incurred not only the disfavour but irefull displeasure of his Sacred *Majesty*. For the first, knowing the innocency and integrity of my heart, that it is free from any such crime either in thought, word or deed against either my gratious *Soveraign*, or my native *Country*, I shall the more easily beare the burthen of the charge, but to groane under the burthen of a most Pious and wise Prince his displeasure, wounds me sore.

Mr. *Speaker*, I humbly desire so much favour of this Honourable House of which I have had the happinesse to be a Member, to speake something of my Innocence in all these Crimes I am charged withall.

This Honourable House, (Mr. *Speaker*) can I hope witnesse for me, the manner of my carriage and disposition in any debate or arguments wherein I have beene one, I hope nothing hath proceeded from me, that can come any wayes within the compasse of Treason.

In all disputes and conclusions of any matter by Vote of the House, my Vote hath commonly agreed with the Major part then I hope my Vote in *Parliament* being free cannot be Treason.

Mr. *Speaker*, The Articles that are exhibited against mee and the other Gentlemen, are of most dangerous and pernitious consequence, if wee should be found guilty of them, which God defend; I would to God these persons that incensed his *Majesty* against us, (which is easily conceived who they are) were as free from thoughts, words, nay actions within the limits of Treason) as I hope we shall prove our selves by Gods blessing.

MASTER *Speaker*, It is alleadged, wee have endeavoured to subvert the fundamentall Lawes of this Land, abridge the Kings power, and deny his Royall *Prerogatives*. Give mee leave I beseech you, to speake concerning this Article. There is (as I conceive) not two Formes or Governement in this Kingdome: there it not two sorts of Fundamentall Lawes: there is but one forme of Government; One sort of Fundamentall Lawes, that is, the Common Lawes of this Land, and acts, Statutes, and Ordinances of Parliament, these two Mr. *Speaker*, depend and

hang

(3)

hang one upon another, so that they cannot bee separated; and he that subverts the one, breaks and infringes the other. Now under favour *Mr. Speaker*, to speake freely in *Parliament* (freely called and assembled by his Majesties most Royal Authority) to Vote freely in the same, upon the conclusion of any Bill to be made a Law by the whole consent of Parliament assented to by his *Majesty*: to agree in Voting with the whole Parliament against Delinquents, and Malefactors in the State, to bring them to condigne punishment for the same: to give my Vote in the House, or removing evill Counsellours from his sacred Majesty, to place loyall and faithfull ones in their place: To assent with the whole State assembled together in Counsell for the setling of peace and tranquillity in the same: To ordaine and enact such wholsome Lawes and Ordinances whereby his Majesties good Subjects may be governed in righteousnesse and good obedience: To Vote with the House for redressing the many grievances of the Common-wealth, If these be to subvert the Fundamentall Lawes of the Land, then Mr. Speaker am I guilty of this Article in giving my Vote against the Earle of *Strafford*; in Voting those acts already made and passed by his Majesty; in Voting against the Bishops; in protesting to maintaine the Fundamentall Lawes of the Land, the true *Protestant* Religion, according to the true Doctrine of the Church of *England*: I say then Mr. *Speaker*, in this am I guilty of high Treason: but if this bee not to subvert the Lawes of the Land; then (as I conceive) am I cleare from beeing guilty of this Article. Which I humbly leave to the consideration of this Honourable House.

Under favour (*Master Speaker*) I come now to the other Articles of the Charge: I will onely recite the substance of them; for they all harpe on one thing: To indeavour to bring in an Arbitrary and tyrannicall Forme of Government: To invite Tumults, and unlawfull resorts of multitudes of people to the *Parliament*, to be a colour for our Designes: to raise Forces and Armies in this Land to assist me in my practises: To invite forraigne Princes to bring an Army into the Land: To endeavour by Declarations, Proclamations, and otherwise to alienate the hearts of his Majesties loyall Subjects from their lawfull Soveraigne thereby to avert their due obedience from him, and having an evill opinion of his sacred Majesty, to side with us, and take our parts to effect our Designes.

Give me leave I beseech you to speake concerning these crimes: And first *Mr. Speaker* to endeavour to bring in an Arbitrary power and tyrannicall Forme of Goverment in the Subject, is to deny Parliamentary proceedings: To oppose the Laws enacted by *Parliaments*: To incense his Majesty against *Parliaments*; to protest and Petition against the proceedings thereof, is to bring in an Arbitrary forme of Government. But to agree with the *Parlia-*

(4)

ment being a Member thereof by Vote, to make and enact Lawes; I conceive this cannot be termed Arbitrary; neither I perswade my selfe can the effects thereof be tyrannicall.

Secondly, concerning the late Tumults about the House, I am innocent thereof; neither came they by my invitation or incouragement: I alwaies thought their resorts in that sort were illegall and riotous: I have Voted with this House for their suppressing; have assented to all Orders for their appeasing; agreed with the *Parliament* in all things concerning their petitions and Requests: Then I hope this *Honourable* House will not conceive me guilty of this Crime: if it be one, and granted; yet I conceive far without the limits of Treason for these Reasons.

1. They came not with Armes to force any thing to be done in *Parliament*; but humbly by Petition shewed their grievances, and desired redresse thereof which is one Priviledge (and one of the greatest) to make their griefs knowne to a *Parliament*, and by them to be relieved.

2. They offered no assault; but (beeing assaulted) preserved themselves and departed.

3. The matter of their clamour was not against the King nor any of his Counsell: It was not against the Lords, nor House of Commons: It was onely against Delinquents, against such as had been the greatest oppressors of them.

Thirdly, I come in a word to the other Articles of the charge which I intend to speake of (under favour) altogether: I pray you who raised any army actually in this Land but the trained Bands, which was done by the *Parliament* for the security of their owne persons in the Kings absence; and in obedience to his commands, at his returne home they were discharged, and afterwards againe raised by his Majesties owne Royal Authority. And for inviting or procuring any forreigne Princes to ayd me with an Army, I am altogether innocent therein; I know of no aid required but from *Scotland*, which is done by the *Parliament*, my Vote as a Member thereof only agreeing with them in the same: And that aid is procured for his Majesties assistance in subduing the Rebellion in *Ireland*, and (as I conceive) for no other purpose. And for the last Article wherewith I am charged, I hope to bee cleared by this whole House for what Declamations or Proclamations have beene published but by Authority of the *Parliament*, joyn'd with his Majesties most Royall Power and assent thereunto. It is manifest to all people that nothing is published by the *Parliament*; or any of the Members thereof, but tendeth to the winning of the hearts of his Majesties Subjects to dutifull obedience and incite love and tender affection towards their gracious Soveraign. And I dare confidently say, that there is none of his Majesties Subjects that are

(5)

are true Protestants, and well affected to Religion; but upon the least command of his Majesties, will spend their dearest bloud in defence of his Sacred Person, his Queene and Princely Issue, of the Lawes and Constitutions of this Kingdome, of *Parliaments* and the Rights and Priviledges thereof; of Religion and the Doctrine of the Church of *England*. And therefore I conceive I am far from intending any Treason against his Majesty or Kingdome. And thus craving pardon for my presumption, and humbly thanking this Honourable House for their patience, beseeching them to have a good opinion of me and my Actions, that I may receive such Tryall as to their wisedomes shall seeme meet, with my hearty Prayers for the happy continuance of this *Parliament*; to effect and finish such great matters both in Church and State, as may advance Gods glory, settle all things in a right frame for the good Governement of this Kingdome, and the everlasting peace and tranquillity of his Majesty and all his Kingdomes.

Master *Pymme* his Speech in *Parliament* on Wednesday the 5. of *January*, 1641.

Concerning the Vote of the House of Commons, for his Discharge upon the Accusation of High Treason, exhibited against himselfe, and others, &c.

Master Speaker,

These Articles of High Treason, exhibited by his Majestie against me and the other Gentlemen in the accusation charged with the same Crime, are of great consequence, and much danger to the State: The Articles in themselves, if proved, are according to the Lawes of this Land High Treason.

First, to endeavour to subvert the Fundamentall Lawes of the Land, is by this present Parliament in the Earle of *Strafords* Case adjudged High Treason.

Secondly, to endeavour to introduce into this Kingdome an Arbytrarie and tyrannicall forme of Government, is likewise Voted High Treason.

Thirdly

(6)

Thirdly, to raise an Army to compell the Parliament to make and enact Lawes without their free Votes, and willing proceedings in the same is High Treason.

Fourthly, to invite a forraigne force to invade this Land, to favour our designes agitated against the King and State, is High Treason.

Fiftly, to animate and encourage riotous Assemblies and tumults about the *Parliament* to compell the King to assent to the Votes of the House is Treason.

Sixtly, to cast aspersions upon his Majesty and his Government, to alienate the affections of His people, and to make his Majesty odious unto them is Treason.

Seventhly, to endeavour to draw his Majesties Army into disobedience, and to side with us in our designes, if against the King, is Treason.

I desire, Master *Speaker*, the favour of this House to declare my selfe, concerning this Charge, shall onely parrallell and similize my actions since the sitting of this *Parliament* with these Articles.

First, Master *Speaker*, if to Vote with the *Parliament*, as a Member of the House, wherein all our Votes ought to be free : it being one of the greatest privledges thereof to have our debates, disputes, & arguments in the same unquestinable, be to endeavour to subvert the Fundamentall Lawes, then am I guilty of the first Article.

Secondly, If to agree and consent with the whole State of the Kingdome by Vote to ordaine and make Lawes for the good government of his Majesties Subjects in peace and dutifull obedience to their lawfull Soveraigne bee to introduce an Arbitrary and tyrannicall forme of government in the state, then am I guilty of this Article.

Thirdly, If to consent by Vote with the *Parliament*, to raise a Guard, or Traine-Band to secure and defend the persons or the Members thereof, being invironed and beset with many dangers in the absence of the King, and by Vote with the House, in willing obedience to the Royall command of his sacred Majesty, at his returne, be actually to levie Armes against the King: then am I guilty of this Article.

Fourthly, If to joyne with the *Parliament*, by free Vote to crave brotherly assistance from *Scotland*, Kingdomes both under obedience to one Soveraigne, both his loyall and dutifull Subjects, to suppresse the Rebellion in *Ireland* which lyes gasping every day in danger to be lost from his Majesties subjection, be to invite and incourage a forraigne power to invade this Kingdome: then am I guilty of High Treason.

Fiftly, If to agree with the greatest and wisest Councell of State, to suppresse unlawfull tumults and riotous assemblies, to agree with the House by

Vote

Vote to all Orders, Edicts, and Declarations for their repelling, bee to raise and countenance them in their unlawfull actions, then am I guilty of this Article.

Sixtly, If by free Vote to joyne with the *Parliament* in publishing of a Remonstrance, in setting forth Declarations against Delinquents, in the State against Incendiaries betweene his Majesties Kingdome, against ill Counsellors which labour to avert his Majesties affection from *Parliaments* against those ill affected Bishops that have innovated our Religion, oppressing painefull, learned and godly Ministers with vexatious, suites and molestations in their unjust Courts, by cruell sentences of Pillory, and cutting off their eares, greatfines, Banishment, and perpetuall Imprisonment, If this Mr. *Speaker* be to cast aspersions on his Majesty and his governement, and to alienate the hearts of his Loyall Subjects good Protestants, and well affected in Religion, from their due obedience to his Royall Majesty, then am I guilty of this Article.

Seventhly, If to consent by Vote with the *Parliament* to put forth Proclamations, to send Declarations to his Majesties Army, to annimate and encourage the same to his Loyall obedience, to give so many Subsidies, raised so many great summes of mony willingly for their keeping on foote to serve his Majesty upon his Royall command on any occasion, to apprehend and attach as Delinquents, such persons in the same as are disaffected both to his sacred Person, his Crowne and Dignity, to the wise and great Counsell of *Parliament* to the true and Orthodox Doctrine of the Church of *England*, and the true Religion grounded on the Doctrine of *Christ* himselfe, and established, and confirmed by many Acts of *Parliament* in the Reigne of *Hen.* 8. *E.* 6. Queene *Elizab.* and King *Iames* of blessed memory, if this Mr. *Speaker* be to draw his Majesties Army into disobedience, and to side with us in our Designes, then I am guilty of this Article.

Now, Master *Speaker*, Having given you a touch concerning these Articles comparing them with my Actions, ever since I have had the Honour to sit in this House as a Member thereof: I humbly crave your consideration, and favourable judgement of them, not doubting, they being weighed in the even scales of your Wisedomes, I shall bee found innocent and cleare from these Crimes laid to my charge.

Master *Speaker*, I humbly crave your further patience to speake somewhat concerning the exhibiting of this Charge which is to propose to your Considerations these propositions, *viz.*

First, whether to exhibit Articles of High Treason by his Majesties owne hands in this House agrees with the rights and priviledges thereof.

Second.

Secondly, Whether for a guard armed, to come into the Parliament to accuse any of the Members thereof, be not a breach of the priviledge of Parliament.

Thirdly, Whether any of the Members of Parliament being so accused may be committed upon such accusation, without the whole consent thereof.

Fourthly, Whether a Parliament hath not priviledge to bayle any Member so accused.

Fiftly and lastly, Whether if any of the Members of a Parliament so charged, and by the House discharged without release from his Majesty may still sit in the House as members of the same. And thus Master *Speaker*, I humbly crave pardon for my presumption in so farre troubling this Honourable House, desiring their favourable consideration of all my Actions, and that I may have such a tryall as to this wise Counsell shall thinke meete, cheerefully submitting my selfe and actions to the righteous judgements of the same.

FINIS.

John Pym's comparable Defense was published with that of AH, and the whole has been retained here, because of interest in comparing the two statements. Pym was the superior politician and legal scholar, relative not only to AH but also to most other members of Commons. Even so, AH's statement does not come off so badly. It is possible, even likely, however, that Pym had a hand in composing it; for their venture was a collective one, and each knew the importance of mutual support and loyalty. A recent historian of the episode, John Adamson, endorsed Edward Hyde's claim that AH gained considerable standing by having been associated in so dramatic a manner with Pym and his already established circle of lawyers and parliamentary officials.[48]

The next document is AH's report to the Council of State for Irish and Scottish Affairs about conditions of the Scottish prisoners at Durham, Newcastle, and elsewhere.

---

[48] John Adamson, *The Noble Revolt* (London: Weidenfeld & Nicolson, 2007), page 492.

A LETTER

From Sir *Arthur Hesilrige*,

To the Honorable Committee

OF THE

Councel of State

FOR

Irish and *Scotish* Affairs at *White-Hall*,

Concerning the

Scots Prisoners.

Die Veneris, 8 Novembr. 1650.

Ordered by the Parliament, That this Letter be forthwith printed and published.

Hen: Scobell, Cleric. Parliamenti.

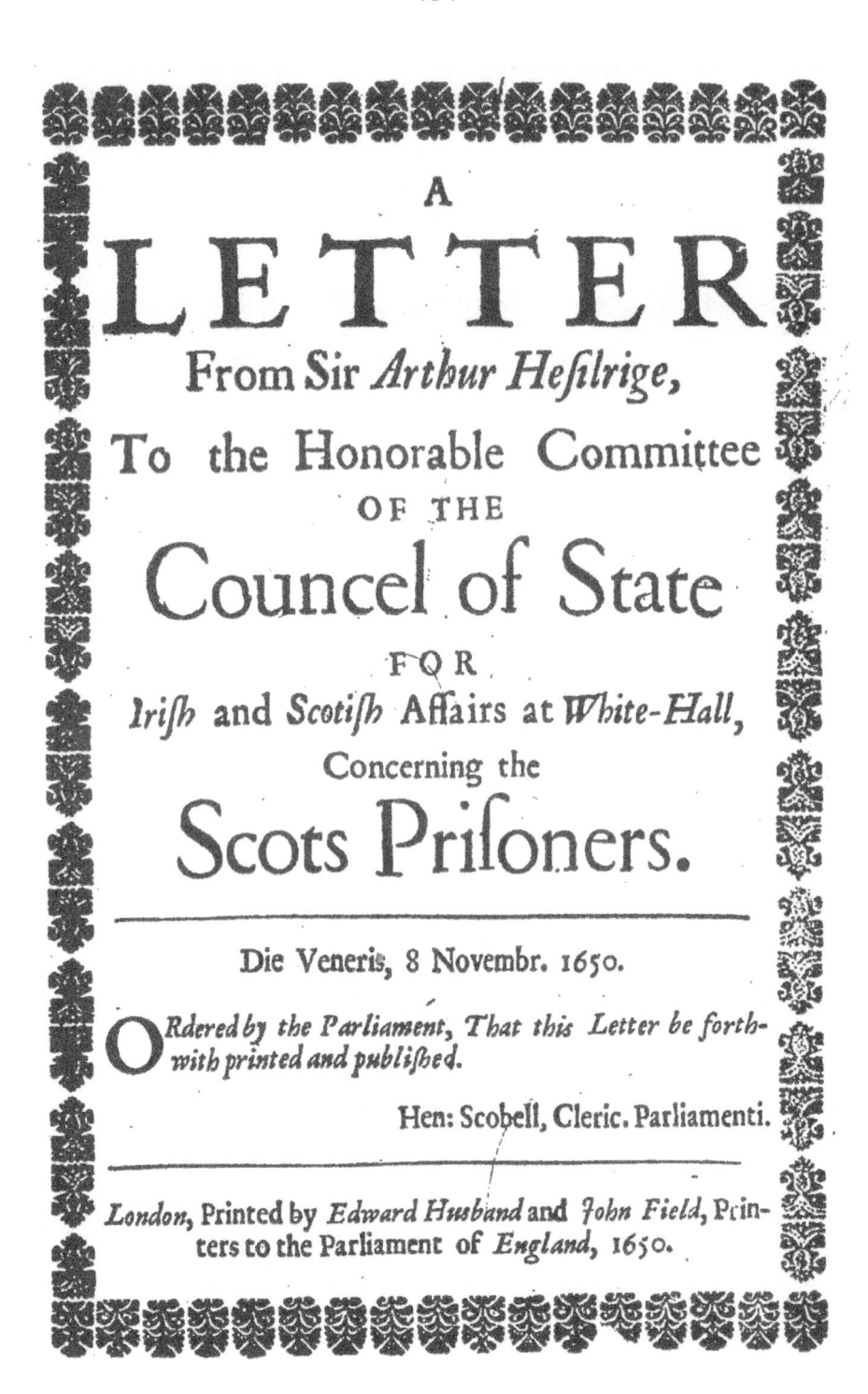

London, Printed by *Edward Husband* and *John Field*, Printers to the Parliament of *England*, 1650.

Exhibit 8.9. Disposition of Scottish Prisoners, 8 November 1650

Gentlemen,

I Received your Letter dated the Twenty sixth of *October*; in that you desire me, That Two thousand three hundred of the *Scotch* Prisoners now at *Durham* or elswhere, able and fit for Foot Service, be selected, and marched thence to *Chester* and *Liverpool*, to be shipped for the South and West of *Ireland*, and that I should take special care not to send any Highlanders.

I am necessitated upon the receipt of this, to give you a full accompt concerning the Prisoners: After the Battel at *Dunbar* in *Scotland*, my Lord General writ to me, That there was about Nine thousand Prisoners, and that of them he had set at liberty all those that were wounded, and, as he thought, disabled for future Service, and their Number was, as Mr. *Downing* writ, Five thousand one hundred; the rest the General sent towards *Newcastle*, conducted to *Berwick* by Major *Hobson*, and from *Berwick* to *Newcastle* by some Foot out of that Garison, and the Troop of Horse; when they came to *Morpeth*, the Prisoners being put into a large walled Garden, they eat up raw Cabages, Leaves and Roots; so many, as the very seed and the labor, at Four pence a day, was valued by sufficient men at Nine pounds; which Cabage, as I conceive, they having fasted, as they themselves said, near eight days, poysoned their Bodies; for as they were coming from thence to

Newcastle, some dyed by the way-side, and when they came to *Newcastle*, I put them into the greatest Church in the Town, and the next morning when I sent them to *Durham*, about Sevenscore were sick, and not able to march, and three dyed that night, and some fell down in their march from *Newcastle* to *Durham*, and dyed; and when they came to *Durham*, I having sent my Lieutenant Colonel and my Major, with a strong Guard both of Horse and Foot, and they being there told into the great Cathedral Church, they could not count them to more then Three thousand; although Colonel *Fenwick* writ to me, That there were about Three thousand five hundred, but I believe they were not told at *Berwick*, and most of those that were lost, it was in *Scotland*; for I heard, That the Officers that marched with them to *Berwick*, were necessitated to kill about Thirty, fearing the loss of them all, for they fell down in great Numbers, and said, They were not able to march; and they brought them far in the night, so that doubtless many ran away. When I sent them first to *Durham*, I writ to the Major, and desired him to take care, that they wanted not any thing that was fit for Prisoners, and what he should disburse for them, I would repay it. I also sent them a daily supply of bread from *Newcastle*, and an allowance equal to what had been given to former Prisoners: But their Bodies being infected, the Flux encreased amongst them. I sent many Officers to look to them, & appointed that those that were sick should be removed out the Cathedral Church into the Bishops Castle, which belongs to Mistris *Blakiston*, and provided

Cooks,

Cooks, and they had Pottage made with Oatmeal, and Beef and Cabages, a full Quart at a Meal for every Prisoner: They had also coals daily brought to them, as many as made about a hundred Fires both day and night, and Straw to lie upon; and I appointed the Marshal to see all these things orderly done, and he was allowed Eight men to help him to divide the coals, and their Meat, Bread and Pottage equally: They were so unruly, sluttish and nasty, that it is not to be believed; they acted rather like Beasts then Men, so that the Marshal was allowed Forty men to cleanse and sweep them every day: But those men were of the lustiest Prisoners, that had some small thing given them extraordinary: And these provisions were for those that were in health; and for those that were sick, and in the Castle, they had very good Mutton Broth, and sometimes Veal Broth, and Beef and Mutton boild together, and old Women appointed to look to them in the several Rooms: There was also a Physitian which let them Blood, and dressed such as were wounded, and gave the sick Physick, and I dare confidently say, There was never the like care taken for any such Number of prisoners that ever were in *England*. Notwithstanding all this, many of them dyed, and few of any other Disease but the Flux; some were killed by themselves, for they were exceeding cruel one towards another: If a man was perceived to have any Money, it was two to one but he was killed before morning, and Robbed; and if any had good clothes, he that wanted, if he was able, would strangle him, and put on his clothes: And the Disease of the Flux still encreasing amongst them,

them, I was then forced, for their preservation, if possible it might be, to send to all the next Towns to *Durham*, within four or five miles, to command them to bring in their Milk; for that was conceived to be the best Remedy for stopping of their Flux, and I promised them what Rates they usually sold it for at the Markets, which was accordingly performed by about Threescore Towns and places, and Twenty of the next Towns to *Durham* continue still to send daily in their Milk, which is boiled, some with Water, and some with Bearsflower, the Physitians holding it exceeding good for recovery of their health.

Gentlemen, You cannot but think strange this long preamble, and to wonder what the matter will be; in short its this, Of the Three thousand prisoners that my Officers told into the Cathedral Church at *Durham*, Three hundred from thence, and Fifty from *Newcastle* of the Sevenscore left behinde, were delivered to Major *Clerk* by Order from the Councel, and there are about Five hundred sick in the Castle, and about Six hundred yet in health in the Cathedral, the most of which are in probability Highlanders, they being hardier then the rest, and other means to distinguish them we have not, and about Sixteen hundred are dead and buried, and Officers about Sixty, that are at the Marshals in *Newcastle*. My Lord General having released the rest of the Officers, and the Councel having given me power to take out what I thought fit, I have granted to several well-affected persons that have Salt-works at *Sheels*, and want Servants, Forty, and they have engaged to keep them to work at their Salt-pans; and I have taken out more

about

(7)

about Twelve Weavers, to begin a Trade of Linnen cloth like unto the Scotch-cloth, and about Forty Laborers. I cannot give you on this sudden a more exact Accompt of the Prisoners, neither can any Accompt hold true long, because they still dye daily, and doubtless so they will, so long as any remain in Prison. And for those that are well, if Major *Clerk* could have believed that they had been able to have marched on foot, he would have marched them by Land; for we perceive that divers that are seemingly healthy, and have not at all been sick, suddenly dye, and we cannot give any reason of it, onely we apprehend they are all infected, and that the strength of some holds it out till it seize upon their very hearts. Now you fully understand the condition and the number of the Prisoners, what you please to direct, I shall observe, and intend not to proceed further upon this Letter, until I have your Answer upon what I have now written. I am,

Gentlemen,

Your affectionate Servant,

Octob. 31. 1650.

Art: Hesilrige.

F I N I S.

The next document (Exhibit 8.10) pertains to the period which would prove to be, for the republican cause, the end game. It comes from Burton's diary (as mentioned earlier), his recording of AH's speech to the House of Commons on 7 February 1658/9. The transcription is direct, without effort to convert spoken words to the (usually) greater consistency of written composition.

Exhibit 8.10. AH's Speech to Commons, 7 February 1658/9

Sir Arthur Haslerigge. I wonder not at this silence in a business of this weight. I have much weakness upon me.

The business that we are about, is the setting up a power over this nation. It will be necessary, for method's sake, to consider what we have been; what we are, and what we shall be I must beg patience to look far back. Time was, this nation had seven kings, and no doubt but the strongest put down the weakest, against the will of the rest. I never knew any single person to have power, willing to lay it down. After it was in one single person, then came in the Conqueror. The Kentishmen stood up for their liberties, and in some sort, preserved liberty to all the rest.

Succeeding Kings, sons and others, began to grow very oppressive to the people's liberties. Then rose up the noble Barons who struggled so long, till with their swords, they obtained our *Magna Charta*. That our Barons were men of great power, appears by what they compelled the King to grant; the whole estate being in them and the Bishops, Abbots, and King. They were so great, and sensible of their greatness.

The Government was then in King and Parliament, Lords and Commons sitting altogether. They withdrew and went into another House, to make a distinct jurisdiction. Thus the Lords had all but the power of the purse, which, to this day, preserved the liberties of the nation. Then the Government was enlarged into three estates, King, Lords, and Commons, and continued thus above three hundred years.

As all governments have their beginning from time, so time puts an end to them. The government, continuing so long, it had contracted rust. The people groaned under great oppression, both as men and Christians.

The Council Table bit like a serpent; the Star Chamber like scorpions. Two or three gentlemen could not stir out, for fear of being committed for a riot. Our souls and consciences were put on the rack by the Archbishop. We might not speak of Scripture, or repeat a sermon at our tables. Many godly ministers were sent to find their bed in the wilderness. The oppression was little less in the lower courts and in the special courts.

Altars were set up, and bowing to them enjoined. Pictures were placed in Church-windows, and images set up at Durham, and elsewhere; with many other exorbitances introduced, both in Church and State. The Archbishop would not only impose on England, but on Scotland, to bring in the Book of Common-Prayer upon them. They liked it not, and, as luck would have it, they would not bear it. He prevailed with the King to raise an army to suppress them. The King prevailed with his nobles to conquer them into it. He went to their country, and finding himself not able to conquer them, came back.

He called a Parliament, which was named the Little, or Broken Parliament, disbanded not his army, but propounded that we should give him a great sum to maintain the war against Scotland. We debated it, but the consequence of our debate made him fear we would not grant it. We had, if he had suffered us to sit. Then did Strafford and his Council advise him to break us and to rule arbitrarily, and that he had an army in Ireland to make it good. For this Strafford lost his head. The King suddenly broke that Parliament. I rejoice in my soul it was so. He raised the gallantest army that ever was, the flower of the gentry and nobility. The Scots raised too, and sent their declaration into England, that by the law of God and nature they might rise up for their own preservation; and thus they came into England. At Newburn the armies met. We were worsted. God was pleased to disperse our army, and give them the day. The Scots passed Newburn, and advanced to Newcastle.

Then some of our nobles, Say, Essex, and Scroop, humbly petitioned his Majesty for a Parliament. He, seeing danger, called a Parliament. This was the Long Parliament. The first proposition was to raise money for the Scots. We gave them a brotherly assistance of 300,000*l.* They showed themselves brethren and honest men, and peaceably returned. Then money was pressed for our own army. The House, considering how former Parliaments had been dealt with, was unwilling to raise money till the Act was passed not to dissolve the Parliament but by their own consent. It passed freely by King, Lords, and Commons. This was wonderful; the very hand of God that brought it to pass; for no man could then foresee the good that Act produced.

The King then practised with the Scots, then with his army, to assist him against this Parliament, and to make them sure to his particular interest. Sir John Conyers discovered it, to his everlasting fame. Mr. Pym acquainted the House. Divers officers of the army, Lord Goring, Ashburnham, Pollard, and others, were examined here. They all absented. The House desired of the King, that they might be brought to justice; but the King sent them away beyond sea.

The King demanded five members, by his Attorney-General. He then came personally to the House, with five hundred men at his heels, and sat in your chair. It pleased God to hide those members. I shall never forget the kindness of that great Lady, the Lady Carlisle, that gave timely notice. Yet some of them were in the House, after the notice came. It was questioned if, for the safety of the House, they should be gone; but the debate was shortened, and it was thought fit for them, in discretion, to withdraw. Mr. Hampden and myself being then in the House, withdrew. Away we went. The King immediately came in, and was in the House before we got to the water.

The Queen, on the King's return, raged and gave him an unhandsome name, "poltroon," for that he did not take others out; and certainly if he had, they would have been killed at the door.

Next day the King went to the City. They owned the members. Thereupon he left the Parliament, and went from step to step, till he came to York, and set up his standard at Nottingham, and declared the militia was in him.

The House of Lords then sent down to declare that the King had broken his trust. The word of the King, seduced by evil counsel, lost us forty lords. The House declared the militia to be in them. That was then a great question. Commissioners were then sent out in the name of the King and Parliament.

Then was there the King against the Parliament, and Parliament against him. There was at this time, no thought to alter Government. We met at Edgehill. The King went to Oxford, and gave thanks for the victory, and we at London gave thanks for the victory: and so it was in many other battles. Thus the English pushed on both sides, and much precious English blood was spilt on the ground. Several propositions, at length, were tendered; but God hardened his heart. He would not accept. Then we came to make a new model, and a Self-denying Ordinance. Thereupon this noble Lord was chosen the Parliament's General. The Commission as to him, was from the Parliament only; the name "King" was left out. I appeal to all the world for the undeniable, the unquestionable victories after that. We had not one doubtful battle. The King after that never gave thanks. In process of time, there were propositions, again and again, seven, eight, or nine times,—at least seven times,— sent to the King, desiring, for ourselves, our ancient liberties with our ancient Government, but his heart was still hardened. Next we shall find him in the Isle of Wight, where the last propositions were tendered to him. He would not consent, though his sword was broken, and he was in the lowest condition. He denied. Many gentleman in this House, of great worth, foreseeing our troubles, apprehended there was enough in the King's condescensions for a well-grounded peace. But the officers of the army were otherwise opinioned. Finding the King not sufficiently humbled, they thought the good cause would be betrayed. The officers seized several members. Those that stayed within, asked for them, but could not have them.

They seized upon the King, demanded justice, and brought him to judgment. He would not answer, not owning our authority, because he was accountable only to God; whereas, God never made such a creature, to govern men, and not to be accountable to men. Yet he received his judgment, and submitted his head quietly to the block. The edge of justice struck it off. See the wonderful hand of God! The King dead, some members of the House, the late General, and Commissary-general Ireton, they would have it determined, (which the wisdom of the House thought meet) that not only this line, nocent and innocent, but that kingship should be abolished, as dangerous useless and burthensome. Then there was an end of one of the three estates. The Lords, most of them being gone, the remainder, amazed and troubled at this, adjourned their House; but never came again unto it. As they had their beginning from themselves, so they had their end from themselves. The Commons approved the Lords' adjournment, and did by them as they had done by the King: and there was an end of that estate. Two of the three estates were thus gone. Then, for the third estate, that, God knows! had been much shattered and broken. Force was much upon us. What should we do? We turned ourselves into the Commonwealth. By advice of the soldiers among us, a declaration to that purpose went out from the Army. We continued four years, before we were put an end to. In which time, I appeal to all, if the nation, that had been blasted and torn, began not exceedingly to flourish. At the end of the four years, scarce a sight to be seen that we had had a war. Trade flourished; the City of London grew rich; we were the most potent by sea that ever was known in England. Our Navy and Armies were never better.

Yet, after these estates were ended, we found a new trouble. The wars were not then ended. Waters broke out. A strong remnant got into Colchester. Our brethren of Scotland were not so firm upon that great shaking of kingship. We sent an army into Scotland, to Colchester, to Wales. This noble Lord went to the gates of Colchester and conquered, and put an end to all the English war. Then a general was sent into Scotland. Our late Protector that died was then general of all our forces. You know the great mercy. There we obtained that memorable victory at Dunbar. What care did the Parliament then take to furnish their army from London with all necessaries, by land and in ships; all provided with the greatest diligence. None but a numerous company of good and honest-hearted men could have done the like. The King of Scots came in with a great army. Twenty thousand men came suddenly and freely to Worcester. The people voluntarily rise and assist, in the greatest numbers that were ever read. The Scotch Army returned, not three in a company. Man by man they returned in rags. This battle, the 3d of

September, 1651, put an end to all the miseries of war in England and Scotland. Our wars in Ireland were then not considerable.

    This done, it is true here was only remaining a little part of that triple cord, and you know what became of them. I heard, being seventy miles off, that it was propounded that we should dissolve our trust, and dissolve it into a few hands. I came up and found it so; that it was resolved in a junto at the Cockpit.* I trembled at it, and was, after, there and bore my testimony against it. I told them the work they went about was accursed. I told them it was impossible to devolve this trust. Next day, we were labouring here in the House on an act to put an end to that Parliament and to call another. I desired the passing of it with all my soul. The question was putting for it, when our General stood up, and stopped the question, and called in his Lieutenant, with two files of musqueteers, with their hats on their heads, and their guns loaden with bullets. Our General told us we should sit no longer to cheat the people. The Speaker, a stout man, was not willing to go. He was so noble, that he frowned and said he would not out of the chair, till he was plucked out; which was quickly done, without much compliment, by two soldiers, and the mace taken: and there was an end of the third estate also. I rejoiced then, from the soul, that the question was not put. But I would have passed the severest sentence upon those that did this horrid business, that ever was passed upon men, and would have been from my heart the executioner of it. But I forgive them now, both the dead and the living. There was no possibility to dissolve this Parliament, the remaining part of the three estates, but by our own officer. He only had power. Our enemies had none.

    Surely all the English blood was not spilled in vain? It was a glorious work of our Saviour to die on the cross for our spirituals. This is as glorious a work for our civils, to put an end to the King and Lords. The right is, originally, without all doubt, in the people. Undeniably and most undoubtedly it reverts to the people: the power being taken away. Like

---

*"Cockpit" refers to an apartment in Whitehall.

the gordian knot, it asked but Hercules's sword to cut this knot. This done, our General, in 1653, looked on himself as having all power devolved upon himself: a huge mistake! The power was then in the people. If by conquest he had come in, he might have had something to say. It was, undoubtedly in the people. It was a mistake in him; you shall see it.

He was pleased to select a number of gentlemen, good, honest men, hither brought. He gave them power. They came into this House, and voted themselves a Parliament. They acted high in some things, and soon cracked. Some of them ran to Whitehall, and returned their power. Whence it came, thither it went. Judge whether power could pass thus, either to or from him.

This not serving the turn, then there was contrived an Instrument of Government, with our General at the head of it. This was first delivered to him in Westminster Hall. The Judges, most that were in town, and the Mayor and Aldermen of the City of London, were summoned, few knowing what it was for. There was an oath in this Instrument, which he took; and after that took upon him the name of Protector.

After that, a Parliament was called to confirm this. I was chosen one of those that the people sent up. Something was put in the writ, concerning our owning of this government in that Parliament; but, come hither, some gentlemen were pleased to say, being in the dark. I remember one learned gentleman, very well read in Scripture, said openly, that "other foundation than that could no man lay," (the latter words left out). Others said that the Parliament and Protector were twins, but the Parliament was the elder brother.

I then said no one Parliament could limit or impose upon me in any other. This doctrine was not well liked by the Protector. We were all turned out. Such a thing as never was done! An oath was made without doors, to be taken by us, and was set at the door. Those that would take it came in. Those that would not, were kept out by pikes. Knowing the privilege, that no power without doors could make an oath, I went away, and divers more gentlemen.

Those gentlemen that did sit, after five months were raised without giving any confirmation. It needed not, if other foundation could no man lay. They did nothing.

Then came the last Parliament, in 1656. I was again chosen, but not for any particular place; but for the whole county. When we came I found pikes again; one set to my breast. I could not pass without a ticket from the Council. I found in the hall above fifty of us. We joined in a letter to the Speaker; declaring our willingness to serve, and that we were kept out. After two or three days attendance we were sent to the Council for a ticket. I durst do no such thing. I had lifted up my hands to God for the privilege of Parliament. I could not do it. Two hundred were kept out. Upon this, divers that had been admitted left the House.

Then the government fell dangerously sick, and it died. Another foundation was laid; a Petition and Advice; and this must be the law and the foundation of all! And these must be the fruits, all we must enjoy, after the spilling of so much blood and so much treasure! Pardon me, if I thus make bare my mind to you.

This was a forced Parliament, because some of us were forced out; an imperfect Parliament, a lame Parliament, so much dismembered. We are here the freest, and clearest, and most undoubted representatives that ever were since the desolation of the three estates, King, Lords, and Commons. I know not one member kept out: if I did, I would on my knees beg his admittance. I hope God will direct us how to get out of this great darkness, as the minister told us that we have been in since this great desolation. What was done in the last Parliament is not a sufficient foundation to bring peace and settlement to this nation. The people of England were never more knowing and sensible of their privileges and liberties, nor better prepared to have a settlement from this free representative. We can do here whatsoever is for the good of the people. We have power over their purses and persons; can take away whole laws, or part of them, or make new ones. I will tell you what we cannot do. We cannot set up any power equal to the people; either in one person, or another House. We are trusted with no such power.

God is the King of this great island, as Mr. Calamy told us. I hope he is King of our hearts. God has done this work. King, Lords, and Commons: it was not in our thoughts at first. Let not us set up what God has pulled down; not plant what God has rooted up, lest we be said to build against God.

We see what a confusion we are in. We have not prospered. Our army at Jamaica prospered not. The trade and glory of the nation are much diminished. The council have been exceedingly bewildered. The government you see twice set up, presently pulled down. The strange oppression by making Acts of Parliament without a Parliament; raising monies; denying *habeas corpus*; sending learned long robe gentlemen to the Tower, for asserting *Magna Charta*, such as all the Kings of England never did; all this because we knew not the good mind of God. We were in darkness. It is God's mercy that we are here to declare ourselves in this place.

I shall now come to speak to the bill, whether to be committed or not. [The bill under consideration called for recognition of Richard Cromwell as Lord Protector. See below.] I confess, I do love the person of the Lord Protector. I never saw nor heard either fraud or guile in him. I wish only continuance of wealth, health, and safety to his family. I wish the greatest of honour and wealth of any man in this nation to him and his posterity; but this bill to recognize is a hard word. I never heard of such a bill but in King James's case; which was to declare him of the undoubted line to the crown, and so having a right to succeed. We must here take for granted the government, the Petition and Advice, which was not done in a free Parliament. It may be skinned over for a time, but will break out. The people are not pleased. What foundation soever is built, let it rise from us that are the clear representatives. For the authority itself, it appears by that Petition that the Protectorate was for his life; but it appears not how he appointed his successor; we must not take that upon trust, but be fully satisfied. I would not have this committed at present; but let it lie here. Never begin with the person first, but agree what trust he shall have. I forget not the great cause of our mischiefs, the influence of the kings over the judges. To make the King judge of necessity; that

> cut all our purses, that brought all our evil upon us. I would have us seriously advise and consider what we may do, as the people's representatives. The way of wisdom is everlasting peace. There is no danger to the nation, so long as this representative sits here. They are the supreme power. The way to prevent fire is to do our duties. We shall be preserved from the fire of hell and the fire of men. Let us let this rest, and consider of foundation stones. If a single person be thought best, to be accountable to the people for mal-administration, I shall submit to the majority.

As noted earlier, some of the published documents of AH are in the form of records of one or another parliament, either as these records exist in the *Journal of the House of Commons* or in a diary—in the present case, the diary of Thomas Burton. The foregoing speech was delivered on the floor of Commons on Monday, 7 February 1658/9, as recorded in Burton's Diary.[49] Footnotes by editors of printed editions, here removed, generally offer cross-references and correspondences from other sources. For instance, the first footnote comes at the end of his first sentence. It reads:

> The bill being read, Sir Arthur Haslerigge, moving himself upon his seat, was called up, as if he had an intention to speak, which it seems he had not, but being called up, and seeing so great a silence, not wondering at it, it being so great a work, and prefacing something of weakness then upon him, yet hoping that if he had anything to deliver, that God would enable him, he began a very long harangue. Goddard MS. p. 124.

This was presumably from the *Journal* of Guibon Goddard, an MP for Castle Rising, Norfolk.

The bill to which AH was referring, entitled "An Act of Recognition of his Highness's right, and title to be Protector and Chief Magistrate of the Commonwealth of England, Scotland, and Ireland, and the dominions and

---

[49]*Diary of Thomas Burton Esq: Volume 3, January - March 1659*, edited by John Towill Rutt (London, 1828), pp. 85-118.

territories thereunto belonging," had just been given its second reading, following which there was a long silence. That bill began:

> "Whereas his Highness, immediately after the death of his Highness's late father, became the lawful successor to succeed to the government of, &c. to the great joy of the people, testified by their general consent and approbation; and that God had invested him with power and authority, and that his Highness hath taken the government upon him. And although this be ample satisfaction, &c yet we, the two Houses of Parliament, do think it our duty to recognize and acknowledge, and pray that it be enacted and declared, that his Highness is the lawful Chief Magistrate and Protector, &c.; and that all the people be commanded to obey him accordingly." *Ibid.* pp. 123, 124. See the Act at large. "Thurloe State Papers," (1742) vii. 603, 604.

AH was, needless to say, opposed. The style of "princely courtesies," as it has been called, was still honoured, if sometimes between gritted teeth, or with a dash of sarcasm.

Sir Arthur's Last Thoughts?

It would not be too much to suppose that by summer of 1660, if not before, AH was struggling with demoralization. Christopher Hill, a prominent historian in recent times, summarized the situation with astute sensitivity when he said, "Those who had been the instruments of the omnipotent God in 1648-49 were now revealed as impotent mortals."[50] Was AH a "true believer"? Every indication says that he was. If there was any distance between his public declarations and his private thoughts about either religion or politics, a distance of skepticism or self-doubt, it remains hidden. His diary, assuming he maintained one, would have told glimmers, at least, had it survived. For those of us born with skepticism in our veins, the degree of self-certainty evinced by a true believer is at once puzzling and a call for skepticism. We more than they understand that a stitch in time is seldom more than a deferral of unraveling. Things change much more quickly now than during the seventeenth century. But however that may be, sympathy for those who suffer demoralization is not alien to us.

Writing in 1920, Farnham and Thompson observed that despite many vicissitudes, the Hazlerigg family "has continued to hold Noseley

---

[50] Christopher Hill, "God and the English Revolution," *History Workshop Journal*, volume 17 (Spring 1984), pages 19-31.

until the present time, and is thus numbered among the very few landed families now existing in Leicestershire which hold property held by their ancestors before 1500 in male descent."[51]   One can easily imagine Sir Arthur, ill in and confined to a cold damp room in the Tower, thinking that he had failed his family in that respect, that Noseley and other holdings would be lost for all time. Perhaps he harbored some hope that Monck's intercession would extend to some portion of the family's estate for benefit to son Thomas. But realism would probably have been trading far more in pessimism than any optimistic glimmer that Noseley could be saved.

In any case, it is clear in retrospect that Farnham and Thompson did not exaggerate when they remarked how unusual the family's good fortune in that regard even to the end of the second decade of the twentieth century. For all sorts of reasons, the odds of good fortune continued to be against the family long after AH's demise, and indeed increasingly against the likelihood of financial feasibility of maintaining a large landed estate as the travails of the twentieth century bore more and more heavily on Britain. In 1920, however, the fifty-year future of agrarian production could hardly be seen with the clarity that retrospection afforded in 1970, by which time it was evident that unless an old manorial estate could be added to the lists of tourism its future was bleak. But even as late as the 1970s in England, the idea of marketing Noseley Hall as one-time home of Sir Arthur Hesilrige, 2nd Bt—one of "The Five Members" of Commons, then one Cromwell's stalwart field generals, then opponent of the Lord Protector's dictatorial tendencies, and avid proponent of republicanism—had virtually no attraction to ardent fans of monarchy, the lodestone and linchpin of English tourism.

---

[51] George Farnham and A Hamilton Thompson, "The Manor of Noseley," *Transactions of the Leicestershire Archæological Society*, volume 12, part 2 (1921-22), pages 214-71, at page 229.

432

~ 9 ~
Recovery and Resumption

According to a famous truism, victors write the history. So it was after the restoration of monarchy. A prime example is Edward Hyde's *History of the Rebellion and Civil Wars*, a work cited on numerous occasions in preceding chapters. Hyde's work stands as one of the best of the post-restoration works of history, arguably the best of the early works in terms of quality of reporting. It had a point of view, of course, but it was open and reasonably well measured. Hyde's view of Sir Arthur Hesilrige's character was probably not so far from the truth as one might like, just as his final description of the 2nd Bt's political position was reasonably appreciative: "sir Arthur Haslerig ... was irreconcileable to monarchy, and looked upon as chief of that republican party, which desired not to preserve any face of government in the church, or uniformity in the public exercise of religion."[1]

Many other works were so atrociously, scandalously biased that they undercut their own credibility. An example is James Heath's *A Brief Chronicle of the late Intestine War in the three Kingdoms of England, Scotland, and Ireland*, first published in 1661. A claim by Heath of particular interest held that Thomas[12f] Hesilrige, the brother to Sir Arthur (previously discussed), had engaged in "suborning witnesses to vilify the King; and he evidently served the Parliament so faithfully as to secure honourable burial within Westminster Abbey, and thus rendered his memory so obnoxious that his remains were included amongst those disinterred after the Restoration, and thrown into a common pit in the Churchyard."[2] Neither Heath nor anyone else has shown evidence to support the charge of suborning witnesses (a legal charge that involves more than simply encouraging witnesses to go forward and tell the truth as they know it). Thomas[12f] indeed was buried in the abbey, 30 October 1651. Ten years later, on orders of Charles II, his remains, together with the remains of eighteen other supporters of the parliamentary cause, were removed from the abbey and reburied in an unmarked pit next door in the churchyard of St Margaret's church. A memorial plaque on the outside of

---

[1] Hyde, *History of the Rebellion and Civil Wars* (Oxford: Clarendon Press, 1826), volume 7, page 440. Hyde was there writing of events of 1660.

[2] The account is from Walter Money's *The First and Second Battles of Newbury*, 2nd edition (London: Simpkin, Marshall, and Co., 1884), page 257. See also Barry Denton, *Only in Heaven* (Sheffield: Sheffield Academic Press, 1997), page 159. Both Money and Denton repeat Heath's charge without question.

the wall to the left of the main west entrance of St Margaret's gives testimony. As for Heath, the entry for him in the *Dictionary of National Biography* (1885-1900, volume 25) says that he was "extremely biassed," his chronicle stating "hardly any facts on his own authority" but "mostly compiled from lying pamphlets and all sorts of news-books," containing "innumerable errors." Morrill has described Heath's tract on Cromwell as "scurrilous, mendacious, malicious."[3] Heath may have been hoping to gain income via the restored royal court's effort to rebrand and re-image the Stuart kingship. But he soon found that he lacked credibility in every quarter.[4]

Exhibit 9.1. Plaque at St Margaret's Church, Westminster

A second example of particular interest to this family's history is the repeated effort of John Musgrave to extract revenge against the 2nd Bt for the latter's unwillingness to approve compensation of Musgrave's claim of losses. A native of Cumberland, Musgrave asserted charges of corruption and/or misfeasance against various officials and landowners of the county. Each time his charges were dismissed for lack of evidence. It is difficult to discern much coherence of rationality in his tracts, but it appears that he believed that Sir Arthur, presumably in his capacity as governor of Newcastle, had been nominating inappropriate persons to serve as commissioners for the northern counties. Musgrave's entry in the *Dictionary of National Biography* (1885-1900; volume 39), which offers greater detail of the aforementioned (and other) instances of his behavior,

---

[3] John Morrill, "Rewriting Cromwell," *Canadian Journal of History*, volume 38 (2003), pages 553-578, at page 564.
[4] See, e.g., Kevin Sharpe, *Rebranding Rule* (New Haven: Yale University Press, 2013).

leaves one with an impression of derangement. In any case, later writers took him at face value. Benjamin Nightingale cited him and his pamphlets as authority against the 2nd Bt in particular, with regard to the sequestration of clerics in accordance to the parliamentary Act of March 1649/50 "for the better propagating of the Gospel in the four Northern Counties"—but as Nightingale apparently saw it, following Musgrave, all in order to further Sir Arthur's material gain.[5]

As we saw in chapter 8, there is abundant evidence that the 2nd Bt "invested heavily in lands of the bishopric of Durham." But there is none that he did so in Cumberland or Westmoreland. In fact, as Gentles found from his detailed study of the records, Sir Arthur, together with several other members of the military and/or parliaments during the years 1649 to 1660, did not acquire any of the crown's extensive lands after the death of Charles I.[6] With regard to the clerics of Cumberland (as was noted in the prior chapter), Sir Arthur did appoint Rowland Nichols in 1650 to the rectorship of Aikton (which included Gamelsby, Biglands, Burgh upon the Sands, and more), his predecessor having been ejected.[7] Conforming after 1660, Nichols served another 34 years, so he must have been both a young man in 1650 and satisfactory to his parishioners as well as to the ecclesiastical authority. A similar ejection and replacement under the 2nd Bt's authority occurred at about the same time in Graystock parish, Leeth Ward, Cumberland. In this case the ejected rector appealed to no avail until 1660, when he was returned to his position. This latter case is the only known instance in which the qualification of Sir Arthur's choice of replacement might have been questioned for legitimate reasons other than the obvious one of conformity versus nonconformity (which mattered in the opposite direction in 1660), and there is no direct evidence of other grounds.

The foregoing claims and charges have been cited merely as a few examples of the continuing efforts to vanquish the memory of Sir Arthur,

---

[5] *The Ejected of 1662 in Cumberland and Westmoreland*, 2 volumes (Manchester: Manchester University Press, 1911), volume 1, pages 83-84, 601-02, 616-17, 627-30; volume 2, pages 825-26.

[6] Ian Gentles, *The Debentures Market and Military Purchases of Crown Land, 1649-1660* (Unpublished PhD dissertation, University of London, 1969). The quotation is of page 171. See also his "The Sales of Crown Lands during the English Revolution," *Economic History Review*, 2nd series, volume 20 (1973), pages 614-635.

[7] William Hutchison, *The History and Antiquities of Cumberland*, 2 volumes (Carlisle: F. Jollie, 1794), volume 2, page 481; Joseph Nicholson and Richard Burn, *The History and Antiquities of the Counties of Westmoreland and Cumberland*, 2 volumes (London: W Strahan and T Cadel, 1777), volume 2, page 201.

and by extension his family, long after his death. They provide glimpses of some of the obstacles that his survivors faced, as they sought to get on with their lives and recover the family's fortunes to the extent possible. It is that recovery and the resumptions that successful recoveries made possible that are the chief topic of this chapter. Our temporal framework will be slightly longer than a century—that is, to approximately 1770—a period that will take us through the lives of the first five of Sir Arthur's successors to the baronetcy. This means that, in view of the repetition of forenames, now especially "Arthur," the use of superscripting will be resumed. The same period will take us through the so-called Glorious Revolution of 1688—which can be seen as a partial vindication of the 2nd Bt's efforts for republicanism—and through the reigns of seven monarchs (counting William III separately, since he reigned alone after Mary's death in 1694) and into the early years of an eighth, George III, who was third of a new monarchal house, the House of Hanover (later renamed as Windsor). The century was also a time of expansion and consolidation of the British Empire, including the first major war of independence against it; some very early glimmers of what would become the industrial revolution; and, in 1752, the kingdom's switch from the Julian to the Gregorian calendar.

While the reforms and accommodations made during 1688 set England on the road to a more stable parliamentary form of monarchism, corresponding settlements of basic issues of religion were not achieved. The official church remained as a bulwark of division, casting "dissenter" and "non-conformist" to the outside, until eventually congregations of the latter came to be known as "the people's churches" in distinction from "the state's church."[8] Royal court and established church alike maintained an attitude of suspicion, continually looking for people who in their view posed threats to public security—which is to say, security of and by the court and church. During the 1670s and 1680s search parties, often led by Anglican clerics, went in search of dissenters, so as to root them out.[9]

Even so, major changes were underway in, as well as at the borders of, religious thought. While dozens of English men and women had been sailing to the Netherlands in search of religious liberty, many of them then crossing the Atlantic, the two countries nonetheless formed a "familiar pair

---

[8] Alison Light, *Common People: The History of an English Family* (London: Penguin, 2014), *passim*.

[9] Neil A Paterson, *Politics in Leicestershire, c1677 to c1716* (Unpublished doctoral thesis, University of Nottingham, December 2007), pages 164-67; Geoffrey Holmes, *Politics, Religion and Society in England, 1679-1742* (London: Hambledon, 1986).

of twins," as a recent historian of the Reformation put it,[10] not only in commercial ventures—both seafaring nations with far-flung colonies—but also in adjustments of religious tradition. Thomas Hobbes was cautiously circumspect when, while broaching the argument that the notion of a God lacking material substance lacked credibility, his sentences easily accommodated the suggestion that Christian doctrine should be viewed skeptically. Across the water in Amsterdam, Baruch Spinoza more boldly doused the fires of Christian Hell and rejected the idea that God cared to intervene in human concerns and hopes. If some readers yet today think these outrageous assaults, imagine the impact felt during the middle or late 1600s. Spinoza's publication in 1670, the *Tractatus Theologico-Politicas*, was banned four years after the ink had dried, for, among other infractions, declaring that the Bible was anything but infallible and should be approached critically as one would any other product of literary output. John Milton had already raised similar doubts in England, though not quite so forcefully and with the added protection that he could be dismissed as a crank, unsound in the head. But already in 1656 there appeared in English translation a work, *Præ-Adamitæ* ("Men before Adam"), written by a French Huguenot, Isaac La Peyrère, living in Amsterdam, who espoused a staunchly millenarian version of Calvinism. Arguing from a logical reading of Old Testament texts, La Peyrère concluded that there must have been human beings, Gentiles, living before Adam, progenitor of the ancient Hebrew people.[11] The institutional conflicts that had regulated the official church's boundaries in England were being supplanted by revisionary readings of received doctrines of religious dogma.

    The principal interests of the present chapter are in the efforts of the Hesilrige family to recover patrimony and standing, after 1660, and then to resume progress in building still greater stability of resource and future value. Residual effects of events of the 1640s and 1650s remained handicaps for some time to come. In addition, however, what might be called the terms of engagement were changing at a more rapid pace, as the economy of the nation shifted increasingly to a mercantilism based far less on land, and far more on trade of commodities and finished goods in a new kind of "world market." The term "globalization" had not yet been coined, but much of the globe was indeed being yoked into a European network of relations of economic power, with efforts of political power in the form of differing versions of colonial governance close behind.

---

[10] Diarmaid MacCulloch, *The Reformation* (New York: Viking, 2003), page 672.
[11] See, e.g., Richard H Popkin, *Isaac La Peyrère (1596-1676): His Life, Works, and Influence* (Leiden: Brill, 1987).

Before turning to the efforts of familial recovery, it will be useful to insert another segment of lineage.

A Segment of Lineage, c1660 to c1770
Five men of the main lineage are primary focal points in this chapter: Sir Thomas[13a], the 3rd Bt, and his son, Sir Thomas[14a], the 4th Bt, followed by Sir Robert[13b], the 5th Bt, and his son, Sir Robert[14a], the 6th Bt, then the latter man's son, Arthur[15a], the 7th Bt.

Recall that Thomas[13a] and Robert[13b] were half-brothers, both of them sons of the 2nd Bt. Rather than reproduce the lineage segment that includes all of the 2nd Bt's children (which can be seen in chapter 6), the present segment begins with the two half-brothers. This trimming results from the fact that the two half-brothers were the only sons of the 2nd Bt to sire offspring, together with the fact that offspring of Hesilrige daughters are seldom traced beyond their own children, if that. It is perhaps useful to remind the reader also that Hesilrige men who are not in the main (or titled) line tend to disappear from records rather quickly. Thus, the lineage shown in chapter 6, to use it as example, includes at least some offspring of the 2nd Bt's brothers John[12e] and Thomas[12f] (but none for brother William[12h], for whom we lack vital dates and marriage information, though we know he was living as late as 1658), but effort to track the offspring of all the daughters and sons was generally unproductive or, in a few instances, so productive as to bend the principal intent of this account.

Thomas[13a] Hesilrige, 3rd Bt.: b. c1625, d. 24 February1679/80; m. c1660 Elizabeth (b. <1640, d. 30 May 1673), elder daughter and coheir of George Fenwick of Brunton Hall, Northumberland, and Alice Boteler (*nee* Apsley)

    L-- **Thomas**[14a] Hesilrige, 4th Bt.: b. 1664, d. 11 July1700 Noseley; never married, died without issue

    L-- Arabella[14b] Hesilrige: b. c1660, d. <1716; m. 11 July 1682 Rawson Hart, esq., of Grantham, Lincolnshire (his will dated 24 May 1716); issue: Mary Hart (b. c1695)

    L-- Mary[14c] Hesilrige: b. >1660, d. <1699; m.(1) (?) Arthur[13d] Hesilrige (son of John[12e] of Alderton), m.(2) Sir Samuel Rolle, knight, Heanton, Devon

∟-- Diane[14d] Hesilrige: b >1661, d. <June 1673
∟-- Elizabeth[14e] Hesilrige: b.>1664, d. <June 1673

∟-- Dorothy[14f] Hesilrige: b<June 1663, d. >1735; m. c1690 Robert Shafto, esq. (b. April 1634, d. 1714) of Benwell Tower, Northumberland; issue: Robert (b. >1690, d. 3 November 1735), Dorothy (d. >October 1735); more below

Robert[13d] Hesilrige of Ilveston (i.e., Illston), 5th Bt: b. Jul 1639 Noseley, d. 22 May 1713; m. 3 May 1664 St Mary's, Islington, Middlesex, Bridget (b. 1642, d. 26 July 1697), daughter of Sir Samuel Rolle, knight, Heanton, Devon; more below

∟-- **Robert**[14a] Hesilrige, 6th Bt: b. <June 1666 Noseley, d. 19 May 1721; m. 29 July 1696 Easton, Essex, Dorothy (b. c1670, d. 11 September 1748 Noseley), daughter of Banastre Maynard and Elizabeth Grey; more below

∟-- **Arthur**[15a] Hesilrige, 7th Bt: b. 28 March 1704 Noseley, d. 23 March 1763 Northampton; m. June 1725 St Peter's church, Northampton, Hannah (b. 1708/9, d. 17 February 1765/6) daughter of Robert and Mary Sturges; more below and in chapter 10

∟-- 16 children (see lineage in chapter 10)

∟-- Dorothy[15b] Hesilrige: b. 1 Dec 1700, d. >1725; m. William Battell, a clergyman of Hertfordshire; both living in Bath 1725

∟-- Samuel[14b] Hesilrige: b. 25 November 1667 Northampton, d. 8 July 1689

∟-- Arthur[14c] Hesilrige: b. 19 April 1669 Northampton
∟-- Mary[14d] Hesilrige: b. >1664, d. <1713

∟-- Bridget[14e] Hesilrige: b. 16 February 1670/1, d. 18 February 1670/1 Noseley

∟-- Bridget[14f] Hesilrige: b. 10 July 1673, d. 10 June 1720
∟-- Frances[14g] Hesilrige: b. 6 August 1674 Noseley

L-- William[14h] Hesilrige: b. 12 August 1675 Noseley, d. >1702; commissioned as captain-lieutenant in Queen's 2nd Regiment of Foot, renewed by Queen Anne 25 June 1702

Initial Consequences and Recoveries
With the death of Sir Arthur[12b] Hesilrige in January 1660/1, the most vulnerable member of the family was son and heir, Thomas[13a], then in his mid-thirties. His vulnerability stemmed not only from parentage but also from the fact that he had served as a captain in the parliamentary army. He was taken prisoner at Daventry in 1660, but release came quickly, as a result of intercession by the duke of Albemarle, George Monck. As titles and seat were reaffirmed, Thomas[13a] returned to gentry life at Noseley, along with wife Elizabeth, coheir of George Fenwick and his wife Alice —a woman who would be remembered in New England centuries later as "Lady Alice Apsley Boteler, widow of Lord John Boteler and daughter of Sir Edward Apsley of Sussex, [who had] married Mr George Fenwick just before he embarked for America," accompanying him to a colony in Connecticut.[12] This was indeed the same George Fenwick, nearly exact contemporary of Sir Arthur[12b] Hesilrige, who had migrated during the late 1630s to Saybrook colony.

Thomas[13a] and Elizabeth had six children at Noseley. Thomas[14a], who succeeded to the baronetcy in 1680 as 4th Bt, died unmarried and without issue during the last year of the century. Arabella[14b], the first-born, married Rawson Hart, by whom she birthed additional lineages of the Hart and the Boddam families. Hart's will, dated 24 May 1716, attested that Thomas[14a] had given to "my late wife Arabella" some interest in the Noseley estate toward her marriage settlement with Hart.

The case of Thomas[13a] and Elizabeth's daughter Mary[14c] was discussed in chapter 6, immediately after the presentation of that lineage segment, because of a curious claim in some records, and nothing more can be added here. Two daughters, Diane[14d] and Elizabeth[14e], are known only as names. Lastly, daughter Dorothy[14f], the youngest child, married Robert Shafto (aka Shaftoe) of Benwell Tower, Northumberland, who, like his ancestors, became high sheriff of the shire. Recall from chapter 4 that the Swarland branch of the Hesilrige family was still active and prospering in Northumberland. For instance, on 14 November 1697 Jane Hazlerig, probably daughter of Robert, was baptized in Felton church, where also she married George Robinson 29 January 1717/8. Thus, in addition to the

---

[12] Thomas Goddard Wright, *Literary Culture in Early New England, 1620-1730* (New Haven: Yale University Press, 1920), page 76.

Fenwick connection, Dorothy[14f] would have had familial support from her father's side as well.

We will return to Thomas[13a] and his children later. For the moment, let's back up to his siblings. Of the dozen children of Sir Arthur[12b] and his two wives, five either were never named or have been forgotten by forename. Three of these five were children by first wife, Frances (one son and two daughters). Of the surviving seven, one we know never married because of death at age 12. This was third son Arthur[13c], a lad whom we met in the previous chapter: he was remembered as of "rare endowments and incomparable learning for his age, both in Hebrew, Greek, Latin and French; of singular wit and judgment; of sweet nature and very pious" (the inscription on his monument in Noseley chapel). The six others all married at least once; four of these were daughters, and we know the names of their husbands. At least three of these marriages occurred after 1660, and given probable birth years it is likely that these were first marriages.

The point of that inventory has to do with a question of possible repercussions on family members, daughters especially, during the years immediately following royal restoration. Given the notoriety of the head of the family, Sir Arthur[12b], one can easily imagine that subsequent affairs of the family would have been adversely shadowed, and one of the most vulnerable arenas would have been arrangements of marriage. Sons in the titular line would have benefited from that fact and its landed wealth. But daughters could not bring title to a marriage; and while Noseley, the home manor, had been restored to the family, other parts of the estate had not been restored; and, as we will see below, recovery through purchases had high priority on liquid assets. We have probably seen in the case of Arabella[14b] one effect of that conjunction of circumstances. In order to gain closure on settlement with the Hart family, her brother Thomas[14a] offered a share of the home manor itself as Arabella's[14b] dowry.

Were Hesilrige daughters shunned because of their forebear in the prior or next prior generation? Ultimately that question must remain open for the obvious reason that evidence of motivations is absent. Even the weaker sort of evidence that might be assembled, comparisons over time of the number of daughters who never married, lacks clarity because in many cases of daughters known to have died unmarried, date of death is absent. As mentioned above, two of Sir Arthur's[12b] granddaughters by Thomas[13a] are known only as names, probably because they never married, but perhaps also because they died young. As we saw in the lineage segment in chapter 6 (and repeated below), Sir Arthur[12b] had four more granddaughters by his son Robert Hesilrige[13d] of Ilveston (i.e., Illston), who succeeded to the baronetcy in 1700. He and his wife Bridget, daughter of Sir Samuel Rolle, knight, of Heanton, Devon, by his second wife, Margaret, daughter of Sir Thomas Wise of Sydenham, Devon, were determined to have a daughter named Bridget. After the first one died at young age, they named a second daughter Bridget, and she survived to marriage. The two other girls died unmarried within their father's lifetime. Since he died in 1713 and his marriage to Bridget Rolle occurred in May of 1664, we are left in somewhat ambivalent territory; but at least one of the two girls, and probably both, would surely have counted as "spinster," or well beyond expected age at marriage, when they died.

Exhibit 9.2. Memorial to Catherine ("Kate") Hesilrige Babington

Another sort of penalty has been documented, but this one came as a consequence of a Hesilrige daughter's choice in good conscience. Sir Arthur's[12b] first child by Dorothea Greville was Catherine[13b], whom we have already met. After her first husband, George Fenwick, died (15 March 1657) she married Philip Babington (b. c1632), first son of William Babington of Ogle castle, Northumberland. Just as George Fenwick had been a member of parliament during the civil wars and then governor of Berwick-on-Tweed, so Philip served Berwick-on-Tweed as governor and as member of parliament; but not during the reign of either Charles II or his brother, James II, rather during the first year of the reign of William and Mary.

At the local level remnants of the code of chivalry prevailed, enabling Philip and Catherine[13b] to live a reasonably good life in the Babington family's Harnham Hall, a small Northumberland estate that remained in the Babington family until 1677. But when Catherine[13b] died she could not be buried in the local parish churchyard—as Mr Forster, the vicar of Bolam explained—because she had been excommunicated from the church of England as a Dissenter.[13] She was thus buried in a sepulcher that Philip had hewn from a stone cliff in a garden at Harnham Hall. Philip inscribed the stone with this: "Here lyeth the Body of Madame Babington, who was laid in this sepulcher on the 9th September 1670." Catherine[13b], known far and wide as "Kate," had penned a quatrain for the occasion, and Philip added it to the stone (as can be seen in Exhibit 9.1):

> My time is past, as you may see,
> I viewed the dead as you do me.
> Or long you'll be as low as I,
> And some will look on thee.

Kate's reputation as a feisty Dissenter (apparently for exquisite physical beauty as well) has remained alive in the area to this day.[14]

Nonetheless, Catherine[13b] did remarry, and quite well, even if it was far north of London. By the same token, her three younger sisters, Dorothy[13e], Frances[13f], and Mary[13g], also married well, all in southern England, and at least two of them after 1661. In sum, the record of marriages, while mixed, shows no clear pattern of resistance to young Hesilrige women during the first decade or two after the 2nd Bt's death.

No doubt motives of "settling scores" did persist for some time, however. They typically found outlets in mixtures of other motivations, some of them deceits spun out for purposed advantage but others worried diversions from the threat of entrapment in memories. An example of the latter was told by Samuel Pepys in his diary entry of 1 November 1660. He had dined with a group of men who included

---

[13] Catherine's[13b] first husband, recall, was son of George Fenwick of Brinkburn, Northumberland, and Dorothy, daughter of John Forster. Was this the same Forster family?

[14] John Gough Nichols, *The Topographer and Genealogist*, 2 volumes (London: John Bowyer Nichols and Son, 1846), volume 1, pages 277-278; John Hodgson, *A History of Northumberland in Three Parts*, part 2, volume 1 (Newcastle upon Tyne: Edw, Walker, 1827), pages 347-347. The Babington estate and Kate's burial site were recalled in a brochure published by the Northumberland County Council, 2002. A marked footpath includes Harnham Hall.

my old school-fellow, with whom I had much talk. He did remember that I was a great Roundhead when I was a boy, and I was much afraid that he would have remembered the words that I said the day the King was beheaded (that, were I to preach upon him, my text should be "The memory of the wicked shall rot"); but I found afterward that he did go away from school before that time.

As an editor of Pepys' diary reminded, "Pepys might well be anxious on this point, for in October of this year Phieas Pett, assistant master shipwright at Chatham, was dismissed from his post for having when a child spoken disrespectfully of the King." Pepys knew that very case, for he was employed as clerk for the Navy Board, and on the 23rd of August he had noted the then impending inquiry into Pett's past.

Traffic in rumor and innuendo has always flowed along byways of social discourse, offering repast to those who hunger for advantage by any means available. What one does not hear exactly can be nevertheless "clarified" through a bit of cultivation here or there, leaving incriminating evidence about the innocent by the vulnerable, or vice versa. Sometimes the alleged evidence needs no tailoring as it is passed on; yet it becomes ambiguous or even nonsensical simply because of the circumstances of its passage. A possible case in point involves an alleged witnessing of overheard conversation centered, for purposes of the witness, on a man named "Thomas Haslerig, kinsman of the late Sir Arthur." According to this piece of "testimony," a man named "Simon Maine, son to Maine one of the late King's judges, and Thomas Haslerig, kinsman of the late Sir Arthur, and Dr Harrington, brother of the late Sir James Harrington," had been overheard in what they thought was private conversation, Thomas Haslerig saying, "(and has often suggested the same to me) that the old King deserved his death for entertaining private conferences with priests and Jesuits and that this King [the present Charles II] exactly followed his father's steps and would assuredly receive his fate."[15] No report of consequences has been found, nor do we know the certain identity of the kinsman "Thomas Haslerig." Assuming such conversation actually took place as reported, the man in question would not have been the son and heir of Arthur[12b] Hesilrige—unless the conversation occurred at least three years before the report in 1683—for Thomas[13a] died in February 1679/80. The overheard man could have been either of two nephews of the 2nd Bt,

---

[15] *Calendar of States Papers, Domestic Series: Charles II (1683)*, page 42.

sons of brother John[12e] and brother Thomas[12f] (the latter's son was born in 1646, while of the former the best we can say is that he was born after 1628). A third possibility, from the standpoint of dates probably the likeliest, is Arthur's[12b] grandson, Thomas[14a], born in 1664. The point is, the alleged conversation might well have occurred; Samuel Pepys was hardly the only boy or young man to have uttered words in public that left him vulnerable on a later day. But then again, of course, the whole episode could have been concocted by the supposed eyewitness. For all we know, one of the court's informants overheard nothing more than the swagger of a tippling braggart grousing with his companions. Even so, the report could have entailed substantial danger to one or another man named "Thomas Haslerig."

The 2nd Bt's eldest son and heir, Thomas[13a], began re-assembling the family estates soon after 1661, as testified by many documents in the Hazlerigg Collection, as well as in other depositories.[16] These efforts of recovery continued well into the 1700s. The process involved various means, including leasings, purchase agreements, and mortgages designed to gain capital liquidity. Purchases ranged from parcels of land to pieces of furniture. Examples of the latter occurred 30 December 1669, when Robert[13d] Hesilrige of Northampton bought items from John Haslewood of London which Haslewood had been granted by Charles II, and on the first day of January following, when Thomas[13a] made similar purchases from Haslewood (DG21/187 & 188). An example of mortgaging, this one involving timber and land, occurred 10 July 1674 by Thomas[13a], the 3rd Bt, in order to increase his income stream. But mortgages could also consume capital, sometimes unexpectedly, as when a mortgage that had been made by the 2nd Bt was presented to his grandson Thomas[14a], 4th Bt, on 23 May 1685. Thomas[14a] settled the debt by payment of £1600. As for leasing, there were several large arrangements, one of them by the 2nd Bt's second eldest surviving son, Robert[13d], who had controlling interests in several properties in Northumberland (the manors of Fawdon, East and West Brunton, Weetslade, etc.) and in an agreement dated 8 June 1664 let them to others for one-year terms (DG21/86). Such actions in aid of recovery continued for some time.

Sales were also arranged among family members, typically across generations, sometimes as a means of minimizing risks or of increasing

---

[16] Relevant documents in the Hazlerigg Collection begin with DG21/85 and follow from there, though somewhat intermittently. Rather than consider each one individually, they will be summarized in their general patterns.

surety of succession. On 21 May 1696, Thomas[14a] Hesilrige, 4th Bt, who, though in only his 32nd or 33rd year of life, may have been experiencing intimations of death, signed an agreement with his uncle Robert[13d], who would succeed him, and with his uncle's son and heir, Robert[14a], selling to the latter men his estate interests, including Noseley, in return for £8500, but with full rights of continued use of the manor of Noseley during his lifetime and with rights of inheritance in tail male, then rights of inheritance to Robert[13d] and his heirs in tail male. (DG21/99, 106-07, 111). Thomas[14a] was dead a little more than four years later. Robert[13d] became the 5th Bt.

During the long process of recovering estates, other obligations on the family patrimony had to be covered, of course. One obligation was noted above, the mortgage that the 2nd Bt had made more than a quarter-century before it was presented to his grandson for settlement. Another instance was a marriage settlement, this one for the marriage between Robert[14a] and the second daughter, Dorothy, of Banastre, baron Maynard, of Easton, Essex, and his wife, Elizabeth Grey, dated 9 June 1698 (DG21/108).[17] Banastre succeeded as 3rd baron Maynard in 1699. (We will encounter the Maynard family repeatedly in this and in the next chapter.)

Still another example of the need to meet other familial obligations while trying to regain the patrimony took place on 25 April 1672. Recall from chapter 5 that Thomas[11c] Hesilrige, almost certainly a son of Edward[10b] Hesilrige (but exact documentation has not been found; see the lineage segment of chapter 5), wed Sarah Dixon in 1633 at St Andrews in Holborn, London. Thomas[11c] and Sarah had at least five children, the last two, Donald[12d] and Thomas[12e], shortly before their father died (the youngest might have been born posthumously) and not long before their mother died. Sir Arthur[12b], the 2nd Bt, became guardian of the youngsters, having arranged an interest in some Durham properties for their mother Sarah. On that April day of 1672, Thomas[12e] Hesilrige of St Andrew, Holborn, gentleman, acting on his own behalf as son, heir, and administrator of the estate of his deceased father, Thomas[11c], and as heir and administrator of the estate of his deceased brother, Donald[12d], asked the 2nd Bt's surviving sons, Thomas[13a] and Robert[13d], to settle an account due from their remaining interests in rents and profits from land and

---

[17] Joseph Lemuel Chester, *London Marriage Licences, 1521-1869*, edited by Joseph Foster (London: Bernard Quaritch, 1887), page 672.

tenements in the Bishopric of Durham and in Gedney, Lincolnshire. This was done, by payment of £1616 in addition to a prior payment of £100.[18]

The record for Thomas[13a], 3rd Bt, and his household with wife Elizabeth (*nee* Fenwick) is rather sparse, but what there is of it suggests that he and Elizabeth were not wholly confident that they would be able to regain and keep full possession of the manor of Noseley, or of other properties of the family in Leicestershire. It appears that they increased their presence in the areas of Northumberland that had been harbor to the family in earlier times. Part of this was probably due to Elizabeth's parental family, and part of it stemmed from the fact that Thomas[13a] had once been lord of the manor of Cornforth, and held related properties, about 30 miles across the Tyne in Durham. But there is also evidence to indicate that Thomas[13a] was concerned to demonstrate cooperation and accommodation toward other Northumberland families. As an example, recall that his father had fought furiously with the Collingwood family for possession of the Eslington manor. Thomas[13a] issued a deed dated 15 July 1663 in which he released his inherited claim to Eslington.[19]

All of the foregoing serves also as context for the fact (mentioned earlier) that Thomas[13a] and Elizabeth's youngest of five daughters, Dorothy[14f], married c1690 Robert Shafto, esq., of Benwell Tower (which was then a few miles west of Newcastle; today, within the city). Dorothy[14f] surely did not remember her mother, Elizabeth, who died 30 May 1673, leaving (as the memorial inscription for her in Noseley chapel says) "one son, three daughters, and a most sorrowful husband." (She was further described as "a woman of singular piety, great prudence, rare for charity, an incomparable mother, and a most admirable wife: ... in a word, she was the Phoenix of her sex.") So far as we know, Thomas[13a], then in his late 40s, did not remarry. Two daughters, Diane[14d] and Elizabeth[14e], had died before their mother,[20] but that left son and heir Thomas[14a], then nine, and daughters Arabella[14b], about 13 years old, Mary[14c], about 11, as well as Dorothy[14f], perhaps an infant. Who cared for them? Perhaps at least Dorothy[14f], the youngest, was left in the care of a Fenwick aunt. That

---

[18] This document, DG21/189 of the Hazlerigg Collection, confirms the relationships among siblings as well as to their parents. It is, not surprisingly, silent as to parentage of Thomas[11c], so the conjectured descent from Edward[10b] must remain conjecture.

[19] John Crawford Hodgson, "On the Medieval and Later Owners of Eslington," *Archæologia Æliana*, 3rd series, volume 6 (Newcastle-upon-Tyne: Andrew Reid & Co., 1910), pages 1-33, at page 23.

[20] One of the two lived long enough to be remembered by friends and future kin; the other, not. This seems the indication from the fact that a published lineage of the Shafto family cites Dorothy[14f] as youngest of four, not five, daughters.

would certainly have increased the likelihood of continuing contact with the Shafto family.[21] But otherwise, one may conjecture, the considerable responsibility of caring for the younger children might have fallen to the oldest daughter, Arabella[14b]. There is no firm evidence to support that conjecture, but it offers a plausible explanation for the fact that Thomas[13a] singled out Arabella[14b] to whom he bequeathed a substantial portion of his estate—excluding, of course, the entailed part, which went to Thomas[14a]. It is also likely that the bequest was at least partly for marriage settlement between Arabella and Rawson Hart, a marriage which occurred 11 July 1682, son after death of her father.[22] Also, however, as will become plain below, there is reason to wonder if Thomas[13a] at times felt overburdened.

As 3rd Bt, Thomas[13a] was remembered as "a man of excellent parts, great learning, and very hospitable." Note that this phrase, "a man of many parts," was a very popular encomium during the seventeenth and eighteenth centuries in England. It was generally intended as signifying a person of many talents, someone talented in many areas of life; and that was usually intended as a compliment. But the meaning could also be turned, and sometimes was, to imply that such a person was, or was capable of being, treacherous, deceptive. This was part and parcel of the notion that "a simple man" was honorable and above board, and that complexity could be dangerous.

For all we know, however, Thomas[13a] had indeed been appreciated as honorable and multi-talented. He had been dealt a difficult hand, and from all accounts, thin though they are, it appears that he had played it well. His times were difficult partly because of his inheritance—memories of his service in the army of rebellion, the gains of land from the bishopric of Durham, and of course most of all the fact that he was son of that much-pilloried Sir Arthur Hesilrige. His times were also difficult in ways that affected a great many people, those who inhabited London and vicinity especially. These difficulties may have lessened some of his burden by inheritance, strangely enough; for they consumed great quantities of attention, grief, and fear during the mid-1660s. First came the Great Plague outbreak of 1664-66; then (foreshortening the plague, some have speculated) the Great Fire, September 1666.

---

[21]Ties between families dated from at least the early 1650s. Recall that in 1651-52 and probably some years thereafter William Shafto, high sheriff of Newcastle, and cousin of the branch residing nearby at Benwell Tower, had served with the 2nd Bt on committees for Northumberland and Durham. Note, too, that Dorothy's[14f] husband, Robert Shafto, was high sheriff of Northumberland in 1696, as his father Robert had been, as his son Robert would be.

[22] Chester, *London Marriage Licences* (1887), page 638.

Outbreaks of the plague had been intermittent since the devastation in 1347, but the mortality rates had generally been relatively small in scale and periods between outbreaks sometimes long. According to published Bills of Mortality, London witnessed 30,000 deaths in the 1603 episode; 35,000 in 1625; and 10,000 in 1636. Estimates of the plague's toll of death from late 1664 to late summer of 1666 have been varied, of course, a main reason for the variation being uneven detection and reporting. In those areas of London in which records appear to have been maintained regularly and then preserved, plague deaths accounted for a third to half of the total population. Most of the victims were poor. People who could afford to flee and had welcoming destinations did just that (as did the king, who took his court to Oxford). The areas of London just cited were probably atypical in that they tended to be the more densely populated central areas. Taking London as a whole, however, it is very likely that at least one-quarter of the population died from this, the last major outbreak.[23]

Just as new incidents of plague had rapidly declined, the Great Fire devastated the city—mostly the City of London proper—during the second through fifth days of September. There are no good estimates of fatalities, because in many areas the fire storm reached temperatures in excess of cremation, sufficient to mix human remains with remains of buildings to an extent that could not be separated by existing technology. Reports that human deaths were in single digits are simply preposterous. The fire began in a bakery east of the City proper—or so said contemporary reports—and winds swept the flames westward. When the firestorm jumped the Fleet River,[24] there was fear it would reach Whitehall, then Westminster. But winds subsided enough that contemporary techniques of "backburning," removal of fuel (buildings), and the like, finally stopped the spread.

One can see the area of destruction in the part of Wenceslaus Hollar's map of 1666 that is reproduced as Exhibit 9.3 on the next page. Note that the wall of the Tower kept the flames away, just as the old city wall to the north mostly stopped the spread.

---

[23] Reasons for this latter fact—that subsequent outbreaks of the plague were far less lethal and less frequent—are still debated. The fact that after the fire London rebuilt with wider streets and somewhat improved means of sewage disposal no doubt helped. See, e.g., A Lloyd Moote and Dorothy C Moote, *The Great Plague* (Baltimore: Johns Hopkins University Press, 2004).

[24] The Fleet River (later converted to a covered culvert) is the dark line (Exhibit 9.3) that runs into the urban area from the northwest, then curves southward and empties into the Thames. Whitehall and Westminster are well to the lower left of this field of view.

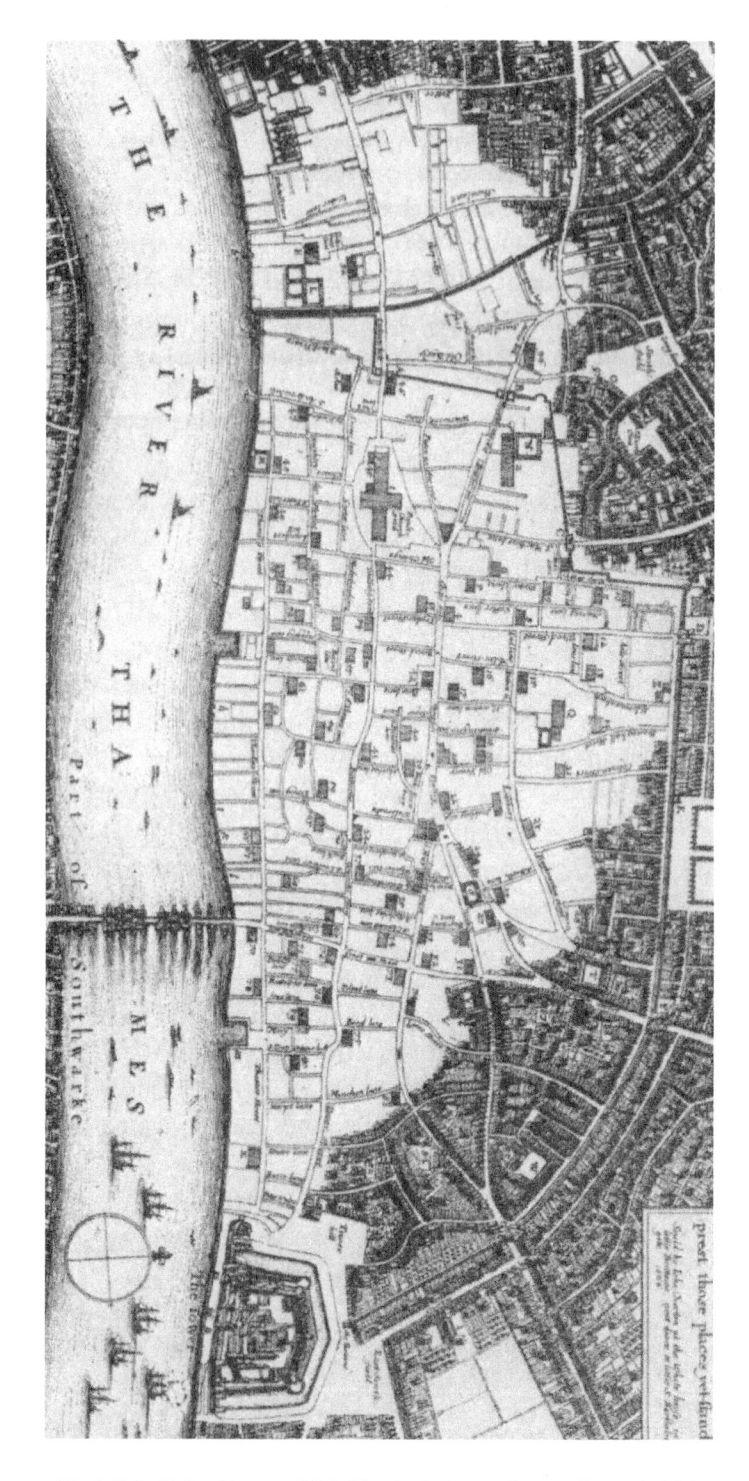

Exhibit 9.3. Part of Hollar's Map of London, 1666

Needless to say, the back-to-back conflagrations long occupied attentions and energies in London and most of England for some time to come. When the baronetcy passed from Thomas[13a] to his son, Thomas[14a], in February 1679/80, memories of the 1640s and 1650s had dimmed. That does not mean, however, that recovery of the family's estate had more than begun. In fact, much remained to be accomplished in that regard.

Thomas[14a], one of six children but lacking a brother as spare, left a small footprint during his short adulthood. He died about 20 years after succeeding to the baronetcy, still in his mid-thirties. Cause of death is not known. He matriculated at Clare College, Cambridge, in 1682, then soon turned his attention to Leicestershire politics. The weight exerted by the center, London and Canterbury, on county politics had grown noticeably during the 1670 and 1680, making exposure at the local level increasingly risky, especially in view of a swelter of rumors about plots against crown and archbishop; and during the first two decades after resumption of monarchy the family had been shy of involvement in politics, local as well as national. With the 4th Bt that began to change. He served as a justice of the peace (i.e., of the commission of the peace) in 1685, 1689-90, and 1694-95; as sheriff in 1686-87; and as deputy lieutenant for Leicestershire in 1690. These experiences were apparently satisfactory all around, so in 1690 he stood as Leicestershire's MP and won, allying himself with the "Whig party" (about which, more below). As we will see later, however, his experience at Westminster apparently was not all that satisfactory to him, and he refused to stand again for election to what would be the Third Parliament of William III and Mary II.[25] His willingness to stand in 1690 surely signaled a resumption of comfort about being in the national arena. However, there had also been a notable change of circumstances within the national arena, which probably facilitated that comfort at least initially, and this merits consideration (greater, in fact, than can be given here).

The "Glorious Revolution" of 1688

What began early in the 1640s (or earlier) as a Great Rebellion, or nothing so much as a revolution, had been both put aside and then transmogrified by 1688 into Revolution—not merely revolution, as a matter of fact, but a Glorious Revolution. Times had changed. But here the main change was due to political theatre and a campaign to remould public opinion of history and current circumstances.[26] In fact, the "glorious revolution" recalled the

---

[25] See document DG21/229, Hazlerigg Collection.
[26] Sharpe, *Rebranding Rule* (2013), drawing on a large material of evidence as well as the work of other historians, has stated the case quite well.

failed revolution of the 1640s and 1650s mostly only for the "anti-popery" theme, now regenerated by actions of the latest Stuart king, James II, who had gained the throne after death of his brother Charles II. The chief event of 1688 and 1689 was an invasion of Britain by a Dutch army led by William of Orange, as a result of which James II fled to France. William of Orange had wed Mary, eldest daughter of James, duke of York (soon to be James II), and Anne, daughter of Edward Hyde, 1st earl of Clarendon (the historian whose work we viewed in prior chapters, and courtier to Charles II as well as to his father). The line of succession from James II was first his daughter Mary, then his daughter Anne, then William of Orange (who was also first cousin to Mary). That is, such was the line of succession until a son was born to James II, who determined to raise his son as Roman Catholic (unlike Mary and Anne, who had been separated from him, for the most part, and, in accord with policy established by their uncle, Charles II, raised Protestant—i.e., Anglican). This revision of the line of succession troubled leading Protestant members of parliament, the city of London, and merchant grandees in general, to the extent that they invited William and Mary to invade, rout the increasingly troublesome king, and assume the throne as co-monarchs, William III and Mary II.

That sequence was in fact how the main intrigues and negotiations turned out. But the popular account and then dominant historiography of the sequence largely presented the sequence as a matter of destiny. And so it endured until recent times. This sort of understanding was what became known as "the Whiggish view of history": one gives an account of a past time as if that time has been destined to become the present (as if all the contingencies and fraught junctions that might well have turned out differently were irrelevant). We can now see in the struggle over James II and his efforts to restore Roman Catholicism the formation of political factions that soon sedimented into (continually evolving) political parties, Whigs and Tories. Each term was initially used by one faction to denigrate the other. Whigs, opposed to James II and any semblance of "divine right" or other version of absolutism, favored constitutional limitations on monarchy, whereas Tories had favored James II not necessarily because of support for Roman Catholicism but because of his hereditary right to the throne. Whigs saw Tories as hopelessly subordinating futures to mythic pasts and traditions no matter how outdated. Tories accused Whigs of "making it up as they went along," in order to achieve some desired end, traditions be hanged. In the context of the late 1600s and early 1700s, Whigs were generally the "party" of landed, aristocratic families and the mercantile-financial urban interests, while Tories generally represented a "party" of country squires, defenders of tradition, and opponents of foreign involvements. Notably, it was a group of Whiggish financiers who established the Bank of England in 1694 as a means of selling government notes in return for bullion from investors, all to the end of enabling William III to rebuild the English navy, which had been crushed in a sequence of defeats by the French navy.[27] In creating the bank, these financiers bridged an age-old debate between two views of "money function": one view says the primary function is to store value (i.e., a stable stock), while the other view says the primary function is to enable exchange (i.e., a regular flow of commerce). The "stock" view was important to large landowners; the "flow" view, to traders, merchants, and of course those same landowners who wanted to sell products. In selling government notes for bullion, the bank created a growing store of value; in allowing buyers to sell their notes in a secondary market (i.e., to issue new notes based of the government-issued notes), market exchange was greatly accelerated.

In any case—to return to the settlement between parliamentary leaders and William III and Mary II—one of its actual consequences was (and remains) the Bill of Rights, passed by the Convention Parliament 16 December 1689. This celebrated document began as a Declaration of Right that was presented to William and Mary the prior March as a condition of their succession to the throne. The main provisions included specific limits on powers of the monarch, agreed rights of parliament to hold regular sessions by free elections with rights of free speech within parliamentary business, and specified rights of a monarch's subjects (e.g., freedom from cruelty of punishment). The result was not a republic. But the agreement began (or resumed) a long process of subordinating powers of monarchy to functions of representation by parliamentary office.

It was within that new context that Thomas[14a] felt comfortable in taking increased visibility of political responsibilities, first within local governance in Leicestershire (though this occurred during James II), then as a county representative to the Second Parliament of William III and Mary II, which held six sessions from 1690 to October 1695, when it dissolved in wake of the death of Queen Mary II. As a brief biography for purposes of the current *History of Parliament* reports, Thomas[14a] was listed

> by Lord Carmarthen (Sir Thomas Osborne) as a Whig. Apart from his nomination to various committees, there is little sign that

---

[27] This project of investment and construction is an often overlooked stimulant to the industrial revolution. Building a massive navy required a large array of supportive manufactures on a large scale, for which new techniques of fabrication were invented.

Hesilrige's involvement in Commons proceedings was anything more than slight. In about April 1691 Robert Harley listed him as a Country supporter, though on 15 Nov. 1692 he in fact seconded Sir Scrope Howe's motion for a supply, the only occasion he is known to have spoken.[28]

The same biographer speculated that the 4th Bt's decision not to stand for election in 1695 "was almost certainly dictated by chronic financial embarrassments," but added that Thomas[14a] had seemingly "grown out of sympathy with Whiggery," demonstrating some affinity for "the Church party." The speculation about "chronic financial embarrassments" was probably on target, though not the whole story. In October 1687 James II had instructed all his lords lieutenant (chief officer of a county) to screen candidates for office and current office holders by their answers to three questions: willingness to repeal laws that had banned Roman Catholics and dissenters from public office, willingness to vote for candidates who would seek to repeal those laws, and willingness to live peaceably with people of all religious views. Whereas some men gave carefully ambiguous answers, Thomas[14a], then sheriff of Leicestershire, answered straightforwardly "no," "no," and "yes."[29] In answering "no" to the two questions of repeal, was he speaking as a dissenter who nonetheless would not support Roman Catholic candidates for office? Probably not. He was probably showing himself to be a "strong Churchman," and here, it should be clear, "Church" meant the Anglican or established church. After James II became, as history writers later declared, England's last Roman Catholic king, the answers Thomas[14a] gave to those three questions would not have been, and were not, a barrier to office holding, including Knight of the Shire (i.e., MP). In refusing to stand for parliament again in 1695, he expressed disappointment in the Whigs (the specific reasons are not clear) and chose to align with "the Church party," or neither Whig nor Tory. One conclusion from that seems clear: "the Puritan moment" had come to a close, at least for this part of the family. Puritan ardor had dampened, and with it the republican interest in separating religion, of whatever kind, from public governance. As we will see below with regard to the Anglican

---

[28] *The History of Parliament: The House of Commons 1690-1715*, edited by Eveline Cruickshanks, Stuart Handley, and D W Hayton (Cambridge: Cambridge University Press, 2002).

[29] For an example of the ambiguous response, see Peter Walker, *James II and the Three Questions* (Bern: Peter Lang, 2010), page 220; also see Paterson, *Politics* (2007), pages 270-72 and appendix 3

church in Northampton, the main or titled line of the family had concluded that conformity offered greater benefit.

Changing Patterns of Familial Organization
Whig and Tory views of history have generally differed on any number of topics, as exemplified above. Curiously, however, one topic on which the two have shared understanding to a remarkable extent is "the family"— that is, the history of family structure or organization. More specifically, the assumption has been that "family" has been the one organization of human life largely exempt from changes that make a history. As a factual matter, this is of course absurd, and recent work by historians has shown it to be so. That the assumption held sway as long as it did is testimony to the strength of a tendency to fix on a current ideal image—in this instance an ideal family structure—and to read it backward into past times as if it had then, too, been the ideal, the goal, and either to ignore actual departures from that ideal or to regard them as aberrations or "deviant forms." This was mainly a European, and Euro-American, phenomenon. Other cultures, "exotic cultures," could be seen as different, typically as primitive or less civilized, perhaps eventually to learn the benefits of "western civilization." For Tory and Whig alike, the ideal image was (and to a noticeable extent still is) what is called the nuclear family: father, mother, children.

The image was maintained mainly from ignorance. Until recent times, very little was known of the social relations within families—thus, even less about variations across families. Most of what little was known consisted in the rudiments of demography—how many inhabitants of a dwelling, their genders, their approximate ages, location of dwelling—and that information was often crude and partial. Efforts to divine more from that base of information typically exceeded its "carrying capacity." In any locality the majority of households, often with weakly defined boundaries, consisted of people of "the lower orders," for whom record keeping was often perfunctory at best even for those families who participated in parish life. The bias resulting from that selectivity of evidence is almost surely important; but the extent and specificity of bias are usually addressable only from ignorance. Consequently, there is a strong bias toward forms and demographies of landed-gentry and aristocratic households; and these, too, have sometimes been forced into inferential service well beyond their capacities. By the same token, absence of evidence is sometimes taken as evidence of absence. An illustration has to do with marriage in families of the gentry or aristocracy. Certainly there was strong familial interest in arranging favorable marriage; unions were a means of building alliances and improving patrimony and standing; whether dowry, bride wealth, and the like, were involved or not, marriage was an institution of exchange. It is often possible to find evidence by which to gauge the economic factors of exchange. It is much more difficult to find evidence of affective factors in mate selection. This latter fact does not mean, however, that affective preferences were unimportant.

In previous chapters we have seen some evidence of changes in the familial organization of the Hesilrige family, but the evidence was limited, usually ambiguous, mostly only suggestive. That remains the case for the present period. As illustration, consider the "heir and spare" relationship. It is tempting to assume clear and stable demarcation in that relationship, such that when time of succession comes, the heir is in clearly dominant position relative to spare, even if, prior to that time, there had been a vacancy-chain upward shift of sons because of death of initial heir. That pattern might be regarded as ideal image, but actual circumstances can be rather messier. Thomas[13a] was eldest son and heir to the 2nd Bt, while next eldest surviving brother Robert[13d] was spare. Whereas heir inherited the manor of Noseley and associated properties, spare inherited lesser properties. Heir looked to his son as heir; so, too, did spare, though as spare he had to consider rights of reversion of estates to the main line. And yet in this relationship of heir and spare, Thomas[13a] and Robert[13d] sometimes acted as if they were equal heirs. An example occurred 10 May 1664, when Thomas[13a] was about 39 with an heir on the way if not already born, and Robert[13d] was almost 25 with no heir in sight. Both, named as "of Noseley," signed leases for one year, conveying to "John Horton, the younger, of Noseley, gent.," and to "Henry Gilford, of Noseley, gent." two bundled properties: (a) the manor of Hardwick, plus some lands in Shangton and Illston, and (b) three-fourths of the manor of West Brunton, plus some other Northumberland properties, "to hold (a) in trust" for Thomas[13a] and his heirs and assignees, and "to hold (b) in trust" for Robert[13d] and his heirs and assignees.[30] In short, the brothers were jointly leasing properties to two other parties for one year, to increase liquidity from those properties. Seemingly, the brothers were acting cooperatively, a behavior that had occurred during earlier periods as well. While it is clear that as of 1664 (and indeed much later) the claim by John Nichols that Thomas[13a] was "restored to all those lands which Sir Arthur enjoyed that did not belong to the church" was far off the mark, he, or he and his

---

[30] See document DG21/85, Hazlerigg Collection. For another example, see DG21/96-97 (1683/4), this one jointly by the 4th Bt and his uncle Robert[13d], to the benefit of the 4th Bt's sister Arabella.

brother jointly, were in possession of some Northumberland properties and Hardwick, Shangton, and Illston, as well as Noseley, in Leicestershire.[31] But it is notable, too, that both men who were leasing the properties were resident at Noseley. Whether they were already leasing messuages on the manor grounds or had previously purchased interests in the manor during the time that the manor was confiscated by the crown is unknown.

If that were the sum, substance, and end of the leasing transaction, one could tentatively conclude that Thomas[13a] and Robert[13d] were indeed engaged in brotherly cooperation for the sake of restoring the family patrimony. However, seen from a later perspective, that transaction takes on a rather different look. Robert[13d] has moved to Northampton, purchased a substantial mansion, become a major presence in local politics and social life, and fathered three sons, all of them still living twenty years after that leasing agreement. At that same point in time, 1684, Thomas[13a] had been dead four years after long struggles to rebuild patrimony, leaving but one son as heir, Thomas[14a], now 20, who also was struggling. The difference is striking. Was it a matter of difference of character, and that in turn perhaps due to difference in parenting by Sir Arthur and/or by different mothers, and/or a difference in household composition? Or was it due at least in part to a "rebranding," so to speak: Thomas[13a], and then Thomas[14a] after him, trying to play the traditional role of lord of the manor, and in this case a manor probably still identified, when an audience heard the name, with a period of English history that many would have sooner be forgotten, while Robert[13d], 14 years younger and more easily able to exercise freedom from such memories, could be more entrepreneurial, more venturesome with his liquid capital, more modern in outlook? If Thomas[13a] had in fact mentally rebelled against his father (rather than have only engaged in mutual theatre), the likeliest direction of rebellion would have been backward, toward the traditional, away from his father's quest for the new. Was Thomas[13a], and then Thomas[14a] after him, less comfortable with the evolving individualism within family life as within society at large, while Robert[13d] was freer to pursue quests of the individual spirit?

Again, of course, this is grasping after possibilities with too little guidance by known facts to enable one even to winnow the more from the less likely. We simply have no good evidence of individual motivations. While the hypothesized difference is plausible and consistent with known facts, we do not know how it aligned with mentalities. Let's return to matters better supported.

---

[31] John Nichols, *The History and Antiquities of the County of Leicester*, volume 2, part 2 (London, 1798), page 748.

We know from records of land transactions that family ties helped to generate capital via inheritance of properties which could then be sold. Prime examples occurred thanks to Sir Arthur[12b] Hesilrige's age-mate confidant and later son-in-law, George Fenwick, who acquired estates in Sussex through his marriage to Alice Boteler. (We met Alice earlier; she was sister to Edward Apsley, who, like George, became a colonel in the parliamentary army.)[32] The chief property was Thakeham Place, a manor located about 50 miles (slightly west of) due south of the City of London. With it came Laybrooke, a small manor within Thakeham parish. Soon thereafter Fenwick acquired the manor house and park of Warminghurst manor, neighbouring Thakeham to the east. At George's death in 1657, these estates passed to his daughters and co-heirs, Elizabeth and Dorothy. Elizabeth brought her share to marriage with Sir Thomas[13a] Hesilrige, while Dorothy did likewise to Sir Thomas Williamson. The two couples sold Warminghurst manor house and park in 1665 to Henry Bigland, who in turn sold it in 1676 to William Penn, the founder of Penn's Colony in North America (Pennsylvania).[33] In 1678 the Williamsons sold their half of Thakeham Place also to Henry Bigland. At an unknown, perhaps later date, Thomas[13a] and Elizabeth similarly disposed of their half. In 1678 an advowson in Thakeham church was settled on their son Thomas[14a], who sold it ten years later to William Deane of Leicester. Thomas[13a] and Elizabeth also held portions of the tenements of Thakeham, Ashurst,

---

[32] See the biography of Fenwick in the *Dictionary of National Biography* (1885-1900), volume 18, page 328. An interesting footnote to the Apsley estate record is reported by Henry F. Waters in his *Genealogical Gleanings of England* (Boston: New England Historic Genealogical Society, 1885), volume 1, pages 78-79). Edward Apsley, who apparently never married, died without an heir in 1651. A will dated 11 October 1651 contained this passage:

> The yearly profits of all my real and personal estate, in Sussex, Middlesex and Kent, to my brother George Fenwick [i.e., his brother-in-law], till my nephew Edward Fenwick attain the age of twenty one years. Then my will is that he should change his name to mine; and so I give to him the said Edward Fenwick als Apsley all mine estate, both real and personal, he paying to his father one hundred pounds per annum during his life.

The document continued with various other specific bequests, several of them quite substantial. On 13 August 1652 a court issued letters of administration to Sir Arthur Hesilrige, 2nd Bt, with regard to this "pretended will" which named no executor and was declared null and void.

[33] The manor house was pulled down by James Butler c1708. As noted earlier, "Butler" and "Boteler" were alternative spellings of the same family name. Thus, this James Butler, c1708, might have been descendant of Fenwick's first wife and her husband, Sir John Boteler.

Ashington, and Warminghurst, which they probably used as income properties until signing quitclaims to Bigland in 1665.[34]

All of that is straightforward enough, and it indicates the continued importance of marital ties in building and maintaining, or in rebuilding, family patrimony. But the record has one curious feature: John Horton and Henry Gilford, presumably the same two men we encountered in the leasing agreement of May 1664, were also involved in the settlement of Thakeham and Laybrooke. Their relationship(s) and role(s) remain quite unclear. One of them could have been, in effect, an "in house" lawyer; but *two* lawyers? Unlikely. Were they Noseley-resident parts of an extended kinship structure? No known record supports that, though one must bear in mind that records of marriages even for this period are spotty, especially for marriages between non-conforming families. Or were they investors, ready to help Thomas[13a] Hesilrige in his effort to recover patrimony, at some profit to themselves, of course? Was the manor of Noseley, thus the household of Noseley, assuming something of a corporate form, a hybrid structure that wove commercial interests into traditional personal-familial concerns? The basic form would hardly have been unprecedented. After all, craft and agrarian production had been mixing commercial and personal-familial activities in the household dwelling for quite a long time.

Northampton's Hazelrigg House

Although the record is not entirely clear on this point, Robert[13d], the 5th Bt, was probably the man who purchased what in Northampton and surrounds came to be known as Hazelrigg House (local spelling), a late sixteenth-century mansion on the south side of Marefair Street, across from the site of Northampton castle. A map of the area as it was during the latter part of the nineteenth century is shown in Exhibit 9.4.[35] As one local historian said, the family became prominent benefactors of the Marefair area, of St Peter's church (next to the mansion; see map and Exhibit 9.5), and of Northampton as a whole.

> A Hesilrige gave a portion of the communion plate of St Peter's; another member of the family was mainly instrumental in the re-hanging of the bells; and the [family] name frequently occurs in

---

[34] This account is based on records abstracted by Edwin H W Dunkin in *Sussex Manors, Advowsons, Etc.* (London: Sussex Record Society, 1915), volume 2, pages 436, 437, and 504.

[35] *Northamptonshire Notes and Queries*, volume 1, edited by Walter D Sweeting (Northampton: Dryden Press, 1886), page 58.

the parochial registers of St Peter's between 1667 and 1763. A portion of the old family mansion still stands in close proximity to the church, shorn, it is true, of its wings and outbuildings; with its gardens and pleasure grounds sadly curtailed, but still ... one of the most interesting buildings in Northampton.[36]

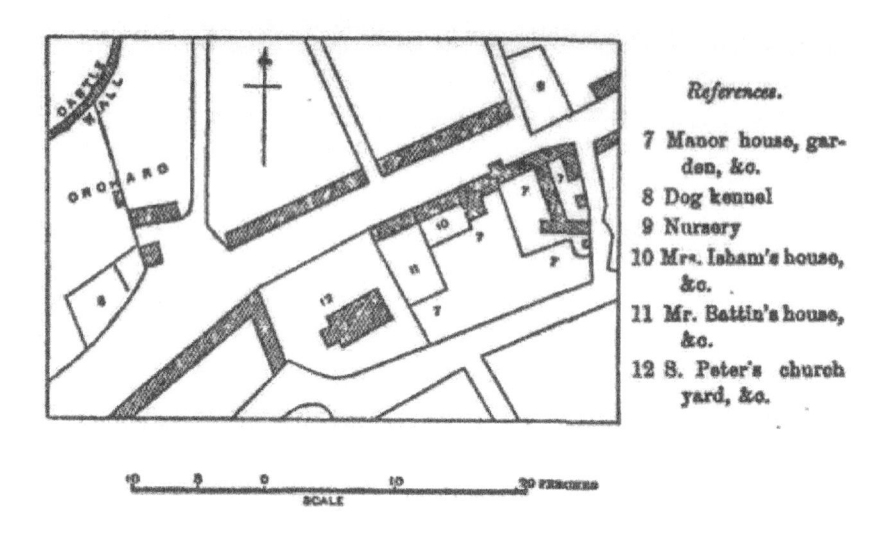

Exhibit 9.4. Map of Marefair District, Northampton, c1880

Indeed, the mansion survived the seventeenth century mainly because of a quick shift in prevailing winds. As in London a decade earlier, the city of Northampton was devastated by fire in September 1675. Reportedly begun as a small open fire near the castle grounds, winds whipped the flame into buildings nearby, which quickly spread into tightly packed structures, street after street. Nearly all buildings were consumed.[37] Hazelrigg House and one other house were reportedly the two major survivors. Robert[13d] Hesilrige was named one of the commissioners to organize the rebuilding of the city, collect donations to that end (one of which was a large quantity of timber from Charles II), and to assist in temporary housing for the estimated 700 families who had lost their homes.

---

[36] R M Serjeantson, *A History of the Church of St Peter, Northampton* (Northampton: William Mark, 1904), page 137.
[37] Edward Pearse, *The State of Northampton from the Beginning of the Fire Sept. 20th, 1675, to Nov. 5th* (Northampton: Jonathan Robinson, 1675) offers an eyewitness report by Pearse himself, a non-conformist minister.

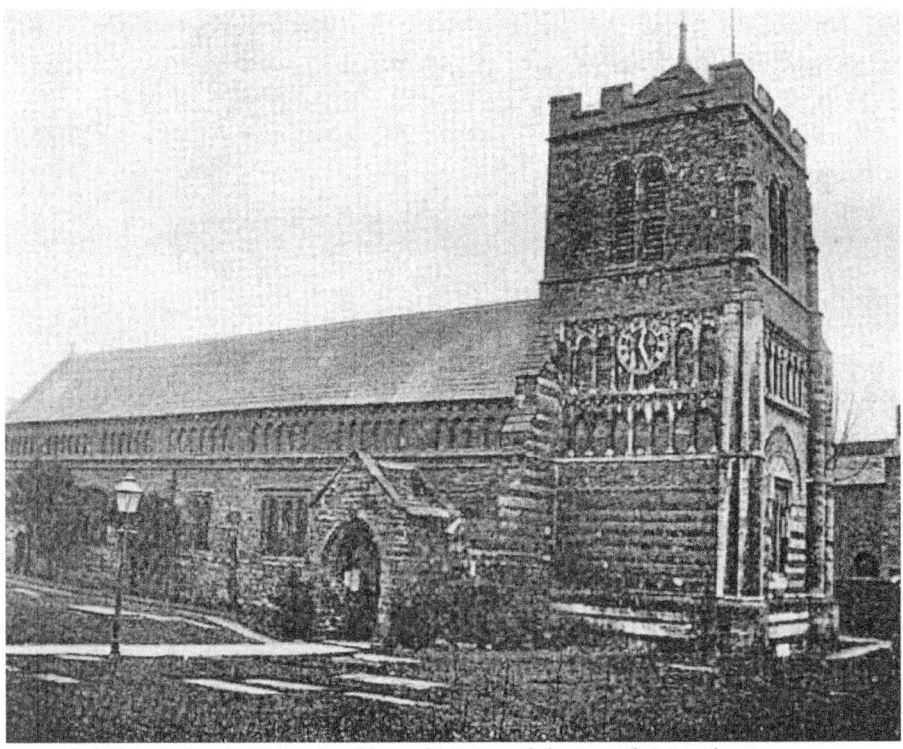

Exhibit 9.5. St Peter's Church, Marefair Road, Northampton

Sir Robert[13d] Hesilrige, 5th Bt, died in 1713, just short of his 74th birthday anniversary. He was the last surviving child of the 2nd Bt, with the possible exception of Mary[13g] (who was about ten years younger than her brother). He had been able to consolidate gains made by half-brother Thomas[13a] and Thomas' son, the 4th Bt, and then add to those gains a rather handsome fortune of his own making. Executors of his estate bought back much of the outstanding debt of Noseley, at a cost of £12,000.[38]

Hazelrigg House, now owned by the city's Borough Council, is an Elizabethan-era construction, now greatly diminished in its footprint. (Previously a front with five dormer gables, for instance, it was narrowed to three, as shown in Exhibit 9.6, during the mid-1800s.) Some accounts say that the mansion was built for the Hesilrige family. That is unlikely. Another account says it was site of Cromwell's night of sleep prior to the battle of Naseby (nearby) in June 1645, which might be correct but is bare of evidence. In any case, it was a main residence of the family during the

---

[38] See Serjeantson, *History of St Peter's Church* (1904), page 141. Measured in terms of relative economic power, a land wealth of £12,000 in 1713 is roughly equivalent to £230 million today.

late 1600s and 1700s. Sir Arthur Hesilrige, 7th Bt, made extensive use of it, living there continuously until 1730, when, placing this advertisement in the local newspaper, *The Mercury*, he moved to Noseley: "To Let – the dwelling house of Sir Arthur Hazelrig, Bart., ... With good gardens, brew-house, stables, coach houses and all other Conveniences fit for a Gentleman's Family." The family sold Hazelrigg House to historian George Baker in 1831.

Exhibit 9.6. Hazelrigg House, 33 Marefair Road, Northampton

Robert[13d] had married at age 24, 3 May 1664 in London, Bridget Rolle, aged 21, of Heanton, Devon.[39] Her mother and father both dead, she was regarded as a legal subject responsible for her own decisions—one of the determinations resulting from advances of individualism. She and Robert[13d] had four sons: Robert[14a], surviving heir who was born at Noseley in 1666; Samuel[14b], born at Hazelrigg House in 1667, dead 22 years later; Arthur[14c], born 1669 at Hazelrigg House, dead before May 1713; and William[14h], born at Noseley in 1675, pursuant of a career in the royal army, but apparently also dead before May 1713. There were four daughters; all dead before May 1721 but one, the second Bridget[14f], who died 10 Jun 1721. This record of mortality is somewhat unusual, in that of the eight children only one, Robert[14a] the heir, lived past age 50; four did not see a fortieth birthday anniversary, and of these one died at two days and the other just short of age 22. Causes of death are unknown. It appears that none of the daughters (and perhaps only one of the sons) had married. Whatever the causes—most likely infectious diseases—the rate at which Robert's[13d] offspring restocked the family tree did not bode well for family longevity.

As mentioned above, Robert[13d] had made a good marriage for his son and heir, Robert[14a], four years prior to the end of the century. Not only was his new father-in-law, Banaster Maynard, due to inherit an Essex barony; his mother-in-law, Elizabeth Grey, was daughter of the 10th earl of Kent, Henry Grey, who had been MP for Leicestershire in the Short Parliament of 1640 (and was succeeded by Sir Arthur[12b] Hesilrige, 2nd Bt).[40] Elizabeth's brother, Anthony, succeeded as 11th earl of Kent, and his son, Henry, became the 1st duke of Kent.

Banaster Maynard, whose forename repeated his mother's surname (Dorothy Banastre), was son and heir of William Maynard, 2nd baron Maynard, of Easton, Essex. William had been in favor of the effort of Presbyterians in parliament to achieve a compromise with Charles I, and when that failed he was soon in favor of bringing Charles II to the throne, for which he was amply rewarded. Young Banaster came of age in good financial circumstances, at a time when the practice of "the Grand Tour" had become established as a sort of "finishing school" in the education of young men of note. Beginning in the spring of 1660—a good time to be

---

[39] Chester, *London Marriage Licences* (1887), page 672.
[40] This is not the same Henry Grey who, as we saw in chapter 7, assaulted Sir Arthur[12b] Hesilrige on one, perhaps two, occasions. The present man was son of Anthony Grey, who, before succeeding to the earldom, was a rector in Aston Flamville, Leicestershire.

out of lines of fire—Banaster set out on his three-year tour of Europe, attended by a man named Robert Moody, who had served other young men as tour guide and could draw on considerable experience in that regard. Many years later Moody composed an account of Banaster's tour, which, given the (mostly accurate) detail must have been based on Moody's own diary of the actual itinerary.[41] Moody reported dates, places, functions attended, persons met, others' impressions of Banaster (all favorable, of course), and much else. There is little observation of Banaster himself, however. If the two of them conversed in a way that told Moody something of Banaster's first-person experiences, Moody apparently thought prudentially about including such recollections, which from all indications had not begun by commission from Banaster or his father and may have been designed by Moody to curry favor. Be that as it may, Moody's report of Banaster's tour is one of the earliest and most detailed of such accounts. As we will see below, Banaster's grandson, Arthur[15a] Hesilrige, undertook his own Grand Tour, perhaps in emulation of Banaster Maynard's journey.

On his return to Essex Maynard was elected MP for the county in 1663, continuing in that capacity to 1679. He succeeded as 3rd baron Maynard in 1699.

Maynard's son-in-law, Robert[14a] Hesilrige, born 1666 at Noseley, succeeded his father in 1713, at age 47. He served as justice of the peace in Leicestershire in 1712, 1715, and 1719. He received commission as deputy lieutenant for Leicestershire 23 July 1715. And he was sheriff of the county beginning 19 December 1715.[42] There is no indication that he gave thought to standing for parliament. Unlike his father who lived well into his seventies, the 6th Bt died while in his mid-fifties, in 1721, leaving the baronetcy and estates to his young son, Arthur[15a] Hesilrige.[43]

The estates directly held by the 6th Bt had increased, possibly quite unexpectedly, the year after his father's death. Recall from chapter 4 the manor of Swarland and smaller estates associated with it; more specifically Robert[S12b] Heselrig of Swarland, who, having inherited most of what he called "the ancient estate" of that branch of the family, found himself

---

[41] The report can be read in *The Origins of the Grand Tour: The Travels of Robert Montague, Lord Mandeville (1649-1654), William Hammond (1655-1658), and Banaster Maynard (1660-1663)*, edited by Michael G Brennan. (London: Hakluyt Society, 2005).

[42] See documents DG21/230 & 231, Hazlerigg Collection.

[43] As is often the case, there is some disagreement about his birth year. Parish records at St Peter's church in Northampton give the year as 1704. Elsewhere the year is stated as 1702 and even c1699.

without an "heir of the body." He thus stipulated in his will, dated 17 August 1714, that his estate, minus bequests, should pass to his cousin at Noseley Hall, Sir Robert[14a] Hesilrige, 6th Bt.

Exhibit 9.7. Dorothy (*nee* Maynard) and Robert[14a] Hesilrige, 6th Bt

Robert[14a] and Dorothy were married almost 25 years. During that time, it appears, they had but two children, Arthur[15a], as already said, and a daughter Dorothy[15b], who was the older. She married a Hertfordshire clergyman, William Battell. Both were living in Bath in 1725; no further information is known of either. Dorothy (*nee* Maynard) Hesilrige lived beyond her husband more than a quarter-century, dying at Noseley in September 1748. She shared the manor house with daughter and son until each married. Her son, Arthur[15a], married in 1725 in Northampton, where he and his wife resided until 1730, when they moved to Noseley, perhaps to aid his mother. But the couple moved back to Hazelrigg House six years later, perhaps because their brood of children had become too boisterous for their grandmother.

Arthur and Hannah

Counting from the first Sir Arthur[12b] and his brother John[12e], there had been at least three efforts to have a surviving son named in his honor. Those efforts surrounded a notable gap during the decades after 1661, for whatever reason. John's[12e] son, Arthur[13d], was the first to survive beyond age 30. The fourth effort was the present man, Sir Arthur[15a] Hesilrige, 7th Bt from 1721 and great-grandson of the first Sir Arthur[12b] Hesilrige.

Exhibit 9.8. Sir Arthur Hesilrige, 7th Bt, 1738

Earlier in the chapter we read a salutation of Thomas[13a] Hesilrige, as "a man of excellent parts." As much could be said of the 7th Bt as well. To quote an anonymous author's description in a Sotheby's catalogue, he

> could step out of a novel by Samuel Richardson or Henry Fielding. He inherited as a minor but by the 1740s he had restored the family finances, rebuilt Noseley, and gathered around him a large family of seventeen children. From his surviving account books (Hazlerigg Collection, Leicestershire Record office) the measure of his busy life can be taken. His wife and children are generously supported by fat allowances. His servant Pursall, his chaplain Mr. Buckley (who in typical 18th Century style marries the younger Miss Hesilrige), his gardener Mr. Bird, John Spence

who mends the clock and the deliciously named John Speeding, his coachman, all pass in and out of the pages. His regular bookseller was John Lacy; his newspapers were supplied by Mr. Samwell; and Mr. James Goodwin made his hats. There are bills for his horses, his tobacco and copious wine, his subscriptions to canal building, and of course to the Lotteries. He is almost like Squire Weston and it is not surprising that Richardson is said to have based his novel Pamela on Sir Arthur's wife, the admirable Hannah Sturges. She emerges as a kindly, loving wife whose milliner's bills are sometimes large and who has to resort to the 'waters' or a visit from the doctor from time to time. The only sadness appears to have been their eldest son, Robert, who, although protesting reform from his profligate life, does not seem to have succeeded.

Eldest son Robert[16a], one could argue, was unfairly singled out in a field of profligacy, but that matter will be left to the next chapter, wherein all of the children of the 7th Bt and his wife Hannah will be considered.

Arthur[15a] performed his civic duties beginning as a very young man: he served as sheriff for Northamptonshire from 29 January 1725/6, as deputy lieutenant for that same county from 6 April 1728 and then in that same capacity for Leicestershire from the next March.[44]

He was prolific in financial matters as well, to the great benefit of the family patrimony. Indeed, in 1739 he repurchased the remainder of the Noseley estate for £13,150.[45] A process that had begun soon after the death of the 2nd Bt was now, 78 years later, complete, or as nearly so as was feasible.

But let's back up a bit and consider the even younger man. In light of the account quoted at length just above, some of his earlier actions bear more than passing attention. For a start, having finished college in 1723 he embarked on his Grand Tour. It was a shorter version than that taken by his father-in-law, concentrated on Italy and mainly the cities Rome, Naples, and Venice. Accompanied by two men, Daniel Pain of Welford and a Mr Cave of Stamford Hall, who presumably offered counsel to his interests in fine arts, he purchased paintings from the studio of Giovanni Paolo Panini (popular for his vistas of Rome, its antiquities in particular), among others, and, together with other objects, brought his collection back to Noseley Hall.

---

[44] See documents DG21/234, 236, and 237, Hazlerigg Collection.
[45] Serjeantson, *History of St Peter's Church* (1904).

Shortly after his return to Noseley Arthur[15a] wed Hannah, daughter of Robert and Mary Sturges. Arthur[15a] was about 20 years of age; Hannah, about 16. Although already heir to the dignity and to a large estate, he was an unusually young groom for a man of his standing and that era. His age alone would have been reason for noting the marriage. But another factor made the marriage surprising, even scandalous in the eyes of many. The leading Tory newspaper of the day, *Mist's Weekly Journal*, took note of the event in its issue of 14 August, uttering a rather condescending report.[46]

Exhibit 9.9. Sir Arthur and Hannah (*nee* Sturges) Hesilrige

Accounts vary. Enough was written at the time, purporting fiction on the basis of or mixed with fact, that one now faces the difficult task of sorting through mixtures in search of "the real Hannah" vis-à-vis fictional versions of her. The root cause of scandal—in the eyes of those who saw a misadventure in youthful exuberance, incontinence, poor form, and worse—was the fact that Hannah was not of a family of the aristocracy or the landed gentry but of the servant class of people. Some accounts say her father was a coach master, whether to the 7th Bt or to another lord is not clear. Some accounts say Hannah herself came to Noseley as a scullery maid and was so employed when the 7th Bt took note of her person. Some accounts say that his mother, Dorothy, and her Maynard family behind her, were so horrified by the marriage that they "did everything they could" to break it apart, but, for all their good effort, failed. Hannah, depicted in

---

[46] Thomas Keymer and Peter Sabor, *'Pamela' in the Marketplace: Literary Controversy and Print Culture in Eighteenth- Century Britain and Ireland* (Cambridge: Cambridge University Press, 2005), page 102.

Exhibit 9.9 along with her husband, must have been a person of uncommon strength of forbearance.[47]

If this reads all too much like an advertisement for an eighteenth-century forerunner of a "bodice-ripping Harlequin romance," the reason is that mixture of fiction and fact, referred to above.[48] Samuel Richardson's epistolary novel, *Pamela*, was published in 1740. It is the story of a young woman, Pamela Andrews, told in her letters to her family. She is in service to a landowning family whose young scion, "Mr B," is determined to seduce her. As she refuses, he plots ever more furiously to succeed, even if by rape. Still, she prevails. The novel's subtitle (*or, Virtue Rewarded*) tells the rest. Mr B realizes his match, proposes marriage; she accepts and then does her best to adapt to a social order from the inside as an outsider, so to speak. The novel was commercially very successful, even as (and because) it raised hackles for being "licentious."

Richardson acknowledged that the broad outlines of the plot had been taken from an actual case, as told to him by another. For a variety of reasons, that "actual case" was soon identified as Sir Arthur and Hannah. The balance of literary investigation has supported that identification, even though there are reasons to doubt it.[49] However that may be, some members of the Hesilrige family embraced the identification, and it mostly stuck in reports of family history.[50]

For purposes here, what is of greater importance about the "Pamela aspect" of Arthur[15a] and Hannah is neither the "scandal" nor the effort to secure the identification but two facts, what should be obvious if simpler facts. First, rape of women no doubt did occur; they did occur when lords of the manor or their scions took advantage of maids in service. That does not mean, however, that women, perhaps especially women of "the lower orders," did not know how to "knock heads" and did not exercise those skills. If in fact Arthur[15a] "had designs" on Hannah, he was probably aware of that simple fact and respected it (since, as the story goes, he did refrain

---

[47] The portraits in Exhibit 9.9 (as in 9.8) were painted by Philip Mercier. See Robert Raines and John Ingamells' exhibition catalogue, *Philip Mercier* (London: Paul Mellon Foundation, 1969), plates 55, 56, and 57.

[48] Regarding Richardson's attention to dynamics of commercial market, see Roger Chartier, *Inscription and Erasure*, translated by Arthur Goldhammer (Philadelphia: University of Pennsylvania Press, 2005), pages 105-125.

[49] See, e.g., Keymer and Sabor, *'Pamela'* ... (2005); Richard Gooding, *Pamela, Shamela*, and the Politics of the *Pamela* Vogue," *Eighteenth-Century Fiction*, volume 7 (January 1995), pages 109-130.

[50] An example is William G D Fletcher's *Leicestershire Pedigrees and Royal Descents* (London: Clarke and Hodgson, 1887), page 13.

from physical attack). The second simple fact is that he did marry Hannah Sturges, a woman of "the lower orders," *despite* the scandal of it, and from all accounts he and Hannah lived a long, handsome, productive marriage.

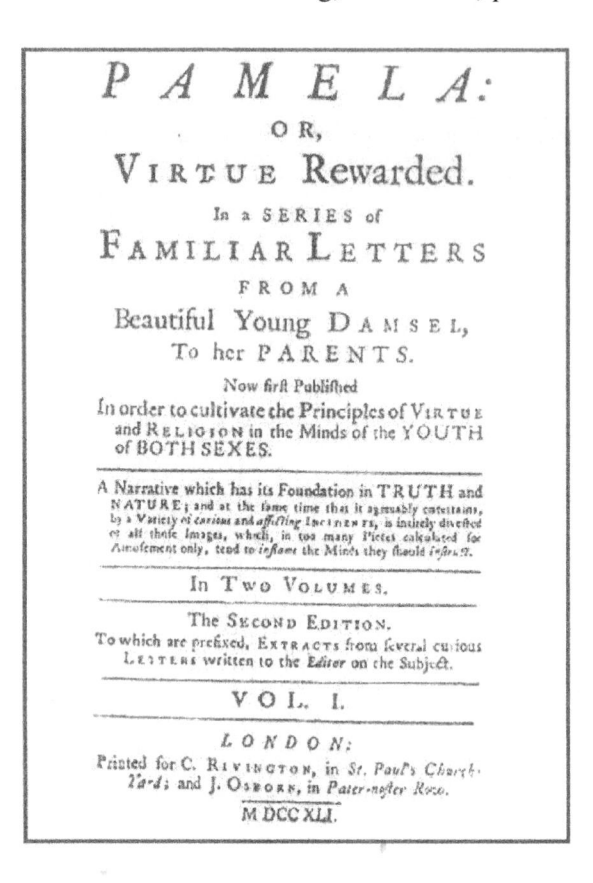

> PAMELA:
> OR,
> VIRTUE Rewarded.
> In a SERIES of
> FAMILIAR LETTERS
> FROM A
> Beautiful Young DAMSEL,
> To her PARENTS.
> Now first Published
> In order to cultivate the Principles of VIRTUE and RELIGION in the Minds of the YOUTH of BOTH SEXES.
>
> A Narrative which has its Foundation in TRUTH and NATURE; and at the same time that it agreeably entertains, by a Variety of curious and affecting INCIDENTS, is intirely divested of all those Images, which, in too many Pieces calculated for Amusement only, tend to *inflame* the Minds they should *instruct*.
>
> In TWO VOLUMES.
>
> The SECOND EDITION.
> To which are prefixed, EXTRACTS from several curious LETTERS written to the *Editor* on the Subject.
>
> VOL. I.
>
> LONDON:
> Printed for C. RIVINGTON, in St. Paul's Church-Yard; and J. OSBORN, in Pater-noster Row.
> MDCCXLI.

Exhibit 9.10. Title Page, Richardson's *Pamela*, 2nd Edition

Both simple facts open onto complex relations, of course, and with regard to the latter of the two facts that complexity has to do with changes in familial organization. Arthur[15a] made his choice of marital partner primarily in terms of personal preference on emotive grounds, rather than on grounds of what traditionally mattered in "arranged marriage," building alliances in furtherance of family resources. That difference surely figured into the apprehensions of scandal. Arthur[15a] was not alone in choosing on the basis of love for a person, however; this emotive face of an individualist mentality had been spreading slowly throughout early modern society, and it was no doubt awareness of this trend that fueled the greater part of the shudder of scandal.[51] Arthur[15a] could not be quarantined, as it were, with realistic aim of halting the spread of infection. *Pamela* was popular not merely because of the titillation. Youngish readers enjoyed the expression of individual liberation in matters of marital selection. This was new and exhilarating for the young; disturbing and preposterous, to their parents.

Exhibit 9. 11. Stonework above Front Entrance, Noseley Hall

Arthur[15a] and Hannah lived busy lives during their nearly forty years of marriage. In addition to raising their sixteen children—all but two of whom lived to maturity, nine of them surviving their father—they kept two mansions in service, Noseley Hall and Hazelrigg House, as well as managed various other properties. They rebuilt and "modernized" Noseley Hall and developed its parkland along with the gardens of the mansion in Northampton. One can see in the left panel of Exhibit 9.9 Arthur[15a] gesturing toward a recently commissioned painting of Noseley, and it was probably he who, in rebuilding part of the front edifice of the hall, had

---

[51] In recommending caution about accepting the nomination of Hannah Sturges as model of Pamela, Keymer and Sabor, *'Pamela'* ... (2005), page 102, observed that "Several other possible models—labouring-class women who married high-born men between 1710 and 1725—can be readily identified."

masons add the basic shield of the family arms above the entrance (see Exhibit 9.11).

Ringtail

Arthur[15a] engaged in business ventures with the aid of his attorney, Mr Timothy Rogers of Northampton, several of which, judging from his account books, reaped major returns. But he also engaged a passion for horse breeding and the sport of racing. One of his favorites, remembered as the epitome of his interest in racing, was a mare named Ring Tail or Ringtail, rather small in stature (at 13 hands 2 inches)—therefore, in the idiom of the day, known as a Galloway—but large in heart. A selection of accounts follows.

According to the *General Stud Book* (here citing the 5th edition, volume 1, page 11):

> Hobby mare, dam of Brocklesby Betty, was got by Lister's Turk out of the Duke of Kingston's Piping Peg. [An appended note says that 'Piping Peg had also a sister to the Hobby mare, which was the dam in 1716 of Mr. Pelham's Hip, by The Curwen Bay Barb.] A sister to Piping Peg had a filly by Hip, which was the dam of Sir A. Hazlerigg's Ringtail Galloway, by The Curwen Bay Barb, which was dam in 1737 of Mr E. O'Brien's Patch or Miss Patch, by Lord Halifax's Justice. Miss Patch was the dam in Ireland of Brutus, by Old England, and *Patty*, by Tim (son of Squirt).

According to Pick's Turf Register (volume 1, page 94):

> Hip was foaled in 1722 [1716; he ran as a six year old in 1722] and bred by Charles Pelham, esq. of Brocklesby, Lincolnshire. He was got by Mr. Curwen's Bay Barb, (sire of Brocklesby Betty, and of the dam of Partner); his dam, (sister to Brocklesby Betty's dam) by Mr. Lister's Turk, (sire of Snake).

Pick's Turf Register also says (volume 1, page 508):

> Miss Patch, bred by Sir Arthur Hasleridge, Bart. of England, and sold to Sir Edward O'Brien, Bart. of Dromoland, in the county of Clare, Ireland. She was a bay mare, foaled in 1737, and got by Lord Halifax's Justice, out of Sir Arthur Hasleridge's famous Ringtail Galloway Mare, by Mr. Curwen's Bay Barb; her dam by

Hip, (son of the said Bay Barb) out of a full sister to Piping Peg, by Mr. Lister's Turk, sire of Snake.

Heber's Racing Calendar (volume 11, 1761, page 143):

Brutus, was bred by Sir Edward O'Brien, and got by Old England, son of the Godolphin Arabian; his dam was a famous Gallaway mare of Sir Edward's, distinguished by the name of *Patch*, she was bred by Sir Arthur Hassleridge, and got by the late Lord Halifax's Justice, son to the Hampton Court Litton Arabian, upon Aldby Jenny, bred by Mr. Brewster, her Grand Dam called Ruby, was got by Mr. Leed's Dragon: Patch's dam was the Ringtail Galloway mare, she was out of a full sister to the Witty mare, being both daughters of Curwen's Bay Barb, and got by Hip, bred by Mr. Pelham, by the same Bay Barb, upon a full sister to Piping Peg, who was got by the Lister Turk.

The foregoing selection of accounts illustrates some of the conventions and vocabularies of horse breeding—and in the process demonstrates via the various inconsistencies that, just as with genealogies of human families, horse lineages can and often do differ according to keepers of the stud books and registers.

An oft-cited painting of Ringtail, mounted near the ceiling of Noseley's great Marble Hall (one of the 7th Bt's constructions) includes on the far right side (but not legible in Exhibit 9.12) her pedigree. As Nichols reported in his *History*, "after having been sold at three years old, in 1727, by a miller (who had used her for his business) for fifty shillings," Ringtail won her first plate (prize) the next year, and then "obtained 21 plates or public prizes before she was beat; and afterwards won the gold cup at Morpeth (in 1733), and twelve other prizes to the value of £1000."[52] Not bad for a miller's cart horse.[53]

---

[52] Nichols, *History and Antiquities* ... (1798), volume 2, part 2, page 749.
[53] As probably any family member can testify from first visit to Noseley Hall during any part of the latter half of the twentieth century, Arthur, the 14th Bt, & 2nd baron Hazlerigg recalled Ringtail's exploits with probably as much enthusiasm as ever had the 7th Bt.

Exhibit 9.12. Painting of Ringtail, Noseley Hall

~ 10 ~
Becoming Citizens of the World

Between 1660 and 1700 Britain's standing in the world increased to an unprecedented degree. If one had to nominate a single nation as standing at the apex of the world's slate of nations toward the end of the sixteenth century, the choice is clear: it would be China. A strong case can be made that one hundred years later the rapidly rising star was Britain—England and Scotland yoked together—and would very soon be, if not already, at the top of the ranks. The engine of that rise was commerce, trade in raw materials, in finished goods, in knowledge and technical skills, and, as millions of victims could have testified, in slave labor. Members of the Hesilrige family played some role in that mixture of processes, beginning with the investments in shipping initiated by the 2nd Bt or perhaps by his father.

In an essay he wrote in 1711, Joseph Addison (1672-1719), a poet, playwright, sometime politician, and co-founder, with Richard Steele, of a magazine called *The Spectator*, fancied himself to be "like the old philosopher, who upon being asked what countryman he was, replied, that he was a citizen of the world."[1] The occasion of that remark was Addison's admiration of the Royal Exchange, center of that square mile known as the City of London and, at least by anticipation, of a nascent empire in the making. What struck him foremost about the Exchange was its declaration that commerce subordinated nationalities. The Royal Exchange was "a great council

> in which all considerable nations have their representatives. Factors in the trading world are what ambassadors are in the politic world; they negotiate affairs, conclude treaties, and maintain a good correspondence between those wealthy societies of men that are divided from one another by seas and oceans, or live on the different extremities of a continent. I have often been pleased to hear disputes adjusted between an inhabitant of Japan and an alderman of London, or to see a subject of the Great Mogul entering into a league with one of the Czar of Muscovy. I am infinitely delighted in mixing with these

---

[1] Joseph Addison, "The Royal Exchange," *The Spectator*, no. 69 (19 May 1711); see the collection of his *Selected Essays* (Boston: Chautauqua Press, 1886), pages 70-74.

several Ministers of Commerce, as they are distinguished by their different walks and different languages: sometimes I am jostled among a body of Armenians; sometimes I am lost in a crowd of Jews; and sometimes make one in a group of Dutchmen. I am a Dane, Swede, or Frenchman at different times.

The myopia of that view (though it did not afflict Addison) was often not perceived as such by the viewer, who simply assumed that Britain was, and would continue to be (one hoped), at the center of this commercial network of nations, the center itself being the adjudicating nation. France, for one, would periodically challenge the occupancy during the next hundred years, until 1815.

It was a Frenchman, in fact, who, having resided in England several years, issued a similar yet notably different view of an equally admired Royal Exchange. In the sixth of his *Letters on England*, published in English in 1733, Voltaire described the Exchange as

a place more venerable than many courts of justice, where the representatives of all nations meet for the benefit of mankind. There the Jew, the Mahometan, and the Christian transact together, as though they all professed the same religion, and give the name of infidel to none but bankrupts.

For this Frenchman it was difference of religion, not of nationality, that had been subordinated by commerce among all nations meeting "for the benefit of mankind."[2]

By the time the children of Arthur[15a], 7th Bt, and Hannah (*nee* Sturges) Hesilrige had come of age, British citizens of the world had traveled most of the world and had planted colonies here and there, though mainly across the Atlantic on the eastern side of the great North American continent. The colonies of British North America were more than a century and a half old, and English and Scottish merchants had made some progress toward the goal of integrating "the British Atlantic Community," to borrow the phrase used as subtitle for a recent book.[3] The Seven Years War with France (known in the USA as the French and Indian War) was underway, diverting attention and other resources from

---

[2] Voltaire, *Letters on England* (London: Cassell and Co., 1894), pages 43-44.
[3] David Hancock, *Citizens of the World: London Merchants and the Integration of the British Atlantic Community* (Cambridge: Cambridge University Press, 1995).

means to that goal, but this diversion proved to be of a piece with a larger pattern: the English crown, suffering its own myopia, too often gave short shrift to the interests and ambitions of the British subjects of North America. There is much evidence in support of the thesis that migration, especially long-distance migration, is a sorting process whereby the most ambitious and most intrepid adventurers are favored to undertake the journey, first of all, and then favored to succeed in their places of destination.[4] Not that Britain was being depleted of ambitious, intrepid people; far from it. For England in particular the outward migrations had been draining away the variety of problems associated with "excess population"—and here, to be clear, "excess" was mainly in terms of insufficiently rapid creation of new urban jobs and accommodations for the waves of people who were continuing to move both *from* farmlands "shrinking" because of enclosures, engrossments, and associated processes, and *toward* the attractions of "modern means and customs" of big cities. But for the recipient colonial outposts the influx of people who were above average in ambition, risk tolerance, and sturdy self-assurance was resulting in a population proportionately higher in such qualities, even after taking into account the winnowing effects of greater hardship of local conditions during the early years.

We have seen in previous chapters the evidence that early movers to North America included members of the Hesilrige family. Some of that evidence will be reviewed here. More to the point, however, we will meet some family members who lived in British North America during the 1700s, including the period of rebellion of predominantly British colonists against the governing offices of the "mother country." The outcome of that rebellion, it is no secret, was a loss of most of Britain's claim to an Atlantic community. The loyalists of what later became the eastern part of the Dominion of Canada remained, to be sure, as did the island colonies of Bermuda, Jamaica, and so forth. But "the thirteen colonies" had accounted for the majority of the market structure which was Britain's promise of imperial benefit.

Already by 1784 other far-flung outposts of English and Scottish endeavor were beginning to flourish, however, and the crown shifted its attention to some of those, most especially the Asian subcontinent of India. These Indian outposts had begun as a joint-stock company, the Honourable East Asia Company, at about the same time, the early 1600s, as the similar joint-stock company known as the Virginia Company of

---

[4] For a recent review of the evidence, see Ian Goldin, Geoffrey Cameron, and Meera Balarajan, *Exceptional People* (Princeton: Princeton University Press, 2011).

London. By the mid-1700s an extensive network of trading posts and mercantilist factories had developed to the point of fielding its own army and civil service. Later in the century the crown exercised increasing influence and then control of the company, until it became formally a part of the British Empire. Also late in the 1700s Britain extended imperial reach into the African continent. Occupying the formerly Dutch colony at the southern Cape in 1795, and then consolidating it as formal territory of the British Empire, Cape Colony was seen as the first step toward colonial rule from the Cape to Cairo and the Suez Canal. Again, members of the Hesilrige family were involved in several of those "adventures," as well as in contingent wars in places such as Afghanistan and China (Canton, Hong Kong). We will meet some of these people, even if only briefly. In some ways similar to the London merchants who form the main cast of Hancock's study of *Citizens of the World*, they, too, can be seen generally as "opportunistic," moving here or there, to locations of better opportunity, and in that sense "restless."[5] But the Hesilrige men who are part of the cast of this chapter more often occupied positions of civil service or military support, as well as investment in trade, less often direct merchandising or shop keeping.

As in previous chapters, our next early stop is a segment of lineage, this one ranging from the 7th Bt (whom, with his wife Hannah, we met in chapter 9) to their grandchildren, among them the 11th Bt. During this period of nearly a century, two recording changes occurred. First was replacement of the Julian by the Gregorian style of calendar, as authorized by the Chesterfield Act of 1750. This had the peculiar effect of reducing the legal year of 1751 to 282 days (that is, 25 March to 31 December) and the legal year of 1752 to 355 days (the calendar advanced eleven days instantaneously, from 2 September to 14 September). The second change occurred 8 July 1818, on which day George III granted a royal licence to Sir Arthur[17b] Grey Hesilrige, 11th Bt, to alter the spelling of the family's surname to Hazlerigg.[6] Was this change a symbolic effort to declare a break with the family's past, even if rather late in the game? The answer cannot be determined. Perhaps the motive came from a desire to "modernize" the spelling. Some time ago we witnessed a shift from "Hes" to "Has," an effect of the general vowel shift, in conjunction

---

[5] See also Emma Rothschild's *The Inner Life of Empires* (Princeton: Princeton University Press, 2011). Rothschild drew upon a rich collection of correspondence as well as other documentary evidence primarily of one Scottish family who spread across the globe during the 1700s.

[6] See document DG21/255 in the Hazlerigg Collection.

with the family's greater presence in the south of England. Perhaps "z" was preferred to "s" by similar reasoning. In any case, it should be noted that not all members of the family, including several if not all of the 11th Bt's siblings, agreed to the change. The prior spelling (Hesilrige) has been maintained by some members to the current day. Usages here will conform to individual preference insofar as it is known.

A Segment of Lineage, c1760 to c1850

Arthur[15a] Hesilrige, 7th Bt: b. 28 March 1704 Northampton, d. 23 March 1763 Northampton; m. June 1725 St Peter's church, Northampton, Hannah (b. 1708/9, d. 17 February 1765/6), daughter of Robert and Mary Sturges

L-- **Robert**[16a] Hesilrige, 8th Bt: b. 27 August 1727 Northampton, d > 1797; m. 21 December 1754 Braintree, MA, Sarah (b. 29 March 1736 Roxbury, Massachusetts, d. 10 May 1775 Boston, MA), daughter of Nathaniel Walter of Roxbury, MA, and Rebecca (*nee* Abbott) Walter of Andover, MA; more below

L-- **Arthur**[17a] Hesilrige, 9th Bt: b. 16 February 1756 Braintree, MA, d. 28 July 1804 Lucknow, West Bengal, India; m(1) Elizabeth Charnaud (b. c1779 Smyrna, Turkey, d. 29 July 1797 Calcutta, India; m(2) 27 February 1798 St John's Anglican church, Calcutta, India, Charlotte Elizabeth (b. 1783, d. 8 January 1817 at sea) daughter of James Gray; no issue either union; more below

L-- Hannah[17b] Hesilrige: b. 20 August 1757 Boston, MA, d. 3 May 1789 MA; m. 18 July 1776 Roxbury, MA, Thomas Abbott (1745 MA, d. 1 November 1789 MA)

L-- Sarah[17c] Hesilrige: b. 26 March 1759 Boston, MA, d. 10 June 1786 Boston, MA; m. 12 March 1782 Boston, MA, David Henley (b. 5 February 1749, d. 1 January 1823 Washington, DC); issue: Arthur Hesilrigge Henley (b. 1783, d. 1849), David Henley, Jr. (b. c1784, d. September 1790)

L-- **Arthur**[16b] Hesilrige: b. 29 July 1728 Northampton, d. 11 April 1791 Kibworth-Beauchamp, Leicestershire; m. >1748; more below

L-- Banaster[16c] Hesilrige: b. 18 August 1729 Northampton, d. <1763

L-- Elizabeth[16d] Hesilrige: b. 4 May 1731 Noseley, d. >1763; m. 5 June 1760 St Wilfrid's parish church, Kibworth-Beauchamp, Richard Buckby of Kibworth (later, Seagoe, county Armagh, Eire); more below

L-- William[16e] Hesilrige: b. 21 July 1732 Noseley, d. <1763

L-- Dorothy[16f] Hesilrige: b. 22 October 1733 Noseley, d. 9 May 1796 Wansford, Cambridgeshire

L-- George[16g] Hesilrige: b. 3 April 1735 Noseley, d. <1763

L-- Mary[16h] Hesilrige: b. 15 May 1736 Northampton, d. young

L-- Hannah[16i] Hesilrige: b. 15 September 1737 Northampton, living at Stamford, Lincolnshire, unmarried, 1797

L-- Bridget[16j] Hesilrige: b. 30 October 1738 Northampton, living at Stamford, Lincolnshire, unmarried, 1797

L-- James[16k] Hesilrige: b. 14 November 1739 Noseley, d. <1763

L-- **Thomas**[16l] Maynard/Hesilrige, 10th Bt: b. 29 December 1740 Noseley, d. 24 April 1817 Upper Brook Street, London; m(1) 1805 Mary, daughter of Edmund Tyrell of Gepping (or Gipping) Hall, Suffolk; m(2) 30 November 1811 Letitia (b. 1774, d. 3 January 1864), daughter of John, 1st baron Wodehouse, of Kimberley, Norfolk and Sophia Berkeley; no issue either union; more below

L-- Harriet[16m] Anne Hesilrige: b. >1738, d. young

L-- Charles[16n] Hesilrige: b. 19 November 1744 Noseley, d. <1800 Boulogne, France; m. Sarah Wall; sheriff, Leicestershire, 1770

L-- Jemima[16o] Hesilrige: b. 19 November 1744 Noseley, d. 1822

L-- Amabell or Arabella[16p] Hesilrige: b. 29 November 1746 Northampton, d. > Aug 1784; m. 11 August 1784 Charles Roberts, esq,, of Thornby, Northamptonshire; issue: Charles Roberts

L-- Grey[16q] Hesilrige: b. 23 November 1748 Noseley, d. October 1810 Noseley; m. Bridget, daughter of Rev Richard Buckby; more below

L-- Dorothy[17a] Hesilrige: bap. July 1789 St Mary's, Lambeth, Surrey, d. >1861

L-- **Arthur**[17b] Grey Hazlerigg, 11th Bt: b. 8 November 1790 Noseley, d. 24 October 1819; m. 25 July 1811 Henrietta Anne (b. 1783 Leighton, Bromwold, Huntingdonshire, d. 25 October 1868 Southfield, Leicestershire), daughter of John Bourne; changed spelling of surname by royal licence, 8 July 1818; more below

L-- Elizabeth[17c] Bridget Hesilrige: b. 3 October 1792, d. 5 December 1851

L-- Thomas[17d] Hesilrige: b. 23 August 1794, d. 1814 troop ship crossing the Atlantic Ocean; unmarried

L-- Robert[17e] Greville Hesilrige: b. 23 October 1796, d. c1820; more below

L-- Isabella[17f] Hesilrige: b. 25 August 1798; m. Fnu McDonnell, esq.

L-- Jemima[17g] Hesilrige: b. 24 July 1800 Hereford, d. 1842; m. William Buckby (b. c1803 Tandragee, d. 28 May 1868 county Armagh, Eire; more below

L-- Charles[17h] Maynard Hesilrige: b. 24 August 1802 Hereford, d. 4 December 1878 Carlton Curlieu, Leicestershire; m. 10 March 1829 Deborah Maria, daughter of Arthur Buckby of Seagoe, county Armagh, Eire; more in chapter 11

L-- Hannah[17i] Hesilrige: b. 28 October 1804 Hereford, d. November 1824

Dorothy[15b] Hesilrige: b. 1 December 1700, d. >1720; m. William Battell, MA, of Comber Grove, Somerset; a clergyman of Hertfordshire; both living in Bath August 1725

British North America
If any one member of the Hesilrige family could have best claim as first of the family to be "citizen of the world," that person would be Robert[16a], eldest son and heir of Sir Arthur[15a], 7th Bt. Granted, the latter fellow undertook his version of a Grand Tour, arguably the first Hesilrige to engage in that once-mandatory phase of a young man's education. But the tour was limited to the continent, and only western parts of that, and usually it did not entail continual circuits of travel and habitation. Robert[16a] appeared in the Massachusetts colony of North America when in his mid-twenties. In 1754 he married the daughter of a Massachusetts minister and during the next few years lived part of the time in the colony, siring a son and two daughters, and part in London.[7]

Not that Robert[16a] was the first member of the family to land on the North American continent and establish a life there. As mentioned earlier, a Thomas Haselrig arrived on the shores of Virginia probably during the 1640s, perhaps the late 1630s, and became progenitor of the family's many generations across the breadth of the USA. His location in the lineages of the family in England has remained elusive, unfortunately, and probably will remain unknown. Thomas arrived under indenture to John Mottrom, a member of a prominent Cheshire family whose interests circulated from London to other ports, until he himself emigrated to Maryland and then to Virginia. The fact that Mottrom's interests were largely in and around London suggests that Thomas probably made contact with him in that area.

Also previously noted was the possibility that this Thomas might not have been the first Hesilrige descendent to have arrived in North America. Recall from chapter 5 that a Raffe Lowle "married _____ Heselrig, descendant of Robert [sic] de Hesilrige, one of the knights who came with William."[8] Raffe was probably born in or near the area of Yardley parish, northeastern Worcestershire, which is about 55 miles

---

[7] More particulars follow, below. Any reader of the companion volume to this one, *Hazelrigg Family History: North America, c1635 to c1935*, 3rd edition, should note that the facts reported here for Robert[16a] and his family include corrections of information.
[8] William Richard Cutter, *Historic Homes and Places and Genealogical and Personal Memoirs Relating to Families of Middlesex County, Massachusetts* (New York: Lewis Historical Publishing Co., 1908), volume 4, page 1466.

slightly south of due west from Noseley. Relevant dates are only broadly known. In fact, reliable birth dates are elusive until we come to the fifth-great grandson of Raffe and his Heselrig wife, Percival Lowell (1571-1664), a prosperous wholesale merchant of Bristol, Somerset, who decided, in protest of the religious strictures of Charles I, to uproot his family and emigrate to Newbury, Massachusetts.[9]

Exhibit 10.1. Memorial to Percival Lowell (1571-1665)

Percival, his wife Rebecca, two of their sons, John and Richard, and daughter Joane, plus the respective households, arrived in Boston 23 June 1639. At that date, Percival would have been 68 years old, an extraordinary age for contemplating and then enduring the event of

---

[9] In addition to the volumes by Cutter, previously cited, sources include Frederic William Weaver, ed., *The Visitations of the County of Somerset in the years 1531 and 1575*. (Exeter: W. Pollard, 1885), pp. 120-121 ("Lowle of Clyvedon"), and Delmar R. Lowell, *The Historic Genealogy of the Lowells of America from 1639 to 1899* (Rutland, VT: The Tuttle Co., 1899), page xiii. However, all three of these (along with other, more recent accounts of the Lowell family) derive from the same source: *Heralds' Visitations of Somersetshire in A.D. 1573, 1591 and 1623* (Harleian ms, 1559, folio 215). Judging from the number of generations between Raffe and Percival, as reported in Lowell records, and assuming an average generational length of 25 years, Raffe would have been born c1400. His mother was a Baskerville, a prominent family of still-remembered Norman ancestry; but that fact also does not yield greater precision of estimate of Raffe's birth year (by which to narrow the list of Heselrig daughters).

transoceanic travel in that era. He quickly re-established his company, again dealing mainly in imported goods, and lived another quarter-century, dying 8 January 1664/5 in Newbury (see marker in Exhibit 10.1). It is possible, perhaps even probable, that Percival was the first, at least earliest known, descendant of a Hesilrige to settle in North America.

From Percival and Rebecca the Lowell family spread slowly down the seacoast toward Boston and inland to an area that encompassed early steps in industrialization (e.g., Lowell, Massachusetts).[10] Their third-great grandson John, born 1743 in the seaport of Newbury, died 1802 in Roxbury (one of the six villages established in the Massachusetts Bay Colony in 1630, southwest of Boston, now a neighborhood of Boston). If he visited Roxbury during the 1760s, John Lowell might well have met the family of Nathaniel Walter, a prominent minister of Second Church in Roxbury (his father, Nehemiah, had been minister of First Church). The Walter family included a daughter Sarah (b. 29 March 1736), who married, 21 December 1754, an Englishman, Robert[16a] Hesilrige, known as the scion of a prominent landowning family of Leicestershire. One can imagine that, had Robert[16a] and John Lowell met, they would have exchanged notes of their joint ancestries.

Exhibit 10.2. Meeting-House Hill, Roxbury, 1790

We will return to consider Robert[16a] and his Massachusetts family momentarily. In the meantime, notice will be given to the possibility of other Hesilrige descendants or relatives in British North America.

---

[10] Lowell, *Historic Genealogy* ... (1899) reports in considerable detail the lineages from Percival and Rebecca (and a brief account of the pre-emigration genealogy).

A few researchers have noticed the fact of some correspondence dated 1647, 1648, and 1650 in which there is indication of cousinship among three households: those of Sir Arthur[12b] Hesilrige, 2nd Bt, Edward Winslow, and Herbert Pelham. In one recent article, for instance, the pseudonymous author reported some research that ended with plausible though unproven linkages.[11] With regard to Sir Arthur[12b], the link to Edward Winslow (a founder and governor of the Plymouth colony), if factual, is probably through the 2nd Bt's second wife, Dorothy, daughter of Fulke Greville and thus sister to the woman who married Kenelm Winslow, whose grandson was Edward Winslow. (We know about Dorothy, of course; but it is not presently clear that either of the two Winslow links has been proven.) The Pelham link has been suggested as due to Mary Copley: she and first husband Capt. Ralph Bosvile, esq., were grandparents of Elizabeth Bosvile, who became second wife of Herbert Pelham and who (Copley) married secondly Fulke Greville, which leads to both Dorothy and to her sister who supposedly married Edward Winslow's grandfather Kenelm Winslow.

A flaw in both of those accounts is the apparent lack of record that Dorothy and Robert Greville, children of Fulke Greville (son of Robert Greville and Blanche Whitney) and Mary Copley, did have a sister. That does not mean that there was not a second daughter; only that record of her is apparently not available, if she did exist.

No other proposal of a link of the 2nd Bt to either Winslow or Pelham seems as likely as the foregoing. An elaborate hypothesis offered during the 1960s, involving fourth- and fifth-cousin linkages, still gains attention, but it is rather implausible even aside from the distance of links.[12] That there was in fact some sort of relationship denoted by the three letter writers as "cousin" is testified in the letters themselves. The letter from the 2nd Bt, with appended note by Dorothy, dated 8 October 1650, was to Winslow, who was addressed in the letter by Sir Arthur[12b] as "my honored cosen" and by Dorothy as "yr affectionate cosen."

Now to Robert[16a] Hesilrige, eldest son and heir of the 7th Bt.

No known record tells us the circumstances in which Robert[16a] and Sarah Walter met. As one source says, we know that Robert[16a],

---

[11] Kenneth W Kirkpatrick, "The 'Loving Cosens': Herbert Pelham, Sir Arthur Hesilrige, and Gov. Edward Winslow," *The New England Historical and Genealogical Register* volume 154 (January 2000), pages 78-108.

[12] Adrienne Welty Boaz, *Specific Ancestral Lines of the Boaz, Paul, Welty and Fishel Families* (Baltimore: Otter Bay Books, 2014), page 521. Kirkpatrick reviewed the hypothesis, as published by John Hunt in the 1960s, and found it to be implausible.

"having engaged in mercantile affairs in Boston, had taken up his residence in Roxbury," but there is no direct evidence that he met Sarah only after he had settled in Roxbury.[13] Boston was a bustling city of more than 15,000 inhabitants in 1754. Roxbury, about five miles southwest of Boston's main marketplace and meeting venue, Faneuil Hall, counted perhaps 1,200 inhabitants at that time. If the attraction of that small town was not the Walter family's daughter, perhaps it was simply the convenience of a respite a short ride from the city center, which in turn was but a quick walk from the noise and odors of the harbor. There is no known indication that Robert[16a] intended permanent immigration to Massachusetts or anywhere else in North America. The habit of alternative abodes—one in the country and another in a major city—had proved both very useful and affordable to men of the family's titled line for quite some time, and this was likely Robert's[16a] intent.

The Atlantic voyage, now usually about seven weeks in duration when weather cooperated, still had its hazards, but the rate of passage had enormously increased since the mid-1600s, to more than 1500 ships a year, bringing thousands of Europeans and three times as many enslaved Africans to the shores each year. This was in spite of the widely known hardships of the voyage even under good sailing conditions. A German schoolmaster who made his way to the port of Philadelphia during the summer season of 1750 recorded in his diary thoughts of the hardship: "terrible misery, stench, fumes, horror, vomiting, many kinds of seasickness, fever, dysentery, headache, heat, constipation, boils, scurvy, cancer, mouth rot, and the like, all of which come from old and sharply-salted food and meat, also from very bad and foul water, so that many die miserably."[14]

> The sale of human beings in the market on board the ship is carried on thus: Every day Englishmen, Dutchmen, and High German people come from the city of Philadelphia and other places, in part from a great distance, say twenty, thirty, or forty hours away, and go on board the newly-arrived ship that has brought and offers for sale passengers from Europe, and select

---

[13] Francis Samuel Drake, *The Town of Roxbury* (Roxbury, 1878), pages 442, 443. The image in Exhibit 10.2 is from Drake.

[14] Gottlieb Mittelberger, *Journey to Pennsylvania in the Year 1750 and Return to Germany in the year 1754*, translated by Carl T Eben (Philadelphia: John J McVey, 1898), page 20, and pages 26-27 for the following quotation. His *Journey* was first published in Germany, 1756.

among the healthy persons such as they deem suitable for their business, and bargain with them how long they will serve for their passage money, which most of them are still in debt for, When they have come to an agreement, it happens that adult persons bind themselves in writing to serve three, four, five, or six years for the amount due by them, according to their age and strength. But very young people, from ten to fifteen years, must serve till they are twenty-one years old.

Robert[16a] paid his own passage, no doubt, and there is reason to think that the ship that brought him to Boston was his own. Indeed, given that his initial arrival was on mercantile business, he was very likely anticipating a continuation of trade, bringing some cargo to Boston and returning with a different cargo. The arriving cargo could have included human migrants, some of them (perhaps most of them) enslaved people of Africa. Cargo to England would have included commodities such as timber, hides, cotton, tobacco, and a few other durable goods.

Robert[16a] and Sarah's first-born child was a son, and thus heir to the title. This was Arthur[17a], born 16 February 1756, which date implies that conception occurred approximately five months after the December wedding. Given that date of conception, together with the much greater hazards of sailing the Atlantic during winter and early spring, it seems well-nigh certain that Robert[16a] had remained in or around Roxbury after the wedding. Because the record says that Arthur[17a] was born in Braintree, it also appears that the young couple had moved their household from Roxbury to this small town, located another ten miles southwest of Boston. Again, we lack information about motivation. One possibility is prestige: not only was Braintree farther into the country; it was also home of the already notable John Adams, John Hancock, and other figures important to circles of political and economic influence.

Arthur[17a] was joined by sister Hannah[17b], born 20 August 1757, and then another sister, Sarah[17c], born 26 March 1759. These dates imply dates of conception of approximately December 1756 and June 1758. The former would have been consistent with a round-trip journey to London during the summer months of 1757; the latter, the summer months of 1758.

At this point we must shift gears and bring another dimension into the story of Robert[16a] and his young family. On the British side of the sea Robert[16a] has been remembered primarily as a "disappointment," to put it mildly. Nichols was discreetly brief in his account, saying only that the then-current 8th Bt "resides in London" and that "the principal part of the estate [was] devised by his father to a younger son."[15] The loudest sound of disapproval was indeed made by the 7th Bt, father of Robert[16a] and four other sons who were living when Sir Arthur[15a] composed his last will and testament. Given the rule of primogeniture and heraldic protocol, the title could only pass to the eldest surviving son, Robert[16a], but Arthur[15a] made very plain his displeasure with his heir by leaving him only a quarterly allowance, to be administered by a stipulated set of guardians, as it were, with (as Nichols said) "the principal part of the estate," Noseley included most conspicuously, going to Charles[16n], second youngest son, for whom Arthur[15a] still had some hope of rectitude at maturity. According to the few accounts that are more forthcoming (about which, more below), the 7th Bt thought his heir to be irresponsible, too much taken with the "high society" life of London.

By the sixth decade of the eighteenth century the life of London was becoming quite unlike anything witnessed even by a man who, thirty years earlier, had experienced the Grand Tour. Arthur[15a] surely did not think of himself as one of "the bourgeoisie," that new class of city dwellers who had been ruling the city, and increasingly its hinterlands and growing parts of the world beyond the British Isles. Although active in commerce and its monetary rewards, his orientation remained some blend of the entrenched cultures of landed gentry and aristocracy. But the aristocracy itself was being divided between those who remained in their own eyes "superior by breeding and nature" to the "upstarts" of London's commercial center, and those who were adapting to that new center in order to remain relevant to this new, rapidly expanding world of commerce. These latter aristocrats, allied with leading figures of the bourgeoisie, were instrumental in rejuvenating England's claim to being *the* world power, commercially and militarily.

As often happens, the main stimulant to that alliance had been the resounding defeat of the English navy of William III by the French navy of Louis XIV at the battle of Beachy Head, off the chalk headlands of East Sussex in 1690. The government of William III lacked sufficient means, including credit standing, to fund major projects of infrastructure, now most especially needed the rebuilding of the navy. Several men stepped forward to create a corporation of subscribers, which gained charter as the Bank of England just before the turn of the century. The subscribers' investments amounted to loans to the government, in return

---

[15] John Nichols, *The History and Antiquities of the County of Leicester*, volume 2, part 2 (London, 1798), page 749. Wooten's *Baronetage* of 1771 was also quiet (page 245).

for exclusive rights to issue bank notes against government bonds, thus creating a multiplier effect in markets. The program raised £1.2 million in less than two weeks. Half of that sum was used to build a new navy, and the process of *that* construction, involving not only new ironworks and the like but also huge investments in provisioning a much larger force, resulted in massive new economic growth. Observers could not but be astonished at this display of financial power in such short order. No family of the landed gentry was threatened with confiscation or subordinated to monarchal taxes under the name of "ships money." No member of the aristocracy had to relinquish a palatial estate for the pleasure of a king. Anyone who had the liquidity was welcome as subscriber. All subscribers were equivalent shareholders, risk takers, and profiteers, in proportion to their shares in this privately held joint-stock company. London as a whole was on the way to hosting one million inhabitants. The City of London proper was widely recognized as the financial hub of the world.

In the meantime, several opulent districts had grown up to the west of the City, centered on the tree-lined streets and squares of Mayfair. High street shops of Bond and Oxford streets offered many fancy new attractions to the well-heeled, as did the carnivalesque entertainments of Piccadilly Circus. Poverty was being pushed outward, to the swamps south of the river and the bogs to the east. There now existed a distinctive "London society," and its attractions to young men and women who were in search of appropriate identity in this new world of accelerating innovation both of "technical know-how" and of "life style" began to act something like the multiplier effect of financial markets. A notion of "self-making"—not just "making one's way in the world" but also, and at least as importantly, "making one's self into a preferred, self-conscious character"—had taken hold, leading young men and women to ask of themselves questions not previously part of routine education: "what sort of person should I become now, now that the world around is again different"? Much of this was good material for William Hogarth's (1697-1764) "painting and engraving modern moral subjects," subjects such as the libertine, the rake, the fop, the antiquary, and the dilettante. Further, art had become its own subject. No longer a preserve of aristocrats' and monarchs' taste for flattering poses and bucolic settings, art had become commercial, sold in shops, offered in newspapers and store-front windows, drawing on itself and sometimes the butt of its own parodic sense of humor.

Arthur[15a] may have found some or all of this curious at a distance, but in his own sons he saw a severe limit to his own tolerance. When time came to write his will, he expressed his disappointment in his heir as furiously as he could, having written Robert[16a] off as a failure. For better or worse, that verdict has been Robert's[16a] destiny. For whatever reason, he has not left to us his own account of who he was, what he did, why the surviving story has been so bleak when not simply dismissive. Remarkably, for a man who traveled as extensively as he did, engaged in commerce over long distances, and supposedly participated in the "high life" of London society, nothing of his correspondence survived. What we are left with is a small set of pictures painted by others.

One of these pictures was in correspondence retained by Richard Price (1723-1791), a philosopher, writer, and nonconformist minister of Newington Green, neighbor to Islington in north London. The following is a letter from Nathaniel Gorham, Boston, Massachusetts, to Price, dated 26 December 1785.[16]

> I want, Sir, to ask your advice on a matter of very considerable importance to an individual here which may be thus stated. Some years ago Sir Arthur Haselrig had an only son who came to this Country and after living a dissolute life for some time married a very worthy and amiable Young Lady, *Daughter* to a Mr Walter the Congregational Minister of Roxbury, by whom he had three children, one son and two daughters and then returned to England and still lived in such a manner as to displease his Father. Old Sir Arthur, being deceived as to the character of his Son's wife and her connections, previous to his Death settled £200 a year on his son who died in the Fleet prison, and by his Will gave all his very great landed Estate to Lord Maynard with limitations if Lord Maynard died without issue to his Lord Maynard several Brothers, and if they all died without issue then to revert to his own family, viz the three children above mentioned, the son first and if he failed of issue to the daughters. The case now is that the several Maynards are all dead without issue except the present Lord Maynard, who is somewhat advanced as I am informed, and his Wife. He has no children. His heir apparent as to the estate in question is the

---

[16] Richard Price, *The Correspondence of Richard Price*, volume 2 (ed. D O Thomas). Durham, NC: Duke University Press, and Cardiff: University of Wales Press, 1991, pages 329-330.

young Arthur Haselrig, about 30 years old, the son of the above marriage, who has been married several years and has no children and who is very infirm Man now in the East Indies. The two daughters reside in this Country, the eldest of which is married to a worthy Man, a Congregational Clergyman who has been dismissed from his Parish and is rather in low circumstances. And it would conduce much to his and his wife's comfort if they could raise a sum of money from their prospect to this estate, which I was informed by a relation of theirs now in England amounts to th[letter torn] thousand sterling per annum laying in all most all the Midland Counties in England. They think as Lord Maynard is very nearly sixty years old, his Wife about 50, and no person between Lord Maynard and them except the Brother in India, that money might be had, provided they engaged to pay a much larger sum if they ever possessed the estate. I shall be exceedingly obliged if you will think on this subject and write me your opinion, directed for me at N. York; if your avocations will admit of your doing it soon, you will exceedingly oblige me, and in the meantime I remain with every sentiment of esteem and regard, Sir,
Your most Humble Servant
   Nathaniel Gorham

Gorham, a Boston-born (1738-1796) merchant and political leader (e.g., signatory to the US Constitution), mis-stated some particulars (Robert[16a] was not only son, nor is there evidence that he died in Fleet prison; the 7th Bt left the estate to his second youngest son, Charles[16n]; etc.). In general, the letter has the appearance of a report by second- or third-hand sources. It seems unlikely that, if Robert[16a] did in fact live "a dissolute life for some time" in Massachusetts, he would not have been welcomed into the Walter household, much less the marriage. But in one particular Gorham's letter is from all known evidence based on the factual situation of Robert's[16a] Massachusetts family. At unknown date between 1758 (probably 1763, the year of his father's death) and 1775 (the year of his wife Sarah's death in Boston), Robert[16a] returned to London, apparently never again to step foot onto North American soil.

   It is not only Gorham's letter that testifies to that apparent fact. We also have letters from an eighteenth-century merchant and shipping agent, Ralph Carr, who had interests in North America as well as Britain, among other places. Copy books of his own business letters (but generally not those of his correspondents) were preserved for the period from 1737 to c1783. These include four letters of interest here.[17]

1768, Apr. 29.—Mr. Ralph Inman is requested to make quest for "a very unfortunate poor lady at Roxbury," Lady Hesilrige, wife of the son [Robert] of Sir Arthur Hesilrige, who is enquired for by Mr. Jonathan Ormston, Sir Arthur's trustee, and who must make proof of her marriage.

1768, Nov. 18.—Letter to Lady Hesilrige at Boston: 120*l*. to be paid to her as the interest due on the 500*l*. legacy from the death of her father[in-law], Sir Arthur Hesilrige, and 20*l*. annually. "I most sincerely lament that your unhappy situation and worth were not known before the death of Sir Arthur; sure I am you and yours would have been provided for, but it is the hand of Providence, which is still able to conduct and assist you. No doubt you heard that Sir Arthur left his estate to the youngest of five sons, and even thought him very unworthy of it, and [I] doubt he has not been mistaken by the accounts I have of him. He is not yet of age; when he is I pray God he may have an inclination equal to his ability to assist you. For your son, as he will have the title, ought to have the estate likewise. I had much talk with Mr. Ormston as to paying you in the 500*l*., but this he apprehends cannot be done till your children are of age, but when they get an estate in this neighbourhood sold for the payment of legacies and the other sons' fortunes, he will consult the nobleman [lord Maynard] who was left joint trustee with him."

1770, July 2.—Letter to Lady Hesilrige, urging her to send her eldest son over to England; he hopes the sight of him would warm lord Maynard (who is 80 years old) into compassion for the unmerited loss of his birthright.

1771, Apr. 4.—Letter to Lady Hesilrige, congratulating her on the reception her son has met with from lord Maynard, who in

---

[17] The copy books were collected by a descendant and published as *The Manuscripts of J R Carr-Ellison, Esq.*, pages 92-100 in *The Manuscripts of Shrewsbury and Coventry Corporation [etc] Fourth Report, Appendix: Part X* (London: HMSO, 1899).

letters to Mr. Ormston "expresses more of a parental fondness for him than my most sanguine wishes could even hope for." Enclosing a copy of a letter of thanks to lord Maynard, dated 30 March.

Bear in mind that Sir Arthur[15a], 7th Bt, died in 1763. Jonathan Ormston was one of the trustees of settlements stipulated in his will. (The others were Charles, baron Maynard, and Sir Thomas Palmer, Bt.) In his letter of 2 July 1770 Carr urged Robert's[16a] wife, Sarah (*nee* Walter) Hesilrige, to send her (only) son, Arthur[17a], then 14 years of age, to England, in the hope that Maynard would become his guardian. This hope was fulfilled. Maynard took Arthur[17a] under his wing, first sending him to school at Chiswick (west side of London), and then to Calcutta, in April 1773, on appointment to the civil service of the East India Company. Sarah lived the rest of her life in a house on Milk Street in Boston, where she died 10 May 1775, the morning of the colonists' rebellion, soon to be a war for independence.

A careful reading of the 7th Bt's will, dated 31 January 1763, offers some clues as to the father-son relationship. In addition to stipulating full benefits to his wife, Hannah, making generous bequests to friends and servants, and naming his sons Charles[16n], Grey[16q], and Thomas[16l] (in that order) as heirs to the Noseley estate upon attaining the age of 25 years, he stipulated annuities to son Arthur[16b] and to daughters Elizabeth[16d], Dorothy[16f], Hannah[16i], Bridget[16j], and Ammabell[16p] (as he spelled her forename). Of the five named daughters, only Elizabeth[16d] was married as of that date, and her husband was recognized by name, Richard Buckby. Ammabell[16p] would marry later. Dorothy[16f], Hannah[16i], and Bridget[16j] apparently never married. The other daughters, unmentioned in the will, had died earlier. Except Jemima[16o], for whom a death date of 1822 has been recorded: she was not mentioned in the will. Perhaps the recorded death date is wrong. She was fraternal twin of Charles[16n], which perhaps entailed neo-natal death. The sequence in which daughters' names were mentioned is seemingly as irregular as the sequence of sons' names. Some have said that Charles[16n] was named as first heir to the Noseley estate because, given his young age at the time, the 7th Bt still had hopes that he would amount to something. Perhaps, though no firm evidence of that or any other motivation has come to light. And why Charles[16n], not Grey[16q], who was younger still?

Notice of the rights of "my dearly beloved wife Dame Hannah Hesilrige" is given first in the will, as one would expect. Closely following is notice of the estate inheritances of the three sons Charles[16n], Grey[16q], and Thomas[16l]. Only later is notice given of the titular heir, Robert[16a], and this is not formally of the title but of an annuity stipulated by the 7th Bt, with some conditions. Robert[16a] is to receive payment of £200 per year, net of the land tax and "all other deductions," to be paid quarterly by the trustees (Maynard, Palmer, and Ormston) to Robert[16a] *in person*; and "not any part thereof to any other by his order." Further, "the said annuity shall be for his support and maintenance during his life and not be applied to any other use or purpose whatsoever." Note that by the date of the will Robert[16a] had already three children, including Arthur[17a], the future 9th Bt. The will does not mention that titular inheritance. But the 7th Bt did include notice of provision for "the first and every other son of his body lawfully to be begotten on the body of any other woman he shall hereafter marry (except his present wife if he be already married)."

    What can one make of all the foregoing but that Sir Arthur[15a], the 7th Bt, was greatly disturbed that his heir had married Sarah Walter and had a son by her? If that is correct, the next question becomes, What was wrong with Sarah? She was not of the landed gentry or aristocracy of England, to be sure; but nor was Hannah Sturges. Was that the rub? Did the 7th Bt feel that his heir was in some degree mocking him, showing lack of respect? It seems more likely that the rub was the fact that Robert[16a] had married a colonist woman, had sired a son and heir by her, and in so doing had put in jeopardy the family's dignity (title) as well as material patrimony. There is one more feature of the 7th Bt's will, not heretofore mentioned, that adds relevant information. In naming the three sons as heirs of the Noseley estate, the 7th Bt stipulated in addition to the above-noted age threshold this proviso: "or be married with the approbation testified in writing of the Right Honourable Charles Lord Maynard, Sir Thomas Palmer, Bt, and Jonathan Ormston of Newcastle-upon-Tyne." It was consideration of the quality of marriage. The 7th Bt was displeased with his heir's marriage, and he was determined to achieve a breach in that marriage. If Robert[16a] wanted to collect his quarterly payment, he had to appear in person, and he had to convince the trustees that he was applying the money only to his own maintenance, not to any other purpose. Finally, the 7th Bt left a not-so-subtle encouragement to marry an English woman and "begin again," sire an heir and even a spare by an English woman, and put Boston behind him evermore.

Robert[16a] may well have led a "libertine life" in London prior to his "adventures" in Massachusetts; he may have engaged or re-engaged that life afterward; he may have been a "libertine" the entire time. While we lack direct evidence of it, we also lack means of disproving the claims; and it bears repeating, we lack any testimony from Robert[16a] himself. But there is a plausible alternative account, whether in place of or as supplement to the story of a "libertine character" that has been his future.

Exhibit 10.3. Sir Robert Hesilrige, 8th Bt

It would be mistaken to attribute the 7th Bt's attitude toward his son's marriage to what became the colonists' war of independence. When Robert[16a] wed Sarah Walter in Massachusetts in 1754, attention in England was focused on the conflict with France, which would become officially declared war in 1756 (known in the USA as "the French and Indian War" but in England as yet another war with France, and after the fact as "the Seven Years War"). At the conclusion of that war, in the Treaty of Paris, 1763, Britain had consolidated a huge expanse of North American territory (from the Atlantic to the Mississippi River, excepting New Orleans), all at the expense of France. The Ordinance of 1763 set a western boundary to colonists' settlement activity, which colonists generally did not like; but the boundary was almost immediately ignored. Most people in England had little conception of or interest in the colonies, and the reverse was also true. While the typical colonial household was materially better off than the typical household in England (i.e., materially richer, more comfortable), few on either side of the Atlantic were aware of that fact—or would have cared much, had they been aware, since the operative standard of comparison in either country was usually local. As animosity toward "the mother country" began to develop among colonists after 1763, its focus was mainly on parliamentary activity in Westminster, not the actions of George III. In fact, a good case can be made that the majority of colonists were monarchist, not republican, in sentiments, right up to the year 1775; and even after, the sentiments often did not sort cleanly along that line.[18]

The letter abstracts in the Carr-Ellison copy books suggest a few conclusions beyond what has already been said. First, it would appear that nothing could be done to restore any part of the material estate to Arthur[17a], Robert's[16a] son and heir. Thus, his best option was to be enrolled as civil servant in the East India Company. We do not know whether any effort was actually made to gain legal redress; but there is no known record of it. This seems rather odd, especially in light of another suggested conclusion from a witness' observation—namely, that the son to whom the bulk of the estate was left (i.e., Charles[16n], the second youngest son, about whom more below) had been failing to meet his father's hopes. Third, apparently nothing was done to alleviate Sarah's penurious condition in Boston, other than try to comfort her with the thought that Charles Maynard had taken her son to his bosom. Presumably one or more of the trustees felt confident in knowing the true intent of the 7th Bt when he composed his will and felt ethically bound to abide by that knowledge. One can only wonder what conversations transpired between the trustees, one or all, and Robert[16a], the 8th Bt. Trapped by terms of his father's annuity from aiding his wife and children, yet—so far as can be determined from English marital

---

[18] See, e.g., Brendan McConville, *The King's Three Faces* (Chapel Hill: University of North Carolina Press, 2006); Eric Nelson, *The Royalist Revolution* (Cambridge, MA: Belknap Press, 2014).

records—refusing the option of obtaining a divorce and marrying an English woman, he must have been tormented, perhaps to the point of a dissolution that then confirmed all the stories of libertinism.

What to Do with Those Rancorous Colonists
Had the 7th Bt lived another dozen years, his attention to North America would surely have changed—with what consequences for Robert[16a] we cannot say. By 1775 it had become apparent that "the colonial situation"—at that date, almost entirely North American in location—had deteriorated, and so quickly after the Treaty of Paris. Westminster's constituents were still fatigued of war, the cost in human casualties and in treasure a living memory. The public mood was an unhappy mixture which parliamentary ministers and backbenchers alike could easily share, regret, and then try to ignore, hoping the more sensible heads among the colonists would prevail. And it was not only trouble in the colonies that disturbed the public mood. There was also worry that maybe England, maybe Great Britain, was in danger of losing position in the world.

An illustration of much of the concerns takes the form of a letter addressed "To the PRINTER" (or, in current idiom, "To the Editor") and published 22 August 1771 in the *London Chronicle*. It is worth noting that far away, in the city of Philadelphia, Benjamin Franklin, following his usual habit of perusing the newspapers of London (and elsewhere), was taken with this letter writer's account and republished the letter in his own *Pennsylvania Gazette* on 12 December of that same year.

To the PRINTER

SIR,
Nothing is more scandalous when the distresses of this unfortunate country are talked of, than to say our neighbours are in a worse condition than ourselves. Such consolation is perfectly similar to the comfort which was once offered to a confined debtor, who was desired not to mind his misfortunes, because an intimate acquaintance of his, lately convicted of highway robbery, was then ordered for speedy execution.

It is the great misfortune of the French to suffer for the guilt of their forefathers; their liberty is lost; and their situation is beyond the reach of relief. But the case is widely different with the people of Great Britain; they are free, and have a right to expect, nay, to require, that their public concerns shall be conducted in the manner most likely to promote their evident prosperity. If this is not done, it is their right to interpose for the dismission, controul, or even punishment of Ministers, whose negligence, or whose tyranny, endangered the public happiness of the kingdom. Mismanagement in other countries is no excuse for mismanagement in this, nor can the miseries of any neighbouring nation ever afford satisfaction to the benevolent bosom of an Englishman.

But though we have heard so much about the distresses of other nations, it does not, from the conduct of any, if we except only the people of France, appear that our neighbours are really in a deplorable state. Ten years are elapsed since the conclusion of the late peace, and the Manilla Ransom is yet unpaid. Nay, Portugal, the creature of our hands, the dependent upon our immediate bounty, violates her treaties with us, and promotes her own partial interests, at the notorious expense of her Protector. Whatever the real situation of our neighbours, therefore, may be, it is obvious that they entertain no very high idea of ours, or they would not thus hazard a rupture with us, in the open face of Europe. As to France, she is a known deceiver in politics, and has often meditated a blow against this kingdom, when she herself appeared to be undone. Who that knows anything of history, can be ignorant how Lewis the Fourteenth kept the united universe at bay, when seemingly tottering on the verge of destruction; and found continual resources within himself to baffle the utmost efforts of his enemies. Let us think of these things, and let us also recollect, that notwithstanding the present imaginary ruin of the French, they have been some time industriously collecting a force at the Island of Mauritius, which is probably intended for a more important purpose than a settlement on Madagascar, though even a settlement on Madagascar is a circumstance which we should prevent by every means in our power. Portugal above all things requires our particular attention; their proceedings have of late been uniformly injurious to us in a variety of ways, and as ungratefully favorable to the trade of our enemies; so that if we should be again plunged into another war, there can be no foundation for supposing she will not take an active part against us. In all other parts of Europe we are wholly without a friend, but such as we must, purchase on terms manifestly prejudicial; at the same time that discontent is raging in England, Ireland, and America; that our affairs are in an evident state of disorder in the East Indies, that population is declining from the insupportable weight of taxes, and the whole system of national resource greatly impaired, so as to leave us almost hopeless in the future day of exigence.

This picture, Mr. Printer, is no flattering representation of our comparative superiority in the political balance of Europe; and should animate us to the utmost exertions, in order, as much as possible, to become prepared for the hour of calamity. –But instead of turning their labours to these essential objects of national felicity, the sole struggle of our Patriots is to harass the Administration; every truly great principle of public good is sacrificed to personal resentment, or interested ambition, and instead of complaining that Government does no more for our preservation, it is really surprising how, amidst the endless wantonness of opposition, they have been able to do so much. –The whole business of Parliament is now a private quarrel about places; the Sessions opens, and the Minister is attacked; the attack produces a defence; the defence opens fresh sources of accusation, and the Prorogation arrives before anything of consequence can possibly be done for the real advantage of the people.

From the specimens which we have received of Lord North's abilities since his appointment to the Treasury, in re-establishing an intercourse with America; in abrogating Parliamentary Privileges to the servants of Members; in electing Representatives during the periods of recess, and in regulating the mode of deciding contested Elections, the most flattering consequences are to be expected; if he is only allowed what the Sportsmen term *fair play*, by the Hounds of Opposition. But if he is to be *run down* the instance he suggests any measure for the general welfare, or to be eternally pursued with a personal cry, merely *because* he is a *Minister*, it will not be in his power, it will not be in any Minister's power, treated thus unfairly, to retrieve our finances from confusion. –An Administration there *must* be, and opposition for the sake of opposition, may make the government cautious not to give any *new* cause of complaint; yet it will wholly incapacitate the servants of the Crown, from effectually establishing the security of the People.

The determination with respect to General Warrants, Mr. Printer, is universally considered as an important acquisition in the favour of Liberty, yet it is by no means so essentially valuable to the subject, as the abrogation of Parliamentary Privilege in cases of debt. –An individual suffered perhaps occasionally by General Warrants, but thousands were hourly injured by the privilege, in cases of debt. –And it really is surprising, that the present reign should be considered as oppressive by popular disclaimers, since no period in our History can shew more instances of exalted attention to the public freedom. –It is fashionable to celebrate the late Prince, by way of reflecting on his successor, but good and venerable as George the Second really was, were the Judges made independent in his time? –Were General Warrants pronounced illegal in his time? –Was Parliamentary Privilege contracted in his time, or was the Press in his time tolerated with a licence unlimited? Our Patriots will feel the force of these

Questions, whatever Answer they may think proper to make, and I shall have justice from their hearts, though their tongues may reproach me with being a Ministerial Hireling.
ARTHUR HASLERIG.

So who was this fellow? Arthur[16b] Hesilrige, second son and namesake of the 7th Bt.

Before pursuing the letter writer, a few notes about context and some specific events will aid in understanding the letter's contents. First of all, to begin with a technical matter, recall that "prorogation" refers to the close of business of a parliamentary session before the term has ended. Presumably all business has been finished; parliament, now "prorogued," may be called back into session under certain specified conditions and rules, until and unless its term ends.

Substantively, one should bear in mind that governmental politics in England during the 1760s and early 1770s were unsettled for internal as well as external reasons. George II had been a rather unpopular king, in part because he was thought to be an ill-tempered boor. His son and heir apparent, Frederick, died in 1751, and that event brought Frederick's son to the throne in 1760 as George III, at age 22. The dominant force in domestic politics had been for quite some time parliament, its ministers and committees. That did not change under George III. What did change, however, was the character of the monarch. This young king, unlike his Hanoverian forebears, had been born in Great Britain and spoke English as his native tongue. He was also fortunate in bringing to successful end in 1763 the contest with France (the Seven Years War). As already said, this victory resulted in Great Britain becoming the dominant imperial power in most of North America and in India—indeed, in most of the western hemisphere. But no sooner had that war ended than troubles with North American colonists began to grow both in proportion and in consequence. Being somewhat at the mercy of contests between Tories and Whigs for the formation of ministerial governments, with power switching back and forth rather quickly, George III failed to apprehend the superior advice of the few ministers who understood the rebellious colonists' legitimate complaints; and the rest of the story is, as the cliché has it, history.[19]

---

[19] A history that can be written rather differently from each of at least four standpoints: that of the rebellious colonists, that of the loyalists (especially those north of the St Lawrence River), that of most of the British public, and that of the Native American or indigenous (Indian) population of North America.

During the last years of the Seven Years War, Britain also tangled with Spain, partly in an expedition to the Philippines as a result of which Manila and a seaport were captured and occupied (1762-64) by the British. The expedition was led by General William Draper and Admiral Samuel Cornish. Having captured a Spanish galleon and other booty, the British demanded a ransom from Spain. This was probably motivated mainly as a personal reward for Draper and Cornish, a plain agreement in which London acquiesced since the ransom could be used to pay expenses as well as personal reward (a not uncommon practice at the time, an all but official piracy). The ransom was never paid. Spain simply refused, and as there were other and much more pressing matters in ministerial government in London, the claim got little attention, none that made the ransom demand worth another fight. But for many people in Great Britain the failure to enforce "the Manilla ransom" was a serious lapse. In his *History of England in the Eighteenth Century*[20] William Edward Hartpole Lecky, describing various proceedings of ministerial governments during the 1760s that were not "fitted to add to their popularity," opined that "Their tame acquiescence in the Spanish refusal to pay the Manilla Ransom offended bitterly the national pride." In the same year that Arthur published his letter, Samuel Johnson published an essay, "Thoughts on the late Transactions respecting Falkland's Islands," in which he refers to the upset over "the Manilla ransom."[21] This episode remained an issue in domestic politics for some time.

Arthur's[16b] citation of "Portugal, the creature of our hands," referred probably to the fact that Britain had supported Portugal after it became independent of Spain in 1640. This support was enhanced when in 1662 the British monarch, Charles II, married a member of Portugal's newly royal House of Braganza, Catherine. But the support continued after the reign of Charles II, mainly because of the continuing contest between Britain and Spain. No doubt the Portuguese people would have objected (then as now) to Arthur's[16b] attribution, "creature of our hands."

Arthur's[16b] apparent defense of Frederick North, 2nd earl of Guilford, chancellor of the Exchequer, and prime minister of Great Britain (1770-82), is perhaps understandable in the sense of a general sentiment of "give the fellow a chance." Hindsight is unavoidable, of course: North proved to be inept in handling the colonists' revolt by

---

[20] (London: Longmans, Green, 1882), volume 3, page 83.
[21] The essay is found in various places in different editions of Johnson's collected works—e.g., pages 96-141 of volume 8 of *The Works of Samuel Johnson*, edited by Arthur Murphy (London, 1810).

proposing ever harsher punitive actions. One could argue that it was clear enough by 1771 that North was not the most adept at dealing with matters of those "rancorous colonists," especially in light of the fact that one of his recent predecessors, William Pitt ("the elder"; i.e., the 1st earl of Chatham) had clearly offered accurate insights into the motivations of rebellious factions and had proposed responses that might well have defused the impending crisis. But such is hindsight.

While it is rather obvious that Arthur[16b] wrote the letter as a missive in domestic politics, his views nonetheless provide some insight into the balance of concerns in public sentiment. Given his offices— captain of the county militia, justice of the peace, part of a commission for setting rates of carriage transport from and to London (e.g., Middlesex sessions 1 May 1781)—his views would not have been far from the typical for those of a similar political persuasion.

An Englishman in India
Born in 1756 in Massachusetts, Arthur[17a] sailed to Calcutta, India, on appointment to the East India Company, after having benefited from schooling, both under the aegis of baron Maynard. The record is a bit choppy with regard to dates, but judging by dates of correspondence in the copy books of Carr-Ellison he probably arrived in London from his birth home in Massachusetts during the summer months of 1770, at age 14. He almost surely made the ocean voyage without accompaniment, on an adventure of much uncertainty. Whatever assurances he may have been told by his mother and others, he could not have been deaf to the tensions due to his father's English family's displeasure. However that may be, we are told by another source that he "landed as a writer [in Calcutta] in 1773," at age 17.[22] There he lived the remaining days of his rather short life, dying during the fourth year of the nineteenth century.

Imagine the contrasting experiences that the young man processed during his adolescence and young adulthood. First living a life of some comfort and standing as heir to a titled Englishman in the Boston area of what was still sometimes called "the New World," he soon must come to terms with the apparent fact that his father had abandoned him, his two sisters, and their mother. He might well have been aware that his father's family regretted his very existence. Next, he is transported to England, where an elderly man takes him under wing, sends him to a prominent

---

[22] W W Hunter, *The Annals of Rural Bengal* (London: Smith, Elder, & Co., 1868), page 79. Note that Calcutta is now known as Kolkata, which is a variant spelling of one of the three villages that coalesced into a trading town and seaport on the river Hooghly.

school, then arranges an appointment for him in the East Indian Company's civil Service. Did he have any contact with his father while in the London area? There is no evidence one way or the other; but if Maynard felt compelled to abide by the wishes of the lad's paternal grandfather, he likely stood between father and son. And then, after three years in and around London, the young man endures another, and longer, ocean voyage, this time to a city of roughly 150,000 inhabitants, located on the east bank of the river Hooghly, north of the Bay of Bengal, in the eastern part of India. It was a city of sharply divided parts: in the central and eastern part, an area known as White Town, occupied mainly by British citizens whose presence was due to the same joint-stock company, now increasingly acting as an imperial power with the full blessings of Westminster, Whitehall, and Canterbury; to the north, another area, known as Black Town. It would be understandable that young Arthur[17a] thought of this contrast on analogy to the contrast known to the typical Massachusetts school boy, between white, European, or British and "redskin" or "Indian." He also would have heard his new place of abode described as "a pestilential town." He would have experienced as never before a tropical climate of alternating wet and dry seasons, with many sweltering summer days of temperatures reaching toward 100°F. It would have required a number of adjustments in living, including, most likely, at least occasional renewals of the feeling of having been abandoned by family. One wonders if anyone informed him of his father's death, which occurred at least 24 years after his arrival in India and at least 22 years after his mother's death in Massachusetts.[23]

Life in India was indeed a new order of colonial empire, different from what he had known in Massachusetts, a fact which Arthur[17a] surely grew to appreciate as his years passed. Fort William, built in 1712 and improved repeatedly thereafter, began as protection of the East India Company's (EIC) trading factory, but became the center of an extensive military force organized and controlled by the EIC, along with its own civil service, until the British crown took control in 1858 and established direct rule, the "British raj." By 1772 Calcutta was headquarters of the

---

[23] The Museum of Fine Arts in Boston has in its collection (but not on display) a small painting of Arthur[17a] as a lad of perhaps 13 years. The image, which is not of very good quality, could be digitally cleaned and clarified by a professional graphics technician, but the legal agreement that would have authorized reproduction of the image for the purposes of this book would have disallowed modifications of the image. Further, that agreement would have entailed unwanted restrictions on the book as a whole. Suffice to say of the image that it depicts a young adolescent who looks much like an immature version of his paternal grandfather, the 7th Bt (Exhibit 9.8).

EIC, later to become capital city of all of India. The volume of trade (which included more than opium) was enormous even before industrial plants began their work in India during the nineteenth century. However, if Rothschild's estimate is more or less correct, Arthur[17a] must have felt a bit estranged, especially in the beginning, for he would have been one of "no more than a few hundred British subjects" employed by the East India Company in all of India (which then included what are today Pakistan and Bangladesh).[24]

Perspective is well-nigh everything, of course, and what one sees varies accordingly, because attention varies accordingly. In one of the first novels written by someone who had direct experience with the EIC service, an early conversation between the novel's central character, Edward Oakfield, and a fellow Englishman who had been in India quite some time includes this passage:

> Well, old fellow, you know best why you came out. I tell you candidly I can't comprehend it. I can understand a boy of sixteen being glad to get away from school, and rush to the gorgeous East to wear a red coat; but why you at one-and-twenty, should have voluntarily abandoned a respectable university career to come to this wretched country, I cannot conceive.[25]

But come they did. Kent, who had studied the phenomenon mainly during the Victorian era (and who quoted most of that passage by Arnold), made the crucial point that it began at home, in England and Scotland, in a distinctive formation of power both commercial and imperial which produced requisite actors who were eager to serve crown and country in far-off reaches of an empire on which the sun never failed to shine.[26] Arthur[17a] probably did not begin as one of those young actors. But he may have grown into one.

If he arrived as "a writer" in 1773, he soon moved into management and collection of accounts. According to one EIC record, vague though it is, he was "appointed Assistant at Dinagepore January 1775." The naming has changed enough that locating "Dinagepore" on

---

[24] Emma Rothschild, *The Inner Life of Empires* (Princeton: Princeton University Press), page 185.
[25] William D Arnold, *Oakfield* (London: Longmans, Brown, Green, and Longmans, 1853), page 2.
[26] Eddy Kent, *Corporate Character* (Toronto: University of Toronto Press, 2014).

available maps from the early 1800s has proved an elusive quest. Apparently the name was of a sizeable district in the vicinity of Burdwan, which is today about 60 miles northwest of Kolkata. It was thus a bit out of the way, probably a typical "breaking in" assignment. The length of Arthur's[17a] stay in that district is not known, nor do we know to what office he was "assistant" or anything of his progression. Hunter reported that he was "assistant and occasionally acting Collector of Beerbhoom or Bishenpore, from 25th April 1786 to 9th July, when he was removed on a charge of embezzlement." He cleared himself and gained appointment as "Collector of Jessore from the 1st May 1793." The interval of about seven years (1786 to 1793) is a blank to us. Surely he cleared himself of the charge much more quickly than that, but we lack any further indication of the charge, its dismissal, or his activity during that interval. The only other known record has Arthur[17a] as "Senior Merchant in the Civil List of 1804," which was but months before his death.[27]

He married twice, first to Elizabeth Charnaud, who was of a family of French Huguenots who had fled during the purges, some to Switzerland and some to Britain, and at least one eventually to Smyrna (today, Izmir), Turkey, and the Levant Company. An English chartered company founded in 1581 for purposes of organizing trade with cities of the Levant, the company established trading posts in several cities that were already commercial centers—chiefly, Aleppo (the company's headquarters), Alexandria, Smyrna, and Constantinople. Agents in each city, known as "factors," were expected to be wholesale merchants, facilitating flows of goods across Levantine networks and with other factories such as those in Bengal, then on to London. The company was hardly a colonial venture like the EIC in India—the Ottoman rulers would not have tolerated such effort—but it monopolized trade between Turkey and Britain, and it planted small cultural enclaves of residents from Britain, France, Greece, and elsewhere in each of the cities. In Smyrna the main influence from northern Europe was probably French, but well-to-do British families were also prominent within the cosmopolitan blend of legal traditions, languages, and other parts of cultural heritages interwoven with Turkic and Arab cultures.[28]

---

[27] Hunter, *Annals* ... (1868), page 79. Beerbhoom is today Birbhum, a district of West Bengal and about 120 miles northwest of Kolkata. Bishenpore, today Bishenpur, is a district of the state of Manipur and more than 900 miles northeast of Kolkata; so Hunter probably meant Beerbhoom, not Bishenpore. Jessore, today a city and district of Bangladesh, is about 80 miles northeast of Kolkata.
[28] See, e.g., Philip Mansel, *Levant: Splendor and Catastrophe on the Mediterranean* (New Haven: Yale University Press, 2010.

Elizabeth's father (still unidentified) was probably a factor in the Levant Company (several Charnaud men were associated with the company in one way or another). How she and Arthur[17a] met is unknown. Perhaps she accompanied her father on a business journey to Calcutta. In any case, the two wed c1796 in what would be a short union: Elizabeth died childless 29 July 1797. The notice of her death said, "At Calcutta, Mrs Hesilrige, wife of Arthur Hesilrige esq. judge and collector of the department of Jessore, only son of Sir Robert H. of Noseley, co. of Leicester, bart." Elizabeth was buried reportedly in a Calcutta cemetery.

Arthur[17a] married secondly Charlotte Elisabeth Gray, daughter of Sir James Gray, 2nd Bt. The wedding occurred 27 Feb 1798 in St John's Anglican church of Calcutta. Judging by the proximity of that date and the death of his first wife, one would conclude that Charlotte had been an acquaintance and a Calcutta resident, which suggests in turn that her father was employed by the East Indian Company. Apparently this union, too, produced no offspring. After Arthur died (1804), she married 1 Aug 1805, in Burdwan, West Bengal, a fellow named Henry William James Wilkinson, by whom she had six children, before dying at sea in 1817, intended destination not known by us.

It may be noted that a pedigree chart compiled for the Hesilrige family lists 1805 as year of Arthur's[17a] death. Other records, including family records of the Grays, indicate a death date of 28 July 1804, which is very likely correct. His death was announced in *The Annual Register of World Events*: "Sir Arthur Hesilrige, bart. of Noseley-hall, in the county of Leicester; by whose death the title devolves to his uncle Thomas H. Maynard, esq. of Hoxne-hall, Suffolk, now Sir Thomas Hesilrige Maynard, bart." The account also reported him as "in the East India company's civil service"; nothing more. [29] He died in Lucknow, where the EIC had a concession (to be much expanded later in the century). Lucknow is more than 650 miles west-northwest of Calcutta. Had his assignment been moved, or was he on circuit? We do not know. Nor do we know the cause or circumstances of his death. Had he suffered bouts of chronic illness? Were they related to the apparent fact that he was unable to sire children? All questions without answers.

Before closing this section note must be taken of a friend and business associate of Arthur[17a] in India. A man named Richard Blechynden, born in Islington in 1790, arrived in India when about 22 years old and set out on a career as surveyor and builder, mostly in and

---

[29]*The Annual Register of World Events: A Review of the Year*, volume 47 (London: Longmans, Green, 1805), page 482. "Hoxne" is pronounced *hok-sən*.

near Calcutta. On arrival, it appears, he took lodgings with Arthur[17a] for a time. When in 1822 Richard died in that city, he left behind a multi-volume diary in which he recorded events of his own life along with extensive accounts of his personal views of life in Calcutta and of people he knew. During his 40 years in India he never married, or so it appears, but lived with a sequence of concubines, some of them Indian, some mixed, and at least one an English daughter of a fellow official. By these various women he had at least seven children, six of them surviving to adulthood. One of the six was a son named Arthur, born in Calcutta 10 February 1790.[30]

Arthur continued his father's business after the latter's death in 1822. He married Josephine Frances de Carrion ("last surviving issue of the late Count de Carrion") 7 December 1813, with whom he had three sons, of whom at least one married and had a daughter, who published an interesting memoir of life in Calcutta in 1905.[31]

Arthur[17a] was godfather to Richard's son Arthur, who was named Arthur Hesilridge Blechynden. (Why Richard used that spelling is not known.) The mother was described as "a Moslem woman." An entry in Richard's diary has him thinking of sending Arthur to England (the date is 21 January 1795) and wondering about his reception: "surely my relations must have more liberality of Sentiment than to refuse to notice him because he is illegitimate—that is not *his* fault it is *mine*." Judging from the Blechynden family records, the "relations" did not include a Hesilrige, so the naming must have been due only to the local connection. Richard left behind an interesting picture of the hardships of English life in India, which very likely pertained to Arthur[17a] Hesilrige as well, including bouts of severe indebtedness (as a result of which, at one point, according to Richard, Arthur[17a] was imprisoned).

Arthur Hesilridge Blechynden died in Calcutta in April 1836 and was buried (11 April) probably in South Park Street Cemetery.

---

[30] Sources in addition to the Blechynden family records include three works by Peter Robb, who has extensively studied the voluminous diary of Richard Blechynden and related materials: "Credit, Work, and Race in 1790s Calcutta," *India Economic and Social History*, volume 37 (2000), pages 1-25; and a two-volume set, *Sex and Sensibility* and *Sentiment and Self* (Oxford: Oxford University Press, 2011).

[31] Katheleen Blechynden, *Calcutta Past and Present* (London: W Thacker, 1905).

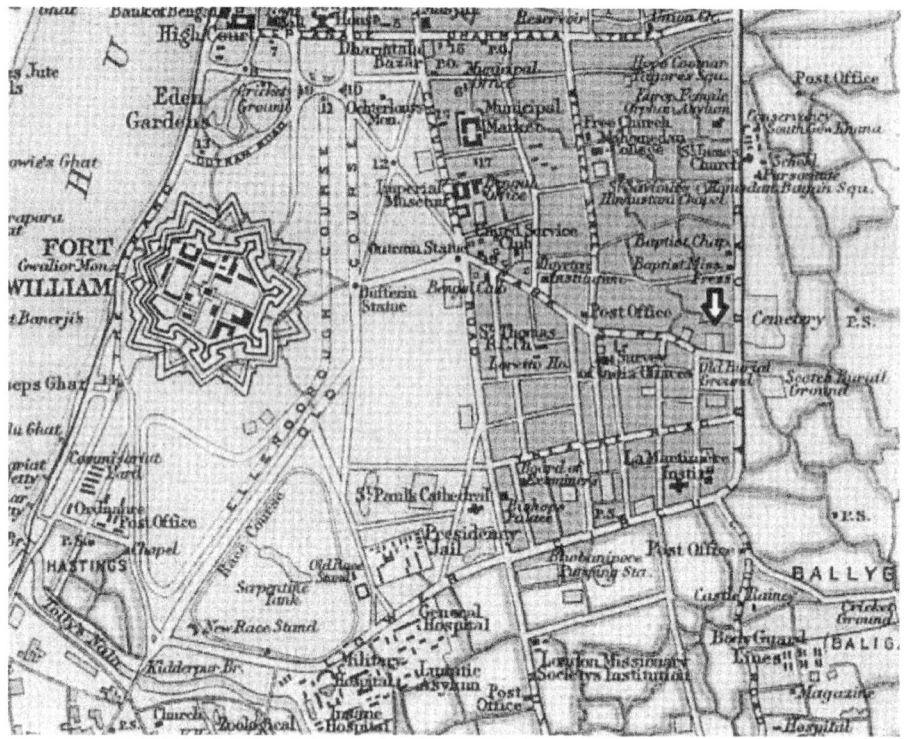

Exhibit 10.4. Map of a Central Area of Calcutta, 1893

The map in Exhibit 10.4 depicts the central area of Calcutta, 1893, from Fort William on the east bank of the river Hooghly eastward toward the Lower Circular Road and beyond. Note the locational arrow at middle right side of the map: it points to "the Old Burial Ground" on Palmer Street, to its right a larger cemetery, and south of that the "Scotch Burial Ground." The cemetery was established in 1766, as final places were needed for the legions of British residents who died of disease (especially dysentery and malaria), problems of childbirth, or, to a far smaller extent, activities of military service. There once were two cemeteries: North Park Street Cemetery, located on the north side of Park Street, and South Park Street Cemetery (both can be seen in Exhibit 10.4). The former was replaced by a church and church hospital. The latter still exists, now surrounded by Calcutta's central commercial district and residential apartments, and schools and colleges. Although in a poor state of repair as the many monuments and tombs have slowly decayed, the cemetery certainly recalls the impact of the British Raj and its predecessor, the EIC, as a large portion of the gravesites proclaim the substantial importance of those persons who found this their last place of rest.

Arthur[17a] might have been buried in the Palmer Street Cemetery, perhaps alongside his first wife; but if either of them had a memorial marker, it has become illegible if not entirely absent. There is no evidence that Arthur[17a] ever returned to England, either on business or to visit family and perhaps explore the possibility of permanent return. Given the parlous state of his finances, he probably could not have afforded the journey.

A few years before the cemetery added its last resident, Rudyard Kipling recorded this description in the last of the articles comprising his *City of Dreadful Night* [32]: go

> up a long and utterly deserted thoroughfare, running between high walls. This is the place, and the entrance to it, with its *mallee* [i.e., Mālī, gardener] waiting with one brown, battered rose for the visitor, its grilled door and its professional notices, bears a hideous likeness to the entrance of Simla churchyard. But, once inside, the sightseer stands in the heart of utter desolation—all the more forlorn for being swept up. Lower Park Street cuts a great graveyard in two. The guide-books will tell you when the place was opened and when it was closed. The eye is ready to swear that it is as old as Herculaneum and Pompeii. The tombs are small houses. It is as though we walked down the streets of a town, so tall are they and so closely do they stand—a town shrivelled by fire, and scarred by frost and siege. They must have been afraid of their friends rising up before the due time that they weighted them with such cruel mounds of masonry. Strong man, weak woman, or somebody's "infant son aged fifteen months"—it is all the same. For each the squat obelisk, the defaced classic temple, the cellaret of chunam, or the candlestick of brickwork—the heavy slab, the rust-eaten railings, the whopper-jawed cherubs and the apoplectic angels. Men were rich in those days and could afford to put a hundred cubic feet of masonry into the grave of even so humble a person as "Jno. Clements, Captain of the Country Service, 1820." When the "dearly beloved" had held rank answering to that of Commissioner, the efforts are still more sumptuous and the verse....
> Well, the following speaks for itself:
> Soft on thy tomb shall fond Remembrance shed

---

[32] (New York: Alex Grosset, 1899), pages 87-89. The articles were composed during the mid- to late-1880s, and first published individually as newspaper articles. Kipling is notorious, of course, for his dismissive attitudes toward most things Indian, especially educated Indian men, but in those he was rather typical.

>The warm yet unavailing tear,
>And purple flowers that deck the honoured dead
>Shall strew the loved and honoured bier.

Failure to comply with the contract does not, let us hope, entail forfeiture of the earnest-money; or the honoured dead might be grieved. The slab is out of his tomb, and leans foolishly against it; the railings are rotted, and there are no more lasting ornaments than blisters and stains, which are the work of the weather, and not the result of the "warm yet unavailing tear." The eyes that promised to shed them have been closed any time these seventy years.

Let us go about and moralise cheaply on the tombstones, trailing the robe of pious reflection up and down the pathways of the grave. Here is a big and stately tomb sacred to "Lucia," who died in 1776 A.D., aged 23. Here also be verses which an irreverent thumb can bring to light.

The Fortunes of Noseley Hall

Whatever the actual case of his first son and heir Sir Robert[16a], it is very clear in retrospect that Sir Arthur's[15a] concern about the future of his estate, an estate which he and Hannah had recovered, restored, and in large measure rebuilt, was not entirely misplaced. In naming Charles[16n], his second youngest son, as heir of Noseley, the 7th Bt was venturing a hope that this young boy would grow into the responsible man that he could not see in Robert[16a], or Arthur[16b], or Thomas[16l], for whatever reason. Note that while a specific story of poor behavior has attended the memory of Robert[16a], we have no details of the 7th Bt's supposed assessment of either Arthur[16b] or Thomas[16l] as deficient in expected qualities.

Not yet to his nineteenth birthday anniversary in 1763, Charles[16n] presumably had not demonstrated the poor behaviors that his father had so regretted in the three surviving older brothers. That alone would not account for the choice of Charles[16n] over his younger brother Grey[16q], but perhaps their father thought Grey[16q] *too* young, too far removed from age of majority. In any case, Arthur[7a] stipulated in his will that the bulk of his material estate would pass first to his widow, Hannah (who survived him by two years), and then to Charles[16n] on attaining his 25th birthday anniversary, with Grey[16q] named as secondary beneficiary at age 25 years. When the calendar turned to that November day in 1769, there was a grand celebration, with the whole of the town of Northampton invited to a party. As reported in local newspaper, the *Mercury*, in early December, "great rejoicings were made here by the ringing of bells at all our churches most of the day, an ox was roasted and given to the poor, and in the evening grand fireworks were played off in [Charles'] gardens in Gold Street in this town." Whether anyone at the time recognized his party as mere preamble is not known.

The taste for profligacy—although he probably did not think of it in that way—was quickly expanded. In 1770 Charles[16n] became sheriff of Leicestershire, and here the arena for performance was much wider. As John Nichols recounted the scene (he was probably an eyewitness of the event), Charles[16n] used a mode of ceremonial transport that surely recalled his third-great grandfather's carriage in London:

> His carriage was drawn by six fine blood chestnut horses, which were said to have cost £500, and were afterwards purchased by Mr Hungerford of Dingley. He had in his suite thirty javelin-men in green coats, with half collars, and buff waistcoats and breeches, to whom he gave stockings, hats, and gloves. The procession was conducted by a marshall; and two trumpeters with silk flags finely emblazoned with the family arms. Two French-horn men also preceded the cavalcade; and two servants out of livery, several footmen, and two pages, in light handsome dresses, on each side of the carriage.[33]

If all of that seems odd, it was in fact customary in that day. A typical ceremonial retinue (including that of a condemned man on his way to the gallows) featured a top-level officer of law (marshall or sheriff or both, plus an undersheriff), followed by a "priest, constable, and javelin-men who were meant to impart solemnity and security to the procession."[34]

Charles[16n] and his wife Sarah (*nee* Wall) lived their private lives in a similar high-consumption style, until they depleted much of the estate's liquidity. Then, sometime after 1786, Charles[16n], apparently alone, fled to France with a train of many creditors close to heel. He died in Boulogne (probably Boulogne-sur-Mer, Pas de Calais), without issue.

Before he fled, Charles[16n] had been induced by his younger brother Grey[16q] to agree to a financial settlement to benefit in separate equal trusts their sisters, Hannah[16i], Bridget[16j], and Ammabell[16p], all of whom were at that date (30 July 1783) unmarried. (Ammabell[16p] married the next year; both other sisters remained unmarried.) The three trusts, based on a principal of £2000, were annuitized at an annual interest rate

---

[33] John Nichols, *The History and Antiquities of the County of Leicester* (London, 1798), volume 2, part 2, page 749 n.3.
[34] V.A.C. Gatrell, *The Hanging Tree* (Oxford: Oxford University Press, 1996), page 33.

of five percent, and held by William Tockington, of Stamford, Lincolnshire (which was place of residence of the three sisters) and by John Adams of Symonds Inn, Chancery Lane, Middlesex.[35]

Their eldest sister, Elizabeth, eldest daughter of the 7th Bt and Hannah, married a clergyman nine years her senior in 1760 at Kibworth-Beauchamp, Leicestershire, and they begat a long lineage of Buckbys several of whom repeated Hesilrige family names. Recall from chapter 9 a discussion of the possibility that female descendants of the 2nd Bt could have faced "obstacles by surname" in local marriage markets (though little if any evidence of it was found). Here we have, if anything to do with events a century earlier, what might be considered celebration of the name. In illustration of the point, an abbreviated segment of the Buckby family lineage immediately follows.[36]

> Rev. Richard Buckby of Kibworth, Leicestershire: b. 8 March 1722, d. 18 January 1796 Seagoe, County Armagh; appointed vicar of Seagoe, County Armagh, 1763; m. 5 June 1760 Elizabeth Hesilrige, eldest daughter of Sir Arthur, 7th Bt, and Hannah (*nee* Sturges) Hesilrige
> ⌞ Hannah Buckby: b. & d. 1762 Kibworth
> ⌞ Hesilrige Buckby: b & d. 1762 (twin of Hannah?) Kibworth
> ⌞ Richard Buckby: b. 7 October 1765 Seagoe, Armagh, d. 2 July 1830
> ⌞ Arthur Buckby: b. 13 November 1768, d. 5 August 1825; m. Elizabeth McDonnell (b. 1768 Tangragee, Armagh)
>   ⌞ Richard Buckby: b. c1800
>   ⌞ William Buckby: b. >1800; m. Jemima Hesilrige, daughter of Grey Hesilrige & Bridget Buckby
>   ⌞ Arthur Grey Buckby: b. 18??, d. >1870; m. 14 October 1852 Catherine Cave-Brown; issue: Arthur Grey Hesilrige Buckby of New Zealand (b. c1854), Dorothy Hesilrige Buckby, Robert Hesilrige Buckby (b. 1856), Charles Maynard Hesilrige Buckby (b. 1858), William Cave Hesilrige Buckby (b. 1864), John Roger Hesilrige Buckby (b. 1861), Catherine Hesilrige Buckby (b. 1864),

---

[35] See document DG21/157, Hazlerigg Collection. Note, again, that there is uncertainty regarding the forename of Ammabell[16p]: in her father's will she is so cited, but in other records she is named "Arabel" or "Arabell." She was probably named after Banastre Maynard's daughter Amabell, sister of Dorothy, wife of Robert[14a] Hesilrige, 6th Bt., both women sisters of Charles, 6th baron Maynard (of whom, more below).

[36] Most of this is taken from William G D Fletcher's *Leicestershire Pedigrees and Royal Descents* (Leicester: Clarke and Hodgson, 1887), pages 63-66.

Thomas Edward Hesilrige Buckby (b. 1867), and two more
       L- and eight others
L- John Buckby: b. 1805
L- Charlotte Buckby: b. c1810, d. 1885
L- Elizabeth Buckby: b. c1810
L- Deborah Maria Buckby: b. c1811 Armagh, Eire, d. Dec 1866 Armagh; m. 10 March 1829 Charles Maynard Hesilrige (b. 24 Aug 1802, d. 4 Dec 1878)

L- John Buckby: b. 13 Oct 1772, d. 17 May 1839

L- Bridget Buckby: b. >1760; m. Col. Grey Hesilrige of Noseley (b. 1748, d. 1810)

L- Charlotte Buckby: b. >1760; m. Fnu Humfrey

L- Dorothy Buckby: b. > 1760; m. Robert Haymes

It is evident from the repeated intermarriages as well as the use of names that some parts of the Buckby family took pride in the relationship.

Exhibit 10.5. Col. Grey Hesilrige

After the fiasco of Charles[16n], the residue was left to Grey[16q], who in the meanwhile had established a reputation for leadership, prudence, and sound judgment in Northamptonshire, where he attained the rank of Colonel as leader of the county militia. Col. Hesilrige, as he was generally styled, and his wife, Bridget Buckby, were parents of at least nine children, including Sir Arthur[17b], the 11th Bt (whom we meet again below), and Charles[17h] Maynard Hesilrige (next chapter).

Grey[16q] and Bridget's second oldest son, Thomas[17d], was lost at sea in 1814 when his ship, carrying him and other soldiers for combat in a war with the USA, was wrecked. Identity of this ship has not been determined. It might have been a troop transport carrying replacement troops for the 58th (Rutlandshire) Regiment, which had been sent from combat in the war with Napoleon to Quebec in May 1814, to defend Canada and engage the forces of the USA. Lacking name of the ship, we cannot determine cause of the ship's loss.

Exhibit 10.6. Robert Greville Hesilrige's Waterloo Medal

Their third oldest son, Robert[17e] Greville, survived the Waterloo campaign, having served in the 2nd Battalion of the 73rd (Highland) Regiment of Foot since mustering in 17 September 1810. But he was wounded during the battle at Quatre Bras, a crossroads about eleven miles south of Waterloo (all today in Belgium). No description of his wound(s) has been found. He was awarded The Waterloo Medal. Although some records show him with rank of captain, his service record shows him as an ensign at the time of the battle and leaving army service as a lieutenant. Robert[17e] died a few years after leaving service, cause unknown, perhaps a delayed result of the wound.[37]

Not only do victors write the histories; a goodly portion of what is written is propaganda. Some of that is conspicuous enough that later readers can filter it out, if they are so inclined. The more insidious part of it, however, is usually less easy to detect, because it is in effect a species of the Whiggish view of history (mentioned earlier). A prime illustration of the point, in Britain and to a considerable extent in the USA as well, concerns the Napoleonic wars. As various scholars have emphasized, the tendency has been to see the outcome as virtually inevitable.[38] It was anything but. The battle at Quatre Bras, for instance, has usually been regarded as a strategic victory for the French forces, even though tactically it was won by the alliance of Britain and Prussia. More generally, England experienced great fright throughout the land—and for very good reason, as rumors of invasion were furthered by rumors of Napoleon's forces using his new air force of balloons to cross the water, then as reconnaissance, and drop that day's version of a gravity bomb. For all the exhortations of the gallantry of a Wellington and a Nelson, there were hordes of soldiers and sailors who had managed to survive despite missing limbs and persistent threat of gangrene, only to be lost at home for lack of medical services. Robert[17e] might well have been one such casualty.

When Sir Arthur[15a] Hesilrige, 7th Bt, wrote his will leaving the bulk of his material estate first to his widow and then to son Charles[16n], followed by son Grey[16q], he had for all practical purposes left son Thomas[16l] out of the queue, which fact Thomas[16l], already 23 years old at the time of the 7th Bt's death, surely considered in regard to his own future. While it was of course possible that both of his younger brothers would die at relatively young ages, he must have known the odds were against it. So his choice was to devise his own fortune as best he could. Why his father considered Thomas[16l] to be unworthy of first inheritance

---

[37] Charles Dalton, *The Waterloo Roll Call*, 2nd edition (London: Eyre and Spottiswoode, 1904), pages 185, 187.
[38] A recent corrective account is Jenny Uglow's *In These Times: Living in Britain through Napoleon's Wars, 1793-1815* (London: Faber and Faber, 2014).

is another of the mysteries of the 7th Bt's motivation. He had been admitted to Emmanuel College, Cambridge, 29 September 1758, and paid his own way. It is true he was unmarried at the time his father composed his will, but at only 23 years of age Thomas[16l] was hardly unusual in that regard.

Thomas[16l] established a good relationship with Charles, the 6th baron and 1st viscount Maynard, perhaps at about the same time that the latter man was being asked to act as a sort of guardian of Robert[16a] Hesilrige's young son, Arthur[17a], by bringing the lad to England from Massachusetts (which he did, as we saw earlier). Maynard was by that time an elderly man, never married, without children, living at Hoxne Hall, in Suffolk. He left his Hoxne estate to Thomas[16l], surely an arrangement that had been agreed prior to Maynard's death in 1775. Probably also, part of the agreement was that Thomas[16l] would assume the Maynard surname, which he did. Or perhaps that decision was solely on his own initiative: it is easy to imagine that Thomas[16l] felt some conflicted emotions about his own recent heritage as a Hesilrige.

For the next quarter-century he lived as lord of the manor of Hoxne, unmarried, with various interesting contacts in London and elsewhere. An early friendship was established with Laurence Sterne, author of one of the classics of English satire—indeed, English literature in general—*The Life and Opinions of Tristram Shandy, Gentleman*, first published as a serial in nine volumes. A surviving letter from Sterne to Thomas[16l] Hesilrige can be read in Exhibit 10.7.[39] Sterne was alerting Thomas[16l] to forthcoming works and soliciting his help with subscriptions, the standard means of financing publication costs.

As mentioned in previous discussions, English arts and letters began during the latter half of the seventeenth century to regale readers and viewers with various forms of satire, among other artistic delights. Following Jonathan Swift's (1667-1745) biting satire in critique of the society of his day, William Hogarth (1697-1764) concocted a series of lampoons of the pomposity and hypocrisy of, and associated with, certain character types. A short time later Laurence Sterne (1713-1768) began another sort of satirical work, this one offering a softer, amusing quality which invited readers to smile at themselves with a touch of irony. This trend told of a newer, more subtle sense of humor, one that could be self-deprecating even while opening perspective to divergent scenarios.

---

[39] First published in Wilbur Lucius Cross, *The Life and Times of Laurence Sterne* (New York: Macmillan, 1909), pages 349-50, 528.

> York, July 5 [1765]
>
> *My dear dear Sir*
>
> *I made a thousand enquiries after you all this last winter and was told I should see you some part of it, in town—pray how do you do? and how do you go on, in this silly world? Have you seen my seven and eight graceless children?—but I am doing penance for them, in begetting a couple of more ecclesiastick ones—which are to stand penance (again) in their turns—in Sheets about the middle September—they will appear in the Shape of the third and fourth volumes of Yorick. These you must know are to keep up a kind of balance, in my Shandaic character, and are push'd into the world for that reason by my friends with as splendid and numerous a List of Nobility &c—as ever pranced before a book, since subscriptions came into fashion—I should grieve not to have your name amongst those of my friends—and in so much good company as it has a right to be in—so tell me to set it down—and if you can—Lord Maynard's—I have no design , my dear Hesselridge, upon your purse—'tis but a crown—but I have a design upon the credit [of] Lord Maynard's name—and that of a person I love and esteem so much as I do you. If any occasions come in your way of adding three or four more to the list, your friendship for me, I know will do it.*
>
> *N.B.—You must take their crowns—and keep them for me till fate does the courtesy to throw me in your way—This will not be, I fear, this year—for in September, I set out Solus for Italy—and shall winter at Rome and Naples. L'hyvere à Londres ne vaut pas rien, pur les poumones—à cause d'humidité et la fume don't l'aire est chargée—Let me hear how you do soon—and believe me ever your devoted and affectionate friend and wellwisher*
>
> *L. Sterne*

Exhibit 10.7. Laurence Sterne to Thomas Hesilrige, 1765[40]

Although we do not know exactly how early began the friendship between Sterne and Thomas[161], it is clear that the two men had exchanged visits as well as correspondence on numerous occasions prior to this letter

---

[40] The French sentence in the letter reads, "Winter in London is not good for the lungs, due to humidity and air filled with smoke." Sterne suffered tuberculosis.

of July 1765. Thomas[16l] was then employed in service to Sir William Maynard, 4th Bt, of Walthamstow, a cousin of Charles, 6th baron and 1st viscount Maynard.[41] William Maynard (1721-1772) was then an MP for Essex (1759-72), and it was probably to him that Sterne referred in his request of aid from Thomas[16l]. Judging from the correspondence with Sterne, one could see added evidence that Thomas[16l], in his mid-twenties, was mostly estranged from his Hesilrige kinfolk: he did not mention them; and, notably, Sterne did not ask him to solicit subscriptions from any of his Hesilrige kin, at least not directly by name. However, that sense of evidence would be only weakly supported, since most of the correspondence did not survive.

It is also notable that, so far as we can tell from the record, Thomas[16l] did not marry until after he succeeded his nephew, Arthur[17a], as 10th Bt. Thomas[16l] was then approaching his 65th birthday anniversary. Why he did not marry during his years as lord Maynard of Hoxne Hall is another question that remains open. Perhaps his sense of personal identity was unsteady or unresolved.

In any case, in 1805 he wed Mary, daughter of Edmund Tyrell (1703-1749) of Gipping Hall, Suffolk. Mary was probably Tyrell's daughter by his first wife, Mary Sparrow, which would have put her birth year sometime between c1730 and 1743. Given that Thomas[16l] was born 1740, Mary's birth year was probably about the same. Whether this was her first marriage is unknown. She died 13 February 1809.[42] Thomas[16l] married secondly, 30 November 1811, Letitia (1774-1864), daughter of John, 1st baron Wodehouse, and his wife, Sarah Berkeley, of Kimberley, Norfolk. Neither union resulted in children.

Land tax records for London, 1692-1932, show Thomas[16l], listed as "Major Haselrige," renting a residence for himself and his wife, Letitia, from James Crompton, Paddington parish, Middlesex, paying a tax on his rent of 10 shillings. By 1815 he and Letitia had moved to a rental on Upper Brook Street, Westminster; in that year his rent was £32 10s and his land tax on the rent was £6 10s. From 1819 on, Letitia was the tax payer, apparently the same rental property, 33 Upper Brook Street. Letitia wed again in 1842, a man named Felix Ferdinand Frederick Fielding (1786-1853). She survived this man, a dozen years her junior, by more than a decade. She died 3 January 1864 at her

---

[41] Walthamstow was then a parish of county Essex; today, a district in the northeast of Greater London.

[42] Her death was announced in *The Gentleman's Magazine*, volume 79, part 1 (1809), page 279.

residence, 23 Upper Brook Street, and was buried six days later at All Soul's, Kensal Green. Like her father, she lived into her early 90s. She had lived well but frugally since the death of Thomas[16l], her estate registry showing that "The Honourable Dame Letitia Maynard Hesilrige" had left nearly £40,000 to her heirs.

Exhibit 10.8. Thomas Maynard Hesilrige, 10th Bt, c1803

Thomas[16l], rendered in a watercolour by Hugh Douglas Hamilton (Exhibit 10.8), had fared rather well as lord of Hoxne, with gratitude to Charles Maynard and despite the doubtful beginning. Upon succeeding to the title he returned to the Hesilrige surname. He did not have many years left to enjoy, however, as he died in April 1817, the title, with Noseley, passing to his nephew Arthur[17b] Grey Hesilrige, who in turn would have an even shorter period, thirty months, in which to enjoy the honor and incumbency.

Thomas[16l] wrote his last will and testament at Hoxne Hall, the eleventh day of September 1816 (with a brief codicil added 12 June 1817, shortly before his death).[43] The will shows every indication that he had developed good habits of financial investment, accounting, and arts of legal protection. It is meticulous, not so much in the writing (a strong hand) but in attention to detail. He made careful provisions for his wife, Letitia, and remembered his first wife, Mary, and her family. Among benefits to Letitia, he directed that £16,000 should be invested, leaving the choice of instruments—government stocks, other funds, real estate—to his executors, and continued at interest during her lifetime. Early notice also went to "my trusty old servant Elizabeth Robwell," to whom he left a cottage and other real estate. He recognized other servants and several friends (Rev. John Saw, Doctor of Divinity, the Rev. Thomas Cowper, among others, each remembered with a bequest of £100). He directed his executors to dispose of a rather large number of real estate holdings, in Norfolk as well as Suffolk. He identified a number of items of wall art, other objects of art, and specific articles of furniture in Hoxne Hall, and how they should be dispersed. To "my nephew Arthur Grey Hesilrige," for instance, he left "the old family seal with the full arms, that portrait of my grandfather which hangs in the dressing room in a black glazed frame," and a bust of his father. (The seal, stamped in red sealing wax, is shown in Exhibit 10.10, magnified for clarity. It dates from the first Bt.)

Exhibit 10.9. Hoxne Hall, c1800

---

[43] Hoxne Hall, later renamed Oakley Park, was pulled down sometime during the 1920s.

Exhibit 10.10. The Hesilrige Seal

Thomas[16l] directed a number of monetary bequests to specifically named persons, either as lump-sum bequests or as annuities. Most of the recipients were nephews and nieces, the main exceptions being annuities for his sisters Hannah Hesilrige and Amabel Roberts and for "children of my late deceased aunt, Mrs Sopwith" (her identity not otherwise known). The nephews were "Lt. Col. Richard Buckby of the 58th Regiment of Foot," £3500; and John Buckby, Arthur Buckby, and "Charles Roberts the younger" (son of Amabel[16p]), each £2500. Two nieces were named, Mrs Charlotte Humfrey and Mrs Dorothy Haymes, each a recipient of £2500. Sisters to each other and to the three Buckby nephews of Thomas[16l], all were children of Elizabeth[16d], his eldest sister.

Now we turn to Arthur[17b] Grey Hesilrige, successor to his uncle Thomas[16l] as the 11th Bt, and successor to his father Grey[16q] as resident lord of Noseley.

During the quarter-century that separated the death of Thomas[16l] from the birth of his successor, Arthur[17b] Hesilrige, rapid advancement in understanding and application of the physical sciences, chemistry and physics especially, surely counts as among the most momentous developments. If one sees beginnings of an industrial revolution prior to the late 1700s—and there are good reasons for it—those developments were a function mainly of the application of mechanical principles that had long been known in practice as well as in theory (levers on pivots, wheels on axles, and the like) to new sources of kinetic energy (steam engines as well as water and wind turbines). The late 1700s were a time when, as someone (probably Kenneth Clark) once said, "science was to some extent an after-dinner occupation." Aside from some presence in universities (a few laboratories but mainly tutorials), "scientist" was not yet the name of a professional occupation. This was an age of the amateur scientist, and names such as Joseph Priestley (1733-1804), Thomas Beddoes (1760-1808), and Humphrey Davy (1778-1829) were champions of a more assertively experimentalist science which would, in rather short order, remake the everyday world to a degree that would have been simply unfathomable a century earlier. Phenomena such as oxidation—in some instances so slow as to be measured in weeks or months and generating so little heat as to be undetectable by human touch (e.g., iron oxide, or "rusting") but in other instances so fast as to erupt in flash fire, generating heat and ultraviolent light, potentially lethal to human observers (as in, e.g., oxidation of magnesium or, still more dangerous, of phosphorous). In 1800 such advances in understanding did not have much application, and it would be anachronistic to evaluate any persons of that time in terms of foresight of applications that were rapidly expanding by 1900. But it would not have been too early for leading men and women of a family to know that wealth and power, both actual and potential, had become largely urban goods, and that the transfer would not cease. Consumption with *rentier* intent had a self-limiting future.

Such was the newly reforming world into which Arthur[17b] entered in 1790, the eldest son of Grey[16q] and Bridget (*nee* Buckby) Hesilrige. He partook very little of it, as noted above. A notice in *The Gentleman's Magazine* told the story: "*Oct. 24.* At the Baths of Tivoli, near Paris, in his 29th year Sir Arthur Grey Hesilrige, baronet, of Noseley-hall" died."[44]

---

[44] Volume 126, part 2 (1819), page 468.

One would like to know the circumstances. Was it death by accident? If his portrait is reliable indication (Exhibit 10.11), he was not suffering a debilitating disease, unless perhaps an aggressive cancer or an advanced stage of tuberculosis.

Exhibit 10.11. Sir Arthur Grey Hazlerigg, 11th Bt, 1819

Like its more famous cousin near Rome, the Tivoli Gardens near Paris were an amusement park, located on the south side of Montmartre at the (then) northern edge of Paris. Its main attractions were a large wheel, slides, roller coasters, pantomimes, and various other spectacles. A bath ("Les eaux thermales et minérales de Tivoli") was established in 1799, but it closed in 1810, along with most of the park. Re-opened soon after as *Folie-Richelieu* (or in England as the "Second Tivoli"), it was popular for its amusements and perhaps the bath (it is not clear that the bath did re-open). In any case, it appears that the bath (unlike Lourdes, for instance) was never touted for medicinal or spiritual purposes. So we are left without even scraps of evidence pertaining to the cause of Arthur's[17b] early death.

    Short though his candle proved to be, it cast enough light for him to leave his marks. Having celebrated his 20th birthday anniversary, and presumably knowing that he was next in line to the title, Arthur[17b] married a woman seven years his senior, Henrietta Anne, daughter and heir of John and Susanna (*nee* Rowland Litchford) Bourne of Stanch Hall, Hampshire.[45] They had four children, including the lad who would soon inherit as the 12th Bt (who will be taken up in the next chapter). Henrietta has been described as a character out of Thackeray, but without indication of which character. Since Thackeray's main works begin in the 1830s, the attributed likeness would have been perceived long after Henrietta had had ample time in which to become a stock character. Given what we mainly know of her behavior, she was probably being likened to Becky Sharp, the engagingly manipulative, "social climbing" chief character of *Vanity Fair*, which was published serially in 1847-48 and remains one of Thackeray's most stylish satires. Perhaps Henrietta only reinforced her young husband's own preference for *rentier* rather entrepreneurial consumption. In any case, the couple began almost immediately after marriage to add to the furnishings of Noseley Hall, especially advancing the collection of elegant furniture and fine paintings. This project came to an abrupt halt with Arthur's[17b] early death. However, Henrietta's taste for finery had been whetted. Another bout of profligacy ensued, as expenses of her lifestyle continued to mount. She was unhappily removed from Noseley Hall in 1835, when her son, the 12th Bt, married and began his own household.

---

[45] Official pedigrees give 25 July 1811 as date of marriage, though another record says the date was 26 November 1811. Little is known of this Bourne lineage.

~ 11 ~
A Millennium of History in Britain

Granted, to announce a millennium of history of the Heselrig/Hesilrige/Hazlerigg family in Britain is a bit of an anticipation—as of this date, by a half-century. There is no reason to doubt that the family will be present in Britain in the year 2066, unless humankind stumbles (or marches) into nuclear incineration. Shorelines will look different in fifty years. The United Kingdom may have been undone. Monarchy might have been consigned to past times—well, no, probably not. It is even possible that Noseley Hall will have been pulled down—a step too far, one thinks, but it could happen. Despite any or all of that (excepting the stumbling or marching), the Hesilrige/Hazlerigg family in Britain—or in England—will celebrate the millennial anniversary of Hastings. We will, one hopes, take justifiable pride in being one of the few English families to have persevered in unbroken agnatic line those thousand years, looking always toward tomorrow for still better successes. Fifty years is a short toss. For those of us who stand sturdily enough to be there, the celebration will be a time of great wonder and promise. For those not, an anticipation across fifty years means much the same.

Most of the presentation in this chapter reflects a truncation of the known record, sometimes by a substantial amount. Reasons for it have to do with concerns of personal privacy and preference, as was indicated in the preface. The manner of presentation will therefore differ, consisting mostly of vignettes, some briefer than others, connected by the threads of a concluding segment of lineage.

Taking One's Kit into the World, and Back
"One's kit" could be thought of as "Little England," though as a matter of fact it was also "Little Scotland," Little Wales," and, in good part, "Little Ireland" or "Little Eire." All four parts were integral to the movement of Westminster, Whitehall, and the City of London out into the larger world in activities of trade, cultural transplantation, military impositions, and designs of governance through plantation or colonial enclaves. The sum of those activities was a complex mixture of good and bad effects, even when intentions were (as conceived by intender) good. This is not the place to argue merits one way or another. Here, the point is simple: over the years various members of the family were involved in those activities. A few of them we met in previous discussions. Here, we will meet

several more. In chapter 10 we attended one man, Sir Arthur[17a] Hesilrige, 9th Bt, who devoted nearly thirty years of his life to colonial administration in eastern India. In this chapter we will witness family members serving as colonial administrators and/or as military officers in Afghanistan, British East Africa (i.e., Kenya, Tanganyika, Uganda), Ceylon, China, Crimea, the Gold Coast (i.e., Ghana), Jamaica, and South Africa, among other places. The density of presence increased during the nineteenth century, then began to decline. While the British Empire struggled through the early decades of the twentieth century, the rate at which members of our family became involved dropped sharply.

As citizens of the British Isles took their kit to faraway places, the effects were felt in the home economies even more than in the colonial economies. Everyone touts the industrial revolution, of course, and one cannot gainsay the weight of that long sequence of technical innovations and developments. Even so, one should not overlook the importance of trade. Raw materials were imported from various outposts of the empire, and some finished goods were exported to those same outposts, sometimes filtering into the native populations of the colonial territories and creating new demand. Again, this is not the place to draw up a balance sheet of pluses and minuses between colonial territories and home country. There can be no denying, however, that Great Britain became a very wealthy spot on the world map. By 1870 productivity in Great Britain was 70 percent higher than in Germany and 30 percent higher than in the USA, a consequence of Britain's more rapid industrialization, fueled by supply and demand in the empire's nexus of trade. That complex process had been underway for many decades, it is plain to see in retrospect, though one would have been very hard-pressed in 1815 to predict results a half-century hence. The year 1815 offers a good perspective forward, in our retrospect, for developments were then substantial yet still relatively slow in both pace and momentum. In that year, for instance, William Smith published an extraordinary work for the time, his *Geological Map of England and Wales, and Part of Scotland*. It was so extraordinary, in fact, that it was hardly appreciated until years later.[1] One of its features was a remarkably accurate identification of coal deposits, not merely those seams that lay open at surface but also the deeper deposits—all of which became highly instrumental in power for concentrations of mechanical equipment far from water power and far more energetic as well as more reliable than wind power. It was also

---

[1] See, e.g., Simon Winchester's study in *The Map that Changed the World* (New York: HarperCollins, 2001).

terribly polluting, of lungs in addition to air, water, flora and fauna, and the great stone facades that had been erected in previous centuries. But the train was unstoppable.

Again, consequences were mixed, but among the greatest of them was (and is) a redistribution of the means of wealth, as more and more adults were shifted into cities and their industrial-factory labor forces of predominantly semi-skilled and unskilled workers. Consequences for such standards as income rates and what incomes will buy are difficult to assess over time, because so many changing factors go into the determination. A useful way in which to assess wage rates over long spans of time is to express a prevailing wage rate—that is, the price of labor—in ratio to the price of some necessity such as a foodstuff. This exercise has been done for us recently, for a long period of English history, by a team of economic historians. They have reported that the price of unskilled labor relative to the price of bread declined after the early 1500s, reaching a low point during the mid-1600s, then slowly recovered during the next 100 years. It declined again during the late 1700s, then began a more rapid ascent, regaining its early-1500s high about 1860 and thereafter rose sharply as industrialization replaced skilled craft work with machine-powered work by less skilled persons. That same technique can be used to track long-term changes in income inequality. Expanding their comparison standard to other staple foods as well, the team of historians found that "between 1500 and 1815 the prices of staple foods rose much more than the prices of what the rich consumed. This greatly magnified the rise in real income inequality. ... The poor needed land-intensive food and housing, and land was owned by the rich. The rich, in turn, hired labor services much more than today, so that the fall in workers' real wages became a fall in the cost of an affluent lifestyle."[2] Population growth increased labor supply and demand for staple foods, thus putting downward pressure on real wages and upward pressure on the price of staples.

During the latter part of that period of time the enclosure acts had concentrated land in fewer hands, and by the mid-1800s productive land, land that could be exploited for economic gain, whether it be by growing crops and/or livestock or by extracting minerals, timber, fish, and similar resources, had become highly concentrated in the hands of the landed aristocracy and upper gentry. As one recent analyst noted, in England

---

[2] See figure 1A and pages 322-323 in Philip T Hoffman, David Jacks, Patricia A Levin, and Peter H Lindert, "Real Inequality in Western Europe since 1500," *Journal of Economic History*, volume 62 (June 2002), pages 322-355.

and Wales combined in 1873 "the most landed 5 percent held 79 percent of all real-estate value." The concentration extended into cities, of course: "land in booming cities [was] concentrated in the hands of a few aristocrats, such as London's Duke of Marlborough (Grosvenor, as in West End) and Duke of Bedford (Russell, as in Bloomsbury and Covent Garden)." In general, the "extreme inequality" of wealth in Victorian England "was rooted in the special economic and political dominance of the English landed aristocracy."[3]

But at the same time, the composition of that wealth was changing enormously, as it was being re-allocated from agrarian to industrial forms of production. One measure of that re-allocation can be seen in the comparison of two trends. First, during the 1800s the total value of all land in agricultural production in Britain declined, in real terms, from being about four times the size of Britain's gross domestic product (GDP) to being less than half the size of its GDP. Of course, GDP grew a lot during that century; but agrarian forms of production were accounting for smaller and smaller proportions of growth. Second, during that same century the total value of all residential property in Britain increased from being a little more than the country's GDP to being about fifty percent greater than its GDP. People were moving into cities, where industrial plants were being built, but the effect of re-allocation of wealth in terms of residential property was slower to develop. Because of serious economic depression and the two world wars, the total value of residential property in Britain declined during the early decades of the twentieth century. But from about 1945 to 2010 that value, again measured in real terms, increased from being slightly less than the GDP to being four times the GDP.[4] This meant that families whose patrimony rested entirely or mostly in land and its support of agrarian production were losing in relative standing. On average the patrimony continued to grow for quite some time; but even then its rate of growth was small as compared to growth of the national economy. Eventually the loss in relative standing translated into a loss in absolute terms, as industrial means of production were applied to agricultural

---

[3] Peter H Lindert, "Unequal Living Standards," in *The Economic History of Britain since 1700*, 3 volumes, 2nd edition, edited by Roderick Floud and Deirdre McCloskey (Cambridge: Cambridge University Press, 1994), volume 1, pages 357-385, at pages 378, 379.

[4] For one set of systematic estimates of these trends, see Thomas Piketty, *Capital in the Twenty-First Century*, translated by Arthur Goldhammer (Cambridge: Belknap Press of Harvard University, 2014), pages 113-120. While the estimates are necessarily rough, the trends are very clear.

production with greater and greater efficiency gains. Commensurate with those changes, but with a sometimes large lag in time, the political power of the landed gentry and most of the aristocracy declined.

Interest here is not in following that decline to its conclusion in the twenty-first century. Rather, our primary attention will remain with members of the Hazlerigg/Hesilrige family during the period from the early 1800s to the early 1900s, as recorded in this next (and for this book, the last) segment of lineage, followed by a sequence of vignettes.

A Concluding Segment of Lineage
The greater length of this segment of lineage is due partly to the fact that the state function of record keeping shifted during the nineteenth century to a much more democratic model. Thus, coverage expanded outward from the titled line and forward to more generations of progeny by men and women whose places of birth were other than Noseley Hall or related sites. One of the ironies following from that expansion is that just as more information is available for a much wider casting of the net, restrictions on the results must here be imposed for reasons already stated. With very few exceptions, for example, specific persons are not followed from census to census, in order to track residences, occupations, household compositions, and the like. Here the "bare facts" remain much as before: names, vital dates, marriages, and, for the earlier unions, progeny.

Grey[16q] Hesilrige: b. 23 November 1748 Noseley, d. October 1810 Noseley; m. Bridget Buckby; more in chapter 10

 L-- Dorothy[17a] Hesilrige: bap. July 1789 St Mary's, Lambeth, Surrey, d. >1861

 L-- **Arthur**[17b] Grey Hazlerigg, 11th Bt: b. 8 November 1790 Noseley, d. 24 October 1819 Paris, France; m. 25 July 1811 Henrietta Anne (b. 1783 Leighton, Bromwold, Huntingdonshire, d. 25 October 1868 Southfield, Leicestershire), daughter of John Bourne.

  L- **Arthur**[18a] Grey Hazlerigg, 12th Bt: b. 20 October 1812 Whitchurch, Hereford, d. 11 May 1890; more below

  L- Thomas[18b] Maynard Hazlerigg: b. 10 April 1815 Noseley, d. c1816

└ Henrietta[18c] Susan Hazlerigg: b. 1817 Noseley, d. 4 September 1901 Billericay, Essex; m. 15 October 1840 Thomas Bell, esq. (1816-1863), Capt. 58th Regiment; issue: 2 sons, 5 daughters

└ Grey[18d] Hazlerigg: b. 13 March 1818, d. 4 October 1912; m. 24 June 1873 Loughborough, Leicestershire, Sarah Ann (b. 1847, d. 27 June 1901), daughter of Thomas Clarke of Forest Road Cottage, Loughborough, Leicestershire

└ Henrietta[19a] Anne Hazlerigg: b. 1874 Leicester, d. 11 June 1934 Hunstanton, Norfolk; never married

└ Caroline[19b] Susan Hazlerigg: b. 1875 Leicester, d. January 1963 Bath, Somerset; m. 11 April 1900 Leicester, Henry Doudney Thompson (1875-1921), solicitor

└ Lilian[19c] Elizabeth Hazlerigg: b. 1877 Leicester, d. 27 September 1948 Leicester; m. 1900 Leicester, Frank Densham (1876-1950); issue: 7 sons and 4 daughters

└ Grey[19d] Hazlerigg: b. 14 January 1879, d. 11 April 1948 London; BA 1900 & LLB 1906 St John's College, Cambridge; m. 8 December 1908 Wangford, Suffolk, Sarah Dorothy, daughter of Herbert Bakewell Whetstone, a Leicester brewer and miller; divorce 1924; m(2) 8 November 1933 Westminster, Fannie Smith (b. 1875, d. 26 November 1949 London)

└ Herbert[20a] William Grey Hazlerigg: b. 13 September 1910 Paddington, London, d. January 1991 Brighton, Sussex; m. 1937 Lewes, Sussex, Gladys Margaret Knighton; issue: 3 sons, 1 daughter

└ Dorothy[20b] Mary Louise Hazlerigg: b. c1912, d. 7 July 2007 Shoreham-by-Sea, Sussex

└ Alexander[20c] Maynard Hazlerigg: b. 23 June 1914 Ceylon (Sri Lanka), d. July 1997 Worthing, Sussex; m(1) 1944 Kettering, Jean Dorothy Rowan, m(2) 1969 Greenwich, Helen M Moore

└ Dorothy[19e] Frances Hazlerigg: b. 9 September 1880 Leicester, d. 1982 Somerset; m. 1903 Leicester, Wilfred Tyler (1872-1943)

└ Thomas[19f] Maynard Hazlerigg: b. 1882 Leicester, d. 6 November 1961 Shrewsbury, Shropshire; m(1) 1905 Violet Isabella (b. 1883, d. 25 October 1941), daughter of H J Price; m(2) December 1941 Fylde, Lancashire, Gladys May (b. 23 Dec 1899, d. 1979), daughter of Thomas Cotton

└ Robert[20a] Maynard Hazlerigg: b. 7 March 1911, d. 26 February 1913

└ Diana[20b] Margaret Hazlerigg: b. 3 January 1914 Leicester, d. 4 December 1977 Lewes, Sussex; m. 14 March 1946 Robert Edward Hope-Falkner (1904-1991)

└ Elizabeth[17c] Bridget Hesilrige: b. 3 October 1792, d. 5 December 1851

└ Thomas[17d] Hesilrige: b. 23 August 1794, d. 1814 troop ship crossing the Atlantic Ocean; unmarried

└ Robert[17e] Greville Hesilrige: b. 23 October 1796, d. c1820; more in chapter 10

└ Isabella[17f] Hesilrige: b. 25 August 1798; m. Fnu McDonnell

└ Jemima[17g] Hesilrige: b. 24 July 1800 Hereford, d. 1842; m. William Buckby (b. c1803 Tandragee, d. 28 May 1868 county Armagh, Eire; more in chapter 10 and below

└ Charles[17h] Maynard Hesilrige: b. 24 August 1802 Herefordshire, d. 4 December 1878 Carlton Curlieu, Leicestershire; m. 10 March 1829 Deborah Maria, (b. c1811, d. 2 December 1866) daughter of Arthur Buckby and Elizabeth (*nee* McDonnell) of Seagoe, county Armagh, Eire

└ Grey[18a] Hesilrige: b. 10 December 1830 Kibworth, Leicestershire, d. 9 February 1848 Carlton Curlieu, Leics.; never married

┕ Hannah[18b] Hesilrige: b. 6 February 1831, co. Armagh, Eire, d. 3 May 1900 Carlton Curlieu, Leics.; never married

┕ Thomas[18c] Maynard Hesilrige: b. 26 September 1832, d. 12 November 1835

┕ Arthur[18d] Hesilrige: b. 20 June 1834, d. 14 February 1863 Bourne, Lincolnshire; m. 4 June 1862 Mary Augusta, daughter of George John Nicholls, esq., FRCS, of Bourne, Lincolnshire

┕ Arthur[19a] George Maynard Hesilrige: b. 5 September 1863 Bourne, Lincolnshire; d. 13 April 1953 Paddington, London; m. 2 July 1889 Hammersmith, London, Amy Florence (b. 1857, d. 29 May 1947), daughter of Michael S Myers of Chiswick

┕ Phyllis[20a] Maynard Hesilrige: b. 16 August 1890, d. June 1968 Middlesex; m. 12 December 1925 Kenneth Leslie Mortimore (b. 1893)

┕ Corrie[20b] Maynard Hesilrige: b. 2 February 1893 Hammersmith, London, d. 1957 Kensington, London; never married

┕ Violet[20c] Maynard Hesilrige: b. 20 April 1900 Hammersmith, London, d. March 1982 Hastings, Sussex; m. 17 March 1943 Westminster, London, George R Jackson

┕ Bridget[18e] Hesilrige: bap. 23 February 1837 Fownhope with Fawley, Herefordshire, d. 4 May 1838

┕ Charles[18f] Maynard Hesilrige: b. 7 May 1838 Billingham, Herefordshire, d. 4 September 1901 Wharfdale, Yorkshire; m. 1871 Tadcaster, Yorkshire, Sarah Hannah Mason (b. 1839, d. 7 January 1902)

┕ Grey[19a] Hesilrige: b. 1872 Leeds, Yorkshire, d. 26 July 1939 Surrey; m. 3 August 1904 Godstone, Surrey, Elizabeth Hannah, daughter of John Shrimpton of Great Haseley, Oxfordshire

┕ Maria[19b] Hesilrige: b. April 1874 Wighill, Yorkshire, d. 27 August 1959 Brighton, Sussex; never married

└ Charles[19c] Hesilrige: b. April 1876 Belper, Derbyshire, d. 14 January 1947 London; m(1) 22 May 1920 Kingston upon Thames, Surrey, Florence Burn; m(2) 25 July 1945 Durham, Doris Rawlings

└ Robert[18g] Hesilrige: b. 14 April 1840 Herefordshire, d. 12 August 1840

└ Thomas[18h] Greville Hesilrige: b. 8 August 1841 Little Birch, Herefordshire, d. 5 August 1906 Market Harborough, Leics.; m. 1871 Barrow upon Soar, Leics., Eliza Ann Preston (b. c1851, d. 3 March 1923 Market Harborough, Leics.)

└ Laura[19a] Hesilrige: b. 1873 Illston on the Hill, Leics., d. November 1950; m. July 1898 John David Wright; issue: David (b. 1900)

└ Deborah[19b] Maria Hesilrige: b. April 1874 Illston on the Hill, Leics., d. 18 June 1928 Shangton, Leics.; m. October 1914, Market Harborough, Leics., Henry James Dilworth

└ Eliza[19c] Ann Hesilrige: b. & d. 15 March 1877

└ Thomas[19d] Greville Hesilrige: b. April 1878 Illston on the Hill, Leics., d. 18 October 1955 Binley, Warwickshire; m(1) 1901 Florence Elizabeth (1879-1919), daughter of Edwin Henry Griffiths of Mount Pleasant, Shrewsbury; m(2) 1921 Gertrude May Downs (1893-1985)

└ Dorothy[20a] Greville Hesilrige: b. 1904 Rugby, Warwickshire, d. >1926; m. 1926 Coventry, Warwickshire, Thomas G Hodgett

└ Robert[19e] Maynard Hesilrige: b. March 1884 Illston on the Hill, Leics., d. 2 February 1951 Merton Cottages, Tur Langton, Leics.; m. October 1914 Market Bosworth, Leics., Dora Cope

└ Dorothy[18i] Hesilrige: b. 5 May 1846 Little Birch, county Hereford, d. 5 June 1920 Wheaton, DuPage County, Illinois; m(1) Fnu Young, m(2) 22 September 1884 Knighton parish, Blaby, Leics., Daniel Foster Hawkes (b. 1 March 1860 Broughton, Huntingdonshire, d.

7 November 1944 Wheaton, DuPage County, Illinois; emigrated to USA 1885; no issue

   L- Robert[18j] Martival Hesilrige: b. 13 July 1847, d. 26 December 1906 Belfast; never married

   L- Octavius[18k] Hesilrige: b. 6 February 1849, d. 1896; never married

  L-- Hannah[17i] Hesilrige: b. 28 October 1804 Herefordshire, d. November 1824

Arthur[18a] Grey Hazlerigg, 12th Bt: b. 20 October 1812 Whitchurch, Herefordshire, d. 11 May 1890; m. 14 July 1835 Henrietta (b. 1814 St Bride's Head, Pembrokeshire, d. 13 December 1883), daughter of Charles Allen Phillips

 L- Arthur[19a] Grey Hazlerigg: b. 10 January 1837, d. 16 July 1880 Pretoria, South Africa; m. 9 January 1878 Janet Edith, daughter of Sir Archibald Orr-Ewing, 1st Bt; more below

  L- **Arthur**[20a] Grey Hazlerigg, 13th Bt: b. 17 November 1878, d. 25 May 1949; m. Summer 1903 Dorothy Rachel (b. 4 December 1883, d. 29 April 1972), daughter of John Henry Buxton of Hunsdon, Hertfordshire; more below

   L- Rachel[21a] Elizabeth Hazlerigg: b. 22 June 1904 Noseley, d. Summer 1989 Winchester, Hampshire; m. Spring 1928 Marylebone, London, Anthony C W Kimpton (1901-1990); issue: Patricia (1940-1965)

   L- Dorothy[21b] Joan Hazlerigg: b. 27 August 1905, d. 10 November 1962 Marylebone, London; m. 25 October 1930 James Nathaniel Bosanquet Alexander (1902-1964); issue: 1 son, 2 daughters

   L- Edith[21c] Bridget Hazlerigg: b. 30 March 1908 Kensington, London, d. 17 April 1984 Leicester, Leicestershire

L- **Arthur**[21d] Grey Hazlerigg, 14th Bt: b. 24 February 1910, d. 30 September 2002; m. 19 September 1945 Patricia Ethel (b. 15 July 1915 Durban, South Africa, d. 21 April 1972 Leicester), daughter of John (b. 19 October 1885 England, d. 5 March 1935 Durban, SA) and Julia (*nee* Edwards) Pullar of Durban, South Africa; issue: 1 son, 2 daughters; more below

L- Thomas[21e] Heron Hazlerigg: b. 17 January 1914 St George, Hanover Square, London, d. 31 July 1998 Norwich, Norfolk; m(1) 1942 Westminster, Audrey Cecil Bates (b. 15 July 1919, d. January 1994 Leicester), m(2) 1957 Westminster, Doussa Cayzar (b. 1917 Ramleh, Egypt, d. 1997 London), m(3) Anne Buxton (b. >1920); issue: 2 sons by Bates

L- Robert[21f] Maynard Hazlerigg: b. 21 July 1916 Kensington, London, d. 12 September 1997 Leicester; m. 1942 Billesdon, Rose Mary Cox (b. c1920, d. 11 January 1979); issue: 2 daughters

L- Henrietta[19b] Louisa Hazlerigg: b. 1839 Noseley, d. 9 April 1923; m. 6 December 1866, Illston on the Hill, George Turner, esq., of Thorpelands, Northhamptonshire; issue: Allen A G (b. c1868), Charles Edward (b. 1870), Gwendoline Mary (b. 1872), Greville H A (b. c1874)

L- Thomas[19c] Maynard Hazlerigg: b. 5 August 1840 Noseley, d. 5 November 1915 Greenwich, Kent; m. 19 July 1869 Margaret (b. 1852 India, d. 1918), daughter of Lt Gen Francis Walker Drummond; Maj Gen, Royal Horse Artillery

L- Gwendoline[20a] Alice Hazlerigg: b. 1870 Peshawar, India, d. 9 December 1933 Greenwich, Kent; never married

L- Henrietta[20b] Mabel Hazlerigg: b. 1871 Noseley, d. 26 January 1955 Worthing, Sussex; never married

L- Arthur[20c] Hazlerigg: b. 31 March 1873, Charlton, Kent, d. 13 May 1900, battle of Mafeking (Second Boer War), South Africa; never married

L- Evelyn[20d] Hazlerigg: b. 1874 Aldershot, Hampshire, d. 22 October 1953 Worthing, Sussex; never married

└ Thomas[20e] Hazlerigg: b. 1 June 1877 Christchurch, Kent, d. 15 March 1935 London; m. 17 March 1903 Marylebone, London, Edith Violet (1879-1959), daughter of Lt Col W H McCheane of the Royal Marine Light Infantry; more below

    └ Arthur[21a] William Hazlerigg: b. 5 February 1904, d. 16 March 1987 Cambridge; m(1) 17 June 1935 Ruby Marjorie Dorothea Turner, m(2) 16 June 1947 Ella Wilson (1908-1977)

└ Greville[20f] Hazlerigg: b. 12 December 1881 Woolwich, Kent, d. 7 March 1944 Worthing, Sussex; m. 1 June 1908 Kensington, London, Helen Margaret (1877-1949), daughter of Maj Gen Needham Thompson Parsons, 103rd Fusiliers

    └ Arthur[21a] Greville Maynard Hazlerigg: b. 7 November 1910, d. December 1990 Yeovil, Somerset; m. Autumn 1941 London, Nancy Ingles; issue: 1 son, 2 daughters

└ Margaret[20g] Hazlerigg: b. 1885 Noseley, d. 19 November 1956 Worthing, Sussex; m. 10 October 1914 Blackheath, Kent, George Okeover Anson (b. 8 August 1880 New Zealand, d. December 1977 Cornwall)

└ Dorothy[19d] Susan Hazlerigg: b. 1842 Billesdon, Leics., d. 9 January 1914 Hastings, Sussex; m. 21 November 1861 Herrick Augustus Palmer (1835-1908), Capt 62nd Regiment, Major Royal Glamorgan Militia (taken prisoner at storming of the Redan 8 September 1855); issue: 7 sons, 3 daughters

└ Gwendoline[19e] Frances Hazlerigg: b. May 1844 Noseley, d. 11 June 1906 Camberwell, Surrey; m. 3 October 1883 Arthur Vores (1857-1910) of Uppingham, MRCS

└ Charles[19f] Cecil Hazlerigg: b. 31 July 1845, d. 31 July 1891 Rockhampton, Queensland; never married; more below

└ William[19g] Greville Hazlerigg: b. 8 June 1847, d. 1 November 1893; m. 20 April 1876 Barbara Mary (1850-1911), daughter of Lt Col

Joseph Walker Pease of Hesslewood House, Yorkshire, and his wife Barbara Catherine Palmer; more below

└ Roger[20a] Greville Hazlerigg: b. 22 January 1877 Hessle, Yorkshire, d. 11 January 1952 Chichester, Sussex; m. 2 September 1919 Esther Rosamond Everett (1900-1976)

└ Jean[21a] Mary Hazlerigg: b. 19 December 1921, d. April 2010 Worcestershire; m. October 1947 Chichester, Kenneth L Perrin (1920-1982); more below

└ Charlotte[20b] Isabel Hazlerigg: b. 1878 Billesdon, Leics., d. 1 January 1942; m. 27 February 1915 Kensington, London, William John Hilyer (1882-1962); more below

└ Barbara[20c] Henrietta Hazlerigg: b. 1880 Billesdon, Leics., d. 13 February 1927 Sussex; m. 22 February 1908 Sir Herbert Castleman Lushington, 6th Bt (1879-1968); issue: 3 sons

└ Eleanor[20d] Frances Hazlerigg: b. 1882 Billesdon, Leics., d. 23 May 1963 Chichester, Sussex

└ Guy[20e] Maynard Hazlerigg: b. 8 February 1887, d. 1962 Perth, Australia; m(1) 15 March 1913 Strand, London, Erna Irene (1889-1924), daughter of Capt R C Heidenreihe, 5th Austrian Hussars, m(2) 1929 Margaret Jennie (1890-1958), daughter of Thomas Austin Francis; more below

└ George[21a] Maynard Hazlerigg: b. 25 August 1915, d. 19 August 1916

└ John[21b] W V Hazlerigg: b. Feb 1921 Paddington, London, d. Spring 1921 Paddington, London

└ Isabel[19h] Cecilia Hazlerigg: b. 1849 Noseley, d. 17 May 1870 Billesdon, Leics.

└ Allen[19i] Martival Hazlerigg: b. 28 October 1855 Noseley, d. 1949; attended Harrow, leaving 1872; m. 24 July 1880 Kensington, London, Adela Louisa Julia Fanny (b. c1870, d. 25 August 1938

Rochford, Essex), daughter of Capt Charles Codrington-Forsyth, Royal Navy C B

L- Ella[20a] Jeannette Hazlerigg: b. 1881, Billesdon, Leics., d. 1881 Billesdon, Leics.

L- Martival[20b] Grey Hazlerigg: b. 9 October 1884 Worsley, Lancashire, d. September 1971 Barnet, Middlesex; Lt, Royal Field Artillery, c1915; m. 31 October 1925 Maidenhead, Berkshire, Marion Ellen Ray (*nee* McAuliffe, 1898-1999); issue: 1 son

Vignettes

In earlier chapters we saw repeated examples of the traditional pattern for sons of a family head, when two or more surviving sons were present. The heir inherited the estate (or the main estate), which left the spare sometimes with a minor estate and usually with a choice of two "standby" positions, either military or clerical service. Third and later sons could also seek position as soldier or clergyman. These alternatives were additional to efforts to attract a well-endowed daughter for marriage.

As Rothschild has illustrated through her detailed study of the Johnstone family, those were still main avenues of placement in the order of eighteenth-century Britain. But another had been added—commerce, especially commerce involving overseas trade.[5] This addition was made possible by several innovations at the juncture of means of transport and overseas plantations or colonies, which created new markets for trade; and soon that juncture resulted in a new addition to military, clerical, commercial, and marital avenues of advancement—namely, foreign civil service. We saw an instance of this in the prior chapter, with the 9th Bt making his way in India via a combination of civil service and commerce. The growth and development of empire during the 1800s entailed considerable expansion of the civil service. Although the line between it and military service in colonial areas was always porous—with relations between functions of the two branches sometimes contentious—exchanges of assignment were usually generational, scions of military officers entering the civil service more often than exchanges in the opposite direction. Conflicts more often occurred between

---

[5] Emma Rothschild, *The Inner Life of Empires* (Princeton: Princeton University Press, 2011).

institutions of commerce and institutions of state, whether military or civil service, and Rothschild has shown how some of those conflicts were lived in the lives of actual persons. We could imagine that corresponding members of the Hazlerigg family had similar experiences of conflict but for the fact that very few of them engaged in commercial activity. The main exception appears to have been the 9th Bt, and in the prior chapter we saw glimpses of conflictive relations in his experiences in India.

While Hazlerigg/Hesilrige men pursued all of the main avenues of advancement during the nineteenth century, they apparently preferred the pursuits of military and civil service in faraway places. The absence of introspective documents such as personal letters and diaries leaves us with only conjectural inferences about motivations and ambitions, but it appears that few if any young men in the family considered commercial enterprise to be a sufficiently attractive alternative. Perhaps traditions meant that commerce was still viewed in terms of the town shopkeeper, even though earlier generations had demonstrated quite well that fortunes could be made in shipping and other entrepreneurial actions. In any case, from all available evidence it is clear that commerce at any notable scale played little if any significant role. Probably the closest activity would have been the role of solicitor, which is of course a form of commerce but one in which the notion and standing of "profession" is put forth.

Nor did marital arrangements play much of a role, by comparison to the importance of strategic alliances during previous centuries when the patrimony was sometimes enhanced very considerably via marital unions. As partial substitution to the older form of marital alliance, the professionalization of military service invigorated what had been a weak or occasional marriage market involving sons and daughters of military families. Because of professionalization of a "regular army" (a newer version of the New Model concept developed by Cromwell and Fairfax during the civil wars of the 1640s and 1650s), grades of officers could be, and were, seen as a sort of extension of heraldic tradition. The networks of social honour did little or nothing to enhance a family's patrimony in a material way, for these were really networks not among landed or commercial wealth but of salaried employees of a governmental agency. They nonetheless served important functions of social standing—as exemplified in later editions of pedigree books such as Burke's Peerage.

Military
Some men were clearly career military in outcome, if not necessarily in first thought, and were defending empire. Three examples follow.

Arthur[19a] Grey Hazlerigg, son of the 12th Bt and Henrietta (*nee* Phillips) Hazlerigg: b. 10 January 1837, d. 16 July 1880 Pretoria, South Africa

The first known record shows that he served in the war in the Crimea, in 1854. As of 1871 he was a captain in the 21st Regiment of Foot, stationed at the district depot in Kent. Eight years later a lieutenant colonel in the Royal Scots Fusiliers (i.e., 21st Regiment of Foot), his regiment was among those reinforcements arriving in South Africa during the Spring of 1879 in preparation for what proved to be the decisive battle of the Anglo-Zulu War, at Ulundi, on 4 July 1879.[6] As many as 19 officers of the combined British forces were wounded in that battle; he might have been one of them. Ulundi is about 340 miles southeast of Pretoria, so it would have been a rough journey for a seriously wounded man. He died in Pretoria at age 43 years, cause unknown. He is shown in uniform as a major, with his bride, Janet Edith Orr-Ewing, in Exhibit 11.1.

Exhibit 11.1. Major Arthur Grey Hazlerigg & Janet Edith Orr-Ewing

---

[6] See the account by Frances E Colenso, *History of the Zulu War and Its Origin* (London: Chapman and Hall, 1880), page 395 *et passim*.

Thomas[19c] Maynard Hazlerigg, another son of the 12th Bt and Henrietta (*nee* Phillips) Hazlerigg: b. 5 August 1840 Noseley, d. 5 November 1915 Greenwich, Kent

Little is known of his youth. As second son, he probably decided early for a career in the army, like his elder brother. He was in India by 1869, for he wed Margaret Drummond that year at a popular hill station of the British Raj, Mussoorie, in northern India. Their first child, Gwendoline[20a] Alice, was born the next year, 570 miles to the northwest, in Peshawar (now in northern Pakistan). In 1891 he was a colonel of Royal Artillery, assigned to the staff of the adjutant general in Woolwich; in 1901, now retired as a major general, Royal Horse Artillery, he was living with Margaret in Greenwich, along with some of their adult children; and again, in 1911, in Greenwich, as a pensioned retired major general. He died in Greenwich, 5 Nov 1915.

Daughter Gwendoline[20a] never married. In 1891 and in 1901 she was living in her aunt's household, Eastend House, in Carmichael, then part of Lanarkshire. (In 1891 her brother Thomas[20e], aged 13, was also living there.) This aunt was Alice T (*nee* Drummond) Carmichael, sister to Margaret Drummond, wife of Thomas[19c] Maynard Hazlerigg. Both Alice and Margaret were born in India (Alice, 6 May 1849; Margaret, about two years later). Their father, Francis, a cavalry officer in Bengal, rose to become a lieutenant colonel. He was second son of Sir Francis Walker Drummond, of the Drummonds of Hawthornden, Midlothian, one of whose ancestors was the poet, William Drummond of Hawthornden (1585-1649), whom we met earlier.

The preceding paragraph was meant to show both the interlocking circles of military families and the repetition of family associations over long spans of time. It also reflects a temptation to suspect evidence of a link between the Drummond and Hazlerigg presences at Carmichael and one or more of several sites in Scotland, sites that have recently carried the Hazlerigg/Hazelrigg name. About sixty miles south-southwest of Carmichael, for instance, lies the small community of Balmaclellan in the Castle Douglas area, and in that small community there is (or was) a place called Hazelrigg House.[7] Then, too, about 30 miles west northwest of Carmichael is the site of an old village called Blacklaw. (It is now a suburban area of Glasgow; the main remnants of the village are a Blacklaw Drive and a Blacklaw public school.) The interest here has to

---

[7] At last inspection the building was in poor repair and might well have been pulled down by this date.

do with a dim memory of a "Hazelrigg Farm" in that area, as recalled by the late Hugh Crauford Rae, who wrote historical fictions and thrillers under various pen names (especially, with co-author Peggy Coghlan, "Jessica Stirling"). In one of those fictions (*The Dark Pasture*) they cited "Hazelrigg Farm." When years later asked about source, he said he only dimly recalled the name from his childhood in Glasgow, and could remember no details of the place or of its naming.[8] One wonders if he remembered the name from visiting kin in Dumfries (home of many members of the Rae family), about 80 miles south of Glasgow. On the southwest side of town there is a short street named Hazelrigg Avenue, angled in a way that suggests it might have been a close. Even more interesting is the fact that as late as the early 1900s there was a farm known as "Hazelrigg Farm" on the Glasgow side of Dumfries, near Amisfield in the old parish of Tinwald. Tax records show that it was a productive farm as far back as August 1797, when the occupant, James Milligan, was taxed for three horses.

Before leaving Glasgow mention must be made of the fact of Edward Haselrig: author of a book entitled *Attic Stories*, Edward reported himself and his older brother (Thomas) to be sons of "the laird of Craigheuch."[9] Perhaps Edward's brief account of his family ancestry was part of his fiction, a means of establishing his credentials as observer of the local scene and, at the same time, nurturing rapport from his readers. No other record of this alleged household in the vicinity of Glasgow, late 1700s to early 1800s, has come to light. Finally—and a very long throw north of Glasgow, even north of Aberdeen—lies the charming town of Wick, on the North Sea; and in the middle of Wick, at 7 Coronation Street, stands an impressive stone house known as Hazelrigg (lately venue of a bed-and-breakfast offer). Now the question: which if any of these namings were due to the family rather than (probably mostly) to botanic scenery?

Thomas[20e] *Hazlerigg*, son of Thomas[19c] Maynard and Margaret (*nee* Drummond) Hazlerigg: b. 1 June 1877 Christchurch, Kent, d. 15 March 1935

Like his father and his uncle Arthur[19a], Thomas[20e] married into a military family, W H McCheane, who retired as a lieutenant colonel of the Royal Marine Light Infantry. Serving in what was then called the Great War—

---

[8] Personal communication; for which, a remembrance of thanks and a tip of the tam to a fine gentleman who left much too soon.
[9] Edward's book is available through a website < publicdomainreprints.org >

for which he was made Companion of the Distinguished Service Order in 1918—Thomas[20e] attained lieutenant colonelcy in the Royal Army Service Corps. He retired from military life to his father's country abode, Holme Lodge, which had been erected c1900 on site of the old glebe house, at Goadby.[10]

Some men might have been on a career track in military service but got cut down early. Two examples, brothers of the just-considered Thomas[20e], are next in the sequence of vignettes.

> *Arthur[20c] Hazlerigg*, son of Thomas[19c] Maynard & Margaret (*nee* Drummond) Hazlerigg: b. 31 March 1873, Charlton, Kent, d. 13 May 1900

As a lad and young man, Arthur[20c] moved about quite a bit, this being one of the contingencies of life as child of a military household. At date of census enumeration, 1881, he was living with his parents and siblings at his grandparents' estate, Noseley Hall. Ten years later he was still with his parents, who now lived in Woolwich, Kent. Ten years later he was dead, having died of a gunshot wound to the stomach while on duty during the siege of Mafeking. He was a trooper in the second division of the Cape Police, South Africa Field Force. His date of arrival in the Cape Colony is still unknown. We know he was there at the beginning of the siege of the town and outpost by forces of the Boer uprising in what to Britain was known as the Second Boer War (to the Afrikaans people, the Second War for Freedom). Given that he did arrive in the Cape Colony, what were the circumstances under which he became a private in the constabulary, as opposed to a unit of the regular army? No answer has been uncovered. What we do know is that on the 213th day of the siege of Mafeking (i.e., four days before the siege was lifted) he was delivering a message to an encampment, was "shot in the stomach" and for some time lay in the middle of what amounted to a "no man's land" until a veterinarian-officer, William Dunlop Smith, reached him and applied some treatment. Arthur[20c] died soon after.[11] His name is on a Mafeking Memorial (Exhibit 11.2)

---

[10] As noted in chapter 5 (page 232), a glebe is a benefice in support of a priest (Roman Catholic or Anglican tradition)—at minimum some land, which sometimes included one or more houses (rentals), one or more farms and/or "factories" (e.g., a pottery), and so forth, in addition to a parsonage or vicarage.

[11] Most of what is known of the event comes from a newspaper of sorts which was published during the siege: *The Mafeking Mail: Special Siege Slip*. Issue number 19 tells us that on Sunday, 26 November 1889, hostilities suspended for the Sabbath, a

>
> **CAPE POLICE.D.2.**
> SERGT.MAJ. J SCHREINER DIED OF DISEASE 22 APR.1900
> PTE. D MACDONALD DIED OF DISEASE 7 MAR.1900
> PTE. S WEBB KILLED 9 MAR.1900
> PTE. C S RICHARDS DIED OF DISEASE 22 APR.1900
> PTE. A HAZLERIGG DIED OF WOUNDS 13 MAY.1900
> **BECHUANALAND RIFLES.**
> LCE.CPL. E IRONSIDE DIED OF WOUNDS 4 MAY.1900
> PTE. J MC CORKINDALE DIED OF DISEASE 6 APR.1900
> **TOWN GUARD**
> POST COMMANDER J DALL KILLED 10 FEB.1900
> POST COMMANDER R H GIRDWOOD (LATE CAPT 3RD. BATT
> ROYAL IRISH RIFLES ATTACHED A.S. CORPS.)
> DIED OF WOUNDS 13 FEB.1900
> PTE. E G PARSLOW KILLED 1 NOV.1899
> PTE. W SMITH KILLED 6 DEC.1899
> PTE. F B SLATER KILLED 1 JAN.1900
> PTE. C MEIL DIED OF DISEASE 9 JAN.1900
> PTE. W WILSON DIED OF DISEASE 9 JAN.1900
> PTE. W DUDLEY DIED OF WOUNDS 12 JAN.1900
> PTE. P GRAHAM DIED OF WOUNDS 17 JAN.1900
> PTE. T J KIDDY DIED OF DISEASE 1 FEB.1900
> PTE. W C JONES DIED OF WOUNDS 3 FEB.1900
> PTE. J J BORTHWICK DIED OF DISEASE 20 FEB.1900
> PTE. J CALVERT DIED OF DISEASE 22 FEB.1900
> PTE. J MC MULLEN DIED OF DISEASE 26 FEB.1900
> PTE. J W ALPEN DIED OF DISEASE 26 MAR.1900
> PTE. R CARTER DIED OF DISEASE 26 MAR.1900
> PTE. J COULSON DIED OF WOUNDS 31 MAR.1900
> PTE. W KIRBY DIED OF DISEASE 13 APR.1900
> PTE. C HEALE KILLED 12 MAY.1900
> PTE. J M SMIT DIED OF WOUNDS 16 MAY.1900

Exhibit 11.2. A Tablet of the Mafeking Memorial

Greville[20f] Hazlerigg, a younger son of Thomas[19c] Maynard and
Margaret (*nee* Drummond) Hazlerigg: b. 12 December 1881
Woolwich, Kent, d. 7 March 1944 Worthing, Sussex

Unlike his brother Arthur[20e], who did not survive long enough to marry, Greville[20f], following in his father's path, married the daughter of another military man, Needham T Parsons, who would be a major general of the 103rd Fusiliers. Prior to his marriage, Greville[20f] served as a junior

---

number of men, including Arthur[20c], enjoyed a game of football. Accounts of his death were published in issues 142 and 143 (14 and 16 May 1900). Command of the garrison, by the way, was under Robert Baden-Powell, who (though doubted by some yet regaled by others) was elevated to major general, and later founded the Boy Scouts.

officer in the 2nd Battalion, Sherwood Foresters (an infantry regiment) in 1902. Nothing more is known of his military service. But according to the 1911 census, he was "Retired Army," living with his parents and his four sisters at their residence in Greenwich. Neither his wife, Helen Margaret, nor their newly born son, Arthur[21a] Greville Maynard Hazlerigg, was present; but nor could either be found elsewhere in the 1911 enumeration. Depending how early his entry muster, he could have been in the latter part of the Second Boer War, the last main battle of which occurred in April 1902. The voyage of about 6,000 miles could have been completed in two weeks (assuming transit by one of the fastest steamers of that day), and we know that the Sherwood Foresters were present in the Second Boer War at least as late as September 1901. Otherwise, the regiment was not engaged in warfare during 1902. One other relevant fact is that whereas the electoral rolls show Greville[20f] in Greenwich during the 1920s and 1930s, Helen Margaret was more than 60 miles to the southwest, in Farnham, Surrey, during those years. Whether there was any connection between the apparent marital separation and his early "retirement" from the army is another unknown. At least much of the time he was living with his sisters Gwendoline[20a] and Evelyn[20d] in Greenwich.

Other young men of the family were clearly engaged in empire defence—whether with intent of military career is not clear, but either decided to muster out after some major engagements or, as in the first of the three cases that follow, died early, perhaps from battle injury.

Arthur[18d] Hesilrige, son of Charles[17h] Maynard and Deborah
Maria (*nee* Buckby) Hesilrige: b. 20 June 1834, d. 14 February
1863 Bourne, Lincolnshire

After attending Sidney College, Cambridge, this young man entered the officer corps of the 59th Regiment of Foot, often called "The Five and Nine," a regiment that had been involved in many postings and battles around the world. It appears that his first major combat experience was at Canton (Guangzhou), China, during the taking of that coastal city in what is often called in English-speaking memory the Second Opium War or the Second Anglo-Chinese War, even though the offensive force was a combination of British and French units. Combat occurred from the end of 1857 through part of the following January. The 59th then shipped to duty in South Africa, not returning to England until 1861.[12] Whether

---

[12] Thomas Carter, *Medals of the British Army* (London: Groombridge and Sons, 1861), pages 180-181.

Arthur[18d] returned to England directly after Canton or stayed with the 59th is unknown. On 4 June 1862 he wed Mary Augusta Nicholls, daughter of a Lincolnshire surgeon, in Bourne. Nine months later he was dead. Had he been one of the 113 men of the allied force who were wounded at Canton? There is no known record by which to answer that question. But his biography in Cambridge records refers to him as "Lieutenant" at the time of his marriage.

Arthur[21a] William Hazlerigg, son of Thomas[20e] and Edith (*nee* McCheane) Hazlerigg: b. 5 February 1904, d. 16 March 1987 Cambridge; Clare College, Cambridge

With this man we have entered wholly into the twentieth century, which means that privacy concerns take priority and entail restrictions of access to information. He attained captaincy, served in the Royal Regiment of Artillery from 5 October 1936; then, certified in long survey theory and practice, on 21 December 1939, he was assigned to General Staff Offices. He advanced to become a major in the Royal Army, then retired as an honorary lieutenant colonel, 21 April 1947. From there he undertook a second career, which will be addressed as continuation of this vignette, under the heading of Teaching.

Herbert[20a] William Grey Hazlerigg, son of Grey[19d] and Sarah (*nee* Whetstone) Hazlerigg: b.13 September 1910 Paddington, London, d. January 1991 Brighton, Sussex

Born in 1910, Herbert's[20a] trajectory in the Royal Army included time in Sudan (c1932-33), at the Royal Military College (1933), and then in India (1 Feb 1935-1936). Beyond those few basic facts, the record remains closed.

As has been noted already, the line between military and colonial civil service could be rather porous at times; some of the foregoing cases exemplified that porosity. Another case is the following, although here there seems little doubt that a military career had not been planned at any point.

Charles[19f] Cecil Hazlerigg, third son of 12 Bt and Henrietta (*nee* Phillips) Hazlerigg: b. 31 July 1845 Billesdon, Leicestershire, d. 13 July 1891 Rockhampton, Queensland, Australia

Named after his mother's father (Charles Allen Phillips) and mother (Cecilia), this fellow attended Harrow, leaving in 1861. He then joined the 26th Regiment of Foot, British Army, which in 1861 had just returned from service in Canada and was stationed in Edinburgh, before shipping out to Bombay in July 1865 and returning from India 10 years later. How long Charles[19f] was in service with the 26th is not known. The entry for him in *The Harrow School Register, 1801-1900*, after noting his service in the 26th Regiment, says "subsequently farmed in Australia."[13] While the entry is silent as to dates, the presumption seems to have been that he was engaged in Australia for some time. However, another record both confirms his presence in Australia and raises doubt about when and how long. Ship records show passage from England to Brisbane, arriving 26 May 1891. This could have been his return after visiting in England, but it could also have been his emigration. Facts are scarce. In addition to the foregoing, we know that he died in Queensland on 13 July 1891. Probate was completed in England a year later (14 July 1892), the record of which refers to him as "of Planet Downs Springsure Rockhampton Queensland." His estate was recorded as £3544 18s 1d, assigned to his brother, "Thomas Maynard Hazlerigg, col. Royal Artillery." There is no indication that he ever married or had any children, but then records in Australia during that period were not always maintained. The geographic location mentioned above was in fact Planet Downs station (i.e., ranch) in the parish of Springsure, diocese of Rockhampton, in central Queensland. There is notice of approved probate in Queensland as well, according to Rockhampton's *Morning Bulletin* for Tuesday, 1 September 1891. This proceeding, completed 17 August, proved a valuation of £820 for the estate of "Charles Cecil Hazelrigg." Little is known of Planet Downs station. It was situated on Planet Creek in a valley described in a local history as a "vast expanse of rich agricultural land." Very little more was said of the station in that history.[14] It appears the station was held by a Frederick Walker in 1860. From then until 1892 the known record is blank. In that year the colonial secretary received a letter from a Brock Hollinshead (aka Holinshed) of Planet Downs. He owned the station until losing all of his stock in a severe drought of 1902, after which the station was acquired by the Logan family. The 1871 census found 18 residents at Planet Downs. All in all, it seems likely that Charles[19f] had not been an owner of the station, or at best had owned a small share of it; that he had probably arrived only recently, though perhaps prior to 1891;

---

[13] (London: Longmans, Green, 1901), page 291.
[14] Matthew J Fox, *The History of Queensland*, 3 volumes (Brisbane: States Publishing Company, 1923). The section on central Australian agricultural places and people begins on page 189 of volume 1.

that he left most of his estate in England, perhaps undertaking, at age 46, the expedition to Australia as a trial. How did he die? We do not know. The land of Planet Downs, however rich it might have been, lay at the border of a tropical climate. Malaria, cholera, influenza, and the lot, were common scourges, and for an Englishman the heat could be unrelentingly torrid.

Charles[19f] might have been the first Hesilrige/Hazlerigg to have settled in Australia, but he was probably not the first descendant to have done so. Tracing all descendants is an impossible task, of course, but one indication of the likelihood of an early emigration to Australia can be seen in the abbreviated segment of Buckby lineage in chapter 10, as well as from the following abbreviation of the descent lineage from Jemima[17g] Hesilrige (daughter of Col. Grey Hesilrige and Bridget Buckby).

Jemima Hesilrige: b. 1800, d. 1842
 + William Buckby: b. c1801 Tandragee, Eire
   ˪ Charlotte Emily Maria Buckby: b. 1842
     +Thomas Edward Shannon: b. c1835 Eire,
        m. 13 Sep 1859 Kilmare, Eire
      ˪ Arthur Grey Hesilrige Shannon: b. Jul 1863
         Grantham, Lincolnshire
        + Emma Maria Townsend: b. 1867 Victoria
           m. 1895 Victoria, d. 1929 NSW
         ˪ Arthur Grey Hazlerigg Shannon: b. 1895
            Victoria, Australia
         ˪ Violet Townsend Shannon: b. 1900, d. 1957

Exhibit 11.3. Arthur Grey Hazlerigg Shannon

Exhibit 11.3 shows Arthur Grey Hazlerigg Shannon in a section of a photograph taken in December 1916, Salisbury, England, of the unit in which he served as a gunner, the 7th Australian Field Artillery Brigade, during World War I.

Who today does not know that the twentieth century was a time of massive warfare, with tens of millions of fatalities—including civilian men, women, and children, along with military combatants and support personnel, in many parts of the world. Men and women of the British Isles were called upon to defend their homelands against the onslaught of "total war." The following were among them.

> *Martival[20b] Grey Hazlerigg*, son of Allen[19i] Martival and Adela (*nee* Codrington-Forsyth) Hazlerigg: b. 9 October 1884 Worsley, Lancashire, d. September 1971 Barnet, Middlesex

He served as a lieutenant in the Royal Field Artillery, from c1915, and in 1917 was awarded the Victory Medal for his service in France. We do not know the conditions of his service, but in general we do know that one did not have to be in a trench to suffer effects of mustard gas, or to be mangled by artillery shells. Martival[20b] survived, dealt with what were surely some gruesome memories, and through the 1930s was living with wife Marion and (in the early 1930s) his mother in Islington.[15] He was nearing his eighty-seventh birthday anniversary when the end came.

> *Arthur[20a] Grey Hazlerigg*, 13th Bt, son of Arthur[19a] and Janet Edith (*nee* Orr-Ewing) Hazlerigg: b. 17 November 1878, d. 25 May 1949

In addition to serving as His Majesty's Lord Lieutenant and *Custos rotularum* (Guardian of the Rolls) of Leicestershire, the 13th Bt was a lieutenant in the Royal Naval Volunteer Reserve, 1915-16, and honorary captain in the Royal Air Force, 1916-18; more below.

> *Arthur[21d] Grey Hazlerigg*, 14th Bt, son of 13th Bt and Rachel (*nee* Buxton) Hazlerigg: b. 24 February 1910, d. 30 September 2002

During World War II the 14th Bt served in the Royal Army, first in North Africa, then in Syria and Palestine, and last in Italy, achieving colonelcy. He was awarded the Military Cross for his service in combat.

---

[15] His parents had separated at unknown date between 1891 and 1901. By 1911 mother and son were living at Awre, Gloustershire, she as "widow," he as "poultry farmer."

British women had major roles during each of the world wars. Examples are:

Charlotte[20b] Isabel Hazlerigg, daughter of William[19g] Greville and Barbara (*nee* Pease) Hazlerigg: b. 1878 Billesdon, Leics., d. 1 January 1942

Charlotte[20b] served in the Voluntary Aid Detachment during 1917 and 1918, receiving the British War Medal and Victory Medal.

Jean[21a] Mary Hazlerigg, daughter of Roger[20a] Greville and Esther (*nee* Everett) Hazlerigg: b. 19 December 1921, d. April 2010 Worcestershire

A book could be written about contributions to the war effort by Jean[21a] and her colleagues. As a matter of fact, books *have* been written about those contributions; but, as was once a common disavowal, "names have been changed" (whether to protect the innocent or to preserve security). While head girl at her school near Bognor Regis, Jean[21a], noted for her unusual ability with crossword puzzles, was recruited to the cryptography operations at the Government Code and Cypher School (GC&CS), a new and larger team assembled by several government officials and academic types during the summer of 1939 at Bletchley Park in Buckinghamshire. This "Ultra secret" operation gained acclaim after the war as "Britain's greatest secret"—although people who had worked there would not be at liberty to speak of their activities until the 1970s. The core of their assignment was breaking codes produced by each new generation of an encrypting machine ("the Enigma") that had been invented in Germany many years earlier. Some versions of the Enigma had been employed in commercial as well as diplomatic work, even though these early codes were broken repeatedly. The German army developed more complex versions, the Abwehr Enigma, with each new edition more difficult to fathom. In March 1940 Jean[21a] was introduced to Professor Alan Turing as his assistant. By this time, the newest available edition of the Enigma coding machine was being taken apart, in search of clues to its coding process, using a device, the "Bombe machine," which Alan Turing had developed from a Polish cryptographic device. Jean[21a] was part of the deciphering crew who unraveled messages of the Italian navy's version of Enigma, as a result of which the Royal Navy was prepared for decisive engagements in November 1940, first at Cape Matapan (Greek coast) and then at Italy's naval base Taranto, destroying much of the ability of the Italian navy to challenge the British fleet in the Mediterranean. Jean[21a] was assigned next to Intelligence Service Knox (ISK), headed by a Cambridge classics professor, Alfred Dillwyn Knox, who had been chief cryptologist at the GC&CS since the end of the Great War. "Dilly," as he was usually called, was in charge of breaking the latest versions of the Abwehr Enigma coding system. Jean[21a], one of the team of "Dilly's girls," wrote trial menus for the Bombe machine. ISK operations yielded more than 140,000 decrypted messages, including some that proved to be important to success of the Normandy invasion.

Exhibit 11.4 Jean Marie Hazlerigg, 1943 and 2009

After May 1945 Jean[21a] continued her work in cryptography, now at the Government Communications Headquarters (GCHQ), at Eastcote and then at Cheltenham. However, having met Kenneth Perrin while at Bletchley Park, Jean[21a] married in 1947, leaving government service. Remaining highly circumspect during the next decades about her wartime activities, Jean[21a] witnessed loss of interest in Bletchley Park and all that it had meant. By the early 1990s the physical property had deteriorated so much that the old mansion was scheduled for demolition, a shopping center its rumored successor. But, no; a few rallied, forming a trust that eventually won recovery and remembrance. In July 2009 Gordon Brown, Prime Minister, addressed Jean[21a], along with other surviving members of the Bletchley Park crew, with official commemoration of their service during the war that had begun 70 years earlier. The following 9th day of

October she received a commemorative badge, presented by the Lord Lieutenant of Worcestershire, Mr Michael Brinton. Nearly a case of "too late," if not also of "too little": Jean[21a], alert, attentive, and appreciative during the short ceremony, died the next April.

The two world wars were not the first occasions in which women were called upon to support a war effort, standing in for husbands sent to the front and sending sons to join others in combat zones and in support functions. Two Hazlerigg daughters who exemplified the willingness to offer support as wives of military men were:

Henrietta[18c] *Susan Hazlerigg*, daughter of 11th Bt and Henrietta (*nee* Bourne) Hazlerigg: b. 1817 Noseley, d. 4 September 1901 Billericay, Essex; m. 15 October 1840 Thomas Bell, esq. (1816-1863), Capt 58th Regiment

Dorothy[19d] *Susan Hazlerigg*, daughter of 12th Bt and Henrietta (*nee* Phillips) Hazlerigg: b. 1842 Billesdon, Leics., d. 9 January 1914 Hastings, Sussex; m. 21 November 1861 Herrick Augustus Palmer (1835-1908), Capt 62nd Regiment, Major Royal Glamorgan Militia (taken prisoner at storming of the Redan, 8 September 1855, during the Crimean War)

And other daughters—as we saw earlier, for instance, Gwendoline[20a] Alice, daughter of Thomas[19c] Maynard & Margaret (*nee* Drummond) Hazlerigg—had little choice in the matter, as they were born into a military household, sometimes in lands that were extremely challenging to one's very survival.

Clergy

The English country clergyman, from the early eighteenth century through the nineteenth, was in some ways an often underestimated figure. He was one of the few who regularly had the learning and then the leisure time to engage in systematic thought and writing. Thomas Bayes was but one example--stellar, to be sure—of the type. Not all who had the position and its advantages did much with them. But quite a few did, serving as tutors to the local youth as well as composing astute observations of local life. There was indeed a "flip side" to the "pleasant image of a bucolic and latitudinarian parson was," as Light put it in her family history: "the fat cleric, clutching his tithe pig, a favourite butt of cartoons of the period."[16] Variation in human character occurred as often, probably, and as great in degree, among those who were "of the cloth" as among men and women in general. Rent-seeking behavior may well be more frequent in clerical occupations than in some others, but there is probably greater difficulty in accurately discriminating it in the daily activities of a cleric than in those of, say, a shop keeper or a farmer.

The clerical vocation was traditionally one of the most common avenues for sons who were not heir apparent. But it seems to have been an avenue less often taken among young men of the Hesilrige/Hazlerigg family during the nineteenth and early twentieth centuries, as indicated by the sum of the following vignettes.

Charles^{17h} Maynard Hesilrige, son of Grey^{16q} and Bridget (*nee* Buckby) Hesilrige: b. 24 August 1802 Herefordshire, d. 4 December 1878 Carlton Curlieu, Leicestershire

Between completing his BA degree in 1828 and his MA in 1831 (Queens College, Cambridge), he wed 10 March 1829 Deborah Maria, daughter of Arthur and Elizabeth (*nee* McDonnell) Buckby of Seagoe, Armagh, Eire (or today, Northern Ireland). In 1846 Charles^{17h} began service as rector of Carleton Curlieu, Leicestershire, completing a new rectory that year at his own expense of about £1,000. His service as rector continued until his death in 1878.[17]

Grey^{18d} Hazlerigg, third son of Arthur^{17b}, 11th Bt, and Henrietta (nee Bourne) Hazlerigg: b. 13 March 1818, d. 4 October 1912

After attending school first at Brighton and then at Eton, he was in 1837 commissioned a junior officer of the 48th Regiment of Foot, and in that same year he was selected as one to carry the colours of the new queen's (Victoria) regiment in procession through Manchester. But a year later Grey^{18d} resigned his commission. Perhaps the decision was due partly to concern about his widowed mother, Henrietta, who was in her mid-fifties at the time and might have been experiencing health problems (although she lived another 30 years).[18] Grey^{18d} himself, later recalling that period of his life, attributed the change in prospect to an inner realization of

---

[16] Alison Light, *Common People* (London: Penguin/Fig Tree, 2014), page 83; and more generally pages 83-93.
[17] John M Lee and Richard A McKinley, *A History of the County of Leicester, volume 5: Gartree Hundred* (Oxford: Oxford University Press, 1964), pages 77-81.
[18] In his preface to a small book of his mother's letters, *Sweet Memories*, which he published in 1869, he referred to her "tendency to bronchitis and heart-disease."

aimlessness, brought to a head by an exchange with a fellow officer at mess one day, which exposed an enormous self-doubt. Fearing for his health, he "sold my commission." But then, bereft of the discipline imposed by army life, he felt himself ever more adrift.[19] According to the 1841 census, he was then living with his mother in the village of Kilby, ten miles west of Noseley. Two years later he matriculated during Michaelmas term at St John's College, Cambridge, reportedly with the intent of taking Anglican orders. However, he gradually came to believe that "the Established Church" could not provide him with the security of a strict discipline which he had been desperately needing, and he shifted to doctrines and practices that made him "nonconformist." In 1846 Grey[18d] was living with his mother, "Dowager Lady Hazlerigg," at Carlton Curlieu Hall, where his uncle, Charles[17h] Maynard Hesilrige, had recently become rector. By 1848 he had declared himself "Calvinistic Baptist," and in 1850 he became minister of the Alfred Street Chapel in Leicester. Twenty years later his congregation suffered a schism, about ninety of the members declaring for the Society of Particular Strict Communion Baptists; and in 1873 they moved to Zion Chapel on Erskine Street, where he continued his ministry until 1912.[20] Much of that time he lived in the Willoughby House at 108 Regent Road, Leicester.[21]

Grey[18d] apparently did not marry until in his mid-fifties, when he wed Sarah Ann, age 26, daughter of Thomas Clarke, a Loughborough (Leicestershire) dyer and trimmer whose firm employed nearly two dozen men and women. Thomas was raised as a Baptist, according to the Nonconformist Register of Loughborough, and his children were probably raised with similar beliefs. Sarah died in 1901, leaving a personal estate of £1065 to her brothers John and William, both dyers in the family firm. She and Grey[18d] raised six children during their 28 years of marriage. Grey[18d] died during his 95th year. His personal estate of £3866 was left to three people, his eldest daughter Henrietta[19a] (never

---

[19] Grey Hazlerigg, *Letters to a Mother* (London: William Wileman, 1886), pages 8-9, 12, 14-20. Throughout this accounting he mentioned members of his family never as guides but as guided by his personal revelations. However, "family" had been reduced mainly to his mother, his father having died when Grey[18d] was an infant, his only sister having married, and his elder brother Arthur[18a] tending to his estate at Noseley. Perhaps he included in his reference to "family" his uncle Charles[17h] and that household.

[20] William White, *History, Gazetteer, and Directory of Leicestershire* (Sheffield: Robert Leader, 1846), page 492.

[21] Other reminders of days gone by in Leicester include a footpath, Hesilrige Walk, which extended from Hungarton Boulevard to Main Street, Humberstone village, now part of Leicester (see chapter 5, pages 232-33).

married), his son-in-law Wilfred Tyler, and his son Thomas Maynard Hazlerigg[19f], a solicitor.

Exhibit 11.5. Grey Hazlerigg, c1890

Grey's[18d] missionary zeal seldom took him beyond Leicestershire geographically, but it generated a series of booklets and larger books in which he plainly hoped to reach many readers beyond his small flock. Reference has already been made to his collection of some of his mother's letters and to his book of homiletics, which begins with a long "sketch of my own experience" and then proceeds to a collection of his letters to his mother, dated from 1856 to 1868. He also published several booklets, one of them a celebration of John Knox and others with titles such as *Thoughts upon God's Words* (1890) and *An Antidote and a Protest against Unsound Teaching* (1889). All of his published writing illustrates the porous border between professions of a cleric and professions of a teacher.

Charles[18f] Maynard Hesilrige, son of Charles[17h] Maynard and Deborah Maria (*nee* Buckby) Hesilrige: b. 7 May 1838 Billingham, Herefordshire, d. 4 September 1901 Wharfdale, Yorkshire; buried Weston, Harrogate

Son of his cleric father and namesake, Charles[18f] could be exemplar of the fact that men of the family who chose a clerical career were not "the fat cleric, clutching his tithe pig" of the once-common cartoon. He and his household lived a simple life while he served as vicar of Weston in Otley, Yorkshire. His preference carried through to the simple cross that marks his grave at the parish church he served. His personal estate, £274, was bequeathed to his and Sarah's son Grey[19a], who was then an assistant master at the Children's Home (see below). .

William[19g] Greville Hazlerigg, fourth son of Arthur[18a], 12th Bt, and Henrietta (*nee* Phillips) Hazlerigg: b. 8 June 1847, d. 1 November 1893

By this time, one may have noticed, school-leaving age for baccalaureate degrees had lengthened a bit, from 19 or 20, as had been the case during earlier generations, to the mid-twenties for men of the early 1800s such as Charles[17h] Maynard Hesilrige and William[19g] Greville Hazlerigg. This was a result of more strenuous curricula, as well as slightly older ages at admission. In addition (as can be seen in each of these cases), more men were adding to that degree the credential of a master's degree, especially when in preparation for one of the liberal professions such as the clerical and teaching professions. The latter man, William[19g] Greville, gained his BA in 1871 when he was 24, his MA two years later, from Pembroke College, Oxford. Not yet 29, he married Barbara Mary Pease, daughter of an army man, and pursued his clerical career, first as Billesdon's vicar. By 1891 they had moved to Hallaton, nearby, where he was rector at St Michael's. Two years later he was dead at age 46, cause unknown.

As mentioned above, two of the traditional liberal professions, cleric and teacher, have been closely linked in heritage, and, although the traffic between them has lessened, in an earlier era young men moved between them rather freely. By the nineteenth century this circulation had become more often generational, rather than by movement within a generation. An example:

Grey[19a] Hesilrige, son of Charles[18f] Maynard and Sarah (*nee* Mason) Hesilrige: b. 1872 Leeds, Yorkshire, d. 26 July 1939 Surrey

When his father died, Grey[19a] was an assistant master at the Church Missionaries' Children's Home in Limpsfield, Surrey (the 1901 census enumeration described him as "tutor"). One of his co-workers, a matron, according to that census, was Elizabeth Hannah Shrimpton, daughter of an Oxfordshire family. On 3 August 1904 she and Grey[19a], now a master at the Home's school, wed at Godstone, Surrey.

Other members of the family combined the lecturing skills of a teacher with interest in colonial service or in the honours traditionally associated with manorial patrimony or in the benefits of teaching for its own sake. We will meet some of them in the following sections.

Colonial Civil Service
From imaginations of "a new empire of universal commerce" during the 1700s, when such luminaries of Enlightenment philosophy as David Hume, Adam Smith, and Immanuel Kant wrote blueprints for a new order, to the complex realities of what had actually resulted weighed more and more heavily during the 1900s, when traditional claims of fair play, proper form, and superior culture were increasingly reflected back by "subaltern peoples" as hybrid progeny of those blueprints, the actions of imperial power were (and continue to be) highly contentious.[22] As citizens of the dominant side of equations of imperial power, men and women of the Hesilrige/Hazlerigg family probably viewed the British Empire firstly and mainly from the default position of simply assuming that the work of the Empire was for the good of the world, not just Great Britain. That tends to be part of the cost of power for anyone who views "the world," including "the other" within it, from a persistently dominant standpoint. After all, powerful actors usually prefer to think of their acts on fair analogy to charity—"taking modern medicine to the ill, poor, and ignorant people," so to speak, whether these people be in backwaters of one's own country or in some faraway place.

Even so, however, dominant actors are likely to catch at least glimmers now and again of views from the other side—from "the natives," from the "subaltern people"—and those contrasting views may register as "second thoughts," reasons for doubt, about motivations and effects of rulership in an empire. It is well known, for instance, that the Indian independence movement soon learned to use British proclamations of the value of fair play, proper form, and similar tributes of conscience, to its own ends, and with growing success, merely by holding up a mirror.[23]

---

[22] Rothschild, *Inner Life* ... (2011), pages 43, 211-12.
[23] Eventually the mirror was incorporated into a famous English novel, E M Forster's *A Passage to India* (1924), even as the author displayed unself-consciously some of the typical imperial assumptions in his own depictions of the society and cultures of India.

Here, unfortunately, we are faced with another set of personal experiences by members of the Hesilrige/Hazlerigg family who did not leave behind any reflective writings—or none that have survived to present inspection.

Grey[19d] Hazlerigg, son of Grey[18d] and Sarah Ann (*nee* Clarke) Hazlerigg: b. 14 January 1879, d. 11 April 1948 London

In contrast to a claim made in the prior section of vignettes, this young man obtained his BA at age 21, in 1900, followed by his LLB in 1906, both at St John's College, Cambridge. We do not know his baccalaureate course of study, but it appears that he trained for a legal career. His activity during the next two years remains unknown, but by 1908 he was district commissioner in the Gold Coast, as Ghana was then called in Britain. A year later he was acting assistant colonial secretary of the Gold Coast. Within that span of time he also returned to Surrey long enough to marry a Suffolk daughter in December 1908, Sarah Dorothy Whetstone, whose father was a justice of the peace. By 1910 Grey[19d] was registrar of the Supreme Court of Ceylon (i.e., Sri Lanka). This rapid progression within Britain's imperial civil service was then interrupted by the call of military duty. Having been commissioned a junior officer (2nd lieutenant) of the Sherwood Foresters regiment by 1901, Grey[19d] served in that capacity during the Great War, although from 1916 to 1919 in the Colonial Office. In 1920 he was invested as an Officer of the Most Excellent Order of the British Empire. Then, from 1920 to 1924, he was back into the external empire, this time as secretary to first one and then another incumbent of the Governor Generalship of South Africa. By the end of this tour of duty strains in the marital relationship had developed to the point that official divorce seemed the best solution. This occurred in 1924, during which time another spell in the Colonial Office had been conveniently arranged. Grey[19d] remained single for several years, but on a November day in 1933, at Westminster, his years of journeying from one part of the empire to another mostly if not entirely behind him, he wed Fannie Smith.

Alexander[20c] Maynard Hazlerigg, son of Grey[19d] and Sarah (*nee* Whetstone) Hazlerigg: b. 23 June 1914 Ceylon (i.e., Sri Lanka), d, July 1997 Worthing, Sussex

Born while his father, the just-considered Grey[19d], and his mother, Sarah, were stationed in Colombo, Ceylon, Alexander[20c], along with his parents and two older siblings (Herbert[20a] and Dorothy[20b]), returned to London on

26 January 1915. According to the passenger record, the plan was for the three children to remain in England (perhaps with her relatives), while Grey[19d] and Sarah returned to a post in one of the "British possessions" (as the form put it), although we know, as stated above, that Grey[19d] was posted in the Colonial Office from 1916 to 1920. In any case, records show that Alexander[20c] began his adult life following in his father's footsteps, with a posting in the colonial civil service in Jamaica in 1935. Two years later he was a sub-inspector in the constabulary of Trinidad. No record has been found of his activities during the years of World War II, until 1944, when he was in Kettering, Northamptonshire, to wed Jean Dorothy Rowan.

> *Thomas[19f] Maynard Hazlerigg*, second son of Grey[18d] & Sarah
> (*nee* Clarke) Hazlerigg: b. 1882 Leicester, d. 6 November 1961
> Shrewsbury, Shropshire

After attaining captaincy in the Royal Army Service Corps during World War I, for which he was awarded the Military Cross in 1919, Thomas[19f] gained the position of assistant crown solicitor in Hong Kong, 1920. A succession of civil service postings in Hong Kong ensued over the next quarter-century, among them: registrar, Supreme Court, 1929; crown solicitor, 1935; special advisor to the government, 1946-47; member of Hong Kong's Executive Council and simultaneously member of Hong Kong's Legislative Council, 1946-47. After death claimed his first wife, Violet, in 1941, he married secondly Gladys May Cotton, who in her own right was awarded a British Empire Medal. During the spring of 1946, she travelled by steamer from the UK to San Francisco, via the Panama Canal, thence to Hong Kong, to be with Thomas[19f], who was installed as Commander, the Most Excellent Order of the British Empire. Following retirement from the colonial civil service, he returned to Leicester and offered his services as a solicitor.

> *Guy[20e] Maynard Hazlerigg*, son of William[19g] Greville and
> Barbara (*nee* Pease) Hazlerigg: b. 8 February 1887 Market
> Harborough, Leicestershire, d. 1962/1963 Perth, Australia

The record for Guy[20e] is very sketchy, even allowing for his birth year, and on some points of information rather perplexing. After schooling, he was commissioned a lieutenant in the Army Service Corps. The first clear record of him shows his return from Durban, South Africa, in September 1909. Two years later he was stationed at the ASC depot in Aldershot, Surrey, still a lieutenant, and two years after that, on 15 March

1913, he was in London for his marriage to Erna Irene (1889-1924), daughter of Captain R C Heidenreihe of the 5th Austrian Hussars. Their son, George[21a] Maynard Hazlerigg, was born 25 August 1915 but lived less than a year. However, Erna, as Mrs Erna Hazlerigg, was on a ship returning from Mombasa, Kenya, arriving in England 15 February 1915. With her was "Master Cecil Hazlerigg," age 5 years. Who was he? The ships' register is silent about relationship, and no known record offers an answer; but one could presume he was an older son, returning with his mother (now pregnant with a second child), having been with his father, Guy[20e], who saw combat in East Africa c1916, for which he was awarded a Military Cross. At unknown date Guy[20e] departed military service as a major in the Reserve Officers of the Army Service Corps. It was perhaps at this time that he reportedly took a posting in the colonial civil service as an assistant district commissioner for British East Africa, apparently stationed in the port city of Malindi, in Kenya. The known record is once again rather murky. In 1921 he and Erna are in Westminster, residing at 93 Lauderdale-mansions, Maida Vale, Middlesex. Had he been posted to the Colonial Office? Perhaps. A ship's roster dated 7 December 1921 includes Mrs Erna I Hazlerigg, age 31, sailing to Cape Town, intending, according to the registry, permanent residency in South Africa (which meant residence for one year or more). Guy[20e] was not on the manifest. Was he was already on station? Perhaps. But a year later, it appears, he arrived in Western Australia by way of Singapore. Given the advantage of hindsight, one suspects that at least some of this travel was undertaken in exploration of possible emigration; for it is unlikely that his arrival in Australia would have been due to a colonial posting. In any case, the next we see of Erna, she is living in Middlesex, where, as "wife of Guy Hazlerigg," she died 19 Jan 1924. Probate was returned 2 June 1924 in Middlesex court, again as "wife of Guy Hazlerigg"; her personal effects, totaling £1219 15s 6d, went to Gordon William Stow, solicitor.

By 1925 Guy[20e] was working as a laborer and residing, apparently alone, at 7 Murray Street.in Perth, Western Australia. In 1929 he married in Perth a woman named Marguerite Jennie, daughter of Thomas Austin Francis. By 1931 she and Guy[20e] are jointly on the electoral rolls. Five years later they are living in Victoria Park, Perth; he is employed as a taxi driver. The same record is repeated in 1943 and again in 1954. Guy[20e] died in Perth in 1962 or in 1963, depending on which record one accepts. There is no indication of children by Marguerite (who was born c1890, died 18 February 1958 in Perth).

Earlier we saw the presence of Charles[19f] Cecil Hazlerigg in eastern Australia, along with Hazlerigg descendants via the Buckby family, among others. One of the consequences of military and colonial civil service for the sake of empire was a rapidly growing family fund of experience with long-distance travel and, via foreign postings for years at a time, residence in other places amidst other cultures. Australia, along with New Zealand, held particular attractions despite the geographic distances, because the cultural distances were considerably smaller as compared with other parts of the British Empire. Judging from named sites in Australia, there might have been other emigrants to Australia, in addition to those just named. A candidate site, for instance, is located in northeastern New South Wales: Hazelrigg Gardens, a prominent if small botanical garden in the Maitland district of the Hunter river valley (41 Belmore Road, Lorn, NSW), was probably named after a connection to the family, although (as of the early 2000s) no one seemed to recall the particulars. Another candidate site is (or was) a vineyard in the Barossa valley of South Australia, Hazelrigg Farm. Again, effort to draw out the naming history was frustrated by too much change in ownership (as well as too little time on site). Think of these candidates as another reason for a family researcher to explore the delightful lands of Australia.

Arthur[21a] Greville Maynard Hazlerigg, son of Greville[20f] and Helen Margaret (*nee* Parsons) Hazlerigg: b. 7 November 1910, d. December 1990 Yeovil, Somerset

With this case we are treading all too close to present times, so little will be said. Arthur[21a] was a mechanical engineer with high reputation. His repeated journeys to Nigeria and back (some of them with members of his household) suggest that he had been at one time a member of the civil service.

Teaching

Traditionally, the connection between future and past was primarily and mainly in familial relationships. Patrimony in general and aristocracy in particular were major organizing principles of family life both spatially and temporally. Familial relationship remains important in the linkages of past to future, but it now has much company in the building and repair of those linkages. One of the thrusts of the Enlightenment movement emphasized a principle of "universal education." This meant not only that everyone is or should be entitled to education; it also meant that the content of the education should be, at least in "basics," universal and public. Impetus for that aim and goal came from the development of the modern nation state: the intent was to knit together the thousands of local communities into a single national fabric, all members of society knowing the same history, engaging the same ceremonial emotions, reading the same traditional literatures, and recognizing the same national paladins of arts and sciences, as well as adding columns of numbers to the same sums. With that, the traditional free (i.e., liberal) profession of teaching became a public civic function, not restricted to private relationships of parents who could afford to hire their own tutors for their children.

As a public civic function, education also expanded beyond the schoolhouse as well as the family household and the parsonage, for there developed at the same time a *business* of enlightenment, which extended well beyond the traditional copyist scribe to the printer, the proofreader, the salon patron, the newspaper editor and reporter, the illustrator, the bookseller, and on and on. In short, teaching become polymorphous, the public civic function diverse in motive and goal.

Some of that diversity can be seen in the activities of several men of the family as considered above. A few other cases follow.

Charles[19c] Hesilrige, son of Charles[18f] Maynard and Sarah (*nee* Mason) Hesilrige: b. April 1876 Belper, Derbyshire, d. 14 January 1947 London

Like his brother Grey[19a] (see above), Charles[19c] chose the profession of teaching, but first he had to survive the ordeals of the Great War, serving as a private in the Royal Fusiliers, 1915-1918, for which he was awarded the Victory Medal and British War Medal. His BA degree was bestowed by the University of London. He became master at Bishop Auckland Grammar School, Durham.

Arthur[21a] William Hazlerigg, son of Thomas[20e] and Edith (*nee* McCheane) Hazlerigg: b. 5 February 1904, d. 16 March 1987 Cambridge

Previously considered in the section of military vignettes, Arthur[21a], after retiring from the army in 1947, began his second career at his alma mater, Cambridge, first as university draftsman (inaugural for Cambridge; 1947-1961) and then as senior assistant registrar (1961-1971). As draftsman he no doubt had instructional duties; in the registrar's office, probably not. An autumn leave of absence enabled him to serve as a lecturer in Nigeria from September to December 1955. With retirement from the army he and his second wife, Ella (*nee* Wilson), made their residence at The Lordship Farm in Melbourn, about ten miles southwest of Cambridge.

Arthur[19a] George Maynard Hesilrige, son of Arthur[18d] and Mary Augusta (*nee* Nicholls) Hesilrige: b. 5 September 1863 Bourne, Lincolnshire; d. 13 April 1953 Paddington, London

From 1887 to 1935 Arthur[19a] was editor of *Debrett's Peerage*; retiring from the position in 1935, he nonetheless remained as consulting editor until his death in 1953. During his long tenure he guided the enterprise into greater diversity of offerings, initiating, for instance, *Debrett's House of Commons and the Judicial Bench* in 1918. While Arthur's[19a] work might not be considered teaching in the traditional sense, it was nonetheless an educational service, and it illustrates one aspect of the increasingly commercial extensions of education as a public civic function. Pedigree books had become a business, seemingly all the more profitable as evidence accumulated that the "age of pedigree" was definitely elderly, perhaps passing.

The sixteenth and seventeenth centuries, recall from earlier chapters, witnessed heraldic visitations of counties. In some portion this activity was due to competition among families for "official" recognition of standing. Royal courts were alert to opportunities for greater revenue both as a result of learning more clearly and systematically the wealth of established families and, from that basis, by engaging in "honours for a fee," with one hand, and subtle (sometimes not so subtle) extortion, with the other hand.

The later eighteenth and nineteenth centuries witnessed "pedigree books," which drew on results of those earlier visitations and brought them up to date. These were commercial ventures, often announced in advanced as subscriptions—rather like the "Who's Who" volumes of the twentieth century ("Purchase a volume and your name, too, will be in it!"). One can imagine that the pedigree books must have required some level of proof of claims, but the proof required often amounted to no more than pointing to one's family record in one of the earlier visitations. The redundancy across records and from edition to edition has the appearance of another version of the dictum that victors write the history.

In an earlier era, the circle of people who would have appeared in such a book, had one been produced, was small enough that virtually all of them knew one another, or at least knew *of* one another. They did not need a book to tell them particulars. Beyond that circle there were few people worth impressing with one's credentials. By the 1900s, however, the circle had become much larger, and as "new" families had been arriving, sometimes replacing "old" ones, it was useful to have an up-to-date guide. In addition, commercial culture offered new sorts of advertisement—literally as well as figuratively—and the audience for "badges, trademarks, and pedigrees" not only had grown in size but also continued to serve as keepers of useful services of influence and power, thus well worth impressing by the latest means available.

One consequence of some of those new services was a new regimen of proofing, an advent not always welcome. Claims to this or that antiquity of pedigree had long been coins of competition. Once established through visitations or other official or quasi-official documentation, their comparative values could circulate through marriage markets, local office holding, and the like. Now, however, partly because of new venues of commerce and partly because traditional deferences had weakened so much, calls for better testing of claims against records previously hidden away in Latin scrolls, and against standards of logic that were unimpressed by question begging and similar errors of reasoning, pedigrees were vulnerable as never before.

The price of vulnerability varied in proportion to the antiquities being asserted. The most expensive, as judged from the consequence of loss, was any claim of descent from a companion of William, duke of Normandy. As was mentioned in chapter 1 with regard to "our Roger," that descent has long been a talisman for a great many people, and the lengths to which many have been willing to go in order to buttress the claim—even to the extent of creating documents—testifies to the status competition driving such pursuits. Yet there is reason to think that the "original" *Roll of Battle Abbey,* in the sense of an inventory by anyone who was in a position to know who did arrive with the duke, never existed. In any case, disputes have been the stuff of new legend. At the beginning of the last century John Horace Round, bane of concocted pedigrees, demonstrated numerous instances in which entries in Burke's Peerage and similar other records of standing have presented claims, and sometimes presumed documentation, that do not survive inspection.[24]

---

[24] John Horace Round, "The Companions of the Conqueror," *The Monthly Review,* volume 3 (June 1901), pages 91-111; *Studies in Peerage and Family History* (Westminster: Archibald Constable, 1901); *Peerage and Pedigree* (London: James Nisbet, 1910). As he stated in the 1901 article (pages 95-96), "we do not hear of such a Roll having even existed at Battle till we come to the days of Elizabeth." Based on his research, he doubted the Roll was older than the fourteenth century, which would be consistent with the Auchinleck "copy" of 1335. Today, Round's investigations are less

Such was the context when Arthur[19a] George Maynard Hesilrige took on the task of serving as editor of Debrett's. Judging by his continued maintenance of the earlier "standard" spelling of the family surname, he was a man who put considerable stock in tradition.

Estate Management

Traditionally, heirs held decisive advantage over spares. "Of course!" one might retort. And so it was: "perfectly obvious." Granted, the heir was saddled with great responsibility by inheritance; but he also inherited great reward, the family patrimony—landed estates, agricultural production on large scale, perhaps a fleet of ships, a chain of mines, acres and acres of valuable timber, to boot. Plus, there was the value of titles, which on their own could carry considerable weight. Spares had to carry the burden of a large ambiguity in time—waiting in the wings for an event that might never come, faced with the obligation to be prepared, never quite free to get on with one's own future, be it as it is. But in the balance?

Another balance was changing, however, not so noticeably during the nineteenth century but increasingly evident during the next. This was the balance between the burden of responsibility and the rewards attending the burden. The number of landed families for whom that balance did not shift, or shifted only slightly, grew smaller and smaller—initially mainly in proportionate terms but then after the early decades of the 1900s smaller also in absolute number. The Cavendish family, the Spencer family, "even" the Russell family, for example, have felt the change.[25] As the examples of Grosvenor Estates and Cadogan Estates most famously testify at present date, estate management has become "big business"—*very* big business.

Thus, while the previous vignettes were focused mainly on sons who were "spares," here the attention turns to heirs, the managers of estates of the family patrimony.

---

disturbing, one suspects, than they were when first published. The democratization of pursuits of family history has been only partly responsible for that difference.

[25] Notably, of the five wealthiest families in Britain today (who collectively have greater wealth than the bottom fifth of all families), only the Grosvenor family and the Cadogan family could be considered "old British families." Of these two, moreover, the Cadogan holdings date from only the 1700s, gaining the entirety of the manor of Chelsea (west end of London) in 1821, whereas the holdings of the Grosvenor family date from the 1600s.

Arthur[17b] Grey Hazlerigg, 11th Bt: b. 8 November 1790 Noseley, d. 24 October 1819 Paris, France

He succeeded when his uncle Thomas[161] died in April 1817. He was lord of the manor two and one-half years.

Arthur[18a] Grey Hazlerigg, 12th Bt: b. 20 October 1812 Whitchurch, Herefordshire, d. 11 May 1890

He succeeded at the death of his father in October 1819, barely (by four days) seven years old. He was lord of the manor more than 70 years (1819 to 1890).

Arthur[20a] Grey Hazlerigg, 13th Bt and 1st baron Hazlerigg: b. 17 November 1878, d. 25 May 1949

He succeeded at age twelve when his grandfather died in May 1890, his father having died ten years earlier. He was lord of the manor 59 years (1890 to 1949). Exhibit 11.6 shows him with his wife, Dorothy Rachel (*nee* Buxton), and in Exhibit 11.7 he, as lord lieutenant, was attending Edward, prince of Wales during a Leicestershire visit.

Exhibit 11.6. Dorothy Rachel (*nee* Buxton) and Arthur Grey, 13th Bt and 1st baron Hazlerigg of Noseley

Exhibit 11.7. Edward, Prince of Wales, and Sir Arthur Hazlerigg

In addition to the offices listed in the military vignette, Sir Arthur[20a] Grey Hazlerigg, succeeding as 13th Bt in 1890, served as chairman of the county council for Leicestershire, 1923-24; as president of the Royal Agricultural Society, 1931; as chairman of the Council of Agriculture for England, 1932. In 1906, after the last of the Manners family left vacant a Leicestershire seat in parliament, he stood for the Melton division of the county, but he was defeated in the election and did not again attempt it, devoting his attention instead to county governance.[26] He underwrote construction of a residence hall, Hazlerigg Hall, on the campus of Loughborough University (see Exhibit 11.8). On 1 January 1945, in recognition of his public service, he was created 1st baron Hazlerigg by George VI. This was the 241st hereditary barony of the United Kingdom.

Exhibit 11.8. Hazlerigg Hall, Loughborough University, Loughborough, Leicestershire

Arthur^{21d} Grey Hazlerigg, 14th Bt and 2nd baron Hazlerigg: b. 24 February 1910, d. 30 September 2002

Succeeding when his father died in May 1949, he was lord of the manor 53 years (1949-2002). In addition to the offices listed above (in the military vignette for him), he qualified as a chartered surveyor and land agent. A successful cricketer in his youth and at Cambridge, he was captain of the Leicestershire Cricket Club during the 1930s. He served the county also as a justice of the peace and as deputy lieutenant.

---

[26] David Cannadine, in his book *The Decline and Fall of the British Aristocracy* (New Haven: Yale University Press, 1990), repeatedly misnamed him "Sir John" (pages 150, 164, 682). He later acknowledged the error (personal communication), saying that should another edition occur he would correct the error.

Exhibit 11.9. Arthur Grey Hazlerigg, 14th Bt and 2nd baron

Arthur[21d] left to his son and heir, Arthur[22b] Grey Hazlerigg, 15th Bt and 3rd baron, the great burden and unpleasant task of managing the Noseley estate to its end as seat of the Hesilrige/Hazlerigg family. In order to spare *his* son and heir, Arthur[23a] William Grey Hazlerigg, continuation of that burden and task, he sold the bulk of the manor of Noseley in October 2014. The lineage continues, however, with the birth (2020) of Arthur Ivor Grey Hazlerigg.

Last Stands

The patrimonial familial form of organization is very old. Its longevity has depended on the ability of family heads to reinvent the form in timely manner as conditions change. Suitable adjustments were made as the rise of functional individualism during the sixteenth and seventeenth centuries recommended adjustments. Continual and often more rapid adjustments were required during the nineteenth century, in accordance with shifts from agricultural to industrial modes of productivity of landed estates. These shifts meant that land in rural areas was losing value relative to land in increasingly populous urban areas—the area of London most conspicuously—since the cities held the concentrated population of mobile workers and support facilities for industrial plants. Families such as the Grosvenors, whose holdings from 1677 included the 500 acres of the old manor of Ebury (the northern part of which they developed from the 1720s as Belgravia), and the Cadogan family, who acquired the whole of the old manor of Chelsea by 1821, enjoyed a formidable head start. So, too, did a few others, but they were not as assiduously foresighted in maintaining presence.[27] The Hesilrige family had presence in Middlesex even before those dates (see chapter 5, pages 193-98), but never on sufficient scale for it to make a decisive difference much later. Traditions of agrarianism remained strong.

It is time to recall an observation made by George Farnham and Hamilton Thompson almost a century ago in their account of the manor of Noseley. Few families can claim a continuous history in one plot of land for more than two or three centuries. The eighteenth and nineteenth centuries saw massive movements of human populations westward across Europe and the Atlantic Ocean into and across the expanse of the North American continent. Then, with the advent of means of personal transport beyond the horse and buggy—trains, automobiles, airplanes—huge numbers of individuals and even entire households were able to "pick up stakes" and try life's chances in a different place—and some years later do it all over again. Such easy mobility meant that rootedness in one patch of land for more than a few decades, much less a few generations, became the rare exception. Imagine, therefore, the change since Farnham and Thompson noticed that "very few landed families" living in Leicestershire in 1920 could claim to have held one patch of land, a few thousand acres, without interruption in continuity of male

---

[27] The state and death taxes also played a part, to be sure. In response, the large landed families transferred the bulk of a family's holdings into limited-liability companies—thus, "estate management" companies such as Cadogan Estates, Grosvenor Estates, etc.

descent, for half a millennium.[28] Very few in 1920. Fewer still today, nearly a century later. It is a remarkable record.

---

[28] George Farnham and A Hamilton Thompson, "The Manor of Noseley," *Transactions of the Leicestershire Archæological Society*, volume 12, part 2 (1921-22), pages 214-217, at page 229.

~~~~~

Printed in Great Britain
by Amazon